Teachings of the Doctrine of Eternal Lives

Some Things to Consider

in their own words, from the scriptures, and teachings and writings of the Prophets, Apostles, and LDS Scholars

Teachings of the Doctrine of Eternal Lives
© Copyright 2011 Digital Legend Publishing

All rights reserved. No part of this book may be reproduced in any form or by any means without permission in writing from the publisher, Digital Legend Press. This work is not an official publication of The Church of Jesus Christ of Latter-day Saints. The views expressed herein are the responsibility of the author and do not necessarily represent the position of the LDS Church or Digital Legend Press.

Send inquiries to:
Digital Legend Press and Publishing
1994 Forest Bend Dr.
Salt Lake City, UT 84121   U.S.A.

Email: info@digitalegend.com
For more copies visit www.digitalegend.com

For a listing of all Digital Legend products, visit www.digitalegend.com or call 801-810-7718

Printed in the United States of America

ISBN: 978-1-934537-96-1

Dedicated to Jan, Tom, Zona, Butch, Stan, Kris, John, Jennifer, and Professor Hugh Nibley

"...they will not search knowledge, nor understand great knowledge, when it is given unto them in plainness, even as plain as word can be." (2 Nephi 32:7)

"When things that are of the greatest importance are passed over by weak-minded men without even a thought, [then] I want to see truth in all its bearings and hug it to my bosom." (*Teachings of the Prophet Joseph Smith*, p. 373)

"The great plan of salvation is a theme which ought to occupy our strict attention, and be regarded as one of heaven's best gifts to mankind" (*Teachings of the Prophet Joseph Smith*, p. 68)

"...the things of God are of deep import; and time, and experience, and careful and ponderous and solemn thoughts can only find them out. Thy mind, O man! if thou wilt lead a soul unto salvation, must stretch as high as the utmost heavens, and search into and contemplate the darkest abyss, and the broad expanse of eternity—" (*Teachings of the Prophet Joseph Smith*, p. 137)

Table of Contents

Introduction 1
Foreword 1
Mysteries 5
Revelation 11
Prayer: The Key to Greater Knowledge 21
The Second Comforter 29
Joseph and Brigham Knew More than They Could Teach 31
On the Potter's Wheel 37
Again 39
From Grace to Grace, From Exaltation to Exaltation 41
Eternal Progression—Eternal Lives 47
Culminating Ordinances 91
Treasures in the Heavens 101
Tried in All Things 103
Born Again 107
To Go No More Out 109
Kingdoms of Glory and the Seven Heavens 111
Joseph Smith and Brigham Young 121
Joseph, Brigham, and Heber Will Finish Their Work 123
Joseph Smith and Some Thought-Provoking Possibilities 129
Elijah and John the Baptist 135
Elias, Elijah, Noah, and John the Baptist 137

GOD HIMSELF SHALL COME DOWN 143
   God May Reside in the Bodies of Some Great Men 150
SERVANTS WHO MAY BE INSTANCES OF GOD'S
CONDESCENSION 153
THE LAW OF CAUSE AND EFFECT 157
THE PISTIS SOPHIA 161
MAN: DIVERSITY AMONG MEN AND SPIRITS 165
UNIVERSAL SALVATION 171
THE GODS 175
   Godliness 178
   The Head God and Godhead 178
   The Father 180
   The Son 186
   The Holy Ghost 188
   Resurrected Beings 189
   Man Is One with God 190
   The Father, Son, and Holy Ghost are One God 194
   Doing the Works of (a) Christ 198
ADAM AND EVE 201
KING AND PRIEST 213
   Kings and Priests in the Last Days 214
SECOND DEATH 217
APPENDICES 223
   Excerpts from Orson F. Whitney's Epic Poem "Elias" 225
   Excerpts from Sermons of Joseph Smith 239
      Sermon Delivered on 14 May 1843 239
      Sermon Delivered on 21 May 1843 241
      Sermon Delivered on 11 June 1843 243
      James Adams Funeral Sermon Delivered on 9 Oct 1843 247
      King Follett Funeral Sermon Delivered on 7 April 1844 249
      Plurality of Gods Sermon Delivered on 16 June 1844 261
   Excerpts from Sermons of Brigham Young 267
      Sermon Delivered on 9 April 1852 267
      Sermon Delivered on 8 August 1852 268
      Sermon Delivered on 27 February 1853 271
      Sermon Delivered on 10 July 1853 277

Sermon Delivered on 12 February 1854 281
  Sermon Delivered on 8 October 1854 287
 Excerpts from Sermons of Heber C. Kimball 313
  Sermon Delivered on 2 April 1854 313
  Sermon Delivered on 25 February 1855 314
  Sermon Delivered on 5 October 1856 316
  Sermon Delivered on 27 September 1857 318
 The Paracletes 321
 Excerpts from 2 Esdras (Also known as 4 Ezra) 325
  2 Esdras, Chapter 2 325
  2 Esdras, Chapter 4 326
  2 Esdras, Chapter 5 328
  2 Esdras, Chapter 7 330
 Robert Matthias 337
 Excerpts from Hugh Nibley 339
  Teachings of the Pearl of Great Price: Lecture 3 339
  Teachings of the Pearl of Great Price: Lecture 4 346
  Teachings of the Pearl of Great Price: Lecture 8 356
  Teachings of the Pearl of Great Price: Lecture 9 357
  Teachings of the Pearl of Great Price: Lecture 11 359
  Teachings of the Pearl of Great Price: Lecture 12 360
  Teachings of the Pearl of Great Price: Lecture 14 361
  Teachings of the Pearl of Great Price: Lecture 16 364
  Teachings of the Pearl of Great Price: Lecture 17 365
  Teachings of the Pearl of Great Price: Lecture 18 366
  Teachings of the Pearl of Great Price: Lecture 19 372
  Teachings of the Pearl of Great Price: Lecture 21 375
  Teachings of the Pearl of Great Price: Lecture 22 375
  The Message of the Joseph Smith Papyri: An Egyptian
   Endowment 376
  An Approach to the Book of Abraham 379
  One Eternal Round 381
FINAL THOUGHTS 385
INDEX 395

INTRODUCTION

The odyssey that brought me to the point in life of publishing this collection of teachings regarding "eternal lives" began on a bright warm summers morning in June of 1969 when I first discovered some of these concepts which eventually led to a concerted effort on my part to study the lives and teachings of the prophets and apostles and the history of the LDS Church. During my ongoing search for truth and knowledge, I have read from the journals, biographies, histories, and teachings of every man who has ever served in the Quorum of the Twelve Apostles or in the First Presidency of the Church in these Latter-days, so far as the materials have been available. Having poured through many hundreds of such volumes, I have come to know as intimately as possible from reading, the men who shoulder the mantle of the Apostleship and First Presidency, and the doctrines which they espouse; and from my readings I have discovered a lost and mostly forgotten world of many surprisingly beautiful and wondrous teachings and doctrines with respect to the plan of happiness that we seldom teach any longer.

During the many years that I have been reading and studying and researching, I have often had startling experiences where I've read from the teachings of the prophets and apostles, significant passages of revelatory insight regarding the more subtle elements of the plan of salvation which have left me breathless, and after many years of such research, I have collected these mostly forgotten teachings together into a single document and I have decided to publish this collection of teachings of the prophets and apostles, so that those who are seeking these things, which have been taught in the Latter-days, might find them.

This document is being published anonymously because I do not have a personal agenda with regard to these things, nor am I seeking any recognition for this work; in fact I want nothing more than to continue to live my unassuming life in anonymity. I am only quoting directly from the prophets, apostles, LDS scholars and Mormon historians, and a very few close associates of Joseph Smith and Brigham Young who have addressed these topics, and I'm not trying to teach or promote anything that has not been taught publicly by the men who have been called of God in these last days to lead His Church. I do not claim any special revelation for anyone or for the Church. I'm just a very simple man who has found some remarkable things from the collective documentary history of the LDS people.

As you will see from this document, some of the brethren have had conflicting points of view on various associated topics, and that is fine. I've simply collected what they've had to say about topics that coincide with the concept of "eternal lives" and you can draw your own conclusions. This is by no means a comprehensive collection of everything pertinent that has ever been said concerning the related topics. Please just keep in mind as you read, that this document is primarily focused on the doctrine of "eternal lives" and the highly related issues as I perceive them, and that this document is not intended to be anything more than simply a collection of the specific teachings of the latter-day prophets and apostles (including the related commentary from trusted associates of the prophets, and from the community of scholars and historians) relating to the doctrine of "eternal lives" and the possibilities entailed in the ideas and understanding which the brethren advocated.

This is a wondrous doctrine that is seldom discussed in the Church these days, thus the lack of many recent comments from the brethren in the last forty years or so. Having said that, there is of course more material from earlier time periods in our Church's history that could have been included in this work (in fact 635 pages of material was originally compiled for this project) but most of the additional material was simply repetitive in nature, and nothing that is considered to be significant or unique has been left out. I've tried to present a fair representation of the beliefs of the various brethren as they expounded their diverse points of view.

Some of the men who discussed these sacred things were obviously blessed with exceptional insights into the inner workings of the plan of salvation for God's children, and they left their testimonies with regard to these things as part of the record of their ministries. If you read carefully, you'll be astonished at the surprising number of supernal gems that have been right here in front of all of us, but perhaps which we failed to read from the vantage point of understanding what the prophets and apostles may have been trying to teach us concerning the possibilities within the concept of "eternal lives." Furthermore, you may be startled by the number of statements often given by the authority and power of apostolic or prophetic testimony as to the absolute truthfulness of the doctrines they were teaching!

I've invited a special friend who is no stranger to these things to write an anonymous foreword to this collection of teachings, and I want to thank my friend for the interest and help with this endeavor. Over the course of the past thirty-three years of my seeking to find these additional truths, I have bumped into many others from the LDS faith who are themselves seeking answers to the greater mysteries of our eternal existence, not yet revealed by God to the Church as a whole, but which He does reveal to many of His children individually from time to time, "To whom he grants this privilege of seeing and knowing for themselves;" (D&C 76:117).

To all of those who have had such an insightful influence on my life, though anonymously, I offer my thanks and I hope that this collection of the teachings of the prophets and apostles "in their own words" will be of great value to those who are searching for these precious doctrines of truth which have been revealed. If this document is of any help to you in your personal journey of searching for truth, then it has been worth all of the effort and sacrifice its creation has required. Perhaps this forum will serve as a springboard for further dialogue within the LDS community with reference to the doctrine of "eternal lives."

In the final assessment of this editor, these words of the prophets and apostles uncover and reveal a gospel message that is more compassionate, more forgiving, more tolerant, more charitable, more ennobling, more uplifting, more inspiring, more merciful, and all inclusive. A message that rings with eternal hope; a hope for everyone, that eventually, through the process of time and the experience of "eternal lives," that all of God's children will partake equally, the intended eternal blessings for which we exist, and the blessings which the atonement of Jesus Christ anticipated.

Editorial Note: When the statements from the brethren were first collected for my own personal use, each passage was placed in quote marks. Later when the numerous statements from the scholars were added to the original collection, they were not placed in quote marks due to the enormity of that effort. The same format has been followed here. Furthermore, for my personal use I bolded all of the passages that were of greatest personal significance to this study, and I've decided to retain that format in the published version. You may be stunned by the difference in interpretation of certain passages when you pay close attention to the bolded selections.

—July 2002

Introduction to the 2004 Revised Edition

In August 2001 when I began compiling the content for this project, I was quite sure that I had discovered all of the applicable material from relevant LDS sources, and yet, as I've continued my studies, I've found numerous additional unique and significant statements that warrant inclusion in this collection. I've added twenty pages of supplementary material that expand on prior understanding and insight.

If I have one regret, it is that Hugh Nibley's final work has not yet been published, because it no doubt will contain analogous and discerning information that will compliment and extend our knowledge of the subject matter contained in this collection. The reader should note the tremendous influence of Hugh Nibley over this project, although vicariously so to speak, and without his direct involvement in its creation. The title of his last great work, "One Eternal Round," speaks to the heart of the doctrine of eternal lives, and this revised edition is dedicated in part to the greatest scholar among the Latter-day Saints.

—July 2004

Introduction to the 2011 Revised Edition

Over the course of many years of study and life experience, one tends to acquire broadened perspectives, deeper insights, and further appreciation for the unfolding miracles, and the unique variance ascribed to a journey of discovery from beginning to end. Things are not what they appeared to be at the outset, nor am I fully certain that we yet understand things as they really are. An approximation of truth may be as close as we can attain in this world, because the seeming normalcy of life, veils and portrays an identity of things, equal to the lowest common denominator of daily experience, yet if we lift the covers sufficiently, our experiential vantage point suddenly reveals a world we had not previously known, and truths leap-out from unexpected places.

One of the most wonderfully unexpected sources of additional brilliant light and insight turned out to be the Holy Scriptures which held stunning surprises at every turn, once our vision adjusted to the outlook of writers whose knowledge of the "greater things," allowed them to obfuscate stunning gems, in the garb of the common and everyday word. No wonder God speaks of having eyes to see! And if surprises of this order of magnitude were not expected at the beginning, just imagine the stunners which revealed a world-view held by the likes of Joseph Smith, Brigham Young, and Heber C. Kimball (among others of the early generations of the restoration) which bare almost nothing in common with current Mormon viewpoints. Their views were far more expansive, and illustrative of the grandeur of the "greater things" which God shared with them, in contrast to our modern diminished Deseret.

As the world rushes headlong to its inevitable destiny, and as an ever-increasing number of community and religious distractions and intrusion clamor for our time and attention, we as individuals are left to seek further light and knowledge by our own effort and choices, enhanced hopefully, by the Holy Spirit and the ministering of Angels, or else we succumb to the herd mentality which is the stock-in-trade of our modern world. There is no corporate body intended to bestow these "greater things" upon us anyway. It is very much an individual undertaking to seek God, once our feet are set upon the path. That is clearly the intention of mortal life, as so aptly described through the life of Abraham, so we had best find ourselves fully engaged regarding this most important endeavor of life. Waiting in a comfortably appointed room, depending on others to guide the way, is the sure sign of a people who have lost their bearings and who do not know their God individually.

Many mentors have journeyed alongside for whom I am deeply indebted. Some of their names are mentioned in the dedication, though most go unrecognized but appreciably valued as friends and associates of the highest order. One for whom I must add an especial and additional thanks and recognition is Brother Nibley. In this latest edition, we were fortunate enough to include additional insights from his last two volumes: *An Approach to the Book of Abraham* and *One Eternal Round*. Hugh Nibley spent much of his sanguine career, sifting-out the applicable notes from history which supported the landscape vistas he had envisioned regarding eternal lives and the course we pursue of one eternal round. His was a lone voice in the wilderness, which the Latter-day Saints hardly appreciated, and certainly didn't understand. Perhaps this volume will help a few among us to really see for the first time, the glorious truths which Nibley tried to bring to our scattered and unfocused attention.

We see in Joseph's, Brigham's, and Heber's words, the same themes, doctrines, and ideas which Hugh extracted from a wide array of ancient sources, and which he spent a lifetime trying to bring into focus. Moreover, we are fortunate to have the recently released five-volume collection of Brigham Young's sermons made available to add significant insight to these things. This collection of teachings is a tribute to those who for generations, tried to point our minds to the inner-workings of God's plan of salvation for us, and the sweet and melodic mysteries revealed through the restoration, but lost now from the corpus of our compendium.

Lastly, I must thank our friend JCO for the encouragement to reissue this burgeoning collection of the most important matters of doctrine espoused in the last days, as well as for the inexorable editorial efforts.

When asked why I published this book anonymously, the answer is very simple. **These sacred things were transmitted directly by God to His Prophets and Apostles through the gift and power of revelation, and they are a gift from God to man.** The prophets and apostles in turn shared their deepest knowing, testimonies, and insights regarding the signal and salient points of salvational truth, which God had revealed to them. This really has nothing to do with me, thus the necessary anonymity. These are not my words, rather, they are the words of Heaven, distilled for our eternal benefit, and brought together here from a lifetime of study and research. Any claim to originality of authorship regarding this material would, in my opinion, distract from the purpose of sharing these wondrous things.

I do not expect to revisit this outpost again, as its remoteness to modern concerns will unlikely require any further editions. Sadly, as Nibley said, he had been shouting about these things for years, but no one was listening.

—January 2011

Foreword

"Treasure these things up in your hearts, and let the solemnities of eternity rest upon your minds." (D&C 43:34)

"Canst thou read this without rejoicing and lifting up thy heart for gladness?" (D&C 19:39)

Who are we? Why are we here? What is our destiny? These are the profound questions addressed in this collection of inspired thoughts of leaders, teachers, and prophets of The Church of Jesus Christ of Latter-day Saints and accompanying scriptures.

These writings reveal our probationary experiences as the path of "becoming," which path does not end at death, nor with the assignment to a particular post-mortal glory, but continues as we progress from one degree to another. In what should point the thoughtful mind to serious consideration, this continual progression is considered as taking place in the context of our own earth.

The ideas are not new. However, they temper contemporary Mormon cultural interpretations imposed on our spiritual cosmology: that our eternal destiny is utterly dependent on our succession in this one probationary experience, and that failure to successfully overcome our trials in this lifetime suggests an eternal and fatal deficiency of spiritual character.

What light is shed by this collection! We and all men and women are experiencing the "Deity within us" (Brigham Young, see p. 55) that will motivate us to grow forever in grace and truth. Indeed, "we are conducted along from this probation to other probations" (Heber C. Kimball, see p. 62). And "if there was a point where man in his progression could not proceed any further, the very idea would throw a gloom over every intelligent and reflecting mind" (Wilford Woodruff, see p. 65).

These ideas illustrate the legitimacy of our faith in others and in God, whose plan of happiness demonstrates such faith in us! Our patience is likewise justified as we allow others around us to experience God's plan of happiness and *his faith in them!* Although we never stop teaching and encouraging, we may set aside feelings of desperation which might lead us to coerce others based on the assumption that mistakes made here may mean their place at the table of heaven will be eternally empty.

As we receive grace for grace, and as we progress and understand, we reach to those around us and offer them encouragement and understanding. Jesus Christ performed this role for us in the salvation of this world and He is our example.

"Thus the children of men will be *continually exalted and drawn up toward God* through the principle of repentance" (George Q. Cannon, see p. 47-48). This is truly the good news of the gospel of Jesus Christ, restored in its fullness in the latter-days.

—L.H., July 2002

"And to make all *men* see what *is* the fellowship of the mystery, which from the beginning of the world hath been hid in God." (Ephesians 3:9)

"The secret *things belong* unto the LORD our God: but those *things which are* revealed *belong* unto us and to our children for ever…" (Deuteronomy 29:29)

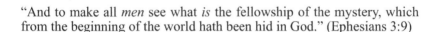

When asked why I published this book anonymously, the answer is very simple. These sacred things were transmitted by God to His Prophets and Apostles through the gift and power of revelation, and they are a gift from God to man. The Prophets and Apostles in turn shared their deepest knowing, testimonies, and insights regarding the signal and salient points of salvational truth, which God had revealed to them. This really has nothing to do with me, thus the necessary anonymity. These are not my words, rather, they are the words of Heaven, distilled for our eternal benefit, and brought together here from a lifetime of study and research. Any claim to originality of authorship regarding this material would, in my opinion, distract from the purpose of sharing these wondrous things.

Chapter 1

Mysteries

David, King of Israel

"The secret of the LORD is with them that fear him; and he will shew them his covenant." (Psalms 25:14)

Apostle Matthew

"He answered and said unto them, Because it is given unto you to know the mysteries of the kingdom of heaven, but to them it is not given." (Matthew 13:11)

Joseph Smith

"I advise all to go on to perfection and search deeper and deeper into the mysteries of Godliness" (*The Words of Joseph Smith*, p. 366)

"If we have any claim on our Heavenly Father for anything, it is for knowledge on this important subject. Could we read and comprehend all that has been written from the days of Adam, on the relation of man to God and angels in a future state, we should know very little about it. **Reading the experience of others, or the revelation given to them, can never give us a comprehensive view of our condition and true relation to God.** Knowledge of these things can only be obtained by experience through the ordinances of God set forth for that purpose. **Could you gaze into heaven five minutes, you would know more than you would by reading all that ever was written on the subject.**" (*Teachings of the Prophet Joseph Smit*h, p. 324)

"It has always been my province to dig up hidden mysteries, new things for my hearers—" (*The Words of Joseph Smith*, p. 366)

"**For he that diligently seeketh shall find; and the mysteries of God shall be unfolded unto them, by the power of the Holy Ghost**, as well in these times as in times of old, and as well in times of old as in times to come; wherefore, the course of the Lord is one eternal round." (1 Nephi 10:19)

"Behold, great and marvelous are the works of the Lord. **How unsearchable are the depths of the mysteries of him**; and it is impossible that man should find out all his ways. And **no man knoweth of his ways save it be revealed unto him**; wherefore, brethren, **despise not the revelations of God.**" (Jacob 4:8)

"Seek not for riches but for wisdom, **and behold, the mysteries of God shall be unfolded unto you**, and then shall you be made rich. Behold, he that hath eternal life is rich." (D&C 6:7)

"And if thou wilt inquire, thou shalt know mysteries which are great and marvelous; therefore thou shalt exercise thy gift, that **thou mayest find out mysteries**, that thou mayest bring many to the knowledge of the truth, yea, convince them of the error of their ways." (D&C 6:11)

"One of the grand fundamental principles of 'Mormonism' is to receive truth, let it come from whence it may." (*Teachings of the Prophet Joseph Smith*, p. 313)

"The great thing for us to know is to comprehend what God did institute before the foundation of the World. Who knows it?...Had I inspiration, revelation, and lungs to communicate what my soul has contemplated in times past, there is not a soul in this congregation but would go to their homes and shut their mouths in everlasting silence on religion till they had learned something. Why be so certain that you comprehend the things of God, when all things with you are so uncertain. You are welcome to all the knowledge and intelligence I can impart to you." (HC 5:530, 531)

"Therefore, if you will ask of me you shall receive; if you will knock it shall be opened unto you. Now, as you have asked, behold, I say unto you, keep my commandments, and seek to bring forth and establish the cause of Zion. **Seek not for riches but for wisdom; and, behold, the mysteries of God shall be unfolded unto you**, and then shall you be made rich. Behold, he that hath eternal life is rich." (D&C 11:5–7)

"Ask that you may know the mysteries of God, and that you may translate and receive knowledge from all those ancient records which have been hid up, that are sacred; and according to your faith shall it be done unto you." (D&C 8:11)

"If thou shalt ask, thou shalt receive revelation upon revelation, knowledge upon knowledge, that thou mayest know the mysteries and peaceable things—that which bringeth joy, that which bringeth life eternal." (D&C 42:61)

"But unto him that keepeth my commandments I will give the mysteries of my kingdom, and the same shall be in him a well of living water, springing up unto everlasting life." (D&C 63:23)

"And to them will I reveal all mysteries, yea, all the hidden mysteries of my kingdom from days of old, and for ages to come, will I make known unto them the good pleasure of my will concerning all things pertaining to my kingdom. Yea, even the wonders of eternity shall they know, and things to come will I show them, even the things of many generations. And their wisdom shall be great, and their understanding reach to heaven; and before them the wisdom of the wise shall perish, and the understanding of the prudent shall come to naught. For by my Spirit will I enlighten them, and by my power will I make known unto them the secrets of my will—yea, even those things which eye has not seen, nor ear heard, nor yet entered into the heart of man." (D&C 76:7–10)

"But great and marvelous are the works of the Lord, and the mysteries of his kingdom which he showed unto us, which surpass all understanding in glory, and in might, and in dominion; Which he commanded us we should not write while we were yet in the Spirit, and are not lawful for man to utter; Neither is man capable to make them known, for they are only to be seen and understood by the power of the Holy Spirit, which God bestows on those who love him, and purify themselves before him; To whom he grants this privilege of seeing and knowing for themselves;" (D&C 76:114–117)

"The power and authority of the higher, or Melchizedek Priesthood, is to hold the keys of all the spiritual blessings of the church—**To have the privilege of receiving the mysteries of the kingdom of heaven, to have the heavens opened unto them**, to commune with the general assembly and church of the Firstborn, and to enjoy the communion and presence of God the Father, and Jesus the mediator of the new covenant." (D&C 107:18–19)

"**It is given unto many to know the mysteries of God**; nevertheless they are laid under a strict command that they shall not impart only according to the portion of his word which he doth grant unto the children of men, according to the heed and diligence which they give unto him. And therefore, he that will harden his heart, the same receiveth the lesser portion of the word; and he that will not harden his heart, **to him is given the greater portion of the word, until it is given unto him to know the mysteries of God until he know them in full**. And they that will harden their hearts, to them is given the lesser portion of the word until they know nothing concerning his mysteries…" (Alma 12:9–11)

"And this greater priesthood administereth the gospel and holdeth the key of the mysteries of the kingdom, even the key of the knowledge of God." (D&C 84:19)

"How vain and trifling have been our spirits, our conferences, our councils, our meetings, our private as well as public conversations—too low, too mean, too vulgar, too condescending for the dignified characters of the called and chosen of God, according to the purposes of His will, from before the foundation of the world!

We are called to hold the keys of the mysteries of those things that have been kept hid from the foundation of the world until now. Some have tasted a little of these things, many of which are to be poured down from heaven upon the heads of babes; yea, upon the weak, obscure and despised ones of the earth. Therefore we beseech of you, brethren, that you bear with those who do not feel themselves more worthy than yourselves, while we exhort one another to a reformation with one and all…" (*Teachings of the Prophet Joseph Smith*, p. 137. HC 3:296)

"Come unto me, O ye Gentiles, and I will show unto you the greater things, the knowledge which is hid up because of unbelief. Come unto me, O ye house of Israel, and it shall be made manifest unto you how great things the Father hath laid up for you, from the foundation of the world; and it hath not come unto you, because of unbelief.

Behold, **when ye shall rend that veil of unbelief** which doth cause you to remain in your awful state of wickedness, and hardness of heart, and **blindness of mind, then shall the great and marvelous things which have been hid up from the foundation of the world from you**—yea, when ye shall call upon the Father in my name, with a broken heart and a contrite spirit, then shall ye know that the Father hath remembered the covenant which he made unto your fathers, O house of Israel. **And then shall my revelations which I have caused to be written by my servant John be unfolded in the eyes of all the people.**" (Ether 4:13–16)

Hyrum Smith

"…**the mysteries of God are not given to all men**; and unto those to whom they are given they are placed under restrictions to impart only such as God will command them…and let the mysteries alone **until by and by.**" (*Times and Seasons,* Vol. 5:474)

Brigham Young

"You often hear people desiring more of the knowledge of God, more of the wisdom of God, more of the power of God. They want more revelation, to know more about the kingdom of heaven, in heaven and on the earth, and they wish to learn and increase. There is one principle that I wish the people would understand and lay to heart. Just as fast as you will prove before your God that you are worthy to receive the mysteries, if you please to call them so, of the kingdom of heaven-that you are full of confidence in God-that you will never betray a thing that God tells you-that you will never reveal to your neighbour that which ought not to be revealed, as quick as you prepare to be entrusted with the things of God, there is an eternity of them to bestow upon you.

Instead of pleading with the Lord to bestow more upon you, plead with yourselves to have confidence in yourselves, to have integrity in yourselves, and know when to speak and what to speak, what to reveal, and how to carry yourselves and walk before the Lord. **And just as fast as you prove to Him that you will preserve everything secret** that ought to be-that you will deal out to your neighbours all which you ought, and no more, and learn how to dispense your knowledge to your families, friends, neighbours, and brethren, **the Lord will bestow upon you, and give to you, and bestow upon you, until finally he will say to you, 'You shall never fall; your salvation is sealed unto you; you are sealed up unto eternal life and salvation, through your integrity…' I say this that you may learn to reveal that which you ought, and to keep the rest to yourselves. By so doing you prove to God that you are His friends, and will keep His secrets**. The world may howl around you and plead for the secrets of the Lord which he has given you, but they will not get them. **When the Lord has proved His children true to what He has given into their charge, and that they will do His bidding, He will tell such persons anything that they should know.**" (JD 4:371–372)

"Men can never search out the mysteries of godliness by the wisdom and learning of this world." (*The Essential Brigham Young*, p. 180)

Chapter 2

Revelation

Joseph Smith

"It is not wisdom that we should have all knowledge at once presented before us; but that we should have a little at a time; then we can comprehend it." (HC 5:387)

"For I design to reveal unto my church things which have been kept hid from before the foundation of the world, things that pertain to the dispensation of the fullness of times." (D&C 124:41)

"There are many things which belong to the powers of the Priesthood and the keys thereof, **that have been kept hid** from before the foundation of the world; **they are hid from the wise and prudent to be revealed in the last times**." (HC 4:209–210)

"God hath not revealed anything to Joseph [calling himself by name], but what He will make known unto the Twelve, and even the least Saint may know all things as fast as he is able to bear them," (HC 3:380)

"That which is of God is light; and he that receiveth light, and continueth in God, receiveth more light; and that light groweth brighter and brighter until the perfect day. And again, verily I say unto you, and I say it that you may know the truth, that you may chase darkness from among you;" (D&C 50:24–25)

"And there are many among us who have many revelations, for they are not all stiffnecked. And as many as are not stiffnecked and have faith, have communion with the Holy Spirit, which maketh manifest unto the children of men, according to their faith." (Jarom 1:4)

"The light shineth in darkness, and the darkness comprehendeth it not; nevertheless, **the day shall come when you shall comprehend even God**, being quickened **in him and by him**." (D&C 88:49)

"Draw near unto me and I will draw near unto you; seek me diligently and ye shall find me; ask, and ye shall receive; knock, and it shall be opened unto you. Whatsoever ye ask the Father in my name it shall be given unto you, that is expedient for you;" (D&C 88:63–64)

"…if you do right [there is] **no danger of going too fast**; he said he did not care how fast we run in the path of virtue. Resist evil and there is no danger." (*The Words of Joseph Smith*, p. 117)

"I want to see truth in all its bearings and hug it to my bosom. I believe all that God ever revealed, and **I never hear of a man being damned for believing too much**; but they are damned for unbelief." (*Teachings of the Prophet Joseph Smith,* p. 373)

"But without faith it is impossible to please God, for he that cometh to God must believe that he is, and that **he is a revealer to those who diligently seek him**." (*The Words of Joseph Smith,* p. 40–41)

"Therefore, he that lacketh wisdom, let him ask of me, and I will give him liberally and upbraid him not." (D&C 42:68)

"…the things of God are of deep import; and time, and experience, and careful and ponderous and solemn thoughts can only find them out. Thy mind, O man! if thou wilt lead a soul unto salvation, must stretch as high as the utmost heavens, and search into and contemplate the darkest abyss, and the broad expanse of eternity—thou must commune with God." (HC 3:295)

"Wherefore murmur ye, because **that ye shall receive more of my word**…And because that I have spoken one word **ye need not suppose that I cannot speak another**; for my work is not yet finished; neither shall it be until the end of man, neither from that time henceforth and forever." (2 Nephi 29:8–9)

"…if we have direct revelations given us from heaven, surely those revelations were never given to be trifled with, without the trifler's incurring displeasure and vengeance upon his own head…" (*Teachings of the Prophet Joseph Smith,* p. 53)

"…verily brethren **there are things in the bosom of the Father, that have been hid from the foundation of the world, that are not Known neither can be except by direct Revelation**. The Apostle says, unto them who have obtained like precious faith with us the apostles through the righteousness of God & our Savior Jesus Christ, through the knowledge of him that has called us to glory & virtue add faith virtue &c. &c. to godliness brotherly kindness—Charity—ye shall neither be barren or unfruitful in the Knowledge of our Lord Jesus Christ. He that lacketh these things is blind—wherefore the rather brethren after all this give diligence to make your calling & Election Sure Knowledge is necessary to life and Godliness. wo [sic] unto you priests & divines, who preach that knowledge is not necessary unto life & Salvation. Take away Apostles &c. take away knowledge and you will find yourselves worthy of the damnation of hell. **Knowledge is Revelation hear all ye brethren, this grand Key**; Knowledge is the power of God unto Salvation." (*The Words of Joseph Smith,* pp. 206–207)

"**It is the privilege of the Children of God to come to God & get Revelation…When any person receives a vision of Heaven, he sees things that he never thought of before**…any person that believes the works I do shall he do also & greater works. The Father could not be glorified in the Son on any other principle than we coming to God, asking, receiving, heavens open visions &c.—They are done away because of unbelief—" (*The Words of Joseph Smith,* pp. 13–14)

"A person may profit by noticing the first intimation of the spirit of revelation; for instance, when you feel pure intelligence flowing into you, it may give you sudden strokes of ideas, so that by noticing it, you may find it fulfilled the same day or soon; (i.e.,) those things that were presented unto your minds by the Spirit of God, will come to pass; and thus by learning the Spirit of God and understanding it, you may grow into the principle of revelation, until you become perfect in Christ Jesus." (HC 3:381)

"It is a great thing to inquire at the hands of God or to come into his presence; and we feel fearful to approach him on subjects that are of little or no consequence to satisfy the queries of individuals, **especially about things the knowledge of which men ought to obtain, in all sincerity, before God, for themselves**, in humility by the prayer of faith; and more especially a teacher or a high priest in the Church." (HC 1:339)

"…one great privilege of the priesthood is to obtain revelations of the mind and will of God." (HC 2:477)

"He will be inquired of by his children. He says: 'Ask and ye shall receive, seek and ye shall find';…who will listen to my voice and to the voice of my servant whom I have sent; **for I delight in those who seek diligently to know my precepts, and abide by the law of my kingdom; for all things shall be made known unto them in mine own due time**, and in the end they shall have joy." (HC 5:136)

"A man is saved no faster than he gets knowledge," (HC 4:588)

"Search the scriptures—search the revelations which we publish, and ask your Heavenly Father, in the name of his Son Jesus Christ, to manifest the truth unto you, and if you do it with an eye single to his glory nothing doubting, he will answer you by the power of his Holy Spirit. You will then know for yourselves and not for another. You will not then be dependent on man for the knowledge of God; nor will there be any room for speculation. No; for when men receive their instruction from him that made them, they know how he will save them." (HC 1:282)

"When things that are of the greatest importance are passed over by weak-minded men without even a thought, [then] I want to see truth in all its bearings and hug it to my bosom." (HC 6:477)

"We believe all that God has revealed, all that He does now reveal, and we believe that He will yet reveal many great and important things pertaining to the Kingdom of God." (9th Article of Faith)

"Many things are insoluble to the children of men in the last days: for instance, that God should raise the dead, and forgetting that things have been hid from before the foundation of the world, which are to be revealed to babes in the last days. There are a great many wise men and women too in our midst who are too wise to be taught; therefore they must die in their ignorance, and in the resurrection they will find their mistake. Many seal up the door of heaven by saying, So far God may reveal and I will believe." (HC 5:424)

"Now what I am after is the knowledge of God & I take my own Course to obtain it" (*The Words of Joseph Smith,* p. 329)

"No one can truly say he knows God until he has handled something, and this can only be in the Holiest of Holies." (Ibid, pp. 119–120)

Brigham Young

"Where is the divine who knows the least thing about that Being who is the Father of our spirits and the author of our bodies?…**I have had many revelations; I have seen and heard for myself, and know these things are true**, and nobody on earth can disprove them…What I know concerning God, concerning the earth, concerning government, **I have received from the heavens, not alone through my natural ability**, and I give God the glory and the praise." (JD 16:46)

"The spirit of revelation can reveal these things to the people. But unless they live so as to have the revelations of the Lord Jesus Christ, they will remain a mystery, for there is a veil before the minds of the people, and they cannot be understood. Some of these principles have been taught to the Latter-day Saints, but who can understand them?" (JD 13:264)

"I tell you this as my belief about that personage who is called the Ancient of Days, the Prince and so on, but I do not tell it because that I wish it to be established in the minds of others, though to me this is as clear as the sun, it is as plain as my alphabet. I understand it as I do the path to go home. **I did not understand so until my mind became enlightened with the Spirit and by the revelations of God, neither will you understand until our Father in Heaven reveals all these things unto you. To my mind and to my feelings those matters are all plain and easy to be understood**." (Brigham Young, April 25, 1855, Church Archives. Also see *Dialogue,* Vol. 15, No. 1, pp. 22–23)

"They must pass through the same ordeals as the Gods, that they may know good from evil, how to succor the tempted, tried and weak, and how to reach down the hand of mercy to save the falling sinner. The Lord has revealed his gospel and instituted its ordinances that the inhabitants of the earth may be put in possession of eternal life. But few of them, however, will accept it. I have preached it to many thousands of them who are naturally just as honest as I am, but through tradition there is an overwhelming prejudice in their minds, which debars them of that liberty I have in my heart. They would be glad to know the ways of God, and to know who Jesus is, and to reap the reward of the faithful, if they had the stamina, I will call it, the independence of mind necessary to embrace the truth, to say, 'I know this is true, and if there is no other person on the face of this earth who will defend it I will to the last.' But this is not in their hearts, it is not in their organization, consequently they do not manifest it…There is no mystery to me in what God has revealed to me, or in what I have learned, whether it has been through Joseph, an angel, the voice of the Spirit, the Holy Ghost or the Spirit of the Lord; no matter how I have learned a thing, if I understand it perfectly it is no mystery to me...Some may say to me, 'Why, Brother Brigham, you seem to know it all.' I say, Oh no, I know but very little, but I have an eternity of knowledge before me, and I never expect to see the time when I shall cease to learn, never, no never, but I expect to keep on learning for ever and ever, going on from exaltation to exaltation, glory to glory, power to power, ever pressing forward to greater and higher attainments, as the Gods do. That is an idea that drowns the entire Christian world in a moment. Let them try to entertain it and they are out of sight of land without a ship, and if they had a ship it would have neither sail, rudder nor compass. 'What,' say they, 'God progress?' Now, do not lariat the God that I serve and say that he cannot learn any more; I do not believe in such a character. 'Why,' say they, 'does not the Lord know it all?' Well, if he does, he must know an immense amount.

No matter about that, the mind of man does not reach that any more than it comprehends the heaven beyond the bounds of time and space in which the Christians expect to sit and sing themselves away to everlasting bliss, and where they say they shall live for ever and for ever. If we look forward we can actually comprehend a little of the idea that we shall live for ever and ever; but you take a rear sight, and try and contemplate and meditate upon the fact that there never was a beginning and you are lost at once. The present and the future we can comprehend some little about, but the past is all a blank, and it is right and reasonable that it should be so. **But if we are faithful in the things of God they will open up, open up, open up, our minds will expand, reach forth and receive more and more, and by and by we can begin to see that the Gods have been for ever and for ever**." (*Deseret Weekly News* 22:308–309, June 18, 1873)

"I know just as well what to teach this people and just what to say to them and what to do in order to bring them into the celestial kingdom, as I know the road to my office. It is just as plain and easy. The Lord is in our midst. He teaches the people continually. **I have never yet preached a sermon and sent it out to the children of men, that they may not call Scripture**. Let me have the privilege of correcting a sermon, and it is as good Scripture as they deserve. The people have the oracles of God continually." (JD 13:95)

"When you see Zion redeemed and built up-when you see the people performing the ordinances of salvation for themselves and for others, (and they will hereafter,) you will see simply this (but I have not time this morning to tell you only a little part of it): about the time that the Temples of the Lord will be built and Zion is established-pretty nigh this time, you will see, (those who are faithful enough,) the first you know, there will be strangers in your midst, walking with you, talking with you: they will enter into your houses and eat and drink with you, go to meeting with you, and begin to open your minds, as the Saviour did the two disciples who walked out in the country in days of old.

About the time the Temples are ready, the strangers will be along and will converse with you, and will inquire of you, probably, if you understand the resurrection of the dead. You might say you have heard and read a great deal about it, but you do not properly understand it; and they will then open your minds and tell you the principles of the resurrection of the dead and how to save your friends: they will point out Scriptures in the Old and New Testament, in the Book of Mormon, and other revelations of God, saying, 'Don't you recollect reading so and so, that Saviours should come up on Mount Zion?' &c.; and they will expound the Scriptures to you.

You have got your Temples ready: now go forth and be baptized for those good people. There are your father and your mother-your ancestors for many generations back-the people that have lived upon the face of the earth since the Priesthood was taken away, thousands and millions of them, who have lived according to the best light and knowledge in their possession. **They will expound the Scriptures to you, and open your minds, and teach you of the resurrection of the just and the unjust, of the doctrine of salvation**: they will use the keys of the holy Priesthood, and unlock the door of knowledge, **to let you look into the palace of truth**. You will exclaim, That is all plain: **why did I not understand it before**? and [sic] you will begin to feel your hearts burn within you as they walk and talk with you…

You will enter into the Temple of the Lord, when by-and-by **here come along brothers Joseph and Hyrum Smith; for instance**; for they will be perfectly capable of coming and staying over night with you, **and you not know who they are**. Or suppose David Patten should come along, and shake hands with some of the Twelve, and want to stay all night with them and **expound the Scriptures and reveal the hidden things of God**. It will not be long before this will be so." (JD 6:294–296)

"Now I want to tell you that which, perhaps, many of you do not know. Should you receive a vision of revelation from the Almighty, one that the Lord gave you concerning yourselves, or this people, but **which you are not to reveal** on account of your not being the proper person, or because it ought not to be known by the people at present, you should shut it up and seal it as close, and lock it as tight as heaven is to you, and make it as secret as the grave. The Lord has no confidence in those who reveal secrets, for He cannot safely reveal Himself to such persons.

It is as much as He can do to get a particle of sense into some of the best and most influential men in the Church, in regard to real confidence in themselves. They cannot keep things within their own bosoms…

If a person understands God and godliness, the principles of heaven, the principle of integrity, and the Lord reveals anything to that individual, no matter what, **unless He gives permission to disclose it, it is locked up in eternal silence**. And when persons have proven to their messengers that their bosoms are like the lock-ups of eternity, **then the Lord says, I can reveal anything to them, because they never will**

disclose it until I tell them to. Take persons of any other character, and they sap the foundation of the confidence they ought to have in themselves and in their God...

If we are His friends, we will keep the secrets of the Almighty. We will lock them up, when he reveals them to us, so that no man on earth can have them, and no being from heaven, unless he brings the keys wherewith to get them legally. **No person can get the things the Lord has given to men, unless by legal authority; then I have a right to reveal them, but not without**. When we can keep our own secrets, **when we can keep the secrets of the Almighty strictly, honestly, truly in our own bosoms, the Lord will have confidence in us**. Will He before? No. Are we going to become secret keepers in any other way than by applying our lives to the religion we profess to believe? No." (JD 4:288–289)

"If God has given me light, if I possess the light of the Spirit of revelation, and bestow that knowledge upon my brethren, that same fountain increases in me; whereas, if I were to shut it up-to close up the vision-and keep it from the people, it would be like the candle lighted and put under the bushel, where of course the want of free air would extinguish it;" (JD 4:265–266)

"Here let me give you one lesson that may be profitable to many. If the Lord Almighty should reveal to a High Priest, or to any other than the head, things that are, or that have been and will be, and show to him the destiny of this people twenty-five years from now, or a new doctrine that will in five, ten, or twenty years hence become the doctrine of this Church and kingdom, but which has not yet been revealed to this people, and reveal it to him by the same Spirit, the same messenger, the same voice, and the same power that gave revelations to Joseph when he was living, it would be a blessing to that High Priest, or individual; but he must rarely divulge it to a second person on the face of the earth, until God reveals it through the proper source to become the property of the people at large." (JD 3:318)

"I am more afraid that this people have so much confidence in their leaders **that they will not inquire for themselves of God whether they are led by him**. I am fearful they settle down in a state of **blind self-security**, trusting their eternal destiny in the hands of their leaders with a reckless confidence that in itself would thwart the purposes of God in their salvation, and weaken that influence they could give to their leaders, **did they know for themselves, by the revelations of Jesus, that they are led in the right way**. Let every man and woman know, by the whispering of the Spirit of God to themselves, whether their leaders are walking in the path the Lord dictates, or not." (JD 9:150)

"I don't care whether the people believe me to be a Prophet, Seer or Revelator or not, I have been very profitable to this people and **I have seen a good many things, and I have revealed many things**." (Brigham Young, *The Complete Discourses of Brigham Young*,

Vol. 1, 1832 to 1852, Ed. Richard S. Van Wagoner, Smith-Petit Foundation, Salt Lake City, 2009, p. 493)

"Sanctification is a mystery to all and the people are left in mystery. **Get the spirit of revelation and then you will understand what the Lord designs**." (Brigham Young, *The Complete Discourses of Brigham Young*, Vol. 2, 1853 to 1856, Ed. Richard S. Van Wagoner, Smith-Petit Foundation, Salt Lake City, 2009, p. 816)

Orson Pratt

"Nephi says—'I ponder upon the things of God continually which he has revealed unto me,' and there is no harm for us to do the same. We should not get into that old sectarian notion, that we have no right to know anything about this, that or the other, and that we must not pry into this, that or the other.

That is an old sectarian notion, which we have fought against all the day long, and we do not want it to creep into the Church of Jesus Christ of Latter-day Saints. It is the privilege of its members to let their minds expand, and to ponder upon the things of God, and to enquire of him, and by and by, when we have prepared ourselves by getting all the knowledge we possibly can from that which is written, God will give us more." (JD 16:336)

John Taylor

"The Scriptures tell us there are 'Gods many and Lords many. But to us there is but one God, the Father.' (1 Cor., viii, 5.) And for this reason, though there were others engaged in the creation of the worlds, it is given to us in the Bible in the shape that it is; **for the fullness of these truths is only revealed to highly favored persons for certain reasons known to God**; as we are told in the Scriptures: 'The secret of the Lord is with them that fear him; and he will show them his covenant.'—Psalms, 25:14." (*The Mediation And Atonement*, p. 93)

"The philosophers in the world understand something of the rules of natural philosophy; but those rules will never lead a man to the knowledge of God; **if he ever obtains this knowledge it must be by the principle of revelation**. All the works of God, whether on the earth or in the heavens, are constructed on strictly philosophical principles. We understand in part the things of earth; **when we see things as God sees them, we shall then understand the philosophy of the heavens: the mysteries of eternity will be unfolded** and the operations of mind, matter, spirit, purposes and designs, causes and effects and all the stupendous operations of God will be developed and they will be found to accord with the strictest principles of philosophy, even the philosophy of the heavens." (JD 10:117–118)

"…the only reason why we do not comprehend many things that are revealed in former times, is because we are not acquainted with the philosophy of the heavens, nor the laws that govern the intelligences in the eternal worlds. The philosophy of man, of the earth, and of the things with which we are surrounded, is deep—it is abstruse; it is difficult of comprehension even by the most enlightened mind and the most comprehensive and enlarged intellect. One great reason why men have stumbled so frequently in many of their researches after philosophical truth is, that they have sought them with their own wisdom, and gloried in their own intelligence, and have not sought unto God for that wisdom that fills and governs the universe and regulates all things." (JD 11:74)

"We believe that it is necessary for man to be placed in communication with God; that he should have revelation from Him, and that unless he is placed under the influence of the inspiration of the Holy Spirit, he can know nothing about the things of God…he cannot understand certain things without the Spirit of God, and that necessarily introduces the principle I before referred to—the necessity of revelation. Not revelation in former times, but present and immediate revelation, which shall lead and guide those who possess it in all the paths of life here, and to eternal life hereafter…If I can not have a religion that will lead me to God, and place me *en rapport* with him, and unfold to my mind the principles of immortality and eternal life, I want nothing to do with it." (JD 16:371)

Wilford Woodruff

"Well, you say, the President of the Church should give revelation. Yes, it is true, the President holds the keys of revelation to the Latter-day Saints. But is he alone to give revelation? No, verily, no! There is not an Apostle in this Church, there is not an Elder in this Church that stands up in this congregation to teach this people, but should be full of revelation. There is where your revelation should come—from those who teach you day by day. **How many revelations did Brigham Young give that were written to the people? Very few. How many has John Taylor given that were written to the people? Very few. How many has Wilford Woodruff given? Very few. We have had some, though not revealed to the people, perhaps, or published.**" (Brian H. Stuy, ed., *Collected Discourses,* 5 vols. [Burbank, Calif., and Woodland Hills, Ut.: B.H.S. Publishing, 1987–1992], Vol. 2, p. 29)

George Q. Cannon

"The genius of the kingdom with which we are associated is to disseminate knowledge through all the ranks of the people, and to make every man a prophet and every woman a prophetess, that they may understand the plans and purposes of God." (JD 12:46)

"Some men are continually prying into doctrine and trying to reveal mysteries, as President Woodruff referred to this morning about the Godhead and other things. **They want to know a great many mysteries. Now, if we will do that which lies before us we will grow in knowledge, and God will give us revelation upon revelation, and nothing will be concealed from us.**" (Brian H. Stuy, ed., *Collected*

Discourses, 5 vols. [Burbank, Calif., and Woodland Hills, Ut.: B.H.S. Publishing, 1987–1992], Vol. 4:308)

Spencer W. Kimball

"Scripture study is commanded. The Lord is not trifling with us when he gives us these things, for 'unto whomsoever much is given, of him shall be much required.' (Luke 12:48) **Access to these things means responsibility for them**. We must study the scriptures according to the Lord's commandment (see 3 Nephi 23:1–5)

One cannot receive eternal life without becoming a 'doer of the word' (see James 1:22) and being valiant in obedience to the Lord's commandments. And one cannot become a 'doer of the word' without first becoming a 'hearer.' **And to become a 'hearer' is not simply to stand idly by and wait for chance bits of information; it is to seek out and study and pray and comprehend…The Lord's teachings have always been to those who have 'eyes to see' and 'ears to hear.' The voice is clear and unmistakable, and against those who neglect so great an opportunity the witness is sure…**

Understanding requires desire and patience. One's faith can be strengthened by a program involving several elements-by reading the scriptures with a happy frame of mind and desire to absorb additional truth. This reading needs to be done with a constructive attitude-a reaching for truth and a ready acceptance of it. As one reads something which does not for the moment seem to have meaning he can put that item on the shelf and move forward with the reading. In most instances the additional information gained and faith developed seem to provide the background so that the un-understandable item falls naturally into place. If anything seems to counter previous concepts, one can read and study and ponder and pray and wait and usually a clarification comes." (*The Teachings of Spencer W. Kimball,* edited by Edward L. Kimball [Salt Lake City: Bookcraft, 1982], pp. 127–136)

Truman G. Madsen

Oral tradition attributes another wise maxim to the Prophet: "Don't climb to the extreme branches of the tree, for there is danger of falling: cling close to the trunk." One translation: Avoid the vain mysteries and the discussion of them. Avoid imaginative speculation. **But Joseph Smith, one must quickly add, made a distinction between the mysteries of godliness-that is, the deeper things that can only be known by revelation to the soul** on the how of living a godly life-and the speculative pursuit of matters that are without profit to the soul. "I advise all to go on to perfection," he said, "and search deeper and deeper into the mysteries of Godliness." The vain mysteries are those of which we know nothing and need not know anything-whether, for example, the pearly gates swing or roll, or what is the ultimate destiny of the sons of perdition. "Cling close to the trunk." (*Joseph Smith the Prophet* [Salt Lake City: Bookcraft, 1989], p. 104)

Chapter 3

Prayer: The Key to Greater Knowledge

David, King of Israel

"Let **the words of my mouth**, and the meditation of my heart, be acceptable in thy sight, O LORD, my strength, and my redeemer." (Psalms 19:14)

"Hear my prayer, O God; **give ear to the words of my mouth**." (Psalms 54:2)

Joseph Smith

"The best way to obtain truth and wisdom is not to ask it from books, but to go to God in prayer, and obtain divine teachings" (HC 4:425)

"Yea, he that repenteth and exerciseth faith, and bringeth forth good works, and prayeth continually without ceasing—unto such it is given to know the mysteries of God; yea, unto such it shall be given to reveal things which never have been revealed;" (Alma 26:22)

"Having a knowledge of God, we begin to know how to approach him, and **how to ask so as to receive an answer**. When we understand the character of God, **and know how to come to him,** he begins to unfold the heavens to us, and to tell us all about it. When we are ready to come to him, he is ready to come to us." (*Teachings of the Prophet Joseph Smith*, p. 349)

"If thou shalt ask, thou shalt receive revelation upon revelation, knowledge upon knowledge, that thou mayest know the mysteries and peaceable things—that which bringeth joy, that which bringeth life eternal." (D&C 42:61)

"He spoke of delivering the keys of the Priesthood to the Church, and said that the faithful members of the Relief Society should receive them with their husbands, that the Saints whose integrity has been tried and proved faithful, **might know *how to ask the Lord and receive an answer*;**" (*Teachings of the Prophet Joseph Smith*, p. 226. Also see D&C 124:94, 97)

"Therefore, if you will ask of me you shall receive; if you will **knock** it shall be opened unto you...**And if thou wilt inquire, thou shalt know mysteries which are great and marvelous**; therefore thou shalt exercise thy gift, that thou mayest find out mysteries, that thou mayest bring many to the knowledge of the truth, yea, convince them of the error of their ways." (D&C 6:5, 11. Compare with 2 Nephi 4:35)

Brigham Young

"The name that was given to Adam was more ancient than he was. The name Adam was given him because he was the first man, but his new name pertained to the Holy Priesthood and, as I before stated, is more ancient than he was. There are 4 penal signs and 4 penal tokens and should I want to address the throne to enquire after ancient things which transpired on planets that rolled away before this planet came into existence I should use my new name which is ancient and referred to ancient things. Should I wish to enquire for present things I should use my own name which refers to present things. And should I want to enquire for future things I would use the 3rd name which refers to the first token of the Melchizedek Priesthood or is the 3rd token that is given and refers to the Son." (28 December 1845. *Brigham Young Addresses*, Vol. 1, 1836–1849. Edited by Elden J. Watson, p. 87. Also see *The Mysteries of Godliness*, pp. 84–85 for additional information about this topic and references to journal entries by William Clayton and John D. Lee regarding Brigham Young's unique teachings about prayer. Also compare with Job 8:8–10; Alma 9:20; D&C 38:2; 88:41; 93:24; 130:7; Moses 1:6)

Spencer W. Kimball

"I have always loved the story of Enos, who had great need. Like all of us—for none of us is perfect—he had strayed. How dark were his sins I do not know, but he wrote, 'I will tell you of the wrestle which I had before God, before I received a remission of my sins.' The account is graphic and his words impressive: 'Behold, I went to hunt beasts in the forests...' But he took no animals.

He was searching his soul, reaching, knocking, asking, pleading. He was being born again. He would have lived all his life in a weed patch, but now he sought a watered garden...After a lifetime of prayers, I know of the love and power and strength that comes from honest and heartfelt prayer. I know of the readiness of our Father to assist us in our mortal experience, to teach us, to lead us, to guide us. Thus, with great love, our Savior has said, 'What I say unto one I say unto all; pray always.' **If we will do so, we shall gain for ourselves personal knowledge that our Father in Heaven truly hears and answers prayers. This knowledge he wants each of us to have. Seek it, my beloved brothers and sisters! Seek it!**" (*Ensign*, Oct. 1981, pp. 3–6)

"However, it is the sad truth that if prophets and people are unreachable, the Lord generally does nothing for them. Having given them free agency, their Heavenly Father calls, persuades, and directs aright his children, but waits for their **up reaching hands, their solemn prayers, their sincere, dedicated approach to him**. If they are heedless, they are left floundering in midnight's darkness when they could have the noonday sun." (*Ensign*, May 1977, p. 76)

Bruce R. McConkie
"We do not give memorized, ritualistic, or repetitious prayers. We seek the guidance of the Spirit and suit every prayer to the needs of the moment, with no thought of using the same words on successive occasions. But it would be appropriate for us to use words that convey such thoughts as these in our prayers: Father, we ask thee, in the name of Jesus Christ, **to hear the words of our mouth**, to discern with thy all-seeing eye the thoughts and intents of our heart, and to grant us our righteous desires. We feel it is a great privilege to come into thy presence, to bow before thy throne, to address thee as Father; and we know thou wilt hear our cries." (*Ensign*, May 1984, pp. 32–33)

"In this setting, then, seeking to learn and live the law of prayer so that we, like him, can go where he and his Father are, let us summarize what is truly involved in the glorious privilege of approaching the throne of grace. **Let us learn how to do so boldly and efficaciously, not in word only but in spirit and in power**, so that we may pull down upon ourselves, even as he did upon himself, the very powers of heaven." (*Prayer,* [Salt Lake City: Deseret Book Co., 1977], p. 8)

Zebedee Coltrin
"Once Joseph gave notice to the school for all to get up before sunrise, then wash themselves and put on clean clothing and be at the school by sunrise, as it would be a day of revelation and vision. They opened with prayer. Joseph then gave instructions to prepare their minds. He told them to kneel and **pray with uplifted hands. (Brother [Zebedee] Coltrin then gave an account of the appearance of the Father and Son** as given in the minutes of the meeting of the 3rd inst.) Jesus was clothed in modern clothing, apparently of gray cloth…He had seen Joseph giving revelation when he could not look on his face, so full was he (Joseph) of the glory of God, and the house was full of the same glory. About the time the school was first organized some wished to see an angel, and a number joined in the circle and prayed. When the vision came, two of the brethren shrank and called for the vision to close or they would perish; they were Brothers Hancock and Humphries. When the Prophet came in they told him what they had done and he said the angel was no further off than the roof of the house, and a moment more he would have been in their midst. Once after returning from a mission, he [Zebedee Coltrin] met Brother Joseph in Kirtland, who asked him if he did not wish to go with him to a conference at New Portage. The party consisted of Presidents Joseph Smith, Sidney Rigdon, Oliver Cowdery and myself [Zebedee Coltrin]. Next morning at New Portage, he noticed that Joseph seemed to have a far off look in his eyes, or was looking at a distance and presently he, Joseph, stepped between Brothers Cowdery and Coltrin and taking them by the arm, said, 'Let's take a walk.' They went to a place where there was some beautiful grass and

grapevines and swamp beech interlaced. President Joseph Smith then said, 'Let us pray.' **They all three prayed in turn**—Joseph, Oliver, and Zebedee. Brother Joseph then said, '**Now brethren, we will see some visions**.' Joseph lay down on the ground on his back and stretched out his arms and the two brethren lay on them. The heavens gradually opened, and they saw a golden throne, on a circular foundation, something like a light house, and on the throne were two aged personages, having white hair, and clothed in white garments.

They were the two most beautiful and perfect specimens of mankind he ever saw. **Joseph said, 'They are our first parents, Adam and Eve.'** Adam was a large, broad-shouldered man, and Eve as a woman, was a[s] large in proportion. (Brother Coltrin was born September 7th, 1804, and was baptized into the church on the 9th of January, 1831.) Meeting adjourned until 3 o'clock this afternoon." (Zebedee Coltrin, Remarks, Salt Lake City School of Prophets, 11 October 1883, p. 69)

"At one of these meetings after the organization of the school, (the school being organized on the 23rd of January, 1833, when we were all together, Joseph having given instructions, and while engaged in silent prayer, kneeling, **with our hands uplifted** each one praying in silence, no one whispered above his breath, a personage walked through the room **from east to west**, and Joseph asked if we saw him. I saw him and suppose the others did and **Joseph answered that is Jesus**, the Son of God, our elder brother. Afterward Joseph told us to **resume our former position in prayer**, which we did. Another person came through; he was surrounded as with a flame of fire. He (Brother Coltrin) experienced a sensation that it might destroy the tabernacle as it was of consuming fire of great brightness. **The Prophet Joseph said this was the Father of our Lord Jesus Christ**. I saw Him.

When asked about the kind of clothing the Father had on, Brother Coltrin said: I did not discover his clothing for he was surrounded as with a flame of fire, which was so brilliant that I could not discover anything else but his person. I saw his hands, his legs, his feet, his eyes, nose, mouth, head and body in the shape and form of a perfect man. He sat in a chair as a man would sit in a chair, but this appearance was so grand and overwhelming that it seemed I should melt down in his presence, and the sensation was so powerful that it thrilled through my whole system and I felt it in the marrow of my bones. The Prophet Joseph said: **Brethren, now you are prepared to be the apostles of Jesus Christ, for you have seen both the Father and the Son and know that they exist and that they are two separate personages**. This appearance occurred about two or three weeks after the opening of the school. After the Father had passed through, Joseph told us to **again take our positions in prayer**. We did so, and in a very short time **he drew our attention and said to us that Brother Reynolds Cahoon was about to leave us, and told us to look at him**. He (Brother Cahoon) was on his knees and **his arms were extended**, his hands and wrists, head, face and neck down to his shoulders were as a piece of amber, clear and transparent, his blood having apparently left his veins.

Upon the attention of the brethren being thus called to Brother Cahoon, the change seemed to pass away and **Joseph said that in a few minutes more, Brother Cahoon would have left us**, but he came to himself again." (Ibid, pp. 58–60)

William Clayton

"The g[rand] key word was the first word Adam spoke and is a word of supplication. He found the word by the Urim and Thummim—it is that key word to which the heavens [are] opened." (William Clayton, 'Journal,' 15 June 1844, Private Custody. Blaine M. Yorgason, *Spiritual Progression in the Last Days* [Salt Lake City: Deseret Book Co., 1994], p. 263)

Hugh Nibley

When Abraham, according to an old and highly respected source, "rebuilt the altar of Adam in order to bring a sacrifice to the Eternal One," as he had been instructed by an angel, he raised his voice in prayer, saying: "El, El, El! Jaoel! [the last meaning Jehovah]…**receive the words of my prayer**! Receive the sacrifice which I have made at the command! Have mercy, show me, teach me, give to the servant the light and knowledge thou hast promised to send him!" Abraham was following the example of Adam, who prayed to God for three days, repeating three times the prayer: "**May the words of my mouth be heard**! God, do not withdraw thyself from my supplication!…Then an angel of the Lord came with a book, and comforted Adam and taught him." When Adam and Eve found themselves cut off from the glory of the Lord, according to the intriguing Combat of Adam, they stood with **up-stretched hands** calling upon the Lord, as "**Adam began to pray in a language which is unintelligible to us.**"

The so-called Coptic Gnostic Writing purports to give us Adam's words on the occasion as being composed of the elements io-i-a and i-oy-el, meaning "God is with us forever and ever," and "through the power of revelation." The Jewish traditions indicate that the story is no Gnostic invention, though of course mysterious names and cryptograms are the stuff on which human vanity feeds, and every ambitious sectary would come up with his own words and interpretations.

Yet, though none of these writings may be taken as binding or authentic, taken all together they contain common elements which go back as far as the church of the apostles. When Mary asks the Lord "tell me your highest name!" "He, standing in the midst of a cloud of light, said, 'He, Elohe, Elohe, Elohe; Eran, Eran, Eran; Rafon, Rafon, Rafon; Raqon, Raqon, Raqon,'" etc., etc. Such mysteries are just the sort of thing unqualified persons love to play around with, and various Gnostic groups took fullest advantage of them. But again, the Jews are way ahead of them, as we see in the huge catalogues of mysterious angelic names in such works as 3 Epoch.

What H. Leclercq calls **"that magnificent gesture" of raising both hands high above the head** with which those in the prayer circle began their prayer was, as he notes, **a natural gesture both of supplication and submission**. It was specifically a conscious imitation of the crucifixion, and that brings to mind the significant detail, mentioned by the Synoptic writers, that the Lord on the Cross called upon the Father in a strange tongue: those who were standing by, though Aramaic was supposed to be their native tongue, disagreed as to the meaning (see Mark 15:33 ff.), and indeed the Mss give many variant readings of an utterance which the writers of the Gospels left untranslated, plainly because there was some doubt as to the meaning. **It recalls the cry of distress of David in Psalms 54:2: "Hear my prayer, O God; give ear to the words of my mouth**," and on Psalms 55:1: "Give ear to my prayer, O God...Attend unto me, and hear me...My heart is sore pained within me: and the terrors of death are fallen upon me."

F. Preisigke, studying the same gesture among the Egyptians (it is none other than the famous "ka" gesture), notes that it represents submission (the "hands up" position of one surrendering on the battlefield) while at the same time calling the attention of heaven to an offering one has brought in supplication. He also points out **that the early Christians used the same gesture in anticipation of a visitation from heaven, to which they added the idea of the upraised arms of the Savior on the cross**. We have already mentioned the prayers of Adam and Abraham calling upon God in a strange tongue in the midst of darkness and distress.

Abraham, says the Zohar, received no message until he built an altar and brought an offering, "**for there is no stirring above until there is a stirring below**...we do not say grace over an empty table"—or altar. Enoch was another **who as he prayed "stretched forth his arms**, and his heart swilled wide as eternity," and to comfort him God sent him the vision of Noah's salvation. (See Moses 7:41 ff.) According to First Enoch, Noah also prayed in his distress, "**calling upon God three times and saying, Hear me! hear me! hear me!**" Let us also recall that when Mary led the prayer circle of the apostles "**she raised her hands to heaven, and began to call upon the Father in an unknown tongue.**"

Suffering is an important theme of the ancient prayer circle. **The rite is always related to the crucifixion**, according to Pulver, which was anticipated by it in the upper room, for "the care of the Lord's Supper is the idea of sacrifice." In the rites "the believer must incur the same sufferings as his god, and therefore he must mourn with him"—hence the peculiar passage in Matthew 11:16–17. Ignatius' Letter to the Romans shows that "real suffering...alone enables one to become a disciple, to learn and gain experience...For Ignatius, the believer must repeat the destiny of his God, he must become an imitator of God, *mimetes tou Theou.*" This is done ritually, as is plainly stated by Cyril of Jerusalem and the author of the Testament of Jesus Christ, cited above: and thou hast stretched forth thy hands in suffering, that they might be freed from such suffering by an act of imitation. The clearest expression of the idea is given in that archetype and model of all initiates and suppliants, Adam. As he and Eve were sacrificing on an altar "**with arms upraised**," an angel came down to accept the sacrifice, but Satan intervened and smote Adam in the side with the sacrificial weapon. Adam fell upon the altar and would have died were it not that God intervened and healed him on the spot, declaring that what Adam had suffered so far was acceptable to him as a true sacrifice, being in the similitude of his own offering: "**Even so will I be wounded!**"

The prayer asks for light and knowledge as well as other aid, and the answer is a teaching situation. Thus the angels who came down in answer to Adam's three-fold appeal, "**May the words of my mouth be heard!**" etc. "came with a book, and comforted Adam and taught him." Or, in another version, when Adam and Eve prayed at their altar three messengers were sent down to instruct them.

The Lord himself appears to teach Abraham as he is studying the heavens, according to Clement, and the valuable Testament of Abraham begins with his receiving instruction at an altar on a holy mountain, surrounded "by men whom I will show you, how they will form a circle around you, being on the mountain of the altars."

Indeed, the main theme of those many ancient writings called "Testaments," and attributed to almost every patriarch, prophet, and apostle of old, is the **journey of the purported author to heaven** during which he receives lessons in the most advanced theology, history, and astronomy. ("The Early Christian Prayer Circle," *BYU Studies,* Vol. 19 (1978–1979), No. 1—Fall 1978 pp. 52–54. Also see *Mormonism and Early Christianity,* edited by Todd M. Compton and Stephen D. Ricks [Salt Lake City and Provo: Deseret Book Co., Foundation for Ancient Research and Mormon Studies, 1987], 56—61. See the article for the numerous associated footnotes)

Column 297–298. Leaving the glorious garden, they (Adam and Eve) were seized with fear and "they fell down upon the earth and remained as if dead." 299. While Adam was still in that condition, **Eve, stretching high her hands, prayed**: 'O Lord...thy servant has fallen from the Garden' and is banished to a desert place. (Genesis 3:18f.) 307–8. The next morning as **Adam prayed with upraised hands**, Satan appeared to him, saying, "Adam, I am an angel of the great God. The Lord has sent me to you." It was his plan to kill Adam and thus "remain sole master and possessor of the earth."

But God sent three heavenly messengers to Adam bringing him the signs of the priesthood and kingship. 309. **And Adam wept because they reminded him of his departed glory**, but God said they were signs of the atonement to come, whereupon Adam rejoiced. 323–24. After a forty-day fast Adam and Eve were very weak, stretched out upon the floor of the cave as if dead, **but still praying**. Satan then came, clothed with light, speaking sweet words to deceive them saying: "I am the first created of God...now God has commanded me to lead you to my habitation...to be restored to your former glory." 325. But God knew that he planned to lead them to far-away places and destroy them.

Adam said, **Who was this glorious old man who came to us**? Answer: He is Satan in human form come to deceive you by giving you signs to prove his bonafides but I have cast him out. 326. Adam and Eve, still weak from fasting and still praying, are again confronted by Satan who, being rebuffed, "is sore afflicted"...329. Again Adam and Eve were sacrificing **with upraised arms in prayer**, asking God to accept their sacrifice and forgive their sins...330. On the fiftieth day, Adam offering sacrifice as was his custom, Satan appeared in the form of a man and smote him in the side with a sharp stone **even as Adam raised his arms in prayer**.

Eve tried to help him as blood and water flowed on the altar. God...sent his word and revived Adam saying: "Finish thy sacrifice, which is most pleasing to me. For even so will I be wounded and blood and water will come from my side; that will be the true Sacrifice, placed on the alter as a perfect offering."...And so God healed Adam. (*Nibley on the Timely and the Timeless* [Provo: BYU Religious Studies Center, 1978], pp. 15–19. See the article for the numerous associated footnotes.)

Chapter 4

The Second Comforter

Joseph Smith

"Now what is this other Comforter? It is no more nor less than the Lord Jesus Christ Himself; and this is the sum and substance of the whole matter; that when any man obtains this last Comforter, he will have the personage of Jesus Christ to attend him, or appear unto him from time to time, and <u>even He will manifest the Father unto him</u>, and they will take up their abode with him, and the visions of the heavens will be opened unto him, and the Lord will teach him face to face, and he may have a perfect knowledge of the mysteries of the Kingdom of God;" (*Teachings of the Prophet Joseph Smith*, p. 150)

"**Now, there is some grand secret here, and keys to unlock the subject**. Notwithstanding the apostle exhorts them to add to their faith, virtue, knowledge, temperance, etc., yet he exhorts them to make their calling and election sure. And though they had heard an audible voice from heaven bearing testimony that Jesus was the Son of God, **yet he says we have a more sure word of prophecy**, whereunto ye do well that ye take heed as unto a light shining in a dark place. **Now, wherein could they have a more sure word of prophecy than to hear the voice of God saying, This is my beloved Son, etc.**

Now for the secret and grand key. Though they might hear the voice of God and know that Jesus was the Son of God, this would be no evidence that their election and calling was made sure, that they had part with Christ, and were joint heirs with him.

They then would want that more sure word of prophecy, that they were sealed in the heavens and had the promise of eternal life in the kingdom of God. Then, having this promise sealed unto them, it was an anchor to the soul, sure, and steadfast. Though the thunders might roll and lightnings flash, and earthquakes bellow, and war gather thick around, yet this hope and knowledge would support the soul in every hour of trial, trouble, and tribulation. **Then knowledge through our Lord and Savior Jesus Christ is the grand key that unlocks the glories and mysteries of the kingdom of heaven**." (HC 5:388–89)

CHAPTER 5

JOSEPH AND BRIGHAM KNEW MORE THAN THEY COULD TEACH

Joseph Smith

"I could explain a hundred fold more than I ever have of the glories of the kingdoms manifested to me in the vision, were I permitted, and were the people prepared to receive them." (*Teachings of the Prophet Joseph Smith*, p. 305)

"Brethren, if I were to tell you all I know of the Kingdom of God, I do not know that you would rise up and kill me…" (As recalled by Parley P. Pratt in *Millennial Star* 55:585)

"If I was to show the Latter-day Saints all the revelations that the Lord has shown unto me, there is scarce a man that would stay with me, they could not bear it" (Ibid, 13:257)

"The design of the great God in sending us into this world, and organizing us to prepare us for the eternal worlds, I shall keep in my own bosom at present." (HC 5:403. Also see *Teachings of the Prophet Joseph Smith,* p. 30)

"People little know who I am when they talk about me, and they never will know until they see me weighted in the balance in the Kingdom of God. Then they will know who I am, see me as I am. I dare not tell them, and they do not know me." (Zebedee Coltrin quoting Joseph Smith. See *Joseph Smith: The Prophet, The Man,* p. 28)

"Brother Brigham, if I was to reveal to this people what the Lord has revealed to me, there is not a man or woman [that] would stay with me." (Brigham Young quoting Joseph Smith, JD 9:294)

"If I were to reveal the things that God has revealed to me, if I were to reveal to this people the doctrines that I know are for their exaltation, these men would spill my blood." (George A. Smith quoting Joseph Smith, JD 2:217)

"I have asked the Lord to take me away. I have to seal my testimony to this generation with my blood. I have to do it for this work will never progress until I am gone for the testimony is of no force until the testator is dead. People little know who I am when they talk about me, and they never will know until they see me weighed in the balance in the Kingdom of God. Then they will know who I am, and see me as I am. I dare not tell them and they do not know me." (Joseph Smith as quoted by Mary Elizabeth Rollins Lightner, plural wife of the Prophet. "Mary Elizabeth Rollins Lightner," *The Utah Genealogical and Historical Magazine* 17 (July 1926), pp. 193-205, 250)

"'Many men,' said he, 'will say, I will never forsake you, but will stand by you at all times', but the moment you teach them some of the mysteries of the kingdom of God that are retained in the heavens, and are prepared for them, they will be the first to stone you and put you to death. It was this same principle that crucified the Lord Jesus Christ, and will cause the people to kill the prophets in this generation. **Would to God, brethren, I could tell you who I am! Would to God I could tell you what I know! But you would call it blasphemy, and there are men upon this stand who would want to take my life**." (Joseph Smith, Jr., as quoted by Heber C. Kimball, *Life of Heber C. Kimball* by Orson F. Whitney, pp. 322–323)

"But there has been a great difficulty in getting anything into the heads of this generation it has been like splitting hemlock knots with a corn dogger for a wedge & a pumpkin for a beetle, Even [sic] the Saints are slow to understand I have tried for a number of years to get the minds of the saints prepared to receive the things of God, but we frequently see some of them after suffering all they have for the work of God will fly to pieces like glass as soon as anything comes that is contrary to their traditions, they cannot stand the fire at all, How [sic] many will be able to abide a Celestial law & go through & receive their exaltation I am unable to say but many are called & few are chosen." (*The Words of Joseph Smith*, p. 319)

"If I should reveal the things that God has revealed to me, there are some on this stand that would cut my throat or take my hearts blood." (Joseph Robinson quoting Joseph Smith. See *Joseph Smith: The Prophet, The Man,* p. 28)

"The Lord deals with this people as a tender parent with a child, communicating light and intelligence and the knowledge of his ways **as they can bear it**." (HC 5:402)

"If a man gets the fullness of God he has to get [it] in the same way that Jesus obtain[ed] it & that was by keeping all the ordinances of the house of the Lord. Men will say I will never forsake you but will stand by you at all times but the moment you teach them some of the mysteries of God that are retained in the heavens and are to be revealed to the children of men when they are prepared, They will be the first to stone you & put you to death" (*The Words of Joseph Smith*, p. 213)

"Behold, he hath heard my cry by day, and he hath given me knowledge by visions in the nighttime. And by day have I waxed bold in mighty prayer before him; yea, my voice have I sent up on high; and angels came down and ministered unto me. And upon the wings of his Spirit hath my body been carried away upon exceedingly high mountains. **And mine eyes have beheld great things, yea, even too great for man; therefore I was bidden that I should not write them.**" (2 Nephi 4:23–25)

"I will from time to time reveal to you the subjects that are revealed by the Holy Ghost to me." (HC 6:366)

"And no tongue can speak, neither can there be written by any man, neither can the hearts of men conceive so great and marvelous things as we both saw and heard Jesus speak; and no one can conceive of the joy which filled our souls at the time we heard him pray for us unto the Father." (3 Nephi 17:17)

"But great and marvelous are the works of the Lord, and the mysteries of his kingdom which he showed unto us, which surpass all understanding in glory, and in might, and in dominion; Which he commanded us we should not write while we were yet in the Spirit, and are not lawful for man to utter; Neither is man capable to make them known, for they are only to be seen and understood by the power of the Holy Spirit, which God bestows on those who love him, and purify themselves before him; To whom he grants this privilege of seeing and knowing for themselves; That through the power and manifestation of the Spirit, while in the flesh, they may be able to bear his presence in the world of glory." (D&C 76:114–118)

"And when they shall have received this, which is expedient that they should have first, to try their faith, and if it shall so be that they shall believe these things then shall the greater things be made manifest unto them. And if it so be that they will not believe these things, then shall the greater things be withheld from them, unto their condemnation. Behold, I was about to write them, all which were engraven upon the plates of Nephi, but the Lord forbade it, saying: I will try the faith of my people." (3 Nephi 26:9–11)

"God shall give unto you knowledge by his Holy Spirit, yea, by the unspeakable gift of the Holy Ghost, that has not been revealed since the world was until now; Which our forefathers have awaited with anxious expectation **to be revealed in the last times**, which their minds were pointed to by the angels, as held in reserve for the fullness of their glory; **A time to come in the which nothing shall be withheld**, whether there be one God or many gods, they shall be manifest." (D&C 121:26–28)

"Behold, ye are little children and ye cannot bear all things now; ye must grow in grace and in the knowledge of truth." (D&C 50:40)

"Behold, I have written upon these plates the very things which the brother of Jared saw; and there never were greater things made manifest than those which were made manifest unto the brother of Jared.

Wherefore the Lord hath commanded me to write them; and I have written them. And he commanded me that I should seal them up; and he also hath commanded that I should seal up the interpretation thereof; wherefore I have sealed up the interpreters, according to the commandment of the Lord. For the Lord said unto me: **They shall not go forth unto the Gentiles until the day that they shall repent of their iniquity, and become clean before the Lord**. And in that day that they shall exercise faith in me, saith the Lord, even as the brother of Jared did, that they may become sanctified in me, **then will I manifest unto them the things which the brother of Jared saw, even to the unfolding unto them all my revelations**, saith Jesus Christ, the Son of God, the Father of the heavens and of the earth, and all things that in them are." (Ether 4:4–7)

"The people cannot bear the revelations that the Lord has for them. There were a great many revelations if the people could bear them." (Brigham Young quoting Joseph Smith. JD 18:242)

"But I beg leave to say unto you, brethren, that ignorance, superstition and bigotry placing itself where it ought not, is oftentimes in the way of the prosperity of this Church; like the torrent of rain from the mountains, that floods the most pure and crystal stream with mire, and dirt, and filthiness, and obscures everything that was clear before, and all rushes along in one general deluge; but time weathers tide; and notwithstanding we are rolled in the mire of the flood for the time being, the next surge peradventure, as time rolls on, may bring to us the fountain as clear as crystal, and as pure as snow; while the filthiness, flood wood and rubbish is left and purged out by the way." (HC 3:296–297)

"It is my meditation all the day & more than my meat & drink to know how I shall make the saints of God to comprehend the visions that roll like an overflowing surge, before my mind. O how I would delight to bring before you things which you never thought of, but poverty & the cares of the world prevent. but [sic] I am glad I have the privilege of communicating to you some things, which if grasped closely will be a help to you when the clouds are gathering & the storms are ready to burst upon you like peals of thunder. lay [sic] hold of these things & let not your knees tremble. nor [sic] your hearts faint." (*The Words of Joseph Smith*, p. 196)

"I will also remark that I am sensible that **no man can speak to a congregation of people upon any subject, only according to the intelligence that is in the people**. There are quite a number of this congregation who knew Joseph Smith the Prophet, and he used to say in Nauvoo that when he came before the people he felt as though he were enclosed in an iron case, his mind was closed by the influences that were thrown around him; he was curtailed in his wishes and desires to do good; there was no room for him to expand, hence he could not make use of the revelations of God as he would have done; **there was no room in the hearts of the people to receive the glorious truths of the Gospel that God revealed to him**." (JD 10:233–234. Heber C. Kimball talking about Joseph Smith.)

"I never have had opportunity to give them the plan that God has revealed to me." (*The Personal Writings of Joseph Smith*, March 15, 1839, pp. 386–387)

"Without a revelation, I am not going to give them the knowledge of the God of Heaven." (HC 6:475)

"Would to God that I had forty days and nights in which to tell you all!" (HC 6:313)

"You don't know me; you never knew my heart. No man knows my history. I cannot tell it: I shall never undertake it." (HC 6:317)

"I wish I could speak for three or four hours…I would still go on, and show you proof upon proofs." (HC 6:479)

"Some people say I am a fallen Prophet, because I do not bring forth more of the word of the Lord. **Why did I not do it? Are we able to receive it? No! not one in this room.**" (HC 4:478)

Brigham Young

"But I would not dare tell you all I know about these matters." (JD 8:208)

"I could tell you much more about this; but were I to tell you the whole truth, <u>blasphemy would be nothing to it</u>, in the estimation of the superstitious and over-righteous of mankind. However, I have told you the truth as far as I have gone." (JD 1:50–51)

"**The life that is within us** is a **part** of an **eternity of life**, and is organized spirit, which is clothed upon by tabernacles, thereby constituting our present being, which is designed for the attainment of further intelligence. The matter composing our bodies and spirits has been organized from the eternity of matter that fills immensity. **Were I to fully speak what I know and understand concerning myself and others, you might think me to be infringing. I shall therefore omit some things that I would otherwise say to you if the people were prepared to receive them.**" (JD 7:285)

"It is said to be eternal life, 'to know the only wise God, and Jesus Christ whom He has sent.' I will tell you one thing, as brother Hyde has said, it would be an excellent plan for us to go to work and find out ourselves, <u>for as sure as you find out yourselves, you will find out God</u>, whether you are Saint or sinner. A man cannot find out himself without the light of revelation; he has to turn round and seek to the Lord his God, in order to find out himself. <u>If you find out who Joseph was, you will know as much about God as you need to at present</u>; for if He said, 'I am a God to this people,' He did not say that He was the only wise God. Jesus was a God to the people when he was upon earth, was so before he came to this earth, and is yet. Moses was a God to the children of Israel, and in this manner you may go right back to Father Adam." (JD 4:271)

"I will now say to my brethren and sisters, that while we were in Winter Quarters, the Lord gave to me a revelation just as much as he ever gave one to anybody. He opened my mind, and showed me the organization of the kingdom of God in a family capacity. I talked it to my brethren; I would throw it out a few words here, and a few words there, to my first counselor, to my second counselor and the Twelve Apostles, but with the exception of one or two of the Twelve, it would not touch a man.

They believed it would come, O yes, but it would be by and by. Says I, 'Why not now?' If I had been worth millions when we came into this valley and built what we now call the 'Old Fort,' **I would have given it if the people had been prepared to then receive the kingdom of God according to the pattern given to Enoch. But I could not touch them**." (JD 18:244)

"You need exhorting rather than teaching. You have been taught doctrine in abundance, and I have sometimes thought it a pity the Lord has revealed quite as much as he has. And I can truly say that I believe, if I am guilty in any one point in my walk before this people, it is in telling them things they are not worthy of—that I have given unto them things that they could not receive. For this reason I deem it mainly needful to stir up your pure minds by way of remembrance." (JD 7:238)

"There are other revelations, besides this (meaning the one on war), not yet published to the world. In the due time of the Lord, the Saints and the world will be privileged with the revelations that are due them. They now have many more than they are worthy of, for they do not observe them. The Gentile nations have had more of the revelations of God than is their just due. And I will say, as I have before said, if guilt before my God and my brethren rests upon me in the least, it is in this one thing—that I have revealed too much concerning God and His Kingdom, and the designs of our Father in heaven. If my skirts are stained in the least with wrong, it is because I have been too free in telling what God is, how he lives, the nature of his providences and designs in creating the world, in bringing forth the human family on the earth, his designs concerning them, etc. If I had, like Paul, said—'But if any man be ignorant, let him be ignorant,' perhaps it would have been better for the people...when a truth is presented to an intelligent person he ought to grasp it and receive it in his faith. There are revelations, wisdom, knowledge, and understanding yet to be proclaimed, and whether they will please the world, or not, is immaterial to me." (*Deseret News*, June 27, 1860; JD 8:58–59)

"How much unbelief exists in the minds of the Latter-day Saints in regard to one particular doctrine which I revealed to them, and which God revealed to me—namely that Adam is our father and God...I told the people that if they would not believe the revelations that God had given he would suffer the devil to give revelations that they—priests and people—would follow after...Have I seen this fulfilled? I have. I told the people that as true as God lived. If they would not have truth they would have error sent unto them, and they would believe it. What is the mystery of it?" (*Deseret Weekly News* 22:308–309, June 18, 1873)

"**...for the heavens have been opened to my views**..." (Brigham Young, *The Complete Discourses of Brigham Young*, Vol. 1, 1832 to 1852, Ed. Richard S. Van Wagoner, Smith-Petit Foundation, Salt Lake City, 2009. p. 354).

Chapter 6

On the Potter's Wheel

David, King of Israel

"Thou shalt break them with a rod of iron; thou shalt dash them in pieces like a potter's vessel." (Psalms 2:9)

Isaiah

"But now, O LORD, thou art our father; **we are the clay, and thou our potter**; and we all are the work of thy hand." (Isaiah 64:8)

Jeremiah

"The word which came to Jeremiah from the LORD, saying, Arise, and go down to the potter's house, and there I will cause thee to hear my words. Then I went down to the potter's house, and, behold, he wrought a work on the wheels. And the vessel that he made of clay was marred in the hand of the potter: so he made it again another vessel, as seemed good to the potter to make it. Then the word of the LORD came to me, saying, O house of Israel, cannot I do with you as this potter? saith the LORD. Behold, as the clay is in the potter's hand, so are ye in mine hand, O house of Israel." (Jeremiah 18:2–6)

Brigham Young

"The Lord said to Jeremiah the Prophet, 'Arise, and go down to the potter's house, and there I will cause thee to hear my words. Then I went down to the potter's house, and, behold, he wrought a work on the wheels. And the vessel that he made of clay was marred in the hands of the potter: so he made it again another vessel, as seemed good to the potter to make it.'

The clay that marred in the potter's hands was thrown back into the unprepared portion, **to be prepared over again**. So it will be with every wicked man and woman, and every wicked nation, kingdom, and government upon earth, sooner or later; **they will be thrown back to the native element from which they originated, to be worked over again**, and be prepared to enjoy some sort of a kingdom." (JD 2:124)

"If I am like a piece of clay, passive in the hands of the potter, the Lord can do something with me; **but if I am like a rude stiff lump of clay, I must be ground over again**." (*The Complete Discourses of Brigham*

Young, Vol. 1, 1832 to 1852, Ed. Richard S. Van Wagoner, Smith-Petit Foundation, Salt Lake City, 2009. p. 96).

Heber C. Kimball
"Elder Heber C. Kimball preached at the house of President Joseph Smith, on the parable in the 18th chapter of Jeremiah, of the clay in the hands of the potter, that when it marred in the hands of the potter it was cut off the wheel and then thrown back again into the mill, to go into the next batch, and was a vessel of dishonor; but all clay that formed well in the hands of the potter, and was pliable, was a vessel of honor; and thus it was with the human family, and ever will be: all that are pliable in the hands of God and are obedient to His commands, are vessels of honor, and God will receive them. **President Joseph arose and said —'Brother Kimball has given you a true explanation of the parable…'**" (Minutes of a meeting of the Twelve in the house of the Prophet. HC 4:478)

"Upon the same principle, supposing I have a lump of clay which I put upon my wheel, out of which clay I want to make a jug; I have to turn it into as many as 50 or 100 shapes before I get it into a jug. How many shapes do you suppose you are put into before you became Saints, or before you become perfect and sanctified to enter into the celestial glory of God? You have got to be like that clay in the hands of the potter. Do you not know that the Lord directed the Prophet anciently, to go down to the potter's house to see a miracle on the wheel?

Suppose the potter takes a lump of clay, and putting it on the wheel, goes to work to form it into a vessel, and works it out this way, and that way, and the other way, but the clay is refractory and snappish; he still trys it, but it will break, and snap, and snarl, and thus the potter will work it and work it until he is satisfied he cannot bring it into the shape he wants, and it mars upon the wheel; he takes his tool, then, and cuts it off the wheel, and throws it into the mill to be ground over again, until it becomes passive, (don't you think you will go to hell if you are not passive?) **and after it is ground there so many days, and it becomes passive, he takes the same lump, and makes of it a vessel unto honor.**

Now do you see into that, brethren? I know the potters can. I tell you, brethren, if you are not passive you will have to go into that mill, and perhaps have to grind there one thousand years, and then the Gospel will be offered to you again, and then if you will not accept of it, and become passive, you will have to go into the mill again, and thus you will have offers of salvation from time to time, until all the human family, except the sons of perdition, are redeemed. The spirits of men will have the Gospel as we do, and they are to be judged according to men in the flesh. Let us be passive, and take a course that will be perfectly submissive." (JD 1:161)

Chapter 7

Again

David, King of Israel

"Thou, which hast shewed me great and sore troubles, shalt quicken me **again,** and shalt bring me up **again** from the depths of the earth." (Psalms 71:20)

Apostle Matthew

"From that time forth began Jesus to shew unto his disciples, how that he must go unto Jerusalem, and suffer many things of the elders and chief priests and scribes, and be killed, and be raised **again** the third day." (Matthew 16:21)

"But after I am **risen again**, I will go before you into Galilee." (Matthew 26:32)

Apostle John

"…I lay down my life, that I might **take it again**. No man taketh it from me, but I lay it down of myself. I have power to lay it down, and I have power to **take it again**." (John 10:17–18)

"**But in the days of the voice of the seventh angel, when he shall begin to sound, the mystery of God should be finished,** as he hath declared to his servants the prophets. And the voice which I heard from heaven spake unto me again, and said, Go *and* take the little book which is open in the hand of the angel which standeth upon the sea and upon the earth. And I went unto the angel, and said unto him, Give me the little book. And he said unto me, Take *it,* and eat it up; and it shall make thy belly bitter, but it shall be in thy mouth sweet as honey. And I took the little book out of the angel's hand, and ate it up; and it was in my mouth sweet as honey: and as soon as I had eaten it, my belly was bitter. And he said unto me, Thou must prophesy **again** before many peoples, and nations, and tongues, and kings." (Revelation 10:7–11)

For other "**again**" scriptures from the New Testament see: Acts 13:33, 37, 17:3; I Corinthians 15:4, II Corinthians 5:15, I Thessalonians 4:14, Matthew 17:9, 23; Romans 4:25, 8:34.

Joseph Smith

"And inasmuch as he is faithful, **I will crown him again** with sheaves." (D&C 79:3)

"And he hath risen **again** from the dead, that he might bring all men unto him, on conditions of repentance." (D&C 18:11–12)

"He suffered temptations but gave no heed unto them. He was crucified, died, and rose **again** the third day;" (D&C 20:22–23)

"If so, wo shall come upon you; but if not so, then cast about your eyes and begin to believe in the Son of God, that he will come to redeem his people, and that he shall suffer and die to atone for their sins; and that he shall rise **again** from the dead, which shall bring to pass the resurrection, that all men shall stand before him, to be judged at the last and judgment day, according to their works." (Alma 33:22)

"Know ye that ye must come to the knowledge of your fathers, and repent of all your sins and iniquities, and believe in Jesus Christ, that he is the Son of God, and that he was slain by the Jews, and by the power of the Father he hath risen **again**, whereby he hath gained the victory over the grave; and also in him is the sting of death swallowed up." (Mormon 7:5)

"God has revealed His Son from the heavens and the doctrine of the resurrection also; and we have a knowledge that **those we bury here God will bring up again**, clothed upon and quickened by the Spirit of the great God; and what mattereth it whether we lay them down, or we lay down with them, when we can keep them no longer? Let these truths sink down in our hearts, that we may even here begin to enjoy that which shall be in full hereafter." (HC 5:362)

"The Lord takes many away, even in infancy, that they may escape the envy of man, and the sorrows and evils of this present world; they were too pure, too lovely, to live on earth; therefore, if rightly considered, instead of mourning we have reason to rejoice as they are delivered from evil, and **we shall soon have them again**." (HC 4:553)

Parley P. Pratt

"Again. In order to enable these organized spirits to take upon them a fleshy tabernacle, physical worlds, with their variety and fullness, would be necessary for their homes, food, clothing, &c., that they might be begotten, sustained, and born, that they might live, die, **and rise again to receive their inheritances on their respective earths**." (Parley P. Pratt, Origin of the Universe, in the *Essential Parley P. Pratt*, p. 195)

Chapter 8

From Grace to Grace, From Exaltation to Exaltation

Apostle Paul

"But we all, with open face beholding as in a glass the glory of the Lord, **are changed into the same image from glory to glory**, *even* as by the Spirit of the Lord." (2 Corinthians 3:18)

Joseph Smith

"God himself was once as we are now, and is an exalted man, and sits enthroned in yonder heavens! That is the great secret…We have imagined and supposed that God was God from all eternity. I will refute that idea, and take away the veil, so that you may see. These are incomprehensible ideas to some, but they are simple. It is the first principle of the Gospel to know for a certainty the Character of God, and to know that we may converse with him as one man converses with another, and that **he was once a man like us; yea, that God himself, the father of us all, dwelt on an earth, the same as Jesus Christ** himself did; and I will show it from the Bible…

The scriptures inform us that Jesus said, as the Father hath power in himself, even so hath the son power —to do what? Why what the Father did. The answer is obvious —in a manner to lay down his body and take it up again. Jesus, what are you going to do? To lay down my life as my Father did, and take it up again. Do you believe it? If you do not believe it you do not believe the Bible. The scriptures say it, and I defy all the learning and wisdom and all the combined powers of earth and hell together to refute it. Here, then, is eternal life —to know the only wise and true God; and you have got to learn how to be gods yourselves, and to be kings and priests to God, the same as all gods have done before you, namely, by going from one small degree to another, and from a small capacity to a great one; from grace to grace, from exaltation to exaltation, <u>until</u> you attain to the resurrection of the dead, and are able to dwell in everlasting burnings, and to sit in glory, as do those who sit enthroned in everlasting power. And, I want you to know that God, in the last days, while certain individuals are proclaiming his name, is not trifling with you or me…What did Jesus Do? 'Why I do the things I saw my father do when worlds came rolling into existence, my Father worked out His kingdom with fear and trembling, and I must do the same; and when I get my kingdom, I shall present it to my father so that He may obtain kingdom upon kingdom, an it will exalt Him in glory, He will then take a higher exaltation, and I will take His place, and thereby become exalted myself.'

So that Jesus treads in the tracks of His father, and inherits what God did before; and God is thus glorified and exalted in the salvation and exaltation of all His children. It is plain beyond disputation, and you thus learn the First Principles of the Gospel, about which so much has been said. When you climb up a ladder, you must begin at the bottom, and ascend step by step, until you arrive at the top...It is not all to be comprehended in this world; it will be a great work to learn our salvation and exaltation even beyond the grave." (Excerpts from the King Follett Discourse, *Teachings of the Prophet Joseph Smith*, pp. 345–348)

"And I, John, bear record that I beheld his glory, as the glory of the Only Begotten of the Father, full of grace and truth, even the Spirit of truth, which came and dwelt in the flesh, and dwelt among us. And I, John, saw that **he received not of the fullness at the first, but received grace for grace; And he received not of the fullness at first, but continued from grace to grace, until he received a fullness**; And thus he was called the Son of God, because he received not of the fullness at the first." (D&C 93:11–14)

Brigham Young

"With regard to the ordinances of God, we may remark that we yield obedience to them because he requires it; and every iota of his requirements has a rational philosophy with it. We do not get up things on a hypothesis. That philosophy reaches to all eternity, and is the philosophy that the Latter-day Saints believe in. Every particle of truth that every person has received is a gift of God. **We receive these truths, and go on from glory to glory, <u>from eternal lives to eternal lives</u>, gaining a knowledge of all things**, and becoming Gods, even Sons of God. These are the celestial ones. These are they whom the Lord has chosen through their obedience. They have not spurned the truth, when they have heard it. These are they that have not spurned the Gospel, but have acknowledged Jesus and God in their true character; that have acknowledged the angels in their true character. These are they that work for the salvation of the human family." (*Discourses of Brigham Young,* selected and arranged by John A. Widtsoe [Salt Lake City: Deseret Book Co., 1954], p. 152. JD 19:50)

"To finite capacity there is much which appears mysterious in the plan of salvation, and there is an eternity of mystery to be unfolded to us; and when we have lived millions of years in the presence of God and angels, and have associated with heavenly beings, **shall we then cease learning? No, or eternity ceases. There is no end. We go from grace to grace, from light to light, from truth to truth**." (JD 6:344)

Neal A. Maxwell

"Just as we can move, step by step, **from faith to knowledge**, so in particular dimensions of living, such as in justice or honesty, some mortals have merited the accolades of prophets 'in that thing.' Significantly, when such spiritually advanced individuals were described as perfect, often their 'justness' was the virtue cited. Little wonder justice is so stressed, in view of this verse: 'He hath shewed thee, O man, what is good; and what doth the Lord require of thee, but to do justly, and to love mercy, and to walk humbly with thy God?' It is clear too that being just not only consists of fair play with one's associates and neighbors, but also reflects **largeness of soul**. In this broadened sense, 'there is not a just man upon earth, that doeth good, and sinneth not.' Jesus Himself did not receive 'of the fullness at first,' but continued 'from grace to grace, until he received a fullness.' **His progress was incomprehensibly more rapid than ours, but the pathway is the same; so can be the pattern of 'grace to grace': 'For behold, thus saith the Lord God: I will give unto the children of men line upon line, precept upon precept, here a little and there a little; and blessed are those who hearken unto my precepts, and lend an ear unto my counsel, for they shall learn wisdom.'"** (*Even As I Am* [Salt Lake City: Deseret Book Co., 1982], p. 15)

"Whether as a spirit son or a spirit daughter of our Heavenly Father, each of us was sent here from our first estate to undergo this joyful yet stressful mortal second estate. Being the literal, premortal spirit children of the Father, each of us can, **by going from grace to grace, eventually receive of the fulness of the Father, as did Jesus** (see D&C 93:20)." (*A Wonderful Flood of Light* [Salt Lake City: Bookcraft, 1990], p. 36)

Dallin H. Oaks

"Perfect worship is emulation. We honor those whom we imitate. The most perfect way of worship is **to be holy as Jehovah is holy**. It is **to be pure as Christ is pure**. It is to do the things that enable us to become like the Father. The course is one of obedience, of living by every word that proceedeth from the mouth of God, of keeping the commandments. How do we worship the Lord? We do it by **going from grace to grace, until we receive the fulness of the Father and are glorified in light and truth as is the case with our Pattern and Prototype, the Promised Messiah**. In the remarkable revelation known as section 93 of the Doctrine and Covenants, the Lord revealed a portion of the truths recorded in the record of John. The Lord explained that he gave this knowledge to his children in this dispensation 'that you may understand and know how to worship, and know what you worship' (D&C 93:19). John recorded the premortal existence of Christ, his role in the creation, his mortal ministry, and his continuing 'from grace to grace, until he received a fulness' (D&C 93:13). John then bore record that the Only Begotten of the Father 'received a fulness of the glory of the Father,' including 'all power, both in heaven and on earth' (D&C 93:16–17).

This knowledge of the exaltation of the Son tells us 'what' we worship. It also tells us 'how' to worship and why we worship: 'That you may come unto the Father in my name, **and in due time receive of his fulness**. For if you keep my commandments you shall receive of his fulness, and be glorified in me as I am in the Father; therefore, I say unto you, you shall receive grace for grace.' (D&C 93:19–20) In truth, as God revealed to his prophet, Moses, 'This is my work and my glory —to bring to pass the immortality and eternal life of man' (Moses 1:39). That is the object and end of worship." (*Pure in Heart* [Salt Lake City: Bookcraft, 1988], p. 135)

Truman G. Madsen

Are you aware that in one experience the Prophet had, the Master approached him and said, in substance, "Joseph, I want you to read this. Then I want to tell you why I want you to read it. It is something John wrote about me." What does it say ? It says something which is blasphemy in relation to the creeds of Christendom. Therefore, so much the worse for the creeds. It says, "**He [Christ] received not of the fulness at the first.**" **He was not always God. He became what He became—and it says it three times**. (D&C 93:12, 13, 14) **But He was called the Son of God because he received not of the fulness at the first, but "continued from grace to grace until he received a fulness.**" (Truman G. Madsen, November 16, 1965, BYU Speeches of the Year, 1965, p. 5)

Susan Easton Black

The role played by grace in the process through which the Lord received a fulness of the glory of the Father was twofold: he received grace for grace, and he went from grace to grace. But what does it mean to receive grace for grace and to go from grace to grace? The answer lies in the very nature of grace. **The word denotes favor, kindness, and goodwill. Out of this comes the theological definition: "the free unmerited love and favor of God," which brings divine assistance to his chosen ones. The key expressions here are love and favor, and unmerited assistance. To receive grace for grace is to receive assistance on the condition of giving assistance. But not just any kind of assistance can be given. What transforms assistance into grace is the kindness and favor felt by the giver which is extended to the receiver, when such service is totally unmerited**. But grace does not have to be given without condition. Indeed, an important aspect of the word is reciprocity.

The scripture states specifically that man receives "grace for grace." (D&C 93:20) Thus, the extension of favor is meant to obligate the recipient so that he will extend the same. As he meets this condition, more grace is extended to him, which further obligates him to greater assistance of others. The possession of light and truth allows one to forsake the evil one and to be protected against his machinations. Further, light and truth enable their recipient to progress toward a fulness of the glory of God. This was the case with the Lord. Through his benevolence he received grace. Additional powers of light and truth were continually being extended to him such that he went from grace to grace. **In other words, he went from one power level to another, from one capacity to a greater, <u>until</u> he received a fulness of the Father**. (Susan Easton Black et al., *Doctrines for Exaltation: The 1989 Sperry Symposium on the Doctrine and Covenants* [Salt Lake City: Deseret Book Co., 1989], pp. 37–39)

Richard O. Cowan

How do we receive "grace for grace" and then continue "from grace to grace"? John testified that we have received of God's fullness "grace for grace" (John 1:16). That phrase may have several meanings. The dictionary in the LDS edition of the Bible defines *grace* as "divine means of help or strength." Perhaps John means that we receive this help "for," or because of, God's goodness and power. The Jerusalem Bible's translation states that "we have, all of us, received—one gift replacing another," the gospel of Christ replacing the law of Moses (p. 1243). The New International Version translates this message in John as, "We have all received one blessing after another" (p. 1593). Latter-day Saint scholar Richard Draper has suggested another possibility. "**To receive grace for grace is to receive assistance on the condition of giving assistance**." "Apparently, it was necessary for the Lord to grow through this process. In order to do so, he first received grace, or divine assistance from the Father. This grace he extended to his brethren. As he did so he received even more grace. The process continued until he eventually received a fulness of the glory of the Father" ('Light, Truth, and Grace,' 37–38) Significantly, we too must receive "grace for grace" (D&C 93:20). Once we have begun receiving God's gifts, **our challenge is to ascend "from grace to grace," or from one gift to another**. Through continued righteousness we progress from one level of holiness to another until we receive a fulness of Godlike attributes. (D&C 93:29–33) (Richard O. Cowan, *Answers to Your Questions About the Doctrine and Covenants* [Salt Lake City: Deseret Book Co., 1996], pp. 114–115)

Chapter 9

Eternal Progression—Eternal Lives

David, King of Israel

"**He brought me up also out of an horrible pit**, out of the miry clay, **and set my feet upon a rock**, *and* established my goings. 3 And he hath put a new song in my mouth, *even* praise unto our God: many shall see *it*, and fear, and shall trust in the LORD." (Psalms 40:2–3)

"*Thou*, which hast shewed me great and sore troubles, shalt quicken me <u>again</u>, and shalt bring me up <u>again</u> from the depths of the earth." (Psalms 71:20)

"They shall perish, but thou shalt endure: yea, all of them shall wax old like a garment; **as a vesture shalt thou change them, and they shall be changed**:" (Psalms 102:26)

"Quicken me, O LORD, for thy name's sake: for thy righteousness' sake bring my soul out of trouble." (Psalms 143:11)

Isaiah

"Behold, **I will make thee a new sharp threshing instrument** having teeth: thou shalt thresh the mountains, and beat *them* small, and shalt make the hills as chaff." (Isaiah 41:15)

Jeremiah

"Alas! for that day is great, so that none is like it: it is even the time of Jacob's trouble; but he shall be saved out of it. For it shall come to pass in that day, saith the LORD of hosts, that I will break his yoke from off thy neck, and will burst thy bonds, and strangers shall no more serve themselves of him: But they shall serve the LORD their God, and **David their king, whom I will raise up unto them**." (Jeremiah 30:7–9)

Ezekiel

"And I will set up one shepherd over them, and he shall feed them, *even* **my servant David; he shall feed them, and he shall be their shepherd**. And I the LORD will be their God, and my servant David a prince among them; I the LORD have spoken *it*." (Ezekiel 34:23–24)

"**And David my servant *shall be* king over them**; and they all shall have one shepherd: they shall also walk in my judgments, and observe my statutes, and do them. And they shall dwell in the land that I have given unto Jacob my servant, wherein your fathers have dwelt; and they shall dwell therein, *even* they, and their children, and their children's children for ever: **and my servant David *shall be* their prince for ever**." (Ezekiel 37:24–25)

Daniel

"And he said, Go thy way Daniel: for the words are closed up and sealed until the time of the end…But go thou thy way till the end be: for thou shalt rest, and stand in thy lot at the end of the days." (Daniel 12:9–13)

The New English version gives a different rendering of that last verse: "But go your way to the end and rest, and you shall arise to your destiny at the end of the age."

Mark

"After that **he (Christ) appeared in another form** unto two of them, as they walked, and went into the country." (Mark 16:12)

Luke

"And Simeon blessed them, and said unto Mary his mother, Behold, this *child* is set for **the fall and rising again** of many in Israel; and for a sign which shall be spoken against;" (Luke 2:34)

Apostle John

"**To him that overcometh** will I grant to sit with me in my throne, **even as I also overcame**, and am sat down with the Father in his throne." (Revelation 3:21)

"Verily, verily, I say unto you, If a man keep my saying, **he shall never see death**." (John 8:51)

"Verily, verily, I say unto you, Except a corn of wheat fall into the ground and die, it abideth alone: **but if it die, it bringeth forth much fruit**." (John 12:24)

Apostle Paul

"Others were tortured not accepting deliverance; **that they might obtain a better resurrection**." (Hebrews 11:35)

"**For I was alive without the law once**: but when the commandment came, sin revived, and I died." (Romans 7:9)

But some *man* will say, **How are the dead raised up? and with what body do they come?** *Thou* fool, that which thou sowest is not quickened, except it die: And that which thou sowest, thou sowest not that body that shall be, **but bare grain**, it may chance of wheat, or of some other *grain:* But God giveth it a body as it hath pleased him, and **to every seed his own body**. (1 Corinthians 15:35–38)

For in this we groan, earnestly desiring to be clothed upon with our house which is from heaven: (2 Corinthians 5:2)

Joseph Smith

"**This is eternal lives**—to know the only wise and true God, and Jesus Christ, whom he hath sent." (D&C 132:24)

"For he that diligently seeketh shall find; and the mysteries of God shall be unfolded unto them, by the power of the Holy Ghost, as well in these times as in times of old, and as well in times of old as in times to come; wherefore, the course of the Lord is **one eternal round**." (1 Nephi 10:19)

"I perceive that it has been made known unto you, by the testimony of his word, that he cannot walk in crooked paths; neither doth he vary from that which he hath said; neither hath he a shadow of turning from the right to the left, or from that which is right to that which is wrong; therefore, **his course is one eternal round**." (Alma 7:20)

"And it may suffice if I only say they are preserved for a wise purpose, which purpose is known unto God; for he doth counsel in wisdom over all his works, and his paths are straight, and **his course is one eternal round**." (Alma 37:12)

"For God doth not walk in crooked paths, neither doth he turn to the right hand nor to the left, neither doth he vary from that which he hath said, therefore his paths are straight, and **his course is one eternal round**." (D&C 3:2)

"Listen to the voice of the Lord your God, even Alpha and Omega, the beginning and the end, **whose course is one eternal round**, the same today as yesterday, and forever." (D&C 35:1)

"And inasmuch as he is faithful, I will **crown him again** with sheaves." (D&C 79:3)

"Let no man be afraid to lay down his life for my sake; for whoso layeth down his life for my sake **shall find it again**." (D&C 103:27)

"For whoso is faithful unto the obtaining these two priesthoods of which I have spoken, and the magnifying their calling, are sanctified by the Spirit unto **the renewing of their bodies**." (D&C 84:33)

"And Abram said, Lord God, how wilt thou give me this land for an everlasting inheritance? 10 And the Lord said, Though thou wast dead, yet am I not able to give it thee? 11 **And if thou shalt die, yet thou shalt possess it**, for the day cometh, that the Son of man shall live; **but how can he live if he be not dead? he must first be quickened**." (JST Genesis 15:9–11)

"But behold, thus saith the Lord God: When the day cometh that they shall believe in me, that I am Christ, then have I covenanted with their fathers that **they shall be restored in the flesh, upon the earth**, unto the lands of their inheritance." (2 Nephi 10:7)

"For, said he, I have repented of my sins, and have been redeemed of the Lord; behold I am born of the Spirit. 25 And the Lord said unto me: Marvel not that all mankind, yea, men and women, all nations, kindreds, tongues and people, **must be born again**; yea, born of God, changed from their carnal and fallen state, to a state of righteousness, being redeemed of God, becoming his sons and daughters; 26 And **thus they become new creatures**; and unless they do this, they can in nowise inherit the kingdom of God." (Mosiah 27:24–26)

"For behold this is my work and my glory —to bring to pass the immortality and eternal life of man." (Moses 1:39)

"Ye were also in the beginning with the Father…" (D&C 93:23)

"…that you may come unto the Father in my name, **and in due time** receive of his fullness." (D&C 93:19)

"And I heard a voice from heaven saying blessed are the dead who die in the Lord for from henceforth they do rest from their labors and their works do follow them—They rest from their labors for a long time **and yet their work is held in reserve for them**, that they are permitted to do the same works after they receive a resurrection for their bodies, but we shall leave this subject of the Terrestrial bodies for another time in order to treat upon them more fully." (*The Words of Joseph Smith,* p. 42)

"And I will show it plainly as I showed it unto my disciples as I stood before them in the flesh and spake unto them saying: As ye have asked me concerning the signs of my coming, in the day when I shall come in my glory in the clouds of heaven, to fulfill the promises that I have made unto your fathers. **For as ye have looked upon the long absence of your spirits from your bodies to be a bondage**, I will show unto you how the day of redemption shall come…" (D&C 45:16–17)

"And after Christ shall have risen from the dead **he shall show himself unto you, my children, and my beloved brethren**; and the words which he shall speak unto you shall be the law which ye shall do." (2 Nephi 26:1. What is Nephi trying to tell his children?)

"And now, behold, **my beloved brethren**, I suppose that ye ponder somewhat in your hearts concerning that which ye should do after ye have entered in by the way. But, behold, why do ye ponder these things in your hearts?…Behold, this is the doctrine of Christ, **and there will be no more doctrine given until after he shall manifest himself unto you in the flesh. And when he shall manifest himself unto you in the flesh**, the things which he shall say unto you shall ye observe to do." (2 Nephi 32:1, 6. Is Nephi trying to tell his brethren that they will be alive again when Christ comes in 600 years?)

"All things are theirs **whether life or death**." (D&C 76:59. Interesting that Celestial person could choose "death" again?)

"Now, **whether there shall be one time, or a second time, or a third time, that men shall come forth from the dead, it mattereth not**; for God knoweth all these things; and it sufficeth me to know that this is the case—that there is a time appointed that all shall rise from the dead." (Alma 40:5)

"And now behold, is the meaning of the word restoration to take a thing of a natural state and place it in an unnatural state, or to place it in a state opposite to its nature? O, my son, this is not the case; **but the meaning of the word restoration is to bring back again** evil for evil, or carnal for carnal, or devilish for devilish—good for that which is good; righteous for that which is righteous; just for that which is just; merciful for that which is merciful." (Alma 41:12–13)

"But if she (Emma) will not abide this commandment, then shall my servant Joseph do all things for her, even as he hath said; and I will bless him and multiply him and give unto him an hundred fold in this world, of fathers and mothers, brothers and sisters, houses and lands, wives and children, and crowns of eternal lives in the eternal worlds." (D&C 132:55)

"The earthly is in the image of the Heavenly shows that is by the **multiplication of lives that the eternal worlds are created and occupied**…" (*The Words of Joseph Smith*, p. 232)

"He showed that the power of the Melchisek P'd [sic] was to have the power of an **endless lives**." (Ibid, p. 247)

"When the word 'ruach' applies to Eve, it should be translated **lives**." (*Teachings of the Prophet Joseph Smith*, p. 301)

"For strait is the gate, and narrow the way that **leadeth unto the exaltation and the continuation of the lives**, and few there be that find it, because ye receive me not in the world neither do ye know me." (D&C 132:22)

"**Joseph said I was his before I came here** and he said all the Devils in hell should never get me from him." (Mary Elizabeth Rollins Lightner quoting Joseph Smith, *The First Mormon* by Donna Hill, p. 351)

"…time passed away with us, and also our lives passed away like as it were unto us a dream…" (Jacob 7:26)

"If Abraham reasoned thus—If Jesus Christ was the Son of God, and John discovered that God the Father of Jesus Christ had a Father, you may suppose that He had a Father also. **Where was there ever a son without a father? And where was there ever a father without first being a son?** Whenever did a tree or anything spring into existence without a progenitor? And everything comes in this way. **Paul says that which is earthly is in the likeness of that which is heavenly**, Hence if Jesus had a Father, can we not believe that He had a Father also? **I**

despise the idea of being scared to death at such a doctrine, for the Bible is full of it." (HC 6:476)

"I would make you think I was climbing a ladder when I was **climbing a rainbow**—who ever revealed it. God never did." (*The Words of Joseph Smith*, p. 211. Do the colors of the rainbow possibly relate to the level of the person's spiritual attainment or the level or grade attained in the spirit world?)

"When his commandments teach us, it is in view of eternity; for we are looked upon by God as though we were in eternity; God dwells in eternity, and does not view things as we do." (HC 6:313)

"All men know that they must die. And it is important that we understand the reasons and causes of our exposure to the vicissitudes of life and of death, and the designs and purposes of God in our coming into the world, our sufferings here, and our departure hence. What is the object of our coming into existence, then dying and falling away, to be here no more? It is but reasonable to suppose that God would reveal something in reference to the matter, and it is a subject we ought to study more than any other. We ought to study it day and night, for the world is ignorant in reference to their true condition and relation. If we have any claim on our Heavenly Father for anything, it is for knowledge on this important subject. Could we read and comprehend all that has been written from the days of Adam, on the relation of man to God and angels in a future state, we should know very little about it. Reading the experience of others, or the revelation given to *them,* can never give us a comprehensive view of our condition and true relation to God. Knowledge of these things can only be obtained by experience through the ordinances of God set forth for that purpose. **Could you gaze into heaven five minutes, you would know more than you would by reading all that ever was written on the subject.**" (HC 6:50)

"All your losses will be made up to you in the resurrection..." (HC 5:362)

Brigham Young

"It is written that God knows all things and has all power. He has the rule and command of this earth, and is the Father of all the human beings that have lived, do live and will live upon it. **If any of his children become heirs to all things, they in their turn can say, by-and-by, that they know all things, and they will be called Supreme, Almighty, King of kings, Lord of lords**. All this and more that cannot enter into our hearts to conceive is promised to the faithful, <u>**and are but so many stages in that ceaseless progression of eternal lives**</u>. This will not detract anything from the glory and might of our Heavenly Father. For he will still remain our Father, and we shall still be subject to him, and as we progress in glory and power, the more it enhances the glory and power of our Heavenly Father. **This principle holds good in either state, whether mortal or immortal**." (*Discourses of Brigham Young,* selected and arranged by John A. Widtsoe [Salt Lake City: Deseret Book Co., 1954], p. 20. JD 10:5)

"**The great and grand secret of salvation, which we should continually seek to understand through our faithfulness, is the continuation of the lives**. Those of the Latter-day Saints who will continue to follow after the revelations and commandments of God to do them, who are found to be obedient in all things, continually advancing little by little towards perfection and the knowledge of God, they, when they enter the spirit world and receive their bodies, will be able to advance faster in the things pertaining to the knowledge of the Gods, **and will continue onward and upward until they become Gods**, even the sons of God. **This I say is the great secret of the hereafter, to <u>continue in the lives forever</u> and forever, which is the greatest of all gifts God has ever bestowed upon his children. We all have it within our reach, we can all attain to this perfected and exalted state** if we will embrace its principles and practice them in our every-day life. How accommodating, how glorious and divine are the dealings of God with his fallen children! We have been called from darkness to light, from the power of Satan to the living God. By obeying the whispering of this Holy Spirit, which we have received by virtue of obedience to the Gospel, which prompts us to purge from within us all sinful desires, we can say we are no more in the world, but we are in Christ, our living head. **The philosophy of our coming out from the world is the putting off the old man sin, and the putting on of the new man Jesus Christ**." (JD 18:260)

"Having fought the good fight we then shall be prepared to lay our bodies down to rest to await the morning of the resurrection when they will come forth and be reunitsd [reunited] with the spirits, the faithful, as it is said, receiving crowns, glory, immortality and eternal lives, even a fullness with the Father, when Jesus shall present his work to the Father, saying, 'Father, here is the work thou gavest me to do.' Then will they become gods, even the sons of God; then will they become eternal fathers, eternal mothers, eternal sons and eternal daughters; being eternal in their organization, they go from glory to glory, from power to power; they will never cease to increase and to multiply worlds without end. When they receive their crowns, their dominions, they then will be prepared to frame earths like unto ours and to people them in the same manner as we have been brought forth by our parents, by our Father and God." (JD 18:259)

"The world may in vain ask the question, 'Who are we?' But the Gospel tells us that we are the sons and daughters of that God whom we serve. Some say, 'We are the children of Adam and Eve.' So we are, and they are the children of our Heavenly Father. We are all the children of Adam and Eve, and they are the offspring of him who dwells in the heavens, **the highest Intelligence that dwells anywhere that we have any knowledge of**. Here we find ourselves, and when infants, the most helpless, and needing the most care and attention of any creatures that come into being on the face of the earth. Here we find in ourselves the germ and the foundation, **the embryo of exaltation, glory, immortality and eternal lives**." (*Discourses of Brigham Young,* selected and arranged by John A. Widtsoe [Salt Lake City: Deseret Book Co., 1954], p. 222. JD 13:311–312)

"When the time came that his First-born, the Savior, should come into the world and take a tabernacle, **the Father came himself and favored that Spirit with a tabernacle instead of letting any other man do it**. The Savior was begotten by the Father and his Spirit, by the same Being who is the Father of our spirits, and that is all the organic difference between Jesus Christ and you and me. And a difference there is between our Father and us consists in that he has gained his exaltation, and has obtained eternal lives.

The principle of eternal lives is an eternal existence, eternal duration, eternal exaltation. Endless are his kingdoms, endless his thrones and his dominions and endless are his posterity; they never will cease to multiply from this time hence forth and forever." (Ibid, p. 50. JD 4:218)

"When the Spirit of revelation from God inspires a man, his mind is opened to behold the beauty, order, and glory of the creation of this earth and its inhabitants, the object of its creation, and the purpose of its Creator in peopling it with his children. He can then clearly understand that our existence here is for the sole purpose of exaltation and restoration to the presence of our Father and God, where we may progress endlessly in the power of godliness. After the mind has thus been illuminated, the ignorance and blindness of the great mass of mankind are more apparent. Yet there is no son or daughter of Adam and Eve who has not incorporated in his organization the **priceless gem of endless life, for the endless duration and endless lives** which they are approaching." (Ibid, p. 37. JD 9:256)

"So, in like manner, every faithful son of God, becomes, as it were, Adam to the race that springs from his loins, when they are embraced in the covenants and blessings of the Holy Priesthood; and in the lapse of eternity, **and in the progress of eternal lives, every true son of God becomes a king of kings, and a lord of lords, and it may also be said of him, as it was written of Jesus Christ, 'Of the increase of his government and peace there shall be no end**.' When death ends the reign of an earthly King, he is stripped of his regal power, which gives place to the habiliments of the tomb; and another wears the crown he wore, sits upon the throne he occupied, and rules over the kingdom he ruled. Not so with the sons of God, when they are crowned and receive their kingdoms; for they have embraced the everlasting Gospel, and have been **regenerated**, and **sanctified** through its institutions, **purified** through the grave, and **raised again** by the power of the resurrection, **to newness of life**, as it is written, 'but is now made manifest, by the appearing of our Savior Jesus Christ, who hath abolished death, and hath brought life and immortality, to light through the Gospel.' We have not yet received our kingdoms, neither will we, until we have finished our work on the earth, **passed through the ordeals**, are brought up by the power of the resurrection, and are crowned with glory and **eternal lives**. Then he that has overcome and is found worthy, will be made a king of kings, and lord of lords over his own posterity, or in other words: A father of fathers." (JD 10:355)

"And when we have passed into the sphere where Joseph is, there is still another department, and then another, and another, and so on to an **eternal progression in exaltation and eternal lives**. That is the exaltation I am looking for. May God bless you. Amen." (JD 3:375)

"We are now, or may be, as perfect in our sphere as God and Angels are in theirs, but the greatest intelligence in existence can continually ascend to greater heights of perfection. **We are created for the express purpose of increase**. There are none, correctly organized, but can increase from birth to old age. What is there that is not ordained after an eternal law of existence? **It is the Deity within us that causes increase**. Does this idea startle you? Are you ready to exclaim, '**What! the Supreme in us!**' Yes. He is in every person upon the face of the earth. **The elements that every individual is made of and lives in, possess the Godhead**. This you cannot now understand, but you will hereafter — **The Deity within us is the great principle that causes us to increase, and to grow in grace and truth**." (JD 1:93)

"You read about a first resurrection. If there is a first, there is a second. And if a second, may there not be a third, and a fourth, and so on?" (JD 7:287)

"The Lord created you and me for the purpose of becoming Gods like Himself; when we have been proved in our present capacity, and been faithful with all things He puts into our possession. We are created, we are born for the express purpose of growing up from the low estate of manhood, to become Gods like unto our Father in heaven. That is the truth about it, just as it is. The Lord has organized mankind for the express purpose of increasing in that intelligence and truth, which is with God, until he is capable of creating worlds on worlds, and becoming Gods, even the sons of God." (JD 3:93)

"To us life is the sweetest of all enjoyments. A man will give all that he has for his life, **yet it is compared to a span length, and is swift to its termination like the shuttle that passeth over the weaver's beam**. Even when denied the enjoyment of health and of worldly comforts and conveniences, still will men cling to life to the last. The kingdom of God secures unto the faithful eternal life, with wives, children, and friends, in glory immortal, and in eternal felicity and bliss. Life eternal in His presence is the greatest gift that God can bestow upon His children. This life is nothing in point of duration in comparison with the life which is to come to the faithful, and for that reason we say that in this life it is the kingdom of God or nothing to us. With the kingdom of God and the facilities it offers for **an everlasting progression in godliness until we know all things as our Father in Heaven knows them, there is no life of greater importance than this life, for there is no life in heaven or on earth to the true followers of Jesus Christ that is not**

incorporated in His gospel. Those who reject the gospel, when it is proclaimed to them by the authority of heaven, cannot know the Father and the Son, and are cut off from the eternal life which this knowledge alone gives." (JD 11:126–127)

"**A few words more upon the subject of the eternal existence of the soul**. It is hard for mankind to comprehend that principle. The philosophers of the world will concede that the elements of which you and I are composed are eternal, yet they believe that there was a time when there was no God. They cannot comprehend how it is that God can be eternal. Let me ask this congregation, **Can you realize the eternity of your own existence? Can you realize that the intelligence which you receive is eternal?** I can comprehend this, just as well as I can that I am now in possession of it. It is as easy for me to comprehend that it will exist eternally, as that anything else will. **I wish to impress upon your minds the reality that when the body which is organized for intelligence to dwell in, dies, and returns to its mother earth, all the feelings, sensibilities, faculties, and powers of the spirit are still alive, they never die**, but in the absence of the body are more acute. They are organized for an eternal existence. If this congregation could comprehend that the intelligence that is in them is eternal in its nature and existence; if they could realize that **when Saints pass through the veil, they are not dead, but have been laying the foundation in these tabernacles for exaltation**, laying the foundation to become Gods, even the sons of God, and for crowns which they will yet receive—they would receive the truth in the love of it, live by it, and continue in it, until they receive all knowledge and wisdom, until they grow into eternity, and have the veil taken from before their eyes, to behold the handiworks of God among all people, **His goings forth among the nations of the earth**, and to discover the rule and law by which He governs. Then could they say of a truth, We acknowledge the hand of God in all things, all is right, Zion is here, in our own possession. I have thus summed up, in a broken manner, that which I desired to speak. We are not able to comprehend all things, but we can continue to learn and grow, until all will be perfectly dear to our minds, which is a great privilege to enjoy—**the blessing of an eternal increase**. And the man or woman who lives worthily is now in a state of salvation." (JD 1:5–6)

"Every person possessing the principle of eternal life should look upon his body as of the earth earthy. Our bodies must return to their mother earth. True, to most people it is a wretched thought that our spirits must, for a longer or shorter period, be separated from our bodies, and thousands and millions have been subject to this affliction throughout their lives. **If they understood the design of this probation and the true principles of eternal life, it is but a small matter for the body to suffer and die**." (JD 7:240)

"We talk about our trials and troubles here in this life: but suppose that you could see yourselves thousands and millions of years after you have proved faithful to your religion during the few short years in this time, and have obtained eternal salvation and a crown of glory in the presence of God; then look back upon your lives here, and see the losses, crosses, and disappointments, the sorrows arising from disobedient children—from wicked parents who have opposed their children who wished to embrace the truth, the persecutions from city to city, from state to state, being hunted and driven, you would be constrained to exclaim, 'But what of all that? Those things were but for a moment, and we are now here. We have been faithful during a few moments in our mortality, and now we enjoy eternal life and glory, **with power to progress in all the boundless knowledge and through the countless stages of progression**, enjoying the smiles and approbation of our Father and God, and of Jesus Christ our elder brother.'" (JD 7:275)

"The Gospel of Jesus Christ is the opening avenue—the open gate in the road or way from earth to heaven, through which direct revelation comes to the children of men in their various capacities, according to their callings and standing in the society in which they live. The Gospel of salvation is a portion of the law that pertains to the kingdom where God resides; and the ordinances pertaining to **the holy Priesthood are the means by which the children of men find access to the way of life, wherein they can extend their travels until they return to the presence of their Father and God**. This no person will dispute, who has faith in the character of the Deity. They will acknowledge that God is true, that his system of salvation is correct, that his law is just, that he is equal in all his ways, and that the ordinances of his house are true and faithful;" (JD 8:159)

"The Spirit of revelation, even **the Spirit of eternal life, is within that person who lives so as to bear properly the yoke of Jesus. The heavens are open to such persons, and they see and understand things that pertain to eternity, and also the things that pertain to this earth**, which will pass away with it; and those who love the things of earth will pass away with it. When death takes them, all is gone. But the person that wears the yoke of Jesus and bears his burden—who loves the cause of truth and righteousness more than all else—'Why,' says he, 'Eternity if full of fathers and mothers. There is my Father enthroned in glory. He is the Father of my spirit.' God our Father, who dwells in eternity, is the Father of our spirits and the God and Father of our Lord Jesus Christ. **The man or woman that lives in the revelations of Jesus Christ can see and understand this**. Here are our earthly fathers, the begetters of our mortal bodies; but there is the foundation of all the life that I or any other person can possess on the face of the earth, even God my Father who dwells in the heavens. There also is my mother. I am not confined to love my father and mother here, if they do not love God, the fountain of all truth. In the heavens are fathers, mothers, sisters, brothers. Unless my father, mother, brother, sister, wife, and child, pertaining to the flesh, love God supremely, embrace the truth, and follow out the dictates of the Holy Ghost, they are not my kindred—I do not own them—I have nothing to do with them; they will perish, die, sink into forgetfulness, and be as though they had never been; they will pass away and return to native element. In heaven dwells my Father. There are the heavenly hosts—my sisters, my brethren, my kindred, and my friends; they are my bosom acquaintances. We behold each other with the natural eye, and that is short-sighted. But had we eyes to see as God sees, we could see our antipodes as well as we can see each other's faces. We could see the uttermost parts of the earth and behold all creation as well at midnight as at noonday. Darkness would be no obstruction, incorporated matter, this Tabernacle, the houses, the earth, and even matter that fills space and prevents our seeing objects at great distances, would be no obstruction to our visions. Then we should behold that God is here, that our Father dwells here. We are in his presence, just as much as those who sit at the farthest side of this congregation are in my presence. **There is much in my presence besides those who sit here, if we had eyes to see the heavenly beings that are in our presence. The person that wears the yoke of Jesus, that has communication with the heavens, finds his yoke easy and his burden light; he is master of it. Wear the yoke of Jesus, bear his burden, and the revelations of the Lord Jesus Christ will show to every individual that you are not servants of anything, but that the principles of eternal life give you the mastery—the supremacy over all things in heaven and on earth.**" (JD 8:206–207)

"It is just so with matter. Take, for instance, a grain of sand. **You can not divide it so small that it can not be divided again—it is capable of infinite division**. We know nothing about how many times it can be divided, and <u>**it is just so with regard to the lives in us**</u>, in animals, in vegetation, in shrubbery. **They are countless**. To illustrate, you take a perfectly ripe kernel of corn—you will have some here perhaps in a few days—and if you get a glass, it does not require a very powerful one, and you take the chit of this corn and open it, you behold distinctly a stalk of corn, in that chit, a perfectly grown stalk of corn, with ears and leaves on it, matured, out in blossom,—there is the tassel, there are the ears and there is the corn! Well, you get a stronger glass and divide again, and you can see that this very chit is the grandfather of corn! We take the scientific world for this. Well, how many lives are there in this grain of corn? They are innumerable, and this same infinity is manifest through all the creations of God. We will operate here, in all the ordinances of the house of God which pertain to this side the vail, and **those who pass beyond and secure to themselves <u>a resurrection pertaining to the lives</u> will go on and receive more and more, more and more, and <u>will receive one after another</u> until they are crowned Gods**, even the sons of God. <u>**This idea is very consoling**</u>." (JD 15:138)

"As for their labor and pursuits in eternity I have not time to take upon that subject; but we shall have plenty to do. We shall not be idle. **We shall go on from one step to another, reaching forth into the eternities until we become like the Gods**, and shall be able to frame for ourselves, by the behest and command of the Almighty. All those who are counted worthy to be exalted and to become Gods, even the sons of God, will go forth and have earths and worlds like those who framed this and millions on millions of others. This is our home, built expressly for us by **the Father of our spirits, who is the Father,**

maker, framer and producer of these mortal bodies that we now inherit, and which go back to mother earth." (JD 17:143)

"This people have embraced the philosophy of eternal lives, and in view of this we should cease to be children and become philosophers, understanding our own existence, its purpose and ultimate design, then our days will not become a blank through ignorance, but every day will bring with it its useful and profitable employment." (JD 9:190-191)

"We might ask, when shall we cease to learn? I will give you my opinion about it; never, never. If we continue to learn all that we can, pertaining to the salvation which is purchased and presented to us through the Son of God, is there a time when a person will cease to learn? Yes, when he has sinned against God the Father, Jesus Christ the Son, and the Holy Ghost—God's minister; when he has denied the Lord, defied Him and committed the sin that in the Bible is termed the unpardonable sin—the sin against the Holy Ghost. That is the time when a person will cease to learn, and from that time forth, will descend in ignorance, forgetting that which they formerly knew, and decreasing until they return to the native element, whether it be one thousand or in one million years, or during as many eternities as you can count. They will cease to increase, but must decrease, until they return to the native element. **These are the only characters who will ever cease to learn, both in time and eternity**." (JD 3:203)

"We **find that there is one eternal resurrection, one eternal change from one state to another, from one degree to another**..." (*The Complete Discourses of Brigham Young*, Vol. 1, 1832 to 1852, Ed. Richard S. Van Wagoner, Smith-Petit Foundation, Salt Lake City, 2009. p. 91)

"Yes, there are millions and millions of them in eternity that have passed through the same ordeals that we are passing through. **There are myriads and myriads of kingdoms** the same as us in this vale of tears." (Ibid, p. 91).

"I would call my friends and take them and lay them away carefully until the morning of the resurrection. I would sow [sic] them, as I would sow [sic] any other grain. You know by experience that **no grain will be quickened, except it die**. Look in your garden and see if any grain will be quickened and grow. It cannot be except it die. **Well, is it not so with mortal bodies? Yes, it is**." (Ibid, p. 92).

"**The Lord will bring every person to their covenant either sooner or later if it must be that they serve a probation in hell, he has to make them atone in hell and bring them back to comply with it**." (Ibid, p. 135).

"**This world is a poor miserable hell**..." (Ibid, p. 329).

"Take up your cross and **prepare yourselves for the regeneration**. No man need think he can go through without losses and crosses." (Ibid, p. 338).

"—in staring point as man **the principle of eternal lives** and every property that pertains to angels—power to produce existence—and then exalt him—no he has not—in eternal light it is power light, excellence and beauty and inseparably connected with Godhead—he is organized in the germ the seed, for the purpose of passing through certain ordeals —with privilege of increasing—**expanding multiplying until he brings up beings similar to himself, and glorifies them in himself**—I view all mankind brought in existence by Him under His watchful care and control—**and he is in all**…" (Ibid, p. 350).

"If I do all the Lord dictates me to do, and I control myself, I do all my Father requires of me and then I do it in and of myself. I was begotten, born, lived, enjoyed – **I have taken a degree of exaltation and am capable of enjoying more, and if I do honor to him that sent me I shall then enjoy more – and do honor to the Father of endless lives**…" (Ibid, p. 351).

"If I do all the Lord dictates me to do, and I control myself, I do all my Father requires of me and then I do it in and of myself. I was begotten, born, lived, enjoyed – **I have taken a degree of exaltation and am capable of enjoying more, and if I do honor to him that sent me I shall then enjoy more – and do honor to the Father of endless lives**…" (Ibid, p. 351).

"…all matter is eternal, all beings are composed of matter whether finer of course material,—**it is one eternal round**." (Ibid, p. 374).

"…the Lord has prepared his kingdom, we are his children naturally – now do just as you please – if you serve me well – right? **If not you shall have no part nor lot with those who shall have eternal lives** – choose whom you will serve, God or Baal – if you serve the devil – the old chief head manager of this world, he is more graceful than you generally imagine – he would want you to pass through the world like a gentleman – and God says do as I tell you and ask no odds of any one – and I will crown you with glory, thrones and dominions – I say to LDS do just as you please – if your eye is single to the glory of God – you will be crowned with blessings – **but if your eye is on your purses then gather up all you can**." (Ibid, p. 383).

"I'm here! Where did I come from? Where am I going to? No person need tell me I was here from eternity but sound **reason taught me this organization must be dissolved** – I was acquainted with the different articles of faith because I read them – but many things I could not comprehend and never shall do – I never did comprehend a heaven beyond the bounds of time and space – but sound sense logic overcame my sensitive powers – I would weigh the others and walk away but **Mormonism touched my heart – it is an eternal increase of knowledge and wisdom – never cease to learn to increase – add and rise – but grow and increase – that is glorious joy, and beauty to my eye**…" (Ibid, p. 384).

"When the spirit enters the body it becomes interwoven together. The spirit hates to leave the body, because a spirit has forgot what has transpired before, and is connected in its passions and life, and cannot bear to leave the old house. **If the spirit knew what it does five minutes after it is let loose you could not rend it back again**, just as quick as we pass through the world, we shall see it is a very happy exchange; and then say Lord as quick as you will, let my wife and children come to me, but I will wait patiently, and it is almost reluctant to let them stay on earth; and when we go I hope we shall go without feeling bad about it." (Ibid, p. 405).

"**God has walked in the same path as we walk in…**" (Ibid, p. 437).

"I will tell whether the messenger sent to brother Kempton was of God of the devil. If the messenger sent was of God, he would know it. If the messenger was [from] anywhere else but here, he must have come from heaven **or from another hell for we are in hell.**" (Ibid, p. 452).

"**…a better stage cannot be than the world, nor better actors than men, to a man of understanding.**" (Ibid, p. 615).

"What is our reward for our labor and faithfulness? It is thrones, kingdoms, principalities, **Eternal Lives**, and a seat among the Gods." (Ibid, p. 630).

"Thank you, Father, **I would rather take a new body**, and then I shall get a good set of new teeth. My sight, too is failing; if I want to read, I cannot do it without using glasses; and if I wish to walk a few miles, I cannot do it without making myself sick; if I wish to go out on a journey, I am under the necessity of taking the utmost care of myself for fear of injuring my health; but **when I get a new body**, this will not be so…" (Ibid, p. 710).

"I will tell you what I believe still further than this; though I do not pretend to say that the items of doctrine, and ideas I shall advance are necessary for the people to know, or that they should give themselves any trouble about them whatever. I believe in the eternities of worlds, saints, angels, kingdoms, and gods: In eternity without beginning. I believe the gods never had a beginning, neither the formation of matter, and it is without end; it will endure in **one eternal round** swimming in space, basking, living, and moving in the midst of eternity. All the creations are in the midst of eternity, and that is one eternity, so they more in **one eternal round**." (Ibid, p. 845)

"**Do we know what hell is? And where hell is?** Who can point it out? In many instances where the apostles have been speaking and likewise Jesus in his communications to the people **this earth is compared to hell**. Well it is in one sense. If we find out really that hell is anything more or less than this earth, this wicked world, we shall find that it is banishment from the from the society and presence of Holy beings." (Ibid, p. 1103).

"**Show me the man who knows enough about his God, and is sufficiently acquainted with the principle of eternal lives to be able to say,** "I can handle the gold and silver , the goods, the chattels, and the possessions of this world, with my heart not more set upon them than it is upon the wind. I know how to use them, to deal out this and to distribute that, and to do all to the glory of my Father in heaven." If there is one in this congregation that knows how to do all this, will you please to rise up? **These are things that I have taught you week after week, and year after year, but do you understand them? No.**" (Ibid, p. 1168).

Heber C. Kimball

"Joseph always told us that we would have to pass by sentinels that are placed between us and our Father and God. Then, of course, <u>we are conducted along from this probation to other probations, or from one dispensation to another</u>, by those who conducted those dispensations." (JD 6:63)

"**What I do not to-day, when the sun goes down, I lay down to sleep, which is typical of death; and in the morning I rise and commence my work where I left it yesterday. <u>That course is typical of the probations we take</u>**. But suppose that I do not improve my time to-day, I wake up to-morrow and find myself in the rear; and then, if I do not improve upon that day, and again lay down to sleep, on awaking, I find myself still in the rear. **This day's work is typical of this probation, and the sleep of every night is typical of death, and rising in the morning is typical of the resurrection**. They are days' labours [sic], and it is for us to be faithful today, tomorrow, and every day. Brethren, this is the course we have to take; **it is a progressive work from one day to another, and from one week to another; and if we advance this year, we are so far advanced in preparation to better go through the next year**." (JD 4:329)

"If you do not cultivate yourselves, and cultivate your spirits in this state of existence, it is just as true as there is a God that liveth, **you will have to go into another state of existence, and bring your spirits into subjection there. Now you may reflect upon it, you never will obtain your resurrected bodies, until you bring your spirits into subjection. I am not talking to this earthly house of mine, neither am I talking to your bodies, but I am speaking to your spirits**. I am not talking as to people who are not in the house. Are not your spirits in the house? Are not your bodies your houses, your tabernacles or temples, and places for your spirits? Look at it; reflect upon it. If you keep your spirits trained according to the wisdom and fear of God, you will attain to the salvation of both body and spirit. **I ask, then, if it is your spirits that must be brought into subjection? It is; and <u>if you do not do that in these bodies, you will have to go into another estate to do it</u>**. You have got to train yourselves according to the law of God, **or you will never obtain your resurrected bodies**. Mark it! You do not think of these things, you only think of to-day…You are talking about heaven and about earth, and about hell, &c.; **but let me tell you, you are in hell now, and you have got to qualify yourselves here in hell to become subjects for heaven; and even when you have got into heaven, yea will find it right here where you are on this earth**. When we escape from this earth, we suppose we are going to heaven? Do you suppose you are going to the earth that Adam came from? that Eloheim came from? where Jehovah the Lord came from? No. When you have learned to become obedient to the Father that dwells upon this earth, to the Father and God of this earth, and obedient to the messengers He sends—when you have done all that, remember you are not going to leave this earth. **You will never leave it until you become qualified, and capable, and capacitated to become a father of an earth yourselves**. Not one soul of you ever will leave this earth, for **if you go to hell, it is on this earth; and if you go to heaven, it is on this earth; and you will not find it anywhere else**. Is it not hard to bring these truths home to you. I tell you I am at home now, and I am in heaven; **but the heaven I have to enjoy is the heaven I make myself**." (JD 1:355–357)

"**Our spirits are entangled in these bodies**—held captive as it were for a season. They are like the poor Saints, who are for a time obliged to dwell in miserable mud shanties that are mouldering away, and require much patching and care to keep them from mingling with mother earth before the time. <u>**They feel miserable in these old decaying tabernacles, and long for the day when they can leave them to fall and take possession of a good new house**</u>." (JD 3:108)

"Now, brethren, you have got a spirit in you, and that spirit was created and organized—was born and begotten by our Father and our God before we ever took these bodies; and these bodies were formed by him, and through him, and of him, just as much as the spirit was; for I will tell you, **he commenced and brought forth spirits; and then, when he completed that work, he commenced and brought forth tabernacles for those spirits to dwell in**. I came through him, both spirit and body. God made the elements that they are made of, just as much as he made anything. Tell me the first thing that is made on earth that God did not organize and place here in this world. Not a thing." (JD 6:31)

Parley P. Pratt

"The very germs of these Godlike attributes, being engendered in man, the offspring of Deity, only need cultivating, improving, developing, and advancing by means of **a series of progressive changes**, in order to arrive at the fountain 'Head,' the standard, the climax of Divine Humanity." (Keys of the Mysteries of the Godhead, in the *Essential Parley P. Pratt*, p. 187)

Orson Pratt

"And thus, all the different portions of the earth have been and will be disposed of to the lawful heirs; while those who cannot prove their heirship to be legal, or who cannot prove that they have received any portion of the earth by promise, **will be cast out into some other kingdom or world, where, if they ever get an inheritance, they will have to earn it by keeping the law of meekness <u>during another probation</u>**." (JD 1:332–333)

John Taylor

"I will go back further, and find the spirits that are existing with him in the eternal world. They came here and obtained bodies, that both bodies and spirits might receive an exaltation among the Gods, **and be capable of eternal increase worlds without end**. I think this agrees more with philosophy and truth, with an intelligent and extensive mind, with true religion, with our fathers, and with God, than any thing else we see abroad." (JD 1:158)

" 'And this is life eternal, that they might know Thee, the only true God, and Jesus Christ whom thou hast sent.' **Hence we have partaken of a portion of eternal lives, and have begun to live forever**." (JD 11:24)

"...**for we have within us the seeds of eternal life**, and no man can take them from us. **We have begun to live forever**, and feel to rejoice and be glad under all circumstances, and to sing 'Hallelujah, for the Lord God Omnipotent reigneth, and will reign until he hath put all enemies under his feet.' We are striving to help God to do that which he desires to do; and what is that? It is to benefit mankind." (JD 11:164)

"**When men leave this earth they leave it to occupy another sphere in another state of existence**. And if, as is the case with Brother Miller, they hold the Priesthood that administers in time and in eternity, having fulfilled this part, as many others have done who have left the world, and as our deceased brother has done, they hold that Priesthood in the eternal worlds, and operate in it there. It is an everlasting Priesthood, that administers in time and in eternity. And the Gospel that we have received unfolds to us principles of which we were heretofore entirely ignorant. **It shows us the relationship that exists between God and man, and it shows us the relationship that exists between men who have dwelt upon the earth before and those who exist to-day**...Since the organization of the world myriads have come and have taken upon themselves bodies, and they have passed away, generation after generation, into another state of existence. And it is so to-day. And I suppose while we are mourning the loss of our friend, others are rejoicing to meet him behind the veil; and while he has left us, others are coming into the world at the same time, and probably in this our territory. **There is a continuous change, and ingress of beings into the world and an egress out of it**. As near as my memory serves me, from one-third to one-fourth of our population to-day are children under eight years of age. **There are thousands of men upon the earth to-day, among the Saints of God, of whom it was decreed before they came that they should occupy the positions they have occupied** and do occupy, and many of them have performed their part and gone home; others are left to still fulfill the duties and responsibilities devolving upon them." (JD 23:176–177)

Wilford Woodruff

"He thought they (those of lower kingdoms) would eventually have the privilege of proving themselves worthy and advancing to the celestial kingdom but it would be a slow progress." (Wilford Woodruff referring to remarks by Brigham Young. *Wilford Woodruff Journal*, August 5, 1855)

"President Young said when some people have little children born at 6 & 7 months from pregnancy & they live a few hours then die they bless them, name them etc[.] but I don't do it for I think that such a spirit has not [had] a fair chance **for I think that such a spirit will have a chance of occupying another tabernacle and develop itself. This is new doctrin [sic] yet it looks Consistent**." (Wilford Woodruff quoting Brigham Young, Susan Staker (ed.) *Waiting for World's End: The Diaries of Wilford Woodruff*, p. 204)

"<u>If there was a point where man in his progression could not proceed any further, the very idea would throw a gloom over every intelligent and reflecting mind</u>. God himself is increasing and progressing in knowledge, power, and dominion, and will do so, worlds without end. It is just so with us. We are in a probation, which is a school of experience." (JD 6:120)

"There is another thing I wish to refer to here. I have heard that in Zion **there are some men who entertain the idea that they inherit the body and spirit of Moses, or Abraham, or David, or Noah, or somebody other than themselves**. I hope none of you here indulge in anything of this kind, because it is a most foolish, nonsensical and false doctrine. You gaze upon a man who professes to have inherited the body or spirit of Moses, or any of those I have named, and I think you will conclude that his appearance does not indicate that such is the case; at any rate, it certainly has not improved him.

Brother Woodruff, Brother Cannon, Brother Smith, Brother Lorenzo Snow, or any of the brethren, **will never inherit anyone's body or spirit but their own, in time or in eternity**, unless the devil gets into them. It is Satan who inspires men to believe in such absurd things. He delights in having any of the brethren entertain false ideas, no matter what they are. I tell you that whoever sees me in time or eternity will see Wilford Woodruff, not Noah, nor Abraham, nor Enoch. Every man has his own identity, and he never will lose that identity. Therefore, when you hear such doctrine as that advanced, do not believe it. There are a good many things Satan would like us to believe; but we must guard against these." (Brian H. Stuy, ed., *Collected Discourses,* 5 vols. [Burbank, Calif., and Woodland Hills, Ut.: B.H.S. Publishing, 1987–1992], Vol. 1: 262–263. See Orson F. Whitney's Diary comments regarding this talk given at Manti, Utah, May 19, 1889).

Lorenzo Snow

"As man is God once was; As God is, man may be."

A revelation given to Lorenzo Snow in Nauvoo prior to his departure to the British Isles as a missionary, and prior to his call to the Apostleship. After arriving in Great Briton, Lorenzo shared this revelation with Brigham Young who responded, "**Brother Snow, that is new doctrine;**

if true, it has been revealed to you for your own private information, and will be taught in due time by the Prophet of the Church; till then I advise you to lay it upon a shelf and say no more about it." (*The Life of Lorenzo Snow* by Thomas C. Romney pp. 34–35)

"**Jesus was a god before he came into the world and yet his knowledge was taken from him. He did not know his former greatness, neither do we know what greatness we had attained to before we came here**, but he had to pass through an ordeal, as we have to, without knowing or realizing at the time the greatness and importance of his mission and works." (Lorenzo Snow Journal, pp. 181–182. Also see *Five Classics* by Truman G. Madsen, p. 197)

"There is just one thing that a Latter-day Saint, as an Elder in Israel should never forget: it should be a bright illuminating star before him all the time—in his heart, in his soul, and all through him—that is, he need not worry in the least whether he should be a deacon or President of the Church. **It is sufficient for him to know that his destiny is to be like his Father, a God in eternity. He will not only be President but he may see himself president of a Kingdom, president of worlds with never ending opportunities to enlarge his sphere of dominion**. I saw this principle after being in the Church but a short time; it was made as clear to me as the noonday sun…**This thought in the breasts of men filled with the light of the Holy Spirit, tends to purify them and cleanse them from every ambitious or improper feeling**. This glorious opportunity of becoming truly great belongs to every faithful Elder in Israel; it is his by divine right and he will not have to come before this or any other quorum to have his status defined. He may be a God in eternity; he may become like his Father, doing the works which his Father did before him and **he cannot be deprived of the opportunity of reaching this exalted state**. I never sought to be a Seventy or a High Priest, because this eternal principle was revealed to me long before I was ordained to the Priesthood. The position which I now occupy [he was then President of the Church] is nothing as compared with what I expect to occupy in the future." (At a meeting of the First Presidency and the Council of the Twelve, recorded in BYU Special Collections, Microfilm Reel number 1, p. 209. Also see *Five Classics* by Truman G. Madsen, p. 199)

"I find in reflecting on life that this world is short compared with eternity; that our intelligence, **the divinity within us, has always existed, was never created, and will always exist through all eternity**. In view of these facts, it becomes us as intelligent beings, to realize that this life closes in a few days, then comes the life which is eternal; and in proportion as we have kept commandments, we have the advantage of those who failed to make those improvements. **Many wonder and become despondent over the question, how can we, feeble creatures of the dust, subject to all temptation, how can we anticipate an advancement to glory and exaltation? Is it not a chimera of the brain? Is there any foundation for this hope?**…the Lord will forgive seventy times seven; and forever and forever, as long as man has weaknesses He will extend mercy towards him. **If all men are eventually to be saved**, what then is the use of all this anxiety and trouble, some may say? **There are vastly different degrees of glory in the kingdom of our God**. Abraham, Isaac and Jacob are now Gods. We are told that Father Smith, the Patriarch, is at His right hand. This glory it is for us to attain. May we so live and order our lives, that we may be worthy to stand in the presence of God, and receive the glory he has prepared is my prayer. Amen." (Brian H. Stuy, ed., *Collected Discourses,* 5 vols. [Burbank, Calif., and Woodland Hills, Ut.: B.H.S. Publishing, 1987–1992], Vol. 2: 259–260)

"If we are in this condition, the trials and afflictions that we have to pass through will not have power to move us, because we are founded upon the revelations of the Almighty. God has fulfilled His promises to us, and our prospects are grand and glorious. Yes, in the next life we will have our wives, and our sons and daughters. **If we do not get them all at once, we will have them some time, for every knee shall bow and every tongue shall confess that Jesus is the Christ**. You that are mourning about your children straying away will have your sons and your daughters. **If you succeed in passing through these trials and afflictions and receive a resurrection, you will, by the power of the Priesthood, work and labor, as the Son of God has, until you get all your sons and daughters in the path of exaltation and glory. This is just as sure as that the sun rose this morning over yonder mountains**.

Therefore, mourn not because all your sons and daughters do not follow in the path that you have marked out to them, or give heed to your counsels. Inasmuch as we succeed in securing eternal glory, and stand as saviors, and as kings and priests to our God, we will save our posterity. When Jesus went through that terrible torture on the cross, He saw what would be accomplished by it; He saw that His brethren and sisters—the sons and daughters of God—would be gathered in, with but few exceptions—those who committed the unpardonable sin. That sacrifice of the divine Being was effectual to destroy the powers of Satan. I believe that every man and woman who comes into this life and passes through it, that life will be a success in the end. <u>It may not be in this life</u>." (Brian H. Stuy, ed., *Collected Discourses,* 5 vols. [Burbank, Calif., and Woodland Hills, Ut.: B.H.S. Publishing, 1987–1992], Vol. 3: 364–365)

"Now I will say what I received in vision, which was just as clear as the sun ever shone. The knowledge that was communicated to me I embraced in this couplet:

>As man now is, God once was.
>As God now is, man may be.

That is a very wonderful thing. It was to me. **I did not know but that I had come into possession of knowledge that I had no business with; but I knew it was true**. Nothing of this kind had ever reached my ears before. It was preached a few years after that; at least, the Prophet

Joseph taught this idea to the Twelve Apostles. Now, however, it is common property; **but I do not know how many there are here that have got a real knowledge of these things in their hearts. If you have, I will tell you what its effects will be.** As John said:

Every man that hath this hope in him purifieth himself, even as God is pure. Now, how is it that God proposes to confer this mighty honor upon us and to raise us to this condition of glory and exaltation? Who are we that God should do all this for us? Why, we are just beginning to find out that we are the offspring of God, **born with the same faculties and powers as He possesses, capable of enlargement through the experience that we are now passing through in our second estate**. Let me illustrate. Here is an emperor sitting upon his throne, governing and controlling his empire wisely and properly. He has an infant son that sits upon the knee of its mother. **That son he proposes to one day set upon his throne, to govern and control his empire**.

Here is that infant, perfectly helpless, not knowing how to sustain its own life, not able to walk alone, without any knowledge, and here is this mighty emperor sitting upon his throne and governing his vast empire. **Who would believe that he could raise that infant up to such a condition as to make it suitable to be placed on his throne? No one would, unless he had seen such things accomplished in his experience**; seen the infant develop into boyhood, and then to manhood, possessing all the powers, faculties and possibilities of its father. Now, we are the sons and daughters of God. He has begotten us in His own image. **He has given us faculties and powers that are capable of enlargement until His fulness is reached which He has promised—until we shall sit upon thrones**, governing and controlling our posterity from eternity to eternity, and increasing eternally.

That is the fact in regard to these matters, **and there are some people who understand distinctly what I am saying**. Does it seem a hard thing that God should raise His posterity and place them upon thrones, to govern and control their posterity from eternity to eternity? **There are a thousand things that might be said in connection with this subject**, but I refrain from saying more because my time has expired. There are many things that we have to attend to, and it would pay us well to attend to them.

God has pointed out the results of traveling upon this road of glory and exaltation and the promises are sure. The Lord knew precisely what He could do. He knew what materials He had to operate with, and He knew just what He said. **If we do the part that He has assigned unto us, and keep our second estate, we shall be sure to realize these promises in every particular, and more than you and I can possibly comprehend**. God bless you, my brethren and sisters. Do not be discouraged. The path may be rough, but much of its roughness arises from our own indifference and carelessness. It would be much smoother if we would diligently observe the commandments of God and keep the Spirit of the Lord continually in our hearts. Yet, after all, there are sacrifices to make, but in making these sacrifices there is a possibility of having enjoyment in the anticipation of what will be the final result. Amen." (Brian H. Stuy, ed., *Collected Discourses*, 5 vols. [Burbank, Calif., and Woodland Hills, Ut.: B.H.S. Publishing, 1987–1992], Vol. 4: 162)

Erastus Snow

"We are in a state of progression, very small beginnings, but onward and upward for a more exalted sphere, in which they move. But I conceive of no stopping place; I conceive of no absolute resting place, but only, as before remarked, a change, a change in our circumstances and conditions, and consequently a change in our labors. I speak now of man as an immortal being, having no reference to this earthly house of our tabernacles; for this mortal house which we occupy for the period of a few short years upon the earth, will not be associated with the immortal man—the god in embryo.

The clothing we wear covers the nakedness of the body; **it answers a good purpose for a little season—until it becomes worn out, when it is cast aside as of no further use for that purpose. So with the outer house of our tabernacles**…It is this spirit that keeps the functions of this tabernacle in motion; when this spirit leaves the body, it is either because the Father calls it away, wishing to use it in another sphere, **considering the time it has spent in this tabernacle sufficient for the purposes required**, and therefore takes it to a higher school, through special design to do a special work; or it may be, it has used its tabernacle until it is so worn out that it has become like a bow which has been long and constantly bent,—it has lost its elasticity; its bones impaired in strength, its muscles stiffened, and the whole frame ready, like our old clothes, to be thrown aside; **and the spirit comes to the conclusion that it has had its run with this old tabernacle and that it is time this old garment were laid aside for a new one**." (JD 21:23–24, 25)

"Joseph Smith said that the faithful elders of Israel, when their labors in the flesh are completed, then they rest from those labors they leave behind, while their spirits are still active upon another class of labor in the spirit world. They rest from earthly labors and pursue spiritual labors **which will qualify them to go on to higher degrees of glory and soar in loftier regions of intelligence**.

"I have thus in short endeavored to present before the people, not a new doctrine to them; but unto many of the rising generation these passages of scriptures may not be understood. Their minds cannot be familiar with these reasons upon which the work of the dead is founded, upon the principles which our faith is founded in relation to the work for the redemption of the dead. I therefore bring these thoughts home to the minds of the rising generation, as well as the more aged and possibly the strangers in our midst who are uninformed, **and to whom this doctrine is marvelously strange**;" (Brian H. Stuy, ed., *Collected Discourses*, 5 vols. [Burbank, Calif., and Woodland Hills, Ut.: B.H.S. Publishing, 1987–1992], Vol. 1: 71–72)

Franklin D. Richards

"Having now observed how Adam, the first man, became God, we inquire why may not millions of his children receive the same God-like knowledge and power? The Apostles, Prophets, and Seers, who have lived on the earth since the days of Adam, have been a succession of intelligences, who by doing the will of the Father receive of His glory, and become the heirs of His increasing dominions. God saw that among His numerous posterity of spirits there were some more noble than others, and therefore capable of assuming greater responsibilities, and performing more important parts in the great work of redemption.

These He foreordained and set apart to the work designed for them, and at the time appointed they appeared on the earth through the lineage of the Priesthood. Having been ordained in the Spirit, and being heirs according to the flesh, they came forth prepared to enter upon the work designed, inherit the fruits thereof, and partake of the same glory and exaltation as the Father.

First among these noble sons stands the Lord Jesus Christ. The heir by birthright of his Father's kingdom, he has proved himself worthy of his high vocation, by nobly offering to become the sacrifice that was necessary for the redemption of his Father's family. Therefore on him the Father has bestowed the keys of salvation, and the powers of the resurrection, to unlock the gates of death. On him devolved the great crowning work of redemption, and the meridian of time was appointed for the sacrifice.

This same Jesus was a man like unto other men, and attained his exaltation by suffering all things, that he might overcome them, and has ascended to power at the right hand of the Father. Next to Jesus Christ in the scale of Godlike intelligences are his brethren—holy men who have faithfully performed the work assigned them in their Father's kingdom, and have received the fruits of their labors as an everlasting inheritance, and thereby become heirs of God and joint heirs with Jesus Christ. These men move and act independent of all others, in their sphere, and are responsible to none but the Lord Jesus Christ who sent them. The Lord has seen fit, in these days, to raise the veil a little which obscures our vision a little, by revealing to us the position now occupied by some of those ancient worthies who lived on the earth previous to his coming.

In a revelation given to the Prophet Joseph, on Celestial Marriage, the Lord, speaking to Abraham, Isaac, and Jacob, says: 'And because they did none other things than that which they were commanded, they have entered into their exaltations, according to the promises, and sit upon thrones; and are not Angels, but are Gods.' All who live on the earth, and faithfully work righteousness, as did those ancient fathers, will receive like blessings of power and dominion, for God is no respecter of persons, but judges all men righteously according to their works.

<u>Thus we have a succession of Gods from Adam down to Christ and his Apostles at least</u>. All men being in the image of their father Adam, even as he is in the image of his father, and possessing a similar knowledge of good and evil, when they receive the keys and powers of the same Priesthood, and by their works attain to its blessings, they will, like Adam, Abraham, Isaac, and Jacob, **bear rule and dominion over their own posterity and have power to redeem, purify, and exalt them, also, to like power and glory.**" (Franklin D. Richards, *Millennial Star* 17:194–196)

"A multitude of our kindred dead await us and our labors here, to know when we can go and tell them what we have done for them here in the flesh, that they, rejoicing with us, may contemplate the glorious anticipations, when they will come rising from the dead triumphant, and rise unto the labors and blessings of a more extended work, which they are now resting from—resting their wearied mortality. The spirit that never dies, that has life and eternal vigor and bloom, is relieved from these cumbrous clods of clay and can look and behold, and can again hear and contemplate that labor to an extent that we know not of in this life.

We, this afternoon, partake of the Sacrament of the Lord's Supper; it is a subject for us to crown the final labors of our Conference with, when we contemplate our existence here, our existence **in the other lives**, before we came and whence we go, we have to bear in mind the one great central figure of this world's existence and character and honor and power;" (Brian H. Stuy, ed., *Collected Discourses,* 5 vols. [Burbank, Calif., and Woodland Hills, Ut.: B.H.S. Publishing, 1987–1992], Vol. 1: 84)

Jedediah M. Grant

"He said to me, brother Heber, I have been into the spirit world two nights in successions, and, of all the dreads that ever came across me, the worst was to have to again return to my body, though I had to do it. But O, says he the order and the government that were there! When in the spirit world, **I saw the order of righteous men and women; beheld them organized in their several grades**, and there appeared to be no obstruction to my vision; **I could see every man and women in their grade and order**. I looked to see whether there was any disorder there, but there was none; neither could I see any death nor any darkness, disorder or confusion. He said that the people he there saw were organized in family capacities; and when he looked at them he saw **grade after grade**, and all were organized and in perfect harmony. He would mention one item after another and say, '**why, it is just as Brother Brigham says it is; it is just as he has told us many a time.**'" (Heber C. Kimball quoting JMG in *Mormon Thunder,* p. 248. Also see JD 4:135–136)

George Q. Cannon

"The Lord our God is working with us; He is trying us, probably with trials of a new sort that He may approve of us in every respect. **If we have set out to obtain celestial glory, the precious and inestimable gift of eternal lives, there is no trial necessary for our purification and perfection as Saints of God that we will not have to meet, contend with and overcome**. Such trials will come in various shapes, on the right hand and on the left, whether they be in having everything move on prosperously, or in adversity, hardship and the laying down of our lives for the truth, until the design is fully accomplished and the dross of our natures is purified and these earthly tabernacles are redeemed from everything that is groveling and low and brought into entire subjection to the mind and will of God." (Oct. 23, 1864, JD 10:346–47. *Gospel Truth: Discourses and Writings of President George Q. Cannon,* selected, arranged, and edited by Jerreld L. Newquist [Salt Lake City: Deseret Book Co., 1987], p. 527)

"It was necessary that a probation should be given to man. The courts of heaven were thronged with spirits that desired tabernacles. They wanted to come and obtain fleshly tabernacles as their Father had done. Their progenitors, the race of Gods with whom they associated and from whom they have descended, had had the privilege of coming on **earthly probations** and receiving tabernacles, which by obedience they had been able to redeem. Hence, I say, the courts of heaven were thronged with spirits anxious to take upon themselves tabernacles of flesh, agreeing to come forth and be tested and tried in order that they might receive exaltation…" (Ibid, p. 21)

"We are the children of God, and as His children **He desires to make us like Himself, to attain to the same glory and enter upon the same career of progress and exaltation that He has entered upon**. Therefore, it is necessary, in His wisdom and according to the laws of exaltation, that we should descend from our heavenly abode and come here and take upon us mortal tabernacles, and forget all that we knew.

The reason of this is that we should be tempted, that we should be tried, that we should be purified, that the dross of our nature should be cleansed by obedience to the laws of God, and that by obedience to His laws these tabernacles which we have received, and which belong to this fallen world, may be redeemed, and be fitted and prepared to dwell in a higher and purer abode—in an element that is far beyond anything that we know anything of at the present time. These tabernacles of ours, which are so full of humanity and its weaknesses, God has given unto us, and He has told us how we can redeem them—by obeying the laws He has taught.

But some will say: 'Why, if God is all powerful, does He not restrain the devil, and why does He allow him to afflict the children of men?' The reason is found in the fact that these things are necessary. **It is necessary that we should be tempted, that we should be tried, that we should be purified by going through these trials and passing**

through this furnace of affliction which this life furnishes. Now, there are some of you, probably, that have had disagreeable missions to perform in your life.

Some of you perhaps have had afflictions. I think there are some here who have been in the penitentiary for carrying out a principle of our religion. You have passed through many severe ordeals. Let me ask you —you men of experience and you women of experience—is it not a fact that those scenes which were the most trying to you and the hardest to bear at the time have been the most profitable to you? Do you not look back to them and feel that they have been the most fruitful in experience to you, and the most beneficial also in the lessons that they have taught you?

I know this is my experience. I look back to the disagreeable parts of my life, that is, the parts that were thought to be disagreeable at the time, and I say to myself, I thank God that I had these things to contend with. …in looking back at those scenes, I am convinced that they have been most profitable to me. The experience was unpleasant at the time. I would have shunned it if I could have had my own way, because human nature shrinks from trials and afflictions.

Human nature desires an easy path to tread. It wants to go with the stream, to float with the current. We therefore avoid the hardships of life if we can. But after we have passed through these trying scenes and endured these afflictions, we look back at them and are thankful, and say they have been more fruitful in profitable experience to us than any other scenes that we have passed through. **This is not only the case in relation to parts of our lives: it is the case in relation to the whole of our lives. When we have passed through this probation, if we have been faithful, we shall look back at all we have experienced and thank God, with all our hearts, that He permitted us to come on the earth and have the opportunities that we had of showing our fidelity to God**, our willingness to keep His commandments, and our determination that we would not be seduced from the path of obedience and rectitude by the blandishments and the temptations of Satan. **It is necessary, I say, to exaltation that we should pass through these scenes**. Some there are who will fail; **but the failure will not produce everlasting damnation. There will be, as the Lord says, few who will walk in the straight and narrow path that leadeth unto lives eternal**." (Brian H. Stuy, ed., *Collected Discourses,* 5 vols. [Burbank, Calif., and Woodland Hills, Ut.: B.H.S. Publishing, 1987–1992], Vol. 2: 144–145)

"**I believe that the religion of the Latter-day Saints shows in the plainest, in the simplest and in the most conclusive manner the relation of man to God**. I do not know any other religion that teaches in a satisfactory manner the object that God has had in placing man upon the earth. I do not know any other religion that teaches concerning the relationship that existed between God and His children prior to the organization of the earth and the placing of man upon it. I do not know any other religion that professes to teach the relationship that will exist between men and women, between parents and children, and between husband and wife, after this mortal career is ended. I do not know of any other religion that gives any distinct idea as to the character of the life beyond the grave, or what shall constitute the glory of man when he becomes immortal, and when he receives the fulness of the blessings that God has promised. I do not know any other religion that throws light upon these questions. **But I do know that there exists at the present time among men a great deal of uncertainty upon all these points**. Some even go so far—and they call themselves intelligent, too—as to doubt the future existence of man, and think that when this mortal career is finished that is the end of man as a living entity.

Now, who is there, with the light that is possessed by the religious world, that can explain in a satisfactory manner how it was that Jesus, our Redeemer, in whose name we approach the Father, existed as God in a previous state—that is, that He existed and exercised power and dominion, and then became a little child, born of a mortal woman? Is there any religion on the earth that can give any explanation of this great event? I have not met with any religion that will answer satisfactorily questions that arise connected with the preexistence and the birth of our Lord and Savior Jesus Christ.

But it is supposed to be clothed in mystery—a mystery that cannot be explained, and that is beyond human ken; and if inquiry arises it is suppressed, because it is considered almost blasphemous to think of such things. So it is with most of these questions that I have briefly alluded to." (Brian H. Stuy, ed., *Collected Discourses,* 5 vols. [Burbank, Calif., and Woodland Hills, Ut.: B.H.S. Publishing, 1987–1992], Vol. 3: 168–169)

"If, brethren and sisters, you want to be happy, you must cultivate happiness within yourselves. You may say, 'Well, if I can only attain the celestial glory, I think my desires will be fully gratified.' **There is no danger but that you will reach it, if you do right, because you are on the path of progression**. You will receive that for which you are qualified and fitted, and no more. Qualify yourselves for the society of angels and of God the Eternal Father and the Lord Jesus Christ, and you will reach it just as sure as you live. <u>**You will go on from one degree to another**</u>, and you will receive all that you live for. You will receive rewards for everything that you do, no matter what it may be, if it is only in the cause of righteousness; and you will receive punishment for your evil deeds. And there is no favoritism with the Lord. He rewards every man according to his works. <u>**Your progress and advancement in the kingdom of God and towards the glory of God depend upon yourselves**</u>.

Of course, when I say that, I mean with God's blessing upon you and His acceptance of your labors. I do not mean that it makes no difference whether the Lord blesses us or not. But our progress in the kingdom of God depends upon our own obedience and faithfulness in keeping the commandments of God. The man that lives up to the light that God has given to him to the very best of his ability will grow and increase, will add light to light, knowledge to knowledge, and power to power, until he will be prepared to enter into the rest of God. The woman or the child that does the same will receive a like blessing. For God is a God of justice, and He fulfills His words and promises, and we need not be afraid." (Brian H. Stuy, ed., *Collected Discourses,* 5 vols. [Burbank, Calif., and Woodland Hills, Ut.: B.H.S. Publishing, 1987–1992], Vol. 4: 16)

"**God has selected all of us to attain to this glory, if we will take the course that He has marked out for its attainment**. He has pointed out the way as plainly before us as this aisle is before me now in which we should walk; He has told us what to do, and warned us of the dangers that beset our pathway, and which we must guard against in order to attain to the end in view." (Brian H. Stuy, ed., *Collected Discourses,* 5 vols. [Burbank, Calif., and Woodland Hills, Ut.: B.H.S. Publishing, 1987–1992], Vol. 4: 311)

"There are different degrees of glory. Some attain to a more exalted glory. They must help those who are lower to rise up to their plane. Then there is another degree below them, and they must labor to lift those who are lower than they. Thus we can go on, every man in his sphere and in his glory endeavoring to lift up others to his height, until eternity will be filled with our labors in this direction; progressing from one degree of glory to another, without end, because there is no end to eternity, no end to glory. And as we progress, of course our capacity becomes enlarged. This will be our heaven. It will be the work in which God is engaged, in which Jesus is engaged; for, as I have said, He forsook the mansions of glory to save us.

It was so great and glorious a labor that in it He felt compensated for leaving heaven and coming to earth. And if we have His spirit we will feel as He does in relation to this, <u>and we shall go on from one degree of perfection to another, advancing as our Father in heaven advances, for there is progress for our Father and for our Lord Jesus. There is no such thing as standing still in the eternal work of our God. It is endless progress, progressing from one degree of knowledge to another degree. Thus the children of men will be continually exalted and drawn up toward God.</u> Of course, I do not refer to those who commit the unpardonable sin, who are sons of perdition; but all others will have the opportunity of progress and of repentance. That is the great word, Repentance! If they will only repent of their sins, God will wash them out. He tells us that though our sins be as scarlet they shall be made white as wool, if we will only repent. That is the great cry that the Elders of this Church are commanded to give unto the inhabitants of the earth; for by means of repentance and obedience to the ordinances which God has revealed, salvation is assured." (Brian H. Stuy, ed., *Collected Discourses,* 5 vols. [Burbank, Calif., and Woodland Hills, Ut.: B.H.S. Publishing, 1987–1992], Vol. 5: 374)

Joseph F. Smith

"I believe that our Savior is the ever-living example to all flesh in these things. He no doubt possessed a foreknowledge of all the vicissitudes through which he would have to pass in the mortal tabernacle...If Christ knew beforehand, so did we." (*Gospel Doctrine*, p. 13)

"'I want to announce that this lady [Lucy Walker Smith] is a wife of the Prophet Joseph Smith, who was sealed to him in his lifetime, and lived with him as his wife in Nauvoo.' Lucy Walker Smith said she wished to relate one incident in the life of the Prophet Joseph that was deeply impressed upon her mind in relation to sealing. On one occasion in the winter of 1830, in a prayer meeting held at Father Joseph Smith's, the Prophet arose to speak, and after speaking a few words he set his eyes upon some object, and remained silent for a few moments, and finally he became beautifully transfigured in appearance.

Then turning from his silence, he said: 'Do you know who that was with us tonight?' Some one present answered, 'Yes, an angel.' He said nothing till Martin Harris spoke, saying, 'I know that Jesus Christ, our Savior, has been in our midst.' 'Yes,' said the Prophet, 'God has revealed this to thee, Martin.' He said further: 'Brethren and sisters, do you know that the Lord has been in our midst tonight, and **He has given me a commandment that I seal you up unto eternal lives, and He has given you all to me, to be with me in my kingdom**, as Jesus is in His Father's kingdom.' This is a principle that was given in that early day, and more has been revealed in detail about it since." (Brian H. Stuy, ed., *Collected Discourses,* 5 vols. [Burbank, Calif., and Woodland Hills, Ut.: B.H.S. Publishing, 1987–1992] Vol. 5: 32)

Francis M. Lyman

"Now, I do not think there are any misgivings in the hearts of the Latter-day Saints this morning in regard to what President Woodruff has said to us concerning the doctrine which he has taken occasion to puncture; **that is, that the spirit of any man now in this probation had been on the earth in a former age, in another body. That doctrine ought to have laid still a score of years ago.** But when a false doctrine is put forth, some unwary person takes hold of it, and then some aspiring individual, later on in life, adopts it as his view. It may be that it savors a little of the mysterious, and some people delight in getting hold of something of that kind, that they may talk of it in private, if not in public, and arouse the curiosity of others. Thus it spreads. Each one says to himself, 'I wonder if this is not something that will turn out to be sound doctrine. It may be put forth a little early; but after a while I think it will be found to be sound doctrine.' This is how they delude themselves. There is so much truth that is plain and simple and easy to be understood by the children and by the Saints, however weak and feeble they may be, that it is a foolish thing for men to indulge in speculative theories." (Brian H. Stuy, ed., *Collected Discourses,* 5 vols. [Burbank, Calif., and Woodland Hills, Ut.: B.H.S. Publishing, 1987–1992], Vol. 1:266)

Heber J. Grant

"**We are living eternal lives, every one of us**, and I want to leave my testimony with you that I do know that, as I know that I live." (President Heber J. Grant, *Improvement Era, 1945*, Vol. xlviii. June 1945. No. 6)

Rudger Clawson

"Apostle J.H. Smith made some remarks respecting men betraying the confidence of the brethren, saying he thought some steps ought to be taken to guard against such things. **Pres. Snow said in reply, he thought the only way it could be done would be by giving men new bodies and eliminating all the material of which they are at present composed.**" (*A Ministry of Meeting: The Apostolic Diaries of Rudger Clawson*, p. 32)

George Albert Smith

"I want to say to many of you that I know personally, I can never repay your kindness and helpfulness to me in many ways. I say never—I'll say I can't do it in this life, **but I believe that we are living eternal lives**, and perhaps some of these failures here may be remedied hereafter." (*Conference Report, April 1946*, Afternoon Meeting, p. 181)

"What a blessed thing it is to know that we are living eternal lives. What a wonderful thing it would be if all the people in the world knew that they are living eternal lives." (*Conference Report, October 1946*, Afternoon Meeting, p. 149)

"Our missionaries are out in the world today trying to explain these things to the learned and other men of the world, and there are many learned men who have access to all of these books who do not believe in God, **who do not know that we are living eternal lives**, but have an idea that when we die that is the end of everything. Yet in the comparatively small organization known as the Church of Jesus Christ of Latter-day Saints, there are thousands of men and women and some children who know that we are the children of our Heavenly Father, **that we are here and now living eternal lives**, that the gospel, the power of God unto salvation to all those who will believe and obey, is on the earth...

All you have to do is to search the scriptures prayerfully. Go where they may be explained to you. Seek the truth, and the beauty of the truth will appeal to you, and perhaps without much of an effort on your part, and I am sure without giving away all your property, you can know as I know that God lives, that Jesus is the Christ, that Joseph Smith is a prophet of the Living God, and that **we are living eternal lives**." (*Conference Report,* October 1948, Afternoon Meeting, pp. 165–166)

Orson F. Whitney

"3 June 1889: This evening I heard that Pres. Woodruff, in a meeting at Manti, a few days ago, publicly declared that the doctrine of reincarnation, that is one spirit having several bodies, to be false; that he was Wilford Woodruff and no one else, &c &c. Alright, bro. Woodruff, if you really said it, it is between you and the Lord. **I believe it to be a true doctrine, & have for the last (a word was cut out of the entry) years**." (Diary of Orson F. Whitney, 3 June 1889, Church Archives. Also see a copy at the University of Utah library).

"8 June 1889: During our talks he (Lorenzo Snow) told me that his sister, the **late Eliza R. Snow Smith was a firm believer in the principle of reincarnation and that she claimed to have received it from Joseph the Prophet, her husband**. He said he saw nothing unreasonable in it, and could believe it, if it came to him from the Lord or his oracle." (Diary of Orson F. Whitney, 8 June 1889, Church Archives. Also copy at the University of Utah library).

"And the glorious thought of the resurrection comes like a balm to our sorrowing spirits, for we have received the promise that though our bodies are laid away in mother earth for a season, they shall come forth clothed upon with immortality and eternal life; that though we die, we shall live again, even as the sun which sets rises on the morrow with a greater and a brighter lustre. We have this hope within us, for God has implanted it there. This is what comforts us, to know that this life is only one among many scenes through which we have passed, and through which we will pass in the future." (Brian H. Stuy, ed., *Collected Discourses,* 5 vols. [Burbank, Calif., and Woodland Hills, Ut.: B.H.S. Publishing, 1987–1992], Vol. 1: 13)

"Mormonism be it true or false, holds out to men the greatest inducements that the human mind can grasp…It takes the humblest child of God, and tells him that he is a son of God; or, if a woman, that she is a daughter of God, and teaches them that they can by growth, by development, by progress and expansion, ascend to those heights where sits enthroned in glory the God of this universe. It teaches men that they can become divine, that man is God in embryo, that God was once a man in mortality, and that the only difference between Gods, angels and men is a difference in education and development.

Is such a religion to be sneered at? It teaches that the worlds on high, the stars that glitter in the blue vault of heaven, are kingdoms of God, that they were once earths like this, that they have been redeemed and glorified by the same laws, the same principles that are applied to this planet, and by which it will ascend to a perfected and glorified state. **It teaches that these worlds are peopled with human beings, God's sons and daughters, and that every husband and father, may become an Adam, and every wife and mother an Eve, to some future planet**. It teaches that all men will be saved except a certain few who are the sons of perdition." (Brian H. Stuy, ed., *Collected Discourses,* 5 vols. [Burbank, Calif., and Woodland Hills, Ut.: B.H.S. Publishing, 1987–1992], Vol. 4:336–337)

"…this great movement nicknamed 'Mormonism' is like a mighty tidal wave rolling up the beach of history, destined to make a higher ripple mark than any wave that has preceded it. Joseph Smith taught men to look up to heaven and conceive of a God in the form of man. He taught them that they could become like their Father and God, who was 'an exalted Man.' And what is more simple and reasonable? Don't you parents expect your children to become like you? Or do you expect your children to be something else than men and women? No. You men will see your sons become men; you women will see your daughters become women. Then God our Father—yes, and our Mother—in heaven, looking down upon this world—this school house in which their children are being educated—expect, and Joseph Smith taught it as a truth, that their children will be exalted, if they pursue the proper course, until they shall become divine beings themselves, worthy to stand upon that plane where stand their Father and their Mother in heaven. Like begets like; and the principle of eternal progress will make of man a God. Joseph Smith also taught the great principle of universal salvation. The Gospel of Jesus Christ saves all men; but saves them according to their merits, in different degrees of glory." (Brian H. Stuy, ed., *Collected Discourses,* 5 vols. [Burbank, Calif., and Woodland Hills, Ut.: B.H.S. Publishing, 1987–1992], Vol. 5: 431)

"The earth upon which we dwell is only one among the many creations of God. The stars that glitter in the heavens at night and give light unto the earth are His creations, redeemed worlds, perhaps, or worlds that are passing through the course of their redemption, being saved, purified, glorified and exalted by obedience to the principles of truth which we are now struggling to obey. Thus is the work of our Father made perpetual, and as fast as one world and its inhabitants are disposed of, He will roll another into existence, He will create another earth, He will people it with His offspring, the offspring of the Gods in eternity, and **they will pass through probations** such as we are now passing through, that they may prove their integrity by their works; that they may given an assurance to the Almighty that they are worthy to be exalted through obedience to those principles, that unchangeable plan of salvation which has been revealed to us." (JD 26:196)

"Deep down, fundamentally, what was it that brought about the death of the Apostle Paul and the death of the Prophet Joseph? The fundamental reason was this: They were servants of God, and Satan wanted them out of the way. They stood as 'lions in the path,' and were building up God's kingdom in His own appointed way. **Both these men had looked upon the face of Deity. Paul had been 'caught up to the third heaven' [2 Corinthians 12:2–5], Joseph to the 'seventh heaven' and there 'heard things unlawful to be uttered.'** [D&C 76:115.] Each was a divinely commissioned preacher of the gospel at the opening of a new dispensation." (Orson F. Whitney, *Conference Report,* October 1912, p. 70)

David O. McKay

"A man's idea of the significance of the words 'eternal progression' will largely determine his philosophy of life...The great secret of human happiness lies in progression. Stagnation means death...The doctrine of eternal progression is fundamental in the Church of Christ." (*Pathways to Happiness*, p. 260)

"Somebody has said, 'Show me a perfectly contented man and I will show you a useless one.' **So there must be some other element with contentment, some other virtue. What is it? Progress**. Contentment and progress contribute to peace. If we are no better tomorrow than we are today, we are not very useful... **so we want to experience two things: contentment and progress**—progress intellectually, progress physically, but above all, progress spiritually; and the cognizance that we grow contributes to peace. **You cannot remain stationary**." (Ibid, p. 292)

James E. Talmage

"...advancement from grade to grade within any kingdom, and from kingdom to kingdom will be provided for." (*Articles of Faith*, 1st Edition, pp. 420–421)

Melvin J. Ballard

"A man who goes to meeting and says long prayers and yet returns home to lose his temper and abuse his wife and berate his loved ones will never get into the kingdom of God until he learns to control his unruly temper. **The very best of us will need a probationary state to finish the work of preparation to go into the presence of the Father. If we do not do it here, just as sure as we live we will have to do it hereafter**, and many of us may lose the chance and opportunity of doing it hereafter." (*Conference Report,* October 7, 1917)

"There are no infant spirits born. **They had a being ages before they came into this life. They appear in infant bodies, but they were tested, proven souls**. Therefore, I say to you that long before we came into this life all groups and races of men existed as they exist today. Like attracts like...The races of today are very largely **reaping the consequence of a previous life**." (Bryant S. Hinckley, *Sermons and Missionary Services of Melvin J. Ballard* [Salt Lake City: Deseret Book Co., 1949], pp. 247–248)

John A. Widtsoe

"Progress means a moving forward from place to place, from knowledge to knowledge, from action to action. It is a process of adding to that which we now possess, by the elimination of errors, by the actual accretion of new truth, and by the development of greater self-mastery. It is a process by which increased power of every faculty is gained. **It is a process of growth and development, a movement toward greater maturity. It is a steady approach to the likeness of God**." (*Evidences & Reconciliations*, p. 179)

"They who so employ their time and talents properly, whether here or hereafter, increase in knowledge. That is the beginning of wisdom. There is no end to knowledge...What then is eternal progress? It is an eternity of active life, increasing in all good things, toward the likeness of the Lord. It is the highest conceivable form of growth...Those in lower kingdoms cannot 'overtake' those in higher kingdoms. What may happen if the man with less power uses it steadily in the spirit of repentance through the eternal years is not known to man. That knowledge rests as yet in the bosom of God." (Ibid, pp. 182–185)

"The essential thing is that man has to undergo experience upon experience, to attain the desired mastery of the external universe; and that we, of this earth, are passing through an estate designed wholly for our further education. Throughout eternal life, increasing knowledge is attained, and with increasing knowledge comes the greater adaptation to law, and in the end an increasingly greater joy. **Therefore, it is, that eternal life, is the greatest gift of God if the great law of progression is accepted, God must have been engaged from the beginning, and must now be engaged, in progressive development. As knowledge grew into greater knowledge, by the persistent efforts of will, his recognition of universal laws became greater until he attained at last a conquest over the universe which to our finite understanding seems absolutely complete.**" (*A Rational Theology* [Salt Lake City: General Priesthood Committee of the LDS Church, 1915], pp. 30–31)

"As more knowledge and power are attained, growth becomes increasingly more rapid. God, exalted by his glorious intelligence, is moving on into new fields of power with a rapidity of which we can have no conception, whereas man, in a lower stage of development, moves relatively at a snail-like, though increasing, pace. Man is, nevertheless, moving on, in eternal progression. In short, man is a god in embryo. He comes of a race of gods, and as this eternal growth is continued, we will approach more nearly the point which to us is Godhood, and which is everlasting in its power over the elements of the universe." (Ibid, pp. 23–25)

Delbert L. Stapley

"As sons and daughters of God, we are required to purify and perfect ourselves in righteousness, otherwise, we cannot be with him nor enjoy **eternal lives** and glory in his kingdom. To become like God we must possess the powers of Godhood. For such preparation there are important covenants, obligations, and ordinances for mankind to receive beyond the requirement of baptism and the laying on of hands for the reception of the Holy Ghost. Every person is to receive his or her endowments in the house of the Lord which permit them, if faithful and true, to pass by the angels who stand as sentinels guarding the way to eternal glory in the mansions of God. The everlasting covenant of marriage ordained of God for man and woman, also is to be entered into and the marriage contract sealed eternally by the authority of the Holy Priesthood of God. Otherwise, the highest degree of the celestial kingdom cannot be attained nor Godhood acquired, **which exalted condition assures continuation of the lives forever**." (*Conference Report,* April 1961, p. 66)

Richard L. Evans

"Be straight and open and honest. Don't permit anything to get into your life's record that will not stand scrutiny under the searching light of day. If you do, it will rise to plague you in the years to come, and your own thoughts will accuse you, even when others do not, for **we ourselves are the record of our eternal lives**." ("The Spoken Word from Temple Square", *Improvement Era,* 1945, Vol. 11-8, September, 1945. No. 9)

Hugh B. Brown

"The time will come when all men will know something of the glory of God. But the time will not come when I or any other man will arrive at a point in knowledge, experience or understanding beyond which we cannot go. In other words, we believe in eternal progression." (*The Abundant Life* [Salt Lake City: Bookcraft, 1956], p. 116)

"When we speak of eternal increase, we speak not only of increase of posterity, we speak of increase of knowledge and the power that comes with knowledge; increase of wisdom to use the knowledge and power wisely; increase of awareness and the joy that comes through understanding; increase of intelligence, which is the glory of God; **increase of all that goes to make up Godhood**." (*Continuing the Quest* [Salt Lake City: Deseret Press, 1961], p. 4)

Gordon B. Hinckley

"I want to give you my testimony of this work and I want to say it in such a way that you can remember that I said it. I know this work is true. I know that God our Eternal Father lives. I am thankful for the knowledge that He loves us as His children. I am grateful that I feel in my heart a great love for Him. I know He lives, my Father in Heaven. I can scarcely comprehend the wonder of it all. He who is the Creator and Governor of the universe knows me, knows you, each of you. He loves you, He is concerned for you. I know that Jesus is my Redeemer, my Lord, my Savior. I know that. I can't comprehend the full meaning of the Atonement, but I know that through His sacrifice **He has made it possible for you and for me to live eternal lives of growth and knowledge and understanding and work, regardless of whether it's on this side of the veil or on the other side of the veil**." (Promontory Branch, Tremonton Utah South Stake, sacrament meeting, Oct. 15, 1995. Messages of Inspiration from President Hinckley, *LDS Church News* 3/2/96. Also see *Teachings of Gordon B. Hinckley* [Salt Lake City: Deseret Book Co., 1997], p. 153)

Neal A. Maxwell

"**When we know who we are, then we know also much more clearly what we might become—and also how and when**. The gospel thereby emancipates us from uncertainty as to our identity. But this precious perspective also brings with it an intensification of our personal accountability, since we know who we are and why we are here." (*A Wonderful Flood of Light*, [Salt Lake City: Bookcraft, 1990], pp. 43–44)

M. Russell Ballard

"Clearly, Jesus and His disciples understood that Heavenly Father's plan included eternal opportunities for spiritual progression. But beyond that, **we don't have many specifics about the next phase of our eternal lives**. That's where our faith comes in. We know that God has promised incredible blessings to those who learn in this life to walk by faith and exercise the moral agency He has given us to make good decisions and choices (including, it should be noted, the choice we all have to believe this eternal plan or not to believe it). That should be enough. We don't have to know all of the details of those promised blessings. We just have to have confidence in them." (M. Russell Ballard, *Our Search for Happiness: An Invitation to Understand The Church of Jesus Christ of the Latter-day Saints* [Salt Lake City: Deseret Book Co., 1993], p. 80)

B.H. Roberts

"…it is said that those of the terrestrial glory will be ministered unto by those of the celestial; and those of the telestial will be ministered unto by those of the terrestrial—that is, those of the higher glory minister to those of a lesser order of glory. We can conceive of no reason for all this administration of the higher to the lower, unless it be for the **purpose of advancing our Father's children along the lines of eternal progression**…But if it be granted that the chief fact about Intelligences is that they have power to add fact to fact and thus build up knowledge, and through knowledge have wisdom, and thus make progress; and if to such intelligences there is granted eternal life—immortality—then it is useless to postulate any limitations for them; for in the passing of even a few thousands of millions of years, even if progress be very slow—**there will come a time when these intelligences**—men and women of even the telestial glory—**may become** very acceptable characters, and **very important personages**." (*Outlines of Ecclesiastical History*, pp. 416–417)

"Even with the possession of [the Holy Spirit] to guide us into all truth, I pray you, nevertheless, not to look for finality in things, for you will look in vain. Intelligence, purity, truth, will always remain with us relative terms and also relative qualities. Ascend to what heights you may, ever beyond you will see other heights in respect of these things and ever as you ascend, more heights will appear, and it is doubtful if we shall ever attain the absolute in respect of these qualities. Our joy will be the joy of approximating them, of attaining unto ever increasing excellence without attaining the absolute. It will be the joy of eternal progression." ("Relation of Inspiration and Revelation to Church Government," *Improvement Era,* 8 March 1905: p. 369)

"God's immutability should not be understood as to exclude the idea of advancement or progress of God…an absolute immutability would require eternal immobility—which would reduce God to a condition eternally static…which from the nature of things, would bar him from participation in that enlargement of kingdom and increasing glory that comes from the redemption and progress of men. And is it too bold of a thought, that with this progress, even for the Mightiest, new thoughts and new vistas may appear, inviting to new adventures and enterprises that will yield new experiences, advancement and enlargement even for the Most High?" (*The Seventy's Course in Theology* [Salt Lake City: Deseret Press, 1911], pp. 69–70)

William W. Phelps

"Again, it not only promises the return of Israel in the latter days, but it declares that they shall seek the Lord their god, and David their King. Seek David their King! Here remember that David had been dead many years, for Hosea prophesied about 175 years before the Babylonish Captivity: It opens the meaning of the latter part of the 37th Chapter of Ezekiel, which speaking of the gathering of Israel, says that they shall dwell in the land that I have given unto Jacob my servant, and they shall dwell therein, they and their children, and their children's children for ever, and my servant David shall be their prince forever. David must have had his eye upon the same thing when he said in the 71st Psalm, '**thou shalt quicken me again, and shalt bring me up again from the depth of the earth**'. No man will attempt to say that the children of Israel have lived in the land of Jacob, governed by David as King or Prince, since God by the mouths of Hosea and Ezekiel declared, that such should be the case, in the latter days! **The secret of the matter is, that God, in his infinite wisdom prepared the children of promise**, the heirs of the Celestial kingdom, **to live twice in the flesh on the earth, once in a state of probation; and once in a state of approbation**, and this is the reason why Job exclaimed: for I know my Redeemer liveth, and he shall stand at the latter day upon the earth: and though after my skin works destroy this body, yet in my flesh shall I see God." (*Evening and Morning Star,* July 1832, p. 14)

"We shall by and by learn that **we were with God in another world** before the foundation of the world, and had our agency, in order that we may prepare ourselves for a kingdom of glory." (*Messenger and Advocate,* June 1835, p. 130)

"If Jesus came to die and rise, to lead captivity captive, so did Joseph come to die and increase the power to bind Satan: **that eternal lives and eternal progression might search the eternal round with out impediment** [*sic*]…The prophet and patriarch have gone to paradise to bear testimony of the wickedness of the world, and help hasten the deliverance of the saints. Joseph goes back among his old associates of the other [?] world, **who have waded through like scenes of affliction** in the several ages past, and being beyond the power of death, as he was mighty for life, liberty and the pursuit of happiness, among good men, to raise and exalt them for eternal lives; how much more almighty will he be with the spirits of just men made perfect, and the Holy ones, to prune the vineyard; remove the bitter branches; and give room for the speedy fulfillment of his great and last revelation?" (The Joseph and Hyrum Smith Funeral Sermon preached by W. W. Phelps. Edited by Richard Van Wagoner and Steven C. Walker, *BYU Studies,* Vol. 23, 1983)

William Clayton

"President Orson Pratt spoke in favor of the suggestions of the Chaplain, and advised the brethren to improve the opportunity while we cross the plains, to get all the information we can. It was finally moved and carried viva vote, [vote by voice] that **the doctrine of the Resurrection be the subject to commence with**, and the following Brethren expressed their views in regard to it viz. Charles Smith, Jesse Turpin, George Mayer, James Park, David Wilkin, Edward Stevenson, and Edward Bunker. The views of these Brethren seemed to differ very materially on the subject, and there was very little or no light manifested by any one. It appears that the great difference in the views, is in regard to what is commonly called the baby resurrection, which idea is, **that instead of the bodies being raised out of the ground &c. we shall again be born of a woman, as we were when we came into this world**. Brother James Park agreed very strongly in favor of this kind of doctrine. This was a matter of astonishment to me, as I had never before heard of such a doctrine to understand it." (*An Intimate Chronicle: The Journals of William Clayton,* pp. 429–430)

Joseph Lee Robinson

"We also heard him (Joseph) say that God had revealed unto him that any man who ever committed adultery in either of his probations that that man could never be raised to the highest exaltation in the celestial glory and that he (Joseph) felt anxious with regard to himself and he inquired of the Lord and the Lord told him that he, Joseph, had never committed adultery (D&C 132:41). This saying of the Prophet astonished me very much. It opened up to me a very wide field of reflection. The idea that we had passed through probations prior to this and that we must have been married and given in marriage in those probations or there would be no propriety in making such an assertion and that there were several exaltations in the Celestial Kingdom of our God, the highest we supposed to be the Godhead and we conclude that there are several grades of exaltations in the servants to the Gods. Be this as it may, this is what he said." (*The Journal of Joseph Lee Robinson,* p. 12)

Benjamin F. Johnson

"In infancy we were fed upon milk, and in childhood by a loving hand, while our mistakes were tenderly admonished. As we became older we began to grasp the principles and issues of physical life and the modes for its sustenance through labors of our hands; while the gospel, as an alphabet, with its possibilities of reaching every principle of truth and light within **the great science of eternal lives**, is given to us as spiritual or intellectual food, through which, by faith, we can forever grow in the knowledge and power of the Gods, to become in reality and fullness even the 'Sons of God,' with glory, exaltation, dominion and **eternal progression, through the procreation of endless lives**..." (Benjamin F. Johnson, Letter to George F. Gibbs, 1903)

Eliza R. Snow

After recounting some of the history of Israel regarding the exoduses that the children of Israel have been forced to endure including the Latter-day Saints, she writes, "But they have been driven from those gathering places from time to time; yes driven farther west. There was the land which God was showing them. At first it was too distant to be seen even by the eye of faith. Too many thousands of miles even for the Spartan heroism of the sisters; too dark a tragedy of expulsion and martyrdoms; **and too many years of exoduses and probations**." (*Women of Mormondom*, p. 72)

Hugh Nibley

...And what is glory? How do you generate that intangible quantity? Glory, we are told, is intelligence. (D&C 93:36). Can we be more specific? That says it all, but what is intelligence? Intelligence is defined as problem-solving ability, i.e., intelligence is as intelligence does. What problem does it solve? **It is the supremely difficult problem of endowing weak and foolish man with immortality and eternal life.** God says this is his "work and his glory—to bring to pass the immortality and eternal life of man" (Moses 1:39)—that we return to his presence and with him partake of eternal life and exaltation. Since his glory is intelligence, he shares it with us. **Glory is shared intelligence.** (*A House of Glory*, transcription online at Maxwell Institute)

While the Apocalypse is Abraham's autobiography, written by himself during his lifetime, the Testament begins with the story of his death—it is a true Book of the Dead, **dealing with the vicissitudes of the soul from the painful experience of dying to the ultimate exaltation and eternal lives in the realms above**. Yet though the two texts deal with different periods in Abraham's life, they both have the same theme— **"the initiation of Abraham into the heavenly mysteries."**

In the closing lines of the Testament, God the Father says, "Take, then, my friend Abraham to the garden (lit. paradise—*eis ton paradeison*), where the tents of my righteous ones and the resting places (*monai*—lit. overnight stops, *mansiones*) of Isaac and Jacob are *in his bosom*." In his earlier cosmic tour in the same book Michael "took Abraham on a cloud, and led him to paradise," the heavenly court. (Rec. B, X.). (*Abraham in Egypt* [Salt Lake City: Deseret Book Co., 1981], p. 25).

This is the principle of subordination, a very important point. Among lights, **none are identical**; **there is a hierarchy (there is a greater and a greater and a greater)**. There is a hierarchy among the many worlds, says the *Pistis Sophia*. Many of these documents are concerned with the elaborate theoretical breakdown of this hierarchy, a favorite theme of the Gnostics: dividing it up into how it broke down, what power was above what, which angel was superior to which—like our friends the Seventh-Day Adventists, who argue as to who has five stars in his crown and who will have six.

The hierarchy among the many worlds is part of a tradition, a good illustration of the individual variations on a general theme. One of the many points of difference between the Gnostics and their rivals was the different way they would put in order and arrange the cosmic hierarchy. All of them, however, share the idea of three main degrees of glory. The *Pistis Sophia* says, "**You can visit the order below you, but not the levels or orders above you**." This is the rule in all worlds: you can go to the lower ones, but not to the ones above you.

The degrees are described in many of these writings. In his early *Epistle to the Trallians*, Ignatius (the second earliest Christian writer we have who is accepted by everyone as authentic) says, "I could write you about the mysteries of the heavens, but I am afraid to, for it would do you harm...

But I am able to understand the orders of the heavens, the degrees of the angels, the variations among them, the differences of dominions, of thrones, of powers—of the Holy Ghost, and of the kingdom of the Lord, and the highest of all—the rule of God over everything else."

"There's an infinite hierarchy in the worlds," says the *Sefer Yetzira*. "Christ rules in the second place, his rule exactly duplicating the Father's, but over a more limited number of cosmoses."

Methodius explains, "If other stars are greater than our world, then it is necessary that they contain life greater than ours, and greater peace, and greater justice, and greater virtue than ours." Of course we think of Abraham: If there is one, there shall be a greater one, and "I am more intelligent than they all" (Abraham 3:16–19). **The hierarchy goes on and on until there's no place to end it, except when it reaches the Father himself.**

These writers were aware of the fact that these doctrines carried over, but they couldn't understand them anymore, so the church Fathers got rid of them in the fourth century. The church Fathers called them "the teachings of the elders" and considered them great mysteries, because they didn't know what to do with them. Methodius says that the spirits are equal in age, but different in power, intelligence, and appearance. They have been so throughout all time.

Why should one be greater than another? This is one of the things the fathers liked to talk about. Origen was greatly intrigued and exercised by the diversity, and especially by the inequality among God's creatures. "Such an inequality," he says, "could not have been arbitrary, or else the Creator would be unjust. He couldn't create a thing small with another great over it—would that be just?"

So he concludes that the levels on which we all find ourselves in this world must somehow have been merited in a former life. However, the later schoolmen, following Aquinas, said that "there is indeed a hierarchy and a diversity simply because God wants it to be that way, and for no other reason." They gave the idea up.

Aquinas had his ideas of the multiplicity of worlds, and the great differences among them, and the hierarchy of worlds. What next? The idea that they are all moving forward. It is not a static system; every world is progressing. "Until Christ opened the way," says the *Gospel of Philip*, "it was impossible **to go from one level to another** [death and resurrection]. He is the great opener of the way because he gave us the plan by which we can progress. He is the way." That's why we call him "the way, the road, or **the gate.**" **The false progress of this world he compared to the ass turning a wheel, going around and around, turning the wheel and getting nowhere at all**. But being the "way," **the Lord himself also advances**.

The *Gospel of Truth* says, "**Thus the Word of the Father advances in the cosmos, being the fruit of his heart and the expression of his will**." Through the ordinances, one makes progress in knowledge, and the ordinances go on and on. "**There are mysteries so much greater than these**," says the *Pistis Sophia*, "that they make these look like a grain of flour, just as the sun looks like a grain of flour from distant worlds." That's in an old Jewish source too. "Everyone here on this earth descends, as it were, to the dregs [earth or dirt] and shares a common substance with all living things."

We are the same matter as the oyster, the cockroach, etc. They will be resurrected too, for they have a spiritual side—another very common teaching. "We share a common substance with all living things, and from here on out we begin to work our way up, step by step, to a knowledge of all things, ever seeking for instruction and carrying out the required ordinances that will lead us to more," says the *Epistle of the Apostles*. This is the idea of progress.

"Thus we move," says *1 Jeu*, "from truth to truth." The farther advanced one is, the faster one moves. The gap broadens as you move in a progression. The more advanced you are, the faster you go, and the more advanced you get in relation to each other—a principle Latter-day Saints also teach. "To them that have shall be given." With exaltation comes an increase and acceleration of exaltation. Thus "we are passed on from hand to hand, from degree to degree!"

Our example is Adam, who, having been established in Christ and God, next established his son Seth in the second order, which was to follow him on up, says the *Pistis Sophia*. "He who has fulfilled all the ordinances and has done good work cannot be held back," says the *Ginza*. "We are taught the principles of salvation, so that we cannot be held back in this world. Those who receive certain teachings and carry out their instructions in this world cannot be held back in this world or the next." "Those who shut the doors against me will be held back in the abode of darkness.

Those that open the doors to me will advance in the place of light." The great blessings pronounced on Adam, according to the same source, say, "**Thou shalt have progress onward.**" (*Temple and Cosmos: Beyond This Ignorant Present,* edited by Don E. Norton [Salt Lake City and Provo: Deseret Book Co., Foundation for Ancient Research and Mormon Studies, 1992], pp. 293–295. See the article for the numerous associated footnotes.)

...we are here as a reward, enjoying an opportunity to achieve yet greater things by being tried and tested **that each one might be promoted**, according to his intelligence and the perfections of his way, **or be retarded according to his wrong-doings**... (*Nibley on the Timely and the Timeless,* p. 53)

Though matter is replaced through an endless cycle of creations and dissolution, only spirit retains conscious identity, so that strictly speaking "only progeny is immortal," each "mounting up from world to world" acquiring ever more "treasure" while "progressing towards his perfection which awaits them all." (Ibid, p. 58)

The Serek Scroll or Manual of Discipline (IQS) from the Dead Sea Scrolls sets forth the beliefs and activities of a community of pious sectaries at Qumran in the desert just before the Christian era—what Professor Frank Cross has called a "church of anticipation." Everything is by way of preparation "for the eternal planting of a Holy Temple for Israel, and the Mysteries (secret ordinances) of a Holy of Holies for Aaron..." (IQS VIII, 5–6). Preparation is the theme; hence, it is not surprising that the specific ordinances referred to are the *initiatory* rites.

But at the same time the Serek scroll makes clear the ultimate objective of its whole operation—exaltation and **eternal lives for the members**—while plainly indicating the general nature of the temple activities to which it looks forward with such eager anticipation. (*The Message of the Joseph Smith Papyri: An Egyptian Endowment* [Salt Lake City: Deseret Book Co., 1975], p. 255).

"The soul (*psyche*) of the man So-and-so of whom I am thinking in my mind (*hit*)...**if it has completed the number of cycles of change (cf. Eg. *khprw*), may it be led to the Virgin of Light...to seal him with the seal of the Ineffable...**" (then the dead will be baptized) and **receive the seal and the sign (*main*) of the Kingdom...and be taken to the degree (*taxis*) of the Light**...Now therefore, let everyone who is worthy receive the ordinances (mysteries) and enter into the light. (277) ...that mankind may not die the death appointed for them by the forces (Archons) of natural law (*heimarmene*). (230) (Christ's message to the world): **Seek constantly and do not give up until you have found the Mysteries of the Light!**...Every man who comes to you (the Apostles) believing and...worthy, give them the mysteries of the light and conceal them not.

And give the higher mysteries to whoever is worthy of them and the lower mysteries to whoever is worthy of them (each should receive to the limit of his capacity). (337) But *hide* this ordinance (of sacrifice), and do not give it to everybody, but only to him who shall do everything which I told you by way of commandment. (Ibid, p. 274).

195: **(In time) all who have repented will come to the Middle Place** (i.e., this world, the transition between premortal and postmortal existence), and those who are in the Middle will baptize them and give them the spiritual anointing, and seal them with the seals of their ordinances (mysteries), and **they shall pass through all the stations (*topos*, degrees) of the Middle...(196)...receiving from each the seal of its mystery...and remaining at each level (*topos*) of ordinances until one finally reaches the Inheritance of Light**.

(291f) **(At each level [*topos*] the soul is examined and tested.) They will all test (*dokimaze*) that soul to find their signs (or tokens, *maein*) in it, as well as their seals and their baptisms and their anointing (*chrisma*).** (292) And the virgin of the Light will seal that soul, and the Workers (*paraleptes*), will baptize it and give it the spiritual anointing...

And then the receptionist (workers) hand it over to the great Sabaoth... at the Gate of Life...**call[ed] "Father."** And to him the soul (fem.) gives...**his seals and his responses, with the seal of each degree (*topos*) in the Right Hand (this is the proper meaning of the word *ounam*); and the soul will give its knowledge (*episteme*, special knowledge) and with the right hand seal of every *topos* with hymns of glory...and all the assistants (*paralptes*) of Melchizedek will seal that soul and lead it to the Treasury of the Light—the *topos* of its inheritance.** (Ibid, p. 275)

CHAPTER 10

CULMINATING ORDINANCES

Hugh Nibley

He who performs that mystery and carries out all the prescribed forms (*schemata*) and figures thereof (*peftypos*), and its steps (*jinaheratou*), will not really come out of the body in doing so...yet when he dies he will not have to go through it all again—the responses and explanations and tokens—on the other side. (Christ has provided the ordinances) (277) that men need not die the death appointed for them by the rulers of Fate [i.e., in the course of Nature]. (246) (It is done figuratively, on a certain level—*chorema*), these things are only types and figures (*schema*)

(291) (**At every station, inspectors) prove the soul and find together their signs in it, and their seals and their baptisms, and their anointing, (whereupon they put their seal on the soul and send it forward to the next inspection point. This goes on to the highest levels**). The Assistants of the Light hand over the soul to the Great Sabaoth the Good, who is at the Gate of Life...who is called Father, who gives the soul his seals...and Melchizedek seals that soul and all the Assistants of Melchizedek seal that soul and lead it into the Treasury of Light (where it is again sealed, and so) goes over into the realm of its Inheritance.

(238–39) (When one receives the Mystery by proxy) he will not be judged, but we will hand him on quickly from one to another, **from order to order** (*topos*) until he reaches the Virgin of Light (Eg. *Maat*) who sees the signs and tokens in him, but holds him back (until he has received complete clearance) then seals him with the holy seal. (276) (For the dead this can be in monthly installments as) every month by month the Virgin seals the candidate with a higher seal. (195)

(**The candidate always moves in a company of his kind**; each *arithmesis*—**set number—of souls has its time and place on earth, and when the number is fulfilled or the initiation completed of** *teleioi psychai*, **the group of souls moves on to**) a higher inheritance in the Light...Everyone must remain in the *topos* in which he is until he is ready to receive the mysteries of the next. (354) (Only) one in

10,000 will ever attain to the Mystery of the First Mystery 258. (357–58) (An important episode of the group initiation is the Prayer Circle, which we have treated elsewhere.)

(188) (**There are mysteries far beyond any known on earth**.) (186) When I lead you to the *topos* of those who have received their inheritance...the Sun will look like nothing but a tiny speck of cornmeal, because of the enormous distance, and **because the new world is so much greater.** (216f) **(These higher mysteries are not for the unqualified, who are terrified of them; they go far beyond mortal comprehension**.) (*The Message of the Joseph Smith Papyri: An Egyptian Endowment* [Salt Lake City: Deseret Book Co., 1975], pp. 277–278. See the article for the numerous associated footnotes)

Even in this short life, we pass through a number of distinct episodes, a number of distinct existences. You could refer to the "lives" of Don Decker, because he had very different lives, as we all have, our own seven stages. Biologically, I am assuredly a very different person from what I was a long time ago. These transitions, these rites of passage, are rites that take us from one state of existence to another; the process is an obsession with the human family, going back to the Stone Age (Don refers to them in a poem of his); and the rites of passage obsess us here and now. Quite literally, too.

A cultural shock occurs when you pass from one state to the other. And the transitions are usually quite abrupt. You are born all of a sudden; you die all of a sudden. Each time you get a new name, a new rank, a new identity, a new function, a new office of priesthood or whatever it may be, you get new duties, new privileges; you become a different person. On many of these occasions, you change your name. You go not into another existence (the Egyptians would say *kheper*).

That implies changing form without changing identity. The classic example with the Egyptians was the butterfly or the frog. A cocoon is not a caterpillar, nor is it a butterfly. The two states are the same creature, but what resemblance would you ever recognize?

Even while we are here, we must give up lives. *Lech lecha,* which means "get up and keep going," is the title of Abraham's life in the chapters of Genesis that describe him. The book of Abraham begins, "At the residence of my fathers...I saw that it was needful for me to obtain another place of residence" (Abraham 1:1). Abraham had to get up and go, and he never settled until the end of his life. He had to buy a grave for his wife and himself from strangers in a strange land. His life was one continual going from one phase to another, **moving from one existence to another all the time**.

So it is with us here: *Lech lecha.* Sometimes it seems cruel. Shakespeare's sonnets are devoted very much to that theme. He treats the passing of youth as a form of death, something you'll never get back again: you are another kind of person; it was another phase of life. Looking back is very romantic. It was hell when you were in it, but as you reflect back, it looks quite nice. We make that common mistake about youth; Shakespeare says it is death.

This is a profound tragedy, because as far as Shakespeare was concerned, there is nothing to it. It is the "baseless fabric of this vision...it...shall dissolve;...and, like the insubstantial pageant faded, leave not a rack behind." That was Shakespeare's last word in the *Tempest*. There is nothing more. It is the end of the show. We are all going home. That is what makes the play so very sad: to have to pass from one phase to another.

But not with us—not with us at all. Passing from one phase is the normal thing; it makes existence more exciting. That is the central theme of the temple—the subject to which my and Don's discussions invariably tended. In each state, the creature must pass through; there is something we couldn't get anywhere else.

But how can a few brief years spent here, born to trouble as we are, have a significant impact on eternal existence? Eternity is a long time; earth life is just a second—a fantastic disproportion. This life, Lehi tells us, is only a probation, only a test (1 Nephi 10:21; 2 Nephi 2:21; Alma 34:32). A test, to be searching and definitive, need last only a few seconds...

...Thus we don't need to go on forever suffering the same nonsense in order to see the things we can be tested for, namely the two things and the only two things we are good at: **we can forgive and we can repent**. These are the two things the angels envy us for...

...Of course, that is the whole thing in the gospel. "Wherefore [the first word to Adam]...thou shalt repent and call upon God in the name of the Son forevermore" (Moses 5:8). When the Lord came to the Nephites, among his first words to them were these: "This is the gospel, that the Father commandeth all men, everywhere, to repent" (3 Nephi 11:32). This is not a popular doctrine.

In my thirty-five years at BYU, I have heard only one sermon (given by Stephen L Richards, incidentally) on repentance. And it was not well received. "Don't tell us to repent. Repentance is for the bad guys."

But Don knew that it was called the gospel of repentance. All must repent constantly, each for himself. You can't repent another person.

Ezekiel 38:18–19 [Ezekiel 33:18–19] defines a righteous man. Who is righteous? Anyone who is repenting. No matter how bad he has been, if he is repenting he is a righteous man. There is hope for him. And no matter how good he has been all his life, if he is not repenting, he is a wicked man. The difference is which way you are facing. **The man on the top of the stairs facing down is much worse off than the man on the bottom step who is facing up. The direction we are facing, that is repentance; and that is what determines whether we are good or bad**.

Don always pondered the problem of repentance. He was aware of it; and how few are. We are expected to commit all kinds of sins here, and also discover them. We are supposed to dig the nitty-gritty out of the rug, so to speak.

We are sent here, going on for eternity (and eternity is a long time), **but we can't go on as defective vessels. If there is anything seriously wrong with our character, we want to find it out and get rid of it before we get launched on that tremendous project we are after.** This is the place to find out all the dirty, nasty, little sides of our nature; it is the only place we can, because we are not in the presence of God and angels here, and it is possible for us to sin. So when God says to Adam, "We shall leave you now, but we shall visit you again"—as soon as he turns, who pops up? Satan. He says, "Aha! Here I am. Now we can really put Adam to the test."

Satan is there to try him and to tempt him and us, but only if we are left here. We are supposed to find out all the dirtiness, the weakness, the sinfulness of our nature; and that is what keeps us repenting all the time until we reach the state of perfect grace and truth. Let us remember, the Only Begotten is full of grace and truth. **When we reach that state**, it will be just dandy. We can stop repenting, I suppose. **But do we realize what that means? What grace, love, complete love for everything, and truth are?**

So it is here that we repent. I remember some of my former lives—my childhood and youth. I was bungling, bemused, wandering in a daze, getting pushed around, trying to push back, and not knowing what was going on. It was not the happy, carefree time we think. But it is profitable to me now. Our lives here will be profitable to us, of tremendous value, at some future time. We are told that spirits enter the other world somewhat in a daze (from the experience of many people—some of whom I know, including myself). The fact is, we are in a daze right here. I go around in a daze most of the time…

But one thing I have learned in the passage from one phase of existence to another is that nothing is lost in the process. (*Approaching Zion, Funeral Address*, edited by Don E. Norton [Salt Lake City and Provo: Deseret Book Co., FARMS, 1989], pp. 298–303)

Here's what we've come out for. "And these are the councils of the spirit for the sons of truth while they are on the earth, and which will be the testing [*pequddah* is a *testing* or a *visitation*; somebody comes and checks up on you, etc.] of all those who walk in this way.

And it is for this: for healing, for increase of peace, for length of days, for the multiplication offspring [these were not celibates out here at all; men, women, and children were buried in the cemetery together] and all the blessings of eternity, and for eternal joy and **lives [plural]** of glory, [this is *netsah*, and it's the same as the Latin word, *nieo*, meaning *to shine*, or *to be glorious*; *nitein*, shining, brilliant, the high glory], and for a crown of exaltation *middat-hadar*, with a garment of glory [*hadar* is white brilliance] in the light of the eternities." A rabbi will tell you, "Well, we don't have eternal life. Heaven is a philosophical concept."

But this is the sort of language we use, isn't it? This is not orthodox Judaism. You can see why they didn't want it. It's not orthodox Christianity either—**this eternal progression thing** and getting the crowns, and being tested while you are here. Then we get to the preexistence, the plan as it was made in the beginning. (*Teachings of the Book of Mormon—Semester 1:* Transcripts of Lectures Presented to an Honors Book of Mormon class at BYU, 1988–1990 [Provo: FARMS], p. 154)

Now it's this name Joseph that they play on, but this is a characteristic thing in genealogy, and Joseph is very special. **But the fact that it should be the same Joseph, leading right down to Joseph Smith, should not surprise you.** (Ibid, p. 277)

In Mosiah 1 he is going to give them a new name and a new identity. See, **every time you get a new life or a new advancement, a new step or initiation, you get a new identity, a new persona**. When a person is born he gets christened. He is not christened until he joins the church. This is the theory in the Christian world. With us it used to be always on the eighth day, circumcision, etc. You have a new name, and when you get married you get another new name. If you get any office, you also get another new name. Then at your funeral you get another identity, etc. **They go through the same ritual every time**.

And, of course, when you reach maturity there's a very important thing —the rites of initiation that come with maturity. In the Christian churches it's when you are confirmed, around the age of fifteen. In all primitive tribes and [other societies] when a person becomes mature— reaches manhood or womanhood—there is that rite. Then they get a new name; they are identified with another group entirely.

Boys are no longer with the women, etc. They now belong to a man's *phratry*. These are the rites of puberty. **So each time you get a new name, a new identity, a new appearance, new marks, and a new title or degree**. (Ibid, pp. 448–449)

See, the Spirit of the Lord guides you. It won't promise you instant prosperity; it will guide you and give you a sense of the things you should be doing. If you don't, you are in a state of "open rebellion against God; therefore he listeth to obey the evil spirit...Therefore if that man repenteth not, and remaineth and dieth an enemy to God, the demands of divine justice..." Notice that he shifts this whole thing to the larger scale. This is on a cosmic pattern and has to do with the other world. That's where atonement takes place. That's where we return to Heavenly Father and are redeemed, bought back again.

See all that re business. You are redeemed, you are resurrected, you are raised up <u>again</u>, you return and go back. Teshûvah means to return and yeshîvah, sit down once you get there. We mentioned the reconciliation. It all has to do with going back to a prior condition that you lived in before you came here—it's very clear.

As I said, the only alternative to that is a simplistic predestination which just stops everything dead cold. "The demands of divine justice do awaken his immortal soul to a lively sense of his own guilt, which doth cause him to shrink from the presence of the Lord [this is what hell is, of course], and doth fill his breast with guilt, and pain, and anguish, which is like an unquenchable fire, whose flame ascendeth up forever and ever." (Ibid, p. 459)

Now concerning that which was to come, remember, the purpose of the year festival was to determine the fortunes of the new age. It was not just launching a new year. *Year* is *gear* and *yule*, the same word as *wheel*. It means "**a turning, a revolution**." It's the same word as *while*. The interesting thing is that in the Arabic world it's *hawl hawla*. It means "**the cycle turned, the wheel revolved**, the year went around." The Greeks call it the *enianton*, "**the here we are again**." Jane Harrison wrote a book about that. **You come back again, and you are in a revolving circle of the time that goes on forever and ever**. (Ibid, p. 461)

They treated John the Baptist the same way. Remember, he was "the mad mullah of the desert." He dressed in camel skin and lived on wild locusts and honey. The people flocked out to see him, etc. **Josephus said an interesting thing about him**. When people asked him who [John the Baptist] was, Josephus didn't know his name. He knew all about him, but he didn't know his name was *John* because he never told anybody his name was *John* . **He said he was *Enoch***, a very interesting thing, and they took him for Enoch Redivivus, "**the returned Enoch**." **And, of course, Enoch is going to return with Elijah**, another one who was treated the same way. (*Teachings of the Book of Mormon—Semester 2:* Transcripts of Lectures Presented to an Honors Book of Mormon class at BYU, 1988–1990 [Provo: FARMS p. 76)

Verse 6: "And after all this, after working many mighty miracles among the children of men, he shall be led, yea, even as Isaiah said, as a sheep before the shearer is dumb, so he opened not his mouth." **He left the celestial circuit to bring us into that celestial circuit, you might say** (verses 6 and 7). The Lord must come down to us to arrange for our removal to a higher realm; we can't go up there to make arrangements. He must come to us to give us a chance to acknowledge him, and accept the offering, and understand what the thing is. It's a sort of martialing area here. Verse 8 tells us that it is a physical breaking of confining bonds, a barrier beyond which life ceases.

The bands of death have to be broken, as we are told in 2 Nephi 9:7 . The second law would be in effect if it weren't for that. That's what Hawking talks about here. Why should the second law [have to] be broken? Why should it ever be there at all? They are all right back where they started, at square one, now. There's no limit to the power of whatever put us here. It could put other people in other places. As Voltaire said long ago, "**Once we get a person born, the idea of getting reborn is just a technical matter**." Just a matter of working out a few bugs. If you've already got him born out of nothing—**all you have to do is repeat the thing.** (Ibid, p. 84)

Mosiah 27:25: "And the Lord said unto me: **Marvel not that all mankind…must be born again.**" Notice that it's nothing less than being born all over again. We are so completely out of it when we are here. **We cannot make the change without leaving the scene. You have to be born again.** See, there's the one world or the other; you can't mix them. It's a very hard thing, as Brigham Young said, as he tried to take the water on both shoulders. "The Latter-day Saint who tries to live in both worlds is torn apart." There's no such agony, no worse experience than that, and it happens to them here. As it explains here, "…yea, born of God, changed from their carnal and fallen state, to a state of righteousness [a complete change], being redeemed of God, becoming his sons and daughters." They become new creatures; it's an entirely different thing, as this explains. (Ibid, p. 191)

This is one of the best-known phenomena of ancient history now. It wasn't a few years ago, but I've been yelling about it for years. As is well known, this is a stock theme. It's a rehearsing of the creation, the refounding, **the rebirth of the human race.** It's the *natalia*, it is the refounding of the kingdom, it's universal. **Everybody is reborn and receives a new name on a particular day**, which is the new year—it's gauged by the sun. And it [this ceremony] is very conspicuous in the documents, and only within the last three or four years, the anthropologists have latched onto it. Finally when they catch up to it, it has become very obvious. You can see that. And this is a very basic theme. I notice the three principal anthropologists writing about this now. They've all got into the act, and they're talking about primitive societies. This is universal. Van Gennep's theory is that society has to regenerate itself by rites of passage. **You know what a rite of passage is—the rite of passage into the other world.**

Then you have to get passage to come back. That's what they're talking about now. There are two worlds. **You go to the one, and then you come back refreshed and renewed to your old world and begin a new cycle of life**. This is what they're saying today. Well, it's been obvious for a hundred years, but they didn't notice it. They've been following Frazier instead, which is a very different pattern. Well, Van Gennep's theory is **regeneration by rites of passage. He says it sometimes takes the form of rites of death and rebirth**. And Victor Turner says the rites all apply to the society and don't affect the individual at all. The society first separates itself from its former life. That is what you do when you drive out a scapegoat, etc. You purge yourself of what you were before. **They separate themselves from their former life. Then there's what he calls the transition; and then there's the reincorporation when you come back to ordinary life and you're good for a new period.** (Ibid, p. 276)

Verse 39: "And Amulek said unto him: Yea, he is **the very Eternal Father** of heaven and of earth, and all things which in them are." He made the whole thing possible. And Hebrews 1:2 says the same thing.

He **made possible the physical resurrection**. "And he shall come into the world to redeem his people." **To redeem something, as we said before, is to bring back somebody who had been there before—to bring him home again.** *Redemptio* **is to buy back again. It's to buy back something that was yours before and got lost; now you buy it back again. Well, we were with Him in the eternities before this. Now we have been separated, and then we go back again.** "And he shall take upon him the transgressions of those who believe on his name; and these are they that shall have eternal life, and salvation cometh to none else." (Ibid, p. 320)

D. Michael Quinn

By the time of his death in 1844, **Joseph Smith had also reversed his prior rejection of the Cabala's doctrine of "transmigration of the souls." Two of the women Smith secretly married as plural wives in the 1840s said that he privately affirmed reincarnation.** Apostle Lorenzo Snow said that "his sister, the late Eliza R. Snow Smith was a firm believer in the principle of reincarnation and that she claimed to have received it from Joseph the Prophet, her husband." Prescindia Huntington Buell (later Kimball) also affirmed her belief in "**plural probations**" referring to a statement "in confirmation" by her polyandrous husband Joseph Smith. (*Early Mormonism and the Magic World View*, p. 302)

Truman G. Madsen

In mankind, the true, the good, the beautiful are not only reflected but come to life. And again the scriptures teach of the inseparable connection-in fact, the eventual union in their highest forms—of light and life. "In [Christ] was life; and the life was the light of men" (John 1:4). And it is His light that "giveth life to all things" (D&C 88:13). And in man the inclusive all refers to the life of the mind and all the creative and responsive forces that are interwoven in him. A modern revelation speaks not only of the classic symbol "eternal life" but also of "**eternal lives**" (D&C 132:22–25), **the plural emphasizing expansion and intensification of the lives within the whole person.** (*The Radiant Life* [Salt Lake City: Bookcraft, 1994], p. 28)

Richard O. Cowan

What is meant by "eternal lives"? Beginning in verse 19 of D&C 132, the Lord outlines the remarkable blessings to be enjoyed by those who are exalted in the celestial kingdom. In verse 24 he paraphrases the well-known statement in John 17:3. President Charles W. Penrose explained that "**eternal lives**" means "more than life, more than mere existence, it means **perpetual increase of posterity, worlds without end**" (in Conference Report, Oct. 1921, 22). President Harold B. Lee reasoned that "if marriage then was for the purpose of the organizing of spirits before the world was formed and for 'multiplying and replenishing the earth' on which we now live, surely there must likewise be a divine purpose in its being continued after the resurrection. This purpose is declared by the Lord to be for 'a continuation of the seeds forever and ever' [D&C 132:19]." (*Teachings of Harold B. Lee,* p. 238). (Richard O. Cowan, *Answers to Your Questions About the Doctrine and Covenants* [Salt Lake City: Deseret Book Co., 1996], p. 147)

Chapter 11

Treasures in the Heavens

Hugh Nibley

We find in the many treasure passages that the treasure is the wisdom and knowledge we left behind us when we came down to this earth. In the premortal existence, we left our treasure in God's treasury, in his keeping. There it is, and by our good works here we can add to it; more will be waiting for us when we go back. So let us not try to pile up wealth and possessions on earth. They're not going to do us any good; we can't take them back there. Let us lay up our treasures there—add to our treasure store. We really do have one there, because we had one before we came. We left it behind, and we're going back to it. It's a very vivid concept, and basic to it is the doctrine of the premortal existence. There's a great treasury in heaven which contains all good things; it is to share in this treasury that all seek. But in the Jewish apocrypha, in the Wisdom of Ben Sira, God orders, by his word, the lights in the heavenly height, and by the utterance of his mouth he opens the treasury, where the righteous have a store of good works preserved. These are good works preserved, already done. And they're being preserved; everything we add to our credit is being preserved in God's treasury. "At that time," says *2 Baruch*, "the treasuries will be opened in which is preserved the number of the souls of the righteous." *Second Enoch* puts another unpopular interpretation on the heavenly treasury. It is the treasure house of the various elements.

We're told, in a recently discovered writing, the Syriac writing called *The Pearl*, how the prince is completely outfitted by his heavenly parents to come down to this earth. He's warned and given final instructions; then with a heavy heart they send him forth. They know he's going to be tested, but it's quite a happy event nevertheless. He's left his treasure behind, and also his special garment, which he will resume when he comes back if he's worthy. So he goes down and lives in the wicked world in Egypt, becomes defiled, forgets his treasure, and has to have a special messenger sent to remind him that he has a treasure, and that he's going to lose it if he doesn't behave himself.

So he reforms his ways and works hard, trying to gain the pearl again so he can bring it back, to put it into the treasury, where his garment is waiting for him. **This idea of a waiting garment occurs many times—**

about a hundred times—in the newly discovered texts. The righteous are completely outfitted by the treasurers with the garments and jewels from the royal treasury, and those God returns. "God has hidden the kingdom as a treasure," says Peter in the *Clementine Recognitions*, "burying it under mountains, where it can only be reached by zealous work. **The righteous attain to it, enjoy the treasure, and want to give it to others.**" In another text, the Lord commands at the creation, "Bring out all the knowledge, bring the books from my storehouse, bring the necessary equipment from my laboratory and my treasury, and bring a reed of quick writing, and give it to Enoch and let's get to work here." These things are in storage. The *Zadokite Fragment* explains that God laid open his hidden things before them, as well as knowledge of the times and the seasons which is kept in his treasury. According to the *Serekh Scroll*, or the *Manual of Discipline*, God in the beginning opened his treasury and poured out his knowledge. That knowledge is being kept there. He poured out his knowledge before the first angels. (This is the time when the world was created in the presence of the first angels.) The writer of the *Thanksgiving Hymns* rejoices constantly in **being able to receive from the treasury of God's secret knowledge.** This is what 2 *Jeu* calls "**the great mystery of the treasury of light,**" **which can be approached only by those who have passed through all the eons and all the places of the invisible God. We return to obtain it, bringing a lot of experience**.

"The treasury of the heavenly king is open," says the *Acts of Thomas*; "and everyone who is worthy takes and finds rest, and when he has found rest he becomes a king." The *Gospel of Thomas* counsels us to "search for the treasure which fails not," and tells us that the kingdom is like a treasure hidden in a field; someone bought the field, found it there, and began lending money to everyone. So also **we want to share the treasure**. (*Temple and Cosmos: Beyond This Ignorant Present*, edited by Don E. Norton [Salt Lake City and Provo: Deseret Book Co., FARMS, 1992], pp. 233–234.)

In coming to earth each man leaves his particular treasure, or his share of *the* Treasure, behind him in heaven, safely kept in trust ("under God's throne") awaiting his return. One has here below the opportunity of enhancing one's treasure in heaven by meritorious action, and also the risk of losing it entirely by neglecting it in his search for earthly treasure. (*Nibley on the Timely and the Timeless*, p. 54)

Chapter 12

Tried in All Things

Joseph Smith

"**My people must be tried in all things**, that they may be prepared to receive the glory that I have for them, even the glory of Zion; and he that will not bear chastisement is not worthy of my kingdom." (D&C 136:31)

"And they shall overcome all things." (D&C 76:60)

"We consider that God has created man with a mind capable of instruction, and a faculty which may be enlarged in proportion to the heed and diligence given to the light communicated from heaven to the intellect; and that the nearer man approaches perfection, the clearer are his views, and the greater his enjoyments, till he has overcome the evils of his life and lost every desire for sin; and like the ancients, arrives at that point of faith where he is wrapped in the power and glory of his Maker and is caught up to dwell with Him.

But we consider that this is a station to which no man ever arrived in a moment: he must have been instructed in the government and laws of that kingdom by proper degrees, until his mind is capable in some measure of comprehending the propriety, justice, equality, and consistency of the same." (*Teachings of the Prophet Joseph Smith*, p. 51)

"You will have all kinds of trials to pass through. And it is quite as necessary for you to be tried as it was for Abraham and other men of God, and (said he) God will feel after you, and He will take hold of you and wrench your very heart strings, and if you cannot stand it you will not be fit for an inheritance in the Celestial Kingdom of God." (Joseph Smith as quoted by John Taylor. JD 24:197)

Brigham Young

"**All intelligent beings who are crowned with crowns of glory, immortality, and eternal lives must pass through every ordeal appointed for intelligent beings to pass through, to gain their glory and exaltation.** Every calamity that can come upon mortal beings will be suffered to come upon the few, to prepare them to enjoy the presence of the Lord. If we obtain the glory that Abraham obtained, we must do so by the same means that he did. If we are ever prepared to enjoy the society of Enoch, Noah, Melchizedek, Abraham, Isaac, and Jacob, or of their faithful children, and of the faithful Prophets and Apostles, **we**

must pass through the same experience, and gain the knowledge, intelligence, and endowments that will prepare us to enter into the celestial kingdom of our Father and God. **How many of the Latter-day Saints will endure all these things, and be prepared to enjoy the presence of the Father and the Son? You can answer that question at your leisure. Every trial and experience you have passed through is necessary for your salvation.**" (*Discourses of Brigham Young,* selected and arranged by John A. Widtsoe [Salt Lake City: Deseret Book Co., 1954], 345. JD 8:150)

"Do you recollect what I told the brethren who came across the plains this season, when they were perplexed by their oxen; and were calling upon God to give you grace to perform the labor which lay before you, **He could not sympathize with you, or know the nature of your trials if He had not passed through the same Himself. He knew just as much about crossing the plains, and the trials connected with it as any of us.**" (*The Essential Brigham Young,* p. 98)

"The disposition, the will, the spirit, when it comes from heaven and enters the tabernacle, is as pure as an angel. The spirit from the eternal worlds enters the tabernacle at the time of what is termed quickening, and forgets all it formerly knew. It descends below all things, as Jesus did. All beings, to be crowned with crowns of glory and eternal lives, must in their infantile weakness begin, with regard to their trials, the day of their probation. They must descend below all things, in order to ascend above all things." (JD 6:333)

"I am a witness that 'Mormonism' is true upon philosophical principles. Every particle of sense I have, proves it to be sound, natural reason. The gospel is true, there is a God, there are angels, there are a heaven and a hell, and **we are all in eternity, and out of it we can never get**, it is boundless, without beginning or end, **and we have never been out of it**. Time is a certain portion of eternity allotted to the existence of these mortal bodies, which are to be dissolved, to be decomposed, or disorganized, **preparatory to entering into a more exalted state of being**. It is a portion of eternity allotted to this world, **and can only be known by the changes we see in the composition and decomposition of the elements of which it is composed**. The Lord has put His children here, and given them bodies that are also subject to decay, to see if they will prove themselves worthy of the particles of which their tabernacles are composed, and of a glorious resurrection when their mortal bodies will become immortalized. **Now if you possess the light of the Holy Spirit, you can see clearly that trials in the flesh are actually necessary**." (JD 2:8)

"Why did Father Adam stretch forth his hand for the forbidden fruit? That you and I might drink the bitter cup—and drink the cup of life eternal—be made happy and increase to all eternity—that is my logic—were it not for the bitter the sweet would be irksome—were it not for darkness light would be weary. I could never know joy or intelligence—our sufferings are perfectly needed—the more we suffer, the more we can appreciate—**and if we do not descend below all things we could**

not ascend above all things." (*The Complete Discourses of Brigham Young*, Vol. 1, 1832 to 1852, Ed. Richard S. Van Wagoner, Smith-Petit Foundation, Salt Lake City, 2009. p. 357)

John Taylor

"If any man or woman expects to enter into the celestial kingdom of our God without being tested to the very uttermost, they have not understood the gospel. **If there is a weak spot in our nature, or if there is a fiber that can be made to quiver or to shrink, we may rest assured that it will be tested**." (*The Kingdom of God or Nothing*, p. 345)

"We are all aiming at celestial glory. Don't you know we are? We are talking about it, and we talk about being kings and priests unto the Lord; we talk about being enthroned in the kingdoms of our God; we talk about being queens and priestesses; and we talk, when we get on our high-heeled shoes, about possessing thrones, principalities, powers, and dominions in the eternal worlds, when at the same time many of us do not know how to conduct ourselves any better than a donkey does.

Notwithstanding our talk and our short comings, there is a reality in these things, and **God is determined, if possible, to make something of us**.

In order to do this, he has to try us and prove us, to manifest principles unto us, to develop the evils that are within ourselves, and to show us, by placing us in various positions and subjecting us to various trials, what we are,—to show us our weaknesses and follies, in order that we may be made to lean and depend upon him alone. He will try men and prove them, to see if their hearts are pure; for he designs to take a course with us that will bring out the evil; and he will touch them in that part that will develop it, for he knows what part to touch in order to make us develop that which is in us." (JD 6:166)

Chapter 13

Born Again

Apostle John

"Jesus answered and said unto him, Verily, verily, I say unto thee, **Except a man be born again**, he cannot see the kingdom of God. Nicodemus saith unto him, **How can a man be born when he is old? Can he enter the second time into his mother's womb, and be born?** Jesus answered, Verily, verily, I say unto thee, Except a man be born of water and *of* the Spirit, he cannot enter into the kingdom of God. That which is born of the flesh is flesh; and that which is born of the Spirit is spirit. **Marvel not that I said unto thee, Ye must be born again**. The wind bloweth where it listeth, and thou hearest the sound thereof, but canst not tell whence it cometh, and whither it goeth: so is every one that is born of the Spirit. Nicodemus answered and said unto him, **How can these things be?** Jesus answered and said unto him, **Art thou a master of Israel, and knowest not these things?** Verily, verily, I say unto thee, **We speak that we do know, and testify that we have seen; and ye receive not our witness**. <u>If I have told you earthly things, and ye believe not, how shall ye believe, if I tell you *of* heavenly things?</u>" (John 3:3–12)

Brigham Young

"Christ's words to Nicodemus seem to have troubled him considerably; he could not understand this **New Birth**. It seems a curious thing, if we have a real translation of what then transpired, that he should have lives as pure as any man possibly could, according to the knowledge he had of the things of God, and yet this was the first time in his life that he had heard the term **New Birth**; and he marveled at the saying, so much so that "he turns round and says how can this be?" Why says Jesus, you must be born of the spirit or you cannot see the kingdom of God. Do you understand this? No I don't see says Nicodemus, it is not according to logic that I who am old should be **born again**…

…To get language to convey my ideas, perhaps would be difficult; but I will try to make you understand me. Nicodemus comes and says how can I be **born again**? How can I understand this **new birth**? I am old, I cannot be born again, but says Jesus, if you and the whole Jewish nation understood things in heaven, you would see how you, and all Israel could be **born again**…

...I tell you he (Nicodemus) might have understood a **New Birth**, if he could have been approached and told to throw down the religion of his fathers and look to the Lord he would have then learned that Jesus was the Christ. Jesus would say to him, "all that is necessary is that you should have the spirit of revelation and see me in my true character and office; that is all that is necessary, enough of that spirit to see me in my humility." Nicodemus had imbibed all of the religion of his fathers and was just as good as a Christian, and was as good a liver as could be found; but something else was necessary, the Birth of the Spirit, and hence said Jesus you must be **born again**, for no man can discern the things of God without the spirit of God...

...Well Nicodemus, all you want is to humble yourself before the Lord, and get his spirit, and then says Jesus you will know that I am the Christ, and this is the only way to obtain this knowledge. It amounts to this; a man must be converted from error to truth, **born again** to see the truth. If he has imbibed error, and is **born again**, and then imbibes errors again, he will be like the old lady, who was about 80 years old, and **who had to be born over and over and over again**, on account of her many [blank] and I don't know but he would want to be **born over and over and over again**." (*The Complete Discourses of Brigham Young*, Vol. 2, 1853 to 1856, Ed. Richard S. Van Wagoner, Smith-Petit Foundation, Salt Lake City, 2009, pp. 871–874)

Hugh Nibley

Mosiah 27:25: "And the Lord said unto me: **Marvel not that all mankind...must be born again**." Notice that it's nothing less than being born all over again. We are so completely out of it when we are here. **We cannot make the change without leaving the scene. You have to be born again**. See, there's the one world or the other; you can't mix them. It's a very hard thing, as Brigham Young said, as he tried to take the water on both shoulders. "The Latter-day Saint who tries to live in both worlds is torn apart." There's no such agony, no worse experience than that, and it happens to them here. As it explains here, "...yea, born of God, changed from their carnal and fallen state, to a state of righteousness [a complete change], being redeemed of God, becoming his sons and daughters." They become new creatures; it's an entirely different thing, as this explains. (*Teachings of the Book of Mormon--Semester 2:* Transcripts of Lectures Presented to an Honors Book of Mormon class at BYU, 1988--1990 [Provo: FARMS pg. 191)

Chapter 14

To Go No More Out

Apostle John

"**Him that overcometh** will I make a pillar in the temple of my God, and **he shall go no more out**." (Revelation 3:12)

Joseph Smith

"And may the Lord bless you, and keep your garments spotless, that ye may at last be brought to sit down with Abraham, Isaac, and Jacob, and the holy prophets who have been ever since the world began, having your garments spotless even as their garments are spotless, in the kingdom of heaven **to go no more out**." (Alma 7:25)

"And now may God grant unto these, my brethren, that they may sit down in the kingdom of God; yea, and also all those who are the fruit of their labors that they may **go no more out**, but that they may praise him forever. And may God grant that it may be done according to my words, even as I have spoken. Amen." (Alma 29:17)

"And this I know, because the Lord hath said he dwelleth not in unholy temples, but in the hearts of the righteous doth he dwell; yea, and he has also said that the righteous shall sit down in his kingdom, **to go no more out**; but their garments should be made white through the blood of the Lamb." (Alma 34:36)

"Yea, we see that whosoever will may lay hold upon the word of God, which is quick and powerful, which shall divide asunder all the cunning and the snares and the wiles of the devil, and lead the man of Christ in a strait and narrow course across that everlasting gulf of misery which is prepared to engulf the wicked—And land their souls, yea, their immortal souls, at the right hand of God in the kingdom of heaven, to sit down with Abraham, and Isaac, and with Jacob, and with all our holy fathers, **to go no more out**." (Helaman 3:29–30)

"And in this state they were to remain until the judgment day of Christ; and at that day they were to receive a greater change, and to be received into the kingdom of the Father **to go no more out**, but to dwell with God eternally in the heavens." (3 Nephi 28:40)

Chapter 15

Kingdoms of Glory and the Seven Heavens

David, King of Israel
24 I said, O my God, take me not away in the midst of my days: thy years *are* throughout all generations. 25 Of old hast **thou laid the foundation of the earth: and the heavens** *are* **the work of thy hands.** 26 They shall perish, but thou shalt endure: yea, all of them shall wax old like a garment; **as a vesture shalt thou change them, and they shall be changed**: (Psalms 102:24–26)

Joseph Smith
"Paul saw to the third heaven, **and I more.**" (*Teachings of the Prophet Joseph Smith,* p. 301. HC 5:392. Also see *The Words of Joseph Smith,* pp. 202, 207, 211–212, 214)

"**I know one who was caught up to the seventh heaven and saw and heard things not lawful for me to utter**" (Joseph Smith as quoted by Mary Elizabeth Rollins Lightner. *Journal and Memoirs of Mary Elizabeth Rollins Lightner,* typewritten copy, BYU Library, p. 4)

Hyrum Smith
"**Those of the Terrestrial Glory either advance to the Celestial or recede to the Telestial**, else the moon could not be a type as it 'waxes and wanes.'" (August 1, 1843. Remarks transcribed by Franklin D. Richards. See F.D.R. Journal.)

Brigham Young
"Who will be saved in the celestial kingdom of God? They that have the oracles of truth and obey them. Where will the rest go? Into kingdoms that God has and will prepare for them and **there are millions of such kingdoms. There is as many degrees of glory as there are degrees of capacity** and to them will be meted out according to their faith, and goodness and the truth that abides in them and according to the light God has imparted to them." (*The Essential Brigham Young,* pp. 139–140)

"**Brethren and sisters, I have a few words to say to you with regard to our present position as connected with future events, future prospects, future kingdoms, glories, and existence**, and the rise, spread, glory, and power of the kingdom of God upon the face of the earth. You know that I am a to-day person in my preaching and exhortations. They are for the time we now live in—not particularly for the millennium, for the resurrection, for the eternities yet to come; for if we can live this day as we ought to live, we shall be prepared for to-morrow, and so on for the next day; and when the eternities come, we shall be prepared to enjoy them. You are constantly taught to live your religion for today. Can you not live it for one hour? Begin at a small point: can you not live to the Lord for one minute? Yes. Then can we not multiply that by sixty and make an hour, and live that hour to the Lord? Yes; and then for a day, a week, a month, and a year? Then, when the year is past, it has been spent most satisfactorily.

We may so live our religion every moment, and so watch our own conduct as to not suffer ourselves in the least to do anything that would infringe upon a good conscience that is formed and regulated by the Priesthood of God, and in all our acts to not permit ourselves to do one act that next year or a few years hence will wound the heart and bring shame and confusion over the countenance; but let every day be filled with acts that will be in our reflections a source of joy and consolation...

This is a world in which we are to prove ourselves. The lifetime of man is a day of trial, wherein we may prove to God, in our darkness, in our weakness, and where the enemy reigns, that we are our Father's friends, and that we receive light from him and are worthy to be leaders of our children—to become lords of lords, and kings of kings,—to have perfect dominion over that portion of our families that will be crowned in the celestial kingdom with glory, immortality, and eternal lives. If we are crowned to become lords of lords and king of kings, it will be to rule and reign over our own posterity pertaining to this flesh—these tabernacles—this commencement in our finite state or being. When I reign king of kings and lord of lords over my children, it will be when my first, second, third, fourth, and so on, son rises up and counts thousands and millions of his posterity, and is king over them; then I am a king of these kings. Our Father, who is Lord of all, will reign a King of kings and Lord of lords over all his children." (JD 8:59–61)

"The President gave it as his opinion that **the earth did not dwell in the sphere in which it did when it was created, but that it was banished from its more glorious state or orbit of revolution for man's sake**." (*The Complete Discourses of Brigham Young*, Vol. 1, 1832 to 1852, Ed. Richard S. Van Wagoner, Smith-Petit Foundation, Salt Lake City, 2009. p. 330)

"**There will be a great many worlds, and enough opportunity for you to enjoy them**...This is the annual [celebration] of the birth day of the saviour of this world; how many such worlds, such saviours and such birth days there has been previous to this and how many there will be in the future is beyond our comprehension, but **I wish you may see a**

great many of them." (*The Complete Discourses of Brigham Young*, Vol. 2, 1853 to 1856, Ed. Richard S. Van Wagoner, Smith-Petit Foundation, Salt Lake City, 2009. p. 749)

Lorenzo Snow

"As soon as the Camp came up different arrangements were entered into in relation to our Fifty. It was concluded not to be wisdom for us to go on as it was at first intended. But for the whole Camp to go to work plowing, fencing and putting up houses. I assisted in chopping and putting up Brother Pratt's house logs and about that time was taken sick with the fever (25th of May.) I never had such a severe fit of sickness before since my recollection. My friends and family had given up most all hopes of my recovery. Father Huntington, the President of the Place, called on his Congregation to pray for me. He also with Gen. Rich and some others clothed themselves in the garments of the Priesthood and prayed for my recovery. I believe it was thro' the continued applications of my family and friends to the throne of Heaven that my life was spared.

In my sickness I went through in my mind the most singular scenes that any man ever did. My family generally believed that I was not in my right mind. **But the scenes thro' which my spirit traveled are yet fresh in my memory** as though they occurred but yesterday. And when my people supposed me in the greatest pain and danger I am conscious of having a great many spiritual exercises sometimes partaking of the most acute suffering that heart can conceive and others the most rapturous enjoyment that heart ever felt or imagination ever conceived. I suppose at first I must have been left in the hands of an evil spirit, in fact I was administered to upon this supposition. I was led into the full and perfect conviction that I was entirely a hopeless case in reference to salvation, that eternities, upon eternities must pass and still I saw my case would remain the same.

I saw the whole world rejoicing in all the powers and glories of salvation without the slightest beam of hope on my part, but doomed to a separation from my friends and family all I loved most Hear to eternity upon eternity. I shudder even now at the remembrance of the torments and agony of my feelings. No tongue can describe them or imagination conceive. Those who were attending me at that time describe me as being in a condition of body. I remained several hours refusing to speak. My body was cool, and my eyes and countenance denoted extreme suffering. After this scene ended I entered another of an opposite character. **My spirit seems to have left the world and introduced into that of Kolob. I heard a voice calling me by name saying, 'he is worthy, he is worthy, take away his filthy garments.'** My cloths were then taken off piece by piece and a voice said '**let him be clothed, let him be clothed.' Immediately I found a celestial body gradually growing upon me until at length I found myself crowned with all its glory and power**. The ecstasy of joy I now experienced no man can tell, pen cannot describe it. I conversed familiarly with Joseph, Father Smith and others, and mingled in the society of the Holy One. I saw my family **all** saved and observed the dispensations of God with mankind **until at last a perfect redemption was effected**, though' great was the sufferings of the wicked, especially those that had persecuted the saints. My spirit must have remained I should judge for days enjoying the scenes of eternal happiness. (*The Iowa Journal of Lorenzo Snow,* edited and introduction by Maureen Ursenbach Beecher, *BYU Studies,* Vol. 24 (1984), No. 2—spring 1984. The spelling has been modernized for use in this document. See the article in the BYU Studies publication from Beecher for original spelling and for the source of the original document from Lorenzo Snow.)

Hugh Nibley

Upon reaching heaven, **Enoch is exalted to the level of the Son of Man** (1 Enoch 70–71); while as a reward, all the righteous may receive "**the secrets of the Son of Man**, who is still a mystery now" (1 Enoch 118). The standard **mounting up to the seventh heaven**, for example, of R. Ishmael, **is an initiation**, reflected in the Hechalot concept. (*Enoch the Prophet,* edited by Stephen D. Ricks [Salt Lake City and Provo: Deseret Book Co., Foundation for Ancient Research and Mormon Studies, 1986], p. 61)

Isaiah is instructed in his Ascension not to worship at any of the six central thrones at any of the *chorostasias* or singing praise-circles, circles he must pass on the way up, since all the others are simply focusing their praise on "**him who sitteth in the Seventh Heaven**." (*Mormonism and Early Christianity,* p. 68)

In 3 Enoch, the Rabbi Ishmael mounting up to heaven must pass through six *hekaloth,* "chamber within chamber," the Halls being arranged in concentric circles. The word *hekal* usually means simply temple (it is the Arabic word for shrine or temple), but in the Enoch literature, it regularly refers to the chambers or rooms of the temple representing various steps of initiation. "Arriving at the entrance of the **seventh hekal.**" (Ibid, p. 71)

Daniel H. Ludlow

2 Enoch is one of the most difficult Jewish writings to date and to understand because it is preserved only in medieval Slavonic manuscripts. It was beloved by the Bogomils, who were shaped by ancient Jewish sources but who also created or reshaped ancient documents. Many scholars trace *2 Enoch* back to a Jew who lived before A.D. 100. After an introduction in which he informs his sons of his impending assumption, Enoch describes his ascent through **the seven heavens** (3–21). Then the Lord reveals secrets to Enoch (22–38), who admonishes his sons (39–66) and is translated into the **highest heaven** (67; chap. 68 is extant only in the long recension). (*Encyclopedia of Mormonism,* 1–4 vols., edited by Daniel H. Ludlow [New York: Macmillan, 1992], p. 460)

Spencer J. Palmer

His second ascension experience took place on Mount Sinai. He then spent forty days in heaven, learning and receiving the Torah. Again **he saw the seven heavens** and the heavenly Temple, as well as the future.

His final ascension came just prior to his death. As with Abraham, an angel was sent, but Moses refused to die until he was allowed to view heaven. He saw the Temple, the Messiah, his brother Aaron, his own throne prepared for him, as well as another vision of the future. He stated at the end of his life: "I ascended heaven and trod out a path there, and engaged in battle with the angels, and received the law of fire and sojourned under [God's] throne of fire, and took shelter under the pillar of fire, and spoke with God face to face; and I prevailed over the heavenly familia, and revealed unto the sons of man their secrets, and received the Law from the right hand of God, and taught it to Israel." (Spencer J. Palmer, ed., *Deity and Death* [Provo: BYU Religious Studies Center, 1978], p. 85)

Donald W. Parry

As the visionary approaches closer to the celestial Holy of Holies and the throne of God, he undergoes a process of ritual initiation and <u>transformation</u> into a being of celestial glory, becoming a member of the heavenly angelic host. Since the angels are frequently described as forming the celestial temple priesthood, initiation into their ranks is closely connected with the reception of priesthood authority, authorizing the visionary to participate in the celestial liturgy and sacrifices. **Two main elements are involved in this transformation: anointing and receiving a celestial robe or garment**. Purification and anointing are the preliminary parts of the initiation. For example, during the ascension of Enoch—a fundamental prototype of all later Hekhalot visionaries—God said to his angels, "**extract Enoch from [his] earthly clothing**, and anoint him with my delightful oil, **and put him into the clothes of my glory.**"

This passage indicates that before entering the celestial temple, the initiate is required to shed his earthly clothes and don celestial robes. These robes are similar to those worn by the angels and God himself. Morton Smith has argued convincingly that the donning of such new garments is symbolic of ritual initiation throughout the Ancient Near East. Likewise, Isaiah is allowed to enter into the presence of God in the innermost sanctuary of the Seventh Heaven only because he has the proper celestial robe or garment: "The Holy Isaiah is permitted to come up here [to the throne of God], for his robe is here."

Gruenwald believes there are two types of celestial garments. There "**are the white garments of the righteous**…[which] are eschatological garments; but we do have another type of heavenly garments:… **mystical garments**. These garments most likely are to protect the mystical visionary from all kinds of dangers [during the ascent]." This suggests that there may have been an actual physical garment that the visionaries wore as part of their ascension rituals, as well as a celestial garment reserved for the righteous in heaven. This interpretation is partially confirmed by the story of Rabbi Yohanan B. Zakkai wrapping himself in his *tallith* garment when studying the mysteries of the chariot, and by the robe used when Christ taught an unnamed initiate the "Mysteries of the Kingdom" according to the *Secret Gospel of Mark*.

An interesting example of this idea comes from a Christian ascension text known as the *Ascension of Isaiah:* "But they [the righteous dead] were not sitting on their thrones, nor were their crowns of glory on them." And I asked the angel who (was) with me, "How is it that they have received these robes, but are not on thrones nor in crowns?" And he said to me…"**They will receive their robes and their thrones and their crowns when he [Christ] has ascended into the seventh heaven**."

In other words, in Christian versions of the celestial ascent, the full exaltation of the righteous dead can only be obtained through the atonement, resurrection, and ascension of Christ. (Donald W. Parry, ed., *Temples of the Ancient World: Ritual and Symbolism* [Salt Lake City and Provo: Deseret Book Co., Foundation for Ancient Research and Mormon Studies, 1994], 454–459. See the article for the numerous associated footnotes)

The *Martyrdom and Ascension of Isaiah* speaks of "the robes of the saints and their going out" and states that "many will exchange the glory of the robes of the saints for the robes of those who love money." But the saints will come with the LORD **with their robes which are stored up in the seventh heaven above**; with the LORD will come those whose spirits are clothed, they will descend and be present in the world, and the LORD will strengthen those who are found in the body, together with the saints in the robes of the saints, and will serve those who have kept watch in this world. And after this they will be turned in their robes upwards, and **their body will be left in the world**. The angel who shows Abraham the heavens speaks to him of the celestial clothing reserved for the patriarch: "**For above all the heavens and their angels is placed your throne, and also your robes and your crown which you are to see**."

[When from the body by the will of God you have come up here], **then you will receive the robe which you see, and also other numbered robes placed [there] you will see, and then you will be equal to the angels who [are] in the seventh heaven**. The angel further spoke to Isaiah regarding the person who would be known on the earth as "the Son": He who is to be in the corruptible world has not [yet] been revealed, nor the robes, nor the thrones, nor the crowns which are placed [there] for the righteous, for those who believe in that LORD who will descend in your form. For the light which [is] there [is] great and wonderful. **Arriving in the seventh heaven**, the angel told Isaiah, "Behold"! From there another voice which was sent out has come, and it says, "**The holy Isaiah is permitted to come up here, for his robe is here**." Of this visit to the **seventh heaven**, we read:

"And there I saw Enoch and all who [were] with him, **stripped of [their] robes of the flesh**; and I saw them in their robes of above, and they were like the angels who stand there in great glory. But they were not sitting on their thrones, nor were their crowns of glory on them."

And I asked the angel who [was] with me, "How is it that they have received these robes, but are not on [their] thrones nor in [their] crowns?" And he said to me, "They do not receive the crowns and thrones of glory—nevertheless they do see and know whose [will be] the thrones and whose the crowns—until the Beloved descends in the form in which you will see him descend." The angel then returned to the subject of Christ to come: And then many of the righteous will ascend with him, whose spirits do not receive [their] robes until the LORD Christ ascends and they ascend with him. Then indeed they will receive their robes and their thrones and their crowns, when he has ascended into the seventh heaven. And I saw many robes placed there, and many thrones and many crowns, and I said to the angel who led me, "Whose [are] these robes and thrones and crowns?" And he said to me, 'As for these robes, there are many from that world who will receive [them] through believing in the words of that one who will be named as I have told you, and they will keep them, and believe in them, and believe in his cross; [for they (are) these] placed [here].'

The angel then told Isaiah, "And you shall return into your robe until your days are complete; then you shall come here." **By "robe," he evidently had reference to mortality, either the body itself or earthly clothing**. Based on these experiences, Isaiah later told King Hezekiah, "But as for you, be in the Holy Spirit that you may receive your robes, and the thrones and crowns of glory, which are placed in the **seventh heaven**." (Donald W. Parry, ed., *Temples of the Ancient World: Ritual and Symbolism* [Salt Lake City and Provo: Deseret Book Co., FARMS, 1994], pp. 683–684. See the article for the numerous associated footnotes.)

Truman G. Madsen

The third metaphor has roots in the Jews' mystical tradition, but it has biblical precedent. They talk about the Sabbath as heaven on earth; as—if you want to be specific and mathematical—one-sixtieth of paradise. You have a foretaste of paradise. **The seventh day, some legends say, is the reflection of the seventh heaven, the highest heaven**. By the way, they also say having dreams is one-sixtieth of being a prophet.

They believe that this is cosmic, that nature herself celebrates the Sabbath. In the Church we have a hymn titled "Come Away to the Sunday School." One of the lines is "Nature breathes her sweetest fragrance on the holy Sabbath day." That's the Jews' feeling. Even the rivers don't work on the Sabbath. They are accustomed to throw up rocks and dirt, so they may be very calm on the Sabbath. Even hell celebrates the Sabbath. People who have been tormented in hell are, for purposes of the Sabbath day, released. The hosts of heaven celebrate the Sabbath. They gather and they sing and they feel tranquility. All the miracles of the six days of creation, say the Jews, are somehow available to us, or should be, on the seventh day. And all creation "resolves itself into melody if we have ears to hear." (*The Radiant Life* p. 74)

Daniel C. Peterson
...the seven heavens were opened to Abraham, up to and including the throne [of God]. (News from Antiquity, *Ensign*, January 1994, p. 19)

Blake Thomas Ostler
J. Rendel Harris points out that the *Odes of Solomon* also contain the ideas of "the preexistent soul that has to leave heaven for earth, and that of the unfallen creation of God, **whose environment is changed from a coat of light to a coat of skins**." The "garment of skins" became the "garment of light" possibly because the Hebrew (coat of skins) so closely resembles, meaning "coat of light."

Even so, the *Apocryphon of James* tells us that when the spirit returns to its heavenly treasure it will become "**as you were first, having clothed yourself, you become the first who will strip himself, and you shall become as you were before removing the garment**." The garment also represents the treasure laid up in heaven awaiting the soul's return, and, in this context, the glory of the resurrected body. An ancient Christian writing known as the *Ascension of Isaiah* states, "**The saints will come with the Lord with their garments which are now stored up in the seventh heaven, with the Lord will come those whose spirits are clothed upon**."

The *Book of Enoch* is replete with references to garments. In connection with the resurrection the *Book of Enoch* says, "And the righteous and elect shall have risen from the earth, and ceased to be downcast in countenance. And they shall be clothed with garments of glory, and they shall be the garments of life from the Lord of Spirits." *The Manual of Discipline*, found among the Dead Sea Scrolls, contains a concept very similar to that of the *Book of Enoch*...The ancient texts make it perfectly clear that the candidate must be properly clothed and possess the "yvwois", or the name of God, in order to pass through the last barrier to the presence of God. **In many documents the prophet passes through seven heavens and must receive a garment of glory to enter into the highest heaven where God dwells. The garment becomes brighter as the prophet passes through each successive heaven. The prophet must also possess the proper identification or sign in order to enter each heaven**. In the *Apocalypse of Paul*, for instance, Paul passes through **seven heavens** and comes to the gate guarded by "principalities and authorities." **The spirit, his guide**, tells Paul, "Give him the sign that you have, and he will open to you. **And I gave him the sign**," **and the seventh heaven opened**. The quasi-canonical *Pastor of Hermas* is a good illustration of the necessity of both the garment and the name:

No man shall enter into the kingdom of heaven except he shall take upon him the name of the "son of God."...**The gate is the Son of God, who is the only way of coming to God**...No man can enter into the kingdom of God except these [virgins] clothe him with their garment. It availeth nothing to take up the name of the "Son of God" unless thou shalt receive the garment...A man shall in vain bear his name unless he is endowed with his powers. **Christ is also represented as the door to the kingdom of heaven** in the *Odes of Solomon.* "He gave me the way of His precepts and I opened the doors that were closed...Nothing appeared closed to me: Because **I am the door of everything**" (Ode 17. 8, 10). **Since** *the gate is Christ*, the scene at the gate is often one of intimate union with Christ, as in the *Apocryphon of James.* After the spirit is clothed again with its garment, Christ tells the Apostle,

Behold, I shall reveal everything to you, my beloved. Know that you come forth just as I am. Behold, I shall reveal to you Him who is hidden. Now stretch out your hand. Now take hold of me...Those who wish to enter and seek to walk in the way that is before the door, open the door through you. The Book of Mormon also refers to the straight way before the gate and identifies the Holy One of Israel with the gatekeeper...the way for man is narrow, but it lieth in a straight course before Him, and the keeper of the gate is the Holy One of Israel, and He employeth no servant there, and there is no way save it be by the gate, for He cannot be deceived, for the Lord God is His name.

The doctrine of the Name of God as a key word runs like red ribbon through the history of revealed religion. Thus, if the *Pistis Sophia* proclaims, "**Thou art the key, O Savior**, which opens the door of all things and shuts the door of all," the author is merely citing Isaiah 22, "I will clothe him with thy robe, and strengthen him with thy girdle...And the key of the House of David will I lay upon His shoulders, so He shall open and none shall shut, and none shall open. And I will fasten Him as a nail in a sure place." One is immediately reminded of the *Pistis Sophia*, where one communicates knowledge to God through certain passwords and signs: And they shall test the soul to find their signs in it, as well as their seals and their baptisms and their anointings...

Ascension of Isaiah 7. 22 explains that each recipient of the garment also receives a crown and a throne: "For above all the heavens and their angels has thy throne been placed, and thy garments and thy crown which thou shalt see." Again, in 8. 14: "When from the body by the will of God thou hast ascended hither, then thou wilt receive the garment which thou seest, and likewise **other numbered garments** laid up [there] thou wilt see, **and then thou wilt become equal to the angels of the seventh heaven.**"

Finally, in 9. 12–13: "How is it that they have received the garments, but have not the thrones and crowns?" And He said unto me: "Crowns and thrones of glory they do not receive, till the Beloved will descend in the form in which you will see Him descend." (See also *Testament of Levi* 8. 5–9; Pastor of Hermas *Similitudes* 8. ii, 1–4; *Odes of Solomon* 1 1–2; and *IQS* 4. 7–8)

"You have received white garments as evidence that **you have been clothed again of the chaste veil of innocence…after being redressed in these garments by the bath of regeneration**." ("Clothed Upon: A Unique aspect of Christian Antiquity, *BYU Studies, Vol. 22 (1982)*, No. 1 —Fall 1982. See the article for the numerous associated footnotes.)

Finally, in the Ascension of Isaiah (about 150 A.D.), Isaiah is overcome by the Holy Spirit as he lies upon a couch and becomes as one dead (6:10); he is then "taken up" in a vision of the heavens (6:14) by "a glorious angel" (7:2–3). Isaiah beholds a throne with angels on the right and on the left (7:14–15; compare 11:32–33). He is then lifted through **the seven heavens** by the angel who interprets their contents to him (7:17–8:28). Isaiah's angel—guide gives him a book wherein is written "the deeds of the children of Israel" (9:22). **In the highest heaven, Isaiah beholds Christ**, who descends through the **seven heavens** to the earth where he is born of the virgin Mary, put to death, descends to the realm of Sheol, and sends out his Twelve Apostles before ascending again through the heavens to be seated on the right hand of God **while the Holy Spirit is seated on the left** (9:7–11:33). Isaiah is then commanded to return to his garment of flesh (11:35) where he tells all present of his vision (11:36–37). ("The Throne-Theophany and Prophetic Commission in 1 Nephi: a Form—Critical Analysis by Blake Thomas Ostler" , *BYU Studies,* Vol. 26 (1986), No. 4—Fall 1986, p. 72)

Chapter 16

Joseph Smith and Brigham Young

Brigham Young
"It is said to be eternal life, 'to know the only wise God, and Jesus Christ whom He has sent.' I will tell you one thing, as brother Hyde has said, it would be an excellent plan for us to go to work and find out ourselves, for as sure as you find out yourselves, you will find out God, whether you are Saint or sinner. A man cannot find out himself without the light of revelation; he has to turn round and seek to the Lord his God, in order to find out himself. If you find out who Joseph was, you will know as much about God as you need to at present; for if He said, 'I am a God to this people,' He did not say that He was the only wise God. Jesus was a God to the people when he was upon earth, was so before he came to this earth, and is yet. Moses was a God to the children of Israel, and in this manner you may go right back to Father Adam." (JD 4:271. Brigham Young talking about Joseph Smith.)

John Taylor
"When Joseph Smith had anything from God to communicate to the children of men or to the Church, what was it he had to fight against all the day long? It was the prejudices of the people; and, in many instances, he could not and dared not reveal the word of God to the people, for fear they would rise up and reject it. How many times has he faltered? It was not that he was particularly afraid; but he had to look after the welfare and salvation of the people.

If the Prophet Joseph had revealed everything which the Lord manifested to him, it would have proven the overthrow of the people in many instances; hence he had to treat them like children, and feed them upon milk, and unfold principles gradually, just as they could receive them. Was all this because it was so hard to comprehend correct principles? No; it was because we were babes and children, and could not understand. How is it now, under the administration of President Young? Much the same, in this respect. He has often found it very difficult to make the people understand things as the Lord has revealed them unto him." (JD: 6:165. John Taylor talking about Joseph and Brigham.)

Wilford Woodruff

"Brother Joseph used a great many methods of testing the integrity of men; and he taught a great many things which, in consequence of tradition, required prayer, faith, and a testimony from the Lord, before they could be believed by many of the Saints. His mind was opened by the visions of the Almighty, and **the Lord taught him many things by vision and revelation that were never taught publicly in his day; for the people could not bear the flood of intelligence** which God poured into his mind…You will see an advance in a great many things; for **the Lord will open the mind of brother Brigham and lead him into many principles that pertain to the salvation of this people; and we cannot close up our minds and say that we will go so far and no farther. This we cannot do without jeopardizing our standing before God**" (Wilford Woodruff referring to Joseph Smith and Brigham Young. JD 5:83–85)

"There is not so great a man as Joseph standing in this generation. **His mind, like Enoch's, expands as eternity, and God alone can comprehend his soul**." (Matthias F. Cowley, Wilford Woodruff, *History of His Life and Labors,* p. 68. Wilford Woodruff referring to Joseph Smith.)

George Q. Cannon

"The Saints could not comprehend Joseph Smith; the Elders could not; the Apostles could not. They did so a little towards the close of his life; but his knowledge was so extensive and his comprehension so great that they could not rise to it." (*Millennial Star* 61:629)

Richard G. Scott

"Brigham Young learned truth by carefully listening to Joseph Smith and striving to understand everything that was taught by word, example, or the spirit. The resulting tutoring has blessed generations. **It conditioned Brigham Young to learn additional truths and to share far more than he had received personally from Joseph Smith. Follow his example**." (*Ensign*, November 1993, p. 81)

Chapter 17

Joseph, Brigham, and Heber Will Finish Their Work

Joseph Smith Will Finish His Work

"Lift up your head and rejoice; for behold! it is well with my servants Joseph and Hyrum. My servant Joseph still holds the keys of my kingdom in this dispensation, and he shall stand in due time on the earth, in the flesh, and fulfill that to which he is appointed…" (A revelation given to Parley. P. Pratt. *Autobiography of Parley P. Pratt*, 1985 Edition, p. 294)

"**So it is with the Prophet Joseph Smith**. He has gone before with the keys of this dispensation, after having lived and conferred them upon the authorities of the Church, even all that was necessary **until he shall come again to build up this kingdom preparatory to the coming of the Lord Jesus Christ**." (Franklin D. Richards referring to Joseph Smith. JD 26:302)

"You will gather many people into the fastness of the Rocky Mountains as a center for the gathering of the people, and you will be faithful because you have been true; and many of those who come under your ministry, because of their much learning, will seek for high positions, and they will be set up and raise themselves in eminence above you, but you will walk in low places unnoticed and you will know all that transpires in their midst, and those that are my friends will be your friends. This I will promise to you, that **when I come again to lead you forth**, for I will go to prepare a place for you, so that where I am you shall be with me." (Quoting the Prophet Joseph Smith, "Diary of John E Forsgren," *Fate of the Persecutors of Joseph Smith*, N.B. Lundwall, p. 154)

"For in that day, for my sake shall the Father work a work, which shall be a great and a marvelous work among them; and there shall be among them those who will not believe it, although a man shall declare it unto them. **But behold, the life of my servant shall be in my hand; therefore they shall not hurt him, although he shall be marred because of them. Yet I will heal him**, for I will show unto them that my wisdom is greater than the cunning of the devil." (3 Nephi 21:9)

"Behold, my servant shall deal prudently; he shall be exalted and extolled and be very high. **As many were astonished at thee—his visage was so marred, more than any man, and his form more than the sons of men**—So shall he sprinkle many nations; the kings shall shut their mouths at him, for that which had not been told them shall they see; and that which they had not heard shall they consider." (3 Nephi 20:43–45)

"No weapon formed against him shall prosper, and **though the wicked mar him for a little season**, he shall be like one rising up in the heat of wine…**Like a sheaf fully ripe, gathered into the garner, so shall he stand before the Lord, having produced a hundred fold**. Thus spake my father Joseph. Therefore my son, I know for a surety that those things will be fulfilled, and I confirm upon thee all these blessings…

Thou shalt stand upon the earth when it shall reel to and fro as a drunken man, and be removed out of its place: **thou shalt stand when the mighty judgments go forth** to the destruction of the wicked: **thou shalt stand on Mount Zion when the tribes of Jacob come shouting from the north**, and with thy brethren, the sons of Ephraim, crown them in the name of Jesus Christ: **Thou shalt see thy Redeemer come** in the clouds of heaven, and with the just receive the hallowed throng with shouts of hallelujahs, praise the Lord. Amen." (Excerpts from Joseph Smith's Patriarchal blessing, given by his Father Joseph Smith Sr. From typescript; p8, F25, photocopy, RLDS Archives; original in Patriarchal Blessings, Vol. 1, pp. 3–4, LDS Archives)

"But verily I say unto you, I have decreed that **your brethren which have been scattered shall return to the lands of their inheritances, and shall build up the waste places of Zion**. For after much tribulation, as I have said unto you in a former commandment, cometh the blessing. Behold, this is the blessing which I have promised **after your tribulations, and the tribulations of your brethren—your redemption**, and the redemption of your brethren, even their restoration to the land of Zion, **to be established, no more to be thrown down. Nevertheless, if they pollute their inheritances they shall be thrown down; for I will not spare them if they pollute their inheritances**. Behold, I say unto you, **the redemption of Zion must needs come by power**; Therefore, **I will raise up unto my people a man, who shall lead them like as Moses led the children of Israel**. For ye are the children of Israel, and of the seed of Abraham, and ye must needs be led out of bondage by power, and with a stretched-out arm. **And as your fathers were led at the first, even so shall the redemption of Zion be**. Therefore, let not your hearts faint, for I say not unto you as I said unto your fathers: Mine angel shall go up before you, but not my presence. But I say unto you: Mine angels shall go up before you, and also my presence, and in time ye shall possess the goodly land. Verily, verily I say unto you, that **my servant Joseph Smith, Jun. is the man to whom I likened the servant to whom the Lord of the vineyard spake in the parable which I have given unto you**." (D&C 103:11–21. See the parable immediately below.)

"And now, I will show unto you a parable, that you may know my will concerning the redemption of Zion. A certain nobleman had a spot of land, very choice; and he said unto his servants: Go ye unto my vineyard, even upon this very choice piece of land, and plant twelve olive-trees; And set watchmen round about them, and build a tower, that one may overlook the land round about, to be a watchman upon the tower, that mine olive-trees may not be broken down when the enemy shall come to spoil and take upon themselves the fruit of my vineyard.

Now, the servants of the nobleman went and did as their lord commanded them, and planted the olive-trees, and built a hedge round about, and set watchmen, and began to build a tower. And while they were yet laying the foundation thereof, they began to say among themselves: And what need hath my lord of this tower? And consulted for a long time, saying among themselves: What need hath my lord of this tower, seeing this is a time of peace? Might not this money be given to the exchangers? For there is no need of these things. And while they were at variance one with another they became very slothful, and they hearkened not unto the commandments of their lord. And the enemy came by night, and broke down the hedge; and the servants of the nobleman arose and were affrighted, and fled; and the enemy destroyed their works, and broke down the olive-trees.

Now, behold, the nobleman, the lord of the vineyard, called upon his servants, and said unto them, Why! what is the cause of this great evil? Ought ye not to have done even as I commanded you, and—after ye had planted the vineyard, and built the hedge round about, and set watchmen upon the walls thereof—built the tower also, and set a watchman upon the tower, and watched for my vineyard, and not have fallen asleep, lest the enemy should come upon you? And behold, the watchman upon the tower would have seen the enemy while he was yet afar off; and then ye could have made ready and kept the enemy from breaking down the hedge thereof, and saved my vineyard from the hands of the destroyer.

And the lord of the vineyard said unto one of his servants: Go and gather together the residue of my servants, and take all the strength of mine house, which are my warriors, my young men, and they that are of middle age also among all my servants, who are the strength of mine house, save those only whom I have appointed to tarry; And go ye straightway unto the land of my vineyard, and redeem my vineyard; for it is mine; I have bought it with money. Therefore, get ye straightway unto my land; break down the walls of mine enemies; throw down their tower, and scatter their watchmen. And inasmuch as they gather together against you, avenge me of mine enemies, that by and by I may come with the residue of mine house and possess the land. And the servant said unto his lord: When shall these things be? And he said unto his servant: When I will; go ye straightway, and do all things whatsoever I have commanded you; And this shall be my seal and blessing upon you —a faithful and wise steward in the midst of mine house, a ruler in my kingdom. And his servant went straightway, and did all things whatsoever his lord commanded him; and after many days all things were fulfilled." (D&C 101:43–62)

"I will now tell you something that ought to comfort every man and woman on the face of the earth. **Joseph Smith, junior, will again be on this earth dictating plans and calling forth his brethren to be baptized for the very characters who wish this was not so**, in order to bring them into a kingdom to enjoy, perhaps, the presence of angels or the spirits of good men, if they cannot endure the presence of the Father and the Son; and **he will never cease his operations, under the directions of the Son of God, until the last ones of the children of men are saved that can be, from Adam till now**.

Should not this thought comfort all people? They will, by-and-bye, be a thousand times more thankful for such a man as Joseph Smith, junior, than it is possible for them to be for any earthly good whatever. **It is his mission to see that all the children of men in this last dispensation are saved, that can be, through the redemption**. You will be thankful, every one of you, that Joseph Smith, junior, was ordained to this great calling before the worlds were.

I told you that the doctrine of election and reprobation is a true doctrine. It was decreed in the counsels of eternity, long before the foundations of the earth were laid, that he should be the man, in the last dispensation of this world, to bring forth the word of God to the people, and receive the fulness of the keys and power of the Priesthood of the Son of God." (JD 7:289. Brigham Young speaking about Joseph Smith.)

"**Joseph, uprisen from the grave-like mound**, His ancient and inglorious battle ground, **Retreads with modern step** the painful path Where erst he fled, a fugitive from wrath;" (Orson F. Whitney's *Elias*, Canto IX)

"And when you have finished the translation of the prophets, you shall from thenceforth preside over the affairs of the church...And this shall be your business and mission **in all your lives**, to preside in council, and set in order all the affairs of this church and kingdom." (D&C 90:13, 16)

"Other Saints preached that 'the day was not far distant when Joseph and Hyrum would be with this people.'" (*The Mormon Reformation,* by Paul H. Peterson, p. 44)

Brigham Young and Heber C. Kimball Will Finish Their Work

"You will be blessed, and you will see the day when Presidents Young, Kimball, and Wells, and Twelve Apostles will be in Jackson county, Missouri, laying out your inheritances. **In the flesh? Of course.** We should look well without being in the flesh! **We shall be there in the flesh, and all our enemies cannot prevent it**. Brother Wells, you may write that. You will be there, and Willard will be there, and also Jedediah, and Joseph and Hyrum Smith, and David, and Parley; and the day will be when I will see those men in the general assembly of the Church of the First-Born, in the great council of God in Jerusalem, too.

Will we want you to be along? **I heard Joseph say twice that brother Brigham and I should be in that council in Jerusalem, when there should be a uniting of the two divisions of God's government.**" (JD 9:27. Heber C. Kimball talking about Brigham and himself and others.)

Chapter 18

Joseph Smith and Some Thought-Provoking Possibilities

Moses

"For Joseph truly testified, saying: **A seer** shall the Lord my God raise up, who shall be **a choice seer** unto the fruit of my loins. Yea, Joseph truly said: Thus saith the Lord unto me: **A choice seer** will I raise up out of the fruit of thy loins; and he shall be esteemed highly among the fruit of thy loins. And unto him will I give commandment that he shall do a work for the fruit of thy loins, his brethren, which shall be of great worth unto them, even to the bringing of them to the knowledge of the covenants which I have made with thy fathers. And I will give unto him a commandment that he shall do none other work, save the work which I shall command him. And I will make him great in mine eyes; for he shall do my work. And **he shall be great like unto Moses**, whom I have said I would raise up unto you, to deliver my people, O house of Israel. **And Moses will I raise up**, to deliver thy people out of the land of Egypt. But a seer will I raise up out of the fruit of thy loins; and unto him will I give power to bring forth my word unto the seed of thy loins —and not to the bringing forth my word only, saith the Lord, but to the convincing them of my word, which shall have already gone forth among them." (2 Nephi 3:6–11)

"Yea, thus prophesied Joseph: **I am sure of this thing, even as I am sure of the promise of Moses**; for the Lord hath said unto me, I will preserve thy seed forever. And the Lord hath said: **I will raise up a Moses**; and I will give power unto him in a rod; and I will give judgment unto him in writing. Yet I will not loose his tongue, that he shall speak much, for I will not make him mighty in speaking. But I will write unto him my law, by the finger of mine own hand; and I will make a spokesman for him." (2 Nephi 3:16–17)

"Therefore, **I will raise up unto my people a man, who shall lead them like as Moses** led the children of Israel. For ye are the children of Israel, and of the seed of Abraham, and ye must needs be led out of bondage by power, and with a stretched-out arm. And as your fathers were led at the first, even so shall the redemption of Zion be. Therefore, let not your hearts faint, for I say not unto you as I said unto your fathers: Mine angel shall go up before you, but not my presence. But I say unto you: Mine angels shall go up before you, and also my presence, and in time ye shall possess the goodly land. Verily, verily I say unto you, that my servant **Joseph Smith, Jun. is the man to whom I likened the servant** to whom the Lord of the vineyard spake in the parable which I have given unto you." (D&C 103:16–21. (**In these provocative verses, is the Lord trying to create a link between Joseph (the Choice Seer) and Moses?**)

"Zion must be led forth out of bondage, as Israel was at the first. In order to do this God has prophesied that he will raise up a man like unto Moses, who shall lead his people therefrom. Whether that man is now in existence, or whether it is someone yet to be born; or whether it is our present leader who has led us forth into these valleys of the mountains, whether God will grant unto us the great blessing to have his life spared to lead forth his people like a Moses, we perhaps may not all know. He has done a great and wonderful work in leading forth this people into this land and building up these cities in this desert country; and I feel in my heart to say, Would to God that his life may be prolonged like Moses, in days of old, who, when he was eighty years old, was sent forth to redeem the people of Israel from bondage. God is not under the necessity of choosing a young man, he can make a man eighty years of age full of vigor, strength and health, and he may spare our present leader to lead this people on our return to Jackson County.

But whether it be he or some other person, God will surely fulfill this promise. This was given before our Prophet Joseph Smith was taken out of our midst. **Many of us no doubt thought when that revelation was given that Joseph would be the man. I was in hopes it would be Joseph**, for I had no idea that he was going to be slain, although I might have known from certain revelations that such would probably be the case, for the Lord had said unto him, before the rise of this Church, that he would grant unto him eternal life even though he should be slain, which certainly was an indication that he might be slain. **But we still were in hopes that he would live and that he would be the man who, like Moses**, would lead this people from bondage<u>. **I do not know but he will yet. God's arm is not shortened that he cannot raise him up even from the tomb**</u>.

We are living in the dispensation of the fulness of times, the dispensation of the resurrection, and **there may be some who will wake from their tombs for certain purposes and to bring to pass certain transactions on the earth decreed by the Great Jehovah**; and <u>**if the Lord sees proper to bring forth that man just before the winding up scene to lead forth the army of Israel, he will do so**</u>. And if he feels disposed to send him forth as a spiritual personage to lead the camp of Israel to the land of their inheritance, all right. But be this as it may, **whether he is the man, whether President Young is the man, or whether the Lord shall hereafter raise up a man for that purpose,** we do know that when that day comes the Lord will not only send his angels before the army of Israel, but his presence will also be there. Do you suppose that the Lord will suffer any unclean thing to be in that army? Not at all, for his angels and he himself are to go before us. God will not dwell in the midst of a people who will not sanctify themselves before him." (JD 15:362-363. Orson Pratt talking about the man "like unto Moses.")

Enoch and Melchizedek
"Or, in other words, let my servant Ahashdah [Newel K. Whitney] **and my servant Gazelam, or Enoch** [Joseph Smith, Jun.] and my servant Pelagoram [Sidney Rigdon] sit in council with the saints which are in Zion;" (D&C 78:9. The code names originally given as part of the revelation from the Lord have been removed from the current edition of the Doctrine and Covenants.)

"Verily, verily I say unto you, that **my servant Baurak Ale [Joseph Smith, Jun.**] is the man to whom I likened the servant to whom the Lord of the vineyard spake in the parable which I have given unto you. Therefore let **my servant Baurak Ale [Joseph Smith, Jun.**] say unto the strength of my house, my young men and the middle aged—Gather yourselves together unto the land of Zion, upon the land which I have bought with money that has been consecrated unto me." (D&C 103:21-22. The code names originally given as part of the revelation from the Lord have been removed from the current edition of the Doctrine and Covenants.)

"Behold, I have commanded my servant **Baurak Ale** [Joseph Smith, Jun.] to say unto the strength of my house, even my warriors, my young men, and middle-aged, to gather together for the redemption of my people, and throw down the towers of mine enemies, and scatter their watchmen;" (D&C 105:16. The code names originally given as part of the revelation from the Lord have been removed from the current edition of the Doctrine and Covenants.)

"Baraq'el is supposed to have been the father of Enoch. That's the name Enoch goes by in the Doctrine and Covenants. Joseph Smith is called Enoch or Baraq'el. A professor in Hebrew at the University of Utah said, 'Well, Joseph Smith didn't understand the word barak meaning 'to bless.'' But Baraq'el means the 'lightning of God.' That was one of the names that Enoch bore. The Doctrine and Covenants is right on target in that, and this confirms it, that he is called Baraq'el here." (*Teachings of the Pearl of Great Price: Lecture 21,* Winter Semester, 1986)

"They are they who are the church of the Firstborn. **They are they into whose hands the Father has given all things**—They are they who are priests and kings, who have received of his fulness, and of his glory; And are priests of the Most High, **after the order of Melchizedek**, which was **after the order of Enoch**, which was **after the order of the Only Begotten Son**. Wherefore, as it is written, **they are gods**, even the sons of God—Wherefore, all things are theirs, whether life or death, or things present, or things to come, **all are theirs and they are Christ's, and Christ is God's**. And they shall overcome all things." (D&C

76:54–60. In this verse, is Joseph trying to create a link from Melchizedek, to Enoch, to Christ beyond just the higher priesthood?)

"In the Secrets of Enoch we are told that **Melchizedek will be priest and king in a place at the center of the earth when the Lord will bring him forth as 'another Melchizedek** of the lineage of the first Melchizedek.' **Here is identity indeed—Melchizedek succeeding himself**! In the Pistis Sophia, **Jesus says that 'the higher mysteries' tell how all 'are to be saved** in the time and in the number of Melchizedek the Great Mediator of the Light, the agent of all who is at the center of the world.'" (*Enoch the Prophet*, pp. 29–30)

Adam through Moses

"It is said to be eternal life, 'to know the only wise God, and Jesus Christ whom He has sent.' I will tell you one thing, as brother Hyde has said, **it would be an excellent plan for us to go to work and find out ourselves, for as sure as you find out yourselves, you will find out God**, whether you are Saint or sinner. A man cannot find out himself without the light of revelation; he has to turn round and seek to the Lord his God, in order to find out himself. **If you find out who Joseph was, you will know as much about God as you need to at present**; for if He said, 'I am a God to this people,' He did not say that He was the only wise God. **Jesus was a God to the people when he was upon earth, was so before he came to this earth, and is yet. Moses was a God to the children of Israel, and in this manner you may go right back to Father Adam**." (JD 4:271. Brigham Young talking about Joseph Smith. Is Brigham trying to tell us that Joseph is God who has come down to earth to minister to the children of men, and is he trying to link Joseph with Moses, with Christ, and with all of the patriarchs of dispensations back to and including Adam???)

Apostle to Joseph

"What is the nature and beauty of Joseph's mission? You know that **I am one of his Apostles**." (JD 5:332. Brigham Young referring to Joseph Smith.)

"I want to talk a little more about the witnesses. I am a witness—of what? I have told it here and in Nauvoo. I know what I am a witness of, and **I know my Apostleship**. I am a witness that Joseph Smith was a Prophet of God. What an uproar it would make in the Christian world to say, **I am an Apostle of Joseph.** Write it down, and write it back to your friends in the east, that **I am an Apostle of Joseph Smith**." (JD 3:212. Brigham Young referring to Joseph Smith.)

"I make this remark, because those words in that connection always made me feel as though I am called more than I am deserving of. **I am Brigham Young, an Apostle of Joseph Smith, and also of Jesus Christ**." (JD 5:296. Brigham Young referring to Joseph Smith and Jesus Christ.)

"How are you going to get your resurrection? You will get it by the President of the Resurrection pertaining to this generation, and that is Joseph Smith Junior. Hear it all ye ends of the Earth; **if ever you enter into the Kingdom of God it is because Joseph Smith let you go there**. This will apply to Jews and Gentiles, to the bond, and free; to friends and foes; **no man or woman in this generation will get a resurrection and be crowned without Joseph Smith says so**. The man who was martyred in Carthage Jail [in the] State of Illinois holds the Keys of Life and Death to this generation. **He is the President of the Resurrection in this Dispensation** and he will be the first to rise from the dead. **When he has passed through it, then I reckon the Keys of Resurrection will be committed to him**. Then he will call up his Apostles. You know I told you last conference **I was an Apostle of Joseph Smith**; and if faithful enough I expect Joseph will resurrect the Apostles; and when they have passed through the change, and received their blessings, I expect he will commit to them the Keys of the Resurrection, and they will go on resurrecting the Saints, every man in his own order." (*The Essential Brigham Young*, p. 99)

"We have just been listening to the testimony of one of the Apostles of the Lord Jesus Christ, **also an Apostle of him whom the Lord has called in our day to establish his kingdom** no more to be overcome by wickedness on the earth. **To say that we are Apostles of Joseph Smith is rather a dark saying to many**. Jesus Christ being sent of the Father to perform a certain work, became an Apostle. It is written in the book called Hebrews, 'Wherefore, holy brethren, partakers of the heavenly calling, **consider the Apostle** and High Priest of our profession, Christ Jesus; who was faithful to him that appointed him, as also Moses was faithful and all his house.' The Saviour called upon a number of men to assist him in the work his Father had sent him to do, and sent them into the world to proclaim his mission and Gospel, instructing them to baptize all believers. **In this way they became the Apostles of Jesus Christ**, and at the day of his coming they will stand at his right hand in a pillar of fire, being clothed with robes of righteousness, with crowns upon their heads, in glory to judge the whole house of Israel. **Joseph Smith was the first Apostle of this Church, and was commanded of Jesus Christ to call and ordain other Apostles** and send them into all the world with a message to all people, and with authority to baptize all who should believe the fulness of the Gospel and sincerely repent of all their sins. **These other Apostles are Apostles of Jesus Christ, and of Joseph Smith the chief Apostle of this last dispensation**." (JD 9:364. Brigham Young referring to Joseph Smith and Jesus Christ.)

Chapter 19

Elijah and John the Baptist

Apostle Matthew

"...Jesus began to say unto the multitudes concerning John...A prophet? yea, I say unto you, and more than a prophet. For this is he of whom it is written, **Behold I send my messenger before my face, which shall prepare thy way before thee.** Verily I say unto you, **Among them that are born of women <u>there hath not risen a greater than John the Baptist</u>**: notwithstanding he that is least in the kingdom of heaven is greater than he...For all the prophets and the law prophesied until John. **And if ye will receive it, this is Elias, which was for to come.**" (Matthew 11:7,9–11,13–14)

The Concordant version translates it as:

"And if you are willing to receive him, he is Elijah..." (Matthew 11, Concordant Literal NT version)

"Why then do our teachers say that Elijah must come first? He replied, Yes Elijah will come and set everything right. But I tell you that **Elijah has already come, and they failed to recognize him**, and worked their will upon him; and in the same way the Son of Man is to suffer at their hands. **Then the disciples understood that He meant John the Baptist.**" (Matthew 17:10–13 New English version. Also see Matthew 17:10–13 KJV)

"When Jesus came into the coasts of Caesarea Philippi, he asked his disciples, saying, Whom do men say that I the Son of man am? And they said, **Some say that thou art John the Baptist: some, Elias; and others, Jeremias, or one of the prophets.**" (Matthew 16:13–14)

Truman Madsen

"A Jewish apocalyptic tradition says that those two prophets who are to one day testify in the streets of Jerusalem to prepare the hearts of the Jews to be turned to the prophets (see D&C 98:16–17), and are then to literally be killed and lie in the streets—martyrs just prior to the coming of the Messiah—are Elijah and Enoch." (*The Radiant Life,* p. 108)

Chapter 20

Elias, Elijah, Noah, and John the Baptist

An Essay That Explores the Relationship Between Elias, Elijah, Noah, and John the Baptist

In this essay I want to look at the scriptural evidence for a link between Elias (Elijah), Gabriel (Noah), and John the Baptist (and others) in terms of eternal lives. I believe that the preponderance of evidence supports this thesis beyond reasonable dispute.

Let's begin with two verses of scripture:

6 And also with Elias, to whom I have committed the keys of bringing to pass the restoration of all things spoken by the mouth of all the holy prophets since the world began, concerning the last days; 7 And also John the son of Zacharias, which Zacharias he (Elias) visited and gave promise that he should have a son, and his name should be John, and he should be filled with the spirit of Elias; (D&C 27:6–7)

Verse 7 offers us an important clue. It tells us that Elias visited Zacharias and promised him a son. In the book of Luke we find the story of Zacharias and the angelic visitor, it reads:

5 ¶ THERE was in the days of Herod, the king of Judaea, a certain priest named Zacharias, of the course of Abia: and his wife *was* of the daughters of Aaron, and her name *was* Elisabeth. 6 And they were both righteous before God, walking in all the commandments and ordinances of the Lord blameless. 7 And they had no child, because that Elisabeth was barren, and they both were *now* well stricken in years. 8 And it came to pass, that while he executed the priest's office before God in the order of his course, 9 According to the custom of the priest's office, his lot was to burn incense when he went into the temple of the Lord. 10 And the whole multitude of the people were praying without at the time of incense. 11 And there appeared unto him an angel of the Lord standing on the right side of the altar of incense. 12 And when Zacharias saw *him,* he was troubled, and fear fell upon him. 13 But the angel said unto him, Fear not, Zacharias: for thy prayer is heard; and thy wife Elisabeth shall bear thee a son, and thou shalt call his name John. 14 And thou shalt have joy and gladness; and many shall rejoice at his birth. 15 For he shall be great in the sight of the Lord, and shall drink neither wine nor strong drink; and he shall be filled with the Holy

Ghost, even from his mother's womb. 16 And many of the children of Israel shall he turn to the Lord their God. 17 **And he shall go before him in the spirit and power of Elias, to turn the hearts of the fathers to the children**, and the disobedient to the wisdom of the just; to make ready a people prepared for the Lord. 18 And Zacharias said unto the angel, Whereby shall I know this? for I am an old man, and my wife well stricken in years. 19 And the angel answering said unto him, **I am Gabriel**, that stand in the presence of God; and am sent to speak unto thee, and to shew thee these glad tidings. (Luke 1:5–19)

Verse 19 names the angelic visitor as "Gabriel" which seems to contradict D&C 27:7 (which names the visitor as Elias). The Bible Dictionary states that Gabriel was the "name of an angel sent to Daniel…to Zacharias…and to Mary. He is identified by latter-day revelation as Noah (HC 3:386)." (Bible Dictionary p. 676)

So it appears that an angelic being with at least two different names (Elias and Gabriel) visited Zacharias.

There is another provocative statement in Luke 1:17 which states, "And he shall go before him in the spirit and power of Elias, to turn the hearts of the fathers to the children" which is almost verbatim what the Lord says to Joseph Smith about Elijah saying,

And also Elijah, unto whom I have committed the keys of the power of turning the hearts of the fathers to the children…(D&C 27:9)

Elias and Elijah seem to be endowed with the same singular priesthood keys. That is because the name Elias, "is the New Testament form (Greek) of Elijah (Hebrew)…Elias in these instances can only be the ancient prophet Elijah whose ministry is recorded in 1 and 2 Kings." (Bible Dictionary p. 663)

Therefore the angelic visitor to Zacharias (Gabriel and Elias) who prophesied of the coming of John the Baptist was none other than both Noah and Elijah at different times in his past eternal lives.

Returning to D&C 27:7, we also learn that the unborn spirit of John the Baptist was credited with visiting Zacharias. Read carefully and note what is said; "**And also John the son of Zacharias**, which Zacharias **he** (Elias) **visited**…" The fascinating thing here is that in this one short sentence, we are given the clues that lead to the discovery that Noah, Elijah, and John the Baptist, were all mortal men whose mortal lives are part of the eternal lives of an angel named Gabriel.

Furthermore we can conclude from D&C 27:7 that when the Lord said to Joseph Smith that John the Baptist was to "**be filled with the spirit of Elias**" that God meant that literally the same eternal spirit which had been Elias (Elijah) would also be John the Baptist.

John the Baptist must be an important character in the Lord's plans. With regard to John the Baptist, the Lord himself said,

7 ¶ And as they departed, Jesus began to say unto the multitudes concerning John, What went ye out into the wilderness to see? A reed shaken with the wind? 8 But what went ye out for to see? A man clothed in soft raiment? behold, they that wear soft *clothing* are in kings' houses. 9 But what went ye out for to see? A prophet? yea, <u>I say unto you, and more than a prophet</u>. 10 For this is *he,* of whom it is written, <u>Behold, I send my messenger before thy face, which shall prepare thy way before thee</u>. 11 Verily I say unto you, <u>Among them that are born of women there hath not risen a greater than John the Baptist</u>: notwithstanding he that is least in the kingdom of heaven is greater than he. 12 And from the days of John the Baptist until now the kingdom of heaven suffereth violence, and the violent take it by force. 13 For all the prophets and the law prophesied until John. 14 <u>And if ye will receive *it,* this is Elias</u>, which was for to come. 15 <u>He that hath ears to hear, let him hear</u>. (Matthew 11:7–15)

10 And his disciples asked him, saying, Why then say the scribes that Elias must first come? 11 And Jesus answered and said unto them, <u>Elias truly shall first come, and restore all things</u>. 12 But I say unto you, That <u>Elias is come already, and they knew him not</u>, but have done unto him whatsoever they listed. Likewise shall also the Son of man suffer of them. 13 **Then the disciples understood that he spake unto them of John the Baptist**. (Matthew 17:10–13)

Now compare these verses with additional evidences from the Joseph Smith Translation. Note the significant differences:

7 And as they departed, Jesus began to say unto the multitudes concerning John, What went ye out into the wilderness to see? Was it a reed shaken with the wind? And they answered him, No. 8 And he said, But what went ye out for to see? Was it a man clothed in soft raiment? Behold they that wear soft raiment are in king's houses. 9 But what went ye out for to see? A prophet? Yea, I say unto you, and more than a prophet. 10 For this is the one of whom it is written, Behold, I send my messenger before thy face, which shall prepare thy way before thee. 11 Verily, I say unto you, Among them that are born of women, there hath not risen a greater than John the Baptist; notwithstanding, he that is least in the kingdom of heaven, is greater that he. 12 And from the days of John the Baptist until now, the kingdom of heaven suffereth violence, and the violent take it by force. 13 But the days will come, when the violent shall have no power; for all the prophets and the law prophesied that it should be thus until John. 14 Yea, as many as have prophesied have foretold of these days. 15 **And if ye will receive it, verily, he was the Elias, who was for to come and prepare all things**. 16 **He that hath ears to hear, let him hear**. (JST Matthew 11:7–16)

10 And Jesus answered and said unto them, Elias truly shall first come, and restore all things, as the prophets have written. 11 And again I say unto you that Elias has come already, concerning whom it is written, Behold, I will send my messenger, and he shall prepare the way before me; and they knew him not, and have done unto him, whatsoever they listed. 12 Likewise shall also the Son of man suffer of them. 13 But I

say unto you, **Who is Elias? Behold, this is Elias, whom I send to prepare the way before me**. 14 Then the disciples understood that he spake unto them of John the Baptist, **and also of another who should come and restore all things, as it is written by the prophets**. (JST Matthew 17:10–14)

We should also compare the following provocative verses from the first chapter of the gospel of John with the JST version of the same verses. The differences with regard to Elias are very enlightening:

19 ¶ And this is the record of John, when the Jews sent priests and Levites from Jerusalem to ask him, Who art thou? 20 **And he confessed, and denied not**; but confessed, I am not the Christ. 21 And they asked him, What then? Art thou Elias? And he saith, I am not. Art thou that prophet? And he answered, No. 22 Then said they unto him, Who art thou? that we may give an answer to them that sent us. What sayest thou of thyself? 23 He said, I *am* the voice of one crying in the wilderness, Make straight the way of the Lord, as said the prophet Esaias. 24 And they which were sent were of the Pharisees. 25 And they asked him, and said unto him, Why baptizest thou then, if thou be not that Christ, nor Elias, neither that prophet? 26 John answered them, saying, I baptize with water: but there standeth one among you, whom ye know not; 27 He it is, who coming after me is preferred before me, whose shoe's latchet I am not worthy to unloose. (John 1:19–27)

20 And this is the record of John, when the Jews sent priests and Levites from Jerusalem, to ask him; **Who art thou? 21 And he confessed, and denied not that he was Elias**; but confessed, saying; I am not the Christ. 22 And they asked him, saying; **How then art thou Elias?** And he said, **I am not that Elias who was to restore all things**. And they asked him, saying, **Art thou that prophet? And he answered, No.** 23 Then said they unto him, Who art thou? that we may give an answer to them that sent us. What sayest thou of thyself? 24 He said, I am the voice of one crying in the wilderness, Make straight the way of the Lord, as saith the prophet Esaias. 25 And they who were sent were of the Pharisees. 26 And they asked him, and said unto him, Why baptizest thou then, if thou be not the Christ, **nor Elias who was to restore all things, neither that prophet?** 27 John answered them, saying, I baptize with water, but there standeth one among you, whom ye know not; 28 He it is of whom I bear record. **He is that prophet, even Elias**, who, coming after me, is preferred before me, whose shoe's latchet I am not worthy to unloose, or whose place I am not able to fill; for he shall baptize, not only with water, but with fire, and with the Holy Ghost. (JST John 1:20–28)

If the foregoing evidence is insufficient, then consider the following additional verse of scripture from the JST which reads,

3 And there appeared unto them **Elias with Moses, or in other words, John the Baptist and Moses**; and they were talking with Jesus. 4 And Peter answered and said to Jesus, Master, it is good for us to be here; and **let us make three tabernacles; one for thee, and one for Moses,**

and one for Elias; for he knew not what to say; for they were sore afraid. (JST Mark 9:3–4)

Joseph Smith clearly knew what he was writing and he understood the link he was creating between Elias (Elijah) and John the Baptist. The writers of the LDS Bible Dictionary have struggled with this obvious linkage and they wrote, "The curious wording of JST Mark 9:3 does not imply that the Elias at the Transfiguration was John the Baptist, but that in addition to Elijah the prophet, John the Baptist was present." (Bible Dictionary p. 663). If this statement was true, then why didn't Peter suggest making four tabernacles? And how could Joseph Smith make this glaring mathematical error if his intention was to separate and segregate Elijah from John the Baptist?

Joseph Smith knew exactly what he was doing!

What else can we learn about Elias?

9 Q. What are we to understand by the angel ascending from the east, Revelation 7th chapter and 2nd verse? A. We are to understand that the angel ascending from the east is he to whom is given the seal of the living God over the twelve tribes of Israel; wherefore, he crieth unto the four angels having the everlasting gospel, saying: Hurt not the earth, neither the sea, nor the trees, till we have sealed the servants of our God in their foreheads. And, if you will receive it, this is Elias which was to come to gather together the tribes of Israel and restore all things. (D&C 77:9)

14 Q. What are we to understand by the little book which was eaten by John, as mentioned in the 10th chapter of Revelation? A. We are to understand that it was a mission, and an ordinance, for him to gather the tribes of Israel; behold, this is Elias, who, as it is written, must come and restore all things. (D&C 77:14)

12 After this, Elias appeared, and committed the dispensation of the gospel of Abraham, saying that in us and our seed all generations after us should be blessed. (D&C 110:12. Could this reference to Elias be referring to either Melchizedek or to Abraham as another instance of the same "Elias" mentioned in D&C 27:7?)

Returning to D&C 27:6 we read,

6 And also with Elias, to whom I have committed the keys of bringing to pass the restoration of all things spoken by the mouth of all the holy prophets since the world began, concerning the last days;

I'll ask a question. To whom did God grant the keys for the restoration in the last days?

13 Unto whom I have committed the keys of my kingdom, and a dispensation of the gospel for the last times; and for the fulness of times, in the which I will gather together in one all things, both which are in heaven, and which are on earth; (D&C 27:13)

7 For I have given him the keys of the mysteries, and the revelations which are sealed, until I shall appoint unto them another in his stead. (D&C 27:8)

18 And I have given unto him the keys of the mystery of those things which have been sealed, even things which were from the foundation of the world, and the things which shall come from this time until the time of my coming, if he abide in me, and if not, another will I plant in his stead. (D&C 35:18)

5 And the keys of the mysteries of the kingdom shall not be taken from my servant Joseph Smith, Jun., through the means I have appointed, while he liveth, inasmuch as he obeyeth mine ordinances. (D&C 64:5)

2 Unto whom I have given the keys of the kingdom, which belong always unto the Presidency of the High Priesthood: (D&C 81:2)

2 Therefore, thou art blessed from henceforth that bear the keys of the kingdom given unto you; which kingdom is coming forth for the last time. 3 **Verily I say unto you, the keys of this kingdom shall never be taken from you, while thou art in the world, neither in the world to come**; (D&C 90:2–3)

16 Therefore, the keys of this dispensation are committed into your hands; and by this ye may know that the great and dreadful day of the Lord is near, even at the doors. (D&C 110:16)

Could it be that the "Elias" spoken of in D&C 27:6 is also the prophet Joseph Smith?

6 to whom I have committed the keys of bringing to pass the restoration of all things spoken by the mouth of all the holy prophets since the world began, concerning the last days; (D&C 27:6)

14 Then the disciples understood that he spake unto them of John the Baptist, and also of another who should come and restore all things, as it is written by the prophets. (JST Matthew 17:14)

Finally, consider this;

5 What is the root of Jesse spoken of in the 10th verse of the 11th chapter? 6 Behold, thus saith the Lord, it is a descendant of Jesse, as well as of Joseph, unto whom rightly belongs the priesthood, and the keys of the kingdom, for an ensign, and for the gathering of my people in the last days. (D&C 113:5–6)

Adam, Enoch, Noah, Melchizedek, Elias, Moses, John the Baptist, Joseph Smith: "Would to God, brethren, I could tell you who I am! Would to God I could tell you what I know! But you would call it blasphemy, and there are men upon this stand who would want to take my life." (Joseph Smith, Jr., as quoted by Heber C. Kimball, *Life of Heber C. Kimball*, by Orson F. Whitney, pp. 322–323)

Chapter 21

God Himself Shall Come Down

Apostle John

"Jesus saith unto him, I am the way, the truth, and the life: no man cometh unto the Father, but by me. If ye had known me, ye should have known my Father also: and from henceforth ye know him, and have seen him. Philip saith unto him, Lord, shew us the Father, and it sufficeth us. Jesus saith unto him, Have I been so long time with you, and yet hast thou not known me, Philip? he that hath seen me hath seen the Father; and how sayest thou *then,* Shew us the Father? Believest thou not that I am in the Father, and the Father in me? the words that I speak unto you I speak not of myself: but the Father that dwelleth in me, he doeth the works. Believe me that I am in the Father, and the Father in me: or else believe me for the very works' sake." (John 14:7–11)

Joseph Smith

"And it came to pass that I saw the heavens open; and an angel came down and stood before me; and he said unto me, Nephi, what beholdest thou? And I said unto him, a virgin, most beautiful and fair above all other virgins. And he said unto me: **Knowest thou the condescension of God?** And I said unto him, I know that he loveth his children; nevertheless, I do not know the meaning of all things. And he said unto me, Behold, the virgin whom thou seest, is the **mother of God**, after the manner of the flesh. And it came to pass that I beheld that she was carried away in the spirit; and after she had been carried away in the spirit for the space of a time, the angel spake unto me, saying, Look!

And I looked and beheld the virgin again, bearing a child in her arms. And the angel said unto me, **behold the Lamb of God, yea, even the Eternal Father**! Knowest thou the meaning of the tree which thy father saw? And I answered him, saying: Yea, it is the love of God, which sheddeth itself abroad in the hearts of the children of men; wherefore, it is the most desirable above all things." (1 Nephi 11:14–22. This version of the scriptures is taken from the original 1830 edition of the Book of Mormon as translated by Joseph Smith and found in the Wilford C. Wood edition, Vol. 1, pp. 24–25)

"Behold, my brethren, do ye not remember to have read the words of the prophet Zenos, which he spake unto the house of Israel, saying:

Hearken, O ye house of Israel, and hear the words of me, a prophet of the Lord. For behold, thus saith the Lord, I will liken thee, O house of Israel, like unto a tame olive-tree, which **a man took and nourished in his vineyard**; and it grew, and waxed old, and began to decay. And it came to pass that **the master of the vineyard went forth**, and he saw that his olive-tree began to decay; and he said: **I will prune it**, and dig about it, and nourish it, that perhaps it may shoot forth young and tender branches, and it perish not.

And it came to pass that **he pruned it**, and digged about it, and nourished it according to his word. And it came to pass that after many days it began to put forth somewhat a little, young and tender branches; but behold, the main top thereof began to perish. And it came to pass that the master of the vineyard saw it, and he said unto his servant: It grieveth me that I should lose this tree; wherefore, go and pluck the branches from a wild olive-tree, and **bring them hither unto me**; and we will pluck off those main branches which are beginning to wither away, and we will cast them into the fire that they may be burned.

And behold, saith the Lord of the vineyard, I take away many of these young and tender branches, and **I will graft them** whithersoever I will; and it mattereth not that if it so be that the root of this tree will perish, I may preserve the fruit thereof unto myself; wherefore, I will take these young and tender branches, and I will graft them whithersoever I will. Take thou the branches of the wild olive-tree, and graft them in, in the stead thereof; and these which I have plucked off I will cast into the fire and burn them, that they may not cumber the ground of my vineyard. And it came to pass that the servant of the Lord of the vineyard did according to the word of the Lord of the vineyard, and grafted in the branches of the wild olive-tree.

And the Lord of the vineyard caused that it should be digged about, and pruned, and nourished, saying unto his servant: It grieveth me that I should lose this tree; wherefore, that perhaps I might preserve the roots thereof that they perish not, that I might preserve them unto myself, I have done this thing. Wherefore, go thy way; watch the tree, and nourish it, according to my words.

And these **will I place** in the nethermost part of my vineyard, whithersoever I will, it mattereth not unto thee; and I do it that I may preserve unto myself the natural branches of the tree; and also, that I may lay up fruit thereof against the season, unto myself; for it grieveth me that I should lose this tree and the fruit thereof. And it came to pass that the Lord of the vineyard went his way, and hid the natural branches of the tame olive-tree in the nethermost parts of the vineyard, some in one and some in another, according to his will and pleasure.

And it came to pass that **a long time passed away**, and the Lord of the vineyard said unto his servant: **Come, <u>let us go down</u> into the vineyard, that we may labor in the vineyard. And it came to pass that <u>the Lord of the vineyard, and also the servant, went down into the vineyard to labor</u>**. And it came to pass that the servant said unto his master: Behold, look here; behold the tree. And it came to pass that the Lord of the vineyard looked and beheld the tree in the which the wild olive branches had been grafted; and it had sprung forth and begun to bear fruit. And he beheld that it was good; and the fruit thereof was like unto the natural fruit.

And he said unto the servant: Behold, the branches of the wild tree have taken hold of the moisture of the root thereof, that the root thereof hath brought forth much strength; and because of the much strength of the root thereof the wild branches have brought forth tame fruit. Now, if we had not grafted in these branches, the tree thereof would have perished. And now, behold, I shall lay up much fruit, which the tree thereof hath brought forth; and the fruit thereof I shall lay up against the season, unto mine own self. And it came to pass that the Lord of the vineyard said unto the servant**: Come, <u>let us go</u> to the nethermost part of the vineyard**, and behold if the natural branches of the tree have not brought forth much fruit also, that I may lay up of the fruit thereof against the season, unto mine own self.

And it came to pass that **<u>they went forth</u> whither the master had hid the natural branches of the tree**, and he said unto the servant: Behold these; and he beheld the first that it had brought forth much fruit; and he beheld also that it was good. And he said unto the servant: Take of the fruit thereof, and lay it up against the season, that I may preserve it unto mine own self; for behold, said he, this long time have I nourished it, and it hath brought forth much fruit. And it came to pass that the servant said unto his master: How comest thou hither to plant this tree, or this branch of the tree? For behold, it was the poorest spot in all the land of thy vineyard.

And the Lord of the vineyard said unto him: Counsel me not; I knew that it was a poor spot of ground; wherefore, I said unto thee, I have nourished it this long time, and thou beholdest that it hath brought forth much fruit. And it came to pass that the Lord of the vineyard said unto his servant: Look hither; behold I have planted another branch of the tree also; and thou knowest that this spot of ground was poorer than the first. But, behold the tree. I have nourished it this long time, and it hath brought forth much fruit; therefore, gather it, and lay it up against the season, that I may preserve it unto mine own self.

And it came to pass that the Lord of the vineyard said again unto his servant: Look hither, and behold another branch also, which **I have planted**; behold that I have nourished it also, and it hath brought forth fruit. And he said unto the servant: Look hither and behold the last.

Behold, **this have I planted** in a good spot of ground; and I have nourished it this long time, and only a part of the tree hath brought forth tame fruit, and the other part of the tree hath brought forth wild fruit; behold, I have nourished this tree like unto the others. And it came to pass that the Lord of the vineyard said unto the servant: Pluck off the branches that have not brought forth good fruit, and cast them into the fire.

But behold, the servant said unto him: Let us prune it, and dig about it, and nourish it a little longer, that perhaps it may bring forth good fruit unto thee, that thou canst lay it up against the season. And it came to pass that the Lord of the vineyard and the servant of the Lord of the vineyard did nourish all the fruit of the vineyard. And it came to pass that a long time had passed away, and the Lord of the vineyard said unto his servant: **Come, <u>let us go down</u> into the vineyard, that we may labor again in the vineyard**. For behold, the time draweth near, and the end soon cometh; wherefore, I must lay up fruit against the season, unto mine own self.

And it came to pass that the Lord of the vineyard and the servant went down into the vineyard; and they came to the tree whose natural branches had been broken off, and the wild branches had been grafted in; and behold all sorts of fruit did cumber the tree. And it came to pass that the Lord of the vineyard did taste of the fruit, every sort according to its number. And the Lord of the vineyard said: Behold, this long time have we nourished this tree, and **I have laid up unto myself** against the season much fruit. But behold, this time it hath brought forth much fruit, and there is none of it which is good.

And behold, there are all kinds of bad fruit; and it profiteth me nothing, notwithstanding all our labor; and now it grieveth me that I should lose this tree. And the Lord of the vineyard said unto the servant: What shall we do unto the tree, that I may preserve again good fruit thereof unto mine own self? And the servant said unto his master: Behold, because thou didst graft in the branches of the wild olive-tree they have nourished the roots, that they are alive and they have not perished; wherefore thou beholdest that they are yet good. And it came to pass that the Lord of the vineyard said unto his servant: The tree profiteth me nothing, and the roots thereof profit me nothing so long as it shall bring forth evil fruit. Nevertheless, I know that the roots are good, and for mine own purpose I have preserved them; and because of their much strength they have hitherto brought forth, from the wild branches, good fruit.

But behold, the wild branches have grown and have overrun the roots thereof; and because that the wild branches have overcome the roots thereof it hath brought forth much evil fruit; and because that it hath brought forth so much evil fruit thou beholdest that it beginneth to perish; and it will soon become ripened, that it may be cast into the fire, except we should do something for it to preserve it. And it came to pass that the Lord of the vineyard said unto his servant: **<u>Let us go down</u> into the nethermost parts of the vineyard**, and behold if the natural branches have also brought forth evil fruit. And it came to pass that they went down into the nethermost parts of the vineyard.

And it came to pass that they beheld that the fruit of the natural branches had become corrupt also; yea, the first and the second and also the last; and they had all become corrupt. And the wild fruit of the last had overcome that part of the tree which brought forth good fruit, even that the branch had withered away and died. And it came to pass that the

Lord of the vineyard wept, and said unto the servant: What could I have done more for my vineyard? Behold, I knew that all the fruit of the vineyard, save it were these, had become corrupted. And now these which have once brought forth good fruit have also become corrupted; and now all the trees of my vineyard are good for nothing save it be to be hewn down and cast into the fire.

And behold this last, whose branch hath withered away, **I did plant** in a good spot of ground; yea, even that which was choice unto me above all other parts of the land of my vineyard. And thou beheldest that **I also cut down** that which cumbered this spot of ground, that I might plant this tree in the stead thereof. And thou beheldest that a part thereof brought forth good fruit, and a part thereof brought forth wild fruit; and because I plucked not the branches thereof and cast them into the fire, behold, they have overcome the good branch that it hath withered away.

And now, behold, notwithstanding all the care which we have taken of my vineyard, the trees thereof have become corrupted, that they bring forth no good fruit; and these I had hoped to preserve, to have laid up fruit thereof against the season, unto mine own self. But, behold, they have become like unto the wild olive-tree, and they are of no worth but to be hewn down and cast into the fire; and it grieveth me that I should lose them. But what could I have done more in my vineyard? Have I slackened mine hand, that I have not nourished it? Nay, I have nourished it, and I have digged about it, and I have pruned it, and I have dunged it; and **I have stretched forth mine hand almost all the day long**, and the end draweth nigh. And it grieveth me that I should hew down all the trees of my vineyard, and cast them into the fire that they should be burned. Who is it that has corrupted my vineyard? And it came to pass that the servant said unto his master: Is it not the loftiness of thy vineyard—have not the branches thereof overcome the roots which are good?

And because the branches have overcome the roots thereof, behold they grew faster than the strength of the roots, taking strength unto themselves. Behold, I say, is not this the cause that the trees of thy vineyard have become corrupted? And it came to pass that the Lord of the vineyard said unto the servant: **Let us go to** and hew down the trees of the vineyard and cast them into the fire, that they shall not cumber the ground of my vineyard, for I have done all. What could I have done more for my vineyard?

But, behold, the servant said unto the Lord of the vineyard: Spare it a little longer. And the Lord said: Yea, I will spare it a little longer, for it grieveth me that I should lose the trees of my vineyard. Wherefore, let us take of the branches of these which **I have planted** in the nethermost parts of my vineyard, and let us graft them into the tree from whence they came; and let us pluck from the tree those branches whose fruit is most bitter, and graft in the natural branches of the tree in the stead thereof. And this will I do that the tree may not perish, that, perhaps, I may preserve unto myself the roots thereof for mine own purpose.

And, behold, the roots of the natural branches of the tree which I planted whithersoever I would are yet alive; wherefore, that I may preserve them also for mine own purpose, I will take of the branches of this tree, and **I will graft them** in unto them. Yea, I will graft in unto them the branches of their mother tree, that I may preserve the roots also unto mine own self, that when they shall be sufficiently strong perhaps they may bring forth good fruit unto me, and I may yet have glory in the fruit of my vineyard. And it came to pass that they took from the natural tree which had become wild, and grafted in unto the natural trees, which also had become wild. And they also took of the natural trees which had become wild, and grafted into their mother tree.

And the Lord of the vineyard said unto the servant: Pluck not the wild branches from the trees, save it be those which are most bitter; and in them ye shall graft according to that which I have said. And we will nourish again the trees of the vineyard, and we will trim up the branches thereof; and we will pluck from the trees those branches which are ripened, that must perish, and cast them into the fire. And this I do that, perhaps, the roots thereof may take strength because of their goodness; and because of the change of the branches, that the good may overcome the evil.

And because that I have preserved the natural branches and the roots thereof, and that **I have grafted** in the natural branches again into their mother tree, and have preserved the roots of their mother tree, that, perhaps, the trees of my vineyard may bring forth again good fruit; and that I may have joy again in the fruit of my vineyard, and, perhaps, that I may rejoice exceedingly that I have preserved the roots and the branches of the first fruit—**Wherefore, go to, and call servants, that <u>we</u> may labor diligently** with our might in the vineyard, that we may prepare the way, that I may bring forth again the natural fruit, which natural fruit is good and the most precious above all other fruit. Wherefore, <u>**let us go** to **and labor with our might this last time**</u>, for behold the end draweth nigh, and this is for the last time that I shall prune my vineyard.

Graft in the branches; begin at the last that they may be first, and that the first may be last, and dig about the trees, both old and young, the first and the last; and the last and the first, that all may be nourished once again for the last time. Wherefore, dig about them, and prune them, and dung them once more, for the last time, for the end draweth nigh. And if it be so that these last grafts shall grow, and bring forth the natural fruit, then shall ye prepare the way for them, that they may grow.

And as they begin to grow ye shall clear away the branches which bring forth bitter fruit, according to the strength of the good and the size thereof; and ye shall not clear away the bad thereof all at once, lest the roots thereof should be too strong for the graft, and the graft thereof shall perish, and I lose the trees of my vineyard. For it grieveth me that I should lose the trees of my vineyard; wherefore ye shall clear away the bad according as the good shall grow, that the root and the top may be equal in strength, until the good shall overcome the bad, and the bad be hewn down and cast into the fire, that they cumber not the ground of my vineyard; and thus will I sweep away the bad out of my vineyard.

And the branches of the natural tree will I graft in again into the natural tree; And the branches of the natural tree will I graft into the natural branches of the tree; and thus will I bring them together again, that they shall bring forth the natural fruit, and they shall be one. And the bad shall be cast away, yea, even out of all the land of my vineyard; for behold, only this once will I prune my vineyard. **And it came to pass that the Lord of the vineyard sent his servant**; and the servant went and did as the Lord had commanded him, and brought other servants; and they were few. And the Lord of the vineyard said unto them: Go to, and labor in the vineyard, with your might.

For behold, **this is the last time that I shall nourish my vineyard**; for the end is nigh at hand, and the season speedily cometh; and if ye labor with your might with me ye shall have joy in the fruit which I shall lay up unto myself against the time which will soon come. And it came to pass that the servants did go and labor with their mights; **and the Lord of the vineyard labored also with them**; and they did obey the commandments of the Lord of the vineyard in all things. And there began to be the natural fruit again in the vineyard; and the natural branches began to grow and thrive exceedingly; and the wild branches began to be plucked off and to be cast away; and they did keep the root and the top thereof equal, according to the strength thereof.

And thus they labored, with all diligence, according to the commandments of the Lord of the vineyard, even until the bad had been cast away out of the vineyard, and the Lord had preserved unto himself that the trees had become again the natural fruit; and they became like unto one body; and the fruits were equal; and the Lord of the vineyard had preserved unto himself the natural fruit, which was most precious unto him from the beginning.

And it came to pass that when the Lord of the vineyard saw that his fruit was good, and that his vineyard was no more corrupt, he called up his servants, and said unto them: Behold, **for this last time have we nourished my vineyard**; and thou beholdest that I have done according to my will; and I have preserved the natural fruit, that it is good, even like as it was in the beginning. And blessed art thou; for because ye have been diligent in laboring with me in my vineyard, and have kept my commandments, and have brought unto me again the natural fruit, that my vineyard is no more corrupted, and the bad is cast away, behold ye shall have joy with me because of the fruit of my vineyard.

For behold, for a long time will I lay up of the fruit of my vineyard unto mine own self against the season, which speedily cometh; and for the last time have I nourished my vineyard, and pruned it, and dug about it, and dunged it; wherefore I will lay up unto mine own self of the fruit, for a long time, according to that which I have spoken. And when the time cometh that evil fruit shall again come into my vineyard, then will I cause the good and the bad to be gathered; and the good will I preserve unto myself, and the bad will I cast away into its own place. And then cometh the season and the end; and my vineyard will I cause to be burned with fire." (Jacob 5:1–77)

"And now Abinadi said unto them: I would that ye should understand that **God himself shall come down** among the children of men, and shall redeem his people. **And because he dwelleth in flesh he shall be called the Son of God**, and having subjected the flesh to the will of the Father, **being the Father and the Son—The Father, because he was conceived by the power of God; and the Son, because of the flesh**; thus becoming the Father and Son—**And they are one God**, yea, the very Eternal Father of heaven and of earth. And thus the flesh becoming subject to the Spirit, or the Son to the Father, being one God, suffereth temptation, and yieldeth not to the temptation, but suffereth himself to be mocked, and scourged, and cast out, and disowned by his people." (Mosiah 15:1–5)

And now, the plan of mercy could not be brought about except an atonement should be made; therefore **God himself atoneth for the sins of the world**, to bring about the plan of mercy, to appease the demands of justice, **that God might be a perfect, just God, and a merciful God also**. (Alma 42:15)

2 But thou, Bethlehem Ephratah, though thou be little among the thousands of Judah, yet out of thee shall he come forth unto me that is to be ruler in Israel; **whose goings forth have been from of old, from everlasting**. (JST Micah 5:2)

GOD MAY RESIDE IN THE BODIES OF SOME GREAT MEN

David, King of Israel

"One *thing* have I desired of the LORD, that will I seek after; that I may dwell in the house of the LORD all the days of my life, to behold the beauty of the LORD, and to enquire in his temple. For in the time of trouble **he shall hide me in his pavilion: in the secret of his tabernacle shall he hide me**; he shall set me up upon a rock." (Psalms 27:4–5. Also see Job 14:13–16)

"**Thou *art* my hiding place**; thou shalt preserve me from trouble; thou shalt compass me about with songs of deliverance. Selah." (Psalms 32:7. Also see 2 Corinthians 6:16; Ephesians 2:2, 4:6)

"**For thou hast been a shelter for me**, *and* a strong tower from the enemy. 4 **I will abide in thy tabernacle for ever**: I will trust in the covert of thy wings. Selah." (Psalms 61:3–4)

"**He that dwelleth in the secret place of the most High** shall abide under the shadow of the Almighty. I will say of the LORD, *He is* **my refuge** and my fortress: my God; in him will I trust." (Psalms 91:1–2)

Isaiah

"Behold, **a king shall reign in righteousness**, and princes shall rule in judgment. And **a man shall be as an hiding place** from the wind, and a covert from the tempest; as rivers of water in a dry place, as the shadow of a great rock in a weary land." (Isaiah 32:1–2)

"**Behold my servant**, whom I uphold; mine elect, *in whom* my soul delighteth; **I have put my spirit upon him**: he shall bring forth judgment to the Gentiles." (Isaiah 42:1)

"**The LORD shall go forth as a mighty man**, he shall stir up jealousy like a man of war: he shall cry, yea, roar; he shall prevail against his enemies. I have long time holden my peace; I have been still, *and* refrained myself: *now* will I cry like a travailing woman; I will destroy and devour at once." (Isaiah 42:13–14)

"Thus saith the LORD, The labour of Egypt, and merchandise of Ethiopia and of the Sabeans, men of stature, shall come over unto thee, and they shall be thine: they shall come after thee; in chains they shall come over, and they shall fall down unto thee, they shall make supplication unto thee, *saying,* **Surely God** *is* **in thee**; and *there is* none else, *there is* no God. Verily **thou** *art* **a God that hidest thyself**, O God of Israel, the Saviour." (Isaiah 45:14–15. Also see 2 Corinthians 6:16; Ephesians 2:2, 4:6)

The Lord hath redeemed his servant Jacob. 21 And they thirsted not; **he** led them through the deserts; **he** caused the waters to flow out of the rock for them; **he** clave the rock also and the waters gushed out. 22 And notwithstanding **he** hath done all this, and greater also, there is no peace, **saith the Lord**, unto the wicked. (1 Nephi 20:21–22)

Chapter 22

Servants Who May Be Instances of God's Condescension

"Nevertheless, the Lord God showeth us our weakness that we may know that it is by his grace, **and his great condescensions unto the children of men**, that we have power to do these things." (Jacob 4:7)

"And behold how great the covenants of the Lord, and **how great his condescensions unto the children of men;** and because of his greatness, and his grace and mercy, he has promised unto us that our seed shall not utterly be destroyed, according to the flesh, but that he would preserve them; and in future generations they shall become a righteous branch unto the house of Israel." (2 Nephi 9:53)

David, King of Israel
"For thou wilt not leave my soul in hell; neither wilt thou suffer thine Holy One to see corruption. **Thou wilt shew me the path of life**: in thy presence *is* fulness of joy; **at thy right** hand *there are* pleasures for evermore." (Psalms 16:10–11. How would David know that there is a fullness of joy at the right hand of God? Is David trying to tell us something about himself?)

"For great *is* thy mercy toward me: and **thou hast delivered my soul from the lowest hell**" (Psalms 86:13). Remember the Joseph Smith taught that: He (Christ) that ascended up on high, as also he **descended below all things**, in that he comprehended all things, that he might be in all and through all things, the light of truth; (D&C 88:6). How could God descend below all things unless he had been delivered from the lowest hell as David taught?)

"David sought repentance at the Hand of God carefully with tears, for the murder of Uriah: **but he could only get it through hell: he got a promise that his soul should not be left in hell.**" (*Teachings of the Prophet Joseph Smith*, p. 339)

"O LORD, thou hast searched me, and known *me*. "Thou knowest my downsitting and mine uprising, thou understandest my thought afar off. Thou compassest my path and my lying down, and art acquainted *with* all my ways. For *there is* not a word in my tongue, *but*, lo, O LORD, thou knowest it altogether. Thou hast beset me behind and before, and laid thine hand upon me. *Such* knowledge *is* too wonderful for me; it is high, I cannot *attain* unto it. Whither shall I go from thy spirit? or whither shall I flee from thy presence? If I ascend up into heaven, thou *art* there: if I make my bed in hell, behold, thou *art there*." (Psalms 139:2–8)

"For thou hast possessed my reins: thou hast covered me in my mother's womb. I will praise thee; for I am fearfully *and* wonderfully made: marvellous *are* thy works; and *that* my soul knoweth right well. My substance was not hid from thee, **when I was made in secret**, *and* curiously wrought in the lowest parts of the earth. Thine eyes did see my substance, yet being unperfect; **and in thy book all *my members* were written**, *which* in continuance were fashioned, when *as yet there was* none of them. How precious also are thy thoughts unto me, O God! **how great is the sum of them!** *If* **I should count them, they are more in number than the sand**: when I awake, I am still with thee." (Psalms 139:13–18)

The Rod of Jesse

"**And there shall come forth a rod out of the stem of Jesse**, and a branch shall grow out of his roots. And the Spirit of the Lord shall rest upon him, the spirit of wisdom and understanding, the spirit of counsel and might, the spirit of knowledge and of the fear of the Lord; And shall make him of quick understanding in the fear of the Lord; and he shall not judge after the sight of his eyes, neither reprove after the hearing of his ears. But with righteousness shall he judge the poor, and reprove with equity for the meek of the earth; and he shall smite the earth with the rod of his mouth, and with the breath of his lips shall he slay the wicked. And righteousness shall be the girdle of his loins, and faithfulness the girdle of his reins." (2 Nephi 21:1–5)

"What is the rod spoken of in the first verse of the 11th chapter of Isaiah, that should come of the Stem of Jesse? 4 Behold, thus saith the Lord: **It is a servant in the hands of Christ**, who is partly a descendant of Jesse as well as of Ephraim, or of the house of Joseph, **on whom there is laid much power**." (D&C 113:3–4)

Now note how Nephi uses the phrase, "the Lord God" when describing the same attributes that Isaiah assigned to the Rod of Jesse.

"And it shall come to pass that **the Lord God** shall commence his work among all nations, kindreds, tongues, and people, to bring about the restoration of his people upon the earth. And with righteousness shall **the Lord God** judge the poor, and reprove with equity for the meek of the earth. And he shall smite the earth with the rod of his mouth; and with the breath of his lips shall he slay the wicked. For the time speedily cometh that **the Lord God** shall cause a great division among the people, and the wicked will he destroy; and he will spare his people, yea, even if it so be that he must destroy the wicked by fire. And righteousness shall be the girdle of his loins, and faithfulness the girdle of his reins." (2 Nephi 30:8–11)

The Root of Jesse

"**And in that day there shall be a root of Jesse**, which shall stand for an ensign of the people; to it shall the Gentiles seek; and his rest shall be glorious. And it shall come to pass in that day that **the Lord shall set his hand again** the second time to recover the remnant of his people which shall be left, from Assyria, and from Egypt, and from Pathros, and from Cush, and from Elam, and from Shinar, and from Hamath, and from the islands of the sea. And he shall set up an ensign for the nations, and shall assemble the outcasts of Israel, and gather together the dispersed of Judah from the four corners of the earth." (2 Nephi 21:10–12)

"What is the root of Jesse spoken of in the 10th verse of the 11th chapter? Behold, thus saith the Lord, it is a descendant of Jesse, as well as of Joseph, unto whom rightly belongs the priesthood, and the keys of the kingdom, for an ensign, and for the gathering of my people in the last days." (D&C 113:5–6)

Now note what is said about Christ:

"And one of the elders saith unto me, Weep not: behold, the Lion of the tribe of Juda, **the Root of David**, hath prevailed to open the book, and to loose the seven seals thereof." (Revelation 5:5)

"**I Jesus** have sent mine angel to testify unto you these things in the churches. **I am the root and the offspring of David**, *and* the bright and morning star." (Revelation 22:16)

Joseph Smith

"It is said to be eternal life, 'to know the only wise God, and Jesus Christ whom He has sent.' I will tell you one thing, as brother Hyde has said, it would be an excellent plan for us to go to work and find out ourselves, for as sure as you find out yourselves, you will find out God, whether you are Saint or sinner. A man cannot find out himself without the light of revelation; he has to turn round and seek to the Lord his God, in order to find out himself. **If you find out who Joseph was, you will know as much about God as you need to at present**; for if He said, 'I am a God to this people,' He did not say that He was the only wise God. **Jesus was a God to the people when he was upon earth, was so before he came to this earth, and is yet. Moses was a God to the children of Israel, and in this manner you may go right back to Father Adam.**" (JD 4:271. Brigham Young speaking about Joseph Smith.)

My Servant

"Ye *are* my witnesses, saith the LORD, and my servant whom I have chosen: that ye may know and believe me, and understand that **I *am* he**: before me there was no God formed, neither shall there be after me." (Isaiah 43:10)

Chapter 23

The Law of Cause and Effect

Mark

"And he said unto them, Take heed what ye hear: **with what measure ye mete, it shall be measured to you**: and unto you that hear shall more be given." (Mark 4:24)

Luke

"Give, and it shall be given unto you; good measure, pressed down, and shaken together, and running over, shall men give into your bosom. **For with the same measure that ye mete withal it shall be measured to you again**." (Luke 6:38)

Apostle Paul

"For we must all appear before the judgment seat of Christ; that **every one may receive the things *done* in *his* body, according to that he hath done**, whether *it be* good or bad." (2 Corinthians 5:10)

"Be not deceived; God is not mocked: for whatsoever a man soweth, that shall he also reap." (Galatians 6:7)

Apostle John

"And I heard a voice from heaven saying unto me, Write, Blessed *are* the dead which die in the Lord from henceforth: Yea, saith the Spirit, that they may rest from their labours; and **their works do follow them**." (Revelation 14:13)

Joseph Smith

"Ye cannot say, when ye are brought to that awful crisis, that I will repent, that I will return to my God. Nay, ye cannot say this; for that same spirit which doth possess your bodies at the time that ye go out of this life, that same spirit will have power to possess your body in that eternal world." (Alma 34:34)

"Therefore, O my son, whosoever will come may come and partake of the waters of life freely; and whosoever will not come the same is not compelled to come; but in the last day **it shall be restored unto him**

according to his deeds. If he has desired to do evil, and has not repented in his days, behold, evil shall be done unto him, according to the restoration of God." (Alma 42:27–28)

"And now behold, is the meaning of the word restoration to take a thing of a natural state and place it in an unnatural state, or to place it in a state opposite to its nature? O, my son, this is not the case; but the meaning of the word restoration is to **bring back again** evil for evil, or carnal for carnal, or devilish for devilish—good for that which is good; righteous for that which is righteous; just for that which is just; merciful for that which is merciful. Therefore, my son, see that you are merciful unto your brethren; deal justly, judge righteously, and do good continually; and if ye do all these things then shall ye receive your reward; yea, ye shall have mercy restored unto you again; ye shall have justice restored unto you again; ye shall have a righteous judgment restored unto you again; and ye shall have good rewarded unto you again. **For that which ye do send out shall return unto you again, and be restored**; therefore, the word restoration more fully condemneth the sinner, and justifieth him not at all." (Alma 41:12–15)

"And may God grant, in his great fulness, that men might be brought unto repentance and good works, **that they might be restored unto grace for grace, according to their works**. And I would that all men might be saved. But we read that in the great and last day there are some who shall be cast out, yea, who shall be cast off from the presence of the Lord; Yea, who shall be consigned to a state of endless misery, fulfilling the words which say: They that have done good shall have everlasting life; and they that have done evil shall have everlasting damnation. And thus it is. Amen." (Helaman 12:24–26)

"He hath given unto you that ye might know good from evil, and he hath given unto you that ye might choose life or death; and ye can do good and be restored unto that which is good, or have that which is good restored unto you; or ye can do evil, and have that which is evil restored unto you." (Helaman 14:31)

"And then cometh the judgment of the Holy One upon them; and then cometh the time that he that is filthy shall be filthy still; and he that is righteous shall be righteous still; he that is happy shall be happy still; and he that is unhappy shall be unhappy still." (Mormon 9:14)

"Fear not to do good, my sons, for **whatsoever ye sow, that shall ye also reap**; therefore, if ye sow good ye shall also reap good for your reward." (D&C 6:33)

"For those that live shall inherit the earth, and those that die shall rest from all their labors, **and their works shall follow them**; and they shall receive a crown in the mansions of my Father, which I have prepared for them." (D&C 59:2)

"And they who remain shall also be quickened; nevertheless, **they shall return again to their own place**, to enjoy that which they are willing to receive, because they were not willing to enjoy that which they might have received." (D&C 88:32)

"...but as they concoct scenes of bloodshead [sic] in this world **so shall they rise** to that resurn." [Resurrection] (*The Words of Joseph Smith*, p. 355)

Russell M. Nelson

Editorial note: The following record is from the journal of A.C. Nelson who was the grandfather of Elder Russell M. Nelson, a current member of the Quorum of the Twelve Apostles. Brother A.C. Nelson recorded a visitation from his deceased father, Mads Peter Nielsen, who confirmed to his son various teachings of the Latter-day Saints. The journal entry was dated April 6, 1891. This record not only provides additional evidence for the doctrine of eternal lives, but there is also provocative evidence for the law of cause and effect (or karma, as some eastern religions refer to it). The reader will note the parallels to the eastern teachings of karma in the twice-repeated statement that spirits cannot avoid being resurrected. In fact, noting that Mads Peter Nielsen taught his son that there were "many spirits in the Spirit world who would to God that there would be no Resurrection" seems to connote that those spirits are reticent to reap the rewards of their past lives. Finally, one cannot help but notice the fascinating definition of resurrection contained in this journal entry that expands well beyond the provincialism of our current Bible Dictionary. A.C. Nelson recorded that his father taught him that, "It is just as natural for all to be Resurrected as it is to be born and die again." Beyond all of this editorial comment, it is personally intriguing that this journal entry would be included in the modern biography of a contemporary, living apostle.

"'Father, is the principle and doctrine of the Resurrection as taught us true?' 'True. Yes, my son, as true as can be. You cannot avoid being Resurrected. It is just as natural for all to be Resurrected as it is to be born and die again. No one can avoid being Resurrected. There are many spirits in the Spirit world who would to God that there would be no Resurrection.'" (Spencer J. Condie, *Russell M. Nelson: Father, Surgeon, Apostle* [Salt Lake City: Deseret Book, 2003], p. 11. The unique capitalization is in the original.)

Chapter 24

The Pistis Sophia

Eternal Lives: A Justification for the Work for the Dead

The quotes used in this essay are taken from the Pistis Sophia [edited by Carl Schmidt and translated by Violet Macdermot, published by E. J. Brill, the Netherlands, 1978] otherwise known as the Askew Codex. The following narrative is portrayed as to why Jesus turned the keys of missionary work among the dead, and why he had the gospel preached to those in the spirit world. The answers provided suggest a parallel for all types of work performed for the dead. The justification of Jesus' work for the dead seems sufficient to also explain the necessity for temple work for the dead (as practiced by members of The Church of Jesus Christ of Latter-day Saints) with regard to the concept of eternal lives as outlined in this book. The ideas contained in the Pistis Sophia suggest that proxy work for the dead is of absolute necessity as Jesus said he "caused the path of their course to be accelerated, so that they might be purified quickly, and they might go upwards quickly. And I lessened their cycles, and I made their path easier, and it was greatly accelerated…" also "…before their power diminished within them, and they declined and they weakened or they became powerless…And their light, which was in their place, ceased. And their kingdom dissolved."

Editorial note: ( ) Parentheses indicate material included by the original editor of the Pistis Sophia. [ ] Square brackets indicate material added by the editor of this book. After Jesus recounts his ministry in the spirit world to his apostles and to Mary Magdalene, the following dialogue is reported on pages 65–79.

It happened when Jesus finished saying these words, Philip sat writing every word as Jesus said them…Philip…spoke to Jesus: "**My Lord, for the sake of what mystery hast thou turned the bondage…?**" Jesus answered…"**I have turned their path for the salvation of all souls. Truly, truly I say to you: unless I had turned their paths a multitude of souls would have been destroyed**…and there would have been delay in the completion of the number of perfect souls, which will be accounted among the inheritance of the height, through the mysteries, and will be in the Treasury of Light…"

Maria [Mary Magdalene according to the translators]…said to Jesus: "**My Lord, in what manner would the souls be delayed outside or in what form will they be quickly purified?**"…Jesus answered and said to Maria: "Excellent, Maria. Thou dost ask well with an excellent question...Now indeed I will not conceal anything from you from this hour, but I will reveal everything to you with certainty and openly. Hear now, Maria, and give ear, all you disciples. Before I preached to all the archons of the aeons, and all the archons of the heimarmene and the sphere [spirits in the spirit world], they were all bound with bonds, in their spheres and their seals, according to the manner in which Jeu [a form of Jehovah], the overseer of the Light, had bound them from the beginning. **And each one of them was continuing in his rank and each one was proceeding according to his course**, according to the manner in which Jeu, the overseer of light, had settled it."

[Next there is a somewhat lengthy dialogue about Melchizedek who is called "the purifier of the light" who removed the bonds by which those spirits were bound, and he "made their cycles turn quickly and he (Melchizedek) took away their power which was in them...and the tears of their eyes..." Incidentally, in the Nag Hammadi Library in the book of Melchizedek pages 439–442, Jesus equates himself with Melchizedek by saying, "I am Melchizedek..." Also see Paul's teachings about the relationship between Melchizedek and Jesus Christ in Hebrews 7:1, 6–7, 15–17, and 24–25. Following this dialogue regarding Melchizedek's work among the spirits in the spirit world, Jesus continues with his narrative as follows:]

"And they cast them into this world of mankind, and they became souls in that place, according to what I have just told you. **These things were now fully completed before their power diminished within them, and they declined and they weakened or they became powerless. It happened when they became weak, their power began to cease within them, and they became weak in their power. And their light, which was in their place, ceased. And their kingdom dissolved. Melchizedek...caused them quickly to abandon their cycles**...and he took their light to the Treasury of the Light. And the matter of their dregs [karma or the law of cause and effect?] was surrounded and swallowed...They now swallowed their matter, that they might not become powerless and weak, that their power might not cease within them and their rulership (kingdom) dissolve. And they swallowed them so that they should not dissolve, but that they should be retarded, and should spend a great time until the completion of the number of perfect souls which would be in the Treasury of the Light...It happened now when I came to go forth for the service for the sake of which I was appointed, through the command of the First Mystery...**I turned their whole path and their whole course, and I caused the path of their course to be accelerated, so that they might be purified quickly, and they might go upwards quickly. And I lessened their cycles, and I made their path easier**, and it was greatly accelerated, and they were confused in their path, and from this time they were not able to swallow the matter of the dregs of what is purified of their light. **And further I lessened their times and their periods**, so that the perfect number of souls which will receive mysteries and which will be in the Treasury of Light should be completed quickly. **And unless I had turned their course and unless I had lessened their periods, they would not have**

allowed any souls to come to the world, on account of the matter of their dregs which they swallowed, and they would have destroyed a multitude of souls. On account of this now, I have said to you at this time: '**I have lessened the times for the sake of my chosen ones, otherwise none of the souls could have been saved**'. **But I have lessened the times and the periods for the sake of the perfect number of the souls which will receive mysteries, which are the chosen ones. And had I not lessened their periods [the atonement and work for the dead?], none of the material souls would have been saved**, but they would have been consumed in the fire which is in the flesh…"

And finally from Book III, Chapter 129, on page 326 of the Pistis Sophia we read, "If they receive the mystery while they are still alive, when they come forth from the body they become beams of light and outpourings of light, and they penetrate every place until they go to the place of their inheritance. But if they are sinners, on the other hand, and they come forth from the body and have not repented, and you perform for them the mystery of the Ineffable, so that they should be returned from all the punishments and **cast into a righteous body** which will become good and inherit the Kingdom of the Light, or else that they should be brought to the last rank of the light: they are not able to penetrate the places because it is not they who perform the mystery."

"Thus saith thy Lord, the Lord and thy God pleadeth the cause of his people; behold, I have taken out of thine hand the cup of trembling, the dregs of the cup of my fury; thou shalt no more drink it again." (2 Nephi 8:22. Also see D&C 104:8–9)

Chapter 25

Man: Diversity Among Men and Spirits

Joseph Smith

"Notwithstanding this congregation profess to be Saints, **yet I stand in the midst of all [kinds of] characters and classes of men**. If you wish to go where God is, you must be like God, or possess the principles which God possesses, for if we are not drawing towards God in principle, we are going from Him and drawing towards the devil. **Yes, I am standing in the midst of all kinds of people**." (HC 4:588)

"All the minds and spirits that God ever sent into the world are susceptible of enlargement. The first principles of man are self-existent with God. God himself, finding he was in the midst of spirits and glory, because he was more intelligent, saw proper to institute laws whereby the rest could have a privilege to advance like himself. The relationship we have with God places us in a situation to advance in knowledge. He has power to institute laws to instruct the weaker intelligences, that they may be exalted with Himself, so that they might have one glory upon another, and all that knowledge, power, glory, and intelligence, which is requisite in order to save them in the world of spirits. This is good doctrine. It tastes good. I can taste the principles of eternal life, and so can you. They are given to me by the revelations of Jesus Christ; and I know that when I tell you these words of eternal life as they are given to me, you taste them, and I know that you believe them. You say honey is sweet, and so do I. I can also taste the spirit of eternal life. I know that it is good; and when I tell you of these things which were given me by inspiration of the Holy Spirit, you are bound to receive them as sweet, and rejoice more and more." (HC 6:311–312)

"So in the other world there are a variety of Spirits." (HC 5:388)

Brigham Young

"In this probation, we have evil to contend with, and we must overcome it in ourselves, or we never shall overcome it anywhere else. Were you to let your minds stretch out, you would learn that the whole kingdom, with its principles, powers, authority, glory, and everything pertaining to it, is combined in the organization of man ready to be developed. We must commence and school ourselves, and so bring our reflections into subjection, that we can make our minds one in faith." (JD 6:99)

"Intelligent beings are organized to become Gods, even the sons of God, to dwell in the presence of the Gods, and become associated with the highest intelligences that dwell in eternity. We are now in the school, and must practice upon what we receive." (JD 8:160)

"Look for instance at Adam. Listen, ye Latter-day Saints! Supposing that Adam was formed actually out of clay, out of the same kind of material from which bricks are formed; that with this matter God made the pattern of a man, and breathed into it the breath of life, and left it there, in that state of supposed perfection, **he would have been an adobe to this day. He would not have known anything**. Some of you may doubt the truth of what I now say, and argue that the Lord could teach him. This is a mistake. The Lord could not have taught him in any other way than in the way in which He did teach him. **You believe Adam was made of the dust of this earth. This I do not believe, though it is supposed that it is so written in the Bible; but it is not, to my understanding**. You can write that information to the States, if you please—that I have publicly declared that I do not believe that portion of the Bible as the Christian world do. I never did, and I never want to. What is the reason I do not? **Because I have come to understanding, and banished from my mind all the baby stories my mother taught me when I was a child**. But suppose Adam was made and fashioned the same as we make adobies; if he had never drunk of the bitter cup, the Lord might have talked to him to this day, and he would have continued as he was to all eternity, never advancing one particle in the school of intelligence. **This idea opens up a field of light to the intelligent mind**." (JD 2:6)

"**Who can define the divinity of man? Only those who understand the true principles of eternity—the principles that pertain to life and salvation**. Man, by being exalted, does not lose the power and ability naturally given to him; but, on the contrary, by taking the road that leads to life, he gains more power, more influence and ability during every step he progresses therein. Mankind have power given them to propagate their species. An exaltation to the celestial kingdom of God by no means lessens that power. On these points the children of men are shrouded in mystery and uncertainty." (JD 7:274)

"If man could have been made perfect, in his **double capacity of body and spirit,** without passing through the ordeals of mortality, there would have been no necessity of our coming into this state of trial and suffering. Could the Lord have glorified his children in spirit, without a body like his own, he no doubt would have done so. We read that there is nothing impossible with God. In a broad sense there is not; but in another sense there are things he never attempted and never will. He will not exalt a spirit to thrones, to immortality, and eternal lives, unless that spirit is first clothed in mortal flesh, and with it, passes through a mortal probation, and overcomes the world, the flesh, and the devil through the atonement made by Jesus Christ and the power of the Gospel. The spirit must be clothed as He is, or it never can be glorified with him. He must of necessity subject his children to the same, through a strict observance of the ordinances and rules of salvation." (JD 11:43)

"Now, understand, all spirits came from God, and they came pure from his presence, and were put into earthly tabernacles, which were organized for that express purpose; and so the spirit and the body became a living soul. If these souls should live, according to the law of heaven, **God ordained that they should become temples prepared to inherit all things**. I wish you to understand that all spirits are pure when they are put into these tabernacles; **but we have not time to explain or set before you the reasons of the variation in appearance in the mortal tabernacles. There are causes for it**. Our spirits fill the tabernacles organized for them; the body is a habitation for the spirit to dwell in; and if the spirit and the body both agree in keeping all the laws and all the commandments that the Lord reveals unto that tabernacle it never shall be destroyed. How many shall be preserved? **All** who do not deny and defy the power and character of the Son of God—**all** who do not sin against the Holy Ghost." (JD 6:291–292)

"If we seek to build up this kingdom, hereafter the Lord will build us up. I don't know that I shall get half through with what I want to say today. **I wish to come back and look at ourselves in the next place. How many glories and kingdoms will there be in eternity? You will see the same variety in eternity as you see in the world**." (JD 6:293)

"We only understand in part why we are required to pass through those various incidents of life. There is not a single condition of life that is entirely unnecessary; there is not one hour's experience but what is beneficial to all those who make it their study, and aim to improve upon the experience they gain. What becomes a trial to one person is not noticed by another. **Among these two thousand persons I am now addressing there cannot be found two that are organized alike**, yet we all belong to the one great human family, have sprung from one source, and are organized to inherit eternal life. **There are no two faces alike, no two persons tempered alike**; we have come from different nations of the world, and have been raised in different climates, educated and traditioned in different and, in many instances, in opposite directions, **hence we are tried with each other, and large drafts are made upon our patience, forbearance, charity, and good will—in short, upon all the higher and godlike qualities of our nature**—For we are required by our holy religion to be one in our faith, feelings, and sentiments pertaining to things of time and eternity, and in all our earthly pursuits and works to keep in view the building up of the kingdom of God in the last days. Our work is to bring forth Zion, and produce the Kingdom of God in its perfection and beauty upon the earth. **The impulses of our different natures present an almost endless variety of pursuit, manner, and expression, yet all this under a wise and judicious direction will accomplish the great end of our existence and calling as ministers of the Most High**." (JD 9:292–293)

"**Can any man tell the variety of the spirits there are**? No, he cannot even tell the variety that there is in the portion of his dominions in which God has placed us, on this earth upon which we live, **for we can see an endless variety on this little spot**, which is nothing but a garden spot in comparison to the rest of the kingdoms of our God. **Again, you may observe the people, and you will see an endless variety of disposition**, and an endless variety of physiognomy. Bring the millions of faces before you, and where can you find two faces precisely alike in every point? **Where can you find two human beings precisely alike in the organization of their bodies with the spirits?** Where can you point out two precisely alike in every particular in their temperaments and dispositions? Where can you find two who are so operated upon precisely alike by a superior power that their lives, their actions, their feelings, and all pertaining to human life are alike? **I conclude that there is as great a variety in the spiritual as there is in the temporal world, and I think that I am just in my conclusion**. You will see people possessed of different spirits; but I will say to you what I have heretofore frequently said, and what brother Joseph Smith has said, and what the Scripture teaches, your spirits when they came to take tabernacles were pure and holy, and prepared to receive knowledge, wisdom, and instruction, and to be taught while in the flesh; so that every son and daughter of Adam, if they would apply their minds to wisdom, and magnify their callings and improve upon every grace and means given them, would have tickets for the boxes, to use brother Hyde's figure, instead of going into the pit. There is no spirit but what was pure and holy when it came here from the celestial world. There is no spirit among the human family that was begotten in hell; none that were begotten by angels, or by any inferior being. They were not produced by any being less than our Father in heaven. He is the Father of our spirits; and if we could know, understand, and do His will, every soul would be prepared to return back into His presence. And when they get there, they would see that **they had formerly lived there for ages, that they had previously been acquainted with every nook and corner, with the palaces, walks, and gardens**; and they would embrace their Father, and He would embrace them and say, 'My son, my daughter, I have you again;' and the child would say, 'O my Father, my Father, I am here again.'

These are the facts in the case, and there are none ticketed for the pit, unless they fill up that ticket themselves through their own misconduct. Are all spirits endowed alike? No, not by any means. Will all be equal in the celestial kingdom? By no means. Some spirits are more noble than others; some are capable of receiving more than others. There is the same variety in the spirit world that you behold here, yet they are of the same parentage, of one Father, one God, to say nothing of who He is. They are all of one parentage, though there is a difference in their capacities and nobility, and each one will be called to fill the station for which he is organized, and which he can fill. We are placed on this earth to prove whether we are worthy to go into the celestial world, the terrestrial, or the telestial, or to hell, or to any other kingdom or place, and we have enough of life given us to do this." (JD 4:268–269)

"Those who come here find a pretty good people, but in their estimation we should be just as holy as angels. We are pretty good, and we are trying to be better; trying to devote ourselves more and more to the building up of the kingdom of God; trying to overcome our passions, subdue our tempers within us; trying to sanctify ourselves, our children, our friends and families, and seeking to become Saints in deed. The people are pretty good, and if they were gathered together so that we could see the difference between those who have been here for years and those who have just come, you would understand the comparison brother Kimball used to make of the clay that is thrown into the mill and has been grinding for years and prepared to make vessels of honor of; but in comes a batch of new clay, and you must grind again; and when it is taken out of the mill it is cut to pieces to see if there is anything in it that should not be. The impurities that are in the clay may destroy the vessel. You will therefore gather all out that should not be in it and throw it away. So it is with the Saints. Some keep leaving and this renders the clay purer and purer." (JD 13:90–91)

"I had this dream, which I will now relate. I thought I had started and gone past the Hot Springs, which is about four miles north of this city. I was going after my goats. When I had gone round the point of the mountain by the Hot Springs, and had got about half a mile on the rise of ground beyond the Spring, whom should I meet but brother Joseph Smith. He had a wagon with no bed on, with bottom boards, and tents and camp equipage piled on. Somebody sat on the wagon driving the team. Behind the team I saw a great flock of sheep. I heard their bleating, and saw some goats among them. I looked at them and thought —'This is curious, brother Joseph has been up to Captain Brown's and got my goats.' There were men driving the sheep, and some of the sheep I should think were three and a half feet high, with large, fine, beautiful white fleeces, and they looked so lovely and pure; others were of moderate size, and pure and white; and **in fact there were sheep of all sizes, with fleeces clean, pure and white. Then I saw some that were dark and spotted, of all colors and sizes and kinds, and their fleeces were dirty, and they looked inferior; some of these were a pretty good size, but not as large as some of the large fine clean sheep, and altogether there was a multitude of them of all sizes and kinds, and goats of all colors, sizes and kinds mixed among them**. Joseph stopped the wagon, and the sheep kept rushing up until there was an immense herd. I looked in Joseph's eye, and laughed, just as I had many a time when he was alive, about some trifling thing or other, and said I —'Joseph, you have got the darndest flock of sheep I ever saw in my life; what are you going to do with them, what on earth are they for?' Joseph looked cunningly out of his eyes, just as he used to at times, and said he—'**They are all good in their places**.' When I awoke in the morning I did not find any fault with those who wanted to go to California; I said, 'If they want to go let them go, and we will do all we can to save them;' I have no more fault to find, the sheep and the goats will run together, but **Joseph says**, '**they are all good in their places**.'" (JD 18:244–245)

"I say to you who are the worst here, go out and gather in some of the damndest rascals you can find **in order that we may have all kinds in the net**. Mormonism is all truth in heaven, earth, or hell." (*The Complete Discourses of Brigham Young*, Vol. 1, 1832 to 1852, Ed. Richard S. Van Wagoner, Smith-Petit Foundation, Salt Lake City, 2009. p. 444)

"**The net has all kinds of fish**. We have some as cursed rascals among us as dwell on the earth, and we find evil here as well as anywhere else. Yet Zion is here. It is in my heart." (Ibid, p. 445)

Chapter 26

Universal Salvation

Joseph Smith

"**God has made provision for every spirit on the eternal world**, and the spirits of our friends should be searched out and saved, Any man that has a friend in eternity can save him if he has not committed the unpardonable sin, **He cannot be dammed through all eternity, there is a possibility for his escape in a little time**, if a man has knowledge he can be saved, if he has been guilty of great sins he is punished for it, when he consents to obey the gospel whether Alive or dead, he is saved. His own mind damns him." (*The Words of Joseph Smith*, pp. 346–347)

Brigham Young

"We have all come from one father even Adam, both the black and the white, the grizzled and the gray; the noble, and the ignoble; and the time will come, when they will all come back again into His presence. When they have behaved themselves, and proved faithful to their calling, and to their God…" (Brigham Young, October 8, 1854 *Conference Report*, Church Archives. Also see *The Essential Brigham Young*, p. 100)

"How many Gods there are, and how many places there are in their kingdoms, is not for me to say; but I can say this, which is a source of much comfort, consolation, and gratification to me: Behold the goodness, the long-suffering, the kindness, and the strong parental feeling of our Father and God in **preparing the way and providing the means to save the children of men—not alone the Latter-day Saints —not those alone who have the privilege of the first principles of the celestial law, but to save all. It is a universal salvation—a universal redemption.**

Do not conclude that I am a Universalist, as the term is generally understood, **although that doctrine is true in part**, like the doctrines or professions of all professing Christians. As was stated yesterday, by one of those who spoke, when he was a Methodist, he enjoyed a portion of the Spirit of the Lord. Hundreds of those now present have had a like experience in a greater or less degree before they joined this Church. Then, when we inquire who will be saved, I answer, **All will be saved, as Jesus said, when speaking to the Apostles, except the sons of perdition. They will be saved through the atonement and their own good works, according to the law that is given to them**. Will the heathen be saved? Yes, so far as they have lived according to the best light and intelligence they had; but not in the celestial kingdom. Who will not be saved? Those who have received the truth, or had the privilege of receiving it, and then rejected it. They are the only ones who will become the sons of perdition, go into everlasting punishment, and become angels to the Devil. The Priesthood of the Lord has again bestowed upon those who will receive it, is for the express purpose of preparing them to become proficient in the principles pertaining to the law of the celestial kingdom. **If we obey this law, preserve it inviolate, live according to it, we shall be prepared to enjoy the blessings of a celestial kingdom.**

Will any others? Yes, thousands and millions of the inhabitants of the earth who would have received and obeyed the law that we preach, if they had had the privilege. When the Lord shall bring again Zion, and the watchmen shall see eye to eye, and Zion shall be established, saviours will come upon Mount Zion and save all the sons and daughters of Adam that are capable of being saved, by administering for them. **Is not this pleasing? Is it not gratifying? Is it not a consoling feeling and influence upon the mind of every intelligent being?** Our former views were that the majority of the inhabitants of the earth would not be saved in any kind of kingdom of glory, but would inherit a kingdom of damnation. Jesus said, 'In my Father's house are many mansions. If it were no so, I would have told you. I go to prepare a place for you, that where I am ye may be also.' In other words, 'I go to prepare a place for you who have received and obeyed the celestial law, which I have committed to you.' The celestial is the highest of all. The telestial and terrestrial are also spoken of; and **how many more kingdoms of glory there are is not for me to say. I do not know that they are not innumerable. This is source of great joy to me**." (JD 8:35)

"The kingdoms that God has prepared are innumerable. Each and every intelligent being will be judged according to the deeds done in the body, according to his works, faith, desires, and honesty or dishonesty before God; **every trait of his character will receive its just merit or demerit, and he will be judged according to the law of heaven as revealed**; and God has prepared places suited to **every class**. The Saviour said to his disciples—'In my Father's house are many mansions: if it were not so, I would have told you. I go to prepare a place for you. And if I go and prepared a place for you, I will come again and receive you unto myself, that where I am, there ye may be also.' How many kingdoms there are has not been told to us: they are innumerable. The disciples of Jesus were to dwell with him. Where will the rest go? Into kingdoms prepared for them, where they will live and endure. Jesus will bring forth, by his own redemption, every son and daughter of Adam, except the sons of perdition, who will be cast into hell. **Others will suffer the wrath of God—will suffer all the Lord can demand at their hands, or justice can require of them; and when they have suffered the wrath of God till the utmost farthing is paid, they will be brought out of prison. Is this dangerous doctrine to preach? Some consider it dangerous; but is it true that every**

person who does not sin away the day of grace, and become an angel to the Devil, will be brought forth to inherit a kingdom of glory...'Go into all the world and preach the gospel to every creature. He that believeth and is baptized shall be saved, and he that believeth not shall be damned; and these signs shall follow them that believe. In my name,' &c. This is the law of the celestial kingdom, and those who hearken to this law, and embrace its truths in their faith, and live them in their **lives**, will be brought to enjoy the presence of the Son, and will dwell with him and the Father.

And all the residue, who do not sin against the Holy Ghost, will be punished according to their deeds, and will receive according to their works, whether it be little or much, good or bad. Jesus will redeem the last and least of the sons of Adam, except the sons of perdition, who will be held in reserve for another time...What say you, ye Latter-day Saints? Is not this the most glorious thought that ever was revealed to mortal man?" (JD 8:154–155)

Hugh Nibley

Thou hast caused me to mount up to an eternal height and to walk in an inconceivable exaltation. **And I know there is hope for everyone** whom thou didst form of the dust in the presence of the eternal assembly...(quoting from the Dead Sea Scrolls; *Nibley on the Timely and the Timeless,* p. 28)

Chapter 27

The Gods

David, King of Israel

"God standeth in the congregation of the mighty; he **judgeth among the gods**." (Psalms 82:1)

"They know not, neither will they understand; they walk on in darkness: all the foundations of the earth are out of course. **I have said, Ye are gods**; and all of you are children of the most High." (Psalms 82:5–6)

Apostle John

"Jesus answered them, Is it not written in your law, I said, **Ye are gods**? If he called them gods, unto whom the word of God came, and the scripture cannot be broken; Say ye of him, whom the Father hath sanctified, and sent into the world, **Thou blasphemest; because I said, I am the Son of God**?" (John 10:34–36)

Joseph Smith

"Wherefore, as it is written, they are gods, even the sons of God —" (D&C 76:58)

"**Then shall they be gods**, because they have no end; therefore shall they be from everlasting to everlasting, because they continue; then shall they be above all, because all things are subject unto them. **Then shall they be gods**, because they have all power, and the angels are subject unto them…and because they did none other things than that which they were commanded, they have **entered into their exaltation, according to the promises, and sit upon thrones, and are not angels but are gods**." (D&C 132:20, 37)

"The elements are the tabernacle of God; yea, man is the tabernacle of God" (D&C 93:35)

Hyrum Smith

"**[there is] a whole train and lineage of gods**…" (Perfection and Progression: Two Complementary Ways To Talk About God by Eugene England, *BYU Studies,* Vol. 29 (1989), No. 3—Summer 1989 p. 33. Original in "George Laub's Nauvoo Journal," ed. Eugene England, *BYU Studies* 18 (Winter 1978): p. 176)

John Taylor

"**What is man**? He is an immortal being. **He is a part of the Deity**. He is the son of God, and God is his Father; and he has come here to work out his salvation and accomplish the thing he came into existence for. We have come here to build up the kingdom of God, to establish correct principles, to teach the world righteousness, and to make millions of the human family happy—even all who will listen to the principles of eternal truth. We are here to introduce correct doctrine, to introduce correct morals, to introduce correct philosophy, to introduce correct government, and to teach men how to live and how to die—how to be happy in this world and in the world which is to come, and **to lay the foundation for eternal lives in the eternal worlds**. What is man? A **god**, even the son of God, possessing noble aspirations, holy feelings, that may be governed by virtuous principles, possessing elevated ideas, wishing to realize everything that God has destined to submit to all his laws, to endure every kind of privation and affliction and suffering, as seeing Him that is invisible, looking for a city that hath foundations, whose builder and maker is God,—feeling to live for that purpose, and that alone. This is what man is, if he lives the religion of heaven, and performs faithfully those things God has appointed him to do, that he may increase from intelligence to intelligence, **and go on with that eternal progression, not only in this world, but in worlds without end**." (JD 8:5)

Erastus Snow

"If we study physiology or anatomy, we are led to exclaim with the Psalmist of old, 'I am fearfully and wonderfully made,' and see a beautiful harmony in all the parts, and a most exquisite design. This is proven by an examination of the various parts of the human form. And every organ adapted to its special use, and for its special purpose, and combining a whole, a grand union—a little kingdom composed of many kingdoms, united and constituting **the grand whole, the being we call man, but which in the language of these Scriptures was called Adam —male and female created he them, and called their name Adam, which in the original, in which these Scriptures were written by Moses, signifies 'the first man.' There was no effort at distinguishing between the one half and the other, and calling one man and the other woman.**

This was an after distinction, but the explanation of it is—one man, one being, and he called their name Adam. But he created them male and female, for they were one, and he says not unto the woman multiply, and to the man multiply, but he says unto them, multiply and reproduce your species, and replenish the earth. He speaks unto them as belonging together, as constituting one being, and as organized in his image and after his likeness. And the Apostle Paul, treating upon this subject in the same way, says that man was created in the likeness of God, and after the express image of his person. John, the Apostle, in writing the history of Jesus, speaks in the same way; that Jesus was in the likeness of his Father, and express image of his person.

And if the revelations that God has made of himself to man, agree and harmonize upon this theory, and if mankind would be more believing, and accept the simple, plain, clear definition of Deity, and description of himself which he has given us, instead of hunting for some great mystery, and seeking to find out God where he is not and as he is not, we all might understand him. There is no great mystery about it; no more mystery about it than there is about ourselves, and our own relationship to our father and mother, and the relationship of our own children to us. That which we see before our eyes, and which we are experiencing from time to time, day to day, and year to year, is an exemplification of Deity.

'What,' says one, '**do you mean we should understand that Deity consists of man and woman?**' **Most certainly I do. If I believe anything that God has ever said about himself, and anything pertaining to the creation and organization of man upon the earth, I must believe that Deity consists of man and woman**. Now this is simplifying it down to our understanding, and the great Christian world will be ready to open their mouths and cry, 'Blasphemy! Sacrilege!' Open wide their eyes and wide their mouths in the utmost astonishment. **What! God a man and woman?**...

Then these Christians—they say he has no form, neither body, parts nor passions. One party says he is a man, and the other says he is a woman. I say he is both. How do you know? I only repeat what he says of himself; that he created man in the image of God, **male and female created he them, and he called their name Adam**, which signifies in Hebrew, the first man. So that the beings we call Adam and Eve were the first man placed here on this earth, and their name was Adam, and they were the express image of God. Now, if anybody is disposed to say that the woman is in the likeness of God and that the man was not, and if vice versa, I say you are both wrong, or else God has not told us the truth. I sometimes illustrate this matter by taking up a pair of shears, if I have one, but then you all know they are composed of two halves, but they are necessarily parts, one of another, and to perform their work for each other, as designed, they belong together, and neither one of them is fitted for the accomplishment of their works alone.

And for this reason says St. Paul, 'the man is not without the woman, nor the woman without the man in the Lord.' In other words, there can be no God except he is composed of the man and woman united, and there is not in all the eternities that exist, nor ever will be, a God in any other way. I have another description: There never was a God, and there never will be in all eternities, except they are made of these two component parts; a man and a woman; the male and the female...As I said, man was created, male and female, and two principles are blended in one; and the man is not without the woman nor the woman without the man in the Lord; and there is no Lord, there is no God in which the two principles are not blended, nor can be; and we may never hope to attain unto the eternal power and the Godhead upon any other principle." (JD 19:268–270, 272)

GODLINESS

Joseph Smith
"For, behold, the mystery of godliness, how great is it!" (D&C 19:10)

"**There are but a very few beings in the world who understand rightly the character of God. The great majority of mankind do not comprehend anything, either that which is past, or that which is to come, as it respects their relationship to God**. They do not know, neither do they understand the nature of that relationship; and consequently they know but little above the brute beast, or more than to eat, drink and sleep. This is all man knows about God or His existence, unless it is given by the inspiration of the Almighty.

If a man learns nothing more than to eat, drink and sleep, and does not comprehend any of the designs of God, the beast comprehends the same things. It eats, drinks, sleeps, and knows nothing more about God; yet it knows as much as we, unless we are able to comprehend by the inspiration of Almighty God. **If men do not comprehend the character of God, they do not comprehend themselves**. I want to go back to the beginning, and so lift your minds into more lofty spheres and a more exalted understanding than what the human mind generally aspires to." (HC 6:303. *Teachings of the Prophet Joseph Smith*, p. 343)

Lorenzo Snow
"**Godliness cannot be conferred, but must be acquired**." (*Biography and Family Record of Lorenzo Snow*, p. 193)

THE HEAD GOD AND GODHEAD

Joseph Smith
"According to that which was ordained in the midst of **the Council of the Eternal God of all other gods** before this world was, that should be reserved unto the finishing and the end thereof, when every man shall enter into his eternal presence and into his immortal rest." (D&C 121:32)

"Thus the head God brought forth the Gods in the grand council…The head God called together the Gods and sat in grand council to bring forth the world…Come here ye learned men, and read, if you can. I should not have introduced this testimony, were it not for the word *rosh* —the head, the Father of the Gods. I should not have brought it up, only to show that I am right." (*Teachings of the Prophet Joseph Smith*, pp. 348–349)

"*'Berosheit baurau Eloheim ait aushamayeen vehau auraits,'* rendered by King James' translators, 'In the beginning God created the heaven and the earth.' I want to analyze the word *Berosheit*. *Rosh*, the head; *Sheit*, a grammatical termination; the *Baith* was not originally put there when the inspired man wrote it, but it has been since added by an old Jew. *Baurau* signifies to bring forth; *Eloheim* is from the word *Eloi*, God, in the singular number; and by adding the word *heim*, it **renders it Gods**. It read first, '**In the beginning the head of the Gods brought forth the Gods**,' or, as others have translated it, '**The head of the Gods called the Gods together**.' I want to show a little learning as well as other fools…

The head God organized the heavens and the earth. I defy all the world to refute me. In the beginning the head of the Gods organized the heavens and the earth. Now the learned priests and the people rage, and the heathen imagine a vain thing. If we pursue the Hebrew text further, it reads, 'Berosheit baurau Eloheim ait aashamayeen vehau auraits'—'**The head one of the Gods said**, Let us make a man in our own image.'

I once asked a learned Jew, 'If the Hebrew language compels us to render all words ending in *heim* in the plural, why not render the first Eloheim plural?' He replied, 'That is the rule with few exceptions; but in this case it would ruin the Bible.' He acknowledged I was right. I come here to investigate these things precisely as I believe them. Hear and judge for yourselves; and if you go away satisfied, well and good.

In the very beginning the Bible shows there is a plurality of Gods beyond the power of refutation. It is a great subject I am dwelling on. **The word *Eloheim* ought to be in the plural all the way through— Gods. The head of the Gods appointed one God for us; and when you take that view of the subject, it sets one free to see all the beauty, holiness and perfection of the Gods. All I want is to get the simple, naked truth, and the whole truth**. They found fault with Jesus Christ because he said he was the Son of God, and made himself equal with God. They say of me, like they did of the apostles of old, that I must be put down. **What did Jesus say**? 'Is it not written in your law, I said, **Ye are Gods**? If he called them Gods unto whom the word of God came, and the scriptures cannot be broken, say ye of him whom the Father hath sanctified and sent into the world, Thou blasphemest because I said I am the Son of God?' It was through him that they drank of the spiritual rock. Of course he would take the honor to himself. **Jesus, if they were called gods unto whom the word of God came, why should it be thought blasphemy that I should say I am the Son of God**?" (*Teachings of the Prophet Joseph Smith*, pp. 369–374. Also see John 10:34–36; Psalm 82:6)

"…any person that has seen the heavens opened knows that their is [sic] three personages in the heavens holding the Keys of Power." (*The Words of Joseph Smith*, p. 213)

Brigham Young

"How has it transpired that theological truth is thus so widely disseminated? It is because God was once known on the earth among his children of mankind, as we know one another. Adam was as conversant with his Father who placed him upon this earth as we are conversant with our earthly parents. The Father frequently came to visit his son Adam, and talked and walked with him; and the children of Adam were more or less acquainted with their Grandfather, and their children were more or less acquainted with their Great-Grandfather." (JD 9:148)

"**Elohim, Yahovah and Michael were father, Son and grandson**. They made this Earth and Michael became Adam." (Brigham Young, as recorded in the Joseph F. Smith Journal, 17 June 1871 entry; Church Archives)

John Taylor

"Our Father in Heaven and who with Jesus Christ, his First Begotten Son, and the Holy Ghost, are one in power, one in dominion and one in glory, constituting **the First Presidency of this system and this eternity**." (The Mediation and Atonement, p. 76)

Edward Stevenson

"Certainly Heloheim [sic] and Jehovah stands before Adam, or else I am very much mistaken. **Then 1st Heloheim [sic], 2nd Jehovah, 3rd Michael-Adam, 4th Jesus Christ**, Our Elder Brother, in the other World from whence our spirits come…Then who is Jehovah? The only begotten Son of Heloheim [sic] on Jehovah's world." (Edward Stevenson Diary, February 28 & March 3, 1896, Church Archives)

THE FATHER

Apostle John

"…he that hath seen me hath seen the Father…" (John 14:9. See John 14:7–11)

Apostle Paul

"For though there be that are called gods, whether in heaven or in earth, **(as there be gods many, and lords many,) But to us there is but one God, the Father**, of whom are all things, and we in him; and one Lord Jesus Christ, by whom are all things, and we by him." (1 Corinthians 8:5–6)

Joseph Smith

"We believe in **God the Father, who is the great Jehovah** and head of all things, **and that Christ is the Son of God**, co-eternal with the Father." (*Times and Seasons* 3:578)

"...the Great God has a name by which He will be called which is Ahman..." (*The Words of Joseph Smith*, p. 64)

"...in the language of Adam, Man of Holiness is his name, and the name of His Only Begotten is the Son of Man, even Jesus Christ." (Moses 6:57)

"Behold, **I am God; Man of Holiness is my name**; Man of Counsel is my name; and Endless and Eternal is my name, also." (Moses 7:35)

"O Thou, who seest and knowest the hearts of all men—Thou eternal, omnipotent, omniscient, and omnipresent **Jehovah—God—Thou Eloheim**, that sittest, as saith the Psalmist, 'enthroned in heaven,' look down upon Thy servant Joseph at this time; and let faith **on the name of Thy Son Jesus Christ**, to a greater degree than Thy servant ever yet has enjoyed, be conferred upon him..." (A prayer of the prophet Joseph. HC 5:127)

"...by the voice of all that is sacred and dear to man, let us plead the justice of our cause; trusting in the arm of **Jehovah, the Eloheim, who sits enthroned in the heavens**; that peradventure He may give us the victory..." (A letter written by Joseph on August 14, 1842. HC 5:94)

"And every one that hearkeneth to the voice of the Spirit cometh unto God, **even the Father**. And **the Father** teacheth him of the covenant which he has renewed and confirmed upon you," (D&C 84:47–48)

"And the angel said unto me, **behold the Lamb of God, yea, even the Eternal Father**! Knowest thou the meaning of the tree which thy father saw? And I answered him, saying: Yea, it is the love of God, which sheddeth itself abroad in the hearts of the children of men; wherefore, it is the most desirable above all things." (1 Nephi 11:14–22. This version of the scriptures is taken from the original 1830 edition of the Book of Mormon as found in the Wilford C. Wood edition, Vol. 1, pp. 24–25)

"And now Abinadi said unto them: I would that ye should understand that **God himself shall come down among the children of men**, and shall redeem his people. **And because he dwelleth in flesh he shall be called the Son of God**, and having subjected the flesh to the will of the Father, being the Father and the Son—The Father, because he was conceived by the power of God; and the Son, because of the flesh; **thus becoming the Father and Son—And they are one God, yea, the very Eternal Father of heaven and of earth**. And thus the flesh becoming subject to the Spirit, or the Son to the Father, being one God, suffereth temptation, and yieldeth not to the temptation, but suffereth himself to be mocked, and scourged, and cast out, and disowned by his people." (Mosiah 15:1–5)

"Teach them that redemption cometh through Christ the Lord, who is the very Eternal Father. Amen." (Mosiah 16:15)

"Behold, I am he who was prepared from the foundation of the world to redeem my people. Behold, **I am Jesus Christ. I am the Father and the Son**. In me shall all mankind have life, and that eternally, even they who shall believe on my name; and they shall become my sons and my daughters." (Ether 3:14)

"…he that will not believe me will not believe the Father who sent me. For behold**, I am the Father**, I am the light, and the life, and the truth of the world." (Ether 4:12)

"…no man knoweth that the Son is the Father, and the Father is the Son, but him to whom the Son will reveal it." (JST Luke 10:22)

"And now, behold, my beloved brethren, this is the way; and there is none other way nor name given under heaven whereby man can be saved in the kingdom of God. And now, behold, this is the doctrine of Christ, and the only and true doctrine of **the Father, and of the Son, and of the Holy Ghost, which is one God**, without end. Amen." (2 Nephi 31:21)

"Now, this restoration shall come to all, both old and young, both bond and free, both male and female, both the wicked and the righteous; and even there shall not so much as a hair of their heads be lost; but every thing shall be restored to its perfect frame, as it is now, or in the body, and shall be brought and be arraigned before the bar of **Christ the Son, and God the Father, and the Holy Spirit, which is one Eternal God**, to be judged according to their works, whether they be good or whether they be evil." (Alma 11:44)

"Behold, I come unto my own, to fulfil all things which I have made known unto the children of men from the foundation of the world, and to do the will, both of the Father and of the Son—**of the Father because of me, and of the Son because of my flesh**." (3 Nephi 1:14)

"And after this manner shall ye baptize in my name; for behold, verily I say unto you, that the Father, and the Son, and the Holy Ghost are one; and I am in the Father, and the Father in me, and the Father and I are one." (3 Nephi 11:27)

"Which Father, Son, and Holy Ghost are one God, infinite and eternal, without end. Amen." (D&C 20:28)

"And that I am in the Father, and the Father in me, and the Father and I are one—**The Father because he gave me of his fulness**, and the Son because I was in the world and made flesh my tabernacle, and dwelt among the sons of men…and the glory of **the Father** was with him, **for he dwelt in him**." (D&C 93:3–4, 17)

Brigham Young

"When you can thus feel, then you may begin to think that you can find out something about God, and begin to learn who he is. He is our Father —**the Father of our spirits, and was once a man in mortal flesh as we are, and is now an exalted Being. How many Gods there are, I do not know. But there never was a time when there were not Gods and worlds, and when men were not passing through the same ordeals that we are now passing through. That course has been from all** eternity, and it is and will be to all eternity. You cannot comprehend this; but when you can, it will be to you a matter of great consolation. It appears ridiculous to the world, under their darkened and erroneous traditions, that God had once been a finite being; and yet we are not in such close communion with him as many have supposed. He has passed on, and is exalted far beyond what we can now comprehend. Eye hath not seen, ear hath not heard, neither hath it entered into the heart of man to conceive all the things of God.

We are not capacitated to receive them all at once; but God, by his Spirit, reveals to our spirits as we grow and become able and capacitated to comprehend, through improving upon every means of grace placed within our power, until we shall be counted worthy to receive all things. 'All is yours,' says the Apostle. Do not become disheartened, give up your labours, and conclude that you are not to be saved. All is yours, if you will but live according to what you know, and increase in knowledge and godliness; and if you increase in these, you will also increase in all things pertaining to the earth; and by-and-by, you will be satisfied that all is the Lord's, and that we are Christ's, and that Christ is God's. All centers in the Father; wherefore let us all be satisfied that he gives to us as we are capacitated to receive." (JD 7:333–334)

"**I believe in one God to us**; as it is written, 'For though there be that are called gods, whether in heaven or in earth (as there be gods many, and lords many); but to us there is but one God, the Father, of whom are all things, and we in Him; and one Lord Jesus Christ, by whom are all things, and we by Him,' and, 'They were called Gods unto whom the word of God came.' **I believe in a God who has power to exalt and glorify all who believe in Him, and are faithful in serving Him to the end of their lives, for this makes them Gods, even the sons of God, and in this sense also there are Gods many**, but to us there is but one God, and one Lord Jesus Christ—one Saviour who came in the meridian of time to redeem the earth and the children of men from the original sin that was committed by our first parents, and bring to pass the restoration of all things through His death and sufferings, open wide to all believers the gates of life and salvation and exaltation to the presence of the Father and the Son to dwell with them for ever more." (JD 11:122)

(Lorenzo Snow put out some principles arguing that Jesus Christ is our father and not our elder brother and asked for light). [Brigham Young continues speaking] "As he was, so are we now. As he is now, so we shall become. Our Father was once born of parents and had a father and mother same as we – he is the Savior of the world – the root of spirit and offspring of flesh only begotten of Father in flesh – **the Father came down and begot him same as we do now** – and Jesus was the only one – it was all told in the Temple although it was run over quick..." (*The Complete Discourses of Brigham Young*, Vol. 1, 1832 to 1852, Ed. Richard S. Van Wagoner, Smith-Petit Foundation, Salt Lake City, 2009. p. 322).

(Lorenzo Snow laid out his opinion as to Jesus Christ being of a different grade that the prophets or more than our brethren – he is God the Father – and not our Elder Brother.) [Brigham Young continues speaking] "…it came to me in England, as God was we shall be – as we are so God was – he is the very eternal Father, because of the creation of God – he is the Son of God the only Begotten, **he is the only one God the Father came down and begat** [him]…" (Ibid, p. 322–323).

"…**who ever has seen Jesus has seen the Father.**" (Ibid, p. 344)

"…**you have not got the glasses that I see through – what's the difference between the Father and Son? The one is a little older than the other.**" (Ibid, p. 359)

"If it would be any satisfaction to you, I would say that God has passed through all the trials and experiences that we have. Jesus Christ has passed through all the trials and experiences the same as we have. **It would not be prudent for me to say that the Father has not the same experiences that His Son had. He had quite as much as his Son had**." (Ibid, p. 479)

John Taylor

"Hence His profound grief, His indescribable anguish, His overpowering torture, all experienced in the **submission to the eternal fiat of Jehovah** and the requirements of an inexorable law." (John Taylor differentiated between Christ and Jehovah. *The Mediation and Atonement,* p. 150)

"Suffice it to say that He bore the sins of the world, and, when laboring under the pressure of those intense agonies, He exclaimed, 'Father, if it be possible, let this cup pass.' But it was not possible. **It was the decree of God; the fiat of the great Jehovah**…" (John Taylor differentiated between Christ and Jehovah. JD 24:34)

Erastus Snow

"We believe in God **the Father, who is the great Jehovah** and head of all things, and that Christ is the Son of God, co-eternal with the Father." (*Times and Seasons* 3:578)

Hugh Nibley

"…**as a Jeu becomes a Father** in a new world, the Fathers then **appoint new Jeus [Jehovahs] for new worlds**, who in turn will **become Fathers**, etc., *ad infintum.*" (*Temple and Cosmos: Beyond This Ignorant Present,* edited by Don E. Norton [Salt Lake City and Provo: Deseret Book Co., Foundation for Ancient Research and Mormon Studies, 1992], p. 286. Read all from pp. 286–317)

"One of the most remarkable of these is 2 *Jeu*. **It tells how one approaches through the stages, passwords, and mysteries in a process which alone qualifies one to return to the Father**. These ordinances cannot be obtained until one first receives baptism. "There are three stages to be passed through and at each one a password or name is required." "There is a series of veils that are drawn before the great king. When you come to this barrier you must recite the mystery and give the proper answer." **The final stage is the complete Adam or Jeu (the name is a form of Jehovah).** (Ibid, pp. 80–81)

Why should the Father be jealous of the Son, or the Son jealous of the Father? This is what glory is for, to be shared. The more it is shared, the greater the glory. It's not like something else—giving out a little of it and not having as much left. No, his glory is this. "For behold, this is my work and my glory—to bring to pass the immortality and eternal life of man" (Moses 1:39). He brings them up, and then his glory is increased. Glory increases the more it is spread around. So this is a different concept. **He comes down himself, but he comes as a Son**. He is the Son of God. Again, we don't argue about the Christological question, the equality, etc. In coming down here and following commandments, he identifies his will with the will of the Father. He does exactly what he is told to do because he is setting the example for us. We must do the same thing; it's going to make this very clear here. **That's why he comes down here, and he is called the Son**. (*Teachings of the Book of Mormon—Semester 2:* Transcripts of Lectures Presented to an Honors Book of Mormon class at BYU, 1988–1990 [Provo: FARMS], p. 82)

Verse 3: "The Father, because he was conceived by the power of God." What does that have to do with it? The status of the Father goes back to another order of existence, obviously way back there. He [the Son] was conceived by the power of God, a godly power which is not of this earth and has nothing to do with this earth at all. This is a place where men dwell in perishable flesh, a condition designated as "the Son." Not second rate, but completely dependent. They are identical species working on different levels. This is the whole point—we are identical species.

We get this in 3 Nephi when the Lord goes and prays. It's the very same thing we have in John 13–17, showing exactly how we are identical. If the Father and the Son are one, we are one with the Son; thereby, we are one with the Father exactly as they are one. Of course, the Bible says that over and over again, and people won't believe it.

They say, "John can't be that naive; this must all be just spirit." So they make John the most ghostly, the most spiritual, the most unreal of all the gospels. They say, "John is the great mystery." (Ibid, p. 83)

"And they are one God, yea, the very Eternal Father of heaven and of earth." That's a very thrilling statement to make—that we are in on that. Then the next verse tells us that the flesh is to the spirit as the Son is to the Father, or the Father is to the Spirit as the Son is to the flesh. It's exactly alike. They both belong to the spiritual order of things.

The flesh is not against the spirit but "subject to the Spirit," we are told. When mortals become totally subject to God, they will have passed the test and are ready to go on. You have to be subject—that's the thing. "… the flesh becoming subject to the Spirit, or the Son to the Father, being one God, suffereth temptation, and yieldeth not to the temptation." This is saying that you belong to this same category. He came to the same category as you. He was tempted just as much as you are, etc. You don't have to give in, but we all do because that was the Fall. That's where Adam did give in. This is necessary for experience, knowing the good from the evil. (Ibid, p. 84)

THE SON

Apostle John

"The Son can do nothing of himself, but what he seeth the Father do: for what things soever he doeth, these also doeth the Son likewise. For the Father loveth the Son, and sheweth him all things that himself doeth." (John 5:19–20)

"He that believeth on me, the works that I do shall he do also." (John 14:12)

"Behold, what manner of love the Father hath bestowed upon us, **that we should be called the sons of God**…Beloved, now **are we the sons of God, and it doth not yet appear what we shall be: but we know that, when he shall appear, we shall be like him; for we shall see him as he is**. And every man that hath this hope in him purifieth himself, even as he is pure." (1 John 3:1–3)

"…he that hath seen me hath seen the Father…" (John 14:9. See John 14:7–11)

Apostle Paul

"For in him [Christ] dwelleth all the fulness of the Godhead bodily." (Colossians 2:9)

Joseph Smith

"We believe in God the Father, who is the great Jehovah and head of all things, and that Christ is the Son of God, co-eternal with the Father." (*Times and Seasons* 3:578)

"…in the language of Adam, Man of Holiness is his name, and the name of His Only Begotten is the Son of Man, even Jesus Christ." (Moses 6:57)

"And it came to pass that I saw the heavens open; and an angel came down and stood before me; and he said unto me, Nephi, what beholdest thou? And I said unto him, a virgin, most beautiful and fair above all other virgins. And he said unto me: Knowest thou the condescension of God? And I said unto him, I know that he loveth his children; nevertheless, I do not know the meaning of all things. And he said unto me, Behold, the virgin whom thou seest, is the **mother of God**, after the manner of the flesh.

And it came to pass that I beheld that she was carried away in the spirit; and after she had been carried away in the spirit for the space of a time, the angel spake unto me, saying, Look! And I looked and beheld the virgin again, bearing a child in her arms. And the angel said unto me, **behold the Lamb of God, yea, even the Eternal Father**! Knowest thou the meaning of the tree which thy father saw? And I answered him, saying: Yea, it is the love of God, which sheddeth itself abroad in the hearts of the children of men; wherefore, it is the most desirable above all things." (1 Nephi 11:14–22. This version of the scriptures is taken from the original 1830 edition of the Book of Mormon as found in the Wilford C. Wood edition, Vol. 1, pp. 24–25)

"And now Abinadi said unto them: I would that ye should understand that **God himself shall come down among the children of men**, and shall redeem his people. **And because he dwelleth in flesh he shall be called the Son of God**, and having subjected the flesh to the will of the Father, being the Father and the Son—The Father, because he was conceived by the power of God; and the Son, because of the flesh; **thus becoming the Father and Son—And they are one God, yea, the very Eternal Father of heaven and of earth**. And thus the flesh becoming subject to the Spirit, or the Son to the Father, being one God, suffereth temptation, and yieldeth not to the temptation, but suffereth himself to be mocked, and scourged, and cast out, and disowned by his people." (Mosiah 15:1–5)

"Teach them that redemption cometh through Christ the Lord, who is the very Eternal Father. Amen." (Mosiah 16:15)

"teach them that redemption cometh through Christ the Lord, which is the very Eternal Father. Amen." (Mosiah 16:15 1830 ed.)

"Behold, I am he who was prepared from the foundation of the world to redeem my people. Behold, **I am Jesus Christ. I am the Father and the Son**. In me shall all mankind have life, and that eternally, even they who shall believe on my name; and they shall become my sons and my daughters." (Ether 3:14)

"…he that will not believe me will not believe the Father who sent me. For behold, **I am the Father**, I am the light, and the life, and the truth of the world." (Ether 4:12)

"…no man knoweth that the Son is the Father, and the Father is the Son, but him to whom the Son will reveal it." (Luke 10:22 JST)

"And now, behold, my beloved brethren, this is the way; and there is none other way nor name given under heaven whereby man can be saved in the kingdom of God. And now, behold, this is the doctrine of Christ, and the only and true doctrine of **the Father, and of the Son, and of the Holy Ghost, which is one God**, without end. Amen." (2 Nephi 31:21)

"Now, this restoration shall come to all, both old and young, both bond and free, both male and female, both the wicked and the righteous; and even there shall not so much as a hair of their heads be lost; but every thing shall be restored to its perfect frame, as it is now, or in the body, and shall be brought and be arraigned before the bar of **Christ the Son, and God the Father, and the Holy Spirit, which is one Eternal God**, to be judged according to their works, whether they be good or whether they be evil." (Alma 11:44)

"Behold, I come unto my own, to fulfil all things which I have made known unto the children of men from the foundation of the world, and to do the will, both of the Father and of the Son—**of the Father because of me, and of the Son because of my flesh**." (3 Nephi 1:14)

"And that I am in the Father, and the Father in me, and the Father and I are one—The Father because he gave me of his fulness, **and the Son because I was in the world and made flesh my tabernacle**, and dwelt among the sons of men…and the glory of **the Father** was with him, **for he dwelt in him**." (D&C 93:3–4, 17)

Brigham Young

(Lorenzo Snow put out some principles arguing that Jesus Christ is our father and not our elder brother and asked for light). [Brigham Young continues speaking] As he was, so are we now. As he is now, so we shall become. Our Father was once born of parents and had a father and mother same as we—he is the Savior of the world—the root of spirit and offspring of flesh only begotten of Father in flesh—the Father came down and begot him same as we do now—and Jesus was the only one—it was all told in the Temple although it was run over quick—(16 February 1849 in Salt Lake City. *The Complete Discourses of Brigham Young* Vol. 1, 1832 to 1852. Edited by Richard S. Van Wagoner, pp. 322)

(Lorenzo Snow laid out his opinion as to Jesus Christ being of a different grade that the prophets or more than our brethren—he is God the Father—and not our Elder Brother.) [Brigham Young continues speaking] It came to me in England, as God was we shall be—as we are so God was—he is the very eternal Father, because of the creation of God—he is the Son of God the only Begotten, he is the only one God the Father came down and begat—(Ibid, pp. 322–323)

Bruce R. McConkie

"Learn of Him—the Man nobody knows! Learn that he was born of Mary in the City of David which is called Bethlehem. Learn that he received not of the fullness at the first, but grew from grace to grace, experiencing, feeling, **undergoing all the needed probations of mortality**." (*The Mortal Messiah,* Vol. 1, p. 15)

THE HOLY GHOST

Joseph Smith

"And by the power of the Holy Ghost ye may know the truth of all things." (Moroni 10:5)

"Joseph also said that the Holy Ghost is now in a state of Probation which if he should perform in righteousness he may pass through the same or similar course of things that the son has." (*The Words of Joseph Smith,* p. 245)

"But the Holy Ghost is yet a Spiritual body and waiting to take to himself a body. As the Savior did or as god did or the gods before them took bodies" (Ibid, p. 382)

"and you shall **receive my Spirit, the Holy Ghost**, even the Comforter, which shall teach you the peaceable things of the kingdom…**I am Jesus Christ**, the Son of God;" (D&C 36:2, 8)

"And in that day **the Holy Ghost fell upon Adam**, which beareth record of the Father and the Son, **saying: I am the Only Begotten of the Father**…" (Moses 5:9)

"God shall give unto you knowledge **by his Holy Spirit**, yea, by the unspeakable gift of **the Holy Ghost**, that has not been revealed since the world was until now;" (D&C 121:26)

Vern G. Swanson

Two little known journal accounts from the Nauvoo period suggest that Joseph Smith may have taken the idea of an anthropomorphic Holy Ghost far, conjecturing that the Holy Ghost is a messiah or savior in training for another world. This notion implies that Jesus Christ was a holy ghost for a previous system or generation. Even though this concept seems new to contemporary Latter-day Saints, there are no official doctrines with which it conflicts…It seems possible that Joseph Smith believed that the members of the Godhead eventually experience each position in the divine presidency as God the third, then God the second, and finally God the first. (Line Upon Line; Essays on Mormon Doctrine, pp. 96–97. See the Joseph Smith quotes regarding the Holy Ghost immediately above.)

RESURRECTED BEINGS

D&C 129

There are two kinds of beings in heaven, namely: Angels, who are resurrected personages, having bodies of flesh and bones—For instance, Jesus said: *Handle me and see, for* ***a spirit hath not flesh and bones****, as ye see me have.* Secondly: the spirits of just men made perfect, they who are not resurrected, but inherit the same glory. When a messenger comes saying he has a message from God, **offer him your hand and request him to shake hands with you. If he be an angel he will do so, and you will feel his hand**. If he be the spirit of a just man made perfect he will come in his glory; for that is the only way he can appear—Ask him to shake hands with you, but he will not move, because it is contrary to the order of heaven for a just man to deceive; but he will still deliver his message. If it be the devil as an angel of light, when you ask him to shake hands he will offer you his hand, and you will not feel anything; you may therefore detect him. **These are three grand keys whereby you may know whether any administration is from God**. (D&C 129:1–9. LDS doctrine teaches us that three messengers or angels visited Adam and Eve after they were expelled from the Garden of Eden. Adam tested the angels, in the manner described above, to his complete satisfaction. What does that tell us about the messengers who visited Adam and Eve?)

MAN IS ONE WITH GOD

Apostle Matthew

"And before him shall be gathered all nations: and he shall separate them one from another, as a shepherd divideth *his* sheep from the goats: And he shall set the sheep on his right hand, but the goats on the left. Then shall the King say unto them on his right hand, Come, ye blessed of my Father, inherit the kingdom prepared for you from the foundation of the world: For I was an hungered, and ye gave me meat: I was thirsty, and ye gave me drink: I was a stranger, and ye took me in: Naked, and ye clothed me: I was sick, and ye visited me: I was in prison, and ye came unto me.

Then shall the righteous answer him, saying, Lord, when saw we thee an hungered, and fed *thee?* Or thirsty, and gave *thee* drink? When saw we thee a stranger, and took *thee* in? or naked, and clothed *thee?* Or when saw we thee sick, or in prison, and came unto thee? And the King shall answer and say unto them, Verily I say unto you, **Inasmuch as ye have done *it* unto one of the least of these my brethren, ye have done *it* unto me**.

Then shall he say also unto them on the left hand, Depart from me, ye cursed, into everlasting fire, prepared for the devil and his angels: For I was an hungered, and ye gave me no meat: I was thirsty, and ye gave me no drink: I was a stranger, and ye took me not in: naked, and ye clothed me not: sick, and in prison, and ye visited me not. Then shall they also answer him, saying, Lord, when saw we thee an hungered, or athirst, or a stranger, or naked, or sick, or in prison, and did not minister unto thee? Then shall he answer them, saying, Verily I say unto you, **Inasmuch as ye did *it* not to one of the least of these, ye did *it* not to me**." (Matthew 25:32–45)

Apostle John

"And I give unto them eternal life; and they shall never perish, **neither shall any *man* pluck them out of my hand**. My Father, which **gave *them* me**, is greater than all; and no *man* is able to pluck *them* out of my Father's hand. **I and *my* Father are one**." (John 10:28–30)

"And now I am no more in the world, but these are in the world, and I come to thee. Holy Father, **keep through thine own name those whom thou hast given me, that they may be one, as we *are*.** While I was with them in the world, **I kept them in thy name: those that thou gavest me I have kept, and none of them is lost**, but the son of perdition; that the scripture might be fulfilled. And now come I to thee; and these things I speak in the world, **that they might have my joy fulfilled in themselves**.

I have given them thy word; and the world hath hated them, because they are not of the world, even as I am not of the world. I pray not that thou shouldest take them out of the world, but that thou shouldest keep them from the evil. **They are not of the world, even as I am not of the world**. Sanctify them through thy truth: thy word is truth. As thou hast sent me into the world, even so have I also sent them into the world. **And for their sakes I sanctify myself, that they also might be sanctified** through the truth. Neither pray I for these alone, but for them also which shall believe on me through their word;

That they all may be one; as thou, Father, *art* in me, and I in thee, that they also may be one in us: that the world may believe that thou hast sent me. And the glory which thou gavest me I have given them; **that they may be one, even as we are one: I in them, and thou in me, that they may be made perfect in one**; and that the world may know that thou hast sent me, and hast loved them, as thou hast loved me.

Father, **I will that they also, whom thou hast given me, be with me where I am**; that they may behold my glory, **which thou hast given me**: for thou lovedst me before the foundation of the world. O righteous Father, the world hath not known thee: but I have known thee, and these have known that thou hast sent me. And I have declared unto them thy name, and will declare *it:* **that the love wherewith thou hast loved me may be in them, and I in them**." (John 17:11–26)

Apostle Paul

"For as we have many members in one body, and all members have not the same office: **So we, *being* many, are one body in Christ, and every one members one of another**." (Romans 12:4–5)

"Know ye not that **ye are the temple of God**, and *that* **the Spirit of God dwelleth in you**? If any man defile the temple of God, him shall God destroy; for the temple of God is holy, **which *temple* ye are**." (1 Corinthians 3:16–17)

"What? know ye not that **your body is the temple of the Holy Ghost** *which is* in you, which ye have of God, and ye are not your own? For ye are bought with a price: therefore **glorify God in your body, and in your spirit, which are God's**." (1 Corinthians 6:19–20)

"But to us *there is but* one God, the Father, of whom *are* all things, and we in him; and one Lord Jesus Christ, by whom *are* all things, and we by him." (1 Corinthians 8:6)

"I speak as to wise men; judge ye what I say. The cup of blessing which we bless, is it not the communion of the blood of Christ? The bread which we break, is it not the communion of the body of Christ? **For we being many are one bread, *and* one body**: for we are all partakers of that one bread." (1 Corinthians 10:15–17)

"For **as the body is one, and hath many members, and all the members of that one body, being many, are one body: so also *is* Christ**. For by one Spirit are we all baptized into one body, whether *we be* Jews or Gentiles, whether *we be* bond or free; and have been all made to drink into one Spirit. For the body is not one member, but many. If the foot shall say, Because I am not the hand, I am not of the body; is it therefore not of the body? And if the ear shall say, Because I am not the eye, I am not of the body; is it therefore not of the body? If the whole body *were* an eye, where *were* the hearing? If the whole *were* hearing, where *were* the smelling?

But **now hath God set the members every one of them in the body, as it hath pleased him**. And if they were all one member, where *were* the body? But **now *are they* many members, yet but one body**. And the eye cannot say unto the hand, I have no need of thee: nor again the head to the feet, I have no need of you. Nay, much more those members of the body, which seem to be more feeble, are necessary: And those *members* of the body, which we think to be less honourable, upon these we bestow more abundant honour; and our uncomely *parts* have more abundant comeliness. For our comely *parts* have no need: but God hath tempered the body together, having given more abundant honour to that *part* which lacked: That there should be no schism in the body; but *that* the members should have the same care one for another. And whether one member suffer, all the members suffer with it; or one member be honoured, all the members rejoice with it. **Now ye are the body of Christ, and members in particular**." (1 Corinthians 12:12–27)

"There is neither Jew nor Greek, there is neither bond nor free, there is neither male nor female: **for ye are all one in Christ Jesus. And if ye be Christ's, then are ye Abraham's seed**, and heirs according to the promise." (Galatians 3:28–29)

"One God and Father of all, who *is* above all, **and through all, and in you all**." (Ephesians 4:6)

"For the perfecting of the saints, for the work of the ministry, for the edifying of the body of Christ: **Till we all come in the unity of the faith**, and of the knowledge of the Son of God, unto a perfect man, unto the measure of the stature of the fulness of Christ:" (Ephesians 4:12–13)

"…Christ is the head of the church: and he is the saviour of the body… For **we are members of his body**, of his flesh, and of his bones." (Ephesians 5:23,30)

"Fulfil ye my joy, that ye be like minded, having the same love, *being* of one accord, of one mind." (Philippians 2:2)

"For both he that sanctifieth and **they who are sanctified *are* all of one**: for which cause he is not ashamed to call them brethren," (Hebrews 2:11)

Joseph Smith

"I am Jesus Christ, the Son of God, who was crucified for the sins of the world, even as many as will believe on my name, that they may become the sons of God, even one in me as I am one in the Father, as the Father is one in me, that we may be one." (D&C 35:2)

"And let every man **esteem his brother as himself**, and practise virtue and holiness before me. **And again I say unto you, let every man esteem his brother as himself**. For what man among you having twelve sons, and is no respecter of them, and they serve him obediently, and he saith unto the one: Be thou clothed in robes and sit thou here; and to the other: Be thou clothed in rags and sit thou there—and looketh upon his sons and saith I am just? Behold, this I have given unto you as a parable, and **it is even as I am. I say unto you, be one; and if ye are not one ye are not mine**." (D&C 38:24–27)

"And the Father and I are one. I am in the Father and the Father in me; and inasmuch as ye have received me, ye are in me and I in you." (D&C 50:43)

"Verily, verily, I say unto you, as I said unto my disciples, where two or three are gathered together in my name, as touching one thing, behold, there will I be in the midst of them—**even so am I in the midst of you**." (D&C 6:32)

"Wherefore, all things are theirs, whether life or death, or things present, or things to come, all are theirs and **they are Christ's, and Christ is God's**." (D&C 76:59)

"Which glory is that of the church of the Firstborn, even of God, the holiest of all, through Jesus Christ his Son—He that ascended up on high, as also he descended below all things, in that he comprehended all things, that **he might be in all and through all things**, the light of truth; Which truth shineth. This is the light of Christ. As also he is in the sun, and the light of the sun, and the power thereof by which it was made.

As also he is in the moon, and is the light of the moon, and the power thereof by which it was made; As also the light of the stars, and the power thereof by which they were made; And the earth also, and the power thereof, even the earth upon which you stand. And the light which shineth, which giveth you light, is through him who enlighteneth your eyes, which is the same light that quickeneth your understandings;" (D&C 88:5–11)

"**Ye were also in the beginning with the Father**; that which is Spirit, even the Spirit of truth;" (D&C 93:23)

"The elements are the tabernacle of God; yea, **man is the tabernacle of God**, even temples; and whatsoever temple is defiled, God shall destroy that temple." (D&C 93:35)

"And the Lord called his people ZION, **because they were of one heart and one mind**, and dwelt in righteousness; and there was no poor among them." (Moses 7:18)

The Father, Son, and Holy Ghost are One God

Apostle John

"Then answered Jesus and said unto them, Verily, verily, I say unto you, **The Son can do nothing of himself, but what he seeth the Father do**: for what things soever he doeth, these also doeth the Son likewise. For the **Father loveth the Son, and sheweth him all things that himself doeth**: and he will shew him greater works than these, that ye may marvel. For as the Father raiseth up the dead, and quickeneth *them;* even so the Son quickeneth whom he will. For the Father judgeth no man, but hath committed all judgment unto the Son: That **all *men* should honour the Son, even as they honour the Father**. He that honoureth not the Son honoureth not the Father which hath sent him. Verily, verily, I say unto you, He that heareth my word, and believeth on him that sent me, hath everlasting life, and shall not come into condemnation; but is passed from death unto life. Verily, verily, I say unto you, The hour is coming, and now is, when the dead shall hear the voice of the Son of God: and they that hear shall live. For **as the Father hath life in himself; so hath he given to the Son to have life in himself**;" (John 5:19–26)

"**I and *my* Father are one**." (John 10:30)

"Jesus saith unto him, I am the way, the truth, and the life: no man cometh unto the Father, but by me. **If ye had known me, ye should have known my Father also: and from henceforth ye know him, and have seen him**. Philip saith unto him, Lord, shew us the Father, and it sufficeth us. Jesus saith unto him, Have I been so long time with you, and yet hast thou not known me, Philip? **he that hath seen me hath seen the Father**; and how sayest thou *then,* Shew us the Father? Believest thou not that I am in the Father, and the Father in me? the words that I speak unto you I speak not of myself: but the Father that dwelleth in me, he doeth the works. Believe me that I *am* in the Father, and the Father in me: or else believe me for the very works' sake." (John 14:6–11)

"For there are three that bear record in heaven, the Father, the Word, and the Holy Ghost: and these three are one." (1 John 5:7)

Apostle Paul

"For though there be that are called gods, whether in heaven or in earth, (as there be gods many, and lords many,) But **to us *there is but* one God, the Father**, of whom *are* all things, and we in him; and one Lord Jesus Christ, by whom *are* all things, and we by him." (1 Corinthians 8:5–6)

"For in him [Christ] dwelleth all the fulness of the Godhead bodily." (Colossians 2:9)

Joseph Smith

"All things are delivered to me of my Father; and no man knoweth that the Son is the Father, and the Father is the Son, but him to whom the Son will reveal it." (JST Luke 10:23)

"And it came to pass that I saw the heavens open; and an angel came down and stood before me; and he said unto me, Nephi, what beholdest thou? And I said unto him, a virgin, most beautiful and fair above all other virgins. And he said unto me: **Knowest thou the condescension of God**? And I said unto him, I know that he loveth his children; nevertheless, I do not know the meaning of all things. And he said unto me, Behold, the virgin whom thou seest, is the **mother of God**, after the manner of the flesh. And it came to pass that I beheld that she was carried away in the spirit; and after she had been carried away in the spirit for the space of a time, the angel spake unto me, saying, Look! And I looked and beheld the virgin again, bearing a child in her arms. And the angel said unto me, **behold the Lamb of God, yea, even the Eternal Father**! knowest thou the meaning of the tree which thy father saw? And I answered him, saying: Yea, it is the love of God, which sheddeth itself abroad in the hearts of the children of men; wherefore, it is the most desirable above all things." (1 Nephi 11:14–22. This version of the scriptures is taken from the original 1830 edition of the Book of Mormon as found in the Wilford C. Wood edition, Vol. 1, pp. 24–25)

"And the angel spake unto me, saying: These last records which thou hast seen among the Gentiles, shall establish the truth of the first, which is of the twelve apostles of the Lamb, and shall make known the plain and precious things which have been taken away from them; and shall make known to all kindreds, tongues, and people, that **the Lamb of God is the Eternal Father and the Saviour of the world**; and that all men must come unto Him, or they cannot be saved; and they must come according to the words which shall be established by the mouth of the Lamb; and the words of the Lamb shall be made known in the records of thy seed, as well as in the records of the twelve apostles of the Lamb; wherefore, they shall be established in one, **for there is one, God and one Shepherd over all the earth**;" (1 Nephi 13:40–41. This version of the scriptures is taken from the original 1830 edition of the Book of Mormon as found in the Wilford C. Wood edition Vol. 1, p. 32)

"And now, behold, my beloved brethren, **this is the way**; and there is none other way nor name given under heaven whereby man can be saved in the kingdom of God. And now, behold, this is the doctrine of Christ, **and the only and true doctrine of the Father, and of the Son, and of the Holy Ghost, which is one God**, without end. Amen." (2 Nephi 31:21)

"And now Abinadi said unto them: I would that ye should understand that **God himself shall come down among the children of men, and shall redeem his people**. And **because he dwelleth in flesh he shall be called the Son of God**, and having subjected the flesh to the will of the Father, **being the Father and the Son—The Father, because he was conceived by the power of God; and the Son, because of the flesh; thus becoming the Father and Son—And **they are one God, yea, the very Eternal Father** of heaven and of earth. And thus the flesh becoming subject to the Spirit, or the Son to the Father, **being one God**, suffereth temptation, and yieldeth not to the temptation, but suffereth himself to be mocked, and scourged, and cast out, and disowned by his people." (Mosiah 15:1–5)

"Teach them that redemption cometh through Christ the Lord, who is the very Eternal Father. Amen." (Mosiah 16:15)

"Now Zeezrom saith again unto him: **Is the Son of God the very Eternal Father**? And Amulek said unto him: **Yea, he is the very Eternal Father** of heaven and of earth, and all things which in them are; he is the beginning and the end, the first and the last;" (Alma 11:38–39)

"Now, this restoration shall come to all, both old and young, both bond and free, both male and female, both the wicked and the righteous; and even there shall not so much as a hair of their heads be lost; but every thing shall be restored to its perfect frame, as it is now, or in the body, and shall be brought and be arraigned before the bar of **Christ the Son, and God the Father, and the Holy Spirit, which is one Eternal God**, to be judged according to their works, whether they be good or whether they be evil." (Alma 11:44)

"Having authority given me of Jesus Christ, I baptize you in the name of the Father, and of the Son, and of the Holy Ghost. Amen…And after this manner shall ye baptize in my name; for behold, verily I say unto you, that the Father, and the Son, and the Holy Ghost are one; and I am in the Father, and the Father in me, and the Father and I are one." (3 Nephi 11:25, 27)

"And this is my doctrine, and it is the doctrine which the Father hath given unto me; **and I bear record of the Father, and the Father beareth record of me, and the Holy Ghost beareth record of the Father and me**; and I bear record that the Father commandeth all men, everywhere, to repent and believe in me. And whoso believeth in me, and is baptized, the same shall be saved; and they are they who shall inherit the kingdom of God. And whoso believeth not in me, and is not baptized, shall be damned. Verily, verily, I say unto you, that this is my doctrine, and I bear record of it from the Father; and **whoso believeth in me believeth in the Father also; and unto him will the Father bear record of me, for he will visit him with fire and with the Holy Ghost**. And thus will the Father bear record of me, and the Holy Ghost will bear record unto him of the Father and me; **for the Father, and I, and the Holy Ghost are one**." (3 Nephi 11:32–36)

"The Father hath made bare his holy arm in the eyes of all the nations; and all the ends of the earth shall see the salvation of the Father; and **the Father and I are one**." (3 Nephi 20:35)

"And for this cause ye shall have fulness of joy; and ye shall sit down in the kingdom of my Father; yea, your joy shall be full, even as the Father hath given me fulness of joy; and **ye shall be even as I am, and I am even as the Father; and the Father and I are one**; And the Holy Ghost beareth record of the Father and me; and the Father giveth the Holy Ghost unto the children of men, because of me." (3 Nephi 28:10–11)

"They were once a delightsome people, and they had Christ for their shepherd; yea, they were led even by God the Father." (Mormon 5:17)

"And he hath brought to pass the redemption of the world, whereby he that is found guiltless before him at the judgment day hath it given unto him to dwell in the presence of God in his kingdom, to sing ceaseless praises with the choirs above, unto **the Father, and unto the Son, and unto the Holy Ghost, which are one God**, in a state of happiness which hath no end." (Mormon 7:7)

"Behold, I am he who was prepared from the foundation of the world to redeem my people. Behold, **I am Jesus Christ. I am the Father and the Son**. In me shall all mankind have life, and that eternally, even they who shall believe on my name; and they shall become my sons and my daughters." (Ether 3:14)

"And whatsoever thing persuadeth men to do good is of me; for good cometh of none save it be of me. I am the same that leadeth men to all good; he that will not believe my words will not believe me—that I am; and **he that will not believe me will not believe the Father who sent me. For behold, I am the Father**, I am the light, and the life, and the truth of the world." (Ether 4:12)

"Which **Father, Son, and Holy Ghost are one God**, infinite and eternal, without end. Amen." (D&C 20:28)

"I am Jesus Christ, the Son of God, who was crucified for the sins of the world, even as many as will believe on my name, that they may become the sons of God, **even one in me as I am one in the Father, as the Father is one in me, that we may be one**." (D&C 35:2)

"and **you shall receive my Spirit, the Holy Ghost**, even the Comforter, which shall teach you the peaceable things of the kingdom…**I am Jesus Christ**, the Son of God;" (D&C 36:2, 8)

"And that **I am in the Father, and the Father in me**, and **the Father and I are one**—4 The Father because he gave me of his fulness, and the Son because I was in the world and made flesh my tabernacle, and dwelt among the sons of men." (D&C 93:3–4)

"And he received all power, both in heaven and on earth, and **the glory of the Father was with him, for he dwelt in him**." (D&C 93:17)

"**God shall give unto you knowledge by his Holy Spirit**, yea, by the unspeakable gift of **the Holy Ghost**, that has not been revealed since the world was until now;" (D&C 121:26)

"And in that day **the Holy Ghost fell upon Adam**, which beareth record of the Father and the Son, **saying**: **I am the Only Begotten of the Father**…" (Moses 5:9)

Doing the Works of (a) Christ

Mark

"And James and John, the sons of Zebedee, come unto him, saying, Master, we would that thou shouldest do for us whatsoever we shall desire. And he said unto them, What would ye that I should do for you? They said unto him, Grant unto us that we may sit, one on thy right hand, and the other on thy left hand, in thy glory. But Jesus said unto them, Ye know not what ye ask: **can ye drink of the cup that I drink of? and be baptized with the baptism that I am baptized with?** And they said unto him, We can. And Jesus said unto them, **Ye shall indeed drink of the cup that I drink of; and with the baptism that I am baptized withal shall ye be baptized**: But to sit on my right hand and on my left hand is not mine to give; but *it shall be given to them* for whom it is prepared." (Mark 10:35–40)

Apostle John

"Verily, verily, I say unto you, He that believeth on me, **the works that I do shall he do also**; and greater *works* than these shall he do; because I go unto my Father." (John 14:12)

"To him that overcometh will I grant to sit with me in my throne, **even as I also overcame**, and am set down with my Father in his throne. He that hath an ear, let him hear what the Spirit saith unto the churches." (Revelation 3:21–22)

Apostle Paul

"I speak as to wise men; judge ye what I say. The cup of blessing which we bless, is it not the communion of the blood of Christ? The bread which we break, is it not the communion of the body of Christ? **For we *being* many are one bread, *and* one body: for we are all partakers of that one bread**." (1 Corinthians 10:15–17. Also see Romans 12:5, and 1 Corinthians 6:15)

"For as the body is one, and hath many members, and all the members of that one body, **being many, are one body: so also *is* Christ**. For by one Spirit are we all baptized into one body, whether *we be* Jews or Gentiles, whether *we be* bond or free; and have been all made to drink into one Spirit. **For the body is not one member, but many**. If the foot shall say, Because I am not the hand, I am not of the body; is it therefore not of the body? And if the ear shall say, Because I am not the eye, I am not of the body; is it therefore not of the body? If the whole body *were* an eye, where *were* the hearing? If the whole *were* hearing, where *were* the smelling? But now hath God set the members every one of them in the body, as it hath pleased him. And if they were all one member, where *were* the body? But now *are they* many members, yet but one body. And the eye cannot say unto the hand, I have no need of thee: nor again the head to the feet, I have no need of you. Nay, much more those members of the body, which seem to be more feeble, are necessary: And those *members* of the body, which we think to be less honourable, upon these we bestow more abundant honour; and our uncomely *parts* have more abundant comeliness. For our comely *parts* have no need: but God hath tempered the body together, having given more abundant honour to that *part* which lacked: That there should be no schism in the body; but *that* the members should have the same care one for another. And whether one member suffer, all the members suffer with it; or one member be honoured, all the members rejoice with it. **Now ye are the body of Christ, and members in particular**." (1 Corinthians 12:12–27. Also see Romans 12:5 and 1 Corinthians 6:15)

Joseph Smith

"Verily, verily, I say unto you, this is my gospel; and ye know the things that ye must do in my church; for the works which ye have seen me do that shall ye also do; for that which ye have seen me do even that shall ye do;" (3 Nephi 27:21)

Brigham Young

" – in the revelation we are to become Sons of God – in [the] New Testament we are to be like Jesus Christ – **we shall wake up in his likeness and be like the Savior – and pas[s] from one station to another** – and be the means of redeeming millions…" (*The Complete Discourses of Brigham Young*, Vol. 1, 1832 to 1852, Ed. Richard S. Van Wagoner, Smith-Petit Foundation, Salt Lake City, 2009. p. 351)

Chapter 28

Adam and Eve

Joseph Smith

"Commencing with Adam, who was the first man, who is spoken of in Daniel as being the 'Ancient of Days,' or in other words, the first and oldest of all, the great, grand progenitor of whom it is said in another place **he is Michael, because he was the first and father of all, not only by progeny**, but the first to hold the spiritual blessings, to whom was made known the plan of ordinances for the salvation of his posterity unto the end, and to whom Christ was first revealed, **and through whom Christ has been revealed from heaven**, and will continue to be revealed from henceforth. **Adam holds the keys of the dispensation of the fullness of times; i.e., the dispensation of all the times have been and will be revealed through him from the beginning to Christ, and from Christ to the end of all the dispensations that are to be revealed**. 'Having made known unto us the mystery of His will, according to His good pleasure which He hath purposed in Himself: that in the dispensation of the fullness of times He might gather together in one all things in Christ, both which are in heaven, and which are on earth; even in him.'" (HC 4:207–208)

Brigham Young

"**Every world has had an Adam, and an Eve**: named so, simply because the first man is always called Adam, and the first woman Eve, and the Oldest Son has always had the privilege of being Ordained, Appointed and Called to be the Heir of the Family, if he does not rebel against the Father, and he is the Saviour of the family. Every world that has been created, has been created upon the same principle. They may vary in their varieties, **yet the eternity is one; it is one eternal round**.

These are things that scarcely belong to the best of this congregation. There are items of doctrine, and principles, in the bosom of eternity that the best of the Latter-day Saints are unworthy to receive. If the visions of their minds were open to look into the vast creations, and gaze upon the Power, and Glory, and Goodness, and Exaltation of the Gods they would exclaim; 'Wo is me, I am undone, I am of unclean lips.'" (Brigham Young, Oct. 8, 1854 *Conference Report,* Church Archives. Also see *The Essential Brigham Young,* p. 93)

"If you look at things spiritually, and then naturally, and see how they appear together, you will understand that when you have the privilege of commencing the work that Adam commenced on this earth, you will have all your children come and report to you of their sayings and acts; and you will hold every son and daughter of yours responsible **when you get the privilege of being an Adam on earth**." (JD 4:271)

"Many of the sisters grieve because they are not blessed with offspring. You will see the time when you will have millions of children around you. If you are faithful to your covenants, you will be mothers of nations. **You will become Eves to earths like this; and when you have assisted in peopling one earth, there are millions of earths still in the course of creation**. And when they have endured a thousand million times longer than this earth, it is only as it were the beginning of your creations. Be faithful, and if you are not blest with children in this time, you will be hereafter. **But I would not dare tell you all I know about these matters**…" (JD 8:208)

"**But I expect, if I am faithful with yourselves, that I shall see the time with yourselves that we shall know how to prepare to organize an earth like this**—know how to people that earth, how to redeem it, how to sanctify it, and how to glorify it, with those who live upon it who hearken to our counsels. The Father and the Son have attained to this point already; **I am on the way, and so are you, and every faithful servant of God**…After men have got their exaltations and their crowns —have become Gods, even the sons of God—are made **Kings of kings and Lords of lords, they have the power then of propagating their species in spirit**; and that is the first of their operations with regard to organizing a world. **Power is then given to them to organize the elements, and then commence the organization of tabernacles. How can they do it**?

Have they to go to that earth? Yes, an Adam will have to go there, and he cannot do without Eve; he must have Eve to commence the work of generation, and they will go into the garden, and continue to eat and drink of the fruits of the corporeal world, until this grosser matter is diffused sufficiently through their celestial bodies to enable them, according to the established laws, to produce mortal tabernacles for their spiritual children. This is a key for you. The faithful will become Gods, even the sons of God; but this does not overthrow the idea that we have a father. Adam is my Father; (this I will explain to you at some future time;) but it does not prove that he is not my father, if I become a God: it does not prove that I have not a father." (JD 6:274–275)

"One thing has remained a mystery in this kingdom up to this day. It is in regard to the character of the well-beloved Son of God…[and] Our God and Father in heaven…When our father Adam came into the garden of Eden, he came into it with a celestial body, and brought Eve, one of his wives, with him. He helped to make and organize this world. He is MICHAEL, the Archangel, the ANCIENT OF DAYS! About whom holy men have written and spoken—He is our FATHER and our GOD, and the only God with whom WE have to do…I could tell you much more about this; but were I to tell you the whole truth, blasphemy would be nothing to it, in the estimation of the superstitious and over-righteous of mankind. However, I have told you the truth as far as I have gone… Jesus, our elder brother, was begotten in the flesh by the same character that was in the Garden of Eden, and who is our Father in Heaven. Now, let all who may hear these doctrines, pause before they make light of them, or treat them with indifference, for they will prove their salvation or damnation. I have given you a few leading items upon this subject, but a great deal more remains to be told…Treasure up these things in your hearts." (JD 1:50–51. Capitals in the original.)

"I tell you, when you see your Father in the Heavens, you will see Adam; when you see your Mother that bore your spirit, you will see Mother Eve." (Brigham Young, Oct. 8, 1854 General Conference Report, Church Archives. Also see *The Essential Brigham Young*, p. 99)

"Eloheim looks round upon the eternity of matter and said to His associates and those that He was pleased to call upon at the time for His counselors, with regard to the Elements, Worlds, Planets, Kingdoms, and Thrones; said He, '**Yahovah Michael**, see that Eternal Matter on all sides, this way and that way; we have already created Worlds upon Worlds, shall we create another World? Yes, go and organize the elements yonder in space…**Yahovah Michael** go and create a world, make it, organize it, form it; and then put upon it everything in all the variety that you have see[n], that you have been in the habit of being associated with in other worlds, of beasts, birds, fowls, fish, and every insect, and creeping thing, and finally, the whole eternity of element is full of life, bring it together and make of it living creatures'. **Yahovah Michael** goes down and does as he is told. **What I am now going to tell you, will no doubt astonish the whole of you**.

When **Yahovah Michael** had organized the world, and brought from another kingdom the beasts, fish, fowl, and insects, and every tree, and plant with which we are acquainted, and thousands that we never saw, when He had filled the Earth with animal and vegetable life, **Michael or Adam goes down to the new made world, and there he stays**." (October 8, 1854 *Conference Report,* Church Archives. Also see *The Essential Brigham Young,* p. 94)

"If Jesus should veil His glory and appear before you as a man, and witness of himself as being the image of his Father, would you believe that he was really Jesus Christ and that he told you the truth? And if you believed His words, would you not wonder exceedingly to hear that our Father and God is an organized being after the fashion of man's organization in every respect? Such, however, is the case. One of the prophets describes the Father of us all, saying, 'I beheld till the thrones were cast down, and the Ancient of days did sit, whose garment was white as snow, and the hair of his head like the pure wool; his throne was like the fiery flame,' etc. The prophet further says, 'thousand thousands ministered unto him, and ten thousand times ten thousand stood before him,' etc. Again, 'and, behold, one like the Son of Man came with the clouds of heaven and came to the Ancient of days, and they brought him near before him.' **Now, who is this Ancient of days?**

You may answer this question at your pleasure, I have already told the people." (JD 11:41–42)

"Is there in the heaven of heavens a leader? Yes, and we cannot do without one and that being the case, whoever this is may be called God. **Joseph said that Adam was our Father and God**" (Brigham Young, *Journal History,* May 14, 1876, Church Archives)

"While it is in all probability true that the gospels were originally written in Aramaic, it is even more certain that the New Testament is based upon an Old Testament-Hebraic culture and religion. This being the case, it is most significant that in the Hebrew language the word for man is Adam, hence in the some-odd 84 passages in the gospels **when Jesus referred to himself as the Son of Man, it can be taken quite literally as a claim on Jesus' part that he was the son of Adam**." (*Teachings of President Brigham Young*, Vol. 3, p. 327)

"Adam is Michael the Archangel and he is the Father of Jesus Christ and is our God and **Joseph taught this principle**." (Brigham Young, December 16, 1867, recorded in Wilford Woodruff Journal)

"If I am not telling you the truth, please to tell me the truth on this subject, and let me know more than I do know. **If it is hard for you to believe, if you wish to be Latter-day Saints, admit the fact as I state it, and do not contend against it. Try to believe it, because you will never become acquainted with our Father, never enjoy the blessings of His Spirit, never be prepared to enter into His presence, until you most assuredly believe it; therefore you had better try to believe this great mystery about God**. I do not marvel that the world is clad in mystery, to them He is an unknown God; they cannot tell where He dwells nor how He lives, nor what kind of a being He is in appearance or character. They want to become acquainted with His character and attributes, but they know nothing of them. This is in consequence of the apostasy that is now in the world. They have departed from the knowledge of God, transgressed His laws, changed His ordinances, and broken the everlasting covenant, so that the whole earth is defiled under the inhabitants thereof. **Consequently it is no mystery to us that the world knoweth not God, but it would be a mystery to me, with what I know, to say that we cannot know anything of Him**. We are His children...

Whether Adam is the personage that we should consider our heavenly Father, or not, is considerable of a mystery to a good many. I do not care for one moment how that is; it is no matter whether we are to consider Him our God, or whether His Father, or His Grandfather, for in either case we are of one species of one family—and Jesus Christ is also of our species...Now to the facts in the case; all the difference between Jesus Christ and any other man that ever lived on the earth, from the days of Adam until now, is simply this, the Father, after He had once been in the flesh, and lived as we live, obtained His exaltation, attained to thrones, gained the ascendancy over principalities and powers, and had the knowledge and power to create—to bring forth and organize the elements upon natural principles. This He did after His ascension, or His glory, or His eternity, and was actually classed with the Gods with the beings who create, with those who have kept the celestial law while in the flesh, and again obtained their bodies. Then He was prepared to commence the work of creation, as the Scriptures teach...

To you who are prepared to enter into the presence of the Father and the Son, what I am now telling will eventually be no more strange than are the feelings of a person who returns to his father's house, brethren, and sisters, and enjoys the society of his old associates, after an absence of several years upon some distant island...Whether you receive these things or not, I tell you them in simplicity. I lay them before you like a child, because they are perfectly simple. If you see and understand these things, it will be by the Spirit of God; you will receive them by no other spirit. No matter whether they are told to you like the thunderings of the Almighty, or by simple conversation; if you enjoy the Spirit of the Lord, it will tell you whether they are right or not..." (JD 4:215–219)

"Some have grumbled because **I believe our God to be so near to us as Father Adam**. There are many who know that doctrine to be true. Where was Michael in the creation of this earth? Did he have a mission to the earth? He did. Where was he? In the Grand Council, and performed the mission assigned him there. Now, if it should happen that we have to pay tribute to Father Adam, what a humiliating circumstance it would be! Just wait till you pass Joseph Smith; and after Joseph lets you pass him, you will find Peter; and after you pass the Apostles and many of the Prophets, you will find Abraham, and he will say, 'I have the keys, and except you do thus and so, you cannot pass;' and after a while you come to Jesus; **and when you at length meet Father Adam**, how strange it will appear to your present notions. If we can pass Joseph and have him say, 'Here; you have been faithful, good boys; I hold the keys of this dispensation; I will let you pass;' then we shall be very glad to see the white locks of Father Adam. But those are ideas which do not concern us at present, although it is written in the Bible—'This is eternal life, to know thee, the only true God, and Jesus Christ whom thou hast sent.'" (JD 5:331–332)

Parley P. Pratt

"On entering this room, a vast and extensive hall was opened before me, the walls of which were white, and ornamented with various figures which I did not understand. In the midst of this hall was a vast throne and white as ivory, and ascended by seventy steps, and on either side of the throne, and of the steps leading to it, there were seats rising one above another. On this throne was seated an aged, venerable looking man. His hair was white with age, and his countenance beamed with intelligence and affection indescribable as if he were the father of the kingdoms and the people over which he reigned.

He was clad in robes of dazzling whiteness, while a glorious crown rested upon his brow: and a pillar of light above his head seemed to diffuse over the whole scene a brilliance of glory and grandeur indescribable. There was something in his countenance which seemed to indicate that he had passed long years of struggle and exertion in the achievement of some mighty revolution, and been a man of sorrows and acquainted with grief. But, like the evening sun after a day of clouds and tempest, he seemed to smile with the dignity of repose.

In connection with this venerable personage sat two others scarcely less venerable, and clad and crowned in the same manner, on the next seat below were twelve personages, much of the same appearances and clad in the same manner, with crowns upon their heads; while the descending seats were filled with some thousands of noble and dignified personages, all enrobed in white and crowned with authority, power and majesty, as kings and presiding among the Sons of God. 'You now behold,' said the Angel of the Prairies, 'the Grand Presiding Council organized in wisdom, and holding the keys of power to bear rule over all the earth in righteousness. And of the increase and glory of their kingdoms there shall be no end…'

'The venerable council which you beheld enthroned in majesty and clad in robes of white, with crowns upon their heads, is the **order of the Ancient of Days**, before whose august presence thrones have been cast down, and tyrants have ceased to rule.'" (Parley P. Pratt, *The Angel of the Prairies*, pp. 13–14, 24. On January 1, 1844 the previous account of Elder Pratt's experience "was read in Nauvoo, in a Council of the Church, in the presence of the Prophet Joseph Smith.")

Orson Pratt

"Now, how are the angels of God after the resurrection? According to the revelations which God has given, there are different classes of angels. **Some angels are Gods, and still possess the lower office called angels. Adam is called an Archangel, yet he is a God**." (JD 13:187)

Wilford Woodruff

"In the first place, I will say that the prophet **Joseph taught us that Father Adam was the first man on the earth to whom God gave the keys of the Everlasting Priesthood**. He held the keys of the Presidency, and was the first man who did hold them. Noah stood next to him. These keys were given to Noah, he being the Father of all living in his day, as Adam was in his day. These two men were the first who received the Priesthood in the eternal worlds, before the worlds were formed. They were the first who received the Everlasting Priesthood or Presidency on the earth. Father Adam stands at the head, so far as this world is concerned. Of course, Jesus Christ is the Great High Priest of the salvation of the human family. **But Adam holds those keys in the world today; he will hold them to the endless ages of eternity**. And Noah, and every man who has ever held or will hold the keys of Presidency of the Kingdom of God, from that day until the scene is wound up, will have to stand before Father Adam and give an account of the keys of that Priesthood, as we all will have to give an account unto the Lord, of the principles that we have received, when our work is done in the flesh." (*Deseret Weekly News* 38:389)

"Before I sit down I want to say a word to the Elders of Israel on another subject. I am called an old man; I guess I am. I was thinking just now, in speaking of the Apostles and Prophets that were with Joseph Smith when he made his last speech, I am the only man living that was with him at that time. The rest are to-day in the spirit world. How much longer I shall talk to this people I do not know; **but I want to say this to all Israel: Cease troubling yourselves about who God is; who Adam is, who Christ is, who Jehovah is. For heaven's sake, let these things alone. Why trouble yourselves about these things?** God has revealed Himself, and when the 121st section of the Doctrine and Covenants is fulfilled, whether there be one God or many gods they will be revealed to the children of men, as well as all thrones and dominions, principalities, and powers. Then why trouble yourselves about these things? God is God. Christ is Christ. The Holy Ghost is the Holy Ghost. That should be enough for you and me to know. If we want to know any more, wait till we get where God is in person. I say this because we are troubled every little while with inquiries from Elders anxious to know who God is, who Christ is, and who Adam is.

I say to the Elders of Israel, stop this. Humble yourselves before the Lord; seek for light, for truth, and for a knowledge of the common things of the kingdom of God. The Lord is the same yesterday, to-day, and forever. He changes not. The Son of God is the same. He is the Savior of the world. He is our advocate with the Father. We have had letter after letter from Elders abroad wanting to know concerning these things. Adam is the first man. He was placed in the Garden of Eden, and is our great progenitor. God the Father, God the Son, and God the Holy Ghost, are the same yesterday, to-day and forever. That should be sufficient for us to know." (Brian H. Stuy, ed., *Collected Discourses,* 5 vols. [Burbank, Calif., and Woodland Hills, Ut.: B.H.S. Publishing, 1987–1992], Vol. 4:292)

B. H. Roberts

"It is generally supposed that Brigham Young was the author of the doctrine which places Adam as the patriarchal head of the human race, and ascribes to him the dignity of future presidency over this earth and its inhabitants, when the work of redemption shall have been completed. Those who read the Prophet's treatise on the Priesthood in the text above will have their opinions corrected upon this subject; for clearly it is the word of the Lord through the Prophet Joseph Smith which established that doctrine. The utterances of President Brigham Young but repeats and expounds the doctrine which the Prophet here sets forth. (HC 3:388) Some of the sectarian ministers are saying that we 'Mormons' are ashamed of the doctrine announced by President Brigham Young to the effect that Adam will thus be the God of this world. No, friends, it is not that we are ashamed of that doctrine. If you see any change come over our countenances when this doctrine is named, it is surprise, astonishment, that any one at all capable of grasping the largeness and extent of the universe, the grandeur of existence, and the possibilities in man for growth, for progress should be so lean of intellect, should have such a paucity of understanding, as to call it into question at all. This is what our change of countenance means —not shame for the doctrine Brigham Young taught." (*The Mormon Doctrine of Deity,* pp. 42–43)

Eliza R. Snow
"These are the sons and daughters of Adam—the Ancient of Days—the Father and God of the whole human family. These are the sons and daughters of Michael, who is Adam, the father of the spirits of all our race. These are the sons and daughters of Eve, the Mother of a world. What a practical Unitarianism is this! The Christ is not dragged from his heavenly estate, to be mere mortal, but mortals are lifted up to his celestial plane. **He is still the God-Man; but he is one among many brethren who are also God-Men. Moreover, Jesus is one of a grand order of Saviours**. Every world has its distinctive Saviour, and every dispensation its Christ." (Eliza R. Snow, *Women of Mormondom,* pp. 191–192)

"Eve—immortal Eve—came down to earth to become the Mother of a race. **How [does she] become the Mother of a world of mortals except by herself again becoming mortal**? How become mortal only by transgressing the laws of immortality? How only by 'eating of the forbidden fruit' by partaking of the elements of a mortal earth, in which the seed of death was everywhere scattered?…**Eve, then, came down to be the Mother of a world**. Glorious Mother, capable of dying at the very beginning to give life to her offspring, **that through mortality the eternal life of the Gods might be given to her sons and daughters**… Did woman hesitate a moment then? Did motherhood refuse the cup for her own sake, or did she with infinite love, take it and drink for her children's sake? **The Mother had plunged down, from the pinnacle of her celestial throne, to earth, to taste of death that her children might have everlasting life…A Goddess came down from her mansions of glory to bring the spirits of her children down after her**, in their myriads of branches and their hundreds of generations! She was again a mortal Mother now…**Eve stands, then, first—the God-Mother**…" (Ibid, pp. 197–200)

The Ultimatum of Human Life

Adam, your God, like you on earth, has been
Subject to sorrow in a world of sin:
Through long gradation he arose to be
Cloth'd with the Godhead's might and majesty.
And what to him in his probative sphere,
Whether a Bishop, Deacon, Priest, or Seer?
Whate'er his offices and callings were,
He magnified them with assiduous care:

**By his obedience he obtain'd the place
Of God and Father of this human race.**
Obedience will the same bright garland weave,
As it has done for your great Mother, Eve,
For all her daughters on the earth, who will
All my requirements sacredly fulfill.
And what to Eve, though in her mortal life,
She'd been the first, the tenth, or fiftieth wife?
What did she care, when in her lowest state,
Whether by fools, considered small, or great?
'Twas all the same with her—she'd proved her worth –
She's now the Goddess and the Queen of the Earth.
Life's ultimatum, unto those that live
As saints of God, and all my pow'rs receive;
Is still the onward, upward course to tread –
To stand as Adam and as Eve, the head
**Of an inheritance, a new-form'd earth,
And to their spirit-race, give mortal birth—**
Give them experience in world like this;
Then lead them forth to everlasting bliss,
Crown'd with salvation and eternal joy
Where full perfection dwells, without alloy.

(*Poems of Eliza R. Snow,* Vol. 2, pp. 8–9; also Eliza R. Snow, *An Immortal,* pp. 188–189)

Hugh Nibley

...as Goyon shows, the document is really Memphite, as the prominence of Atum and Ptah makes clear: indeed, in the Memphite theology **"Atum is Ptah the Ancient,"** (*The Message of the Joseph Smith Papyri: An Egyptian Endowment* [Salt Lake City: Deseret Book Co., 1975], pp. 131–132)

In the beginning, we are told, "...all the gods assembled in the presence" of Ptah, who "made a division between Horus and Seth, and forbade them to quarrel," giving each his assigned portion. Then for some reason he decided that his first-born, Horus, should be his unique heir, and solemnly announced to the assembled gods, pointing to Horus, "I have chosen thee to be the first, thee alone; my inheritance shall be to this my heir, the **son of my son**...the first-born, opener of the ways, a son born on the birthday of Wep-wawet," that is, on the New Year, the Day of Creation. Thus, instead of being two portions, they were both united under Horus, while the controversy with Seth was patched up for the duration of the festival. The entire middle portion of the Shabako Text is obliterated, but from countless other Egyptian sources, we know that the conflict between Horus and Seth never ceased on this earth, the combat and victory of Horus being ritually repeated at every coronation...

After rites dealing with a baptism, resurrection and the building of the temple at Memphis, the texts break off completely to resume with a catalogue of **Ptah's titles** as "**he who sitteth upon the great throne, heavenly father who begot Atum, heavenly mother who bore Atum, the great one, the mind and mouth [heart and tongue] of the council of the gods** [the ennead]." "In the heart [of Ptah] was conceived the image [form, likeness] of Atum, on the tongue [by the word] was the image of Atum. **Great and mighty is Ptah through whose mind and word all the spirits were brought forth**. And through the mind and word [of God] all physical members were invested with power, according to the doctrine that he [God] is as that which is in every body [i.e., the heart] and in every mouth [i.e., the tongue] of every god, of every human, of every animal, of every creeping thing, of whatsoever possessed life; for whatever is thought and whatever is uttered is according to his will.

The council of the gods brought forth the seeing of the eyes, the hearing of the ears, the breathing of the nose, that these might convey information to the heart, which in turn became aware of things, to which awareness the tongue gives expression, giving utterance to the mind. In such a way were all the gods brought forth…The king, representing Osiris, who is the dead king, his own predecessor, "goes through the secret gates in the splendor of the lord of Eternity, in the footsteps of Re of the great throne, to enter the courts on high and become united with the gods and **with Ptah, the ancient of days** [lord of years]." In the concluding scene the earthly king publicly embraces his son and heir, declaring his calling and succession, even as the god did in the beginning. (*Nibley on the Timely and the Timeless* [Provo: BYU Religious Studies Center, 1978], pp. 24–26. See the article for the numerous associated footnotes)

It is hard in some of these associations to avoid hearing the name of Adam for that of Atum. And indeed, E. Lefebure, noting how closely Atum resembles Adam in his attributes and finding no philological obstacles to equating the names, asked, "**Why not identify him with the biblical Adam?**" (*Bibl. Arch. Soc. Trans.*, 9:176). Moret later pointed out that the first inhabitant of the first place on earth, "the anthropomorphic god Atoum," had "a name which is equated (rapproché) with *Adam*" (A. Moret, *Hist. de l'Orient*, I, 209, n. 32). The name Atum signified, according to Moret, both the Creator and "**the collective sum of all future beings**" (*loc. cit.*). More recent studies have concluded that **Atum means "All-embracing," "the Sum of everything** (Inbegriff des Alls)" (J. Spiegel, *Auferstehungsritual*, p. 2), or the uniting of many in one, of combining all *pre*existent beings in a single archtype who thereby represents all beings here*after* (R. Anthes, *ZA*, 80:86; 82:1–8, *JNES*, 18:177)

This suits with Joseph Smith's definition of Adam in the Pearl of Great Price: "And the first man of all men have I called Adam, which is *many*" (Moses 1:34). What complicates the picture is that **Atum is also the creator** (Pyr. 578, #1587; C.T. 132, II, 152),

specifically the creator of man (C.T. 75, I, 372–76); **he is "the Ancient One"** par excellence, "the first hypostasis of the demiurge at the time of the Creation...the Word of Ptah incarnate" (Goyon, *L. 3279*, pp. 63–64). Yet the breath of life comes from *his* mouth as well (C.T. 75, I, 364). In the Breathing literature, the heart which alone can give a man possession of eternal life is Atum, but only as a hypostasis of Ptah, who created man in the first place (Goyon, *op. cit.*, pp. 64–66). **Since this business of launching men into eternity must begin with a repetition of the creation, a new life (Goyon, p. 65), all the greatest creator-gods are understandably present on the scene**. As in the story of the Foredoomed Prince, any deity *not* invited to contribute could cause real trouble! When Re comes down he *is* Atum, as we have seen, while Amon and Ptah together form the body of man and place breath in his body. Whose body? That can be complicated too, but the preferred candidate is Atum, by far the most human of the four:

"I am Ptah, I have opened thy mouth...Thy body is the body of Atum eternally..." (Lefebure, *An. Serv.*, 20:230). "Thou arisest with thy father Atum," the dead king is told; "thou art raised up with thy father Atum..." (Spiegel, *An. Serv.*, 53:370). Atum as the rising and the setting sun, "Re on the horizon," "Re coming down, Atum in the evening" is necessarily the *red* sun as it passes between the upper and the lower worlds. Atum wears the red crown as "the King comes out of Buto, red (*dshr*) as the flame" (Zandee, *ZA*, 99:54, C.T. I, 386ff, P.T. 697 a.d.). This certainly suggests the well-known meaning of Adam as "red." In a Coffin Text the initiate describes himself as vindicator of his father Re at the dawn, i.e., as Re-Atum, but specifically "in my name of *Admw*," where the Semitic form of the name with nominative ending is used (C.T. 148, II, 224)

Ptah is creator pure and simple, the great god of Memphis; he always retains that as his one mark and calling. In the Shabako drama it is Ptah who does the creating, and the one whom he creates is *Atum*—another reason for equating the latter with Adam. Ptah of Memphis is the very old creator god who made all things (Sethe, *Dramat. Texte*, I, 68), and "begot Atum and the other gods" (I, 66). (*The Message of the Joseph Smith Papyri: An Egyptian Endowment* [Salt Lake City: Deseret Book Co., 1975], pp. 133–134. See the article for the numerous associated footnotes.)

Let us consider our Adam. What kind of being is he? The same kind as ourselves—but what is that? **He plays a surprising number of roles**, each with a different persona, a different name, a different environment, a different office and calling: (1) he was a member of the presidency when the earth project was being discussed; (2) he was on the committee of inspection that came down from time to time to check up on the operation; (3) then he changed his name and nature to live upon the earth, but it was a very different earth from any we know; it had to be a garden place specially prepared for him. (4) When he left that paradise, he changed his nature again and for the first time began to reckon the passing of time by our measurements, becoming a short-lived creature subject to death. (5) In this condition, he began to receive instructions from heavenly mentors on how to go about changing his condition and status, entering into a covenant that completely changed his mentality and way of life. "The first man Adam was made a living soul; the last Adam was made a quickening spirit," when "that which is natural" became spiritual. (1 Corinthians 15:45–46) **The man Adam passes from one state of being to another, and so do we: "as we have borne the image of the earthly, we shall also bear the image of the heavenly**." (1 Corinthians 15:49) (6) In time he died and became a spirit being, the head of all his spirit children in the waiting-place, according to common Christian tradition as well as our own. (7) Then he became, after Christ, the first fruits of the resurrection and returned triumphantly to his first and second estates (8) **to go on to glory and eternal lives**. (*Old Testament and Related Studies,* edited by John W. Welch, Gary P. Gillum, and Don E. Norton [Salt Lake City and Provo: Deseret Book Co., Foundation for Ancient Research and Mormon Studies, 1986], p. 77)

And one of our biggest stumbling blocks is not knowing how Adam relates to other beings, earthly and heavenly. That is the root of the Adam-God misunderstanding. (Until we care to look into the matter seriously, I will keep my opinions in a low profile.) (Ibid, p. 82)

Chapter 29

King and Priest

Apostle John

"And hath made us **kings and priests unto God** and his Father…" (Revelation 1:6)

Joseph Smith

"They are they who are **priests and kings**, who have received of his fulness, and of his glory;" (D&C 76:56)

That of Melchisedec who had still greater power even power of an endless life of which was our Lord Jesus Christ which also Abraham obtained by the offering of his son Isaac which was not the power of a Prophet nor apostle nor Patriarch **only but of King & Priest to God** to open the windows of Heaven and pour out the peace & Law of endless Life to man & No man can attain to the Joint heirship with Jesus Christ with out being administered to by one having the same power & Authority of Melchisedec. (*The Words of Joseph Smith*, p. 245)

What was the power of Melchizedek? 'Twas not the Priesthood of Aaron which administers in outward ordinances, and the offering of sacrifices. **Those holding the fullness** of the Melchizedek Priesthood **are kings and priests of the Most High God**, holding the keys of power and blessings. In fact, that priesthood is a perfect law of theocracy, and stands as God to give laws to the people, **administering endless lives to the sons and daughters of Adam**. (HC 5:555)

Here, then, is eternal life—to know the only wise and true God; and you have got to learn how to be gods yourselves, and to be **kings and priests to God**, the same as all gods have done before you, namely, by going from one small degree to another, and from a small capacity to a great one; from grace to grace, from exaltation to exaltation, until you attain to the resurrection of the dead. (HC 6:306)

Brigham Young

For any person to have the fullness of that priesthood, he must be a king and priest. (HC 5:527)

A man cannot sin against the Holy Ghost until the Holy Ghost has revealed unto him the Father and [the] Son and knowledge of eternal things, in a great degree. (*The Complete Discourses of*

Brigham Young, Vol. 1, 1832 to 1852, Ed. Richard S. Van Wagoner, Smith-Petit Foundation, Salt Lake City, 2009. p. 467)

Heber C. Kimball

This brings to my mind the vision that Joseph Smith had, when he saw Adam open the gate of the Celestial City and admit the people one by one. He then saw Father Adam conduct them to the throne one by one, when they were crowned **Kings and Priests of God**. (JD 9:41)

Lorenzo Snow

"Brother Snow, as the Patriarch of his house, bestowed blessings upon the heads of many members of his large family, intending to continue before they separated for their respective homes, to lay his hands upon and bless them until all received his administrations, as it is unlikely that they will ever enjoy another re-union of this kind in this state of existence. But in the great eternity before us all, they expect a re-union of a far more extensive and pleasing character. When the head of this family, having gained his exaltation, and holding the keys of **eternal lives and endless increase**, will gather around him all that belongs to his house, saved, redeemed, resurrected, glorified to reign over them as a **king and a priest unto God** for ever." (*Biography and Family Record of Lorenzo Snow* [Salt Lake City: Deseret News, 1884], pp. 463–464)

Franklin D. Richards

Those holding the fullness of the Melchisedek Priesthood are kings and priests of the Most High God, holding the keys of power and blessings! In fact, that Priesthood is a perfect law of theocracy, and stands as God to give laws to the people, **administering endless lives to the sons and daughters of Adam**. (Franklin D. Richards and James A. Little, *Compendium of the Doctrines of the Gospel* [Salt Lake City: Deseret Book Co., 1925], pp. 279–280)

Hugh Nibley

In the Secrets of Enoch we are told that **Melchizedek will be priest and king in a place at the center of the earth when the Lord will bring him forth as** "another Melchizedek of the lineage of the first Melchizedek." **Here is identity indeed—Melchizedek succeeding himself**! In the Pistis Sophia, **Jesus says that "the higher mysteries" tell how all "are to be saved** in the time and in the number of Melchizedek the Great Mediator of the Light, the agent of all who is at the center of the world." (*Enoch the Prophet*, pp. 29–30)

KINGS AND PRIESTS IN THE LAST DAYS

"[January 1, 1845. Wednesday.]…The organization of the Kingdom of God on 11th March last is one important event. This organization was called the Council of Fifty or Kingdom of God, and was titled by revelation as follows. 'Verily thus saith the Lord, this is the name by which you shall be called, the Kingdom of God and his Laws, with the Keys and power thereof, and judgment in the hands of his servants, Ahman Christ.'...**In this Council was President Joseph chosen our Prophet, Priest and King** by Hosannas." (George D. Smith, *An Intimate Chronicle: The Journals of William Clayton,* p. 153. Also see D. Michael Quinn, *The Mormon Hierarchy: Origins of Power*, p. 229 for more information about Joseph being ordained a "King" of the Kingdom of God by the Council of Fifty.)

"Brother Brigham Young, I pour this holy, consecrated oil upon your head, and anoint thee a King and a Priest of the Most High God over the Church of Jesus Christ of Latter Day Saints, and unto all Israel..." (Heber C. Kimball ordaining Brigham Young a Priest and a King to Israel. *The Mysteries of Godliness*, p. 88)

"Bro. Heber Chase Kimball in the name of Jesus Christ we poor upon thy head this Holy oil a Priest & we anoint thee a King & unto the most High God in & over the Church of Jesus Christ of Latter Days Saints and also Israel..." (Brigham Young ordaining Heber C. Kimball a Priest and a King to Israel. *The Mysteries of Godliness,* p. 87)

Chapter 30

Second Death

Joseph Smith

"...that ye may not be cursed with a sore cursing; and also, that ye may not incur the displeasure of a just God upon you unto the destruction, yea, **the eternal destruction of both soul and body**." (2 Nephi 1:22)

"And now behold, I say unto you then cometh a death, even **a second death**, which is **a spiritual death**; then is a time that whosoever dieth in his sins, as to a temporal death, shall also die **a spiritual death**; yea, he shall die as to things pertaining unto righteousness. Then is the time when their torments shall be as a lake of fire and brimstone, whose flame ascendeth up forever and ever; and then is the time that they shall be chained down to an everlasting destruction, according to the power and captivity of Satan, he having subjected them according to his will. Then, I say unto you, they shall be as though there had been no redemption made; for they cannot be redeemed according to God's justice; and they cannot die, seeing there is no more corruption." (Alma 12:16–18)

"Therefore God gave unto them commandments, after having made known unto them the plan of redemption, that they should not do evil, the penalty thereof being **a second death**, which was an everlasting death as to things pertaining unto righteousness; for on such the plan of redemption could have no power, for the works of justice could not be destroyed, according to the supreme goodness of God." (Alma 12:32)

"And now, my brethren, behold I say unto you, that if ye will harden your hearts ye shall not enter into the rest of the Lord; therefore your iniquity provoketh him that he sendeth down his wrath upon you as in the first provocation, yea, according to his word in the last provocation as well as the first, to **the everlasting destruction of your souls**; therefore, according to his word, unto the last death, as well as the first." (Alma 12:36)

"And may the Lord grant unto you repentance, that ye may not bring down his wrath upon you, that ye may not be bound down by the chains of hell, that ye may not suffer **the second death**." (Alma 13:30)

"Yea, and it bringeth to pass the condition of repentance, that whosoever repenteth the same is not hewn down and cast into the fire; but whosoever repenteth not is hewn down and cast into the fire; and there cometh upon them again **a spiritual death, yea, a second death**, for they are cut off again as to things pertaining to righteousness." (Helaman 14:18)

"...all your losses will be made up to you in the resurrection provided you continue faithful. By the vision of the almighty I have seen it. **More painful to me the thought of annihilation than death**." (*The Words of Joseph Smith*, p. 196)

"Salvation for all men who have not committed a certain sin can save any man who has not committed the unpardonable sin...Why, Must commit the unpardonable sin in this world. **Will suffer in the eternal world until he will be exalted**." (Ibid, p. 342)

"Broad is the gate, and wide the way that leadeth to **the deaths**..." (D&C 132:25)

"...but those who Sin agt. the H.G. cannot be forgiven in this world or in the world to come but **they shall die the 2nd Death**—but as they concoct scenes of bloodshed in this world **so they shall rise to that resurn**. Which is as the lake of fire and brimstone—some shall rise to the everlasting burnings of God & **some shall rise to the dn. of their own filthiness –**" (*The Words of Joseph Smith*, p. 355)

"...those who commit the unpardonable sin are doomed to **Gnaolom**." (Ibid, p. 343)

"Notwithstanding this congregation profess to be Saints, yet I stand in the midst of all [kinds of] characters and classes of men. If you wish to go where God is, you must be like God, or possess the principles which God possesses, for **if we are not drawing towards God in principle, we are going from Him and drawing towards the devil**. Yes, I am standing in the midst of all kinds of people...**As far as we degenerate from God, we descend to the devil** and lose knowledge, and without knowledge we cannot be saved, and while our hearts are filled with evil, and we are studying evil, there is no room in our hearts for good" (HC 4:588)

Brigham Young

"A man cannot sin against the Holy Ghost until the Holy Ghost has revealed unto him the Father and [the] Son and a knowledge of eternal things, in a great degree. When he has a knowledge of these things, [and] with his eyes wide open, he rebels against God and defies His power, [then] he sins against all three." (*Teachings of President Brigham Young*, Vol. 3, p. 8)

"If you suffer the opposite of this to take possession of your tabernacles, it will hurt you, and all that is associated with you, and blast, and strike with mildew, until your tabernacle, which was created to continue throughout an endless duration, **will be decomposed, and go back to its native elements, to be ground over again** like the refractory clay that has spoiled in the hand of the potter, it must be worked over again until it shall become passive, and yield to the potter's wish." (JD 2:135–136)

"The rebellious will be thrown back into their native element, there to remain myriads of years **before their dust will again be revived, before they will be re-organized**, Some might argue that this principle would lead to the re-organization of Satan, and all the devils. I say nothing about this, only what the Lord says, that when he comes 'he will destroy death, and him that has the power of it.'" (JD 1:118)

"They will be decomposed, both soul and body, and return to their native elements. I do not say that they will be annihilated; **but they will be disorganized, and will be as if they had never been...**" (JD 7:57)

"Now understand, to choose life is to choose principles that will lead you to an eternal increase, and nothing short of them will produce life in the resurrection for the faithful. Those that choose death, make choice of the path which leads to the end of their organization. The one leads to endless increase and progression, the other to the destruction of the organized being, ending in its entire decomposition into the particles that compose the native elements." (JD 1:352)

"Hear it, all ye Latter-day Saints! Will you spend the time of your probation for naught, and fool away your existence and being? You were organized, and brought into being, for the purpose of enduring forever, if you will fulfill the measure of your creation, pursue the right path, observe the requirements of the Celestial law, and obey the commandments of God. It is then, and then only, you may expect that the blessings of eternal lives will be conferred upon you. It can be obtained upon no other principle. Do you understand that you will cease to be, that you come to a full end, by pursuing the opposite course? ... everything else tends to decay, separation, annihilation; no not annihilation, as we use the English term, there is no such principle as this, but dissolution or decomposition." (JD 1:113–114)

"Suppose that our Father in heaven, our elder brother, the risen Redeemer, the Saviour of the world, or any of the Gods of eternity should act upon this principle, to love truth, knowledge, and wisdom, because they are all-powerful, and by the aid of this power they could send devils to hell, torment the people of the earth, exercise sovereignty over them, and make them miserable at their pleasure; **they would cease to be Gods**; and **as fast as they adopted and acted upon such principles, they would become devils, and be thrust down in the twinkling of an eye; the extension of their kingdom would cease, and their God-head come to an end.**" (JD 1:117)

"If you adhere to the spirit of the Lord strictly it will become in you a fountain of revelation. After awhile the Lord will say to such, 'My son, you have been faithful, you have clung to good, and you love righteousness, and hate iniquity, from which you have turned away, now you shall have the blessing of the Holy Spirit to lead you, and be your constant companion from this time henceforth and forever.' Then the Holy Spirit becomes your property, it is given to you for a profit and an eternal blessing. It tends to addition, extension and increase, to immortality and eternal lives. **If you suffer the opposite of this to take**

possession of your tabernacles, it will hurt you, and all that is associated with you, and blast, and strike with mildew, until your tabernacle, which was created to continue throughout an endless duration, will be decomposed, and go back to its native elements, to be ground over again like the refractory clay that has spoiled in the hands of the potter, it must be worked over again until it shall become passive and yield to the potter's wish. One power is to add, to build up, and increase; the other to destroy and diminish; one is life, the other is death. **We might ask, when shall we cease to learn? I will give you my opinion about it: never, never.**

If we continue to learn all that we can, pertaining to the salvation which is purchased and presented to us through the Son of God, is there a time when a person will cease to learn? Yes; when he has sinned against God the Father, Jesus Christ the Son, and the Holy Ghost—God's minister, when he has denied the Lord, defied Him and committed the sin that in the Bible is termed the unpardonable sin—the sin against the Holy Ghost. That is the time when a person will cease to learn, and from that time forth, will descend in ignorance, forgetting that which he formerly knew, and decreasing until he returns to the native element, whether it be in one thousand or in one million years, or during as many eternities as you can count. Such will cease to increase, but must decrease until they return to the native element.

These are the only characters who will ever cease to learn, both in time and in eternity. We shall never cease to learn unless we apostatize from the religion of Jesus Christ. Then we shall cease to increase, and will continue to decrease and decompose, until we return to our native element. Mankind are organized of element designed to endure to all eternity; it never had a beginning and never can have an end.

There never was a time when this matter, of which you and I are composed, was not in existence, and there never can be a time when it will pass out of existence; it cannot be annihilated. It is brought together, organized, and capacitated to receive knowledge and intelligence, to be enthroned, to be made angels, Gods—beings who will hold control over the elements, and have power by their word to command the creation and redemption of worlds, or to extinguish suns by their breath, and disorganize worlds, hurling them back into their chaotic state. **The thought of being annihilated, of being blotted out of existence, is most horrid even to that class called infidels. The intelligence that is in me to cease to exist, is a horrid thought**! This intelligence must exist; it must dwell somewhere. If I take the right course and preserve it in its organization, I will preserve to myself eternal life. This is the greatest gift that ever was bestowed on mankind, to know how to preserve their identity. Shall we forge our own fetters through our ignorance?

Shall we lay the foundation to build the bulwarks for our own destruction through our wickedness? I trust that we are laying the foundation to endure eternally. If we do, we must be the friends of God —the friends of the principles of life and salvation; and we must adhere to those principles, and shape our lives according to them, or else we lay the foundation for our own destruction. Talk about liberty anywhere else! What liberty is there in anything that will be dissolved and return to its native element? What liberty can any intelligence enjoy that is calculated to be destroyed? There is no liberty, no freedom there. The principles of life and salvation are the only principles of freedom; for every principle that is opposed to God—that is opposed to the principles of eternal life, whether it is in heaven, on earth or in hell—the time will be when it will cease to exist, cease to preserve, manifest and exhibit its identity; for it will be returned to its native element.

If the Lord sees that we need to be afflicted, he can apply the rod. I do not say this to urge you to do your duty, for if you will not live your religion for the blessings that God bestows upon it, you will not live it anyhow; and the man who will not live his religion ought to be damned. **Never serve God because you are afraid of hell; but live your religion because it is calculated to give you eternal life.** It points to that existence that never ends, while the other course leads to destruction, to dissolution, when they will be destroyed from the earth and from the eternities, and return back to the native elements. We will maintain the kingdom of God living; and if we do not maintain it, we shall be found dying not only a temporal, but also an eternal death. Then take a course to live.

We place the principles of life before you. Do as you please and we will protect you in your rights, though you will learn that the system you have chosen to follow brings you to dissolution—to being resolved to native element. To see people running after this and that which is calculated to destroy them spiritually and temporally—to bring upon them the first death, and then the second, so that they will be as though they had not been—is enough to make the heavens weep." (*Contributor*, Vol. 10 (November 1888–October 1889), Vol. X, September, 1889. No. 11, pp. 401–402)

"He had not the power of endless life in him, and he will be decomposed, and the particles which compose his body and spirit will return to their native element. I told you some time ago what would become of such men. But I will quote the Scriptures on this point, and you can make what you please of it. Jesus says, he will DESTROY *death* and *him* that hath the power of it. What can you make of this but decomposition, the returning of the organized particles to their native element, after suffering the wrath of God until the time appointed. That appears a mystery, but the principle has been in existence from all eternity, only it is something you have not known or thought of. When the elements in an organized form do not fill the end of their creation, they are thrown back again, like brother Kimball's old pottery ware, to be ground up, and made over again.

All I have to say about it is what Jesus says—I will *destroy* Death, and him that hath the power of it, which is the devil. And if he ever makes '*a full end* of the wicked,' what else can he do than entirely disorganize them, and reduce them to their native element? Here are some of the mysteries of the kingdom. On the other hand, let us take the affirmative of the question; and inquire what is life and salvation? It is to take that course wherein we can abide for ever and ever, and be exalted to thrones, kingdoms, governments, dominions, and have full power to control the elements, according to our pleasure to all eternity; the one is life, and the other is death, which is nothing more or less than the decomposition of organized native element. There can be no such thing as power to annihilate element. There is one eternity of element, which can be organized or disorganized, composed or decomposed; it may be put into this shape or into that, according to the will of the intelligence that commands it, but there is no such thing as putting it entirely out of existence." (JD 1:275–276)

"**A man cannot sin against the Holy Ghost until the Holy Ghost has revealed unto him the Father and [the] Son and knowledge of eternal things, in a great degree.**" (*The Complete Discourses of Brigham Young*, Vol. 1, 1832 to 1852, Ed. Richard S. Van Wagoner, Smith-Petit Foundation, Salt Lake City, 2009, p. 467)

Orson Hyde

The following is quoted from the author of a biography about Orson Hyde during Orson's temporary apostasy from the Church: "One answer to his prayers came as a vision. In it he received graphic instructions, he narrates that, 'If I did not make immediate restitution to the Quorum of the Twelve, I would be cut off [from the Church and everlasting blessings] with all my posterity.' More terrifying, **the vision revealed, after death he would be cast among the Satanic host, a consequence of his denial, in essence, of his past immense spiritual enlightenment**." (*Orson Hyde: the Olive Branch of Israel* by Myrtle Hyde, p. 104)

Erastus Snow

"One thing is taught clearly in all the revelations, ancient and modern, that **there is a class on whom the second death shall pass; and the thought of their returning to their native element is the thought which all intelligent beings shrink from**. The instinct within us is to cleave to life—to cleave to our organization; and the greatest joy we feel is in the certain hope of a resurrection from the dead. **The idea of the second death, or dissolution of the spirit, is that which is the most terrifying to the soul**. But our Father has so ordained that our spiritual organizations, as well as our tabernacles, can only be maintained and perfected through obedience to the laws of eternal life." (JD 7:359)

Appendices

Appendix A
Excerpts from Orson F. Whitney's Epic Poem "Elias"

Elias is an epic poem written by Orson F. Whitney that covers much of the religious history of the world from the LDS perspective, but more importantly, Elder Whitney describes his encounter with an angelic messenger and the sublime truths this messenger taught him. The following excerpts are from the revised and annotated edition published in 1914.

> **Progress eterne! Thou goest hand in hand**
> **With Life eterne, and naught but death e'er dies.**
> (quoted from the title page)

Excerpts from Canto I

> I slept and dreamed no more; I was awake!
> **And saw and heard with other eyes and ears,**
> **Which taught me things unseen, unheard before;**
> **Things new and old—old as eternity,**
> Old e'en to time, though new and strange to me.
> **Rejoicing in my new-found strength, I gave**
> Glory to Him, the source and Sire of all;
> That God whom I had neither loved nor feared,
> That God whom now I worshipped and adored;
> Who girdled me with light, truth's triple key,
> Unlocking has been, what yet shall be,
> **Probing death's gloom, life's three-fold mystery,**
> **Solving the secret—whither, Whence, and Why.**

> O wondrous transformation! When with wand,
> Of wakening might, that all uplifting power
> Waved o'er the cross where hung fond hopes impaled,
> Waved o'er the tomb where loved ambitions lay

Touched the strewn fragments of my shattered dream,
Bidding the dead arise in bodies new,
Building, on ruined hope, faith's battlement,
Love's palace, peace—domed, pinnacled in light—
In glory greater than earth's grandest dream,
Than glittering fame's most splendid spectacle;
Ideal transcending ideality,
Ideal made real past all reality!

Whose earth-dimmed eye could see what then I saw?
Whose earth-dulled ear such harmonies could hear?
When the all-searching Spirit tore the veil
Of things that seem, and showed me things that are.
Revealing life in hues of hopefulness;
Eternal life demands a selfless love.
Hampered by pride, greed, hate, what soul can grow?
Conceive a selfish God! Thou canst not, man!
Then let it shame thee unto higher things.
Fare on, full sure that greatest glory comes,
And swiftest growth, from serving humankind.
So spake the Spirit of the Infinite;

Some men I found embodiments of all
The goodness, all the greatness I had dreamed;
Men seeming gods, bestowing benefits
As suns their beams, as seas and skies their showers;
Others as dwarfs, as despots by compare,
Devoured with greed, consumed with jealousy.

But truth taught charity, gave me to see,
As face to face one sees familiar friend,
Why men are not alike in magnitude,
Some souls, than others, have more summits climbed,
More light absorbed, more moral might evolved;
Dowered are they with wealth from earlier spheres;
Hence wiser, worthier than those they lead
Through precept's vale, up steep example's height,
To where love, beauty, wealth, power, glory, reign

While some, innately noble, are borne down
By weight of weaknesses inherited,
By passions fierce, propensities depraved,
Malefic legacy of Centuries,
That much of their true worthiness obscures,
While spirit strives with flesh for mastery,
For higher culture and for added might.

And yet anon such souls effulgent shine,
As bursts the April beam through banks of cloud,
In glory from which envy shades its eyes,
While stands detraction staring, stricken dumb;
The glory of a great intelligence,
Which mortal mists can dim but for a time;

Spirits, like stars, all differ in degree,
And cannot show an even excellence,
Unequal in their first nobility.
Great tells of greater—littleness of less;
Time's hills and vales but type eternity,
Whose glories fixt, essential, evermore.
Truth taught me more, but bade me silent be;

Excerpts from Canto II

Vast, voiceless oracles, **whose intelligence**
Sleeps in the caverns of each stony heart,
Yet breathes o'er all a boundless eloquence,
What wealth historic might your words impart!

But like the laboring brain that burns to speak
Mind's inmost thought, deep in its dungeons pent;
Or liker still to inward boiling peak
Of fires volcanic, vainly seeking vent
Where adamantine bolts and bars prevent;—
Thou'rt doomed to utter stillness, and shalt keep
The burden of thy bearing, till is rent
Yon heavenly veil, and earth and air and deep
Tell secrets that shall rouse the dead from solemn sleep.

And must I be as mute, O silent mount!
Muse of all melody, shall I not sing?—
Burst these dumb bars, when e'en yon babbling fount
May find in every breeze a wafting wing,
Afar its lightest murmured word to fling?
Where art thou, ancient soul of solemn song?
Asleep? Then wake! Wherefore art slumbering?
The world hath need of thee, and waiteth long.
Strike—strike again thy harp, and thrill the listening
throng!

Amazed I listened. Did I more than dream?
Had random word aroused unhoped reply?
Or was it sound whose import did but seem?
Hark!—for again it rolls along the sky:
Then question hast thou none? Or none wouldst ply,
Save to thy soul in meditative strain,
Or heedless winds that wander idly by?
So be it; still to me thy purpose plain,
Thy hidden wish revealed, nor thus revealed in vain.
While freshing waves of woodland-scented air
Widened the spell of that immortal tone;
While, as on threshold of a lion's lair,
Speechless I stood, as stricken into stone;
Me thought the sun with lessening splendor shone,
As if some wandering cloud obscured his gaze.
Then burst a glory from his midday throne!
Turning, mine eye beheld, in rapt amaze,
What memory ne'er would lose were life of endless days.

And thou, O pensive crier in the waste,
Invoker of the Voice now visible!
Prepared art thou a mystery to taste,
Whose fruit is joy or woe ineffable?
Pluck not of wisdom's branches bending full,
Drink not of that divine philosophy,
Save thou canst bravely suffer wrong's misrule,
Thy best intent thought ill; save thou canst be
What men deem "fool," real fools despising, pitying thee.

List while I tell, for I am one by whom
Future and past as present shall appear.
In me behold Messiah's minister,
Ancient of time and of eternity,

Sing, poet, sing! but not of new—of old,
Of old and new—Eternal Truth thy theme,
That holdeth past and future in her fold,
That maketh present but a passing dream,
While time and earth and man as trifles seem;
That knoweth not of new, or old, or strange;
Whose everduring, all-redemptive scheme,
Fixt and immutable 'mid worlds of change,
On, on, from universe to universe doth range.

Faint not, nor fear, for all shall fare thy way—
My way—His way, the Master evermore.

East shall seem West, rethrown the rising ray,
Shining afar from this most ancient shore;
And man shall rise e'en where man fell before.
Fools may deride, may jeer at destiny;
They mock to mourn; oblivion earths them o'er;
While they that champion truth, by truth shall be
Exalted, e'en in time, to live eternally.

Silent, he towered above me, harp in hand,
Was it a dream? Could dream so vivid be?
And with his mantle's fold my forehead fanned.
Then leapt to life the flame of poesy!
Was it a vision of my destiny?
Upon the mount, as erst, I stood alone,
And naught was there of muse or minstrelsy;
Save that afar still trembled that strange tone,
And something said within: "That harp is now thine own."

Excerpts from Canto III

Declare, O Muse of mightier wing,
Of loftier lore than mine!
Why God is God, and man may be
Both human and divine;
Why Sons of God, 'mid sons of men,
Unrecognized may dwell,
So masked in dense mortality
That none their truth can tell.
Give me to lead to this lorn world,
When wandered from the fold,
Twelve legions of the noble ones
That now thy face behold;
Tried souls, 'mid untried spirits found;
That captained these may be,
And crowned the dispensations all
With powers of Deity.

Excerpts from Canto IV

All oracles of light, all arms of power,
Preparers of the way one face before;
Their strength but part of His omnipotence,
Their fault God-given lest man be defied,

And pride in him dethrone humility.

Declare His truth, His generations tell,
O'er whom the many marveled, some to say
Elias, slain of Herod, lives again,
While some said Jeremias. Whom say ye,
Man-hated, though God-missioned ministers,
Unctioned with fire, anointed from on high!
Guardians yet watchful o'er the widening fold!
Whom say ye was your Master, Teacher, Friend?

Word that was God, is God, and shall be aye;
Sire by the spirit, and by flesh the Son;
In glory with the Father ere the world,
And now with that same glory glorified;
Image and likeness of creation's cause,
Mirror and model of humanity,
Of man the parent and the prototype;
Lover of light, hating and righting wrong;
Anointed Lord of Lords, and Sire 'mid Sons.
The Sole—begotten, He that doeth here
All He hath seen erstwhile the Father do;
Elias? Nay, Messiah, Saviour, King,
The Greater whom Elias said would come

Excerpts from Canto V

Once more the ancient tidings among men!
Once more the sign and seal of heavenly power!
Renewal of an endless covenant,
Elias, restitution, unity!

His burden! Hear it, nations! Hear it, isles!
Ere falls an hour, nights darkest hour of doom.
The trial ends, the judgment now begins.
Out, out of her, my people, saith your God!

Who towers aloft, as mountain girt with hills,
Amid be strength of Ephraim's stalwart sons,
To trumpet thus the closing act of time?
Speak, oracle! what sayest thou of thyself?
Who art thou, man of might and majesty?

"Would God I might but tell thee who I am!
Would God I might but tell thee what I know!"

**Then was he of thee Mighty?-one with those
Descended from the Empire of the Sun,
Adown the glowing stairway of the stars;
Regnant and ruling ere they left the realms
Of life supernal, left their sovereign thrones,
To wander oft as outcasts of mankind,**
Unknown, unhonored, e'en like One who came
Unto His own, by them spat on and spurned;
Avails it aught, their name or nations here?
Their state and standing there, the vital tale.

Peers of that Empire nobles of the skies,
The sceptred satraps of the King of Kings;
The royal retinue of Him who reigns
First-born of many brethren; Gibborim,
Great ones worthy the Word that was to come;
Foreknown, elect, predestined, preordained,
**Sons of the Gods, the saviours of mankind.
Building the highway for Messiah's feet,**
And wheresoe'er He fareth following.

**I saw in vision such a one descend,
And garb him in a guise of common clay;
His glory veiling from the gaze of all,
Who wist not that a great one walked with men;
Nor knew it then the soul incarnate there,**
Betwixt the temporal and spirit spheres
So dense forgetfulness doth intervene;
Yet learned his truth betime by angel tongues,
By voice of God, by heavenly whisperings.

But who remains the mystery to solve?
His letter to unlock with spirit key?
The veil to lift by death and silence thrown
O'er all the splendors of that life sublime?

A living prophet unto dying time
Heralding the dispensation of the end;
When Christ once more His vineyard comes to prune,
When potent weak confound the puny strong,
Rending the Kingdoms with a word of flame;
That here the Fathers work may crown the Son's,
And earth be joined a holy bride to Heaven,
A queen 'mid queens, crowned, throned, and glorified.
Wherefore came down this angel of the dawn,
In strength divine, a stirring role to play

In time's tense tragedy, whose acts are seven.
His part to fell the false, replant the true,
To clear away the wreckage of the past,
The ashes of its dead any dying creeds,
And kindly newly on earth's ancient shrine
The Light that points to Life unerringly;
Crowning what has been with what now must be;
A mighty still bespeaking mightier.
Players, immortal twain and mortal one,
Standing but fourteen steps upon life's stair,
An unlearned boy, thinker of thoughts profound,
Boy and yet man, dreamer of lofty dreams.

He holds aloof from those degenerate sects,
Bewildering Babel of conflicting creeds,
And pondering the apostolic line:
"Let any lacking wisdom, wisdom ask
And God will freely give, upbraiding none,"
He puts the promise to the utter test.

What pen can paint the marvel that befell?
What tongue the wondrous miracle portray?
Than theirs, the Vision's own, what voice proclaim
Whose dual presence dimmed the noonday beam,
Communing with him there, as friend with friend,
And giving to that prayer reply of peace?

Wane the swift years; the boy a youth now grown;
And on his brow, woe-carved, a world of care.
Bending an Atlas, 'neath the titans load,
Daily he climbs the hill of sacrifice,
Viewing from far the mount of martyrdom.

Nor marvel at his lot; hath he not told,—
A crime man ne'er forgave in fellow man,—
Told the wise world that God hath spoke again?

"Twas from below," thus bigotry, in rage.
"Nay, from above," the meek though firm reply.
"No vision is there now—the time is past."
"But I have seen," affirms truth's constancy.
"God is a mystery, unknowable."
"God is a Man—I saw Him, talked with Him."?
"Man"?—"Ay, of holiness,—exalted Man."

"Elias comes, Messiah's messenger,

God's host to summon, and His house to save—
First by persuasion's pleading; that contemned,
By voice of wrath and stroke of violence.
He speaks—the mountains kneel, the valleys rise,
Rolls to the north the land—dividing wave;
Equality—nay, justice, holds the helm,
Each hath his own; the lost lamb finds the fold.
Elias comes! 'tis restitution's reign,
And order hurls disorder from the throne.

Excerpts from Canto VI

Thence oft above that mount of mystery,
Of buried lore the solemn sepulchre,
Meet modern seer and ancient oracle;
And while Humility at Wisdom's feet
Expectant waits, where truth from earth shall spring,
Comes, as from riven tomb, this wondrous tale:
Where Joseph, where wast thou, that time when torn
Was earth asunder,—ocean's cleaving sword
The wedded lands wide severing,—Where, when borne
Safe through the watery world, as there devoured
By wind and wave that harmless o'er them roared;
The pilgrim sons of Shinar, favored band,
From that far clime where Babel's folly towered,
And language foundered on confusion's strand,
Won here a precious heritage, this promised land.

Preserver of the pure and primal tongue,
Most faithful found 'mid living sons of men,
Their leader looked on God; then wrestling wrung
By spirit might, and paged with fiery pen,
The full of what should be, of what had been;

Sealing the secret till an hour should chime
When faith as mighty unto mortal ken
Would bring the marvel of a book sublime,
Bridging with lightful lore the shadowy gulf of time.

The favored son of that prophetic sire-
Favored because most faithful and most just—
Hath soared to sacred mysteries yet higher,
And to the elder scions tongued the trust.

Excerpts from Canto VII

The all-creating, all-controlling chain
Whereby the Gods perpetuate their reign,
Whereby the higher, bending, lift the lower,
Wielding the scepter of almighty power;
Stainless save mortal links their lustre stain,
And plunged through fire are purified again;
Behold them coming, coming as they came
Whene'er was kindled here the beacon blaze
By each Elias of the olden days!
A message marvelous to eyes and ears,
The Rythmic message of the songful spheres.
"Truth is eternal!"—Thus the solemn voice—
Twas not her birth made morning stars rejoice;
Nay, but her mission to a new-born sphere,
Whither, as oft, her shining bark would steer
With spirit crew, kin to the kingly race
Peopling the burning orbs of bourneless space.
Truth is eternal, endless as its God,
Author and Framer of the changeless code,
Ever-returning, oft-repeating plan,
Redeeming from all worlds the race of man.
Life-saving line, far flung from heaven to earth,
To rescue souls, God's wealth, supremest worth—
Rescue the fallen, and the penitent,
Who else must bide in hopeless banishment,
Unending were their mortal prisonment,
Did ne'er truth's sunlight gild the gloomy sod,
Gospel of mercy, gift of the gracious God.

Man a divinity in embryo,
Who, ere he reign above, must serve below;
His spirit in earth element baptize;
For birth and death are baptism to the wise.
The space that parts the lower from the higher,
Spaned by development of son to Sire,
Of daughter unto Mother's high estate;
Where man and woman are inseparate.

Time a probation; earth, through time, a school,
Where justice reigns, though oft the unjust rule.
Pain, trouble, toil, preceptors of the soul;
Death, birth, but portals to and from life's goal—
Life's fount, where earth an infant spirit sprang,
And sons of God in countless chorus sang,

Unheeding earthly sorrow—parent pang
Of after joy, o'er which their triumph rang.

Second estate here interlinked with first,
For godliness where spirit life was nurst,
And Satan's rebel host, heaven's third, were sent
To unentabernacled banishment,
Tempters, beguilers, triers of the true,
Who here reap greater gain, or sadly rue
The loss of all, surrendering to him,
Who warreth endlessly 'gainst Elohim,
And, shorn of glory, would all light bedim
Where many, wrecked, to awful depths go down,
While few return to wear the waiting crown,
Reigning where others serve.
Each woe, each bliss,
In after worlds, the yield of life in this;
Here garnered are the fruits from fields of yore'
And sown the harvest of the evermore
The called are not the chosen past mischance;
The sanctified to glorified advance
And stewardship becomes inheritance.
Redemption free, for God hath paid the price;
All else man wins by toil and sacrifice.

Twofold is death, but life hath threefold sway;
What ne'er created was must be alway;
The organized disorganized may be,
But not the life that lives undyingly.
Nothing bides nothing; that which is shall be;
Though form, not essence, change unceasingly.
Space, spirit, matter, all eternal are;
And death but on creation wages war.
What'er beginning had may have an end,
But life eternal doth itself defend.

Souls there above who once below all things
All things inherits and are priests and kings,
Pillars immovable, princes unto God,
No more outgoing, from that high abode,
Where past and future present are alway,
And years a thousand even as a day.

Nor this the tithe of what those tongues unfold,
Nor tithe of tithe of what can ne'er be told.
As unto Judah's one and Joseph's three

Who tasted of translation's ecstacy;
Or him who, spared from Babel's doom, beheld
Messiah's unclothed spirit, faith compelled;
Or him of Tarsus, tranced, **the triple seer
Of things unlawful to be uttered here—
As unto souls like these was given to see
The marvel past, the mystery to be,
So upon him, their peer of modern days,
The Source of all-revealing sends its rays.**

Broken the fountains of the upper deep;
Opened the sepulchers where ages sleep;
The past, the future, now the present leaven;
With truth from earth blends righteousness from heaven;
Welding the parted links of being's chains
Old making new, **the dead live again.**

Excerpts from Canto VIII

A pledge, a token, of millennial rest,
An earnest of the Commonweal to come;
But no fulfillment of the promise old,
No ripe fruition of the ancient oath,
To Enoch sworn, through Moses re-affirmed
By Ephraim's prophet made to live again.

But who art thou that lookest forth sublime,
A soul upsoaring as from sepulture,
Body and spirit pure and free from stain,
As gold and silver tried by seven-timed fire?

Speak! Art not thou the Woman Wonderful,
Summoned from out the silent Wilderness,
Arisen from the grave of centuries,
No more to be despoiled or trodden down?
A symbol of exalted sanctity,
The consecration of the contrite heart;
Of ancient types the modern complement,
Chief splendor of time's sparkling firmament,
Whose silver stars bespoke this sun of gold.

Excerpts from Canto IX

For last is first and old is new once more,

And nations rise where nations fell before!

Joseph, uprisen from the grave-like mound,
His ancient and inglorious battle ground,
Retreads with modern step the painful path
Where erst he fled, a fugitive from wrath;
Fated to flee till ebbs that westward flow,
Bearing from Japeth bitter curse and blow,
While patient heaven holds off the woeful fate
That cometh swift and layeth desolate
The powers that prey on Jacob—all that hate
The God of Joseph, and the just decree
That builds him here a boundless destiny.

Excerpts from Canto X

"Nor marvel at my mood. Could you but gaze
Upon the wonders of the worlds of God,
Where burn, amid the universal blaze,
The Fathers fullness and the Son's abode,
Won by their feet who walked the rightful road,
Nor weary in well-doing; 'twere alone
Reward for all that here hath been your load.
Forgive—leave all to heaven, whose highest Throne
Made endless love to endless life **the stepping stone**.

And there be living now who then shall live and see.
More would I tell that in my bosom burns,
But bigot fires would flame as ne'er before;
For truth, rejected, friend to traitor turns,
And damns where fain 'twould save. Six mounting o'er,
My spirit to a seventh realm did soar,
And saw and heard—ah, would that I might say!
Though memory but renewed a former lore,
What all may learn when full the dawning day,
When twinkling, twilight faith to knowledge shall give way.

Hope not till then to have my history,
What life hath scribed to scan. Nor tongue nor pen
Can tell the tale, dispel the mystery
That hides me from the dim, dull gaze of men.
Sojourning here, within this shadowed scene,
A medial stage, a mortal compromise,
The spirit's might, the body's weight, between,

Deem not that e'en earth's wisest can be wise,
Till heaven the blindness touch that seals all human eyes.

"One little fold I lift of that vast veil:
How came he God, to whom all gods must bow—
The very Sire, whom all the sons now hail
As mightiest of the mighty? I avow
That even He was once as we are now;
That we like him can be—yea, by degrees,
Mount unto loftiest heights, till on each brow
Be writ the name of names. Not angles these,
But Gods, e'en Sons of God, through all eternities.

Weighed in the balance here, nor wanting found;
Tried in the fire, triumphant from the test;
Though wrung their hearts, their finest feelings ground,
Betwixt life's upper, nether millstones prest,
Till proved, of good and brave, the bravest, best.
Less faith than theirs, who follow Abraham,
Honoring o'er all Jehovah's high behest,
Uplifts no gate of that Jerusalem—
The Bosom of the Gods—the Glory of I AM.

Appendix B

Excerpts from Sermons of Joseph Smith

Sermon Delivered on 14 May 1843

Sunday, 14.—Meeting at Yelrome, where I preached. [The following is a synopsis, reported by Elder Woodruff.]

Salvation through Knowledge

It is not wisdom that we should have all knowledge at once presented before us; but that we should have a little at a time; then we can comprehend it. President Smith then read the 2nd Epistle of Peter, 1st chapter, 16th to last verses, and dwelt upon the 19th verse with some remarks.

Add to your faith knowledge, &c. The principle of knowledge is the principle of salvation. This principle can be comprehended by the faithful and diligent; and **every one that does not obtain knowledge sufficient to be saved will be condemned. The principle of salvation is given us through the knowledge of Jesus Christ**.

Salvation is nothing more nor less than to triumph over all our enemies and put them under our feet. And when we have power to put all enemies under our feet in this world, and a knowledge to triumph over all evil spirits in the world to come, then we are saved, as in the case of Jesus, who was to reign until He had put all enemies under His feet, and the last enemy was death.

Perhaps there are principles here that few men have thought of. No person can have this salvation except through a tabernacle.

Now, in this world, mankind are naturally selfish, ambitious and striving to excel one above another; yet some are willing to build up others as well as themselves. **So in the other world there are a variety of spirits**. Some seek to excel. And this was the case with Lucifer when he fell. He sought for things which were unlawful.

Hence he was sent down, and it is said he drew many away with him; and the greatness of his punishment is that he shall not have a tabernacle. This is his punishment.

So the devil, thinking to thwart the decree of God, by going up and down in the earth, seeking whom he may destroy—any person that he can find that will yield to him, he will bind him, and take possession of the body and reign there, glorying in it mightily, not caring that he had got merely a stolen body; and by-and-by some one having authority will come along and cast him out and restore the tabernacle to its rightful owner.

The devil steals a tabernacle because he has not one of his own: but if he steals one, he is always liable to be turned out of doors.

Now, there is some grand secret here, and keys to unlock the subject. Notwithstanding the apostle exhorts them to add to their faith, virtue, knowledge, temperance, &c., yet he exhorts them to make their calling and election sure.

And though they had heard an audible voice from heaven bearing testimony that Jesus was the Son of God, yet he says we have a more sure word of prophecy, whereunto ye do well that ye take heed as unto a light shining in a dark place.

Now, wherein could they have a more sure word of prophecy than to hear the voice of God saying, This is my beloved Son, &c.

Now for the secret and grand key. Though they might hear the voice of God and know that Jesus was the Son of God, this would be no evidence that their election and calling was made sure, that they had part with Christ, and were joint heirs with Him. They then would want that more sure word of prophecy, that they were sealed in the heavens and had the promise of eternal life in the kingdom of God.

Then, having this promise sealed unto them, it was an anchor to the soul, sure and steadfast. Though the thunders might roll and lightnings flash, and earthquakes bellow, and war gather thick around, **yet this hope and knowledge would support the soul in every hour of trial, trouble and tribulation**.

Then knowledge through our Lord and Savior Jesus Christ is the grand key that unlocks the glories and mysteries of the kingdom of heaven.

Compare this principle once with Christendom at the present day, and where are they, with all their boasted religion, piety and sacredness while at the same time they are crying out against prophets, apostles, angels, revelations, prophesying and visions, &c. Why, they are just ripening for the damnation of hell.

They will be damned, for they reject the most glorious principle of the Gospel of Jesus Christ and treat with disdain and trample under foot the key that unlocks the heavens and puts in our possession the glories of the celestial world. Yes, I say, such will be damned, with all their professed godliness.

Then I would exhort you to go on and continue to call upon God until you make your calling and election sure for yourselves, by obtaining this more sure word of prophecy, and wait patiently for the promise until you obtain it, &c." (HC 5:387–389)

Sermon Delivered on 21 May 1843

I do not think there have been many good men on the earth since the days of Adam; but there was one good man and his name was Jesus. Many persons think a prophet must be a great deal better than anybody else. **Suppose I would condescend—yes, I will call it condescend, to be a great deal better than any of you, I would be raised up to the highest heaven; and who should I have to accompany me?** I love that man better who swears a stream as long as my arm yet deals justice to his neighbors and mercifully deals his substance to the poor, than the long, smooth-faced hypocrite. I do not want you to think that I am very righteous, for I am not. God judges men according to the use they make of the light which He gives them. 'We have a more sure word of prophecy, whereunto you do well to take heed, as unto a light that shineth in a dark place. We were eye witnesses of his majesty and heard the voice of his excellent glory.' And what could be more sure? When He was transfigured on the mount, what could be more sure to them? Divines have been quarreling for ages about the meaning of this.

The Prophet's Characterization of Himself

I am like a huge, rough stone rolling down from a high mountain; and the only polishing I get is when some corner gets rubbed off by coming in contact with something else, striking with accelerated force against religious bigotry, priestcraft, lawyer-craft, doctor-craft, lying editors, suborned judges and jurors, and the authority of perjured executives, backed by mobs, blasphemers, licentious and corrupt men and women—all hell knocking off a corner here and a corner there. Thus I will become a smooth and polished shaft in the quiver of the Almighty, who will give me dominion over all and every one of them, when their refuge of lies shall fail, and their hiding place shall be destroyed, while these smooth-polished stones with which I come in contact become marred. There are three grand secrets lying in this chapter [2 Peter 1] which no man can dig out, unless by the light of revelation, and which unlocks the whole chapter as the things that are written are only hints of things which existed in the prophet's mind, **which are not written concerning eternal glory.**

I am going to take up this subject by virtue of the knowledge of God in me, which I have received from heaven. The opinions of men, so far as I am concerned, are to me as the crackling of thorns under the pot, or the whistling of the wind. **I break the ground**; I lead the way like Columbus when he was invited to a banquet, where he was assigned the most honorable place at the table, and served with the ceremonials which were observed towards sovereigns. A shallow courtier present, who was meanly jealous of him, abruptly asked him whether he thought that in case he had not discovered the Indies, there were not other men in Spain who would have been capable of the enterprise? Columbus made no reply, but took an egg and invited the company to make it stand on end. They all attempted it, but in vain; whereupon he struck it upon the table so as to break one end, and left it standing on the broken part, illustrating that when he had once shown the way to the new world nothing was easier than to follow it.

Paul ascended into the third heavens, and he could understand the three principal rounds of Jacob's ladder—the telestial, the terrestrial, and the celestial glories or kingdoms, where Paul saw and heard things which were not lawful for him to utter. I could explain a hundred fold more than I ever have of the glories of the kingdoms manifested to me in the vision, were I permitted, and were the people prepared to receive them. The Lord deals with this people as a tender parent with a child, communicating light and intelligence and the knowledge of his ways as they can bear it. The inhabitants of the earth are asleep: they know not the day of their visitation. The Lord hath set the bow in the cloud for a sign that while it shall be seen, seed time and harvest, summer and winter shall not fail; but when it shall disappear, woe to that generation, for behold the end cometh quickly.

Calling and Election to Be Made Sure

Contend earnestly for the like precious faith with the Apostle Peter, 'and add to your faith virtue,' knowledge, temperance, patience, godliness, brotherly kindness, charity; 'for if these things be in you, and abound, they make you that ye shall neither be barren nor unfruitful in the knowledge of our Lord Jesus Christ.' Another point, after having all these qualifications, he lays this injunction upon the people 'to make your calling and election sure.' He is emphatic upon this subject—after adding all this virtue, knowledge, &c., 'Make your calling and election sure.' **What is the secret—the starting point? 'According as His divine power hath given unto us all things that pertain unto life and godliness.' How did he obtain all things? Through the knowledge of Him who hath called him. There could not anything be given, pertaining to life and godliness, without knowledge**. Woe! woe! woe to Christendom!—especially the divines and priests if this be true.

Salvation is for a man to be saved from all his enemies; **for until a man can triumph over death, he is not saved**. A knowledge of the priesthood alone will do this. The spirits in the eternal world are like the spirits in this world. When those have come into this world and received tabernacles, then died and again have risen and received glorified bodies, they will have an ascendency over the spirits who have received no bodies, or kept not their first estate, like the devil. The punishment of the devil was that he should not have a habitation like men. The devil's retaliation is, he comes into this world, binds up men's bodies, and occupies them himself. When the authorities come along, they eject him from a stolen habitation. **The design of the great God in sending us into this world, and organizing us to prepare us for the eternal worlds, I shall keep in my own bosom at present**. We have no claim in our eternal compact, in relation to eternal things, unless our actions and contracts and all things tend to this end. But after all this, you have got to make your calling and election sure. If this injunction would lie largely on those to whom it was spoken, how much more on those of the present generation!

1st key: Knowledge is the power of salvation. 2nd key: Make your calling and election sure. 3rd key: It is one thing to be on the mount and hear the excellent voice, &c., &c., and another to hear the voice declare to you, You have a part and lot in that kingdom." (HC 5:401–403. This synopsis was compiled by Willard Richards.)

Sermon Delivered on 11 June 1843

The following report is from the journals of Elders Willard Richards and Wilford Woodruff:

Sunday, 11.—Ten a.m., meeting at the stand.

The Prophet's Discourse—The Purpose of the Gathering of Israel

A large assembly of the Saints met at the Temple stand. Hymn by the choir. Prayer by Elder Parley P. Pratt, and singing.

President Joseph Smith remarked—'I am a rough stone. The sound of the hammer and chisel was never heard on me until the Lord took me in hand. **I desire the learning and wisdom of heaven alone**. I have not the least idea, if Christ should come to the earth and preach such rough things as He preached to the Jews, but that this generation would reject Him for being so rough.'

He then took for his text the 37th verse of 23rd chapter of Matthew—'O Jerusalem, Jerusalem, thou that killest the prophets and stonest them which are sent unto thee; how often would I have gathered thy children together, even as a hen gathereth her chickens under her wings, and ye would not.'

This subject was presented to me since I came to the stand. What was the object of gathering the Jews, or the people of God in any age of the world? I can never find much to say in expounding a text. **A man never has half so much fuss to unlock a door, if he has a key, as though he had not, and had to cut it open with his jack-knife**.

The main object was to build unto the Lord a house whereby He could reveal unto His people the ordinances of His house and the glories of His kingdom, and teach the people the way of salvation; for there are certain ordinances and principles that, when they are taught and practiced, must be done in a place or house built for that purpose.

It was the design of the councils of heaven before the world was, that the principles and laws of the priesthood should be predicated upon the gathering of the people in every age of the world. Jesus did everything to gather the people, and they would not be gathered, and He therefore poured out curses upon them. Ordinances instituted in the heavens before the foundation of the world, in the priesthood, for the salvation of men, are not to be altered or changed. **All must be saved on the same principles**.

It is for the same purpose that God gathers together His people in the last days, to build unto the Lord a house to prepare them for the ordinances and endowments, washings and anointings, etc. One of the ordinances of the house of the Lord is baptism for the dead. God decreed before the foundation of the world that that ordinance should be administered in a font prepared for that purpose in the house of the Lord. 'This is only your opinion, sir,' says the sectarian.

If a man gets a fullness of the priesthood of God, he has to get it in the same way that Jesus Christ obtained it, and that was by keeping all the commandments and obeying all the ordinances of the house of the Lord.

Where there is no change of priesthood, there is no change of ordinances, says Paul, if God has not changed the ordinances and the priesthood. Howl, ye sectarians! If he has, when and where has He revealed it? Have ye turned revelators? Then why deny revelation?

Many men will say, 'I will never forsake you, but will stand by you at all times.' But the moment you teach them some of the mysteries of the kingdom of God that are retained in the heavens and are to be revealed to the children of men when they are prepared for them, they will be the first to stone you and put you to death. It was this same principle that crucified the Lord Jesus Christ, and will cause the people to kill the prophets in this generation.

Many things are insoluble to the children of men in the last days: for instance, that God should raise the dead, and forgetting that <u>things have been hid from before the foundation of the world, which are to be revealed to babes in the last days</u>.

There are a great many wise men and women too in our midst who are too wise to be taught; therefore they must die in their ignorance, and in the resurrection they will find their mistake. Many seal up the door of heaven by saying, So far God may reveal and I will believe.

All men who become heirs of God and joint-heirs with Jesus Christ will have to receive the fullness of the ordinances of his kingdom; And those who will not receive all the ordinances will come short of the fullness of that glory, if they do not lose the whole.

I will say something about the spirits in prison. There has been much said by modern divines about the words of Jesus (when on the cross) to the thief, saying, 'This day shalt thou be with me in paradise.' King James' translators make it out to say paradise. But what is paradise? It is a modern word, it does not answer at all to the original word that Jesus made use of. Find the original of the word paradise. You may as easily find a needle in a haymow. Here is a chance for battle, ye learned men. There is nothing in the original word in Greek from which this was taken that signifies paradise; but it was—**This day thou shalt be with**

me in the world of spirits: then I will teach you all about it and answer your inquiries. And Peter says he went and preached to the world of spirits (spirits in prison, I Peter, 3rd chap., 19th verse), so that they who would receive it could have it answered by proxy by those who live on the earth, etc.

The doctrine of baptism for the dead is clearly shown in the New Testament; and if the doctrine is not good, then throw the New Testament away; but if it is the word of God, then let the doctrine be acknowledged; and it was the reason why Jesus said unto the Jews, 'How oft would I have gathered thy children together, even as a hen gathereth her chickens under her wings, and ye would not!'—that they might attend to the ordinances of baptism for the dead as well as other ordinances of the priesthood, and receive revelations from heaven, and be perfected in the things of the kingdom of God—but they would not. This was the case on the day of Pentecost: those blessings were poured out on the disciples on that occasion. God ordained that He would save the dead, and would do it by gathering His people together.

It always has been when a man was sent of God with the priesthood and he began to preach the fullness of the gospel, that he was thrust out by his friends, who are ready to butcher him if he teach things which they imagine to be wrong; and Jesus was crucified upon this principle.

I will now turn linguist. There are many things in the Bible which do not, as they now stand, accord with the revelations of the Holy Ghost to me.

I will criticize a little further. **There has been much said about the word hell**, and the sectarian world have preached much about it, describing it to be a burning lake of fire and brimstone. **But what is hell?** It is another modern term, and is taken from hades. I'll hunt after hades as Pat did for the woodchuck. Hades, the Greek, or Shaole, the Hebrew: these two significations mean a world of spirits. Hades, Shaole, paradise, spirits in prison, are all one: **it is a world of spirits**.

The righteous and the wicked all go to the same world of spirits until the resurrection. 'I do not think so,' says one. If you will go to my house any time, I will take my lexicon and prove it to you.

The great misery of departed spirits in the world of spirits, where they go after death is to know that they come short of the glory that others enjoy and that they might have enjoyed themselves, and they are their own accusers. 'But,' says one, 'I believe in one universal heaven and hell, where all go, and are all alike, and equally miserable or equally happy.'

What! where all are huddled together—the honorable, virtuous, and murderers, and whoremongers, when it is written that they shall be judged according to the deeds done in the body? But St. Paul informs us of three glories and three heavens. He knew a man that was caught up to the third heavens. Now, if the doctrine of the sectarian world, that there is but one heaven, is true, Paul, what do you tell that lie for, and say there are three? Jesus said unto His disciples, 'In my Father's house are many mansions, if it were not so, I would have told you. I go to prepare a place for you, and I will come and receive you to myself, that where I am ye may be also.'

Any man may believe that Jesus Christ is the Son of God, and be happy in that belief, and yet not obey his commandments, and at last be cut down for disobedience to the Lord's righteous requirements.

A man of God should be endowed with wisdom, knowledge, and understanding, in order to teach and lead the people of God. The sectarian priests are blind, and they lead the blind, and they will all fall into the ditch together. They build with hay, wood, and stubble, on the old revelations, without the true priesthood or spirit of revelation. **If I had time, I would dig into hell, hades, shaole, and tell what exists there**.

There is much said about God and the Godhead. The scriptures say there are Gods many and Lords many, but to us there is but one living and true God, and the heaven of heavens could not contain him; **for he took the liberty to go into other heavens**. The teachers of the day say that the Father is God, the Son is God, and the Holy Ghost is God, and they are all in one body and one God. Jesus prayed that those that the Father had given him out of the world might be made one in them, as they were one; [one in spirit, in mind, in purpose]. If I were to testify that the Christian world were wrong on this point, my testimony would be true.

Peter and Stephen testify that they saw the Son of Man standing on the right hand of God. Any person that had seen the heavens opened knows that there are three personages in the heavens who hold the keys of power, and one presides over all.

If any man attempts to refute what I am about to say, after I have made it plain, let him beware.

As the Father hath power in Himself, so hath the Son power in Himself, to lay down His life and take it again, so He has a body of His own. The Son doeth what He hath seen the Father do: then the Father hath some day laid down His life and taken it again; so He has a body of His own; each one will be in His own body; and yet the sectarian world believe the body of the Son is identical with the Father's.

Gods have an ascendancy over the angels, who are ministering servants. In the resurrection, **some are raised to be angels; others are raised to become Gods**.

These things are revealed in the most holy place in a Temple prepared for that purpose. Many of the sects cry out, 'Oh, I have the testimony of Jesus; I have the Spirit of God: but away with Joe Smith; he says he is a prophet; but there are to be no prophets or revelators in the last days.' Stop, sir: The Revelator says that the testimony of Jesus is the spirit of prophecy; so by your own month you are condemned. But to the text. Why gather the people together in this place? For the same purpose that

Jesus wanted to gather the Jews—to receive the ordinances, the blessings, and glories that God has in store for His Saints.

I will now ask this assembly and all the Saints if you will now build this house and receive the ordinances and blessings which God has in store for you; or will you not build unto the Lord this house, and let Him pass by and bestow these blessings upon another people? I pause for a reply." (HC 5:423-427)

James Adams Funeral Sermon Delivered on 9 Oct 1843

"All men know that they must die. And it is important that we should understand the reasons and causes of our exposure to the vicissitudes of life and of death, and the designs and purposes of God in our coming into the world, our sufferings here, and our departure hence. What is the object of our coming into existence, then dying and falling away, to be here no more? It is but reasonable to suppose that God would reveal something in reference to the matter, and it is a subject we ought to study more than any other. We ought to study it day and night, for the world is ignorant in reference to their true condition and relation. If we have any claim on our Heavenly Father for anything, it is for knowledge on this important subject. Could we read and comprehend all that has been written from the days of Adam, on the relation of man to God and angels in a future state, we should know very little about it. Reading the experience of others, or the revelation given to *them,* can never give *us* a comprehensive view of our condition and true relation to God. Knowledge of these things can only be obtained by experience through the ordinances of God set forth for that purpose. Could you gaze into heaven five minutes, you would know more than you would by reading all that ever was written on the subject.

We are only capable of comprehending that certain things exist, which we may acquire by certain fixed principles. If men would acquire salvation, they have got to be subject, before they leave this world, to certain rules and principles, which were fixed by an unalterable decree before the world was.

The disappointment of hopes and expectations at the resurrection would be indescribably dreadful.

The organization of the spiritual and heavenly worlds, and of spiritual and heavenly beings, was agreeable to the most perfect order and harmony: their limits and bounds were fixed irrevocably, and voluntarily subscribed to in their heavenly estate by themselves, and were by our first parents subscribed to upon the earth. **Hence the importance of embracing and subscribing to principles of eternal truth by all men upon the earth that expect eternal life**.

I assure the Saints that truth, in reference to these matters, can and may be known through the revelations of God in the way of His ordinances, and in answer to prayer. The Hebrew Church 'came unto the spirits of just men made perfect, and unto an innumerable company of angels, unto God the Father of all, and to Jesus Christ, the Mediator of the new covenant.' What did they learn by coming of the spirits of just men made perfect? Is it written? No. **What they learned has not been and could not have been written. What object was gained by this communication with the spirits of the just? It was the established order of the kingdom of God: the keys of power and knowledge were with them to communicate to the Saints**. Hence the importance of understanding the distinction between the spirits of the just and angels.

Spirits can only be revealed in flaming fire or glory. Angels have **advanced further**, their light and glory being tabernacled; and hence they appear in bodily shape. The spirits of just men are made ministering servants **to those who are sealed unto life eternal**, and it is through them that the sealing power comes down.

Patriarch Adams is now one of the spirits of the just men made perfect; and, if revealed now, must be revealed in fire; and the glory could not be endured. Jesus showed Himself to His disciples, and they thought it was His spirit, and they were afraid to approach His spirit. Angels have advanced higher in knowledge and power than spirits.

Concerning Brother James Adams, it should appear strange that so good and so great a man was hated. The deceased ought never to have had an enemy. But so it was. Wherever light shone, it stirred up darkness. Truth and error, good and evil cannot be reconciled. Judge Adams had some enemies, but such a man ought not to have had one. I saw him first at Springfield, when on my way from Missouri to Washington. He sought me out when a stranger, took me to his home, encouraged and cheered me, and gave me money. He has been a most intimate friend. I anointed him to the patriarchal power—to receive the keys of knowledge and power, by revelation to himself.

He has had revelations concerning his departure, and has gone to a more important work. **When men are prepared, they are better off to go hence**. Brother Adams has gone to open up a more effectual door for the dead. The spirits of the just are exalted to a greater and more glorious work; hence they are blessed in their departure to the world of spirits. Enveloped in flaming fire, they are not far from us, **and know and understand our thoughts, feelings, and motions, and are often pained therewith**.

Flesh and blood cannot go there; but flesh and bones, quickened by the Spirit of God, can.

If we would be sober and watch in fasting and prayer, God would turn away sickness from our midst.

Hasten the work in the Temple, renew your exertions to forward all the work of the last days, and walk before the Lord in soberness and righteousness. Let the Elders and Saints do away with lightmindedness, and be sober.

Such is a faint outline of the discourse of President Joseph Smith, which was delivered with his usual feeling and pathos, and was listened to with the most profound and eager attention by the multitude, who hung upon his instructions, **anxious to learn and pursue the path of eternal life**.

After singing by the choir, and prayer by the President, Conference adjourned *sine die,* with the benediction of the President." (HC 6:50–52)

King Follett Funeral Sermon Delivered on 7 April 1844

"Conference of the Church, April 1844 (Continued)—The King Follett Sermon—The Character of God—Religious Freedom—God an Exalted Man—Eternal Life to Know God and Jesus Christ—Everlasting Burnings—Meaning of the Hebrew Scriptures—A Council of the Gods —Meaning of the Word Create—The Immortal Intelligence—The Relation of Man to God—Our Greatest Responsibility—The Unpardonable Sin—The Forgiveness of Sin—The Second Death.

Sunday, April 7, 1844.—[Conference Report Continued.]

At quarter past three, P.M., the President having arrived, the choir sang a hymn, Elder Amasa Lyman offered prayer.

President Joseph Smith delivered the following discourse before about twenty thousand Saints, being the funeral sermon of Elder King Follett. Reported by Willard Richards, Wilford Woodruff, Thomas Bullock and William Clayton.

Beloved Saints: I will call [for] the attention of this congregation while I address you on the subject of the dead. The decease of our beloved brother, Elder King Follett, who was crushed in a well by the falling of a tub of rock, has more immediately led me to this subject. I have been requested to speak by his friends and relatives, but inasmuch as there are a great many in this congregation who live in this city as well as elsewhere, who have lost friends, I feel disposed to speak on the subject in general, and offer you my ideas, so far as I have ability, and so far as I shall be inspired by the Holy Spirit to dwell on this subject.

I want your prayers and faith that I may have the instruction of Almighty God and the gift of the Holy Ghost, so that I may set forth things that are true and which can be easily comprehended by you, and that the testimony may carry conviction to your hearts and minds of the truth of what I shall say. Pray that the Lord may strengthen my lungs, stay the winds, and let the prayers of the Saints to heaven appear, that they may enter into the ears of the Lord of Sabaoth, for the effectual prayers of the righteous avail much. There is strength here, and I verily believe that your prayers will be heard.

Before I enter fully into the investigation of the subject which is lying before me, I wish to pave the way and bring up the subject from the beginning, that you may understand it. I will make a few preliminaries, in order that you may understand the subject when I come to it. I do not calculate or intend to please your ears with superfluity of words or oratory, or with much learning; but I calculate [intend] to edify you with the simple truths from heaven.

The Character of God

In the first place, I wish to go back to the beginning—to the morn of creation. There is the starting point for us to look to, in order to understand and be fully acquainted with the mind, purposes and decrees of the Great Eloheim, who sits in yonder heavens as he did at the creation of the world. **It is necessary for us to have an understanding of God himself in the beginning. If we start right, it is easy to go right all the time; but if we start wrong we may go wrong, and it will be a hard matter to get right**.

There are but a very few beings in the world who understand rightly the character of God. The great majority of mankind do not comprehend anything, either that which is past, or that which is to come, as it respects their relationship to God. They do not know, neither do they understand the nature of that relationship; and consequently they know but little above the brute beast, or more than to eat, drink and sleep. This is all man knows about God or His existence, unless it is given by the inspiration of the Almighty.

If a man learns nothing more than to eat, drink and sleep, and does not comprehend any of the designs of God, the beast comprehends the same things. It eats, drinks, sleeps, and knows nothing more about God; yet it knows as much as we, unless we are able to comprehend by the inspiration of Almighty God. **If men do not comprehend the character of God, they do not comprehend themselves**. I want to go back to the beginning, and so lift your minds into more lofty spheres and a more exalted understanding than what the human mind generally aspires to.

I want to ask this congregation, every man, woman and child, to answer the question in their own hearts, what kind of a being God is? Ask yourselves; turn your thoughts into your hearts, and say if any of you have seen, heard, or communed with Him? This is a question that may occupy your attention for a long time. I again repeat the question—What kind of a being is God? Does any man or woman know?

Have any of you seen Him, heard Him, or communed with Him? Here is the question that will, peradventure, from this time henceforth occupy your attention. The scriptures inform us that 'This is life eternal that they might know thee, the only true God, and Jesus Christ whom thou hast sent.'

If any man does not know God, and inquires what kind of a being He is —if he will search diligently his own heart—**if the declaration of Jesus and the apostles be true, he will realize that he has not eternal life; for there can be eternal life on no other principle**. My first object is to find out the character of the only wise and true God, and what kind of a being He is; and if I am so fortunate as to be the man to comprehend God, and explain or convey the principles to your hearts, so that the

Spirit seals them upon you, then let every man and woman henceforth sit in silence, put their hands on their mouths, and never lift their hands or voices, or say anything against the man of God or the servants of God again.

But if I fail to do it, it becomes my duty to renounce all further pretensions to revelations and inspirations, or to be a prophet; and I should be like the rest of the world—a false teacher, be hailed as a friend, and no man would seek my life. But if all religious teachers were honest enough to renounce their pretensions to godliness when their ignorance of the knowledge of God is made manifest, they will all be as badly off as I am, at any rate; and you might just as well take the lives of other false teachers as that of mine.

If any man is authorized to take away my life because he thinks and says I am a false teacher, then, upon the same principle, we should be justified in taking away the life of every false teacher, and where would be the end of blood? And who would not be the sufferer?

The Privilege of Religious Freedom

But meddle not with any man for his religion: all governments ought to permit every man to enjoy his religion unmolested. No man is authorized to take away life in consequence of difference of religion, which all laws and governments ought to tolerate and protect, right or wrong. Every man has a natural, and, in our country, a constitutional right to be a false prophet, as well as a true prophet. If I show, verily, that I have the truth of God, and show that ninety-nine out of every hundred professing religious ministers are false teachers, having no authority, while they pretend to hold the keys of God's kingdom on earth, and was to kill them because they are false teachers, it would deluge the whole world with blood.

I will prove that the world is wrong, by showing what God is. I am going to inquire after God; for I want you all to know Him, and to be familiar with Him; and if I am bringing you to a knowledge of Him, all persecutions against me ought to cease. You will then know that I am His servant; for I speak as one having authority.

God—An Exalted Man

I will go back to the beginning before the world was, to show what kind of a being God is. What sort of a being was God in the beginning? Open your ears and hear, all ye ends of the earth, for **I am going to prove it to you by the Bible**, and to tell you the designs of God in relation to the human race, and why He interferes with the affairs of man.

God himself was once as we are now, and is an exalted man, and sits enthroned in yonder heavens! That is the great secret. If the veil were rent today, and the great God who holds this world in its orbit, and who upholds all worlds and all things by His power, was to make himself visible,—I say, if you were to see him today, you would see him like a man in form—like yourselves in all the person, image, and very form as a man; for Adam was created in the very fashion, image and likeness of God, and received instruction from, and walked, talked and conversed with Him, as one man talks and communes with another.

In order to understand the subject of the dead, for consolation of those who mourn for the loss of their friends, it is necessary we should understand the character and being of God and how He came to be so; for **I am going to tell you how God came to be God**. We have imagined and supposed that God was God from all eternity. I will refute that idea, and take away the veil, so that you may see.

These are incomprehensible ideas to some, but they are simple. It is the first principle of the gospel to know for a certainty the character of God, and to know that we may converse with Him as one man converses with another, **and that He was once a man like us; yea, that God himself, the Father of us all, dwelt on an earth, the same as Jesus Christ Himself did; and I will show it from the Bible**.

Eternal Life to Know God and Jesus Christ

I wish I was in a suitable place to tell it, and that I had the trump of an archangel, so that I could tell the story in such a manner that persecution would cease forever. What did Jesus say? (Mark it, Elder Rigdon!) The scriptures inform us that Jesus said, as the Father hath power in himself, even so hath the Son power—to do what? Why, what the Father did. The answer is obvious—in a manner to lay down his body and take it up again. Jesus, what are you going to do? To lay down my life as my Father did, and take it up again. Do you believe it? If you do not believe it you do not believe the Bible.

The scriptures say it, and I defy all the learning and wisdom and all the combined powers of earth and hell together to refute it. **Here, then, is eternal life—to know the only wise and true God; and you have got to learn how to be gods yourselves, and to be kings and priests to God, the same as all gods have done before you**, namely, by going from one small degree to another, and from a small capacity to a great one; <u>**from grace to grace**</u>, <u>**from exaltation to exaltation**</u>, <u>**until you attain to the resurrection of the dead**</u>, and are able to dwell in everlasting burnings, and to sit in glory, as do those who sit enthroned in everlasting power. And I want you to know that God, in the last days, while certain individuals are proclaiming His name, is not trifling with you or me.

The Righteous to Dwell in Everlasting Burnings

These are the first principles of consolation. How consoling to the mourners when they are called to part with a husband, wife, father, mother, child, or dear relative, to know that, although the earthly tabernacle is laid down and dissolved, they shall rise again to dwell in everlasting burnings in immortal glory, not to sorrow, suffer, or die any more, but they shall be heirs of God and joint heirs with Jesus Christ. What is it? To inherit the same power, the same glory and the same exaltation, **until you arrive at the station of a god**, and ascend the throne of eternal power, **the same as those who have gone before. What did Jesus do? Why, I do the things I saw my Father do when worlds came rolling into existence.**

My Father worked out His kingdom with fear and trembling, and I must do the same; and when I get my kingdom, I shall present it to My Father, so that He may obtain kingdom upon kingdom, and it will exalt Him in glory.

He will then take a higher exaltation, and I will take His place, and thereby become exalted myself. So that Jesus treads in the tracks of His Father, and inherits what God did before; and God is thus glorified and exalted in the salvation and exaltation of all His children. It is plain beyond disputation, and you thus learn some of the first principles of the gospel, about which so much hath been said.

When you climb up a ladder, you must begin at the bottom, and ascend step by step, until you arrive at the top; and so it is with the principles of the gospel—you must begin with the first, and go on until you learn all the principles of exaltation. But it will be a great while after you have passed through the veil before you will have learned them. It is not all to be comprehended in this world; it will be a great work to learn our salvation and exaltation even beyond the grave. I suppose I am not allowed to go into an investigation of anything that is not contained in the Bible. If I do, I think there are so many over-wise men here that they would cry 'treason' and put me to death. So I will go to the old Bible and turn commentator today.

I shall comment on the very first Hebrew word in the Bible; I will make a comment on the very first sentence of the history of creation in the Bible—*Berosheit*. I want to analyze the word. *Baith*—in, by, through, and everything else. *Roch*—the head, *Sheit*—grammatical termination. When the inspired man wrote it, he did not put the baith there. An old Jew without any authority added the word; he thought it too bad to begin to talk about the head! It read first, 'The head one of the Gods brought forth the Gods.' That is the true meaning of the words. *Baurau* signifies to bring forth. If you do not believe it, you do not believe the learned man of God. Learned men can teach you no more than what I have told you. **Thus the head God brought forth the Gods in the grand council**.

I will transpose and simplify it in the English language. Oh, ye lawyers, ye doctors, and ye priests, who have persecuted me, I want to let you know that the Holy Ghost knows something as well as you do. The head God called together the Gods and sat in grand council to bring forth the world. The grand councilors sat at the head in yonder heavens and contemplated the creation of the worlds which were created at the time. When I say doctors and lawyers, I mean the doctors and lawyers of the scriptures. I have done so hitherto without explanation, to let the lawyers flutter and everybody laugh at them. Some learned doctors might take a notion to say the scriptures say thus and so; and we must believe the scriptures; they are not to be altered. But I am going to show you an error in them.

I have an old edition of the New Testament in the Latin, Hebrew, German and Greek languages. I have been reading the German, and find it to be the most [nearly] correct translation, and to correspond nearest to the revelations which God has given to me for the last fourteen years. It tells about Jacobus, the son of Zebedee. It means Jacob.

In the English New Testament it is translated James. Now, if Jacob had the keys, you might talk about James through all eternity and never get the keys. In the 21st. of the fourth chapter of Matthew, my old German edition gives the word Jacob instead of James.

The doctors (I mean doctors of law, not physic) say, 'If you preach anything not according to the Bible, we will cry treason.' How can we escape the damnation of hell, except God be with us and reveal to us? Men bind us with chains. The Latin says Jacobus, which means Jacob; the Hebrew says Jacob, the Greek says Jacob and the German says Jacob, here we have the testimony of four against one.

I thank God that I have got this old book; but I thank him more for the gift of the Holy Ghost. I have got the oldest book in the world; but I have got the oldest book in my heart, even the gift of the Holy Ghost. I have all the four Testaments. Come here, ye learned men, and read, if you can. I should not have introduced this testimony, were it not to back up the word *rosh*—the head, the Father of the Gods. I should not have brought it up, only to show that I am right.

A Council of the Gods

In the beginning, the head of the Gods called a council of the Gods; and they came together and concocted [prepared] a plan to create the world and people it. When we begin to learn this way, we begin to learn the only true God, and what kind of a being we have got to worship. Having a knowledge of God, we begin to know how to approach Him, and how to ask so as to receive an answer.

When we understand the character of God, and know how to come to Him, he begins to unfold the heavens to us, and to tell us all about it. When we are ready to come to him, he is ready to come to us.

Now, I ask all who hear me, why the learned men who are preaching salvation, say that God created the heavens and the earth out of nothing? The reason is, that they are unlearned in the things of God, and have not the gift of the Holy Ghost; they account it blasphemy in any one to contradict their idea. If you tell them that God made the world out of something, they will call you a fool. But I am learned, and know more than all the world put together. The Holy Ghost does, anyhow, and he is within me, and comprehends more than all the world; and I will associate myself with him.

Appendix B—Excerpts from Joseph Smith's Sermons

Meaning of the Word Create

You ask the learned doctors why they say the world was made out of nothing, and they will answer, 'Doesn't the Bible say He *created* the world?' And they infer, from the word create, that it must have been made out of nothing. Now, the word create came from the word *baurau*, which does not mean to create out of nothing; it means to organize; the same as a man would organize materials and build a ship.

Hence we infer that God had materials to organize the world out of chaos—chaotic matter, which is element, and in which dwells all the glory. Element had an existence from the time He had. The pure principles of element are principles which can never be destroyed; they may be organized and re-organized, but not destroyed. They had no beginning and can have no end.

The Immortal Intelligence

I have another subject to dwell upon, which is calculated to exalt man; **but it is impossible for me to say much on this subject. I shall therefore just touch upon it, for time will not permit me to say all. It is associated with the subject of the resurrection of the dead—namely, the soul—the mind of man—the immortal spirit**. Where did it come from? All learned men and doctors of divinity say that God created it in the beginning; but it is not so: the very idea lessens man in my estimation. I do not believe the doctrine;

I know better. Hear it, all ye ends of the world; **for God has told me so**; and if you don't believe me, it will not make the truth without effect. I will make a man appear a fool before I get through; if he does not believe it. **I am going to tell of things more noble**.

We say that God Himself is a self-existing being. Who told you so? It is correct enough; but how did it get into your heads? Who told you that man did not exist in like manner upon the same principles? Man does exist upon the same principles. God made a tabernacle and put a spirit into it, and it became a living soul. (Refers to the Bible.) How does it read in the Hebrew? It does not say in the Hebrew that God created the spirit of man. It says, 'God made man out of the earth and put into him Adam's spirit, and so became a living body.'

The mind or the intelligence which man possesses is co-equal [co-eternal] with God himself. I know that my testimony is true; hence, when I talk to these mourners, what have they lost? Their relatives and friends are only separated from their bodies for a short season: their spirits which existed with God **have left the tabernacle of clay only for a little moment**, as it were; and they now exist in a place where they converse together the same as we do on the earth,

I am dwelling on the immortality of the spirit of man. Is it logical to say that the intelligence of spirits is immortal, and yet that it has a beginning? The intelligence of spirits had no beginning, neither will it have an end. That is good logic. That which has a beginning may have an end. There never was a time when there were not spirits; for they are co-equal [co-eternal] with our Father in heaven.

I want to reason more on the spirit of man; for I am dwelling on the body and spirit of man—on the subject of the dead. I take my ring from my finger and liken it unto the mind of man—the immortal part, because it had no beginning. Suppose you cut it in two; then it has a beginning and an end; but join it again, and it continues one eternal round. So with the spirit of man. As the Lord liveth, if it had a beginning, it will have an end.

All the fools and learned and wise men from the beginning of creation, who say that the spirit of man had a beginning, prove that it must have an end; and if that doctrine is true, then the doctrine of annihilation would be true. But if I am right, I might with boldness proclaim from the house-tops that God never had the power to create the spirit of man at all. God himself could not create himself.

Intelligence is eternal and exists upon a self-existent principle. It is a spirit from age to age and there is no creation about it. All the minds and spirits that God ever sent into the world are susceptible of enlargement.

The first principles of man are self-existent with God. God himself, finding he was in the midst of spirits and glory, because he was more intelligent, saw proper to institute laws whereby the rest could have a privilege to advance like himself. The relationship we have with God places us in a situation to advance in knowledge. He has power to institute laws to instruct the weaker intelligences, that they may be exalted with Himself, so that they might have one glory upon another, and all that knowledge, power, glory, and intelligence, which is requisite in order to save them in the world of spirits.

This is good doctrine. It tastes good. I can taste the principles of eternal life, and so can you. They are given to me by the revelations of Jesus Christ; and I know that when I tell you these words of eternal life as they are given to me, you taste them, and I know that you believe them. You say honey is sweet, and so do I. I can also taste the spirit of eternal life. I know that it is good; and when I tell you of these things which were given me by inspiration of the Holy Spirit, you are bound to receive them as sweet, and rejoice more and more.

The Relation of Man to God

I want to talk more of the relation of man to God. I will open your eyes in relation to the dead. All things whatsoever God in his infinite wisdom has seen fit and proper to reveal to us, while we are dwelling in mortality, in regard to our mortal bodies, are revealed to us in the abstract, and independent of affinity of this mortal tabernacle, but are revealed to our spirits precisely as though we had no bodies at all; and **those revelations which will save our spirits will save our bodies.** God reveals them to us in view of no eternal dissolution of the body, or tabernacle.

Hence the responsibility, the awful responsibility, that rests upon us in relation to our dead; for all the spirits who have not obeyed the Gospel in the flesh must either obey it in the spirit or be damned. Solemn thought!—dreadful thought! Is there nothing to be done?—no preparation—no salvation for our fathers and friends who have died without having had the opportunity to obey the decrees of the Son of Man? **Would to God that I had forty days and nights in which to tell you all!** I would let you know that I am not a 'fallen prophet.'

Our Greatest Responsibility

What promises are made in relation to the subject of the salvation of the dead? and what kind of characters are those who can be saved, although their bodies are moldering and decaying in the grave? When His commandments teach us, it is in view of eternity; for we are looked upon by God as though we were in eternity; God dwells in eternity, and does not view things as we do.

The greatest responsibility in this world that God has laid upon us is to seek after our dead. The apostle says, 'They without us cannot be made perfect'; for it is necessary that the sealing power should be in our hands to seal our children and our dead for the fulness of the dispensation of times—a dispensation to meet the promises made by Jesus Christ before the foundation of the world for the salvation of man.

Now, I will speak of them. I will meet Paul half way. I say to you, Paul, you cannot be perfect without us. It is necessary that those who are going before and those who come after us should have salvation in common with us; and thus hath God made it obligatory upon man. Hence, God said, 'I will send you Elijah the prophet before the coming of the great and dreadful day of the Lord: he shall turn the heart of the fathers to the children, and the heart of the children to their fathers, lest I come and smite the earth with a curse.'

The Unpardonable Sin

I have a declaration to make as to the provisions which God hath made to suit the conditions of man—made from before the foundation of the world. What has Jesus said? All sins, and all blasphemies, and every transgression, except one, that man can be guilty of, may be forgiven; and there is a salvation for all men, either in this world or the world to come, who have not committed the unpardonable sin, there being a provision either in this world or the world of spirits.

Hence **God hath made a provision that every spirit in the eternal world can be ferreted out and saved unless he has committed that unpardonable sin** which cannot be remitted to him either in this world or the world of spirits. **God has wrought out a salvation for all men, unless they have committed a certain sin**; and every man who has a friend in the eternal world can save him, unless he has committed the unpardonable sin. And so you can see how far you can be a savior.

A man cannot commit the unpardonable sin after the dissolution of the body, and there is a way possible for escape. Knowledge saves a man; and in the world of spirits no man can be exalted but by knowledge. So long as a man will not give heed to the commandments, he must abide without salvation. If a man has knowledge, he can be saved; although, if he has been guilty of great sins, he will be punished for them. **But when he consents to obey the gospel, whether here or in the world of spirits, he is saved**.

A man is his own tormentor and his own condemner. Hence the saying, They shall go into the lake that burns with fire and brimstone. The torment of disappointment in the mind of man is as exquisite as a lake burning with fire and brimstone. I say, so is the torment of man.

I know the scriptures and understand them. I said, no man can commit the unpardonable sin after the dissolution of the body, nor in this life, until he receives the Holy Ghost; **but they must do it in this world**. Hence the salvation of Jesus Christ was wrought out for all men, in order to triumph over the devil; for if it did not catch him in one place, it would in another; for he stood up as a Savior. All will suffer until they obey Christ himself.

The contention in heaven was—Jesus said there would be certain souls that would not be saved; and the devil said he would save them all, and laid his plans before the grand council, who gave their vote in favor of Jesus Christ. So the devil rose up in rebellion against God, and was cast down, with all who put up their heads for him. (Moses 4:1–4; Abraham 3:23–28).

The Forgiveness of Sins

All sins shall be forgiven, except the sin against the Holy Ghost; for **Jesus will save all except the sons of perdition**. What must a man do to commit the unpardonable sin? He must receive the Holy Ghost, have the heavens opened unto him, and know God, and then sin against him. After a man has sinned against the Holy Ghost, there is no repentance for him. He has got to say that the sun does not shine while he sees it; he has got to deny Jesus Christ when the heavens have been opened unto him, and to deny the plan of salvation with his eyes open to the truth of it; and from that time he begins to be an enemy. This is the case with many apostates of the Church of Jesus Christ of Latter-day Saints.

When a man begins to be an enemy to this work, he hunts me, he seeks to kill me, and never ceases to thirst for my blood. He gets the spirit of the devil—the same spirit that they had who crucified the Lord of Life —the same spirit that sins against the Holy Ghost.

You cannot save such persons; you cannot bring them to repentance; they make open war, like the devil, and awful is the consequence.

I advise all of you to be careful what you do, or you may by-and-by find out that you have been deceived. Stay yourselves; do not give way; don't make any hasty moves, you may be saved. If a spirit of bitterness is in you, don't be in haste. You may say, that man is a sinner. Well, if he repents, he shall be forgiven. Be cautious: await. When you find a spirit that wants bloodshed or murder, the same is not of God, but is of the devil. Out of the abundance of the heart of man the mouth speaketh.

The best men bring forth the best works. The man who tells you words of life is the man who can save you. I warn you against all evil characters who sin against the Holy Ghost; for there is no redemption for them in this world nor in the world to come.

I could go back and trace every object of interest concerning the relationship of man to God, if I had time. I can enter into the mysteries; I can enter largely into the eternal worlds; for Jesus said, 'In my Father's house are many mansions; if it were not so, I would have told you. I go to prepare a place for you.' (John 14:2). Paul says, 'There is one glory of the sun, and another glory of the moon, and another glory of the stars; for one star differeth from another star in glory. So also is the resurrection of the dead.' (1 Corinthians 15:41). What have we to console us in relation to the dead?

We have reason to have the greatest hope and consolation for our dead of any people on the earth; for we have seen them walk worthily in our midst, and seen them sink asleep in the arms of Jesus; and **those who have died in the faith are now in the celestial kingdom of God.** And hence is the glory of the sun.

You mourners have occasion to rejoice, speaking of the death of Elder King Follett; for your husband and father is gone to wait until the resurrection of the dead—until the perfection of the remainder; for at the resurrection your friend will rise in perfect felicity and go to celestial glory, while many must wait myriads of years before they can receive the like blessings; and your expectations and hopes are far above what man can conceive; for why has God revealed it to us?

I am authorized to say, by the authority of the Holy Ghost, that you have no occasion to fear; for he is gone to the home of the just. Don't mourn, don't weep. I know it by the testimony of the Holy Ghost that is within me; and you may wait for your friends to come forth to meet you in the morn of the celestial world. Rejoice, O Israel! Your friends who have been murdered for the truth's sake in the persecutions shall triumph gloriously in the celestial world, while their murderers shall welter for ages in torment, even until they shall have paid the uttermost farthing. I say this for the benefit of strangers. I have a father, brothers, children, and friends who have gone to a world of spirits. They are only absent for a moment. They are in the spirit, and we shall soon meet again. The time will soon arrive when the trumpet shall sound. When we depart, we shall hail our mothers, fathers, friends, and all whom we love, who have fallen asleep in Jesus. There will be no fear of mobs, persecutions, or malicious lawsuits and arrests; but it will be an eternity of felicity.

A question may be asked—'Will mothers have their children in eternity?' Yes! Yes! Mothers, you shall have your children; for they shall have eternal life, for their debt is paid. There is no damnation awaiting them for they are in the spirit. But as the child dies, so shall it rise from the dead, and be forever living in the learning of God. It will never grow [in the grave]; it will still be the child, in the same precise form [when it rises] as it appeared before it died out of its mother's arms, but possessing all the intelligence of a God. Children dwell in the mansions of glory and exercise power, but appear in the same form as when on earth. Eternity is full of thrones, upon which dwell thousands of children, reigning on thrones of glory, with not one cubit added to their stature.

I will leave this subject here, and make a few remarks on the subject of baptism. The baptism of water, without the baptism of fire and the Holy Ghost attending it, is of no use; they are necessarily inseparably connected. An individual must be born of water and the spirit in order to get into the kingdom of God. In the German, the text bears me out the same as the revelations which I have given and taught for the past fourteen years on that subject. I have the testimony to put in their teeth. My testimony has been true all the time. You will find it in the declaration of John the Baptist. (Reads from the German.) John says, 'I baptize you with water, but when Jesus comes, who has the power (or keys) He shall administer the baptism of fire and the Holy Ghost.' Great God! Where is now all the sectarian world? And if this testimony is true, they are all damned as clearly as anathema can do it. I know the text is true. I call upon all you Germans who know that it is true to say, Eye. (Loud shouts of 'Aye.')

Alexander Campbell, how are you going to save people with water alone? For John said his baptism was good for nothing without the baptism of Jesus Christ. 'Therefore, *not* leaving the principles of the doctrine of Christ, let us go on unto perfection; not laying again the foundation of repentance from dead works, and of faith towards God, of the doctrine of baptism, and of laying on of hands, and of resurrection of the dead, and of eternal judgment. And this will we do, if God permit.' (Hebrews 6:1–3)

There is one God, one Father, one Jesus, one hope of our calling, one baptism. All these three baptisms only make one. Many talk of baptism not being essential to salvation; but this kind of teaching would lay the foundation of their damnation. I have the truth, and am at the defiance of the world to contradict me, if they can. I have now preached a little Latin, a little Hebrew, Greek, and German; and I have fulfilled all. I am not so big a fool as many have taken me to be. The Germans know that I read the German correctly.

The Second Death

Hear it, all ye ends of the earth—all ye priests, all ye sinners, and all men. Repent! Repent! Obey the gospel. Turn to God; for your religion won't save you, and you will be damned. I do not say how long.

There have been remarks made concerning all men being redeemed from hell; but I say that those who sin against the Holy Ghost cannot be forgiven in this world or in the world to come; they shall die the second death. Those who commit the unpardonable sin are doomed to *Gnaolom*—to dwell in hell, worlds without end. As they concocted scenes of bloodshed in this world, so they shall rise to that resurrection which is as the lake of fire and brimstone. Some shall rise to the everlasting burnings of God; for God dwells in everlasting burnings and some shall rise to the damnation of their own filthiness, which is as exquisite a torment as the lake of fire and brimstone.

I have intended my remarks for all, both rich and poor, bond and free, great and small. I have no enmity against any man. I love you all; but I hate some of your deeds. I am your best friend, and if persons miss their mark it is their own fault. If I reprove a man, and he hates me, he is a fool; for I love all men, especially these my brethren and sisters.

I rejoice in hearing the testimony of my aged friends. **You don't know me; you never knew my heart. No man knows my history. I cannot tell it: I shall never undertake it.** I don't blame anyone for not believing my history. If I had not experienced what I have, I would not have believed it myself. I never did harm any man since I was born in the world. My voice is always for peace. I cannot lie down until all my work is finished. I never think any evil, nor do anything to the harm of my fellow-man. When I am called by the trump of the archangel and weighed in the balance, you will all know me then. I add no more. God bless you all. Amen." (HC 6:302–317)

Plurality of Gods Sermon Delivered on 16 June 1844

"Sunday, June 16, 1844—I preached at the stand at 10 A.M. Before I closed my remarks it rained severely. The following synopsis was reported by Elder Thomas Bullock, whom I had transferred from the duties of clerk of the *Maid of Iowa* to my office.

Sermon by the Prophet—The Christian Godhead—Plurality of Gods.

Meeting in the Grove, east of the Temple, June 16, 1844.

Prayer by Bishop Newel K. Whitney.

Choir sang, 'Mortals Awake.'

President Joseph Smith read the 3rd chapter of Revelation, and took for his text 1st chapter, 6th verse—'And hath made us kings and priests unto God and His Father: to Him be glory and dominion forever and ever. Amen.'

It is altogether correct in the translation. Now, you know that of late some malicious and corrupt men have sprung up and apostatized from the Church of Jesus Christ of Latter-day Saints, and they declare that the Prophet believes in a plurality of Gods, and, lo and behold! We have discovered a very great secret, they cry, 'The Prophet says there are many Gods, and this proves that he has fallen.'

It has been my intention for a long time to take up this subject and lay it clearly before the people, and show what my faith is in relation to this interesting matter. **I have contemplated the saying of Jesus** (Luke 17th chapter, 26th verse)—'**And as it was in the days of Noah, so shall it be also in the days of the Son of Man.**' And if it does rain, I'll preach this doctrine, for the truth shall be preached.

I will preach on the plurality of Gods. I have selected this text for that express purpose. I wish to declare I have always and in all congregations **when I have preached on the subject of the Deity, it has been the plurality of Gods**. It has been preached by the Elders for fifteen years.

I have always declared God to be a distinct personage, Jesus Christ a separate and distinct personage from God the Father, and that the Holy Ghost was a distinct personage and a Spirit, and these three constitute three distinct personages and three Gods. If this is in accordance with the New Testament, lo and behold! We have three Gods anyhow, and they are plural: and who can contradict it?

Our text says 'And hath made us kings and priests unto God and His Father.' **The Apostles have discovered that there were Gods above**, for Paul says God was the Father of our Lord Jesus Christ.

My object was to preach the scriptures, and preach the doctrine they contain, there being a God above, the Father of our Lord Jesus Christ. I am bold to declare I have taught all the strong doctrines publicly, and always teach stronger doctrines in public than in private.

John was one of the men, and apostles declare they were made kings and priests unto God, the Father of our Lord Jesus Christ. It reads just so in the Revelation. Hence, the doctrine of a plurality of Gods is as prominent in the Bible as any other doctrine. It is all over the face of the Bible. It stands beyond the power of controversy. A wayfaring man, though a fool, need not err therein.

Paul says there are Gods many and Lords many. I want to set it forth in a plain and simple manner; **but to us there is but one God—that is *pertaining to us*;** and he is in all and through all. But if Joseph Smith says there are Gods many and Lords many, they cry, 'Away with him! Crucify him! crucify him!'

Mankind verily say that the scriptures are with them. **Search the scriptures, for they testify of things that these apostates would gravely pronounce blasphemy**. Paul, if Joseph Smith is a blasphemer, you are. I say there are Gods many and Lords many, **but to us only one**, and we are to be in subjection to that one, and no man can limit the bounds or the eternal existence of eternal time. Hath he beheld the eternal world, and is he authorized to say that there is only one God? He makes himself a fool if he thinks or says so, and there is an end of his career or progress in knowledge. He cannot obtain all knowledge, for he has sealed up the gate to it.

Some say I do not interpret the scripture the same as they do. They say it means the heathen's gods. Paul says there are Gods many and Lords many; and that makes a plurality of Gods, in spite of the whims of all men. **Without a revelation, I am not going to give them the knowledge of the God of heaven**. You know and I testify that Paul had no allusion to the heathen gods. I have it from God, and get over it if you can. **I have a witness of the Holy Ghost**, and a testimony that Paul had no allusion to the heathen gods in the text. I will show from the Hebrew Bible that I am correct, and the first word shows a plurality of Gods; and I want the apostates and learned men to come here and prove to the contrary, if they can. An unlearned boy must give you a little Hebrew. *Berosheit baurau Eloheim ait aushamayeen vehau auraits*, rendered by King James' translators, 'In the beginning God created the heaven and the earth.' I want to analyze the word *Berosheit. Rosh,* the head; *Sheit,* a grammatical termination, The *Baith* was not originally put there when the inspired man wrote it, but it has been since added by an old Jew. *Baurau* signifies to bring forth; *Eloheim* is from the word *Eloi,* God, in the singular number; and **by adding the word *heim,* it renders it Gods**. It read first, 'In the beginning the head of the Gods brought forth the Gods,' or, as others have translated it, '**The head of the Gods called the Gods together**.' I want to show a little learning as well as other fools—

> A little learning is a dangerous thing.
> Drink deep, or taste not the Pierian spring.
> There shallow draughts intoxicate the brain,
> And drinking largely sobers us up again.

All this confusion among professed translators is for want of drinking another draught.

The head God organized the heavens and the earth. I defy all the world to refute me. In the beginning the heads of the Gods organized the heavens and the earth. Now the learned priests and the people rage, and the heathen imagine a vain thing. If we pursue the Hebrew text further, it reads, *'Berosheit baurau Eloheim ait aashamayeen vehau auraits'—*

'**The head one of the Gods said**. Let us make a man in our own image.' I once asked a learned Jew, 'If the Hebrew language compels us to render all words ending in *-heim* in the plural, why not render the first *Eloheim* plural?' He replied, 'That is the rule with few exceptions; but in this case it would ruin the Bible.' He acknowledged I was right. I came here to investigate these things precisely as I believe them. Hear and judge for yourselves; and if you go away satisfied, well and good.

In the very beginning the Bible shows there is a plurality of Gods beyond the power of refutation. It is a great subject I am dwelling on. The word *Eloheim* ought to be in the plural all the way through—Gods. The heads of the Gods appointed one God for us; and when you take [that] view of the subject, it sets one free to see all the beauty, holiness and perfection of the Gods. All I want is to get the simple, naked truth, and the whole truth.

Many men say there is one God; the Father, the Son and the Holy Ghost are only one God! I say that is a strange God anyhow—three in one, and one in three! It is a curious organization. 'Father, I pray not for the world, but I pray for them which thou hast given me.' 'Holy Father, keep through Thine own name those whom thou hast given me, that they may be one as we are.' All are to be crammed into one God, according to sectarianism. It would make the biggest God in all the world. He would be a wonderfully big God—he would be a giant or a monster. I want to read the text to you myself—'I am agreed with the Father and the Father is agreed with me, and we are agreed as one.' The Greek shows that it should be agreed.

'Father, I pray for them which Thou hast given me out of the world, and not for those alone, but for them also which shall believe on me through their word, that they all may be agreed, as Thou, Father, art with me, and I with Thee, that they also may be agreed with us,' and all come to dwell in unity, and in all the glory and everlasting burnings of the Gods; and then we shall see as we are seen, and be as our God and He as His Father. I want to reason a little on this subject. I learned it by translating the papyrus which is now in my house. I learned a testimony concerning Abraham, and he reasoned concerning the God of heaven. 'In order to do that,' said he, 'suppose we have two facts: that supposes another fact may exist—two men on the earth, one wiser than the other, would logically show that another who is wiser than the wisest may exist. Intelligences exist one above another, so that there is no end to them.'

If Abraham reasoned thus—If Jesus Christ was the Son of God, and John discovered that God the Father of Jesus Christ had a Father, you may suppose that He had a Father also. Where was there ever a son without a father? And where was there ever a father without first being a son? Whenever did a tree or anything spring into existence without a progenitor? And everything comes in this way. Paul says that which is earthly is in the likeness of that which is heavenly, Hence if Jesus had a Father, can we not believe that *He* had a Father also? I despise the idea of being scared to death at such a doctrine, for the Bible is full of it.

I want you to pay particular attention to what I am saying. Jesus said that the Father wrought precisely in the same way as His Father had done before Him. **As the Father had done before. He laid down His life, and took it up the same as His Father had done before**. He did as He was sent, to lay down His life and take it up **again**; and then was committed unto Him the keys, &c. **I know it is good reasoning**.

I have reason to think that the Church is being purged. I saw Satan fall from heaven, and the way they ran was a caution. All these are wonders and marvels in our eyes in these last days. So long as men are under the law of God, they have no fears—they do not scare themselves.

I want to stick to my text, to show that when men open their lips against these truths they do not injure me, but injure themselves. To the law and to the testimony, for these principles are poured out all over the scriptures. When **things that are of the greatest importance are passed over by weak-minded men without even a thought**, I want to see truth in all its bearings and hug it to my bosom. I believe all that

God ever revealed, and **I never hear of a man being damned for believing too much; but they are damned for unbelief.**

They found fault with Jesus Christ because He said He was the Son of God, and made Himself equal with God. They say of me, like they did of the apostles of old, that I must be put down. What did Jesus say? 'Is it not written in your law, I said, **Ye are Gods? If He called them Gods** unto whom the word of God came, and the scriptures cannot be broken, say ye of Him whom the Father had sanctified and sent into the world, Thou blasphemest, because I said I am the Son of God?'

It was through Him that they drank of the spiritual rock. Of course He would take the honor to Himself. Jesus, **if they were called Gods unto whom the word of God came**, why should it be thought blasphemy that I should say I am the son of God?

Oh, poor, blind apostates! Did you never think of this before? These are the quotations that the apostates take from the scriptures. They swear that they believe the Bible, the Book of Mormon and the Doctrine and Covenants and then you will get from them filth, slander, and bogus-makers plenty. One of the apostate Church official members prophesied that Joseph would never preach any more, and yet I am now preaching.

Go and read the vision in the Book of Covenants. There is clearly illustrated glory upon glory—one glory of the sun, another glory of the moon, and a glory of the stars; and as one star differeth from another star in glory, even so do they of the telestial world differ in glory, and **every man who reigns in celestial glory is a God to his dominions**. By the apostates admitting the testimony of the Doctrine and Covenants, they damn themselves. Paul, what do you say? They impeached Paul and all went and left him. Paul had seven churches, and they drove him off from among them; and yet they cannot do it by me. I rejoice in that. My testimony is good.

Paul says, 'There is one glory of the sun, and another glory of the moon, and another glory of the stars; for one star differeth from another star in glory. So is also the resurrection of the dead.' They who obtain a glorious resurrection from the dead, are exalted far above principalities, powers, thrones, dominions and angels, and are expressly declared to be heirs of God and joint heirs with Jesus Christ, all having eternal power.

The scriptures are a mixture of very strange doctrines to the Christian world, who are blindly led by the blind. I will refer to another scripture. 'Now,' says God, when He visited Moses in the bush, (Moses was a stammering sort of a boy like me) **God said, 'Thou shalt be a God unto the children of Israel.'** God said, '**Thou shalt be a God unto Aaron**, and he shall be thy spokesman.' **I believe those Gods that God reveals as Gods to be sons of God**, and all can cry, 'Abba, Father!' **Sons of God who exalt themselves to be Gods, even from before the foundation of the world, and are the only Gods I have a reverence for.**

John said he was a king. 'And from Jesus Christ, who is the faithful witness, and the first begotten of the dead, and the Prince of the kings of the earth. Unto Him that loved us, and washed us from our sins in His own blood, **and hath made us kings and priests unto God, and His Father**; to him be glory and dominion forever and ever Amen.' Oh, Thou God who art King of kings and Lord of lords, the sectarian world, by their actions, declare, 'We cannot believe Thee.' The old Catholic church traditions are worth more than all you have said. Here is a principle of logic that most men have no more sense than to adopt. I will illustrate it by an old apple tree. Here jumps off a branch and says, I am the true tree, and you are corrupt. If the whole tree is corrupt, are not its branches corrupt? If the Catholic religion is a false religion, how can any true religion come out of it? If the Catholic church is bad, how can any good thing come out of it? The character of the old churches have always been slandered by all apostates since the world began.

I testify again, as the Lord lives, God never will acknowledge any traitors or apostates. Any man who will betray the Catholics will betray you; and if he will betray me, he will betray you. All men are liars who say they are of the true Church without the revelations of Jesus Christ and the Priesthood of Melchisedek, which is after the order of the Son of God. It is in the order of heavenly things that God should always send a new dispensation into the world when men have apostatized from the truth and lost the priesthood; but when men come out and build upon other men's foundations, they do it on their own responsibility, without authority from God; and when the floods come and the winds blow, their foundations will be found to be sand, and their whole fabric will crumble to dust.

Did I build on any other man's foundation? I have got all the truth which the Christian world possessed, and an independent revelation in the bargain, and God will bear me off triumphant. I will drop this subject. **I wish I could speak for three or four hours**; but it is not expedient on account of the rain: **I would still go on, and show you proof upon proofs; all the Bible is equal in support of this doctrine, one part as another**." (HC 6:473–479)

Appendix C

Excerpts from Sermons of Brigham Young

Sermon Delivered on 9 April 1852

"My next sermon will be to both Saint and sinner. One thing has remained a mystery in this kingdom up to this day. It is in regard to the character of the well-beloved Son of God, upon which subject the Elders of Israel have conflicting views. Our God and Father in heaven is a being of tabernacle, or, in other words, He has a body, with parts the same as you and I have; and is capable of showing forth His works to organized beings, as, for instance, in the world in which we live, it is the result of the knowledge and infinite wisdom that dwell in His organized body. His son Jesus Christ has become a personage of tabernacle, and has a body like his father. The Holy Ghost is the Spirit of the Lord, and issues forth from Himself, and may properly be called God's minister to execute His will in immensity; being called to govern by His influence and power; but *He* is not a person of tabernacle as we are, and as our Father in Heaven and Jesus Christ are. The question has been, and is often asked, who it was that begat the Son of the Virgin Mary. The infidel world have concluded that if what the Apostles wrote about his father and mother be true, and the present marriage discipline acknowledged by Christendom be correct, then Christians must believe that God is the father of an illegitimate son, in the person of Jesus Christ! The infidel fraternity teach *that* to their disciples. I will tell you how it is. Our Father in Heaven begat all the spirits that ever were, or ever will be, upon this earth; and they were born spirits in the eternal world. Then the Lord by His power and wisdom organized the mortal tabernacle of man. We were made first spiritual, and afterwards temporal.

Now hear it, O inhabitants of the earth, Jew and Gentile, Saint and sinner! When our father Adam came into the garden of Eden, he came into it with a *celestial body*, and brought Eve, *one of his wives*, with him. He helped to make and organize this world. He is MICHAEL, *the Archangel*, the ANCIENT OF DAYS! about whom holy men have written and spoken—HE *is our* FATHER *and our* GOD, *and the only God with whom* **WE** *have to do*. Every man upon the earth, professing Christians or non-professing, must hear it, and *will know it sooner or later*. They came here, organized the raw material, and arranged in their order the herbs of the field, the trees, the apple, the peach, the plum, the pear, and every other fruit that is desirable and good for man; the seed was brought from another sphere, and planted in this earth. The thistle, and thorn, the brier, and the obnoxious weed did not appear until after the earth was cursed.

When Adam and Eve had eaten of the forbidden fruit, their bodies became mortal from *its effects*, and therefore their offspring were mortal. When the Virgin Mary conceived the child Jesus, the Father had begotten him in his own likeness. He was *not* begotten by the Holy Ghost. And who is the Father? He is the first of the human family; and when he took a tabernacle, it was begotten by *his Father* in heaven, after the same manner as the tabernacles of Cain, Abel, and the rest of the sons and daughters of Adam and Eve; from the fruits of the earth, the first earthly tabernacles were originated by the Father, and so on in succession. I could tell you much more about this; but were I to tell you the whole truth, blasphemy would be nothing to it, in the estimation of the superstitious and over-righteous of mankind. However, I have told you the truth as far as I have gone. I have heard men preach upon the divinity of Christ, and exhaust all the wisdom they possessed. All Scripturalists, and approved theologians who were considered exemplary for piety and education have undertaken to expound on this subject, in every age of the Christian era; and after they have done all, they are obliged to conclude by exclaiming 'great is the mystery of godliness' and tell nothing.

It is true that the earth was organized by three distinct characters, namely Eloheim, Yahovah, and Michael, these three forming a quorum, as in all heavenly bodies, and in organizing element, perfectly represented in the Deity, as Father, Son, and Holy Ghost. Again, they will try to tell how the divinity of Jesus is joined to his humanity, and exhaust all their mental faculties, and wind up with this profound language, as describing the soul of man, 'it is an immaterial substance!' **What a learned idea! Jesus, our elder brother, was begotten in the flesh by the same character that was in the garden of Eden, and who is our Father in Heaven. Now, let all who may hear these doctrines pause before they make light of them, or treat them with indifference, for they will prove their salvation or damnation**. I have given you a few leading items upon this subject, **but a great deal more remains to be told**. Now remember from this time forth, and for ever, that Jesus Christ was not begotten by the Holy Ghost…**Treasure up these things in your hearts**. In the Bible, you have read the things I have told you to-night; but you have not known what you did read. I have told you no more than you are conversant with; but what do the people in Christendom, with the Bible in their hands, know about this subject? Comparatively nothing." (JD 1:50–52. Capitals in original.)

Sermon Delivered on 8 August 1852

"Man is made an agent to himself before his God; he is organized for the express purpose, that he may become like his master. You recollect one of the Apostle's sayings, that when we see Him, we shall be like Him;

and again, we shall become Gods, even the sons of God. Do you read anywhere that we shall possess all things? Jesus is the elder brother, and all the brethren shall come in for a share with him; for an equal share, according to their works and calling, and they shall be crowned with him. Do you read of any such thing as the Savior praying, that the Saints might be one with him, as he and the Father are one? The Bible is full of such doctrine, and there is no harm in it, as long as it agrees with the New Testament.

I will continue the point I am now at. The Lord created you and me for the purpose of becoming Gods like Himself; when we have been proved in our present capacity, and been faithful with all things He puts into our possession. We are created, we are born for the express purpose of growing up from the low estate of manhood, to become Gods like unto our Father in heaven. That is the truth about it, just as it is. The Lord has organized mankind for the express purpose of increasing in that intelligence and truth, which is with God, until he is capable of creating worlds on worlds, and becoming Gods, even the sons of God.

How many will become thus privileged? Those who honor the Father and the Son; those who receive the Holy Ghost, and magnify their calling, and are found pure and holy; they shall be crowned in the presence of the Father and the Son. Who else? Not anybody. **What becomes of all the rest**. Are you going to cast them down, and sink them to the bottom of the bottomless pit, to be angels to the devil? Who are his angels? **No man nor woman, unless they receive the Gospel of salvation, and then deny it, and altogether turn away from it, sacrificing to themselves the Son of God afresh. They are the only ones who will suffer the wrath of God to all eternity**.

How much does it take to prepare a man, or woman, or any being, to become angels to the devil, to suffer with him to all eternity? Just as much as it does to prepare a man to go into the celestial kingdom, into the presence of the Father and the Son, and to be made an heir to His kingdom, and all His glory, and be crowned with crowns of glory, immortality, and eternal lives. **Now who will be damned to all eternity? Will any of the rest of mankind? No; not one of them…**

…Where are the spirits of the ungodly? They are in prison. Where are the spirits of the righteous, the Prophets, and the Apostles? They are in prison, brethren; that is where they are. **Now let us notice a little experience, lest some of you should be startled at this idea**. How do you feel, Saints, when you are filled with the power and love of God? You are just as happy as your bodies can bear. What would be your feelings, suppose you should be in prison, and filled with the power and love of God; would you be unhappy? No. I think prisons would palaces prove, if Jesus dwelt there. This is experience. I know it is a starling idea to say that the Prophet and the persecutor of the Prophet all go to prison together. What is the condition of the righteous?

They are in possession of the spirit of Jesus—the power of God, which is their heaven; Jesus will administer to them; angels will administer to them; and they have a privilege of seeing and understanding more than you or I have, in the flesh; **but they have not got their bodies yet, consequently they are in prison. When will they be crowned, and brought into the presence of the Father and the Son? Not until they have got their bodies; this is their glory**.

What did the holy martyrs die for? Because of the promise of receiving bodies, glorified bodies, in the morning of the resurrection. For this they lived, and patiently suffered, and for this they died. In the presence of the Father, and the Son, they cannot dwell, and be crowned, **until the work of the redemption of both body and spirit is completed**. What is the condition of the wicked? They are in prison. Are they happy? No. They have stepped through the vail, to the place where the vail of the covering is taken from their understanding. They fully understand that they have persecuted the just and Holy One, and they feel the wrath of the Almighty resting upon them, having a terrible foreboding of the final consummation of their just sentence, to become angels to the devil; just as it is in this world, precisely.

Has the devil power to afflict, and cast the spirit into torment? No! We have gained the ascendency over him. It is in this world only he has power to cause affliction and sickness, pain and distress, sorrow, anguish, and disappointment; but when we go there, behold! The enemy of Jesus has come to the end of his chain; he has finished his work of torment; he cannot come any further; we are beyond his reach, and the righteous sleep in peace, while the spirit is anxiously looking forward to the day when the Lord will say, 'Awake my Saints, you have slept long enough;' for the trump of God shall sound, and the sleeping dust shall arise, and the absent spirits return, to be united with their bodies; and they will become personages of tabernacle, like the Father, and His Son, Jesus Christ; yea Gods in eternity.

They look forward with great anxiety to that day, and their happiness will not be complete—their glory will not attain to the final consummation of its fulness, until they have entered into the immediate presence of the Father and the Son, to be crowned, as Jesus will be, when the work is finished. When it is wound up, the text is preached, in all its divisions, pertaining to the redemption of the world, and the final consummation of all things; then the Savior will present the work to the Father, saying, 'Father, I have finished the work thou gavest me to do;' and the Son will give it up to the Father, and then be subject to Him, and then he will be crowned, and that is the time you and I will be crowned also.

We will notice, by this, that all the nations of the earth, with the exception of those who have apostatized from the Gospel salvation; every son and daughter of Adam, except those who have denied the Holy Ghost, after having received it, are placed in prison with the rest of them, with Prophets, Priests, and Saints. Suppose we quote a little Scripture on this point. Jesus died to redeem the world. Did his body lay in the tomb? Did his spirit leave his body? Yes. Where did his spirit go, you may inquire?

I do not know that I can tell you any better than what the ancient Apostle has told it; he says he went to preach to the spirits in prison. Who are they to whom he went to preach? The people who lived in the antediluvian world. He preached the Gospel to them in the spirit, that they might be judged according to men in the flesh." (JD 3:93, 95–96)

Sermon Delivered on 27 February 1853

"Hear it, all ye Latter-day Saints! **Will you spend the time of your probation for naught**, and feel away your existence and being? **You were organized, and brought into being, for the purpose of enduring forever**, if you fulfill the measure of your creation, pursue the right path, observe the requirements of the Celestial law, and obey the commandments of our God. It is then, and then only, you may expect that the blessing of **eternal lives** will be conferred upon you. **It can be obtained upon no other principle. Do you understand that you will cease to be, that you come to a full end, by pursuing the opposite course?**

The privileges and blessings of the Saints of the Most High God are many. Yes! All there is in heaven, and on the earth—kingdoms, thrones, principalities, powers, heights, depths, things present, and things to come; with all you can see, hear, or think of, realize or contemplate; everything in heaven; earth, or hell, is for your glory, exaltation, and excellence, **if by your lives** you honor the Priesthood Which has been conferred upon you; and, in the proper time, all will become subservient unto you, but not until then. But if you submit to serve your own feelings, and if you desire not to build up the kingdom of God, and sanctify your hearts, they will lead you down to be eternally subject thereunto—subject to the power that will afflict and torment you, **and eventually bring you to destruction**; whereas, if you pursue the opposite course, those feelings and passions will become subject unto you; you will be enabled to govern and control them, and cause them to serve you, and sub serve the object and design for which they were planted in your bosoms.

Often have I looked at individuals passing to and fro through our Territory, and heard them say, 'These are the jolly Mormons; these are the merry Mormons, I never saw such a society!' Why is this? Simply because they enjoy themselves, because they take so much comfort.

Is a man a Saint, who comes into the Church of God under such influences, merely because the Saints appear to be happy? No, he is not. No person can be a Saint, unless he receives the Holy Gospel, for the purity, justice, holiness, and eternal duration of it. **Everything else tends to decay, separation, annihilation; no, not annihilation as we use the English term, there is no such principle as this, but dissolution or decomposition**.

Now, you Elders who understand the principles of the kingdom of God, what would you not give, do, or sacrifice, to assist in building up His kingdom upon the earth? Says one, '**I would do anything in my power,**

anything that the Lord would help me to do, to build up His kingdom.' Says another, '**I would sacrifice all my property.**' Wonderful indeed! Do you not know that the possession of your property is like a shadow, or the dew of the morning before the noonday sun, that you cannot have any assurance of its control for a single moment! It is the unseen hand of Providence that controls it. **In short, what would you not sacrifice? The Saints sacrifice everything; but, strictly speaking, there is no sacrifice about it**. If you give a penny for a million of gold! a handful of earth for a planet! a temporary worn out tenement for one glorified, that will exist, abide, and continue to increase throughout a never ending eternity, **what a sacrifice to be sure!**

Many, no doubt, would consider it a great sacrifice to be called to go on a mission a few years; to leave wife, children, friends, comfortable homes, travel perhaps on foot, encounter storms on the sea, be in perils on land among mobs, and be hated of all men. It is true we might consider this a great sacrifice, and yet men do all this, and more—they risk their own lives upon their venture to get gold, to follow the allurements of pleasure. And should not the Saints of the Most High God be more willing, more anxious to promote the cause of their holy religion, devoting themselves, their influence, property, and, if necessary, their existence, than the votaries of fashion, the devotees of wealth and pleasure, and to merely sensual, temporary objects of worldly gain or aggrandisement? Verily I say unto you, if you are not, and if you have a spirit to seek after the giddy, vain, foolish vanities of the world, the things pertaining only to the gratification of present feelings, passions, and selfish desires, and have no spirit of prayer and supplication, cannot and do not feel to, exercise an interest above all others, for the cause of truth, my advice and counsel is for all such, to go straightway to the gold mines of California, and seek for gold, for rest assured, as many as have this spirit, will run as their unrighteous feelings prompt or dictate. Yes! Go to the gold region, and do not come and seek my counsel about it, whether I am willing that you should go or not, for I am not only willing that you should leave, but anxious that you may as soon as possible.

If you do not love God, and His cause, better than everything else besides, and cannot with a good heart and willing hand, build it up upon the earth; if you will not repent of your follies, and get the Spirit of truth in you, so as to love it, and feel willing to sacrifice all for it, you cannot build up the kingdom of God...

It needs the language of angels to express our ideas, to converse with each other in a manner to be perfectly understood. When we see and comprehend things in the Spirit, we ofttimes realize an utter inability to simplify and tell them in our language to others; though we may receive principles, and convey the same to others, to some extent.

It would be a great consolation to me, inasmuch as faith comes by hearing the word of God, if I had language to express my feelings. No man can tell all that he can see in the Spirit, when the vision of the Spirit is upon him. **He can see and understand in the Spirit only. He cannot tell it, yet many things may be given, in part, to others.**

I thought, while brother Rich was speaking upon certain principles, how beautiful, how satisfactory it would be to the Saints, could they converse in a pure language; if they could have the language of angels with which to communicate with each other. **I have contemplated the principles that pertain to salvation—the principles which I have been trying to lay before you**; the acts of men, and how they should be ordered before their God. I would simply say, we must attend to the duties which are laid upon us, before we enjoy our privileges.

What principle does this convey to your minds? None, unless your minds are open, and enlightened by the visions of the Holy Spirit. The principles of truth are eternal. The mind would ask at once, what is truth? It is any thing, principle, or fact that actually has an existence. If a falsehood, yet it is true that falsehood exists. It is as true that devils exist, as that Gods exist.

Jesus says, 'I am the way, the truth, and the life.' The devil also says, 'I am, I exist;' and consequently, by the same rule, 'I am, Truth.' How far short is this of what the Lord reveals by His Holy Spirit! Jesus Christ, his Father before him, all the faithful, the Gods of eternity, and all organized elements, have been organized for the express purpose of being exalted to an eternal increase; or suppose I say to eternal truth. Would this convey to your minds that the devil, Because it is a truth that he exists, could attain to the same power and exaltation? Suppose that we admit the idea that we shall see the time when we can combine and organize elements, bring worlds into existence, redeem, and bring them up to eternal glory, by merely saying—'I am Truth.' **As before quoted, 'Jesus is the way, the truth, and the life.' We can turn round and say—Satan is the way, the truth, and the death; or the way, and the falsehood. Can you perceive the difference? But to say that Jesus Christ is the way, the truth, and the life is equivalent to saying that he is the only continued or eternal existence. The Lord Jesus Christ works upon a plan of eternal increase of wisdom, intelligence, honor, excellence, power, glory, might, and dominion, and the attributes that fill eternity. What principle does the devil work upon? It is to destroy, dissolve, decompose, and tear in pieces. The principle of separation, or disorganization, is as much an eternal principle, as much a truth, as that of organization. Both always did and will exist.** Can I point out to you the difference in these principles, and show clearly and satisfactorily the benefit, the propriety, and necessity of acting upon one, any more than the other? I will try in my own way, as briefly as I can. It is plain to me, but can you understand it?

In the first place, matter is eternal. The principle of annihilation, of striking out of existence anything that has existed, or had a being, so as to leave an empty space which that thing occupied, is false, there is no such principle in all the eternities. What does exist? Matter is eternal. We grow our wheat, our fruit, and our animals, there they are organized, they increase and grow; but, after a while, they decay, dissolve, become disorganized, and return to their mother earth. No matter by what process, these are the revolutions which they undergo; but the elements of the particles of which they were composed, still do, always have, and always will exist, and through this principle of change, we have an eternal increase.

But Satan works upon the opposite principle; he seeks to destroy, would annihilate if he could, but only decomposes, disorganizes. Permit me to inquire what was his curse? It was, that he should not increase any more, but come to an end.

When I came to the door of the tabernacle this morning, I heard brother Rich telling about one third part of the heavenly host revolting from the government of Jehovah. This was their curse—to never have tabernacles to dwell in. They now exist in Spirit, but shall never have a body, nor be exalted; they shall have no further addition to their existence; whilst those who did not rebel, could have tabernacles, and, through the resurrection, become personages of tabernacle in the eternal world. There it is, on the one hand, and on the other. **You can now see the benefit, the propriety of obeying the principles which lead to eternal lives, exaltations, and increase**; and why it is that Jesus Christ has so much more power than Satan. The power of the evil one is beyond the conception of man; his cunning craft, and winning ways to insinuate and introduce himself into a community, an individual.

This is to obtain, if possible, a tabernacle, which, although a borrowed one, yet increases his power, so long as he can wield it to suit his purposes; and if he fails in this, and in enticing unto evil, then, his object is to decompose, to destroy, that the good power, the good influence, may, like himself, become bereft of the power pertaining to an embodied spirit.

The Lord operates upon the principles of continuing to organize, of adding to, gathering up, bringing forth, increasing and spreading abroad; while the opposite power does not. It shows the nature of his opposition to that peculiar trait of Christianity, based upon the principles of eternal duration, increase, power, glory, and exaltation; and points out the difference between the two adverse powers.

Again, what do you love truth for? Is it because you can discover a beauty in it, because it is congenial to you or because you think it will make you a ruler, or a Lord? If you conceive that you will attain to power upon such a motive, you are much mistaken. It is a trick of the unseen power, that is abroad amongst the inhabitants of the earth, that leads them astray, binds their minds, and subverts their understanding.

Suppose that our Father in heaven, our elder brother, the risen Redeemer, the Saviour of the world, or any of the Gods of eternity should act upon this principle, to love truth, knowledge, and wisdom, because they are all powerful, and by the aid of this power they could send devils to hell, torment the people of the earth, exercise sovereignty over them, and make them miserable at their pleasure; they would cease to be Gods; and as fast as they adopted and acted upon such principles, they would become devils, and be thrust down in the twinkling of an eye; the extension of their kingdom would cease, and their God-head come to an end.

Language, to convey all the truth, does not exist. Even in the Bible, and all books that have been revealed from heaven unto man, the language fails to convey all the truth as it is. Truth, wisdom, power, glory, light, and intelligence exist upon their own qualities; they do not, neither can they, exist upon any other principle. Truth is congenial with itself, and light cleaves unto light, it seeks after itself, and clings thereto. It is the same with knowledge, and virtue, and all the eternal attributes; they follow after and attract each other. Mercy cleaves to mercy, because it is mercy; light to light, because it is light, and there is no darkness, no deception, no falsehood in it. Truth cleaves unto truth, because it is truth; and it is to be adored, because it is an attribute of God, for its excellence, for itself. It is upon this principle, that these principles should be held, esteemed, practised. Any persons, men or women, who do not receive these principles for the love which they bear towards them, because of their beauty, excellence, and glory; and because they are congenial to their feelings upon this principle, are not Saints! They exist upon their own basis, and rest upon their own foundation. **Eternal justice, mercy, love, and truth, never can be moved; they are attributes that correspond, and are congenial with each other; they promote each other, fortify the heavens, the Gods, and that which the Gods possess.**

Now look upon the opposite side of these principles. Suppose you say, 'We will give up the pursuits of our holy religion. We are not Latter-day Saints. Let us go and seek after the things of the world, speculate, get unto ourselves riches, turn away from our duties, neglect the things pertaining to our salvation, go with the giddy, the frivolous, the seeker after gold to California, Australia, or elsewhere, for the purpose of acquiring wealth.' I tell you the result of that course. **You would cease to increase in all the attributes of excellence glory, and eternal duration, from that very moment.** So soon as you conceive such ideas, they find a soil within you prepared to nurture them, and it brings forth their direful effects; from that very moment you cease to increase. **The opposite principle seizes you, fastens itself upon you, and you decrease, lessen, diminish, decay, and waste away in quality, excellence, and strength, until your organization becomes extinct, oblivion covers you, your name is blotted out from the Book of Life, from the heavens, from the earth, and from under the earth and you will return, and sink into your natural element, which cannot be destroyed, though many read the Bible as conveying such an idea, but it does not.**

The principle opposite to that of eternal increase from the beginning, leads down to hell; the person decreases, loses his knowledge, tact, talent, and ultimately, in a short period of time, is lost; he returns to his mother earth, his name is forgotten. **But where, Oh! where is his spirit?**

I will not now take the time to follow his destiny; but here, strong language could be used, for when, the Lord Jesus Christ shall be revealed, after the termination of the thousand years' rest, he will summon the armies of heaven for the conflict, he will come forth in flaming fire, he will descend to execute the mandates of an incensed God, and, amid the thunderings of the wrath of Omnipotence, roll up the heavens as a scroll, and destroy death, and him that has the power of it. **The rebellious will be thrown back into their native element, there to remain myriads of years before their dust will again be revived, before they will be re-organized. Some might argue that this principle would lead to the re-organization of Satan, and all the devils. I say nothing about this, only what the Lord says—that when he comes, 'he will destroy death, and him that has the power of it.' It cannot be annihilated; you cannot annihilate matter**. If you could, it would prove there was empty space.

If philosophers could annihilate the least conceivable amount of matter, they could then prove there was the minutest vacuum, or empty space; but there is not even that much, and it is beyond the power of man to prove that there is any.

Brethren, what is it that you love the truth for? Is it because it gives you the power, the authority of the Priesthood? Is it because it makes you rulers, kings, and priests unto our God, and gives you great power?

Men should act upon the principle of righteousness, because it is right, and is a principle which they love to cherish and see practised by all men. They should love mercy, because of its benevolence, charity, love, clemency, and of all of its lovely attributes, and be inspired thereby to deal justly, fairly, honorably, meting out to others their just deservings.

If selfishness prompts you to embrace the truth, if it is merely to exalt yourself and your friends that you covenant to serve your God, and that is your only motive, you had better pass on the northern route, for we can do you no good if you wait, or remain with us; not but that God has regard for all His children; but He loves those who love all the principles of righteousness, because they are righteous, and have a delight in the exercise of pure principles, of virtue, of excellence and truth, of meekness, long-suffering, and self denial, mercy, and charity.

I am aware that my language fails to convey my ideas to you as I could wish. But I will proceed a little further. A great promise was made to Abraham, which was—you shall have seed, and unto your increase there shall be no end. The same promise was made unto the Saviour; and unto every true and faithful man who serves God with all his heart, and whose delight is in keeping the law of the Lord, obeying the behests of Jehovah, and building up His kingdom upon the earth…

The man who has proved himself before God, has been faithful, has gone through and performed everything the Lord has laid upon him to do, for the purpose of building up and sustaining His kingdom, has proved himself before men, angels, and his Father in heaven, he is the only character that will increase, and obtain a celestial glory. Others may seem to prosper, to increase for a season, but by and by they are left in the shade, their glory is clipped, and their house is left unto them desolate.

Pray the Lord to inspire your hearts. Ask for wisdom and knowledge. It is our duty to seek after it. Let us seek, and we shall find; knock, and it will be opened unto us. But as for His coming down here to pour His Spirit upon you, while you are aiming after the vain and frivolous things of the world; indulging in all the vanity, nonsense, and foolery which surrounds you; drinking in all the filthy abomination which should be spurned from every community on the earth—so long as you continue this course, rest assured He will not come near you.

I will not enter into particulars. You already know enough about them. I ask that you would leave it off; refrain, purify, and sanctify yourselves before your God, and get so much of the spirit of truth that you may become filled with it, so that you can shout aloud with all your might to the praise of God, and feel your hearts clear as the noon-day sun. Then you can dance, and glorify God; and as you shall abide in the truth, God will raise you up, and add to your numbers, so that your train will fill the Holy Temple, as it was said of the Lord by one of old. May the Lord bless you. Amen." (JD 1:113–120)

Sermon Delivered on 10 July 1853

"Life and death are set before us, and we are at liberty to choose which we will.

I have frequently reflected upon these two principles, but were I to explain in full my own views upon them, they might perhaps come too much in contact with the feelings and views of many people.

To me, these principles are like the vision of open day upon this beautiful earth. Life and death are easily understood in the light of the Holy Ghost, but, like every thing else, they are hard to be understood in its absence.

To choose life is to choose an eternal existence in an organized capacity: to refuse life and choose death is to refuse an eternal existence in an organized Capacity, and be contented to become decomposed, and return again to native element.

Life is an accumulation of every property and principle that is calculated to enrich, to ennoble, to enlarge, and to increase, in every particular, the dominion of individual man. To me, life would signify an extension. I have the privilege of spreading abroad, of enlarging my borders, of increasing in endless knowledge, wisdom, and power, and in every gift of God.

To live as I am, without progress, is not life, in fact we may say that is impossible. There is no such principle in existence, neither can there be. **All organized existence is in progress, either to an endless advancement in, eternal perfections, or back to dissolution.** You may explore all the eternities that have been, were it possible, then come to that which we now understand according to the principles of natural philosophy, and where is there an element, an individual living thing, an organized body, of whatever nature, that continues as it is? IT CAN NOT BE FOUND. All things that have come within the bounds of man's limited knowledge—the things he naturally understands, teach him, that there is no period, in all the eternities, wherein organized existence will become stationary, that it cannot advance. in knowledge, wisdom, power, and glory.

If a man could ever arrive at the point that would put an end to the accumulation of life—the point at which he could increase no more, and advance no further, we should naturally say he commenced to decrease at the same point.

Again, when he has gained the zenith of knowledge, wisdom, and power, it is the point at which he begins to retrograde; his natural abilities will begin to contract, and so he will continue to decrease, until all he knew is lost in the chaos of forgetfulness. As we understand naturally, this is the conclusion we must come to, if a termination to the increase of life and the acquisition of knowledge is true.

Because of the weakness of human nature, it must crumble to the dust. But in all the revolutions and changes in the existence of men, in the eternal world which they inhabit, and in the knowledge they have obtained as people on the earth, there is no such thing as principle, power, wisdom, knowledge, life, position, or anything that can be imagined, that remains stationary—**they must increase or decrease**.

To me, life is increase; death is the opposite. When our fellow-creatures die, is it the death we talk about? The ideas we have of it are conceived in the mind, according to a false tradition. Death does not mean what we naturally think it means. Apparently it destroys, puts out of existence, and leaves empty space, but there is no such death as this. Death, in reality, is to decompose or decrease, and life is to increase.

Much is written in the Bible, and in the other revelations of God, and much is said by the people, publicly and privately, upon this subject. Life and death are in the world, and all are acquainted with them more or less. We live, we die, we are, we are not, are mixed up in the conversation of every person, to a lesser or a greater degree.

Why is it so? Because all creation is in progress; coming into existence, and going out of existence, as we use the terms; but another form of language fits this phenomenon of nature much better, (viz.) forming, growing, increasing, then begins the opposite operation—decreasing, decomposition, returning back to native element, &c. These revolutions we measurably understand.

But to simply take the path pointed out in the Gospel, by those who have given us the plan of salvation, is to take the path that leads to life, to eternal increase; it is to pursue that course wherein we shall NEVER, NEVER lose what we obtain, but continue to collect, to gather together, to increase, to spread abroad, and extend to an endless duration. **Those persons who strive to gain ETERNAL LIFE gain that which will produce the increase their hearts will be satisfied with. Nothing less than the privilege of increasing eternally, in every sense of the word, can satisfy the immortal spirit.** If the endless stream of knowledge from the eternal fountain could all be drunk in by organized intelligences, so sure immortality would come to an end, and all eternity be thrown upon the retrograde path.

If mankind will choose the opposite to life held out in the Gospel, it will lead them to dissolution, to decomposition, to death; they will be destroyed, but not as it is commonly understood…

He has caused us to forget every thing we once knew before our spirits entered within this vail of flesh. For instance, it is like this: when we lie down to sleep, our minds are often as bright and active as the mind of an angel, at least they are as active as when our bodies are awake. They will range over the earth, visit distant friends, and, for aught we know, the planets, and accomplish great feats; do that which will enhance our happiness, increase to us every enjoyment of life, and prepare us for celestial glory; but when we wake in the morning, it is all gone from us; we have forgotten it. This illustration will explain in part the nature of the vail which is over the inhabitants of the earth; they have forgotten that they once knew. This is right; were it different, where would be the trial of our faith? In a word, be it so; it is as it should be.

Now understand, to choose life is to choose principles that will lead you to an eternal increase, and nothing short of them will produce life in the resurrection for the faithful. Those that choose death, make choice of the path which leads to the end of their organization. The one leads to endless increase and progression, the other to the destruction of the organized being, ending in its entire decomposition into the particles that compose the native elements. Is this so in all cases? you inquire. Yes, for aught I know. I shall not pretend to deny but what it is so in all cases. This much I wanted to say to the brethren, with regard to life and death.

As to the word annihilate, as we understand it, there is no such principle as to put a thing which exists, entirely out of existence, so that it does not exist in any term, shape, or place whatever. It would be as reasonable to say that ENDLESS, which is synonymous to the word eternity, has both a beginning and an end…

The whole object of my existence is to continue to live, to increase, to spread abroad, and gather around me to an endless duration. What shall I say? You may unite the efforts of the best mathematicians the world can produce, and when they have counted as many millions of ages, worlds, and eternities, as the power of numbers within their knowledge will embrace, they are still as ignorant of eternity as when they began. Then ask people of general intelligence; people who understand in a great degree the philosophical principles of creation, which, they have studied and learned by a practical course of education, and what do they know about it? It is true they know a little, and that little every other sane person knows, whether he is educated or uneducated; they know about that portion of eternity called TIME. Suppose I ask the learned when was the beginning of eternity? Can they think of it? No! And I should very much doubt some of the sayings of one of the best philosophers and writers of the age, that we call brother, with regard to the character of the Lord God whom we serve. I very much doubt whether it has ever entered into his heart to comprehend eternity. **These are principles and ideas I scarcely ever meddle with**. The practical part of our religion is that which more particularly interests me. Still my mind reflects upon life, death, eternity, knowledge, wisdom, **the expansion of the soul**, and the knowledge of the Gods that are, that have been, and that are to be. What shall we say? We are lost in the depth of our own thoughts.

Suppose we say there was once a beginning to all things, then we must conclude there will undoubtedly be an end. Can eternity be circumscribed? If it can, there is an end of all wisdom, knowledge, power, and glory—all will sink into eternal annihilation.

What is life to you and me? It is the utmost extent of our desires. Do you wish to increase, to continue? Do you wish to possess kingdoms and thrones, principalities and powers; to exist, and continue to exist; to grow in understanding, in wisdom, in knowledge, in power, and in glory throughout an endless duration? Why, yes, is the reply natural to every heart that has been warmed with the life-giving influences of the Holy Ghost. And when we have lived, and gathered around us more kingdoms and creations than it is possible for the mind of mortals to comprehend, (just think of it, and how it commenced like a grain of mustard seed, cast into the ground!) then, I may say we could comprehend the very dawning of eternity, which term I use to accommodate the idea in my mind, not that it will at all apply to eternity. **When you have reached this stage in the onward course of your progression, you will be perfectly satisfied not to be in a hurry**.

The inquiry should not be, if the principles of the Gospel will put us in possession of the earth, of this farm, that piece of property, of a few thousand pounds, or as many thousand dollars, but, if they will put us in possession of principles that are endless, and calculated in their nature for an eternal increase; that is, to add life to life, being to being, kingdom to kingdom, principle to principle, power to power, thrones to thrones, dominions to dominions, and crowns to crowns.

When we have lived long enough by following out the principles that are durable, that are tangible, that are calculated in their nature to produce endless life—I say, when we have lived long enough in them to see the least Saint, that can be possibly called a Saint, in possession of more solar systems like this, than it is possible for mortals to number, or than there are stars in the firmament of heaven visible, or sands on the sea shore, **we shall then have a faint idea of eternity, and begin to realize that we are in the midst of it**.

Brethren, you that have the principles of life in you, be sure you are gathering around you kindred principles, that will endure to all eternity. I do not desire to talk any more at this time." (JD 1:349–353. Capitals in original.)

Sermon Delivered on 12 February 1854

"When I contemplate the subject of Salvation, and rise before a congregation to speak upon that all-important matter, it has been but a few times in my life that I could see a beginning point to it, or a stopping place. There is such a multiplicity of principles, and circumstances all interwoven so closely that it seems to be one eternity. I suppose this is the case in reality. To be Saved, to be Redeemed, and to have a right to the Celestial Kingdom of God is to be infinitely connected with the principles of Eternity.

I recollect once when I was preaching, a question was asked me: 'What is Priesthood?' The answer was ready, and perfectly simple in its nature, plain to be understood, and is couched in a short sentence (viz.): Priesthood is a perfect system of Government that rules and reigns in Eternity.

A question at once arises in the mind: 'Where is Eternity?' The answer is at hand: Eternity is here:—we are in Eternity just as much so as any other beings in Heaven or on Earth. Heavenly beings are no more in Eternity than we are. We are in the midst of Eternity; and when we become acquainted with the system of government and the laws that rule in Eternity, we shall then know [that] it [is] calculated to endure; to govern and control all things which are in Heaven, and on the Earth.

The Eternal Priesthood of God—the Government of God—the Laws of Eternity—is a pure and perfect system of government!

While meditating this morning upon what we are here for—why man is acted upon as he is, and the cause of what we see continually exhibited before us—which is referred to in hundreds of passages of scripture, for the ancient prophets and apostles could see the darkness, ignorance, wickedness and blindness of mankind in the midst of Eternity. Made as they are, they seem to be governed and controlled—or were we to speak without reflection, at a glance over the face of the living masses of the human family, we might say with some show of truth: 'they are compelled to do as they do, and be what they are by some power unknown to them, and over which they have no control.' Men in general seem not to know what is the cause of action, and why it is we do as we do. While these thoughts pass through my mind, the question: 'What are we here for,' was answered very nigh as Brother Taylor spoke this morning. We came here to serve God, to be Saints, and help build up the Kingdom of God. Yet we see many things that do not tend to righteousness; we then consider the Lord must be the controller of all things, and it is His hand that rules and overrules, that He has His way, fulfilling the counsels of His own will, setting bounds to man that he cannot pass. Though He governs, and controls the children of men, it is but to a certain extent; for numerous powers, principles, and spirits operate in as great a variety of ways upon them which is seen in their actions, feelings and impressions. The variety is very great. We behold this variety not only in the human creature but in all the other works of God. We may examine the Earth, the elements in which it floats, the planetary system, the starry heavens, and a thousand other things common to natural philosophy, and the same principle of endless variety presents itself to our notice.

What is natural philosophy? We may illustrate this question by saying: If we plow the ground, and properly prepare it for the reception of seed, and then sow it with good wheat it will produce wheat. This is natural philosophy. Every seed will bring forth its own kind. All the reasonable doings, and labors of man have been performed upon the principles of natural philosophy.

While we see this great variety in nature we ask philosophers how many elements they count, for they say the elements can be numbered with ease. This is vain philosophy. I do not believe that any man by the science of natural philosophy has discovered all the elements, and numbered them. They are so interspersed, and operate in such an endless variety of ways; creating an endless variety of new forms, and results. It has not come within the capacity of the most able philosopher to arrange, number, and classify them, to do which is the province of natural philosophy.

When we read the scriptures we read the letter, or that which we know naturally, that we see with our eyes, hear with our ears, handle with our hands, and understand with our natural mind as natural beings. The Apostles when speaking of a certain class of unbelievers, wisely said, 'They were like brute beasts made to be taken and destroyed.' That is, they (the beasts) know naturally as we do when they are hungry; when they want to eat and drink, when they are uneasy from the effects of cold, or over much heat.

What we can see, hear, smell, taste, feel, and understand is embraced in natural philosophy. But without something more than we can gather from natural philosophy—from the natural organization of the human system it all tends to death. As it is written the letter killeth but the spirit giveth life.

That God fills immensity is a true principle to me. There is no portion of space where He is not. **There is no element in existence that does not contain Him**; no matter whether it be in its primitive, or in an organized state, He is through it and round about it. God fills immensity.

Can any person make it plain to our understanding why things are as they are? What produces that which seems natural, and rational to us, and perfectly congenial to our feelings? But our feelings are wholly the result of tradition. As a general thing, what we individually see and understand appears right to us, though we come in contact with things we call wrong—like men's acts, and thoughts, we are very apt to call wrong—but that which we do, and that which we think, and that which we consider to be right, to us is perfectly right. People can be traditionated to think, and act, in every possible way, and justify themselves therein. For instance, refer to the traditions of the world, and ask those who profess Christianity if they can believe it is right for a wife to go on to the funeral pyre to be burnt alive with her dead husband. In some parts of the world, if a husband dies they make what they call a 'funeral pyre,' which is composed of fine dry wood mingled with other inflammable combustibles, which they set fire to, and the beautiful healthy young woman is consumed with the dead body of her husband?

Does the Christian consider this right? It appears almost impossible for us to believe that any human being could be traditionated to do what we often read in history. I will relate another circumstance that transpired upon one of the southern islands. A missionary who had made some considerable progress in his labors on one of these islands was much annoyed by the practice of polygamy among the natives. One of them who had become a member of the Church told his priest that he had two wives. This, of course, appeared to the clergyman [as] an unpardonable sin, who told the savage if he remained a member of the Church he must have but one wife.

The native went from the presence of the priest and in a while returned again saying, 'Me good Christian, me one wife.' The priest inquired what he had done with the other one. 'Me kill her and eat her up.' He believed he had done just right. Is it not strange how people can be traditionated to believe and practice such enormities. That is, to us it appears strange. Some of the old people in this Church, who have been brought up in what we call the blue states, or the Eastern States, are influenced continually by the habits of their youth. To this day the old woman of 80 years of age considers it decidedly wrong to take up her knitting after sundown on Saturday evening. Were she to do it under any pretext whatever, her conscience would be stung with guilt, while another individual would not consider it wrong to run his mill on Sunday but feel perfectly justified in the act. But the good old lady could not take up her knitting after sundown on Saturday night without feeling condemned. Why is this? Because her father, and her mother, and her priest taught her so. They told her it was not right to work after sundown on Saturday. The influence of this teaching follows her to this day. Mormonism rubs off a great deal of this old rust, and causes them to judge, and think for themselves.

Again, I ask this congregation a question, which if I do not answer, I want you should sometime, when you choose, or I should like some of the Elders [to] answer it when they preach to us here. I shall not try to answer it myself. The question is, 'How many spirits has the Lord got?' Many spirits are gone out into the word. We hear of spirits that rap, and spirits that knock, and spirits that write, and numerous others that perform as great a variety of other things. Who can tell how many spirits the Lord has? Perhaps the rapping spirit is one the Lord has sent. The

Apostle in one place enumerates up spirits of God. In another place he says, 'Try the spirits for many false prophets are gone out into the world.' He also speaks of three spirits like frogs, that are the spirits of devils working miracles, which go forth to the kings of the Earth, and of the whole world, to gather them to the battle of that great day of God Almighty. Add to these another quotation, (viz.) 'And then shall that wicked be revealed, whom the Lord shall consume with the spirit of his mouth, and shall destroy with the brightness of his coming; even him whose coming is after the working of Satan, with all power, and signs, and lying wonders. For this cause God shall send them strong delusion, that they should believe a lie, that all might be damned who believe not the truth, but had pleasure in unrighteousness.' How many spirits the Lord has sent into the world I do not pretend to say, but if any man among you knows, let him tell the number.

You may now inquire if the Lord has any spirits but what are good spirits. Are they not all good that He controls, and sends forth to do His pleasure? How shall we answer this question? Shall we say they are all good, or that some are good, and some are evil? Were I to answer it and leave out all modifications, I would say at once, the Lord has control over all spirits, influences, and powers within the confines of His dominions, whether these dominions extend throughout eternal space, or only occupy a portion of it. All within His dominions, good, and bad, clean, and unclean, noble and ignoble, great or small, every spirit in His dominions is controlled by Him.

He gives them their ability, He endows them with the knowledge, power, understanding, and every other attribute they possess according to their worthiness or unworthiness; all they possess they have received from that God who owns, governs, and controls these dominions of which we form a part. I have answered the question in part.

A thousand different queries will arise in the minds of the people upon this and other subjects, each shade of thought being prompted by the spirit they have received from some quarter. All people have received intelligence, either more or less, or a spirit, or an impression that causes the variety in manner, expression, thought, and action which we see manifested among the multitudes that compose the nations of the Earth. This variety is caused, chiefly, by the spirit they have received.

I observe that natural philosophy, or in other words, the letter killeth, but the spirit giveth life. **Now, it is clear to the mind, by the external operations of spirits, there is a tangible something that is invisible to the natural eye. But if a person has the gift of seeing spirits, they see a body, or the body of a spirit. They however do not see with the natural eye. Many are endowed with this natural gift. They are natural seers, and if the spirit should present itself behind them, in an opposite direction to the natural vision, they can see it there as well as in any other position, although they may not turn round to see it. In the visible operations of spirits, we see the affects of an invisible agency**. And as varied are the effects we see as the spirits that produce these affects. Among the many spirits that are sent into the world, we read that the Lord God sent his seven spirits into all the Earth —it confounds and puzzles the children of men to know what spirit to follow to secure to themselves the object of their pursuit. Have you ever felt yourselves in a quandary to know the right from the wrong; the course you ought to pursue, and the one you ought to avoid, in order to gain the object of your pursuit, whatever it might be? Your own minds will echo an affirmative to this question, and each one of you can judge of it for yourselves...

...Are these the spirits of the Lord, sent forth into all the Earth, or are they not? Are the people governed, and controlled by good spirits or evil ones? Can they tell? These are intricate matters to the human family. It is hard for them to discriminate between the good and the evil. It is impossible for them to know the spirits unless the Lord opens the vision of their minds, to give them understanding of things that are not seen with the natural eye. See the present commotions, and hear the loud rumors of war that are spreading like a dark cloud over the world! Who can understand it? No man or woman that now lives or that ever did live can understand the operations of spirits, why things are as they are, and the cause of the endless variety and the sentiments, feelings, and actions of the inhabitants of the Earth, **unless God opens the visions of their minds, and unveils eternity to them, revealing what is in the next, or in the previous world if you please**.

But I said we are in eternity. It is true, but could we look beyond this mortality we should see that which is unclothed. We are now clothed upon with mortal flesh which veils the vision of the eternal spirit, that we cannot perceive what is going on in those eternal elements that have passed through a routine of changes until they have secured to themselves an eternal organization both in body and spirit, in the tabernacle, and out of it. Who can understand these deep matters unless the Lord reveals them? No one!

Then Brethren and Sisters, it is all important that we make this the subject of our consideration, and deep thought, when we rise from our couch, and it ought to be the last thing contemplated when we retire to rest. Our God—our religion—the Way of Life and Salvation—what the Lord wishes of us, to learn our daily actions, thoughts and feelings, to ascertain if we are pursuing the right path, should be the first and foremost, and most prominent thing in our minds. And for this very potent reason, except the Lord is continually with us, guiding us by the light of His Holy Spirit, we are liable to be overtaken by the enemy, drawn away from the right path, lose our faith and confidence in God, and be led captive by the Devil at his will. How important it is that every Latter-day Saint should live their religion. Is it not necessary that every person should know for themselves that they are governed, and controlled by the spirit of the Lord Jesus?

I will make a remark here that will perhaps reflect a little light on the minds of some. We are taught to ask the Father when we pray, in the name of Jesus Christ. The ancients as well as the modern revelations ascribe honor, praise, and glory to Christ. We render praise, and honor, and thanksgiving to the Father, and the Son, and the Holy Ghost; or in other words, Holy Spirits. **This idea may give you a particle of light**. I do not, however, pretend to say how many spirits the Lord has sent forth; but the Holy Spirit that Jesus promised to his disciples, the ancients enjoyed, and so does every man who understands the way of the Lord and has had committed to him the Keys of the Everlasting Priesthood; they are exhorted to seek and enjoy a Holy Spirit.

It is not a matter of moment to me how many other spirits there are; but, brethren and sisters, let you and I seek diligently to possess the Holy Spirit of the Lord Jesus, and then if there are myriads of unholy spirits around us we are prepared to discern the difference. As I observed in the beginning of my remarks, I never know where to begin, or where to leave off in the subject of Salvation. **But I wish to say touching the mysterious presentations that are made in this day, let no man marvel at them**. If Joseph Smith is a prophet he has told us the truth, and Mormonism is the work of the Most High. We believe the time is fast approaching, according to the words of other prophets, as well as Joseph Smith; and according to the words of Jesus Christ, and His Apostles, when the veil of the covering will be taken from the nations of the Earth, for there has been a veil of darkness and ignorance over them. It will be taken off, and all flesh will behold the glory of God, Saint and Sinner, the righteous and the unrighteous; those that believe in Jesus Christ, and those who do not believe in him, all flesh must see the glory of God, and the hand of God manifested to the degree that every knee shall bow, and every tongue confess to the glory of the Father, and that His son Jesus Christ whom He sent into the world is the Savior of the world.

Therefore do not be astonished at the marvelous manifestations from the spirit world, nor be afraid, but let your feelings be calm, for you will see every kind of spirit that ever was in the world manifested among the children of men in the last days. The Priesthood of God is no sooner revived, and in operation, in every age of the world, than the Devil introduces his priesthood in opposition to it; for the Devil has got a priesthood, which many of you have seen illustrated here. He says, 'I have got power, and the Earth is mine, and I rule.' So he will as long as he can; but there are bounds set to his power. He has power to take natural life, and there his power is at an end. Death will yet be driven from the Earth and him that hath the power of it which is the Devil.

When you see spiritual manifestations that you do not understand be quick to see, quick to hear, and then be quick to understand, but slow to judge. I give you this advice for a safeguard, that you may always be upon safe ground, and not be led away, when you may be distant from the body of the Church…

…There is no philosopher that can tell how many elements there are, for there is an eternity of them. Go to the forests of Europe and America, and see if you can find two leaves alike. Go into the meadows and see if you can find two blades of grass exactly alike. We can see an eternity of variety, and there is an eternity of elements to cause that variety, and **an** eternity of spirits and lives to those elements..." (*Teachings of President Brigham Young*, Vol. 3, 1852–1854 [Salt Lake City: Collier's Publishing Co., 1987], pp. 230–45. Also see *The Essential Brigham Young*, pp. 74–86)

Sermon Delivered on 8 October 1854

"**I propose to speak upon a subject that does not immediately concern yours or my welfare**. I expect in my remarks I shall allude to things that you search after as being absolutely necessary for your salvation in the Kingdom of God. It is true **if you are faithful, and diligent there are things that will be fully made known to you in due time at the proper time, according to the will of the Lord**. But so many among us are preaching, lecturing, contemplating upon, and conversing about things away beyond our reach, sometimes I wish to gratify the people by speaking upon these subjects; for I think upon them as well as you; I meditate upon the future and the past as well as you, and I now gratify myself by gratifying the people.

In the first place, I wish to say to all men and women who believe in the Lord Jesus Christ, in the Holy Bible, and in the revelations that have been given at sundry times from the days of Adam to the present, I request that I may have your faith and prayers united with mine that whatever the Lord is pleased to give to the Latter-day Saints through your humble servant this afternoon, He may give it, and that He does not wish to give He may retain, and keep from you. I make this request of the Saints for this reason; **I know by my experience, by the visions of eternity that God reveals things to individuals that does not belong to the Church at large at present**, or that does not yet belong to the Mass. That I know.

It is natural for the people to desire that which is not beneficial to them. It is so in temporal things, and it is so in things that are spiritual. That I know. Again, the Lord blesses His people with temporal things in abundance, and wishes to bless them with knowledge and understanding that is not for the world of mankind who do not believe in Him. That I also know.

I may say things this afternoon that does not belong to the world. What if I do? I know the Lord is able to close up every person's mind who have eyes but see not, hearts but do not understand; so I may say what I please with regard to the Kingdom of God on the Earth, for there is a veil over the wicked that they cannot understand the things which are for their peace.

Jesus said at one time, 'It is not meet to take the children's bread and give it to dogs.' This saying applies to all the dispensations that has been brought forth to the children of men from the days of Adam until now.

I wish the congregation to understand in connection with my sayings thus far, that the Latter-day Saints believe in God the Father, in Jesus Christ His son, in the Holy Ghost[,] God's minister, and in the Celestial

Law, or, in other words, the ordinances of the House of God, which, if obeyed, are calculated to save intelligent beings, exalt them, and bring them back into the presence of their God.

I will tell you what I believe still further than this; though I do not pretend to say that the items of doctrine, and ideas I shall advance are necessary for the people to know, or that they should give themselves any trouble about them whatever. I believe in the eternities of worlds, saints, angels, kingdoms, and gods: In eternity without beginning. I believe the gods never had a beginning, neither the formation of matter, and it is without end; it will endure in one eternal round swimming in space, basking, living, and moving in the midst of eternity. All the creations are in the midst of eternity, and that is one eternity, so they move in one eternal round.

Consequently, when you hear philosophers argue the point how the first god came, how intelligence came, how worlds came, and how angels came, they are talking about that which is beyond their conception; about that which never was, and never will be worlds without end. It manifests their folly. It shows they know nothing of such matters; and if they do know some things they have a right to know, there are things they have no right to know. This applies to all classes of mankind.

These are my views with regard to the gods, and eternities. Do you wish I should particularize?

Then, can you by any process of reasoning or argument, tell whether it was an apple that bore the first seed of an apple, or an apple seed that made the first apple? Or, whether it was the seed of a squash that made the first squash, or a squash that bore the first squash seed? Such abstruse questions belong to the philosophy of the world; in reality there never was and never will be a time when there was not both the apple and the apple seed.

(You must be patient with me, as I am not well enough to preach to such a large congregation in the open air, and labor onward without cessation; you must allow me to take my own time.) I will proceed a little further with my preliminaries before I commence my subject. Inasmuch as I have taken the ground that there never was a beginning, nor end—I wish to say further; there is an eternity of elements, and an eternity of space and there is no space without a kingdom; neither is there any kingdom without a space. Were the best mathematician to multiply figures from the time he first commenced to learn at five or ten years of age, until he is one hundred years old, or until he has exhausted the capacity of figures known to man, he can then tell no more about the number of the creations of God in comparison than a mere child who knows nothing whatever of figures. There is no beginning, no end; there is no bounds, no time, when the elements will cease to be organized into bodies with all the variety you have a faint specimen of on this Earth.

There are philosophers who believe that this Earth upon which we stand has been in existence for millions of ages. I wish to advance a few items that will open the minds of these philosophers, that they may be like well instructed scribes who treasure up in their hearts the mysteries of the Kingdom of God, the Principles of Eternity.

Those who wish to be taught eternal principles, and become true philosophers[,] their minds can reach forth into the unlimited fields of eternity and still discover no end to the boundless expanse, and to its fullness.

There is no necessity of creating a world like this and keeping it in one unalterable state or condition for the express purpose of bringing intelligent beings upon it, while there is an eternity of matter yet to be organized; and when we have lived as long as the best mathematicians among you can figure by millions, billions, trillions, etc., when [you have] exhausted all your wisdom and knowledge, and figures[,] you are then in the midst of eternity where you began.

A true philosopher wishes to grow, and increase continually; he wishes his mind to expand and reach forth, until he can think as God thinks; as angels think, and behold things as God beholds them.

You recollect I told you in the commencement, I should talk about things that did not particularly concern you and me; but the people want to hear something in advance of their present knowledge; they want to find out if there is anything more for us to learn. When you have lived through eternities to come, learning continually, you may then inquire, 'Brother Brigham, is there anything more for me to learn.' My reply to such an inquiry would be, yes there is an eternity of knowledge yet to learn.

Search after wisdom, get knowledge, and understanding, and forget it not; and be not like the fool whose eyes are in the ends of the Earth, or like the misers who are around us here; they are so craving, and anxious after property, that if they saw a picayune on the wall opposite to me there, they would run over forty dollars to secure that picayune; their eyes are on earthly riches to the neglect of riches that are more enduring.

There are a great many persons who are so anxious to learn about eternity, gods, angels, heavens, and hells, that they neglect to learn the first lessons preparatory to learning the things they are reaching after. They will come short of them.

I wish to speak a few words about the Bible as I have hinted at it. The Ordinances of the Kingdom of God on the Earth are the same to the children of Adam from the commencement to the end of his posterity pertaining to the carnal state on this Earth, and the winding up scene of this mortality. With regard to the Bible we frequently say, we believe the Bible, but circumstances alter cases, for what is now required for the people may not be required of a people that may live a hundred years hence. But I wish you to understand, with regard to the Ordinances of God's House to save the people in the Celestial Kingdom of our God, there is no change from the days of Adam to the present time, neither will there be until the last of his posterity is gathered into the Kingdom of God.

Those who are not acquainted with our doctrine are astonished, and say, 'That is strange indeed; we thought no such thing as preaching faith, repentance, and baptism was practiced in ancient, or Old Testament times.' I can tell you that no man from the days of Adam, no woman from the days of Eve to this day, who have lived, and who are now living upon the Earth will go into the Kingdom of their Father and God, to be crowned with Jesus Christ, without passing through the same Ordinances of the House of God, you and I have obeyed. I wish you distinctly to understand that.

There are many duties, and callings spoken of in the scriptures, and there are many not written, those for instance which are handed out to you by your President as circumstances require. Those imposed by the President of the Church of God, or by the president of any portion of it, are duties as necessary to be observed as though they were written in the Bible; but these requirements, duties, callings etc. change with the circumstances that surround the people of God. But when you speak of the system of Salvation to bring back the children of Adam and Eve into the presence of our Father and God, it is the same in all ages, among all people, and under all circumstances worlds without end[.] Amen.

I think these preliminaries will satisfy me, and I feel prepared to take my text; it is the words of Jesus Christ, but where they are in the Bible I cannot tell you now, for I have not taken pains to look at them. I have had so much to do, that I have not read the Bible for many years. I used to be a Bible student; I used to read and study it, but did not understand the spirit and meaning of it;

I knew well enough how it read. I have read the Book of Mormon, the book of Doctrine [and] Covenants, and other revelations of God which [He] has given to His people in latter times; I look at them, and contrast the spirit and power of them with my faithfulness. My clerks know how much time I have to read, it is difficult for me to snatch time enough even to eat my breakfast and supper, to say nothing of reading.

I tell you my text is in the Bible and reads as follows. 'And this is Life Eternal, that they might know Thee the only true God, and Jesus Christ whom thou hast sent.' I will now put another text with this and then offer a few remarks, it is one of the sayings of the Apostle Paul. 'For though there be that are called gods, whether in Heaven, or in Earth (as there be gods many and lords many) but to us there is but one God, the Father, of whom are all things, and we in Him; and one Lord Jesus Christ, by whom are all things, and we by him.' This God is the Father of our Lord Jesus Christ and the Father of our spirits. I feel inclined here to make a little scripture. (Were I under the necessity of making scripture extensively I should get Brother Heber C. Kimball to make it, and then I would quote it. I have seen him do this when any of the Elders have been pressed by their opponents, and were a little at a loss; he would make a scripture for them to suit the case, that never was in the Bible, though none the less true, and make their opponents swallow it as the words of an Apostle, or one of the Prophets.

The Elder would then say, 'Please turn to that scripture, gentlemen and read it for yourselves.' No they could not turn to it but they recollected it like the Devil for fear of being caught.) I will venture to make a little [scripture]. This God is the God and Father of our Lord Jesus Christ precisely as He is our Father varying from mortality to immortality, from corruptible to incorruptible, and that is all the difference. He is the God and Father of our Lord Jesus Christ, both body and spirit; and He is the Father of our spirits, and the Father of our flesh in the beginning. You will not dispute the words of the Apostle, that He is actually the God and Father of our Lord Jesus Christ, and the Father of our spirits[.] You may add these words to it, or let it alone, it is all the same to me, that He is not only the Father of our spirits, but also of our flesh, He being the founder of that natural machinery through which we have all obtained our bodies.

Do you wish me to simplify it? Could you have a father without having a grandfather; or a grandfather without having a great grandfather? I never heard of [but] one circumstance that varied from this rule, and that was a son of the Emerald Isle who said he was born of one of his aunts. Does this unlock to your understandings how the Lord Almighty is our natural Father; He set the great machine to working. If you cannot see this truth now, you will if you are faithful, and patient. I will now quote another scripture. 'And hath made of one blood all nations of men for to dwell on all the face of' the Earth, and hath determined the times before appointed, and the bounds of their habitations.' From these words we understand that God has made of one blood all the inhabitants that are upon the Earth [—all] that has been, and that will be in the future will be of the same blood as those that have been. Do you believe that scripture? I do with all my heart. I believe we are all of one flesh, blood, and bones. We are made of the same matter, the same elements, we have sprang from one mother, Earth.

Matter was brought together from the vast eternity of it that exists, and this terra firma upon which we stand was organized, then comes the world of mankind, the beasts, fishes, fowls, and every living thing to dwell upon the Earth after its kind; and vegetation of every kind to support the animal life upon it, until the organization of this world was perfected in all its variety; being brought from the eternity of matter, and prepared for intelligent beings to dwell upon, wherein to prepare themselves to dwell eternally in the presence of their Father and God. Those who keep this their second estate, and do honor to their being, and answer the design of their creation, shall be exalted to inhabit the Earth, and live upon it when it shall be Celestial, and brought back into the presence of God, there to dwell forever and ever.

Before I proceed any further, I will ask a question. And I would like the men, and women of intelligence, to understand and watch well, to see if I keep the thread of truth, whether I preach to you according to the law, and the testimony, according to the words of the Prophets, of Jesus Christ and his Apostles, and according to the words of angels. Mark ye well my sayings, and see if you can pick any flaw in them. If you think you can so do, when you come to the proper place to be corrected, you may then receive instructions that will do you good.

The question I wish to ask is simply this; and I put it to all the Elders of Israel, and to all the men and women of intelligence in Israel which pertains to the Kingdom of God on Earth; and if the whole world were before me I would ask them the same question. Can any man, or set of men officiate in dispensing the laws, and administering the ordinances of the Kingdom of God, or of the kingdoms and governments of the world legally, without first obeying those laws, and submitting to those ordinances themselves. Do you understand me? If a foreigner wishes to become a citizen of the United States he must first become subject to this government; must you not first acknowledge and obey the laws of this government? Certainly you must.

Then, to apply this to the Kingdom of God on Earth, and ask yourselves if any man has the power, the influence[,] the right, the authority, to go forth and preach this gospel, and baptise for the remission of sins unless he himself has, in the first place, been baptised, ordained and legally called to that office? What would the Elders of Israel and every other sensible man say to this? They would all decide at once with me, that no man can lawfully officiate in any office in the Kingdom of God, or in the governments of men, he has not been called to, and the authority of which has not been bestowed upon him. I am not going to talk a thousand things to you, but I wish to tell you a few, and desire you to understand them, and connect them together.

There are a few more questions I would like to ask, for the simple reason of bringing the minds of the people to bear upon certain items of principle, and the philosophy of the Kingdom of God on Earth, that they may know how heavenly things are. But I will pass on, and notice some of the texts I have quoted. Before I proceed however, I will put one more question, at the same time I wish you [to] bear in mind the one I have just asked, do not forget th[at] no man has authority to officiate in the ordinances of heavenly or earthly governments only so far as he has obeyed them himself. Now to know the only wise God and Jesus Christ whom He has sent, will put the man, woman[,] congregation, or nation in possession of Eternal Life.

Are the hearts of the Latter-day Saints prepared to have Eternal Life given to them in mass, and say there shall be no more apostacy, but bring them all up that they may know and understand the Gods, Eternities[,] Creations, Heavens, Hells, Kingdoms, Thrones, Principalities, and Powers? It cannot be done. The sheep and goats are together; the wheat and the tares are growing together; the good and the bad are mixed; and they must so remain until the time when Jesus Christ will say, 'gather my sheep into my fold; gather my wheat into my garner, and let the tares, and chaff, and stubble be burned.['] That is not yet.

Now if you believe what you have heard me say you will believe there is lords many, and gods many; and you will believe that unto us, the inhabitants of this Earth there is but one God with whom we have to do;

APPENDIX C—EXCERPTS FROM BRIGHAM YOUNG'S SERMONS

and according to the tenor of the Bible, we believe there are many[,] very many who have entered into Power, Glory, Might, and Dominion, and are gathering around them Thrones, and have power to organize elements, and make worlds, and bring into existence intelligent beings in all their variety, who if they are faithful and obedient to their calling and creation will in their turn be exalted in Eternal Kingdoms of the Gods. Do you believe that? You and I have only one God to whom we are accountable, so we will let the rest alone, and search after the one we have to do with; let us seek diligently after Him, the very being who commenced this creation. (asked blessing on bread)

We will now make our inquiries with regard to our position with the God with whom we have to do. You will please recollect all ye Elders in Israel, for I want you to be instructed, by my remarks, that you may not fall into errors, that you have tested the question in your own minds with regard to the rights of officiating in ordinances.

Now I wish to ask you if you have any conception or idea as to the creation of the world? 'Oh yes,' you reply, 'A great many of us have a tolerable idea of it, but still there are mysteries we do not understand; there are some things in the Bible about the creation that seem to be dark: we have learned some things in this Kingdom we do not understand, and that do not correspond with the reading of the Bible.' **Let me open the eyes of your understanding**.

There has never been a time when the creations of worlds commenced, they are from eternity to eternity in their creations and redemption. After they are organized they experience the good and the evil; the light, and the dark, the bitter and the sweet, as you and I do. There never was a time when there were not worlds in existence as this world is, and they pass through similar changes in abiding their creation preparatory to exaltation. **Worlds have always been in progress, and eternally will be.**

Every world has had an Adam, and an Eve: named so, simply because the first man is always called Adam, and the first woman Eve; and the Oldest Son has always had the privilege of being Ordained, Appointed and Called to be the Heir of the Family, if he does not rebel against the Father, and he is the Saviour of the family. Every world that has been created, has been created upon the same principle.

They may vary in their varieties, yet the eternity is one; it is one eternal round. These are things that scarcely belong to the best of this congregation. There are items of doctrine, and principles, in the bosom of eternity that the best of the Latter-day Saints are unworthy to receive. If the visions of their minds were opened to look into the vast creations, and gaze upon the Power, and Glory, and Goodness, and Exaltation of the Gods they would exclaim; 'Wo is me[,] I am undone, I am of unclean lips.'

But we will look at it a little. Do any of you know anything about the creation of this world? 'Oh yes, we understand a good deal about it from the account given in the Bible.' So you read in the Bible of there being three persons in one god; many religionists in the woad believe in a three [in] one god, however, I do not wish to spend time to deliberate upon the notions adopted by the sectarians, the world is full of them. There are lords many and gods many according to the Bible; it does not contradict the doctrine, neither can you find a single passage that does away with that idea.

But let us turn our attention to the God with which we have to do. I tell you simply, He is our Father; the God and Father of our Lord Jesus Christ, and the Father of our spirits. Can that be possible? Yes, it is possible, He is the Father of all the spirits of the human family.

All things are first made spiritual, and brought forth into His kingdom. **The spirits of all the human family were begotten by one Father**. Now be watchful, for if I have time, and feel able, I shall communicate something in connection with this you are not expecting. Yes, every son and daughter of Adam according to the flesh can claim one parentage; the Heathen, and the Christian, the Jew and the Gentile, the high and the low, the king and the beggar, the black and the white, all who have sprung from Adam and Eve have one father.

'Then you make it out we are brethren and sisters.' Certainly for the whole human family are made of one blood of the same material; they are all begotten and brought forth by one parentage, and from one generation to another they are of one flesh and blood, and of one kindred. The God and Father [of] our Lord Jesus Christ is the Father of our spirits.

I began at the end, and shall probably finish at the beginning of my discourse; but it is no matter which end a man begins at, for the first shall be last, and the last first; which proves it is one eternal round; it is one eternity. Eloheim looks round upon the eternity of matter, and said to His associates, and those that He was pleased to call upon at that time for His counselors, with regard to the Elements[,] Worlds, Planets, Kingdoms and Thrones; **said He, 'Yahovah Michael, see that Eternal Matter on all sides, this way and that way; we have already created Words upon Worlds, shall we create another world? Yes, go and organize the elements yonder in space'; not empty space for there is no such thing, once in a while, earth quakes, and the extensive destruction of combustible matter by fire will come nigh making empty space for perhaps the millionth part of a second. 'Yahovah Michael go and create a world, make it, organize it, form it; and then put upon it everything in all the variety that you have see[n], that you have been in the habit of being associated with in other worlds, of beasts, birds, fowls, fish, and every insect, and creeping thing, and finally, [when] the whole eternity of element is full of life, bring it together and make of it living creatures.'**

Yahovah Michael goes and does as he is told. What I am now going to tell you, will no doubt astonish the whole of you. When Yahovah Michael had organized the world, and brought from another kingdom the beasts[,] fish, fowl, and insects, and every tree, and plant with which we are acquainted, and thousands that we never saw, when He had filled the Earth with animal and vegetable life, Michael or Adam goes down to the new made word, and there he stays.

Do you suppose he went there alone. Moses made the Bible to say his wife was taken out of his side, was made of one of his ribs. I do not know anything to the contrary of my ribs being equal on both sides. The Lord knows if I had lost a rib for each wife I have, I should have had none left long ago. Some try to say how many wives the Governor of Utah has, but if they can tell, they can tell more than I can, for I do not know how many I have; I have not counted them up for many years. I did not know how many I had before I left the United States I had so many. I heard that I had ninety. Why bless your souls, ninety is not a beginning. You might ask me if I have ever seen them all; I answer no; I see a few of them I pick up myself here. I have lots, and scores I never see nor shall not until the morning of the resurrection.

Now about the rib. As for the Lord taking a rib out of Adams side to make a woman of, He took one out of my side just as much.

'But, Brother Brigham, would you make it appear that Moses did not tell the truth?'

No not a particle more than I would that your mother did not tell the truth, when she told you that little Billy came from a hollow toad stool. I would not accuse your mother of lying, any more than I would Moses; the people in the days of Moses wanted to know things that was not for them, the same as your children do, when they want to know where their little brother came from, and he answered them according to their folly, the same as you did your children.

Now some will be ready to say, 'We always heard these Mormons did not believe the Bible.' I believe all the truth that is there and that is enough for me, and for you to believe.

'Then the Lord did not make Adam out of the dust of the earth.'

Yes he did, but I have not got to that part of my discourse yet. Adam was made of the dust of the earth.

'Was he made of the dust of this earth.'

No[,] but of the dust of the earth where on he was born in the flesh; that is the way he was made; he was made of dust.

'Did the Lord put into him his spirit.'

Yes, as the Lord put into you your spirit, he was begotten of a father, and brought forth as you and I were; and so are all intelligent beings brought forth from eternity to eternity. Man was not mad[e] the same as you make an adobe to put in a wall. Moses said Adam was made of the dust of the ground, but he did not say of what ground. I say he was not made of the dust of the ground of this Earth, but he was made of the dust of the earth where he lived, where he honored his calling, believed in his Saviour, or Elder Brother, and by his faithfulness, was redeemed, and got a Glorious Resurrection. All creatures that dwell upon this Earth are made of the elements that compose it; which are organized to see if they will abide their creation, and be counted worthy to receive a resurrection. 'What[,] every flesh.'

Yes every flesh, for all flesh pertaining to this world is made of the dust of this Earth; it is all made from the same material, according to the will and pleasure of Him who dictates all things. Our bodies are composed of the same material that composes this Earth; they are composed of the water, air, and solid earth, either of which will resolve back to their native fountain.

How many elements are there I do not know anymore than you. They have never all been classified by science, though scientific gentlemen have tried to do it.

I tell you more, Adam is the Father of our spirits. He lived upon an earth; he did abide his creation, and did honor to his calling and Priesthood; and obeyed his Master or Lord, and probably many of his wives did the same, and they lived, and died upon an earth, and then were resurrected again to Immortality and Eternal Life.

'Did he resurrect himself,' you inquire. I want to throw out a few hints upon the resurrection as it seems to come within the circuit of my ideas whether it ought to come within the circuit of my remarks or not.

I believe we have already acknowledged the truth established that no person can officiate in any office he has not been subject to himself and been legally appointed to fill. That no person in this Kingdom can officiate in any ordinance he himself has not obeyed; consequently no being who has not been resurrected possesses the Keys of the Power of Resurrection. That you have been told often. Adam therefore was resurrected by someone who had been resurrected.

I will go a little further with this lest some of you will be querying, doubting, and philosophizing this away. It is true, Jesus said 'I lay down my life that I might take it again. No man taketh it from me, but I lay it down of myself. I have power to lay it down, and I have power to take it again.' I do not doubt the power of Christ; but did he prove that in his resurrection? No. But it is proved that an angel came and rolled away the stone from the door of the sepulchre, and did resurrect the body of the Son of God.

'What angel was this.'

It is no[t] for me to say. I do not know him. If I ever did know him it is so long since I have entirely forgotten who it was. That Jesus had power to lay down his life, and power to take it up again I do not dispute. Neither do I dispute, but what an angel came, that was sent by the Father of our Lord Jesus Christ, to roll away the stone from the sepulchre, and resurrect the Son of God. **Suffice it to say that he was some character who had himself been resurrected.**

'Is there any further proof with regard to this sacred order of the Kingdom of God on the Earth.'

Oh yes, you can find it in all the scriptures. For instance when the Saviour appeared to Paul of Tarsus, on the road, in answer to the question, 'Lord what wilt thou have me do,' he was told to go into the city of Damascus, and it should be told him there what to do. In the mean[time] one Ananias was sent to him, who Baptized and Ordained him. Jesus would not do this, because he had servants on Earth whose special duty it was to administer these ordinances.

Again the angel that appeared to Cornelius would not operate in the ordinances of the Gospel, but told him to send men to Joppa to the house of one Simon the Tanner, and call for one Peter etc. whose duty it was to do it, he being called and ordained to that power. Many more instances of this kind might be quoted but the above will suffice to illustrate the principle.

Now, many inquiries will be made about the Saviour, such as, 'Who is he? Is he the Father of Adam? Is he the god of Adam?[']When Christ has finished his labor and presented it to his father, then he, Adam will receive a fullness. That is all easily understood by me. He cannot receive a fullness of the kingdoms He has organized until they are completed. If He sends His servants off to the right and to the left to perform a certain labor[,] His kingdom is not complete, until His ministers have accomplished everything to make His kingdom complete and returned home again. **Many inquire, who is this Saviour?** I will tell you what I think about it, and as the [Southerners] say I reckon, and as the Yankees say I guess; but **I will tell you what I reckon. I reckon that Father Adam was a resurrected being, with his wives and posterity, and in the Celestial Kingdom they were crowned with Glory[,] Immortality and Eternal Lives, with Thrones, Principalities and Powers: and it was said to him[, '] It is your right to organize the elements; and to your Creations and Posterity there shall be no end, but you shall add Kingdom to Kingdom, and Throne to Throne; and still behold the vast eternity of unorganized matter.[']**

Adam then was a resurrected being; and I reckon, Our spirits and the spirits of all the human family were begotten by Adam, and born of Eve.

'How are we going to know this?'

I reckon it.

And I reckon that Adam came into the Garden of Eden, and did actually eat of the fruit that he himself planted; and I reckon there was a previous understanding, and the whole plan was previously calculated, before the Garden of Eden was made, that he would reduce his posterity to sin, misery, darkness, wickedness, wretchedness, and to the power of the Devil, that they might be prepared for an Exaltation, for without this they could not receive one.

I reckon that all things were first made spiritual preparatory to the natural organization. 'What was the use of all this[,] could not spirits be happy?' Yes, as far as they could. These Indians that roam upon the plains, and upon the mountains are comparatively happy in their degraded condition, because they do not know the comforts of civilized life. They can lay upon the ground; pull up sage brush to form a temporary shield against the cold, and get plenty of lizards, and crickets to eat, and they are happy. We would want a comfortable house to live in and something comfortable to eat; something that is suited to our nature, ability, taste, and appetite. We would not be happy and satisfied short of that. So our spirits are as happy as they know how to be. Were you now to live without a house you could not be happy; neither could the spirit be happy without a tabernacle which is the house of the spirit. Whe[n] the spirit enters the body it is pure, and good, and if the body would be subject to the spirit it would always be taught to do the will of the Father in Heaven. But the spirit is interwoven with the flesh and blood; it is subjected to the body, consequently Satan has power over both. **I reckon the Father has been through all this**.

Do you recollect what I told the brethren who came across the plains this season, when they were perplexed by their oxen; and were calling upon God to give you grace to perform the labor which lay before you, **He could not sympathize with you, or know the nature of your trials if He had not passed through the same Himself. He knew just as much about crossing the plains, and the trials connected with it as any of us**.

The inquiry will arise, among those who are strenuous, and tenacious for the account given by Moses, as to Adam.

'Did not Adam die.'

Yes he died.

'Does not the Bible say he died.'

I do not know nor care, but I think it would be hard I think to find where he died; or where Moses died though I have no doubt Moses died, and Adam also; how? just as you and I have to die, and be laid away in the bowels of Mother Earth; that, however, Moses did not see fit to tell us.

Adam planted the Garden of Eden, and he with his wife Eve partook of the fruit of this Earth, until their systems were charged with the nature of Earth, and then they could beget bodies, for their spiritual children. If the spirit does not enter into the embryo man that is forming in the womb of the woman, the result will be false conception, a living, intelligent being cannot be produced. Adam and Eve begat the first mortal bodies on this Earth, and from that commencement every spirit that was begotten in eternity for this Earth will enter bodies thus prepared for them here, until the winding up scene, and that will not be until the last of these spirits enters an earthly tabernacle.

Then I reckon that the children of Adam and Eve married each other; this is speaking to the point. I believe in sisters marrying brothers, and brothers having their sisters for wives. Why? Because we cannot do otherwise. There are none others for me to marry but my sisters.

'But yo[u would] not pretend to say you would marry your father and mother's daughter.'

If I did not I would marry another of my sisters that lives over in another garden; the material of which they are organized is just the same; there is no difference between them, and those who live in this garden. Our spirits are all brothers and sisters, and so are our bodies; and the opposite idea to this has resulted from the ignorant, and foolish traditions of the nations of the Earth. They have corrupted themselves with each other, and I want them to understand that they have corrupted their own flesh, blood, and bones; for they are of the same flesh, blood, and bones, as all the family of the Earth. I am approaching the subject of our marriage relations Brother Hyde lectured upon, but I shall not have time, or strength to say much about this. But, I reckon that Father Adam, and Mother Eve had the children of the human family prepared to come here and take bodies; and when they come to take bodies, they enter into the bodies prepared for them, and that body gets an exaltation with the spirit, when they are prepared to be crowned in Father[']s Kingdom.

'What, into Adam's Kingdom?'

Yes.

As to my talking what I want to say at this time I shall not do it. I am exhausting myself; I have to speak loud, and it is hard labor.

I tell you, when you see your Father in the Heavens, you will see Adam; when you see your Mother that bear your spirit, you will see Mother Eve. And **when you see yourselves there you have gained your Exaltation;** you have honored your calling here on the Earth; your body has returned to its mother Earth; and somebody has broken the chains of death that bound you, and given you a resurrection.

How are you going to get your resurrection? You will get it by the President of the Resurrection pertaining to this generation, and that is Joseph Smith Junior. Hear it all ye ends of the Earth; if ever you enter into the Kingdom of God it is because Joseph Smith let you go there. This will apply to Jews and Gentiles, to the bond, and free; to friends and foes; no man or woman in this generation will get a resurrection and be crowned without Joseph Smith says so. The man who was martyred in Carthage Jail [in the] State of Illinois holds the Keys of Life and Death to this generation. He is the President of the Resurrection in this Dispensation and he will be the first to rise from the dead. When he has passed through it, then I reckon the Keys of Resurrection will be committed to him. Then he will call up his Apostles. You know I told you last conference I was an Apostle of Joseph Smith; and **if faithful enough I expect Joseph will resurrect the Apostles; and when they have passed through the change, and received their blessings, I expect he will commit to them the Keys of the Resurrection, and they will go on resurrecting the Saints, every man in his own order**.

I want to say a little more about marriage relations, so that you may understand what my views are. **When you get your resurrection, you**

are not yet exalted; but by and by, the Lord Jesus Christ, our Elder Brother, the Saviour of the world, the Heir of the Family; when he has put down Satan, and destroyed death; then he will say, come let us go home into the presence of the Father.

What will become of the world then? It will be baptized with fire. I[t] has been baptized with water, and it will then be cleansed by fire, and become like a sea of glass, and be made Celestial; and Jesus Christ our Elder Brother will take the whole Earth, with all the Saints and go with them **to the Father even to Adam**; and you will continue to receive more and more Intelligence, Glory, Exaltation, and Power.

I want to tell you a thing with regard to parents, wives, brothers and sisters etc. The time will come when it will be told where this man, and that woman shall be placed; The real blood of Joseph will be selected out from among the tribes of Israel, and every man and woman will be put in their places, and stand in their order where the Lord designs them to be. When you get back into the presence of God, and the Lord should say [']Who have you brought with you?['] Your reply would be, [']My wife and children;' but in reality you have only with you your brothers and sisters.

The Father would say, 'These are my children.['] When you meet your Father in Heaven you will know Him, and realize that you have lived with Him, and rested in His bosom for ages gone passed, and He will hail you as His sons and daughters, and embrace you, and you will embrace Him, and [']Hallelujah[,] thank God I have come to Father again, I have got back home['] will resound through the Heavens. **There are ten thousand things connected with these ideas…I could stand here and tell you what I reckon but it would take an age for me to tell you all there is about it**.

We have all come from one father even Adam, both the black and the white, the grizzled and the gray; the noble, and the ignoble; **and the time will come, when they will all come back again into His presence**. When they have behaved themselves, and proved faithful to their calling, and to their God the curse will be removed, from every class, and nation of men that desires to work the work of God. This [has] been told you[,] that saviours would come upon Mount Zion, and judge the Mount of Esau. Let me read it for you, [']There shall saviours come upon Mount Zion, and Save the Mount of Esau.['] What does gentile signify? Disobedience. What does Israel signify? Obedience. What is the name of the first man[?] Adam, which signifies first man, and Eve signifies first woman. And when Michael the Archangel shall sound his trump and the Ancient of Days shall come, all things that we have once been familiar with will come back again to our memory…" (*Teachings of President Brigham Young*, Vol. 3, 1852–1854 [Salt Lake City: Collier's Publishing Co., 1987], pp. 343–368. Also see *The Essential Brigham Young,* pp. 86–104)

Sermon Delivered on 25 April 1855

Naturally it falls my lot this evening to speak to the congregation. Probably but very little [is] known or [has] been said with regard to this association, the Deseret Theological Institute. The constitution is short and I believe comprises all that we could wish it to. If it is carried out I don't think there will be any lack with regard to the good order and progress of the institution, and above all things I would like to have the last clause of the constitution observed by the officers of the association and its members and have it most strenuously observed so that they may never do or speak or touch or introduce anything to the association derogatory to the instructions and spirit of our Lord Jesus Christ. If this be observed and is carefully carried out there is no danger in the world of the institution being led wrong but there are many times, I will acknowledge, that people's minds may be overcharged through a multitude of business, and they may not feel the same influence of the divine spirit that they would upon other circumstances. If people are destitute of a full flow of the spirit of revelation they should endeavor to act according to their judgment and the best reasoning faculties they are in possession of so as to govern and control themselves to as not to do anything derogatory to the spirit of wisdom. I sometimes feel as though I could exercise myself upon those grounds for eternity. My mind is almost daily overcharged with business and the heaviest task that is upon me is to talk about that which I should not be called to talk about or observe in the least: the business of others, which I should not be troubled with. I do not think that I was ever tired in my life talking or thinking about any matter of business that really had to be attended to. My body has been wearied many times but I have never felt as though my spirit were getting weary. I do not think I was ever weary one moment in my life in reflecting, concerning, calculating, directing, planning, or doing anything that pertained to the building up of the Kingdom of God, or anything that pertained to good and that was my duty to attend to. But when I am flooded with matters that do not belong to me, matters that I should not be troubled with in the least, then my mind gets weary and I get a little perplexed and it makes my head ache, but it never did in my life to do the business that directly belonged to me to attend to. This is the case with many, perhaps, that may be perplexed, worried and harassed into unnecessary things.

I design laying before the congregation this evening some of my views that are incorporated in our constitution. To have my mind filled with the same degree of light and intelligence that I otherwise would have, I can excuse myself through the multiplicity of little things that are upon me: thousands of questions asked me every day, my mind turned from one subject to another as it were like lightning and hence it is difficult to bring my ind to bear on any particular subject as I would wish to do, to lay before the congregation things that would be interesting. **I will say at least to myself, the foundation of my remarks this evening I wish to be placed in the minds of the congregation as the foundation of all theology, and of all knowledge, heavenly and earthly, which incorporates principalities and powers, thrones and dominions, time space and time and times again and of all eternity, and it is simply the words by the apostles when Jesus says, "This is life eternal to know thee, the only true God and Jesus Christ whom thou hast sent."** It is true we might turn around and ask if evil spirits, if the prince and power of the air, Lucifer, the devil, do[es] not know God? I will merely answer the question briefly by saying if he had known even himself, he never would have risen with the power and influence that he possesses to try and dethrone the Almighty God. If he had understood himself, the extent of his knowledge, the ability he possessed, he never would have presumed to have taken such a course. That satisfies me that he did not know God as much as he would have done had he been obedient to his requirements. To know the only wise God as the apostle directed his speech in the influence thereof, to his brethren, and to know that God Almighty that they serve, not in a partial manner, but to the extent that the apostle directed supposes as much as to believe that there is a God and that that God did inhabit eternity and did make the worlds, and that he is the supreme ruler of the universe whom the human family are called upon to acknowledge with their faith, with their mouths, by their acts and influence. Thousands and millions of our fellow creatures, notwithstanding the knowledge they had in the days of the apostles, opposed the work that was then commenced. They opposed the people of God from the commencement of the preaching of the gospel. Thousands knew God partially and heard his voice and saw and understood his miracles that were performed amongst them, yet they did not know that God, whom to know is life eternal. Had they known him they never would have opposed him. This subject I realize perfectly, in the fullness, and the ideas and in the extent there are to be understood by men, them that incorporate all salvation, all intelligence, all power, every knowledge of every class and of every degree we have any knowledge of. As for my explaining and setting the subject before the people in its fullness, I do not undertake the task this evening, but wish to hint at a few leading ideas so that we may learn how to learn and know God, and what we shall know if we do know him. Still further, I wish to hint at a few of the leading principles pertaining to the knowledge of God and the influence of his spirit upon the people and they do not understand it.

In the first place to know God is a subject of the deep interest. We turn and say it is very intricate. It is so in our feelings. It is hard for us to know our God and after we have talked about it and talked again and heard ministers preach about it. I read their writings, and the views of the best theologians of our day, we read the history of those in ancient days, their views upon the subject. We have the history or a portion of the history, of this very God by those that did actually see and sojourn with him in the flesh, did talk and eat and drink and travel and sleep with him in the preach, teach, and did converse with him from day to day and from month to month and from year to year. They knew him in his birth, childhood, youth, and in his ministry, and they said we are acquainted with his brothers and sisters in the flesh. **And this is their God pertaining to the incarnation of this very character as far as the son-ship is concerned, and the relationship and the understanding of the son to the father. We have the knowledge of that very character which if we know him and understand him is to us eternal life. We turn round [that is the enquirer] and saw we do believe that Jesus Christ, the son of God was upon the earth, but who knows the Father? Well now, let me answer this question right here in simplicity, for Jesus did tell his disciples when speaking to them when he said, "he that hath seen me hath seen the father also." I turn round and say, who understood that language? Jesus says in another place, "I am in the father and the father is in me and I and my father are one, and whosoever hath seen me hath seen the father for he is in me and I in him." You know the sectarian world have explained this away and have made out that the father came and did, but if we can learn what he (Jesus) was upon the earth and in eternity, we will know what the father was.** When I let these subjects rest on my mind and I contemplate upon them, I will say for your satisfaction and for mine, that when these subjects are before me and the light that I have in me, the spirit that rests on me, apparently I understand just as well what Jesus wished to convey to his apostles as I do when I talk to you and see you before me. It appears to me I understand his mind and character and who he is and who he came from. And we can learn who he is from the prophets and what character he was at the time of his incarnation and when he went to his father. **But this is for you to believe or disbelieve as you please, for if I were to say who he was I have no doubt but there would be many that would say perhaps it is so and perhaps it is not.** Well I am so liberal that I wish every person could have the privilege, which they certainly enjoy, of learning Jesus Christ whom the father has sent. This can be learned by a close appreciation to the science of theology. **No man can understand theology unless that man is filled with the light of eternity.** They may study till doomsday and then not understand for when they study they mix in all the superstitions of the world instead of being ruled and controlled by the spirit that inhabits eternity.

If I should undertake to tell the people what I believe in my heart and what seemeth to me (I do not say it is so) but what seemeth to me to be eternal truth, how would they know unless they had the spirit of revelation to say to them whether it was a truth or an untruth.

We can read the history of Adam and Eve in the garden of Eden and that after they transgressed the Lord came along and they run scampering away into the bushes. How did they know it was him? Just as well as my family know mine, for they had lived with him and had a long experience with him. Just as soon as my family hear my footsteps they know that I am coming, and so did Adam and Eve know the footsteps of the Lord. Just as quick as they heard his footsteps they knew who was coming as though they had seen his face because they were acquainted with him. But this is no knowledge to you and I. He came along and said, where are you, what have you been doing? They had hid themselves. It is evident from this that they knew his footsteps, but what advantage is that to you? Would you know the footsteps of the Lord if you heard them coming into this hall from merely reading this account? The Lord is capable of coming in at that door and sitting down and should it was some stranger.

Well, how can we learn by reading the history of Adam and Eve to know the Lord? If you were to hear the footsteps of the Lord would you know from the history of Adam and Eve that it was the Lord coming? They knew the Lord and his footsteps for they had lived with him and had been in eternity with him, and what I have upon this subject I now say: **Adam had been with the Lord and had lived with him upon an earth like this and had been faithful and overcome, and had received his body and was resurrected and was well acquainted with the Lord and was one of his mess mates. He had eaten and drunk with him and had lived with him from generation to generation and in many worlds, probably while many had come into and gone out of existence.** And he helped to make this earth and brought the seeds with him that you see springing up spontaneously. And when he called, the elements came rolling together.

Well you see from this when you and I have been with and lived with the Lord we shall know his voice. If father Adam was to come into this house and you were to see him go back and forth, would you know him? No, you would never mistrust it was him unless he revealed himself. But by the time that you have lived with him as long as Adam had before he came here you will know him and recognize his footsteps, but reading the history will not teach you these things, consequently I come right down to ourselves and say we cannot know the only wise God and Jesus Christ whom he has sent. No man can have this knowledge but those to whom God reveals it. Has he revealed it to you, who he is, what he has to do with this world and the relationship that he sustains to it? You must not be astonished when I tell you that the whole world, with the exception of the Latter-day Saint for they do know something about God, but the whole world besides are as far from that knowledge as the east is from the west. Thou they read it in the bible yet it never enters into their hearts that the apostle told the truth when he said, "there is but one living and true God, the father of our spirits." Well now who is the father of our spirits?

I did take the liberty to tell this once and I told it in a way that I did not get to their understandings and I suppose I take the same course this evening and you do not understand. But you have the spirit of the Almighty with you to enable you to appreciate. Or shall I talk it right out as one man talketh and reasoneth with another and in this manner communicate to you my ideas upon the subject? For instance: we begin with the father of our Lord Jesus Christ and our spirits. Who is he? Do you know anything about him? Can you find out who he is? Suppose we go to the scriptures and enquire who he is. At one time he says, "I am that I am." At another time when the question was proposed by someone he replied, "I am the Lord your God." At another time he is spoken of as "a man of war", "a general", and so on. You may trace the scriptures through and you will find that he is known to one people [by] one title today and tomorrow and the next day by another and there he leaves it. If I were to set before you the principle directly to the truth and yet precisely as I understand pertaining to him with whom we have to do, I have no question or doubt but what it would be opposed to your transitions and the feelings of many of you. I will tell you what I think about some who will have something to do with us by and by, when Michael blows his trumpet and calls the world together we shall then be before him and we shall be perfectly satisfied that he can pass all the judgment that we shall want, and that the dominions of the wicked will want. And I have no doubt but the Saints that live and have lived from the days of Adam will be satisfied that he can give them kingdoms and power, thrones and dominions and influence in eternity. And when they get all that he can give they will be satisfied and say, "it's enough." If we can get to him, the ancient of days, whose hair is like wool, a man of age, a man of experience, and can learn of him to understand "I am that I am" we shall then hear him say, "I am your father and your leader. I will be your front and your rearward. I understand what this world is. I understand all about it. I have the government of the world in my hands although to a certain extent my opposer, my enemy, has gained a certain influence in the world." You will hear him say, "I am in the whirlwind at my pleasure. I ride upon the storms and I govern worlds. I set up one king and put another down and organize empires and overthrow them at my pleasure. I the Lord do all these things." When we come to that great and wise and glorious being that the children of Israel were afraid of, whose countenance shone so that they could not look upon him, I say when we get to him whom we could not look upon, to that man, that is I conclude he was a man for it says that he had hands and you know men have hands. And it says that he put his hands out before Moses in the cleft of the rock until his glory passed by and would not suffer Moses to see his face but his parts only. Seeing then that he had parts I conclude that he was a man. When we can see that very character and talk and live with him in our tabernacles, if we are so fortunate as to get there, into his society, then we can say that to use there is but one living and true God and he is the father of our Lord Jesus Christ and of our spirits. And when we get back to him and learn that he is actually our father we shall not feel any anxiety to call upon anybody else for the blessings we are in need of. It is a subject I am aware that does not appear so clear to our understandings at present as we could wish it or as it will some day, and it is one that should not trouble us at all. All such things will become more clear to our minds by and by.

I tell you this as my belief about that personage who is called the ancient of days, the prince, and so on. But I do not tell it because that I wish it to be established in the minds of others, though to me it is as clear as the sun. It is as plain as my alphabet. I understand it as I do the path to go home. I did not understand so until my mind became enlightened with the spirit and by the revelation of God, neither will you understand until our father in heaven reveals all these things unto you. To my mind and to my feelings those matters are all plain and easy to understand.

Now this is the foundation for my remark and which I consider to be all that I wish to hear lectured upon in this society. Now if I could hear lectures, say every evening in the week from persons, and they will actually speak upon their feelings upon whatever subject they may treat upon. We will say it is a joiner and he commences to give us an explanation of what he knows and then we bring up a mason after the joiner has given us a lecture on architecture and he takes up his portion and lectures on that. And finally the farmer comes up, and by and by we find a man that will give us a lecture on physiology and anatomy. And then we will call upon the mechanics and have them set before the people the principles of machinery. And next we find a lecturer that will tell us how to bottle up lightning and carry it about with us in our pockets. And another will tell us how to put up a railroad about the tenth of an inch in diameter and he will tell that by putting up certain wires he can speak with men on the other side of the world and that by extending those wires around the whole earth he could bring intelligence from the remotest parts of this earth in a second or a second and a half. Again, get a man among us that will give us a lecture on mechanics and a lecture upon chemistry. Another will tell us when the first carding machine and the first spinning machine were invented and by and by all the inventions of men upon the whole earth will be brought into the society. And we will get each man up to speak according to his trade or profession and in that way every man will shine in the sphere in which he acts, for every man will, if he understands his business, shine best in his own orbit.

Suppose we get a mechanic up to lecture and tell the origin of our moon or some of the planets. Would he be a proper person to throw light on such a subject? Then you take a person that understands for instance how to manufacture aprons from the raw materials and then go along from him that cut the cloth into this shape with the other till you come to the man who can make copper, take it out of the native bed, and tell how to make saucepans, kettles and plates etc. Then he goes on and tells how to take the metal from the native bed and convert and make it into everything that he wants almost. So it has been from the days of Adam to the present time. **Things have been revealed to man each in its own time and in its season**. One man making one discovery and another one another. One man taking the iron ore and making it into railroads, then another man making the telegraph from here to the States, or China, or back to England, and by it sending messages as quick as light. One lecture to us upon one according to his talents, another upon another and so on. And when they had explained all these I would turn round and say these are all embraced in our text. "To know God" circumscribes the whole of it. But when this knowledge or the discoveries that have been made or that is given to the children of men, they have in every instance taken the honor and glory to themselves. It is said that such a man, a philosopher, has made this discovery. Oh yes, they have discovered so much that they can take this earth and go millions and billions and octillions and every other kind of tillions of miles up into space and weigh the planets, and all these great and important discoveries are attributes to the knowledge of those learned and wise men.

No man knew anything about those worlds or astronomy, mechanics, mathematics or anything else, only what he had learned. You never knew anything but what you learned from some source. I have heard a great many men and women ask when they have heard a man lecture or speak upon some subject, "What a deep and eloquent and sublime discourse. What a very learned man he must be." I would like to know if he had not borrowed it from someone else. "Oh, but," says one, "he has brought it out for himself. We expect it is his own production." Well now let me tell you that I have no knowledge and you have none but what we have received from others. You have no knowledge of this earth or the elements that compose it, or of its resources, none but what you have learned from others. Did you know this? Why yes, a moment's reflection will tell you this; it is easily seen if you only consider for a short time. I look to those things and as things appear to me the source, the influence by which we learn all things is one." [JVL] (*The Complete Discourses of Brigham Young*, Vol. 2, 1853 to 1856, Ed. Richard S. Van Wagoner, Smith-Petit Foundation, Salt Lake City, 2009, pp. 934–938).

Sermon Delivered on 8 February 1857

"…It is one of the first principles of the doctrine of salvation to become acquainted with our Father and our God. **The Scriptures teach that this is eternal life, to 'know Thee, the only true God, and Jesus Christ whom thou hast sent;' this is as much as to say that no man can enjoy or be prepared for eternal life without that knowledge**.

You hear a great deal of preaching upon this subject; and when people repent of their sins, they will get together, and pray and exhort each other, and try to get the spirit of revelation, try to have God their Father revealed to them, that they may know Him and become acquainted with Him.

There are some plain, simple facts that I wish to tell you, and I have but one desire in this, which is, that you should have understanding to receive them, to treasure them up in your hearts, to contemplate upon these facts, for they are simple facts, based upon natural principles; **there is no mystery about them when once understood**.

I want to tell you, each and every one of you, that you are well acquainted with God our heavenly Father, or the great Eloheim. You are all well acquainted with Him, for there is not a soul of you but what has lived in His house and dwelt with Him year after year; and yet you are seeking to become acquainted with Him, when the fact is, you have merely forgotten what you did know. I told you a little last Sabbath about forgetting things. There is not a person here to-day but what is a son or a daughter of that Being. In the spirit world their spirits were first begotten and brought forth, and they lived there with their parents for ages before they came here. This, perhaps, is hard for many to believe, but it is the greatest nonsense in the world not to believe it. If you do not believe it, cease to call Him Father; and when you pray, pray to some other character.

It would be inconsistent in you to disbelieve what I think you know, and then to go home and ask the Father to do so and so for you. The Scriptures which we believe have taught us from the beginning to call Him our Father, and we have been taught to pray to Him as our Father, in the name of our eldest brother whom we call Jesus Christ, the Saviour of the world; and that Saviour, while here on earth, was so explicit on the point that he taught his disciples to call no man on earth father, for we have one which is in heaven. He is the Saviour, because it is his right to redeem the remainder of the family pertaining to the flesh on this earth, if any of you do not believe this, tell us how and what we should believe. If I am not telling you the truth, please to tell me the truth on this subject, and let me know more than I do know. **If it is hard for you to believe, if you wish to be Latter-day Saints, admit the fact as I state it, and do not contend against it. Try to believe it, because you will never become acquainted with our Father, never enjoy the blessings of His Spirit, never be prepared to enter into His presence, until you most assuredly believe it; therefore you had better try to believe this great mystery about God.**

I do not marvel that the world is clad in mystery, to them He is an unknown God; they cannot tell where He dwells nor how He lives, nor what kind of a being He is in appearance or character. They want to become acquainted with His character and attributes, but they know nothing of them. This is in consequence of the apostacy that is now in the world. They have departed from the knowledge of God, transgressed His laws, changed His ordinances, and broken the everlasting covenant, so that the whole earth is defiled under the inhabitants thereof. Consequently it is no mystery to us that the world knoweth not God, but it would be a mystery to me, with what I now know, to say that we cannot know anything of Him. We are His children.

To bring the truth of this matter close before you, I will instance your fathers who made the first permanent settlement in New England. There are a good many in this congregation whose fathers landed upon Plymouth Rock in the year 1620. Those fathers began to spread abroad; they had children, those children had children, and their children had children, and here are we their children. I am one of them, and many of this congregation belong to that class. Now ask yourselves this simple question upon natural principles, has the species altered? Were not the people who landed at Plymouth Rock the same species with us? Were they not organized as we are? Were not their countenances similar to ours? Did they not converse, have knowledge, read books? Were there not mechanics among them, and did they not understand agriculture, &c., as we do? Yes, every person admits this.

Now follow our fathers further back and take those who first came to the island of Great Britain, were they the same species of beings as those who came to America? Yes, all acknowledge this; this is upon natural principles. Thus you may continue and trace the human family back to Adam and Eve, and ask, 'are we of the same species with Adam and Eve?' Yes, every person acknowledges this; this comes within the scope of our understanding.

But when we arrive at that point, a vail is dropt, and our knowledge is cut off. Were it not so, you could trace back your history to the Father of our spirits in the eternal world. He is a being of the same species as ourselves; He lives as we do, except the difference that we are earthly, and He is heavenly. He has been earthly, and is of precisely the same species of being that we are. Whether Adam is the personage that we should consider our heavenly Father, or not, is considerable of a mystery to a good many. I do not care for one moment how that is; it is no matter whether we are to consider Him our God, or whether His Father, or His Grandfather, for in either case we are of one species—of one family—and Jesus Christ is also of our species.

You may hear the divines of the day extol the character of the Saviour, undertake to exhibit his true character before the people, and give an account of his origin, and were it not ridiculous, I would tell what I have thought about their views. Brother Kimball wants me to tell it, therefore you will excuse me if I do. I have frequently thought of mules, which you know are half horse and half ass, when reflecting upon the representations made by those divines. I have heard sectarian priests undertake to tell the character of the Son of God, and they make him half of one species and half of another, and I could not avoid thinking at once of the mule, which is the most hateful creature that ever was made, I believe. You will excuse me, but I have thus thought many a time.

Now to the facts in the case; all the difference between Jesus Christ and any other man that ever lived on the earth, from the days of Adam until now, is simply this, the Father, after He had once been in the flesh, and lived as we live, obtained His exaltation, attained to thrones, gained the ascendancy over principalities and powers, and had the knowledge and power to create-to bring forth and organize the elements upon natural principles. This He did after His ascension, or His glory, or His eternity, and was actually classed with the Gods, with the beings who create, with those who have kept the celestial law while in the flesh, and again obtained their bodies. Then He was prepared to commence the work of creation, as the Scriptures teach. It is all here in the Bible; I am not telling you a word but what is contained in that book.

Things were first created spiritually; the Father actually begat the spirits, and they were brought forth and lived with Him. Then He commenced the work of creating earthly tabernacles, precisely as He had been created in this flesh himself, by partaking of the course material that was organized and composed this earth, until His system was charged with it, consequently the tabernacles of His children were organized from the coarse materials of this earth.

When the time came that His first-born, the Saviour, should come into the world and take a tabernacle, **the Father came Himself and favoured that spirit with a tabernacle instead of letting any other man do it**. The Saviour was begotten by the Father of His spirit, by the same Being who is the Father of our spirits, and that is all the organic difference between Jesus Christ and you and me. And a difference there is between our Father and us consists in that He has gained His exaltation, and has obtained eternal lives. **The principle of eternal lives is an eternal existence, eternal duration, eternal exaltation**. Endless are His kingdoms, endless His thrones and His dominions, and endless are His posterity; they never will cease to multiply from this time henceforth and forever.

To you who are prepared to enter into the presence of the Father and the Son, what I am now telling will eventually be no more strange than are the feelings of a person who returns to his father's house, brethren, and sisters, and enjoys the society of his old associates, after an absence of several years upon some distant island. Upon returning he would be happy to see his father, his relatives and friends. So also if we keep the celestial law when our spirits go to God who gave them, we shall find that we are acquainted there and distinctly realize that we know all about that world.

Tell me that you do not know anything about God! I will tell you one thing, it would better become you to lay your hands upon your mouths and them in the dust, and cry, 'unclean, unclean.'

Whether you receive these things or not, I tell you them in simplicity. I lay them before you like a child, because they are perfectly simple. If you see and understand these things, it will be by the Spirit of God; you will receive them by no other spirit. No matter whether they are told to you like the thunderings of the Almighty, or by simple conversation; if you enjoy the Spirit of the Lord, it will tell you whether they are right or not.

I am acquainted with my Father. I am as confident that I understand in part, see in part, and know and am acquainted with Him in part, as I am that I was acquainted with my earthly father who died in Quincy, Illinois, after we were driven from Missouri. My recollection is better with regard to my earthly father than it is in regard to my heavenly Father; but as to knowing of what species He is, and how He is organized, and with regard to His existence, I understand it in part as well as I understand the organization and existence of my earthly father. That is my opinion about it, and my opinion to me is just as good as yours is to you; and if you are of the same opinion you will be satisfied as I am.

I know my heavenly Father and Jesus Christ whom He has sent, and this is eternal life. And if we will do as we have been told this morning, if you will enter into the Spirit of your calling, into the principle of securing to yourselves **eternal lives**, eternal existence, eternal exaltation, it will be well with you..." (JD 4:215–219)

Appendix D

Excerpts from Sermons of Heber C. Kimball

Sermon Delivered on 2 April 1854

"Comparing us to clay that is in the hands of the potter, if that clay is passive, I have power as a potter to mould it and make it into a vessel unto honor. Who is to mould these vessels? Is it God Himself in person, or is it His servants, His potters, or journeymen, in company with those He has placed to oversee the work? The great Master Potter dictates His servants, and it is for them to carry out His purposes, and make vessels according to his designs; and when they have done the work, they deliver it up to the Master for His acceptance; and if their works are not good, He does not accept them; the only works He accepts, are those that are prepared according to the design He gave. God will not be trifled with; neither will His servants; their words have got to be fulfilled, and they are the men that are to mould you, and tell you what shape to move in. I do not know that I can compare it better than by the potter's business. It forms a good comparison. This is the course you must pursue, **and I know of no other way that God has prepared for you to become sanctified, and molded, and fashioned, until you become modeled to the likeness of the Son of God**, by those who are placed to lead you. This is a lesson you have to learn as well as myself. When I know that I am doing just as I am told by him who is placed to lead this people, I am then a happy man, I am filled with peace, and can go about my business with joy and pleasure; I can lie down and rise again in peace, and be filled with gladness by night and by day. But when I have not done the things that are right, my conscience gnaws upon my feelings. This is the course for me to take.

If it is the course for me to take, it is the course for every other Elder in Israel to take—it does not matter who he is, or where he came from whether he be an American, an Englishman, Irishman, Frenchman or German, Jew or Gentile to this you have got to bow, and you have got to bow down like the clay in the hands of the potter, that suffers the potter to mould it according to his own pleasure. **You have all got to come to this and if you do not come to it at this time, as sure as the sun ever rose and set, you will be cut from the wheel, and thrown back into the mill. You have come from the mill, and you have been there grinding. For what purpose? To bring you into a passive condition**. You have been gathered from the nations of the earth, from among the kindreds, tongues, and peoples of the world, to the Valley of the Great Salt Lake, to purify and sanctify yourselves, and become like the passive clay in the hands of the potter. Now suppose I subject myself enough, in the hands of the potter, to be shaped according as he was dictated by the Great Master potter, that rules over all things in heaven and on earth, he would make me into a vessel of honor. **There are many vessels that are destroyed after they have been molded and shaped**. Why? Because they are not contented with the shape the potter has given them, but straightway put themselves into a shape to please themselves; therefore they are beyond understanding what God designs, and they destroy themselves by the power of their own agency, for this is given to every man and woman, to do just as they please. That is all right, and all just. **Well, then, you have to go through a great many modeling and shapes, then you have to be glazed and burned; and even in the burning, some vessels crack**.

What makes them crack? Because they are snappish; they would not crack, if they were not snappish and willful. If you go to the potteries in Staffordshire, England, where the finest chinaware is manufactured, you will see them take the coarsest materials about the pottery, and make a thing in the shape of a half-bushel; then put the finest ware in these to secure it from danger in the burning operation. All the fine ware made in Europe and in China is burnt in this kind of vessels. After they are done with, they are cast away—they are vessels of wrath fitted for destruction. **So God takes the wicked, and makes them protect the righteous, in the process of sanctifying, and burning, and purifying, and preparing them, and making them fit for the Master's use**. These saggars, as they are called, are compounded of refuse articles that have been cast out; so even they are good for something. The wicked are of use, for they are a rod in the hands of the Almighty to scourge the righteous, and prepare them for their Master's use, that they may enter into the celestial world, and be crowned with glory in His presence." (JD 2:151–152)

Sermon Delivered on 25 February 1855

"The spirits of the Saints will be gathered in one, that is, of all who are worthy; and those who are not just will be left where they will be scourged, tormented, and afflicted, until they can bring their spirits into subjection and be like clay in the hands of the potter, that the potter may have power to mould and fashion them into any kind of vessel, as he is directed by the Master Potter.

When the Lord spoke to Jeremiah He told him to go down to the potter's house, and there he would cause him to hear His words. When he went down to the potter's house, 'Behold, he wrought a work on the wheels.' The potter tried to bring a lump of clay in subjection, and he worked and tugged at it, but the clay was rebellious, and would not submit to the will of the potter, and marred in his hands. Then, of course, he had to cut it from the wheel and throw it into the mill to be ground over, in order that it might become passive; after which he takes it again and makes of

APPENDIX D—EXCERPTS FROM HEBER KIMBALL'S SERMONS

it a vessel unto honor, out of the same lump that was dishonored, because it would not be subject to the potter, and was, therefore, cut from the wheel, and put through another grinding until it was passive. There may ten thousand millions of men go to hell, because they dishonor themselves and will not be subject, and after that they will be taken and made vessels unto honor, if they will become obedient, and God will make us, who are His servants, bring about His purposes. Can you find any fault with that?

The Lord said to Jeremiah, 'O, house of Israel, cannot I do with you as the potter? Behold as the clay is in the potter's hand, so are ye in mine hand.' They dishonored themselves and were rebellious, and I have cut them off and thrown them in the mill, and they shall grind until they are passive. And **I have taken a gentler lump, to see if I cannot make a vessel unto honor**. By and by that lump will dishonor itself, and be thrown back into the mill, and God will take Israel and make of them a vessel unto honor.

Some time ago, when I spoke to the congregation in words of rebuke, it made a wonderful stir with a few men, that is, with those who were hit, and with those who were filled with sympathy for them, because they were such fine, accomplished gentlemen. After I went home from the council that same evening, I dreamed that I was at work at my old trade of making pots, that I had a kiln, and that brothers Brigham, Grant, and others were there. The kiln was full of earthen vessels, and we had burnt wood in the arches until it became red hot, but the blaze was coming out of the flues. It did not draw as we wished it to, for the wood was not sufficiently dry. We went and got some good, dry wood, but were gone sometime, and when we came back the kiln got considerably low in heat. We put in some dry wood, and soon brought it back to the same heat it had before we left it. But when I began to look around, I saw a great many vessels, off on one side, that were not good for anything, they would not stand the fire and began to fall in when nobody was touching them; a whole tier of them fell in at a time. Said I, 'Why have you made these vessels so thin? You have made them two thirds larger than they ought to be, with the amount of clay that is in them. Their skin is too thin, you have stretched them too far, and not given them the thickness in proportion. What shall we do with them? Let us break them up and put them into the mill, and grind them up again. The material is good, but they all need making over.'

Do you understand that dream? The Elders or somebody else, had stretched those vessels too much; they had got the big head, that is, their heads were larger than the substances would sustain, and they fell in— the vessels fell in. The clay was good, but the vessels were made too big in the start; we must not stretch them too much. Potters always work according to the amount of clay on hand; if it is a small lump they make a small vessel, and make it all the way of a thickness, as near as possible.

In the dream, I discovered that there were many just such thin characters all around us, and they fell in because we touched some

of them. I have touched many people here, both men and women, who profess to be Latter-day Saints, and I hurt them just as bad as I hurt some strangers. But I never hurt the feelings of a true Saint, nor of a stranger who is a gentleman, no, not one of them." (JD 3:161–163)

Sermon Delivered on 5 October 1856

"We have not as yet any durable location; **we are merely probationers in this present state, and we shall always be so, until we obtain a permanent exaltation**, by following in the footsteps of our God. He is our Father and our God, and His Son Jesus Christ is our Savior, and the Holy Ghost is to be our comforter, and will comfort all those who will prepare their tabernacles as fit temples for him to dwell in.

When the Holy Ghost dwells in us it will enable us to discern between right and wrong, will show us things to come, and bring things to our remembrance, and will make every one of this people prophets and prophetesses of God.

We have acknowledged brother Brigham to be our leader, and he holds the keys of the kingdom of heaven here on the earth. Whether people believe it or not, he is God's representative in the flesh, and is the mouth-piece of God unto us.

Brother Joseph Smith many a time said to brother Brigham and myself and to others, that he was a representative of God to us, to teach and direct us and reprove the wrong doers. He has past [passed] behind the veil, but there never will a person in this dispensation enter into the celestial glory without his approbation.

Brother Brigham is brother Joseph's rightful successor, and he has his Counselors, and together they are an earthly pattern of the divine order of government. Those men are God's agents, His servants, and are witnesses of your covenants, which you will have to fulfill. **And what you do not fulfil in this year you will have to do in the next; and what are not then fulfilled will have to be in some future time**.

Some people think that because they have passed through a great many troubles, have been to the nations to preach the Gospel, and have been robbed and plucked up several times, that will make an atonement for their sins. What you have passed through has nothing to do with atonement for sins. If you have sinned you have got to make an atonement for that sin, and the trials you have passed through in doing your duty are not the atonement. Trials are to test you, to prove whether you will do those things that are right. Some try to make out that their trials will answer as an atonement, but I tell you that they will not. If you commit sin there must be an atonement to satisfy the demands of justice, and then mercy claims you and saves you. But, as brother Grant has said, many of our old men think because they were in the Church in the first beginning that they can now lay upon their oars, that is, that they can sit down in the ship and not use the oars any more. **But God requires every man and woman** to be faithful; and if they have sinned, they have got **to make an atonement for that sin**, and your trials do not make that atonement.

God says that we shall be tried in all things, even as was Abraham of old. He was called upon to offer up, his son, and was found willing to offer him up, but, as the sin was not sufficient to require the shedding of his son's blood, a lamb was provided, and its blood atoned for the sin that Abraham's son was to be offered up for, and saved the son.

If you are ever saved, you have got to take a course to draw near to the throne of God; and how can you draw near to the throne of God, except you draw near to those men who are placed as His representatives in the flesh? The same principles, the same order, the same Priesthood, the same gifts, and the same powers are instituted, established and organized in our day as they were in the days of Jesus, and all the reason that people do not see it is because of their traditions; the veil of darkness is over their minds, and they cannot see it…

Brother Dan Jones has been talking to you about the clay in the hands of the potter. If you get hold of a lump of clay that is snappish and willful, and not willing that you should twist it into any shape or form, what is the use of working it? You throw it back into the mill and let it be ground again, and then take it out and make of it a vessel unto honor. Perhaps some do not really believe that when a man is thrown back into the mill, or goes into the spirit world, that he ever will be redeemed, but he will, if he has not sinned against the Holy Ghost. He will be ground and worked up until he becomes passive, and then God, through His servants, will redeem him, and make him a vessel unto honor.

A great many will go to hell, and the very men that are preaching to you now will visit you and offer you salvation, after you have laid there, perhaps thousands of years, for you must stay in the mill until you are passive and obedient.

Jeremiah, at the command of God, went to the potter's house where the potter was molding the clay, and when he went to turn it on the wheel it was refractory and rebellious; and he worked at it and sweat over it, but after all it was rebellious, and fell down on the wheel.

What did he do then? He cut it off from the wheel and threw it back into the mill, and after he had ground it awhile, he took it out and made of it a vessel unto honor; so of the same lump he made a vessel unto dishonor, and one unto honor.

Did the potter make it dishonorable? No, the vessel made itself unto dishonor; and the next time it was pliable and passive, and the potter made of it a vessel unto honor, because it was honorable and submissive.

I wished to make these few remarks, because they touch upon things that are on my mind all the time. **And if you wish to be Saints, for God's sake be Saints, and if you wish to be devils, be devils,** and get out of this place; and let those that will be Saints, be Saints; and let them commune together and carry out the purpose of God." (JD 4:119–121)

Sermon Delivered on 27 September 1857

"My tabernacle that is now standing before you, that you see with your eyes, I expect will decay, just like an old house. When it is done with, it decays, and turns back to the mother earth, from whence it was taken; and it is so with my body; it is so with yours; but **it is not so with my spirit, if I live my religion.**

If I do not live my religion, but turn away from the principles of light and life, my spirit will die. You have heard me speak of that a great many times, and so you have brother Brigham. There are thousands upon thousands whose bodies will die by the power of the second death; and then they never will return again. Many call that annihilation.

It is just the same with that as it is with this pitcher: it was made in England; it was once in its mother element, and it was taken out of the earth, and went through a certain process. It was then modeled and fashioned into the shape in which you now see it.

Now, will the day come when this pitcher will return to its mother earth? It will; and it may be thrown into some part of the earth where it may be thousands and millions of years **before that pitcher or the elements of which it is composed will be brought back again; and so it will be with thousands and millions of the people: they never will be brought back into the shape they were in once.**

Some men enquire, 'Why?' Simply because they have dishonoured the spirit and bodies that God gave them; therefore God will make a desolation of those bodies and spirits, and he will throw them back into the earth; that is, that portion that belongs to the earth will go back there. And so it will be with our spirits: they will go back into the elements or space that they once occupied before they came here.

Now, you may believe what you have a mind to about it; it is just as easy to conceive of a dissolution as to conceive of anything else. Chemists take elements and dissolve them and separate them, and can it not be done with our bodies? I answer yes, and with our spirits too, just as easy as a chemist can take a five-dollar piece and dissolve it into an element that is like water. Can that be restored again? It can: it can be dissolved, and it can be brought back again. And upon the same principle can our bodies be dissolved and restored again…

I frequently talk about the clay in the hands of the potter. The Lord said to Jeremiah, 'I will show you a thing that I cannot tell you. Go down to the potter's house, and I will be there, but you shall not see me; and I will make that potter mar a vessel.' Jeremiah went down to the potter's house, and the Lord showed him the very thing he had promised; for the potter undertook to make a vessel, and the clay marred in his hands, and he cut it off the wheel and threw it into the mill; 'and now,' says he, 'take it out again and shape it into a ball, and turn it into a vessel of honor.'

He did that very thing, though it is not written. The Scriptures say that out of the same lump he made a vessel first unto dishonor, and then unto honor. **I used to preach upon that in Nauvoo, and Joseph said it was the true interpretation**. Now, Jeremiah was a man like brother Brigham, brother Heber, Amasa, and thousands of the servants of God that were valiant. There are thousands here that have never seen a potter's house. But if I was in one, I could take a lump of clay and show you; and perhaps, being out of practice, it would mar in my hands: then I would throw it back into the mill and grind it, and afterwards I would take it up again and make a vessel unto honor. And thus the Lord said to Jeremiah, 'As you see that clay mar in the hands of the potter, so shall it be with the house of Israel. They shall go and be in prison till I bring them out and make them vessels unto honor.' That is to be done in the latter days, when the Lord is to say to the dry bones, 'Come forth,' and so on. Go and read the Bible, and you will learn about it. **It will be just so with thousands and tens of thousands who will embrace 'Mormonism:' they will go back into the mill again, through disobedience**." (JD 5:271–274)

Appendix E

The Paracletes

(It is unknown whether this was written by Joseph Smith prior to his death, or whether the author was someone else such as Brigham Young. John Taylor was the editor of the *Times and Seasons* at the time this was published.)

"Once upon a time, the most honorable men of the creations or universes met together to promote the best interest of the great whole. The 'head' said to his oldest son, you are the rightful heir to all, but you know I have many kingdoms and many mansions, and of course it will need **many kings and many priests** to govern them. Come you with me in solemn council, and let us and **some of the 'best' men we have had born in the regions of light** to rule in those kingdoms and set them in order by exhibiting good, that evil may be manifest. It was said and done, for every thing there was adopted from the 'head' by common consent. As free agency gave the sons of the 'head' a fair chance to choose for themselves, the most noble of the hosts came forward and selected a world or kingdom, and a time or a season, when he would take his chance, at winning the hearts of the multitude, a kingdom, crown, and never ending glory.

The innumerable multiplicity of kingdoms, or spheres for action, with beings and animals in proportion, and **time, times, eternity and eternities**, for a full development of the qualities and powers of each, would so far exceed the common comprehension of mortals, that I can only say eye hath not seen, ear hath not heard, nor hath a natural heart yet been able to calculate either. I then shall content myself for this time to sketch but one. Idumia is the one as interesting as any, and being situated at an i**mmense distance from the center or 'head's' residence**, and many eternities from the birth of the 'Son of the morning' or even the great holy day when the 'morning stars sang together,' because so many worlds had been wrought out and left 'empty and desolate,' as places for 'all the sons' of God to multiply and replenish the earth, I select that.

Time being divided into seven parts, the following men agreed to leave the mansions of bliss, and spiritually help (organize) every thing necessary to fill a kingdom for the space of many of the Lord's days, viz: **Milauleph, Milbeth, Milgimal, Mildauleth, Milhah, Milvah and Milzah.**

Now after they had organized the kingdom of Idumia spiritually, **then one at a time, was to come temporally and open the door of communication with the spiritual kingdom**, that all that would, might return to their former estate; for, for this reason, all the regions created and to be created were filled with a variety of beings: agents to themselves but accountable to the 'head' for promises made when they agreed 'to go' and be born of the flesh as they had been of the spirit; that they might know the evil, and choose the good: and then be born **(again)** of the spirit and the water, and enter into the mansions prepared for them before the foundations of the worlds.

Milauleph, being the eldest and first chosen for Idumia, came on when 'there was not a man to till the ground'—that is, there was not a 'man of flesh' to labor temporally; and his elder brethren who had wrought out their salvation, upon worlds or realms or kingdoms, ages, yea even eternities before, formed him a temporal body like unto their spiritual bodies, and put the life of his spiritual body into it, and gave him the power of **endless lives**.

Now the acts of his spiritual body while he was a child with his father and mother in heaven, and his acts while he was in the spiritual councils of the Gods for millions of years; and his acts upon Idumia, while he named, arranged, and prepared every thing upon it to fulfil [sic] the end and aim of their creation, behold they are written in 'the books' of the 'head,'—which are to be opened when the judgment comes for just men to enter into the joys of a 'third existence,' which is spiritual.

Milauleph had one thousand years to account for, as well as to be 'archangel' of Idumia after he laid down his temporal body. Behold here is wisdom, he that hath ears to hear let him hear, for Milauleph as yet had not been tempted with evil that he might (know) the good.

He had not exercised the power of **endless lives** that he might (do) the works that his father had done: and he had not 'fell that men might be.' Although he had seen his eldest brother create worlds and people them; and had witnessed the course and conduct of that world and people, as free agents, 'sinning and being sinned against,' while 'death' who held a commission from the 'Son of the morning,' to end the first partnership between the spirit and the body, yet, with all this knowledge, and a liberal education in the great college of the nobles of heaven, wherein all perfection was taught, all science explained from first to last, and all that was, is, or will be, was exhibited on **the great map of perpetual systems and eternal lives, Milauleph had to take his wife or one of the 'Queens of heaven,' and come upon Idumia**, and be tempted, overcome, and driven from the presence of his Father, **because it had been agreed by the Gods and grand council of heaven that all the family of the 'head' that would do as he or his eldest son did, should be exalted to the same glory.**

This was to be accomplished by the power of **'perpetual succession' in eternal lives**, wherein there was no 'remission of sin without the shedding of blood;' no forgiveness without repentance; and no glory without perfect submission to the 'head.'

The foundation was (truth): and **the continuation, perpetual succession by revelation**. Milauleph, then, knew that he and his wife would sin and be troubled; but as the eternal spirit in him was the candle of the Lord, he knew also that the light thereof upon the eyes of his understanding would show some of the way marks to the original 'truth,' whereby he might work out his salvation with fear and trembling. **That none of the work of the hands of the 'Son' might be lost or any souls which his father had given him might be left in prison, angels were commissioned to watch over Idumia, and act as (spiritual guides) to every soul, 'lest they should fall and dash their feet against a stone.' They were denominated the angels of our presence**.

But I must stop, Mr. Editor: **my story of the whole (seven) who managed the seven dispensations of Idumia** will be too long for one communication. And let me say that I have began this story of the **'Paracletes,' or Holy Ones,** to counterbalance the foolish novel reading of the present generation. My story is not revelation, but the innuendoes relate to holy transactions **which may lead good people to search after truth and find it**. If this meets the approbation of virtuous minds, I shall write more.

—Joseph's Speckled Bird" (1845, *Times and Seasons* 6:891–892)

"Paracletes (continued)

To continue the history of **the seven holy ones,** who agreed to take upon them bodies of flesh, **and work out a more exceeding and eternal crown of glory** upon Idumia, it will be necessary to premise that Milauleph, and his first companion in the flesh knew before they left their 'first estate' what their father's will was; and that when they should begin to replenish the earth, Satan, who had been raised and educated with them in their father's family, would descend from heaven like lightning to tempt them, that they might know to choose good and reject evil. These two, who had engaged to people Idumia: to subdue it, and to return, having (kept the faith) once delivered to the chosen seed, were informed when they agreed to go and labor their hour that, besides the comforter to bring all things to their remembrance, **the angels which attended them on high should attend them below to preserve them from the secret of unforeseen snares of those angels who kept not their first estates**, but were left in their sins to roam from region to region, and in chains of darkness, until the great day of judgment. It was written in the law of the Lord on high that they that overcome by obedience should be made kings and queens, and priests and priestesses to God and his Father, through the atonement of the eldest son, and **that natural eyes should not see**, nor natural ears hear, neither should the natural heart conceive the great, glorious, and eternal things, honors, and blessings that were then in the Father's dominions and mansions, prepared in the beginning for them that kept the faith to the end, and entered triumphantly into their third estates: (**the eternal life**).

It was also written in the law of the Lord on high that when the Lord punished men for their sins, he would 'punish the hosts of the high ones on high,' and the 'kings of the earth upon earth,'—that spirit might judge spirit, and flesh judge flesh; for this honor have all the just, and this honor have all the saints. Having this understanding Idumia was placed in its space, but was 'desolate and empty.' and **the life organizing power of the Gods, or sons of the** '**head**,' moved over the matters and then the land and water separated. And the Gods called 'light, and light came' and they went on and organized a world, and created every thing necessary to beautify and adorn it, with life and the **power of lives** to sustain it, until it should fill the measure of all designed, from a mite to a mammoth; from a man to a God; and Milauleph's and his wife's spirits, clothed in heavenly garments, and learned in eternal wisdom, witnessed the creation **as the spirits of the Gods had witnessed their Father: for even the elder brother could do nothing but what he had seen his Father do in eternities before**.

Perhaps this subject may excite the curiosity of some: as it will lead the mind back among the worlds that have been organized and passed away —and among the Gods and angels that have attended to execute the laws and decrees of one universe after another, from eternity to eternity, from the beginning till (now); and, to increase the curiosity of having this present world pass away with a great noise, when there is no place found for it;—and of having organized a new heaven and a new earth, wherein dwelleth 'righteousness' and as our fathers cannot be perfect without us, nor we without them; and as the man is not without the woman, neither the woman without the man in the Lord, perhaps Milauleph and his wife, as king and queen to God, and all the sons and daughters of the 'head' will shout for joy, and the morning stars sing together again, at the 'third' entrance of Idumia and sanctified millions! —Who knows?

—Joseph's Speckled Bird" (1845, *Times and Seasons* 6:917–918)

Appendix F

Excerpts from 2 Esdras (Also known as 4 Ezra)

2 Esdras, Chapter 2

16: And I will raise up the dead from their places, and will bring them out from their tombs, because I recognize my name in them. (2 Esdras 2:16)

23: When you find any who are dead, commit them to the grave and mark it, **and I will give you the first place in my resurrection**. (2 Esdras 2:23)

26: **Not one of the servants whom I have given you will perish**, for I will require them from among your number. (2 Esdras 2:26)

31: Remember your sons that sleep, because I will bring them out of the hiding places of the earth, and will show mercy to them; for I am merciful, says the Lord **Almighty**. (2 Esdras 2:31)

39: **Those who have departed from the shadow of this age have received glorious garments from the Lord**. 40: **Take again your full number, O Zion, and conclude the list of your people who are clothed in white, who have fulfilled the law of the Lord**. 41: The number of your children, whom you desired, is full; beseech the Lord's power that your people, who have been called from the beginning, may be made holy. 42: I, Ezra, saw on Mount Zion a great multitude, which I could not number, and they all were praising the Lord with songs. 43: In their midst was a young man of great stature, taller than any of the others, and on the head of each of them he placed a crown, **but he was more exalted than they**. And I was held spellbound. 44: Then I asked an angel, **"Who are these, my lord?"** 45: He answered and said to me, **"These are they who have put off mortal clothing and have put on the immortal, and they have confessed the name of God; now they are being crowned, and receive palms."** 46: Then I said to the angel, **"Who is that young man who places crowns on them and puts palms in their hands?"** 47: He answered and said to me, **"He is the Son of God, whom they confessed in the world."** So I began to praise those who had stood valiantly for the name of the Lord. 48: Then the angel said to me, "Go, tell my people how great and many are the wonders of the Lord God which you have seen." (2 Esdras 2:39–48)

2 Esdras, Chapter 4

1: Then the angel that had been sent to me, whose name was Uriel, answered 2: and said to me, "**Your understanding has utterly failed regarding this world, and do you think you can comprehend the way of the Most High?**" 3: Then I said, "Yes, my lord." And he replied to me, "I have been sent to show you three ways, and to put before you three problems. 4: If you can solve one of them for me, I also will show you the way you desire to see, and will teach you why the heart is evil." 5: I said, "Speak on, my lord." And he said to me, "Go, weigh for me the weight of fire, or measure for me a measure of wind, or call back for me the day that is past." 6: I answered and said, "Who of those that have been born can do this, that you ask me concerning these things?" 7: And he said to me, "If I had asked you, 'How many dwellings are in the heart of the sea, or how many streams are at the source of the deep, or how many streams are above the firmament, or which are the exits of hell, or which are the entrances of paradise?' 8: Perhaps you would have said to me, 'I never went down into the deep, nor as yet into hell, neither did I ever ascend into heaven.' 9: But now I have asked you only about fire and wind and the day, things through which you have passed and without which you cannot exist, and you have given me no answer about them!" 10: And he said to me, "You cannot understand the things with which you have grown up; 11: how then can your mind comprehend the way of the Most High? And how can one who is already worn out by the corrupt world understand incorruption?" When I heard this, I fell on my face 12: and said to him, "**It would be better for us not to be here than to come here and live in ungodliness, and to suffer and not understand why**." 13: He answered me and said, "I went into a forest of trees of the plain, and they made a plan 14: and said, 'Come, let us go and make war against the sea, that it may recede before us, and that we may make for ourselves more forests.' 15: And in like manner the waves of the sea also made a plan and said, 'Come, let us go up and subdue the forest of the plain so that there also we may gain more territory for ourselves.' 16: But the plan of the forest was in vain, for the fire came and consumed it; 17: likewise also the plan of the waves of the sea, for the sand stood firm and stopped them. 18: If now you were a judge between them, which would you undertake to justify, and which to condemn?" 19: I answered and said, "**Each has made a foolish plan, for the land is assigned to the forest, and to the sea is assigned a place to carry its waves**." 20: He answered me and said, "**You have judged rightly, but why have you not judged so in your own case? 21: For as the land is assigned to the forest and the sea to its waves, so also those who dwell upon earth can understand only what is on the earth, and he who is above the heavens can understand what is above the height of the heavens**." 22: Then I answered and said, "I beseech you, my lord, why have I been endowed with the power of understanding? 23: For I did not wish to inquire about the ways above, but about those things which we daily experience: why Israel has been given over to the Gentiles as a reproach; why the people whom you loved has been given over to godless tribes, and the law of our fathers has been made of no effect and the written covenants no longer exist; 24: **and why we pass from the world like locusts, and our life is like a mist**, and we are not worthy to obtain mercy. 25: But what will he do for his name, by which we are called? It is about these things that I have asked." 26: He answered me and said, "**If you are alive, you will see, and if you live long, you will often marvel, because the age is hastening swiftly to its end**. 27: For it will not be able to bring the things that have been promised to the righteous **in their appointed times**, because this age is full of sadness and infirmities. 28: For the evil about which you ask me has been sown, **but the harvest of it has not yet come**. 29: If therefore that which has been sown is not reaped, and if the place where the evil has been sown does not pass away, the field where the good has been sown will not come. 30: For a grain of evil seed was sown in Adam's heart from the beginning, and how much ungodliness it has produced until now, and will produce **until the time of threshing comes!** 31: Consider now for yourself how much fruit of ungodliness a grain of evil seed has produced. 32: When heads of grain without number are sown, how great a threshing floor they will fill!" 33: Then I answered and said, "**How long and when will these things be? Why are our years few and evil?**" 34: He answered me and said, "**You do not hasten faster than the Most High, for your haste is for yourself, but the Highest hastens on behalf of many**. 35: Did not the souls of the righteous in their chambers ask about these matters, saying, '**How long are we to remain here? And when will come the harvest of our reward?** 36: And Jeremiel the archangel answered them and said, '**When the number of those like yourselves is completed**; for he has weighed the age in the balance, 37: and measured the times by measure, and numbered the times by number; and he will not move or arouse them until that measure is fulfilled.'" 38: Then I answered and said, "O sovereign Lord, **but all of us also are full of ungodliness. 39: And it is perhaps on account of us that the time of threshing is delayed for the righteous—on account of the sins of those who dwell on earth**." 40: He answered me and said, "Go and ask a woman who is with child if, when her nine months have been completed, her womb can keep the child within her any longer." 41: And I said, "No, lord, it cannot." And he said to me, "**In Hades the chambers of the souls are like the womb**. 42: For just as a woman who is in travail makes haste to escape the pangs of birth, **so also do these places hasten to give back those things that were committed to them from the beginning. 43: Then the things that you desire to see will be disclosed to you**." 44: I answered and said, "If I have found favor in your sight, and if it is possible, and if I am worthy, 45: **show me this also: whether more time is to come than has passed, or whether for us the greater part has gone by**. 46: For I know what has gone by, but I do not know what is to come." 47: And he said to me, "**Stand at my right side, and I will show you the interpretation of a parable**." 48: So I stood and looked, and behold, a flaming furnace passed by before me, and when the flame had gone by I looked, and behold, the smoke remained. 49: And after this a cloud full of water passed before me and poured down a heavy and violent rain, and when the rainstorm had passed, drops remained in the cloud. 50: And he said to me, "Consider it for yourself; for as the rain is more than the drops, and the fire is greater than the smoke, so the quantity that passed was far greater; but drops and smoke remained." 51: Then I prayed and said, "**Do you think that I shall live until those days? Or who will be alive in those days?**" 52: He answered me and said, "Concerning the signs about which you ask me, I can tell you in part; but I was not sent to tell you concerning your life, for I do not know. (2 Esdras 4:1–52)

2 Esdras, Chapter 5

1: "Now concerning the signs: behold, the days are coming when those who dwell on earth shall be seized with great terror, and the way of truth shall be hidden, and the land shall be barren of faith. 2: And unrighteousness shall be increased beyond what you yourself see, and beyond what you heard of formerly. 3: And the land which you now see ruling shall be waste and untrodden, and men shall see it desolate. 4: **But if the Most High grants that you live, you shall see it thrown into confusion after the third period**; and the sun shall suddenly shine forth at night, and the moon during the day. 5: Blood shall drip from wood, and the stone shall utter its voice; the peoples shall be troubled, and the stars shall fall. 6: **And one shall reign whom those who dwell on earth do not expect**, and the birds shall fly away together; 7: and the sea of Sodom shall cast up fish; and one whom the many do not know shall make his voice heard by night, and all shall hear his voice. 8: There shall be chaos also in many places, and fire shall often break out, and the wild beasts shall roam beyond their haunts, and menstruous women shall bring forth monsters. 9: And salt waters shall be found in the sweet, and all friends shall conquer one another; then shall reason hide itself, and wisdom shall withdraw into its chamber, 10: and it shall be sought by many but shall not be found, and unrighteousness and unrestraint shall increase on earth. 11: And one country shall ask its neighbor, 'Has righteousness, or any one who does right, passed through you?' And it will answer, 'No.' 12: And at that time men shall hope but not obtain; they shall labor but their ways shall not prosper. 13: These are the signs which I am permitted to tell you, and if you pray again, and weep as you do now, and fast for seven days, you shall hear yet greater things than these." 14: Then I awoke, and my body shuddered violently, and my soul was so troubled that it fainted. 15: But the angel who had come and talked with me held me and strengthened me and set me on my feet. 16: Now on the second night Phaltiel, a chief of the people, came to me and said, "Where have you been? And why is your face sad? 17: Or do you not know that Israel has been entrusted to you in the land of their exile? 18: Rise therefore and eat some bread, so that you may not forsake us, like a shepherd who leaves his flock in the power of cruel wolves." 19: Then I said to him, "Depart from me and do not come near me for seven days, and then you may come to me." He heard what I said and left me. 20: So I fasted seven days, mourning and weeping, as Uriel the angel had commanded me. 21: And after seven days the thoughts of my heart were very grievous to me again. 22: Then my soul recovered the spirit of understanding, and I began once more to speak words in the presence of the Most High. 23: And I said, "O sovereign Lord, from every forest of the earth and from all its trees thou hast chosen one vine, 24: and from all the lands of the world thou hast chosen for thyself one region, and from all the flowers of the world thou hast chosen for thyself one lily, 25: and from all the depths of the sea thou hast filled for thyself one river, and from all the cities that have been built thou hast consecrated Zion for thyself, 26: and from all the birds that have been created thou hast named for thyself one dove, and from all the flocks that have been made thou hast provided for thyself one sheep, 27: and from all the multitude of peoples thou hast gotten for thyself one people; and to this people, whom thou hast loved, thou hast given the law which is approved by all. 28: And now, O Lord, why hast thou given over the one to the many, and dishonored the one root beyond the others, and scattered thine only one among the many? 29: And those who opposed thy promises have trodden down those who believed thy covenants. 30: If thou dost really hate thy people, they should be punished at thy own hands." 31: When I had spoken these words, the angel who had come to me on a previous night was sent to me, 32: and he said to me, "**Listen to me, and I will instruct you; pay attention to me, and I will tell you more.**" 33: And I said, "Speak, my lord." And he said to me, "Are you greatly disturbed in mind over Israel? Or do you love him more than his Maker does?" 34: And I said, "No, my lord, but because of my grief I have spoken; for every hour I suffer agonies of heart, while I strive to understand the way of the Most High and to search out part of his judgment." 35: And he said to me, "You cannot." And I said, "**Why not, my lord? Why then was I born? Or why did not my mother's womb become my grave, that I might not see the travail of Jacob and the exhaustion of the people of Israel?**" 36: He said to me, "Count up for me those who have not yet come, and gather for me the scattered raindrops, and make the withered flowers bloom again for me; 37: open for me the closed chambers, and bring forth for me the winds shut up in them, or show me the picture of a voice; and then I will explain to you the travail that you ask to understand." 38: And I said, "O sovereign Lord, **who is able to know these things except he whose dwelling is not with men?** 39: As for me, I am without wisdom, and how can I speak concerning the things which thou hast asked me?" 40: He said to me, "Just as you cannot do one of the things that were mentioned, **so you cannot discover my judgment, or the goal of the love that I have promised my people.**"

41: And I said, "Yet behold, O Lord, thou dost have charge of those who are alive at the end, but what will those do who were before us, or we, or those who come after us?" 42: He said to me, "I shall liken my judgment to a circle; just as for those who are last there is no slowness, so for those who are first there is no haste." 43: Then I answered and said, "Couldst thou not have created at one time those who have been and those who are and those who will be, that thou mightest show thy judgment the sooner?" 44: He replied to me and said, "The creation cannot make more haste than the Creator, neither can the world hold at one time those who have been created in it." 45: And I said, "How hast thou said to thy servant that thou wilt certainly give life at one time to thy creation? If therefore all creatures will live at one time and the creation will sustain them, it might even now be able to support all of them present at one time." 46: He said to me, "Ask a woman's womb, and say to it, 'If you bear ten children, why one after another?' Request it therefore to produce ten at one time." 47: I said, "Of course it cannot, but only each in its own time." 48: He said to me, "Even so have I given the womb of the earth to <u>those who from time to time are sown in it</u>. 49: For as an infant does not bring forth, and a woman who has become old does not bring forth any longer, so have I organized the world which I created." (2 Esdras 5:1–56)

2 Esdras, Chapter 7

1: When I had finished speaking these words, the angel who had been sent to me on the former nights was sent to me again, 2: and he said to me, "Rise, Ezra, and listen to the words that I have come to speak to you." 3: I said, "Speak, my lord." And he said to me, "There is a sea set in a wide expanse so that it is broad and vast, 4: but it has an entrance set in a narrow place, so that it is like a river. 5: **If any one, then, wishes to reach the sea, to look at it or to navigate it, how can he come to the broad part unless he passes through the narrow part?** 6: Another example: There is a city built and set on a plain, and it is full of all good things; 7: but the entrance to it is narrow and set in a precipitous place, so that there is fire on the right hand and deep water on the left; 8: **and there is only one path lying between them, that is, between the fire and the water, so that only one man can walk upon that path**. 9: **If now that city is given to a man for an inheritance, how will the heir receive his inheritance unless he passes through the danger set before him?**" 10: I said, "He cannot, lord." And he said to me, "**So also is Israel's portion**. 11: For I made the world for their sake, and when Adam transgressed my statutes, what had been made was judged. 12: And so the entrances of this world were made narrow and sorrowful and toilsome; they are few and evil, full of dangers and involved in great hardships. 13: **But the entrances of the greater world are broad and safe, and really yield the fruit of immortality**. 14: **Therefore unless the living pass through the difficult and vain experiences, they can never receive those things that have been reserved for them**. 15: But now why are you disturbed, seeing that you are to perish? And why are you moved, seeing that you are mortal? 16: **And why have you not considered in your mind what is to come, rather than what is now present?**" 17: Then I answered and said, "O sovereign Lord, behold, thou hast ordained in thy law that the righteous shall inherit these things, but that the ungodly shall perish. 18: The righteous therefore can endure difficult circumstances while hoping for easier ones; but those who have done wickedly have suffered the difficult circumstances and will not see the easier ones." 19: And he said to me, "You are not a better judge than God, or wiser than the Most High! 20: Let many perish who are now living, rather than that the law of God which is set before them be disregarded! 21: **For God strictly commanded those who came into the world, when they came, what they should do to live, and what they should observe to avoid punishment**. 22: Nevertheless they were not obedient, and spoke against him; they devised for themselves vain thoughts, 23: and proposed to themselves wicked frauds; they even declared that the Most High does not exist, and they ignored his ways! 24: They scorned his law, and denied his covenants; they have been unfaithful to his statutes, and have not performed his works. 25: "Therefore, Ezra, **empty things are for the empty, and full things are for the full**. 26: For behold, the time will come, when the signs which I have foretold to you will come to pass, that the city which now is not seen shall appear, and the land which now is hidden shall be disclosed. 27: And every one who has been delivered from the evils that I have foretold shall see my wonders. 28: **For my son the Messiah shall be revealed with those who are with him**, and those who remain shall rejoice four hundred years. 29: And after these years my son the Messiah shall die, and all who draw human breath. 30: And the world shall be turned back to primeval silence for seven days, as it was at the first beginnings; so that no one shall be left. 31: And after seven days the world, which is not yet awake, shall be roused, and that which is corruptible shall perish.

32: **And the earth shall give up those who are asleep in it, and the dust those who dwell silently in it; and the chambers shall give up the souls which have been committed to them**. 33: And the Most High shall be revealed upon the seat of judgment, and compassion shall pass away, and patience shall be withdrawn; 34: but only judgment shall remain, truth shall stand, and faithfulness shall grow strong. 35: And recompense shall follow, and the reward shall be manifested; righteous deeds shall awake, and unrighteous deeds shall not sleep. 36: **Then the pit of torment shall appear, and opposite it shall be the place of rest; and the furnace of hell shall be disclosed, and opposite it the paradise of delight**.

37: Then the Most High will say to the nations **that have been raised from the dead**, 'Look now, and **understand whom you have denied, whom you have not served, whose commandments you have despised**! 38: Look on this side and on that; here are delight and rest, and there are fire and torments!' Thus he will speak to them on the day of judgment—39: a day that has no sun or moon or stars, 40: or cloud or thunder or lightning or wind or water or air, or darkness or evening or morning, 41: or summer or spring or heat or winter or frost or cold or hail or rain or dew, 42: or noon or night, or dawn or shining or brightness or light, but only the splendor of the glory of the Most High, by which all shall see what has been determined for them. 43: For it will last for about a week of years. 44: This is my judgment and its prescribed order; and to you alone have I shown these things." 45: I answered and said, "O sovereign Lord, I said then and I say now: Blessed are those who are alive and keep thy commandments! 46: But what of those for whom I prayed? **For who among the living is there that has not sinned, or who among men that has not transgressed**

thy covenant? 47: And now I see that the world to come will bring delight to few, but torments to many. 48: For an evil heart has grown up in us, which has alienated us from God, and has brought us into corruption and the ways of death, and has shown us the paths of perdition and removed us far from life—**and that not just a few of us but almost all who have been created**!" 49: He answered me and said, "**Listen to me, Ezra, and I will instruct you, and will admonish you yet again**. 50: **For this reason the Most High has made not one world but two**. 51: For whereas you have said that the righteous are not many but few, while the ungodly abound, hear the explanation for this. 52: "**If you have just a few precious stones, will you add to them lead and clay?**" 53: I said, "Lord, how could that be?" 54: And he said to me, "Not only that, but ask the earth and she will tell you; defer to her, and she will declare it to you. 55: Say to her, 'You produce gold and silver and brass, and also iron and lead and clay; 56: but silver is more abundant than gold, and brass than silver, and iron than brass, and lead than iron, and clay than lead.' 57: Judge therefore which things are precious and desirable, those that are abundant or those that are rare?" 58: I said, "O sovereign Lord, what is plentiful is of less worth, for what is more rare is more precious." 59: He answered me and said, "**Weigh within yourself what you have thought, for he who has what is hard to get rejoices more than he who has what is plentiful.** 60: So also will be the judgment which I have promised; for I will rejoice over the few who shall be saved, because it is they who have made my glory to prevail now, and through them my name has now been honored. 61: And I will not grieve over the multitude of those who perish; for it is they who are now like a mist, and are similar to a flame and smoke—they are set on fire and burn hotly, and are extinguished." 62: I replied and said, "O earth, what have you brought forth, if the mind is made out of the dust like the other created things! 63: For it would have been better if the dust itself had not been born, so that the mind might not have been made from it. 64: **But now the mind grows with us, and therefore we are tormented, because we perish and know it.** 65: Let the human race lament, but let the beasts of the field be glad; let all who have been born lament, but let the four-footed beasts and the flocks rejoice! 66: For it is much better with them than with us; for they do not look for a judgment, nor do they know of any torment or salvation promised to them after death. 67: For what does it profit us that we shall be preserved alive but cruelly tormented? 68: For all who have been born are involved in iniquities, and are full of sins and burdened with transgressions. 69: **And if we were not to come into judgment after death, perhaps it would have been better for us.**" 70: He answered me and said, "When the Most High made the world and Adam and all who have come from him, he first prepared the judgment and the things that pertain to the judgment. 71: And now understand from your own words, for you have said that the mind grows with us. 72: For this reason, therefore, those who dwell on earth shall be tormented, because though they had understanding they committed iniquity, and though they received the commandments they did not keep them, and though they obtained the law they dealt unfaithfully with what they received. 73:

Appendix F—Excerpts from 2 Esdras (4 Ezra)

What, then, will they have to say in the judgment, or **how will they answer in the last times?** 74: **For how long the time is that the Most High has been patient with those who inhabit the world**, and not for their sake, but because of the times which he has foreordained!"

75: **I answered and said, "If I have found favor in thy sight, O Lord, show this also to thy servant: whether after death, as soon as every one of us yields up his soul, we shall be kept in rest until those times come when thou wilt renew the creation, or whether we shall be tormented at once?"** 76: He answered me and said, "**I will show you that also**, but do not be associated with those who have shown scorn, nor number yourself among those who are tormented. 77: **For you have a treasure of works laid up with the Most High; but it will not be shown to you until the last times.** 78: Now, concerning death, the teaching is: When the decisive decree has gone forth from the Most High that a man shall die, as the spirit leaves the body to return again to him who gave it, first of all it adores the glory of the Most High. 79: And if it is one of those who have shown scorn and have not kept the way of the Most High, and who have despised his law, and who have hated those who fear God—80: **such spirits shall not enter into habitations, but shall immediately wander about in torments, ever grieving and sad, in seven ways**. 81: The first way, because they have scorned the law of the Most High. 82: The second way, because they cannot now make a good repentance that they may live. 83: The third way, they shall see the reward laid up for those who have trusted the covenants of the Most High. 84: The fourth way, they shall consider the torment laid up for themselves in the last days. 85: The fifth way, they shall see how the habitations of the others are guarded by angels in profound quiet. 86: The sixth way, they shall see how some of them will pass over into torments. 87: The seventh way, which is worse than all the ways that have been mentioned, because they shall utterly waste away in confusion and be consumed with shame, and shall wither with fear at seeing the glory of the Most High before whom they sinned while they were alive, and before whom they are to be judged in the last times. 88: **"Now this is the order of those who have kept the ways of the Most High, when they shall be separated from their mortal body. 89: During the time that they lived in it, they laboriously served the Most High, and withstood danger every hour, that they might keep the law of the Lawgiver perfectly.** 90: Therefore this is the teaching concerning them: 91: First of all, they shall see with great joy the glory of him who receives them, **for they shall have rest in seven orders**. 92: The first order, because they have striven with great effort to overcome the evil thought which was formed with them, that it might not lead them astray from life into death. 93: The second order, because they see the perplexity in which the souls of the ungodly wander, and the punishment that awaits them. 94: The third order, they see the witness which he who formed them bears concerning them, that while they were alive they kept the law which was given them in trust. 95: The fourth order, they understand the rest which they now enjoy, being gathered into their chambers and guarded by angels in profound quiet, and the glory which awaits them in the last days. 96: The fifth order, they rejoice that they have now escaped what is corruptible, and shall inherit what is to come; and besides they see the straits and toil from which they have been delivered, and the spacious liberty which they are to receive and enjoy in immortality. 97: The sixth order, when it is shown to them how their face is to shine like the sun, and how they are to be made like the light of the stars, being incorruptible from then on. 98: **The seventh order, which is greater than all that have been mentioned, because they shall rejoice with boldness, and shall be confident without confusion, and shall be glad without fear, for they hasten to behold the face of him whom they served in life and from whom they are to receive their reward when glorified**. 99: **This is the order of the souls of the righteous, as henceforth is announced; and the aforesaid are the ways of torment which those who would not give heed shall suffer hereafter**." 100: I answered and said, "**Will time therefore be given to the souls, after they have been separated from the bodies, to see what you have described to me?**" 101: He said to me, "They shall have freedom for seven days, so that during these seven days they may see the things of which you have been told, and **afterwards they shall be gathered in their habitations**." 102: I answered and said, "If I have found favor in thy sight, **show further to me, thy servant, whether on the day of judgment the righteous will be able to intercede for the ungodly** or to entreat the Most High for them, 103: fathers for sons or sons for parents, brothers for brothers, relatives for their kinsmen, or friends **for those who are most dear**." 104: He answered me and said, "Since you have found favor in my sight, I will show you this also. The day of judgment is decisive and displays to all the seal of truth. Just as now a father does not send his son, or a son his father, or a master his servant, or a friend his dearest friend, to be ill or sleep or eat or be healed in his stead, 105: **so no one shall ever pray for another on that day, neither shall any one lay a burden on another; for then every one shall bear his own righteousness and unrighteousness**." 36(106): I answered and said, "How then do we find that first Abraham prayed for the people of Sodom, and Moses for our fathers who sinned in the desert," 37(107): "and Joshua after him for Israel in the days of Achan," 38(108): "and Samuel in the days of Saul, and David for the plague, and Solomon for those in the sanctuary," 39(109): "and Elijah for those who received the rain, and for the one who was dead, that he might live," 40(110): "and Hezekiah for the people in the days of Sennacherib, and many others prayed for many?" 41(111): "If therefore the righteous have prayed for the ungodly now, when corruption has increased and unrighteousness has multiplied, why will it not be so then as well?" 42(112): "He answered me and said, "**This present world is not the end; the full glory does not abide in it; therefore those who were strong prayed for the weak**." 43(113): "**But the day of judgment will be the end of this age and the beginning of the immortal age to come**, in which corruption has passed away," 44(114): "sinful indulgence has come to an end, unbelief has been cut off, and righteousness has increased and truth has appeared." 45(115): "Therefore no one will then be able to have mercy on him who has been condemned in the judgment, or to harm him who is victorious." 46(116)": I answered and said, "This is my first and last word, that it would have been better if the earth had not produced Adam, or else, when it had produced him, had restrained him from sinning." 47(117): **"For what good is it to all that they live in sorrow now and expect punishment after death?"** 48(118): "O Adam, what have you done? For though it was you who sinned, the fall was not yours alone, but ours also who are your descendants." 49(119): **"For what good is it to us, if an eternal age has been promised to us, but we have done deeds that bring death?"** 50(120): **"And what good is it that an everlasting hope has been promised to us, but we have miserably failed?"** 51(121): "Or that safe and healthful habitations have been reserved for us, but we have lived wickedly?" 52(122): "Or that the glory of the Most High will defend those who have led a pure life, but we have walked in the most wicked ways?" 53(123): "Or that a paradise shall be revealed, whose fruit remains unspoiled and in which are abundance and healing, but we shall not enter it," 54(124): "because we have lived in unseemly places?" 55(125): "Or that the faces of those who practiced self-control shall shine more than the stars, but our faces shall be blacker than darkness?" 56(126): "For while we lived and committed iniquity we did not consider what we should suffer after death." 57(127): **"He answered and said, "This is the meaning of the contest which every man who is born on earth shall wage,"** 58(128): **"that if he is defeated he shall suffer what you have said, but if he is victorious he shall receive what I have said."** 59(129): "For this is the way of which Moses, while he was alive, spoke to the people, saying, 'Choose for yourself life, that you may live!'" 60(130): "But they did not believe him, or the prophets after him, or even myself who have spoken to them." 61(131): **"Therefore there shall not be grief at their destruction, so much as joy over those to whom salvation is assured."** 62(132): "I answered and said, "I know, O Lord, that the Most High is now called merciful, because he has mercy on those who have not yet come into the world;" 63(133): "and gracious, because he is gracious to those who turn in repentance to his law;" 64(134): **"and patient, because he shows patience toward those who have sinned, since they are his own works;"** 65(135): "and bountiful, because he would rather give than take away;" 66(136): **"and abundant in compassion, because he makes his compassions abound more and more to those now living and to those who are gone and to those yet to come,"** 67(137): **"for if he did not make them abound, the world with those who inhabit it would not have life;"** 68(138): "and he is called giver, **because if he did not give out of his goodness so that those who have committed iniquities might be relieved of them, not one ten-thousandth of mankind could have life;"** 69(139): "and judge, **because if he did not pardon those who were created by his word and blot out the multitude of their sins,"** 70(140): **"there would probably be left only very few of the innumerable multitude."** (2 Esdras 7:1–140)

(All of the above material from 2 Esdras was quoted from the Revised Standard Version.)

Appendix G

Robert Matthias

Joseph Smith

"*Tuesday, November 10*[, 1835]—I resumed conversation with Matthias, and desired him to enlighten my mind more on his views respecting the resurrection.

He said that he possessed the spirit of his fathers, that he was a literal descendant of Matthias, the Apostle, who was chosen in the place of Judas that fell; that his spirit was resurrected in him; and that this was the way or scheme of eternal life—this transmigration of soul or spirit from father to son.

I told him that his doctrine was of the devil, that he was in reality in possession of a wicked and depraved spirit, although he professed to be the Spirit of truth itself; and **he said also that he possessed the soul of Christ**.

He tarried until Wednesday, 11th, when, after breakfast, I told him, that my God told me, that his god was the devil, and I could not keep him any longer, and he must depart. And so I, for once, cast out the devil in bodily shape, and I believe a murderer." (HC 2:307. What was Joseph trying to say? Was he saying that the entire concept was false, or was he saying that for Robert Matthias to have the spirit of the Apostle Matthias "was of the devil"? This was in 1835, and by 1844 at Joseph's death, many of his views had changed dramatically as evidenced by the items of doctrine contained in this document.)

Appendix H

Excerpts from Hugh Nibley

Teachings of the Pearl of Great Price: Lecture 3

The earliest texts are the pyramid texts, aside from the Shabako Stone. These are the oldest books in the world, and they are huge. Incidentally, as Professor Edwards tells me (he is the authority on the pyramids, and he is here now), they are working on the pyramids of the fifth and sixth dynasty now, and they are discovering new pyramid texts everyday.

We have thousands of them, and this is all back before 2400 B.C. This comes from the Old Kingdom. This is what they believed way back there. These are the oldest documents in the world, and it isn't just a few fragments; it's a library.

In the pyramid texts we read this, for example: "The pharaoh was conceived by his father when there was as yet no heaven, nor earth, nor people, nor birth of the gods, nor were there any dead. And every individual existed when the plan of the ancient Lord of heaven was not yet formulated."

It speaks of a primordial mother, **how the one became three**, and how before all that we were together in his presence. "My name is the son of the Primordial God." These are from the pyramid texts and go right over into the coffin texts without a break here. "**I existed before I was born**, when the gods did not exist, when as yet there was no bird trap, when the cattle were not yet lassoed. I was formerly; I was of yesterday, a great one among the great and noble ones."

The ordinary person puts this on his coffin (well, this is nobility here). One thinks of Abraham 3:23 . He saw many that were great and noble. "Thou art one of them," the Lord tells Abraham. Well, you get this all through the Egyptian stuff. Here is a coffin text:

"**Before I was born by hand or born of woman, he created me in the midst of his perfection, which caused to jubilate those who shared in the secrets**." When we were created in the preexistence, remember the sons of God shouted for joy and all the morning stars sang together. That's the creation hymn, and it's often referred to in these writings.

The thing most often referred to in early writings is this creation hymn —the hymn of joy that was sung at the creation to celebrate the plan which was now accepted and would begin to be operative. And we were there. There's also a great deal of that in the Dead Sea Scrolls. **But the fact that this is in the very earliest Egyptian stuff is interesting**.

We mentioned the Clementine Recognitions before. When Peter is explaining the gospel to Clement for the first time, he tells about the plan "which He of his own good pleasure announced in the presence of all the first angels which were assembled before Him. Last of all He made man whose real nature, however, is older and for whose sake all this was created." That's the preexistent man. Moses 6:51 says, "I made the world and men before they were in the flesh." And so we have many passages of this from the early writings. Going back to the Clementine Recognitions, "**This world was made so that the number of spirits predestined to come here when their number was full could receive their bodies and again be conducted back to the light.**" So if they were conducted back after they finished their testing here, they must have been there before...

Another passage: "All that have seen me were amazed. And I was regarded by them as a strange person. He who brought me up is the most high in all his perfection. He who brought me down from on high also brought me up from below. Grace of the elect, and who shall receive it save those who trust it from the beginning. The love of the elect, and who shall put it on except those who possessed it in the beginning. Then they tried to slay me. But I did not perish because I was not their brother. Nor was my birth like theirs. For I was older than they could remember. In vain they attacked me. They fought to destroy the memorial of him who was before them. And while I praised among the praising ones, I was great among the mighty ones. For according to the greatness of the most high, so he made me in his own likeness. And in his own newness he renewed me. And he anointed me from his own perfection. Hallelujah! All who see me will be astonished. **For from another world, from another race am I**."

Then chapter 41 is the creation hymn, hailing the Messiah. You compare it with early Christian liturgy from the eighteenth volume of the Patrologia. We have the Oriental Patrologia too which is very valuable, in which the congregation identifies itself with preexistent design. And the Sophia Christi, "**All spirits are ageless and equal as to creation, but differ in degrees of power.**" **The fact that one person is as old as another doesn't mean that one can't be greater than another**. That's a very interesting thing that's explained in the Pearl of Great Price when we get to that. You think it isn't fair if one person came first? **No, nobody came first**. Intelligence never was created, neither can be. "Man also was in the beginning with God." Then why is God so much greater? Well, that's a very interesting problem in the Pearl of Great Price. I've been quoting here from the Sophia Christi and the Gospel of Truth. These are all very old and very recent findings. "**One's true name is that given to him by the Father in the preexistence.**" **That's the name by which you will be known when you go back**. "How can anyone understand whose name was not called out in the beginning? He remains ignorant to the end, is a plasma of forgetting and will pass away with it."

And here is the doctrine of anamnesis too. If anybody has the true knowledge, it is certain that he is from above because when he is called, he hears, he understands, he answers, and he turns toward the one who calls him. There is this recognition, you see. You recognize the voice of the Father if you are righteous. This is a Platonic doctrine of anamnesis. Again we don't want to get sidetracked. There's a wonderful passage from the Gospel of Thomas about all the sufferings you have to go through in the church, all the beatings you have to take. And this you also find in the Hodayot, the Thanksgiving Scroll of the Dead Sea Scrolls. **You have to suffer a lot, but when you get a chance to know what you were before and how much is at stake, you would look upon this with nothing but rejoicing**. It's your big chance and you wouldn't miss it. You're so glad to come here. And the Gospel of Thomas says, "When you come to know yourselves, then you will be known, and you will know that you are the sons of the living Father. But if you do not know yourselves, then you are in poverty." Jesus says in this same writing, "Blessed is he who was before he came into being, and blessed are the solitary elect. For you shall find the kingdom because you came from it. **You shall go there again**."

Incidentally, this is the Gospel of Thomas which contains sayings of Jesus that are not in the Bible, and all churches, Protestant and Catholic, have accepted at least fourteen of these sayings as authentic. **These are original, authentic sayings of Jesus that were lost, and now they are found**. And in the latest Revised Standard translation of the Bible, they are included. So go to the Gospel of Thomas to find out what they used to believe...

You will find an interesting article by John Allegro who was one of the most insightful students of the Dead Sea Scrolls. He lost his job at Harvard for this article that was in the *Atlantic Monthly* in 1960. The scrolls were discovered at the end of the 1940s. In the 1950s there was a big excitement about them. And then all of a sudden, nothing. **They were suppressed. Were they actually suppressed? Yes, they were**, and that's what Allegro shows in this article. The Jews don't like him, and the Christians don't like him. Nobody likes him because it isn't what they had been teaching. For the Jews, it is much too Christian. You don't have Jews with the sacrament, and a presidency of three, and **twelve apostles before the time of Christ**. That's what Professor Cross at Harvard, who has lectured here a good deal, calls the "church of anticipation." It's as if the whole Christian church was there ahead of time. Well, you get that in the Book of Mormon. The Jews were offended to find out that there was so much Christianity in Judaism, and the Christians were offended to find out that the Jews were doing these things before Christ came.

The Catholics were especially offended because it robbed them of their originality. They felt that Christ had to be original. He had to bring something that wasn't known before. Well, Christ fulfills the prophets and brings more. In the Book of Mormon is where you find that beautiful blending of the two.

And so in the Gospel of Thomas, there are all sorts of things that people don't like today. "When you come to know yourselves, then you will be known and you will know that you are the sons of the living Father…" And then he says down here, "Blessed are the solitary elect; you shall find the kingdom because you came from it."

And Jesus said, "If they say to you from where do you have your origin, say to them [this is one of the unwritten sayings of Jesus], 'We have come from the light where the light has originated through itself. It stood and revealed itself in their image.' Lord, do I and man belong to the material world? The answer is you and your children belong to the Father who existed from the beginning. Your spirit came down from above from the imperishable light; for this reason the lower powers cannot approach you. But all who have known this road are immortal amidst mortal men." You have this satisfaction.

And then there is the Gospel of Philip which is equally old and equally important. From the aspect of the temple, it is very important. "The Lord said, 'Blessed is he who was before he came into being, for he who is and was shall be.'" It continues, "**The exalted nature of man is not revealed but in secret to those who have been initiated and who know**." This is an important thing.

When these new writings turn up, so many of them begin with the title "The Secret Teachings of the Lord to the Apostles After the Resurrection." He taught them secretly after the resurrection, and they did not divulge these things. They were not shouted from the housetops, as the Jesuits insist. You see the Christian world can't admit that there had been any secret teachings, let alone any lost teachings— because if there were, where are they now? Whatever happened to them? Now they admit that there was a great deal and now it is possibly turning up.

From the Gospel of Philip again, this is the Cabalistic teaching: "**At the Council in Heaven every spirit appeared before God in the very same form they were later to take in the human body. God examined them one by one, and many hesitated to come here and to be exposed to contamination**." They knew it would be a hard life, and they didn't want to risk the test. They didn't feel good about it. There's a great deal about that, incidentally. I have some good ones here. Two weeks ago I had occasion to go through the old Slavonic text. It was a very good refresher course for me. In the Second Book of Enoch (remember Enoch was the great scribe), "**Write all the souls of men, however many of them are born, for all souls are prepared to eternity before the foundation of the world**."

In 1912 R. H. Charles got together all the writings that were known before the Dead Sea Scrolls and Nag Hammadi. This is a standard collection of Old Testament apocryphal writings. It is on reserve here. If you have any questions about the Old Testament, look up R. H. Charles,

The Apocrypha and Pseudepigrapha of the Old Testament, Vol. 2. He says, "**The Platonic doctrine of preexistence of souls is here taught. We find that it had already made its way into Jewish thought in Egypt**." So through Egypt, Christians and Jews, he says, both adopted this. But the fact is they had it independently; though, as we saw, it was an Egyptian doctrine.

The doctrine was accepted and further developed by Philo. We mentioned Philo before; he is the one that shows how the Jews lost literalism. He turned everything into the abstractions of the schools. Josephus says it was an Essene doctrine, so it would belong to the Dead Sea Scrolls which were unknown at the time this was written. The idea is that spirits are immortal and endure forever and ever. Man is a spiritual, eternal being without beginning or end. And he gives a number of examples here, "He says it became the prevailing doctrine in later Judaism [the doctrine of preexistence] until modern normative Judaism got rid of it. You will find it in the Beresheit Rabbah and the Tanhuma, etc. "The doctrine of preexistence as taught by the Essenes, by Philo, the Talmud, and the Cabala," says Meyer, talking about that.

The Apocalypse of Baruch is a very valuable one that goes way back. You'll find that in R. H. Charles. It says, "**The multitude of those who should be born was numbered and for that number a place was prepared where the living might dwell**." And this is another view: What are we here for then? Was our coming down here a fall or a calamity? Well, the Gnostic doctrine was that we are here in prison. We are being punished. "Man's descent from heaven at the moment of conception with his human form and divine seal (showing that he had existed before)..." But unlike Origen and the Gnostic schools, the Cabala does not regard life as a fall or exile but as a means of education and a beneficial trial. As Nephi says, "**Our time here became a time of probation**." That's what the Cabala teaches. But Origen, the Gnostics and the Christians went off in this direction—that it is a fall, an imprisonment, and a curse. Well, just like "Adam brought the curse of man's first disobedience and the fruit of that forbidden tree whose bitter taste brought death into the world and all our woes." It was utter calamity that brought us here. In the Jewish teaching that was not so. **It's a benefit, a time of education and learning, and a time of testing**. So in the third chapter of the Book of Abraham we read, "**We will make an earth whereon these may dwell, and we will prove them herewith to see if they will do all the things whatsoever we shall command them. They who keep their first estate shall be added upon...**"

Another book we are going to cite is from the Zohar. This is a very important writing which has been neglected by the Jews; they come back to it. They used to think it was just an invention of Moses of Leon in 1240 A.D., a work of the Middle Ages, but now they know it is very old. It has come out in a number of editions. I have a beautiful, complete Hebrew edition of the Zohar that just came out. It's full of not just biblical teachings, but things that might have been in the Bible. Remember the canon of the Bible is a very arbitrary sort of thing. Many things are in there that shouldn't be, and things are left out that should be there. But the Zohar tells us here: "All men before they lived on earth were present in heaven in the identical form they possess in this life, and everything they learn on earth they knew already before they came to this world." That's an interesting thing; how could you be tested if you knew it already. This becomes a very interesting problem in physics. According to the Talmud, this world is only a marshaling area, a sort of freeport, while that world above is the true dwelling. We have just left it temporarily to be tested here. "All spirits which are to enter into the body exit from the day of creation of the world until the earth shall pass away."

Now a powerful passage in the Zadokite Document from the Dead Sea Scrolls tells how God condemned the wicked in the preexistence by not counting them among those chosen. "From of old, from the days of eternity and before they were established, he knew them and abhorred their generations. With exactitude he set out their names, but those whom he hated he caused to stray." Remember in the Pearl of Great Price, Satan was a liar from the beginning.

This expression that is used is another important one: "from eternity to eternity." In the Serek Scroll of the Dead Sea Scrolls 2:1, it uses the expression me'olam le'olam. It's more than an ecstatic outbreak "from ever to ever." The Christians use it, and Barnabas uses it in his epistle eight. Barnabas—remember, he is one of the seven apostolic fathers, one of the earliest fathers after the New Testament—he says, "From eons unto the eons means that you come out of the eons and you go into the eons." **You have an eternity behind you, and you have an eternity before you. This is the bottleneck you pass through to determine for a long time to come which way you will take hereafter.** He says, "The way of light is the Lord from eons into the eons; the way of life leading from one eternity up to the other one to come. The eschatology is inconceivable without the protology. Typical of this common background to Jews and early Christians is the prayer of Anna in the Pseudo-Philo. "Hast thou not, O Lord, examined the heart of all generations before thou formedst the world?" In the Secrets of Enoch in the Slavonic Enoch (this is one very close to the Joseph Smith Enoch), the Lord says to Enoch, "Sit down and write the names of those who are not yet born and the places which are prepared for them forever; for all the spirits were prepared before the foundation of the earth." Enoch speaks here, "I swear unto you, my children, that before man was made in the womb of his mother, he was prepared; **and how each has sojourned in this age that a man might be tested in the balance while he was here." There's your probation and preexistence too. "There has indeed been prepared in advance a place for every human soul.**"

We'll go back to our friend Gregory of Nyssa again. "The soul had a previous existence and a life of its own where, even as in this life, it was given its free agency by the Creator. **And such as grew weary at doing good entered this life at a disadvantage, having passed the test less**

APPENDIX H—EXCERPTS FROM HUGH NIBLEY

satisfactorily than others." Now this is writing which is accepted by Origen, the earliest Christian theologian, and he says that this is what the brethren taught. "I don't believe it," he said, "but the brethren in the early church taught it." **Now the fact is when we are born into this world it's with unequal advantages, isn't it?** Some are born blind, lame, crippled; it's terrible. Some are born into poverty; some into riches. He says, "How does that happen? **They used to teach that before we came here life was a test too, and when we passed the test, we came into this world. Our life here is a reward for our performance before we came here.**" He says that would certainly explain the inequality of people being born. Or as Gregory of Nyssa says here, "The soul had a previous existence for even as in this life, it was a free agent." Remember there was a Council in Heaven. They voted and some preferred this and some preferred that. You were perfectly free to take your way there. You had your free agency.

And such as grew weary in doing good entered this life at a disadvantage because they passed the test all right, but less satisfactorily than others passed it. Well, there's an interesting thesis that Origen developed. Needless to say, it was slapped down.

Well, Basilides, also a contemporary, says that suffering in this life is punishment for sins in the preexistence, not by way of denying that there was preexistence, by insisting that the opportunity to suffer here, even martyrdom, is rather a reward earned before, **an opportunity for greater glory.** Persecutions are not to punish the saints but to sanctify them. Then back to Origen again, "The spirit stands for progress and by definition evil is refusal to accept progress. This is the principle of apostasy that you refuse to progress, and when you dug in your heels in the other world, you came here at a lower level. "Learn this one thing," wrote Cyril of Jerusalem, "that before coming to this cosmos, the spirit did not sin, but that we came down sinless here and now. And now we sin by choice."

Well, which is it? Is it a matter of sin up there? We had to come down here and take on flesh, I suppose, to be tested in a particular way. No, it's the level of performance that we are judged on in coming down here. And that's another interesting thing—that wonderful passage where the Lord says that one will be more intelligent than another. **Don't resent it, because you know perfectly well why you are not more intelligent than you are.** We only use one thousandth of our potential anyway. So **you can't complain that somebody is ahead of you. You might be far far better than you are. So don't worry about him; just improve yourself. And this is the gospel of repentance.** Well, the time is up and we are still bogged down in these fundamentals. But they are the fundamentals that are treated with peculiar address and clarity in the Pearl of Great Price, and as far as I know, nowhere else. (*Teachings of the Pearl of Great Price:* Lecture 3, Winter Semester, 1986)

Teachings of the Pearl of Great Price: Lecture 4

In the first volume of the Patrologia there is an interesting note by Migne. He edited it. He speaks for the fathers of the church on this subject, I Clement 1:28. "Clement asserts that the spirit is older than the body, according to one of the four interpretations of the fathers." He says the fathers interpret this four ways. Did we preexist or not? Remember this is all essential to our **handbook of terrible questions** which is the Pearl of Great Price. The first thing that Migne says is one school taught that the spirit was before the body (it was preexistent); a second that the body came first and the spirit after that; still others that they came into existence together. That school has a special name. And still others that are not willing to make any assertion at all. Along with which opinion should be mentioned the errors of Pythagoreans, the Platonists, the Gnostics, and the Origenists (the Hermetic School). Origen for a time firmly believed in the preexistence, and then he changed his mind. Pythagoreans believed in reincarnation, metempsychosis, that you did exist before but it was in another shape or being, an animal or something.

This is no satisfaction because if you change your identity completely, you are somebody else and you really haven't continued to exist. I may have been a chair in the preexistence, but that doesn't give me any satisfaction now. Or to think that I will be a cockroach hereafter gives me no great comfort either. That is not me continuing. They feel that very strongly. The Egyptians are particularly strong on this. That's why this emphasis on the name. It was the name to help preserve his identity. It was himself and nobody else that continued. You had to have hereafter, but you had to preserve your identity as well.

But Plato really believed that we existed before and that we still have dim memories of it. How do you know it was good, beautiful, and true? Because you saw it before. You have a memory of it when you come here. **Every recognition of truth is a recognition of something you knew and learned before**, and we are moving toward that state…

…**So the early church believed in the preexistence**; the later churches and the official churches today do not believe in it. But we do because it was restored by Joseph Smith. Incidentally, the most beautiful and moving description of this is the oldest. I brought the text here, but I haven't been into Syriac for a long time. So I'm going to use translations. Five different people have made translations besides me, so all I can do is pass the buck to them. I compare the various translations carefully. **This is a thing called The Pearl**. It was found in 1906 by Rendel Harris way up east of the Tigris. Its dating is interesting because Alfred Adam, a Catholic scholar and very able Orientalist who lives in Jerusalem, dates it between 50 and 70 A.D. That means it could have been written within 25 years of the Crucifixion. Walter Crum, who is the great authority on Coptic documents, places it right there in the first century. You can't get an older Christian document than this. The Pearl is meant to be a romanticized thesis, something like the story *Added Upon*. Now we have rather mediocre (that's a flattering word) musicals about the preexistence. We sentimentalize it. I don't know how much the author of The Pearl cleared on this, but it is the oldest Christian hymn we have and it is certainly the most remarkable.

It starts out, "In my first primeval childhood (he's in heaven, you see, before he came here), I was nurtured (quoting Eliza R. Snow, you recognize) in the royal house of my father with loving care in the midst of abundance and glory." This is where he came from. "My parents sent me forth from our home in the East, the source of light, supplied with all necessities." So he comes down to get the pearl and bring it back with him. The pearl is the integrity which he preserves during the trials and tests of this life so he can continue hereafter to be a member of the royal family and assume his throne and crown above. "...making a packet for me from our rich storehouse. It was sizable but light enough for me to carry. I came from the house on high as a great treasure, bringing with me precious stones from India and Kushan and gold and silver, and they girt me with a diamond.

There's an interesting footnote on adamus, on the diamond here. You see, the word Adam was associated with diamond. Adamantis means that which cannot be damaged, that which is immortal. There's a long story behind that. Diamond is the urim and thummim, the sacred stone that was given to Adam when he came down. So the name Adamantis was given to him—the prince of stones.

Continuing with The Pearl: "**They removed from me the garment of light which they made for me above**." The idea is that when you lived in heaven you had a heavenly garment; and when you left, it was put aside, carefully folded and put under the Father's throne to be kept there until you came back **if you were worthy to receive it again**. A good deal is said in this Syriac stuff, for example, about the great tragedy of sinning in this life because you lose all that you invested. What you have up there represents long terms of investment and work to achieve such a state. You left it all there on reserve, on deposit, the crown and the garment carefully folded and deposited (**in the throne, some say**) in a special chest, for you to resume when you return. And if you can't take it back, **you have lost all that you worked for before, which makes this earthly trial a key experience**, a terrifying sort of thing if we miss it. You can miss it, and it's so important not to. Continuing: "They removed from me the garment of light which they had made for me and my **purple robe** made exactly to fit me." And it would fit no one else. This is interesting. It is your robe, and it has certain marks on it. "They made a covenant with me and **wrote it in my heart** lest I go astray." So you have covenanted with your parents above in this test. He was instructed to go down to Egypt and bring back the pearl—this integrity.

It's in the sea guarded or surrounded by a fire or poisonous snorting serpent—the dragon. This was the dragon or the serpent of the Garden of Eden guarding this thing. But he has to get it away from him. **He has to outwit the dragon and get the pearl**. "Returning the pearl, he may resume his garment of light and his outer priestly mantle and become heir to our kingdom along with our Second One." The Second One is the second heir to the throne. He will become an heir along with the Son. Not the second born, it says, but the next or second in line to the throne, second in glory, successor. That is the first born, Christ, the elder brother.

So if you perform properly when you go down there, you can come back and resume your garment and "become heir to our kingdom along with our Second One." So when he comes down, **he has two guides or guardians**. Remember **they always come in threes**. They are official couriers who know the way and are sent down with him up to the point where they bid him goodbye and he is on his own. Remember, the two guides say, "We will leave you now, but we will return later." Then the minute Adam finds himself alone, that is the time Satan strikes and tries to win him over. That's what happens here. The two guardians are sent with him. That's standard; in the eighteenth chapter of Genesis, the **Lord appears with the three men, always the three**...

Well, there **the guides** leave him on his own, and he goes on toward Egypt. As in the Book of Tobit here, Egypt means the spiritual Sodom. In Egypt he immediately looks up the serpent who has the pearl (it's quite homey; quite like a novel). The serpent is staying at an inn. So he goes to the inn and checks in to keep an eye on the serpent and catch him while he is still asleep. This could be a spy thriller with the dragon just a name given to the odious person who is going to try to get the best of him—who does, as a matter of fact. He shouldn't be doing this dangerous thing the way he does. Don't try to go to the dragon; you'll be in trouble. There he meets a young nobleman from his own country who was born in the covenant and with whom he shares full confidence. He warns him against the temptations and defilements of Egypt. He says, "You're going into dangerous country; I can help you out here."

This is also part of the spy thriller, isn't it? He meets up with Agent X or the fat man, or something like that. Isn't LeCarre writing the best spy thrillers now? To avoid arousing suspicion as a stranger, he adopts the dress of the Egyptians. He can't get away with it because he's not that clever about it. He gives himself away in speech and all sorts of things. **He doesn't really belong to this world**. You see, this is a member of the Church, one who has accepted the covenant. His behavior is different, and they suspect that he is not really one of them. They notice that he is an alien, and so what do they do? They invite him in, make friends with him, and ask him to enter some of their deals. They invite him to dinner. The wine flows freely and before you know he's one of the boys, which is exactly where they want him. "Whereupon, **he forgot that he was the son of the king and served their king**." Well, they got him over to their side. And what's more, he enjoyed the life. We've read about a half dozen spies within the last few weeks that have gone over, and they all did it for money. It's the same thing here. He liked the high lifestyle, the rich foods dulled his senses, and he fell into a deep sleep. Well, the poor guy is helpless now.

So what is going to happen now? Meanwhile, the heavenly parents are aware of what has happened. They call a family council up above.

"**We've got to do something to save the boy. He's making a fool of himself.**" All the great and noble relatives come together, and they decide it's time to act. They must do something, so they draft a letter and they all sign it. "This letter might stir him up, but if this doesn't do any good, we'll have to do something else." I'm sure we've all slipped at some time or other, and then there is some reminder from home. The letter is addressed "to our son in Egypt from thy Father, the King of Kings, and thy Mother, the Queen of the East, and our Second One, thy Brother."

And this was the letter: "Awake and arise from thy sleep. Heed this letter. Remember that you are the son of the King, and **take a good look at your present master. Remember your mission to fetch the pearl**. Remember the garment and robe that are awaiting you so you can put them on again when your name is called out from the book of those who were valiant [this is interesting because in D&C 76 it speaks of those who were valiant] and you will become the heir to our kingdom along with your brother, the successor to our throne." And we read in D&C 76:76–79: "These are they [terrestrial] who receive of his glory, but not of his fullness. These are they who receive of the presence of the Son, but not the fullness of the Father...These are they who are not valiant in the testimony of Jesus; wherefore, they obtain not the crown over the kingdom of our God." It uses the same imagery exactly that we are finding here in The Pearl. "Then the king with his right hand sealed the letter against the evil children of Babylon and the rebellious spirits of Sarbug lest they open and read it or destroy it." Notice that there has to be revelation; there has to be authority in these things. The sealing is very important in the early Christian writings. The seal protects it and keeps it out of contact with the world. That's why we seal people, so they won't revert. If you seal a thing, you put a fix on it. Khatum is the regular word in Egyptian and Arabic. Khatum is the seal or stamp you put on something, and then it can't be opened by anybody else.

"The letter was brought by an eagle, the king of the birds." This is a very rich theme in the East. King Solomon sent a letter to the Queen of Sheba, and it was carried by the eagle. The neser, sea eagle, flew through her window while she was asleep and dropped it upon her bosom. She saw the seal of Solomon on it, opened and read it, and was duly impressed. But it was delivered by the eagle. **The eagle stands for revelation—a dream, a spirit, or something like that. It comes to them while they are asleep.** So we go on, "It alights by his side and [the letter] becomes all speech whereupon he awakes and rises from his sleep." He was sleeping like the queen was. This is what stirs him up again. So there is contact with the other world. "He kisses the letter, breaks the seal, and reads. Lo, it is the same letter which he brought with him from on high." They gave him a letter to carry with him, **but it was written in his heart**. A very common theme in ancient literature is the matching of the two parts of the tessera. You break the tessera, which is usually a coin of clay or metal. You cut it in two and keep half. Another person keeps half, and **when you put the two together, then it is complete**. The stick of Joseph and the stick of Judah are joined the very same way. He matches them up, and it's the same letter that was written in his heart and he brought it with him from on high. "Then he remembers that he is a king's son and his royal nature asserts itself."

From this point on, everything is in reverse. He does an about face and everything reverses. **He remembers the pearl, and he has to get it, so he sets about lulling the serpent to sleep, invoking over it the name of the Father. He does it by prayer**. Having seized the pearl, he does an about-face wholly drawn in one direction toward his Father's house, having at this point reached the uttermost depths. First, he sheds his filthy garments for cleaner ones. Then he leaves them behind in the world where they belong. His sets his course undeviatingly toward the light of our home in the East. The letter that woke him also leads the way both as a guiding voice and as a guiding light. And there were the two birds, the hudhud and the neser, were the two guide birds that take you to the presence of Solomon. It was a real document written on paper or silk of high sheen with red ink. I wish I had the tangible document here. "...encouraged the traveler by its guiding voice and instructions [which fork of the road to follow, etc.] and drawing him on with love. He successfully passed through Sarbug and left Babylon on his left. And so he reached Maishan, the port of the merchants where you cross the division line on the shore of the sea. There his garment and his outer robe were waiting for him."

Now he is entering the temple or going into the new phase. "They had been sent ahead from home by his parents in the custody of the **two faithful guides**." They had left him at that point. They are waiting for him and have the garment ready for him. Everything is ready to resume now. "He had forgotten how glorious the clothing was, having lost his childhood memories of home. Yet it all came back to him the moment he saw it. He saw himself as he was as if in a mirror. He and the garment completely identified with each other for the garment would fit nobody else. They were a single individual though they were separate. He noticed the same phenomenon with **the guides** that brought the garment. There were two of them, but each bore the identical token of the King. By this sign he also reclaimed his own inheritance, namely the garment with the gold and the precious stones which adorned it, fastened everywhere with diamond clasps. And the image of the King of Kings covered the whole thing." Then he saw the whole thing begin to stir and set in motion. Before he could go any farther, he gave certain signs and tokens at the veil. "And I clothed myself with it and mounted up to the gate of greeting." He comes to the gate finally, and the whole family is there to greet him. The first person to embrace him was the last person to embrace him as he left. It was his Heavenly Mother.

You notice that we don't have a lot of Heavenly Mother in our teachings because the **Heavenly Mother has her particular job, which is to keep the store while the others go forth on missions. You notice that all the angels and all the missionaries are male**. The mother is the eternal hearth and home. She has her work to do there. She is the last to greet him as he goes and the first to greet him as he comes back. Those

Appendix H—Excerpts from Hugh Nibley

marvelous lines by Sappho: "The evening brings back to the mother all the creatures that the bright sun of morning has scattered [around 10:00 a.m.]. It brings back the little sheep and goats, and brings the little boy back to his mother." Everybody goes out on their bright adventures.

Odysseus goes forth into the world for his thirty years of adventure, but he always wants to get home. In the end it's his Penelope that he has in mind. It's the same thing. He goes back to home. It's interesting that the Heavenly Mother greets him along with the Father. It says here, "At the gate of his princes, I mingled with the great ones." The oldest book in the world ends with this. He gets back to heaven and mingles with the great ones there. As Virgil says in his Fourth Eclogue, "I mingled with the great ones."

The Pearl continues: "At the doors of the palace which was from the beginning, I mingled among them. He who received me joyfully, I was with him in his kingdom." And then the Kephalia. There are the five greetings he receives. The first greeting of peace the gods and angels gave to the first man as he departed from the eon of light. This same greeting ceremony took place with Adam we are told right at the beginning. The second greeting is the greeting of the right hand, the clasp of the right hand-that which the mother of life gave to the first man when he went forth to the contest. The first embrace, the aspasmos, (the embrace through the veil which is so important in Egypt) is that which the mother of life gave to the first man as he separated himself from her in order to come down to the earth to be tested (for the agon, the testing). She wishes him luck and hopes he will be able to carry on, covers him with love, etc.

As they embrace, as he separates in order to come down to the earth for testing. Also, all the gods and angels embraced him on that occasion, and all who were to be of the Church hereafter embraced him with love. The word is aspazein, which means grasp, embrace. The final verse is, "The first honoring [the first good wish] is that which Adam received when he left for the abyss below. He bowed the knee, worshipped the God of truth and of all the eons of light."

These are remarkable documents that come from the early church. As I said, this one was discovered in 1906, and everybody accepts it as the earliest Christian document we have. It's much earlier than the others, going way back there to the middle of the first century. So the preexistence was a very important part of the early church, but now we need to get to cosmology. What you should notice as we go along are the preexistence passages in the Book of Abraham and the Book of Moses. They are very clear in there. Remember, Abraham comes down in the same way. "...Abraham, thou art one of them; thou wast chosen before thou wast born." (*Teachings of the Pearl of Great Price*: Lecture 4, Winter Semester, 1986. The Pearl can be found in Brother Nibley's *Message of the Joseph Smith Papyri: An Egyptian Endowment* [Salt Lake City: Deseret Book, 1976], Appendix III.)

Teachings of the Pearl of Great Price: Lecture 7

Interestingly, as Bonnet says, the creation of man doesn't enter into the story. "We have no problem about the creation of man," he says, "because that is going on every day. If you want to know how people are produced, you ask your old man." But we know how that happens, so he says we don't have to have mysteries. They don't have mysteries and stories about that at all. Mary, the great sage, said, "**All persons are images of the creator, who have come out of his own members**. Man is in his express image." So that didn't bother them. That wasn't part of the creation. In other words, it's not part of cosmogony. Man is there too, like the other stuff. And then he becomes Ptah-Tenen, as I said. Here it's a very strong demonstrative Ptah pen pel. A person by the name of Stolk quite a few years ago wrote a book on Ptah. Among the other theories that have been very popular is that the name Ptah is the same as PTH. You will recognize what that is, you Hebrew students, patah, pateah. The Arabic is fataha. The opening line of the Koran is called the Fatihun, "the opener." Fataha means "to open," you see. A thing that opens is a mifte'ah, "a key." The Arabic word is miftah. It's cognate with Latin. We have patio, which means "open to expand." It's related to pando, "to expand, to open up," and Pandora. It has also been related to father too. But Patah, our "father," is probably related to the word feeder, food provider, something like that. But anyway, it has been suggested that it means "**the beginning, the opener, the one who started everything going.**" **That's why this name Ptah is given to him**. It's a universal, international name. You're going to find it in lots of things like that.

He is always represented in human form. In all this creation story, you will find no idols, no animal gods, or anything like that at all. This is all strictly human.

And here Sander-Hansen says that Nun, the primal material, the urstoff from which things were made, existed before the creation was universally believed in the ancient world. Nobody believed in creation out of nothing. There was a primal substance that existed before the creation, and the creation was the organizing of that substance. That, he says, was the universal view of the Egyptians, especially of the early times.

We will see a lot about Ptah-Tenen. Notice, he is being acclaimed on the throne. **He is the father**. Ptah-Tenen is a rare form (oh, you run into that a lot), but **Ptah-Tenen means Ptah's office translated down to earth. It means the exalted one**. It refers to the hill, among other things, the exalted hill. It refers both to the first land that emerged after the flood and the first land that emerged in the beginning when waters and darkness covered the earth. There was the later flood, and these are the waters the Egyptians are referring to as you learn from the Pearl of Great Price. Remember, when she discovered the land, it was under water. She went there after the flood. But emerging from the flood is a very important thing. And Ptah-Tenen is the land that first emerged. But it is also the person who first occupied it and first lived in it. It means the exalted one, the exalted or uplifted land. This Ptah-Tenen always belongs to the earth. He is the earthly representative of the heavenly order. Everything about him is earthy, and so he is chthonian. Chthon is the Greek word for "like earth." The solar is the light, and the dark is the chthonian. A perfect example of that is in our Facsimile No 2. Notice all these deities are solar deities. They all have suns, **and they are moving forth in glory**. All these are chthonian, the cow, the female, and including the inscription which tells us this is the dark place where everything comes to a halt. But you have to have both if you are going to create. This is the womb; that's why the cow. That's Hathor, the mother—the womb from whom all life comes. And the four figures in front of her are, as Joseph Smith says, the four elements—the four regions of the earth from which physical bodies must be compounded.

So it tells us here, this is Ptah on the throne of Ptah-Tenen. Wolf has written a good study on Ptah-Tenen. "He stirs the earth out of her lethargy, which is called Nen, a state of inertia, a heat death. That is to say out of her condition of chaos. It is Ptah-Tenen who visits the earth and organizes the earth here below." Out of its condition of chaos, he puts things into order. But he does not give it life or force. He depends on another for that. And he's not a vegetation god. Now, you would think the earth god would be the vegetation god and all that sort of thing, but he isn't. When the waters were divided, he joined the lands together and made the earth habitable; and he sets the pattern for the king, for Horus Ptah-Tenen. He is Ptah's earthly counterpart. He is almost a byword for Ptah. His name is almost a synonym for Ptah's name—Ptah above, Ptah-Tenen below. But he carries things out. He never loses his identity as the exalted one, and his form is purely human. He never takes any form but human. **He wears the same crown as the two sun figures wear**. It's being worn by Abraham in Facsimile 3.

It's the Atef-crown. He wears that crown which is the same as Amon wears. So we get Ptah-Tenen and Ptah. That's the people that begin the play, and Act One ends here.

Then the place, the setting, is the division between the north and the south. This is the northland; this is the southland. They are united here at this particular place where the two thrones are joined in one and the king of the North deseret and the king of the South sut (of the sedge) are united in a single glory. Deseret and the bee are the symbol of the North king. His name is bit nu, meaning "belonging to the bee" which is feminine. They knew that the queen-bee was a queen already. They say in a single glory, Kha, which is a picture of the sun rising over a mound which represents the king mounting the throne. The two thrones are placed side by side: the throne of the king of the South with the sedge; the other with the king of the North with the bee. The king is shown underneath wearing the white crown; the other king wearing the red crown. Everything is divided between the two, and this division is preserved throughout all of Egyptian life. This is a very important thing. In fact it is the main theme of this document, namely the importance of coexistence here. The two thrones are together, and they are as one.

Now, you're never going to get rid of evil in the world. The Egyptians knew that because that was part of the plan. This is why Egypt has been the most stable of all civilizations. They didn't try to wipe out all opposition. They could put up with things. Later, they are less tolerant, however. Notice, they wiped out the name of Shabako here. **The theme is eternal life by eternal generation**. The Gospel of Philip tells us nothing is eternal except progeny. All worlds pass away, as we are told in the Pearl of Great Price. They come into existence and pass away. What doesn't come into existence and pass away? Well, it is the individual. I wish I could find that statement of Brigham Young. It's really a nice one.

We'll go on to the next line. So here they are on the single throne. Now, we come to the theme here. There is much discussion about these lines and what they mean. **Who begot Atum in the beginning? It was Ptah. Atum is the big thing**. At Heliopolis he is everything. It's very interesting. In the very old Coffin Texts, he is called Adamu, using the Canaanite ending u and also the soft d instead of t. In fact, Lefebure, the famous French Egyptologist went to quite a great length to show that **this is the same as Adam, and he obviously is Adam here**. So it says here, **Atum who was begotten and who then became the father of the pesedj or the Great Council**. The pesedj is always translated Ennead, but is it the Ennead? I notice how Sethe sums it up here. Ennead doesn't have to be nine or eight, or any particular number. It means the vast number. **The numberless Council of the Gods is what it means**. I wish I could see how he put ennead here. (Well, who cares?) But it's important though. **There are the nine gods, but there are dozens of lists of them. Sometimes they will add one or take some off, or add five or six. Originally, half should be female and half male, with Ptah making the odd number, you see. It breaks down into couples** such as Shu and Tefnut and Geb and Neith.

But first Atum. His name is a very important one. Rudolf Anthes has written several long articles and monographs about **the name of Atum. It means "many,"** as we are told in Moses 1:34. And, of course, it means "many" here. I notice that even Siegfried Lawrence, a very prejudiced character, says what it means is a gesammtheit—a gathering, a compound, or a complex. It includes everything in itself, and you will see why. The word is very productive in Egypt. It's a word that means almost anything. You just draw a sled, and this is *tm*. It's a regular verb meaning "to be," but it also means "not to be." **It means "to complete, to complete a circle."** Immediately, you think of the Hebrew word for perfect. Job was an upright man, yashar watamim, upright and perfect. Tamim means a perfect circle. It comes right back to the beginning where it started. Of course, tamam is the standard Arabic word for perfect or complete. Well, Atum is the one who is perfect and complete. Oh, there are all sorts of things. When we get to the Atum literature, we may talk about them.

But in Egyptian it means "to be complete, to be everything, to be nothing, and not to be." The basic meaning they give is mes-tm, "**one**

who begot all." Well, that's what it's written as here. The father of all. Mes is like Moses, etc. It means "to beget, to have a child." And Mes-tm is the one who begot all. And Anthes says **the name of Adam represents all that has gone before himself and all that comes after himself.** He is the great bottleneck. **As to his own origin, we are told it is deliberately left unrevealed or unreported.** There are various theories, of course. But in the Pyramid Texts, the oldest writings we have after this, he is the primal god who comes down to earth—the first one to set foot on the primal hill when the waters divide. When the land becomes habitable, Atum is the first one to occupy it. We are told in one text he needed no magic because he came first. He was a real fact. He doesn't need to create something. He has a companion, Amun's pallakida, his mate. That's a very interesting way of putting it, as Bonnet does. This was his companion, his helpmeet. This was Hathor, the woman who settled the land. The priestesses of the Atum temple were always called Hathors. That goes back, he thinks, to a tree cult because they have this tree of life business here.

In spite of any magic background, the creation was an act of mind. But at Heliopolis there was a real marriage we are told. Right where the rivers meet, this is Heliopolis. I said that's where the airport is today. It is right here. It's the On of the Bible, and Unell meaning the stone pillars. It's the old megalithic foundation. It's very important in the New Testament. That's where Moses lived, where Joseph married the daughter of the high priest, where Abraham taught and was taught. Everybody went to Heliopolis, and the earliest Christian accounts say that's where Jesus's parents took him when they went there. There were two temples: the temple at Jerusalem and the temple at Heliopolis. In the Bible they are in frequent contact with each other. We'll get to more of that.

So he brought forth the first pair, which bringing together became the source of all life on earth. They were the first flesh. But it is an interesting thing. **He does not create, he begets. He is a father.** He does not create; others do that. And then there's this idea "who begot himself." What is it talking about there? Diodorus tells us "the seed not the womb contains the life of the child. Therefore, Adam contained within himself the life as in the womb, and so he is both father and mother." Bonnet insists that there is nothing offensive about this.

No lust is involved. It was really a compromise with matriarchy. Whatever form the child may have in the seed, without the mother it cannot enter into this stage of existence. And that's what we're after. This may seem like a mystery, but remember in the Book of Mormon Christ says, "I am the Father and the Son." Well, I think President Joseph Fielding Smith explained that very well when he said, "Who made it possible for us to be resurrected and live in bodies hereafter? Jesus Christ. Without him it wouldn't have been possible. He is the father of our everlasting, eternal bodies—not the bodies we have here. That's something else. But when we are resurrected, he has made that possible. So he is the Father and the Son. Of course, anybody can be a father and a son at the same time; I've achieved that difficult feat."

Now, the conflict between the patriarchy and matriarchy about which a lot has been written. This is dissolved in the very simple question, namely with this. Which one is it, the father or mother, who makes birth possible? You leave one of them out, and birth is impossible. Well, it's a silly question. When Atum's son Shu separated the earth and heaven, male and female, **it was really Atum himself who was doing it all. So Atum comes down here, and he is the father of the human race in every sense**. He comes down and transfers it. But you say, "Oh, this is getting sort of complicated. What have we got here?" **So Ptah begot Atum who was the father of the Council of the Gods**. (*Teachings of the Pearl of Great Price:* Lecture 7, Winter Semester, 1986)

Teachings of the Pearl of Great Price: Lecture 8

The whole purpose of this is to show that the king at Memphis (Shabako in this case) holds the same authority that was held by God and was handed down to man through Atum and through the heavenly council to the spirits and brought down to earth. That's what he is going to tell us about here. So we now proceed here, and **Ptah is the main thing**. But it's now Ptah-Tenen which means the uprising, the lifting up, the exalted. The rising of the land, the rising of the earth, the first pyramid, the first burial mound, the rising of resurrection—all that is together along with the name Ptah-Tenen. His name is Ptah-Tenen, the first person to put life upon the earth. **So this is Ptah coming down to earth** (Ptah means earth, you see). But it's earthy. The problem is how are we going to transmit the powers and forces of the universe to this one little planet? This is the way we do it. Well, this is the land; this is the setting. This is the land of the Mekhy of the North and of the Resy of the South. And it is the joining place of the two glorious ones. These are thrones of glory. That was originally a sunburst coming out here. It's very finely, very beautifully carved, but they were already conventionalized. It was the hill with the sunrise over it. So you had this form like this and then like this. That's what this is, called the Kha, which means to arise in glory. It's a regular word used for coronation or crowning of the king. Enthronement was his rising in glory, of course, being compared with the sun.

Notice he is wearing the white crown of the South; and North, the red crown of the North. There were always two crowns, always two thrones, even two graves for the king. Everything was double. Every ordinance was carried out four times really, but there was the white and the red and they were always mixed. We see they are mixed here. "**And he was who begot Atum.**" **Now here is our friend Atum again who in turn is the father or the begetter of the pesedj. The writing on this pesedj here, that means the nine.** (*Teachings of the Pearl of Great Price:* Lecture 8, Winter Semester, 1986)

Appendix H—Excerpts from Hugh Nibley

Teachings of the Pearl of Great Price: Lecture 9

Now, let's review what we said before. Remember this is the oldest document in the world [the Shabako Stone], oldest writing in the world, and there are many to back it up.

They have found a Demotic copy of this quite recently, so it is confirmed by other sources. We were just able to get started with it. We have to go fast because you are going to find this on many other very old documents. We will refer to them perhaps a little later. This is all very close to our Pearl of Great Price. This is the situation: Ptah-Tenen is going to establish the heavenly order on a new world. The setting is this, and they are going to be united in the United Kingdom of Egypt. **And so he begets Atum; Atum begets the Council of the Gods.** They are all identical. Now there are two things that are mentioned. Remember that Zabkar said, and many others have said (everybody has noted this), including Breasted. (You may have read that article in *The Monist* by now.) They have noted that this is very close to the Gospel of John and Genesis for two reasons. It emphasizes two things that you will find all over in John and Genesis—**namely, the work of identification**. John chapters 14 through 17, "I am in the Father, and they are in me, and I am in them. Those that listen to us, **they are in us.**" **What does it mean by "in us"?** And "I am out of the Father ek Theou." These are the expressions that are used here in the same sense. And the other, the theme of conflict of Genesis, is the theme of creation. Well, this is John 2. The logos, the mystery of the word, the doctrine of creation by the word, the Word of God. And in Genesis God spake, and it's the word. And it uses the very same word: the Old Testament uses sepet which means "lips." Here it is ushepet which is the very same thing, by his lips.

First the situation: now we can begin. The most high god who is acclaimed decides to establish Ptah-Tenen here, and this is the situation in Egypt. **He is the father of Atum, and through Atum, and through himself also, the father of all the Council of the Gods**. He calls the Council of the Gods and they discuss a division between Seth and Horus. Seth is mentioned first here. But when he settles the land, he settles Seth first. Seth is the plaintiff here. He has always been making trouble, and that's going to be a very important element here. Seth is our Satan, of course. But the land is divided between them, the kings of the North and the South, and they are equal. This ends here. He sends each one to his part of the hall and says, "Let there be no more argument between you." And each one takes his place. But then he does a strange thing. He decides to give the whole inheritance to Horus. Why is that? Why did he change his mind? For two reasons made very clear here. First of all, he was very much disturbed. Geb's heart was troubled at the fact that he had given...Now Ptah doesn't change his mind here. It's his plan, but Geb's business (remember Geb represents the earth and everything on the earth) is to implement the divine plan down here. And he saw that it would never work with this equal division here. Therefore, he is troubled that the division was equal between Horus and Seth. So

Geb gave his own entire portion to Horus, the son of his son who was his firstborn. Well, what the theme is here is priesthood and kingship as well as land...

...So now we go to the important part of it which is the creation episode, the second half. Yes, that's the way it should be. Notice, here you **see the house of the old man, the house of the Ancient of Days**. Now we come to this, and this is the theology of the creation. These three are met together (this is why they couldn't read it because it is written backwards). It should read this way by the direction the figures are facing, but actually it's read this way, which Breasted discovered. These are the forms that Ptah bestowed upon all life—how Ptah extended himself and was able to put his life, his nature, and his stamp upon all that was created. The gods who came into existence in or through Ptah. And first of all there is Ptah upon the great throne. He's the first Ptah. These are different Ptahs, you see.

Then there is Ptah-Nun, the heavenly Ptah (incidentally, he is standing in the shrine of the temple of the South here), who is the father of Atum. Then there is Ptah-Naunet who is the mother who bore Atum. And then there is the great Ptah who is the mind, the lips, and the tongue of the Pesedjet of all the gods-whose mind and heart are in all the gods. You notice you have a matter of degrees here. You have a transmission of power, and what is it? Identity? That's what you have in John. The nineteenth chapter of 3 Nephi is the same thing. He goes aside and prays that I may be in you and you, Father, in me; and those that follow me may be in me as you are in me, Father; and that those who follow them (their converts) may also be one as we are one.

This idea of being in others and being identified. That's what we have here, and it's one of the keys of Egyptian, this doctrine of identity...

..."And it came to pass that Horus and Djehuty-Thoth cooperated with him." There are three that are going to operate then. There is Ptah. You notice Geb waits down below to take things over. Atum is the one who transmits the seed. But at the creation **these three made the main council: Ptah, Horus, and Djehuty-Thoth**. As you know, he is Hermes, the secretary of the gods, the spirit, the revealer, the one who keeps all the records, the one who has all knowledge. He is the god of knowledge, the god of wisdom, the god of counsel. He is always rendered in the Greek by Hermes, so that's where you get hermetism, the source of all wisdom, etc. So these three. And, of course, Horus is the son; he is always the son. Horus the son and Djehuty, who is represented in the abstract (well, so is Horus for that matter), by the ibis. They came into existence; they were in Ptah, with Ptah. They cooperated with Ptah in all this...

...We are told when Adam was cast out of the garden and was dying, he sent Seth and Eve back to the garden **to get the oil of anointing** to anoint his eyes, ears, nose, etc. so that he would not lose their function —so that he would not die. **They were met on the way by an angel (this is very well established; you will find this in your R. H. Charles** book) who told them they couldn't have it yet. **Until the Son of Man came with redemption, they couldn't have this ordinance**. And so they had to go back without the oil of anointing. But it was to reverse the order of death. But at the funeral the rabbi angrily strikes the ears because they won't hear anymore, the eyes because they won't see anymore. Well, these were the blows of death inflicted by Satan. Cain learned them from Satan. That's a long story, but these things are all related. You'd be surprised how they tie in together. (*Teachings of the Pearl of Great Price:* Lecture 9, Winter Semester, 1986)

Teachings of the Pearl of Great Price: Lecture 11

The pressure is on all the time—the hopeless disproportion, the hopeless imbalance between our capacity and our performance. See, I know I could do a lot better than this.

I know I wouldn't fumble and stumble, mix my words up, and stray off in all directions. I could do better than that. Why don't I? **What we are and what we could be are so different**. John Eccles tells us that we don't use one ten thousandth of our brain power. We have it, but we never use it. Think of the capacity we have for enjoyment. I lie on my bed and fret when I look up and see all the books on the wall there. There's an Arabic book I would just love to read, but I don't have time. I knock my head off trying to learn to read this stuff, and when I get to it I can't use it because I am doing something else. All this stuff with Egyptian on it. I don't have any time for that stuff. Well, it's pretty sad, isn't it, that you can't begin to use it. There must be a reason for this. **The solution must be found in other times and places because the time is too short here**. We can't play a game of baseball in three minutes or in a closet. We don't have time enough in three minutes, and the closet doesn't give us space enough. That's the situation we are in here. We are time bound. We're in a time box. We can't move in any direction without bumping into something, but we don't have time for that. Of course, we don't have space for that either because we can't think of everything at once. **In this life we are condemned to concentrate always on one thing at a time**. The rest, if you see it at all, makes just sort of a background, side issues, etc. You are aware of it, of course, but you concentrate on only one object and you concentrate, as Eccles also says, on the object you choose to. **That makes this life a time of probation. That shows what the desire of your heart is.**

With the possibility of thinking of a billion things, you prefer to think of one particular thing. You have judged yourself then. This is what I wanted among all these things.

So we are trapped in this time box with a limited horizon. We have tunnel vision only. I can just see this; I can't see all those other places at once, and that's just too bad. So we feel cheated, and quiet desperation is our lot...

...Well, there are three major plots, or rather eight major plots or possibilities, that confront us—past, present and future. Three lives to consider: is there a past, present, and future? This gives us eight possibilities of the I Ching. If you read Fritjof Capra's book on the subject, you know something about that. This is what the plots are, then. This is the past (preexistence), this is the present (this life), and then we have the future life. We will say they are either dark or light. I'll use D for dark and L for light. The past (preexistence) is dark; we know nothing about it. It's mysterious and it's lost. Plot number one is the commonest plot actually. There are eight possibilities, and there are philosophies based on each one (important world philosophies and religions). There's a little fun in this life, so it's light. But what comes after is darkness. The story of the conversion of King Oswy, the first English king to accept Christian missionaries, is the story of that. They are having the banquet in the hall. It's light and bright, and they are celebrating. Either end of the great hall is open to let the smoke out.

A swallow comes in and is completely dazzled and frightened by the light. It flies around awhile, makes itself at home, and then flies out again. King Oswy sees it and he says, "Well, that is our life. We come out of this great darkness. We see a little moment of light, and then we fly out again." He says to the Christian missionaries, "If you can give me anything better than that, I'll listen to you." So he does because that is what Christianity promises, something better hereafter, but nothing before.

So this is the standard scenario. It's really an evasion. **We accept this life because we have to. We can't deny it**. But for the rest, we just deny them. That's what most people do. (*Teachings of the Pearl of Great Price:* Lecture 11, Winter Semester, 1986)

Teachings of the Pearl of Great Price: Lecture 12

We have the Zohar. What does that say? "**God creates worlds and destroys worlds, and you too will be able to create worlds and to destroy worlds**." This was a doctrine common to both the Jews and the Mandaeans. We find it in Bin Gorion. So the Zohar is definitely for it. Not only that God creates and destroys worlds (as in the Pearl of Great Price), **but you too can become a creator of worlds if you follow a certain line**. This is an interesting theory. "Other worlds have disappeared," says the Zohar, "because God did not dwell in their midst regularly and constantly or [as the text reads] because God had not come down to them." They must be visited by God, so they just withered and perished in time. There were unworthy worlds that passed away. That's an interesting thing because they do talk about unworthy races and pre-human races that weren't able to make the grade. Of course, we know that civilizations do pass away. Well, why shouldn't it happen with worlds too, if God hadn't visited them or if they rejected him? So the Jews worked on that.

There's a very famous work by the brethren Ahwan of Basra, edited by Dieterici. I have one of the few copies in existence of the text of this, and it's great. Back in the ninth century at Basra, where all the oil bombing is going on now, there was a society of the holy brethren. They were scientifically advanced. They knew all about microbes and molecules and everything else. They had a marvelous encyclopedia, and in it they say, "The business of the angels is to coordinate the operations between the worlds, to keep them all functioning according to the same plan. There are many worlds. They are all coordinated, and they all work together in one big scheme." This is a very bold concept which, of course, we find in the Pearl of Great Price. (*Teachings of the Pearl of Great Price:* Lecture 12, Winter Semester, 1986)

Teachings of the Pearl of Great Price: Lecture 14

'**At a new creation there is a reshuffling of elements**...' Incidentally, that's a quotation, the last one, and that's from Ben Sirach, one of the most old venerable and universally accepted of all writings. It belongs in the Bible. It's in the Odes of Solomon; it's in the Ginza; it's in the Mandaean Johannesbuch; it's in Berlin Manichaean; it's in the Pistis Sophia, the oldest and best of all the Coptic writings. So this is a common teaching here. '**At a new creation there is a reshuffling of elements**' [that's what you would expect], like the rearranging of notes in the musical scale to make a new composition. It has even been suggested, as we have noted, that **old worlds may be dismantled to supply stuff for the making of newer and better ones.**'...

This is how it happens (quoting from "Treasures in the Heavens" by Nibley): 'Beginning with a very old Egyptian idea, recently examined by E. A. E. Reymond, that the creation of the world was really a re-creation by 'transforming substances' that had already been used in the creation of other worlds, the **Jewish and Christian apocryphal writers envisage a process by which the stuff of worlds is alternately organized into new stars and planets, and when these have served their time, scrapped, decontaminated, and re-used in yet more new worlds.**' As we know today, this world wouldn't exist if a star hadn't exploded. It had to explode after it had gone through its life cycle and done all the pretty things it should do. Bam, it was blown to smithereens.

That alone produced the heavy elements that are necessary to make a world like this. **So as one world completes its cycle, the whole thing has to be re-cycled again into a new one, and then goes through the same process again. Newer stuff is constantly re-cycled** is the tohu wabohu (which the Egyptians call the hu) of the Jewish teachers who saw the ultimate forms of matter in fire and ice. It was either complete energy as it is in the photon period when there's nothing but light, nothing but energy. No particles have any weight, no mass whatsoever —nothing but fire or nothing but ice. Nothing moves at the completion of the cycle of entropy when everything dies down to a dead unit, nothing but a pile of ash. So it is either completely cold or it's completely hot.

According to Jewish teachings, these are the two ultimate forms of matter. 'Likewise,' according to the same authority, 'the world holocaust of the Stoics was merely a necessary preparation for the making of new worlds from old materials. The whole thrust of Weiss's book is that until the early Christian Apologists [in the fourth century] we find no trace anywhere of a doctrine of creation out of nothing.' Well, we've seen that before. So this is interesting.

'And so we have in the Pistis Sophia, continuing the Egyptian teachings, the picture of a constant remixing (kerasmos) [it uses the Greek word kerasmos, mixing up all the time] going on in the universe in which old, worn-out, contaminated substance—the refuge [or garbage] of worn-out worlds and kingdoms—is first thrown out on the scrap-heap and returned to chaos as dead matter [what do you do with it then?] **then melted down in a dissolving fire for many years, by which all impurities are removed from it, and by which it is 'improved,' and is ready to be 'poured from one kind of body into another.'** This whole process by which the souls as well as substances are 'thrown back into the mixing' is under the supervision of Melchizedek, **the great reprocessor, purifier, and preparer of worlds**.

He takes over the refuge of a defunct world or souls, and under his supervision the five great Archons [**they are the five principles**; they are always talking about the five principles; this is Egyptian too] process it...each one specializing in particular elements, which they thus recombine in unique and original combinations, **so that no new world or soul is exactly like any other**.'

Well, they get it going by going into something like a spiral nebula. 'In this full blown pleniarism there is no waste and no shortage: If there were any superfluous or any lacking, the whole body would suffer, for the worlds counterpoise one another like elements of a single organism.'

The worlds go on forever: '**They come and come and cease not, they ever increase and are multiplied, yet are not brought to an end nor do they decrease**.'" Well they took that answer to the three questions: Is the universe expanding so slowly that gravity will finally take hold and draw it back together into another singularity? Is it growing so fast that it will go on forever? Or is it balanced in equilibrium so it will get so large and never get any smaller? So this says it is eternal expansion. **The whole process is thrown back into the mixing. 'It is essentially the Plan that all physical things should pass away.' Well, that's the way it goes. The mere mechanics are quite astonishing**.

We go on to a new world now. This is important too. 'The mere mechanics of the creation process described in our 'treasure' texts display truly remarkable scientific insight. For the making of the world the first requirements, we are told, are a segment of empty space [for there is space there, first of all], pure and unencumbered, and a supply of primordial matter [matter unorganized] to work with.' Those are the two things you need according to this doctrine; again, both of them well documented here. (We will go down for there is space there, and we will take of these substances and we will make a world; 'yonder is matter unorganized.')

'Mere empty space and inert matter are, however, forbidding and profitless things in themselves, disturbing and even dangerous for humans to be involved with—contemplating them, the mind is seized with vertigo until some foothold is found in the void [you go crazy]. The order and stability of a foundation are achieved through the operation of a 'Spark.' [The Spark is very important; it is what starts this inert matter into life again.] **'The Spark is sometimes defined as 'a small idea' that comes forth from God and makes all the difference between what lives and what does not...' Remember the thought of his heart in the Shabako text. It was conceived in the mind of God and then on the tongue of God, and that brought it about.** But first 'it is this idea that makes all the difference between what lives and what does not.'

The Vision of Kenaz is very interesting. It was the Prophet Zenos who lived between Moses and Isaiah, and he gave the prophecy about the vineyard. The Book of Jacob in the Book of Mormon tells the story of the vineyard at great length as it was accounted by the old prophet Zenos. Of course, Zenos wasn't discovered until 1906. So the Book of Mormon knows about Zenos too. But Zenos says that. 'Compared with it all the worlds are but as a shadow, since it is the Spark whose light moves all (material) things.' It is the ultimate particle, the 'ennas, which came from the Father of those who are without beginning,' emanating from the Treasure-house of Light from which all life and power is ultimately derived. Thanks to the vivifying, organizing power of the Spark [we'll call it that; we don't know anything better to call it. It's a very good word because of the electrical analogy. What is the spark that jumps the gap; nobody knows—unsatisfied electron, I suppose], we find throughout the cosmos an infinity of dwelling places, topoi, either occupied or awaiting tenants.

These are colonized by migrants from previously established 'toposes' [topos, a place in space] or worlds, all going back ultimately to a single original center. The colonizing process is called 'planting' [they always use plant; you will plant another world; you will take the seeds down and plant; you will plant Adam there], and those spirits which bring their treasures to a new world are called 'Plants,' or more rarely 'seeds,' of their Father or 'Planter' in another world. Every planting goes out from the Treasure-house, either as the essential material elements or as the colonizers themselves who come from a sort of mustering area called the 'Treasure-house of Souls.'' Always there's that in-between place which the early Christians called the refrigarium or the anapausus, the place where you stop and rest between worlds, a sort of pressure chamber to accustomize yourself. When you came into this world, there was the birth shock; and when you go out, you'll be left in a pleasant garden (a greenhouse) to rest and collect your senses and get ready for the next step—get over the shock. Back in the old times with the ritual dramas, you had the greenhouse for that purpose. You pass from one act, one phase, to another. The actor goes to the greenhouse where you rest, refresh yourself, and get ready for the next strenuous act that is to follow. These things run throughout everything. 'With its 'planting' completed, a new world is in business, a new Treasury has been established from which new Sparks may go forth in all directions to start the process anew in ever new spaces; God wants every man to 'plant a planting'...

This is a very interesting quotation, incidentally. It's from that second Gnostic work I mentioned before and Reymond and the Gospel of Philip (that's a good one, you know). He says, '**God wants every man to 'plant a planting.' Nay, he has promised that those who keep his Law may also become creators of worlds**.' Now that's a flat statement from the earliest gospel we know, even earlier than the Gospel of Philip , after the New Testament.

That's the Gospel of Thomas. That's the Gospel of Philip. **If you keep his law, you may also become creators of worlds. He wants you to be. 'But keeping the Law requires following the divine pattern at every point; in taking the Treasure to a new world**, the Sent One (who follows hard on the heels of the colonists) [He goes to teach them. The teacher is sent to teach Adam after he is in the world.] seeks nothing so much as complete identity with the one who sent him; hence, from first to last one mind alone dominates the whole boundless complex.' ('Call upon God in the name of the Son forever more.') But you call upon God, and God only, in the name of the Son.

'Because each planting is completely dependent on its Treasure-house or home base, the system never breaks up into independent systems; in this patriarchal order all remains forever identified with the Father from whom all ultimately come forth.'" (*Teachings of the Pearl of Great Price:* Lecture 14, Winter Semester, 1986. See also *Nibley on the Timely and the Timeless,* pp. 49–62.)

Teachings of the Pearl of Great Price: Lecture 16

This is from the Joseph Smith papyrus: "That he might enter the horizon along with his father Re (the sun)." "If the essence of cult and festival is transition, **the rite of passage, succession of lives**...[that's quoting a famous work by Mowinckel]." See, the rite de passage, **you pass from one state of existence to another**." **That's what we are interested in more than anything else—transition, the rite of passage, and succession of lives**. "**Now the great exponent of such meaningful motion is the sun which rises and sets everyday**." We quoted Catullus on that. "The sun sets and rises everyday, and it keeps up, and that's an example. But we, unfortunately, can't follow it," he says. The disc is directly observable under normal conditions only on the horizon. That's when you can see it clearly. The Book of the Dead says, "Thou passest over the sky. Every faith watches thee in thy course. Thou thyself are hidden from their gates..." except when you show yourself at dawn and at eventide. Then they can look at your disc, and they can see it. It turns red, and you can view the sun. Otherwise, you'd better look through smoked glasses.

This is from Erik Hornung, an Egyptologist and very good authority on this business: "The gate of heaven or the underworld between the earthly and the other-worldly spirits was from the earliest times localized in the aakhut." That is the seam or juncture, the Nahtstelle, **the interface between the other world and this world**. *(Teachings of the Pearl of Great Price:* Lecture 16, Winter Semester, 1986)

Teachings of the Pearl of Great Price: Lecture 17

Then the Lord says to Moses, "And behold, thou art my son…" After the aretology, He says, this is where you come in: you are my son. In the Gospel of Philip it says an astonishing thing. It says, do you want to know what God is? A horse begets a horse, a dog begets a dog, a bull begets a bull. **What does a god beget, if a god has a son? What can it possibly be except a god?** This is the problem here. If you are the son of such a being, there is a lot of explaining to do here. And, therefore, you're qualified and I'm going to show you a few things. "…look and I will show thee the workmanship of mine hands; but not all, for my works are without end, [There is your En Sof again. His works are without end. His presence is without end. His knowledge is without end. Everything about him is without end.] and also my words. [Remember that the works and the words always go together. The words are to communicate and the works are what's done, but it doesn't happen in a vacuum.] for they never cease [they go on and on—spaceless, timeless]. Wherefore no man can behold all my works, except he behold all my glory…" So **his works are his glory** to behold. Remember that he says, "This is my work and my glory." My work is my glory. That is what it is: to share this with others to bring about the immortality of man. "Wherefore no man can behold all my works, except he behold all my glory; and no man can behold all my glory, and afterwards remain in the flesh on the earth."

Then: Why am I telling you this? Because I have work for you to do. I am going to give you an assignment. **The Prophet Joseph says every one of us received an assignment before we came here. You'd better find out what it is and do it.** "And I have a work for thee, Moses, my son; and thou art in the similitude of mine Only Begotten; [Now, not only is he His son, but in the similitude and the likeness as the Son in the similitude of the Father. He is in the likeness of the Only Begotten.] and mine Only Begotten is and shall be the Savior, for he is full of grace and truth. [That is very interesting because He refers to the Book of Ether 3:8–9 . We won't go into that.] but there is no God beside me…" (verse 6). It tells us later on in the Book of Moses that he is commanded to "call upon God in the name of the Son forevermore." He says to call upon God and God only, but always in the name of the Son. He is full of grace and truth, and of course, those are the qualities.

How do you define grace? That's charis; that's everything good. **Charis is your attitude toward others, toward everything else. It is an attitude of complete love.** It is related to our word cheer and the Latin, gratia which means "thanks, grace," etc. We just described Mephistopheles as all negative, all willing to destroy. This is the absolute opposite of that. There is no shadow of that in it at all. Full of grace and truth—nothing false, nothing deceiving, nothing phony. Whereas Satan, on the other hand, is the one who loves and makes a lie. He was a liar in the beginning. He is the deceiver as well as Apollyon, "the Destroyer." He works by trickery and by lies. He is called "the father of lies." And this is the opposite. The Lord is full of grace and truth. So to what point do we repent in this life, or any other life? **Repent until you are full of grace and truth.** So I think we all need some repentance. Don't call upon anyone else to repent until you have repented. That will be when you are full of grace and truth. That's a long ways off for some people. We can't even conceive of what that would be like, but that is the object. That's what we are after. (*Teachings of the Pearl of Great Price:* Lecture 17, Winter Semester, 1986)

Teachings of the Pearl of Great Price: Lecture 18

"And the first man of all men have I called Adam, which is many [that is the meaning of the Egyptian word Adam]." Rudolf Anthes has proven that. Adam means all that's gone before and all that comes after. Like Eve, which means everybody, "because she is the mother of all living."

"…For behold, there are many worlds that have passed away by the word of my power. And there are many that now stand, and innumerable are they unto men, but all things are numbered unto me, for they are mine and I know them." Then Moses says, All right, I see it now. Tell me just about this world, and I will be content. What the Lord tells him in verse 31 following is that there is more to it than you can ever know. Take care of your sector of the front and leave the rest alone. That's all you can handle. It's assigned to you because you can handle it, and at present it is all you can handle. That's all for anybody. **You have a particular assignment. You fill it to the full and then it will expand**, but don't ask for more. Don't ask to command the whole front. You may not know what is going on in your sector; nobody else may know either, but it is very important not to take things in hand and start giving orders. We have no business doing that.

And so he says, "…O God, and tell me concerning this earth, and the inhabitants thereof, and also the heavens, and then thy servant will be content." He is willing to settle for just this earth (modest man), so he accepts.

Notice that then the Lord goes on and repeats again that this world has to be understood in its setting, in its proper perspective, in its larger picture along with the other worlds. We have seen that again and again. We start out by putting the earth itself in its perspective, which requires a much larger picture actually. It does require an awareness of Moses's own limited scope. He has to be made aware of that by being shown the big picture and also the nature of the earth and the creation. He has to be given an idea of the plan, that he is not the only one. So he settles for that. Starting with verse 40 is the end part. This is a very important part of Moses's assignment to keep the record. We owe more records to Moses than anyone else. It's recognized quite widely now that the "little Genesis" was really originally a book of Abraham.

Moses has just re-edited the story of the creation we find in Moses in the Old Testament. It is a re-edition from an older book of Abraham. It's interesting. He hands it on, and he puts it all together. There are going to be other editions. The classic study of how these things are handed down and re-edited and commentated as they go (as all documents are) is the Book of Mormon. We have this build-up of many records with comments by the builders. So he tells here, this is it. "...I will speak unto thee concerning this earth upon which thou standest;..." That's the formula he uses so often with Abraham too. This is the earth that concerns you. Does that make you clear now? And you write the things I speak. These things are to be recorded because I can't talk to everybody. I'm not going to. They can't qualify; they can't abide my glory.

You are to be the recorder (and he is). And this is the reason: "And in a day when the children of men shall esteem my words as naught and take many of them from the book which thou shalt write [and this is what has happened because they are coming back now; we are finding all sorts of things], behold, I will raise up another like unto thee; and they shall be had again among the children of men—among as many as shall believe." But these are to be kept secret it tells us in the last verse. The record is not to be given to everybody. It wouldn't be appreciated, and it is a special blessing. But Moses was to hand it down, and this is the way apocrypha and apocalyptic are handed down. This is the real meaning of apocrypha: a thing that has been "kept under wraps." Apocalyptic is another form of the same word. It is only revealed to those who are ready to receive it. Of course, it is the same in any subject really. You are not going to profit by going into some class that's ten years ahead of what you should be doing. You won't know what they are talking about. You have to take things as they go. It's the same thing with the scriptures. **They are revealed to the children of men when they are ready to receive them and they are ready to believe them**. Notice this last verse, 42, they have actually put in parentheses to show that it is in red ink. Parentheses are our red ink, aren't they, our rubrics? "These words were spoken unto Moses in the mount..." You don't know which mount so don't argue about that. It's a good thing not to know. Probably way up north there. Now they are spoken unto you. **This is to the Prophet Joseph. He is another like unto him who is raised up**. But there were others after who did the same thing. The prophets had such revelations. "...Show them not unto any except them that believe. Even so. Amen."

Now we come to the second chapter, which we skip. This is repeated in Abraham, and it is in Genesis and it's in the temple too. It's the creation story. We have discussed it in this thing called "**Before Adam**." There are copies of this on reserve. You can look it up over there and see another approach to the creation thing. Though there are some questions that have been asked by people here that we should come into. They come in chapter two, where we are dealing with the creation of man, with primitive man, etc. I have underlined in red in my book here all the passages that are not found in the Bible. This is a very substantial addition to the Biblical account. This says, in Moses 3:4, "And now, behold, I say unto you that these are the generations of the heaven and of the earth when they were created..." That's very interesting. In the Bible it says "of the heavens," and here it says, "of heaven and earth" because every earth has its heaven. "...when they were created, in the day that I, the Lord God, made the heaven and the earth..." So notice this: the generations of the heavens and earth in the day when he made it.

Now the fifth chapter of Genesis starts out saying, "This is the book of the generations of Adam. In the day that God created man..." **That's at a different level. That's another creation**. That's another story; we get to that later. It doesn't say created him. It says called apart, blessed him, and gave him a name. We get to that next time. But these are the generations of heaven. **Notice, generation (an organic process) generates and begets. We are dealing with stages and episodes**. We have mentioned this before. One generation leads to the next. The whole thing comes in distinct and discreet acts. You don't get it all, as the Lord told Moses. Notice, the generations of heaven and earth. The generation, that is the organic process, **the stages or episodes**, the generations by which it comes. This whole scene, this whole chapter, is the most baffling thing about the creation story. **It distinctly tells us about two creations**. Genesis does too. "It had not yet rained upon the earth [a spiritual creation]." What are we going to do about that? Well, here we see again (and this shouldn't bother us at all) that the whole thing is on a different level from the generations of Adam which begin in chapter five. **So it's not the idea of just one act, one creation, everything all at once. It doesn't happen in one flash, instantaneously and simultaneously, not at all. It is spread out all over the place**...

...What light does the Pearl of Great Price throw on primitive man? Here we have a recent article (*National Geographic*, November 1985) with this hologram picture of the skull of this little "Taung child" they call it. It's supposed to be two million years old. It has some nice diagrams, and here's one that unfolds and shows the development of skeletons and the like, supposedly. They put the skeletons together in this order. **This is talked about in this "Before Adam" thing**.

I brought it up pretty well to date. But it says, "stepping on the road to humanity." Now, the whole question that comes up is namely **when does he step across the line that makes him a man? Only when he steps across that line can he be called an Adam or human**. This was the subject of the big conference in 1979 at Nairobi when all the paleontologists in the world got together and thought about the question, when can you say it's a man and when can you say it isn't? There are dozens of different specimens running around now that look like humans, but we know they aren't. **When is he starting to be a man?** I think there is a comment here about the Nairobi conference. "Last September, 150 of the world's leading paleontologists met at the Eighth Pan African Congress of Prehistory and Quaternary Studies in Nairobi. The main issue discussed was what is the definition of homo. Or if you are speaking in Hebrew, what is the definition of Adam?" Ha-Adam is the regular Hebrew word today for man. It's the only one used (Adam and enosh). What is the definition of homo? How do you know a true man when you see him? Well, he looks like a man. Again, there are creatures in the zoo that look like men. Then quoting one of them, "In recent years the old concept of a single steadily evolving lineage from ape to man has been completely replaced by at least three [possibly more] different forms of early man evolving simultaneously in Africa. Which one is the true man?"

...**Now, how many Adams are there? You can think of them. I've got ten here**. There was a Council in Heaven; but before the council, Adam was on hand because he was summoned to the council. Jehovah, Michael; their attention is called and a program is suggested to them by Elohim. **Elohim, of course, is the Council of the Gods, as we learn in the Book of Abraham. That's what the word Elohim means; it's plural. You can't get away from it**. That's the way it is referred to throughout the Book of Abraham. Before the council there was Adam there.

We don't know how long he has been there, a very long time you can be sure, but they are not measuring time our way. The second Adam is when he joins the council and we've seen a lot about that. The Council in Heaven is when they plan the earth, its plan, its purpose, etc. And Michael (he is not Adam yet) is very active in that. Then he goes down as a building inspector. He visits the earth from time to time to see how it is going. He is on the building committee. He and Jehovah go down and visit the earth from time to time then come back and report. According to some of the early Church fathers, this is where he gets his name Adam, from Adamantinos. Adamantine means "diamond." The word diamond comes from Adamantinos. Damao is "to break, to crush, to destroy." Adamanto means it cannot be destroyed. That negates it.

Adam means "to be indestructible." It's the same as our word dam, to stamp down. The word is damno in Greek. It means to injure in any way or to hold down. That can't be done to Adam in his original state. They say when he visited the earth during its construction, it was not a safe place to be. You had to be Adamantinos or you'd never get away from it. There were tremendous temperatures, whirling dust storms, and all the rest. It was in formation. So there's the Adamantinos, the indestructible building inspector.

Then he comes down and changes his name, personality, and everything else—wipes out everything and becomes as a little child. He receives a new name and is now Adam. He is now man; he is now on this earth. Of course, Adam means "red earth," and it means all those other things. We have a lot of names for Adam. We may mention them later on. This is one of the most important periods of all. This is the one that accounts for that time when he was a primitive and all that. We go on here for now.

Then he wakes again. He wakes from a sleep and is blanked out like a little child, and then he goes to sleep again. He wakes up and marries Eve under the covenant. That's number five. That's before they enter the Garden of Eden. In the next phase he enters the Garden of Eden and is an immortal being. He's in paradise now. He's a food gatherer, but he hasn't fallen. He's a spiritual being and would live forever. "Of every tree of the garden thou mayest freely eat."

We cannot conceive of what it was like there in Eden except that it was infinitely delightful. He could have gone on forever without it being boring. But he does leave Eden and ends up in a totally different world. He's outcast, just like Moses in the beginning here. He's flat. There are very dramatic early Christian and Jewish accounts about how Adam, after he was cast out of the garden, found himself desperate. He didn't think the sun would ever rise again. He'd sinned; he was cast out. He was in a dark and dreary world. He despaired of ever being forgiven or of ever living. We are told when he was cast out of Eden, his life became shorter and he became smaller in stature.

So he's another one, but he doesn't stay that way. Because he has been following the rules, an angel comes to visit him. **Not an angel, but angels (we are told three men in the literature) come and start instructing him**. He hears the voice of the Lord, but the angels visit him and bring books and instructions and tell him what he is to do to get back into the presence of God. He now enters the covenant and becomes one of the fold. He becomes one who is receiving instructions and is on the way back to salvation, a very different state from what he was before he received that. In receiving the covenants and receiving the signs and tokens from the angels, he receives a new name too. This is an important thing. (That's eight.)

Then he dies, of course. According to all accounts, like the very famous "Harrowing of Hell," the earliest Christian account we have of what happens after, he goes down and preaches to the spirits in prison, his children whom he is going to deliver. That doesn't just go back to the "Harrowing of Hell" in the fifth century, which became the standard mystery drama of the Middles Ages. It was dramatized on a stage in front of the cathedral at Easter time when the Lord goes down and delivers the children of Adam who are being held below. But it is Adam who leads out the parade of his children.

As we mentioned before, way back in the Apocalypse of Abraham there's the same thing. When Abraham reaches the other side, the first thing he does is look up Michael. He has a great feeling for the human race. He wants to save all of them. He doesn't want these people to be lost. He says, "I don't want any of them to be lost. I can't bear thinking about it." So he and Michael get together and go to Elohim and petition him for permission to establish a system of work or ordinances by which all these fallen people may be redeemed. That's very old. It goes back to the first or second century at least.

But then the most interesting is these verses 19 and 20. People ask about primitive man, etc. Remember it's timeless. We are told in Abraham 5:13 here, "...Now I, Abraham, saw that it was after the Lord's time, which was after the time of Kolob, for as yet [he's talking about the time that they were cast out of the garden] the Gods had not appointed unto Adam his reckoning." It was not reckoning time, so you are wasting time talking about years and periods here. But this is a very important state of things.

This gives us a little vignette on another type of world. "And out of the ground I, the Lord God, formed every beast of the field, and every fowl of the air..." And Adam was formed out of the ground too. He is the same substance that they are. The Lord has commanded that they should come to Adam to see what he would call them. During this period Adam lives on a genial level with the animals. He gets along famously with them. And **they are also living souls**. They don't speak his language, but they are in his community. On the pragmatic level you can exchange signals with animals very well. "...for I God breathed into them the breath of life and commanded that whatsoever Adam called every living creature, that should be the name thereof" (Moses 3:19). Notice, this is a **program of awareness**, of getting acquainted.

Adam gets acquainted with all the other creatures in the world because it is a multiple-use world we are living on. They have a right to it as much as anybody else, as we read in the Doctrine and Covenants. So he gives names. Levi-Strauss's great work shows that the naming and classifying of animals reaches a point of sophistication among the so-called primitives far excelling that which any anthropologist or even biologist ever dreamed up. They really know the animals they are talking about, and they know how to classify them. You must read Claude Levi-Strauss's great work on that.

But as for Adam, there was not found a helpmeet for him. Well, what is he doing alone? He has no helpmeet. **The word "helpmeet" is a very important one. It's spelled various ways. It's the same as "meet," "mate," "match." It means "equal." When you have a game, you don't have a match unless the two sides are equal**. The person who is on the team with you is a mate. When you come together, you have a meet. All these words are together. You and your mates come together for a meet, for a match. But it is always with equals. It's always working together and cooperating. It's very interesting. It's still kept here in its old English form as "helpmeet," which is quite right.

But what is he doing all this time then? Remember, he is a little child. **According to the Hebrew tradition, which is very early and very**

widely testified, he had a wife at this time, and she was Lilith. She represents promiscuity. She didn't like Adam. She did everything she could to keep him from entering into the covenant and marrying in the covenant. **Eve wasn't around then**. Her name means "night," Layla. Way back in the Alphabet of Rabbi Aqiba, a very early writing, we are told about her. She was his mate, but she stands for everything that is promiscuous. She doesn't want to get married, but she wants to play around; that's Lilith. **Adam was living in an animal state of innocence.**

He had become as a little child. I guess he would be a pushover for Lilith. But she is a sinister character because she is irresponsible. She is married to him and she has children, but she doesn't want to be responsible for them, or anything like that. She is regarded as the woman who tries to do everything she can to prevent marriage, to prevent childbirth, and to kill babies in their cribs.

That's Lilith.

There are all sorts of early charms from Babylon and elsewhere against Lilith to keep her from her shenanigans. She's a rather important figure. She represents the sort of sexual license we have in the world today—the anything goes, just have fun. But don't feel under any obligations, and whatever you do, don't enter into any covenants because that will bind you. She does everything she can to frustrate marriage and to keep Adam from it. There are all sorts of stories told about her and her sons. She represents the old matriarchy too. But there is this gap because he hasn't been married yet.

And then there is another deep sleep. He woke from a deep sleep in the first place when **he woke up being Adam after being Michael. And now he goes into another deep sleep. Then he wakes up and finds Eve there**. Now it's time to be properly married. This life ends with another sleep. Notice, it says a deep sleep, a passage. He marries Eve in the covenant, verse 22 following. They are very close, as close as you can get here. The rib in Arabic is the urka or silka. It is the expression for anything as close to you as a thing can possibly be.

What can get closer to your side than your rib? Your rib is your side. You might be able to get along without it, but the rib is about as close to a person as you can get. It is a usage. The metaphor is used in language: As close as my rib and as intimate. It means "bone of my bone and flesh of my flesh," as intimate as you can be. (*Teachings of the Pearl of Great Price:* Lecture 18, Winter Semester, 1986)

Teachings of the Pearl of Great Price: Lecture 19

This puts us into the picture. Everybody gets into the act. That is God's desire. We didn't emphasize enough those two verses, 38 and 39, at the end of First Moses, where he says, "...there is no end to my works, neither to my words...For behold, this is my work and my glory —to bring to pass the immortality and eternal life of man." **It is to**

APPENDIX H—EXCERPTS FROM HUGH NIBLEY

spread it around, to share the glory. Glory is shared intelligence, and it's to be shared here. Here's the way we get in on it. Repent and call upon God in the name of the Son forevermore. Now, you see, we are going to get the Father, Son, and Holy Ghost. We are told if he yields to temptation, they will send a sacrifice for him. This is provided. This is explained here. "And in that day the Holy Ghost fell upon Adam, which beareth record of the Father and the Son, saying: I am the Only Begotten [**You notice the Holy Ghost says, "I am the Only Begotten**." Well, he is bearing record; that's his business to bear record of the Father and the Son from the beginning.] "...henceforth and forever, that as thou hast fallen **thou mayest be redeemed, and all mankind** [but not automatically], **even as many as will**." (Not if you don't want to; not if it's against your will.) In Moses 4:4 it says, "And he became Satan, yea even the devil, the father of all lies, to deceive and to blind men, and to lead them captive at his will, even as many as would not hearken unto my voice." If you want to follow someone else, that's your prerogative. We have the law of free agency here. That's what we are being tested for, after all.

"...henceforth and forever, that as thou hast fallen thou mayest be redeemed, and all mankind, even as many as will." He has fallen but can be redeemed. Of course, this is the good news. This is the gospel. We have Adam fallen here as Moses was in the first chapter (down, hopeless, out). But the good news is that it doesn't have to end here. **You can go back again.** "And **return again** to our presence and with us partake of eternal life and exaltation." We call this the gospel, evangelion, the good news. Notice how they rejoice at the good news which they receive. "And in that day Adam blessed God and was filled, and began to prophesy concerning all the families of the earth..." How can you bless God? Does he need blessing? Does he ask you for a blessing?

A blessing can go in both ways. A blessing is full approval and full acceptance of another. Well, lots of people don't accept God. They don't approve of God all the way, or they would accept him. Bless has a double etymology. One says it's from the Old English word, blotsian, connected with our word blood. To make a blood sacrifice; to bless in that sense. But bless is also connected with the word bliss, a complete approval. (There's the eschatology of bliss and the eschatology of woe.) It's a complete approval, a complete acceptance when you bless God. So people can bless each other. You can bless your father or your mother as well as they can bless you. So he blessed God "and was filled, and began to prophesy concerning all the families of the earth [these are the fathers], saying: Blessed be the name of God, for because of my transgression my eyes are opened..."

What were his eyes opened to? All sorts of things. They have eaten the fruit already and their eyes were opened. They became what the Old Testament calls piqeakh. **A piqeakh is a person whose eyes are open, and he sees things that other people don't see.** Laman and Lemuel accused their father of being a visionary man. That's the way it is nearly always rendered in the Bible. A visionary man is a piqeakh. Like the attendants of Elisha who see the horses there when other people can't see them, **you see things that really are there but others can't see them**. There is such a condition. But this is not what he refers to. When they ate the fruit, they became piqeakh. Their eyes were opened; they saw themselves in a different world. They saw things they had never seen before. They were in a totally different ambience. Here because of his transgression, his eyes are open to his vulnerability. His eyes are open to his condition now. He knew he was in a bad condition, but his eyes were opened to the real situation. There is a whole series of eye openings here. Moses said, "...Now for this cause I know that man is nothing which thing I never had supposed." He had come down to this earth.

His eyes were opened, and he realized how low he could get. That had never occurred to him. His eyes were opened again. Then it says, "He lifted up his eyes, and again he saw God on his throne." So we see different things that are there or that aren't. "...Because of my transgression my eyes are opened..." Just ten years ago they said it was absolutely impossible to create such a thing as a hologram. I showed you that thing in the front of the *National Geographic* last time. That was a hologram. You could see right around this skull very nicely. That's impossible on a two dimensional surface. You can't do that. But you can do it. **When you go into some new phase, your eyes are opened. So be ready for all sorts of surprises**.

...Perdition means lost. It means losing something that you had. It means **one fallen from high estate**. You can't be Perdition; you can't be lost unless you were found. **And you can't be fallen unless you were high, fallen from high estate**. Perditio means that which is lost. "Nine days [as Milton says] he fell in hideous ruin and combustion down, down, down." **You have to be high. He was among the highest in heaven up there, and down he fell**. That means perdition, the one who is lost and fallen and gone (too bad)...for thou wast also before the world." This refers back to the time in the Council in Heaven, in glory. Satan is not going to say, you brought me into this world and put me in this terrible jam, and I had nothing to say about it. Oh no, you were in the preexistence too.

You were high up there because you are perdition now. "...for thou wast also before the world." You had your preexistence and your chance, and all the rest of it. He has his anamnesis too, as Plato would have said. "And it shall be said in time to come—[and this is the theme that all these evils that come into the world really go back to Cain and follow in a single tradition], That these abominations were had from Cain; for he rejected the greater counsel which was had from God [this is what happened: the two plans were put forward, and he rejected God's counsel or plan]; and this is a cursing, which I will put upon thee, except thou repent."

It's still not too late. This is the gospel of repentance. As long as you are in this earth, you can still repent. As long as we are in this earth, there is no one who doesn't need to repent. As long as you are here, it's not too late to repent. The door is open to everyone here. We mustn't judge people and divide them into the good guys and the bad guys. As Ezekiel says in chapter eighteen, it's never too late. **However wicked the bad guys have been all their days, they can still repent and become the righteous. And however righteous the good guys have been all their days, they can still fall and become the wicked.** The door is open right to the end. Never, never claim that you are saved. No one is saved here (beyond sinning). And again, no one is damned. You are not damned on this earth. You are damned in the judgment in the hereafter. And you are not saved on this earth. **You are in between and you are being tested.** Therefore, this life became, as Nephi says, **a time of probation**. (*Teachings of the Pearl of Great Price:* Lecture 19, Winter Semester, 1986)

Teachings of the Pearl of Great Price: Lecture 21

And Mahijah said, "Baraq'el, my father, was with me." That Baraq'el is interesting too because Baraq'el is supposed to have been the father of Enoch. That's the name Enoch goes by in the Doctrine and Covenants. **Joseph Smith is called Enoch or Baraq'el**. A professor in Hebrew at the University of Utah said, "Well, Joseph Smith didn't understand the word barak meaning 'to bless.'" But Baraq'el means the "lightning of God." That was one of the names that Enoch bore. The Doctrine and Covenants is right on target in that, and this confirms it, that he is called Baraq'el here. (*Teachings of the Pearl of Great Price*: Lecture 21, Winter Semester, 1986)

Teachings of the Pearl of Great Price: Lecture 22

The classic theme that comes in here (it usually comes a little later) is **the Watchers**.

They had this crash program that begins here when Satan had great dominion and the gospel began to be preached. Holy angels were sent forth from the presence of God, and by his own voice and the gift of the Holy Ghost and his prophets. In this crash program they sent down angels to preach and put the people right. Now this is a tradition that you will find spread everywhere, including in non-Jewish sources, at a very early time. These were the Watchers, the agregoroi. They came down to observe and then went back to report as to how things were going. They came down to instruct the human race and put them back on the plan of the gospel again, but many of them (200 of them according to tradition) fell away, were tempted by the daughters of men, joined with them, and sinned terribly (these were the terrible Watchers). They knew too much, and that made them very dangerous. The Watchers are responsible for a lot of trouble here. You are going to run into them all the time.

We are told that they came down on the top of Mt. Hermon, the highest mountain in Palestine, which means the "mountain of the oath." Two hundred of them came down there and took their oaths and covenants.

They gave away the rites of the temple, and they perverted them. The whole thing is a rite of perversion. They had all the same things, but they perverted them and claimed that they were being holy, that they had the priesthood, that they had the covenants. This was their great crime, of course, that they perverted the real thing. Fortunately, we are told they didn't have enough knowledge. Their knowledge was limited, so they weren't able to destroy everything. "They knew not the mind of God," as we are told in this book. So their system was not the system God gave Adam...

...Then this passage in verse 59: "...**thou hast made me, and given unto me a right to thy throne**..." This is the one that really knocked Professor Black over. He said, "This is it." This is the one thing he thought he had discovered—**that God gave Enoch a right to His throne**. Here it is. When he saw this here, it really staggered him. **Enoch is promised the throne (this is a very important thing). Enoch is called Metatron. That's commonly interpreted today as meaning "the one with the throne.**" (*Teachings of the Pearl of Great Price:* Lecture 22, Winter Semester, 1986)

The Message of the Joseph Smith Papyri: An Egyptian Endowment

The following quotes from *The Message of the Joseph Smith Papyri: An Egyptian Endowment* seem to refer to the concept of eternal lives which Nibley espoused throughout his incisive and dynamic career, especially when Nibley's numerous other related statements are taken into consideration (see Chapter 9 in this volume for a collection of Nibley's associated writings). Furthermore, Nibley appears to have used this forum to disseminate his remarkable insights regarding the higher mysteries, cleverly disguised and seemingly obfuscated in the garment of Egyptian theology and cited liberally with discerning intellectual erudition and riveting sophistication.

"Every system, no matter how dynamic, must have certain unchanging constants to give it structure: with Einstein, it was the speed of light; with the Egyptians, it was the unchanging identity of the individual. Life was an **endless series of exciting episodes** through which the individual passes undergoing many changes to match every changing environment; but he never loses his identity. **It is our modern dynamic faith that binds the individual to a single stereotype and gives him only one life, chopped off at both ends as neatly as a piece of dough** in an ITT bakery. In the more exalted realms of higher thought, however, modern thinking moves steadily closer to the Egyptians." (in the Explanation, p. xiii)

"...renewal of life..." (p. 8)

"...that he may live again..." (p. 73)

"...designed to initiate the dead into a new and eternal life..." (p. 78)

"By being reborn, 'the dead wins a new life'..." (p. 78)

"...rebirth which in a way repeats the creation itself..." (p. 78)

"...rebirth and rejuvenation..." (p. 79)

"...as though he were creating us afresh...resurrection is a rebirth and so the dead is treated as a newborn babe..." (p. 79)

"...by which he received new life...regarded as his new birth..." (p. 79)

"One of the peculiar traits of Egyptian culture and belief is, surprisingly enough, an obsession with the idea of eternal progression..." (p. 80)

"...a relationship of father to son in a succession to kingships." (p. 80)

"The Ba of an exalted father may be with his living son on earth..." (p. 82. Ba is translated from the Egyptian as "soul." Jan Assmann, *The Search for God in Ancient Egypt*, p. 42)

"To be reborn in resurrection, the King must enter again into his mother's womb..." (p. 84, 241)

" 'I no longer know my first mother whom I knew before'...Thus he wins a new life..." (p. 84)

"...put off their former nature and put on a new one, becoming renewed and reborn..." (p. 85)

"...as the body is moved from one degree of its progress to another, represent[s] the passages both of conception and of birth, by which the dead is both begotten for his rebirth and delivered into his new life..." (p. 85)

"If hiding mysteries from others makes one a cabalistic esoteric, then the Egyptians were just that, as were the Jewish sectaries, and the early Christians." (p. 86)

"When he lives again, having been proven effective countless... times." (p. 88, 89)

"To enjoy the blessings of Osiris—eternal life—one must do the works and suffer the vicissitudes of Osiris...one becomes an Osiris only 'by literally undergoing all of the experiences of Osiris'...man becomes the peer of the gods. Again and again he identifies himself with the victors over death, more especially with Re and Osiris...The Mystery of eternal life is identical for men and gods in every respect..." (p. 92)

"...the living as well as the dead become *nefer*—'renewed'—through the ordinances of *wa'b*—'immersion in the waters of the abyss'..." (p. 94)

"...being reborn with a new and mysterious body..." (p. 94)

"...the baptism by which the Egyptian becomes regenerated like a god...is simply the image of the real baptism, which can only be acquired by death..." (p. 95)

"...mysteriously reborn..." (p. 98)

"...renewal and rebirth..." (p. 99)

"Osiris is resurrected as the newborn Horus...who rejuvenated himself..." (p. 105)

"I am the Lord of life, renewing life eternally!" (p. 107)

"I am the Ba of Shu...who leaves heaven when I please and go down to earth when I please..." (p. 126)

"Atum, father of the gods..." (p. 131)

"...the Chief primal god and creator was Atum..." (p. 131)

"Egyptian gods can be readily combined in a father-son relationship..." (p. 132)

"Atum is unique as one who is a creator yet human, equally at home in heaven and on earth..." (p. 132)

"Atum is the greatest of gods: 'I am Atum who created the great ones...'" (p. 133)

"...the 'Atum theology' give[s] him priority as creator: 'I am the living one, the master of years, who lives for eternity, Lord of eternity; whom Atum created in his splendor when he was one and became three...'" (p. 133)

"It is hard in some of these associations to avoid hearing the name of Adam for that of Atum...Atum resembles Adam in his attributes...'Why not identify him with the biblical Adam?'...The name Atum signified... both the Creator and 'the collective sum of all future beings'...Atum means 'All-embracing,' 'the sum of everything...or the uniting of many in one, of combining all preexistent beings in a single archtype who thereby represents all beings hereafter'...This suits with Joseph Smith's definition of Adam in the Pearl of Great Price: 'And the first man of all men have I called Adam, which is many...'" (p. 133)

"deities who occupy themselves with his new physical body more than with the body he had before." (p. 142)

"Thou sleepiest that thou mayest awake; thou diest that thou mayest live...one awakes into a new life and a new world...In coming down to earth, the subject changes his name and his identity." (p. 146)

"...he had seen the Father in his sleep...I have seen my Father in every form...I have seen my Father in all his forms...I have seen my Father in all his 'transformations' he is ready to be reborn at a higher level..." (p. 147)

"...leading to a repetition of his own rebirth..." (p. 148)

"...we return to be born again..." (p. 173)

"...to be born in a new form..." (p. 180)

"...they shall be changed into every form they desire..." (p. 184)

"...passing from one existence to another..." (p. 185)

"...it is in the capacity of 'the Son' that he is absorbed into the Father..." (p. 192, 202, 204)

"The Gate of Psalm 24:2 refers to the supernatural grades (lit. steps) by and through which alone a knowledge of the Almighty is possible to man." (p. 211–212)

"14 steps or degrees" [Ed. note: From a caption for an Egyptian drawing of 14 steps. This is reminiscent of Orson F. Whitney's line "fourteen steps upon life's stair" from Canto V of Whitney's epic poem Elias, in Appendix A.] (p. 212)

"...the candidate may assume any roll or name necessary, 'feeling himself in each part'...what renders such substitution possible and plausible is the profound identity of Father and Son: 'The apparently illogical aspect of the metamorphosis is explained by the divine renewal in the Son (Horus). 'That is the great Mystery'..." (p. 216)

"...the completion of a life cycle..." (p. 234)

"...who dies and is reborn periodically..." (p. 237)

"...the skin or garment of rebirth...the skin garment of royal rebirth and rejuvenation..." (p. 239–240)

"...his token of rebirth..." (p. 247)

"...there could be no cheating or cutting of corners; to prepare for eternity, one must be willing to go all the way." (p. 255)

"...guarantees that his progress shall be eternal, ad incrementum ad aeternum..." (p. 268)

"There is a time to die and a time to be born..." (p. 281)

An Approach to the Book of Abraham

...since death itself passes as 'repetition of life' and the dead participate actively... (*An Approach to the Book of Abraham,* CWHN Vol. 18, edited by John Gee, Deseret Book Company and Foundation for Ancient Research and Mormon Studies, 2009, p. 180)

It says here that the death chamber is also the birth chamber, or rather "the place where Osiris is begotten...**where he dies to be reborn**." Here "**death is conceived as the beginning of a new life.**" In other words, the man on the couch is both dead king Osiris, and the living king Horus...**Some say it is his own soul returning to him, and it can be that also**. (p. 185)

But that isn't the whole story—let us read on: "But **he only dies in order to be reborn**; he falls beneath the blows of his enemies only to triumph with greater splendour...below the bed there are spread out the royal regalia...of which the king would presently take possession **after his rebirth**." (pp. 187–188)

...Yes, what could he do if he was dead?...**Well, he would just get up again, renewed and invigorated, succeeded by himself in the person of his son, in whom we has reembodied**. It was "abdication followed by replacement...a renewal," says Professor Alexandre Moret. According to Professor Frankfort, we should not even use the word succession. "It is not succession," he said, "**but a renewal...a true renewal** of kingly potency, a rejuvenation of rulership." (pp. 190–191)

The king must pass through some sort of underworld before he can emerge triumphant...**where a cycle of transformation is going to begin**. (p. 202)

A "very rare" vignette from the Book of the Dead shows such "**rites of rebirth**" using three lion couches in succession. (p. 203)

Equally reassuring is the example of the sun, who "**only dies to be reborn**" at the New Year, **and of the grain which springs up anew** from the fallow earth, as you see in these so-called Osiris beds—real beds with real grain growing on them in the form of a man, life-sized: these have been found perfectly preserved in some tombs. The same text that announces the death of the King are quick to give encouragement—he is justified, qualified to become a divine youthful Osiris, **eligible for renewal**. If he has run and hidden from his relentless enemy, he will soon return younger and stronger than ever, to certain victory. Even as they weep for the King in the tomb, the mourners diligently search for him—they haven't given up hope after all. Everyone has a premonition that the show is not over; he perishes only that he may live...**and so he wants to die in order to be born!** (pp. 207–208)

The living king had been permitted to "suffer serious physical damage," as Edouard Naville put it, "for the sake of the experience that it will give him;"...His narrow escape quickly followed by a magnificent coronation scene, "a great one falls on his side," but rises like a god and takes the crown when the Two Ladies order him to arise and mount the throne. By passing the tests he has shown himself "justified"—qualified to take the throne. "Our play proclaims that at the coronation...whatever harm he may have suffered is undone," writes Frankfort, "with [his Eye], Horus has regained his full strength." As Miss Thausing puts it, "**The period of transition end up on a new plane of existence**," with body and spirit on a higher level than before. (pp. 212–213)

Here in the tomb of Tutankhamen we have three real life-sized couches which represent, according to our guidebook, "**three stages of processes of rebirth**," the final stage being that of the lion couch. Professor Moret noted that in the mysteries "a dead person is reborn when he lays himself down, clothed in a skin or a shroud, on a bed." The bed is important, but which bed—a bed of (re)birth, conception, suffering, healing, death, or resurrection?...Yes the same bed changes roles, **just as the people do, from one episode to the next**. (pp. 217–222)

On this theme the Zohar (Sperling and Simon's translation) is full of remarkable hints and suggestions. It tells us that Abraham is building his alters "proceeded **from grade [or step] to grade until he reached his own rightful grade**." Thus when Abraham entered Canaan, "God appeared to him and he received a *nefesh* [became a living body], and built an alter **to the corresponding grade (of divinity)**." Then he went on southward and received a *ruah* (spirit); the he rose to the "medium of the *neshama*," **which is the highest degree**. After this it was necessary for him **to recapitulate all three steps "to test himself,"** and this was represented by his journey into Egypt. It was only after his returning from Egypt **and reviewing all the rights over again "so as to fix all in its proper place" and keep the whole system united that Abraham was "fully endowed, and he became the lot and the portion of God in real truth,"** (p. 457)

One Eternal Round

The one subject which is the raison d'être for religion is studiously avoided by the clergy, who see refuge and comfort in the formalities. The Neo-Freudians have finally recognized "the rediscovery of modern psychology: that death **is man's peculiar and greatest anxiety**," outranking even sex. In his prize winning book, Ernest Becker finds that "All historical religions address themselves to this same problem of how to bear the end of life. Religions like Hinduism and Buddhism performed the ingenious trick or *pretending* **not to want to be reborn**." Not so our Egyptians; Siegfried Morenz has pointed out the complete contrast between the Egyptians' "eternity of the individual" and the Indians' "transmigration of the soul," the one determined to be himself forever and the other resigned to becoming anything you please—a drop of water in an Ocean of Being.

If modern scholars are depressed by the mortuary atmosphere of Egyptian culture, our modern world has an even more demoralizing message—the absolute scientific certainty that man "goes back into the ground a few feet in order blindly and dumbly to rot and disappear forever," taking with him his vast unrealized potential. No wonder a full apprehension of mans' condition would drive him insane." Mircea Eliade concludes his book *Cosmos and History* with the observation that **only in the freedom found in faith "a new formula for man's collaboration with creation**;…only such a freedom…is able to defend modern man from the terror of history." The Egyptians did not look upon the face of death with anymore complacency than other people do. The terror is always there, from the Pyramid Texts, down to the Coptic hagiography. "O-ReAtum…save me from that god whose face is that of a hound but whose skin is human, who lives by butchery, who is in charge of the windings of the Lake of Fire, who swallows corpses, who controls hearts, who inflicts injury unseen." **These are no figures of speech; it is all too real.**

The Egyptians frankly express their hated of going into the long night. Though all men have to suffer death, like children at a party when we all hate going to bed; "the King hates sleep and detests inertness." Kings and commoners plead passionately for an extension of time: "O you who take away years and bring days to an end, do not take away my years or bring my days to an end, for I am Horus...I will not die in the abyss...I will not die a second time!" The final act is too awful. The sand thrown in the face; the cold and motionless obstruction; the rotting, purification, stench, and decay; and finally, the foul and choking dust of the tomb—the Egyptians spare us no detail: "You shall have no purification, O King; you shall have no sweat; you shall have no efflux, O King; you shall have no dust, O King!"

The final response to these horrors was flat denial—the whole thing was simply unacceptable: "I will not be seized. My corpse will not be constrained!" **"I died but I have returned alive." "I disintegrated yesterday but I returned today...I died yesterday, I raised myself today, I returned today."** These people are thinking in terms of millions of years, repeated millions of times. **But even that is not enough; they want to go on living "like Re, from eternity in the past to eternity in the future." What they want is life eternal: "I will not die; I have no end!"** (pp. 31–33)

The dead body was taken below **to regenerate itself**, "not to remain permanently, but to emerge again from the depths that had been opened." (p. 37)

It is most singular that the hypocephalus emphatically shows us as an actual physical reality, Re and Osiris, past and present, yesterday and tomorrow, **as one and the same entity and yet distinctly two beings**, as explained by the Egyptian scribe. Such a conjuncture is only possible, of course, when both meet at Harakhty—Horus on the horizon, the place of transition with the sun-disk exactly on the line between the upper and lower worlds, being in both at once for the usual magical moment. The Egyptian scribe of Book of the Dead 17 explains that the one Janus head is yesterday, Osiris, and the other is tomorrow, Re at his rising." (p. 41)

Finally, by these initiatory ordinances, the eye receives the power to see, and all the members of the body are restored, "that he may walk and not faint." Then he is greeted by his fellows who declare that "he is like Re on the day of his birth." **He has been born again** like a little child and has been given a chance of eternal progression with a promise, "His possessions will never be less, nor his way ever blocked. As a son he receives all the powers of the Father. (pp. 79–80)

We learn that this is not the first such council and that there have been other and older gods before. (p. 81)

The timing is all important to the great event. The occasion was, of course, the end of one age or *saeculum* and the beginning of what the Greeks called the *eniautos*—"**here we are again," the ending of one cycle and the beginning of the next.** (p. 108)

That **the cycle of resurrection and rebirth** is represented is apparent from the Cairro hypocephalus SR 10700, "O Great God, who rises from the primordial waters and illuminates the Two Lands on the day of his birth." (pp. 208–209)

Thus we see in figure 3 how all things represent a process, change, motion from one state or condition to another, **constantly changing form but ever preserving identity**, which the Egyptologist designated as *hpwr*. It must be clearly understood that this term has nothing to do with metempsychosis, or transmigration of souls. As in the seven ages of man, **the changes of form and appearance do not mean that the old identity is lost**; on the contrary, the *hpr* is a voluntary change of form—with the individual always in control—and thus a heightened assertion of individual identity. It is not the loss, but the intensifying of the ego; **the initiate can change his form to match his environment or stage of the journey precisely because he is master of the situation**. The main purpose of transformation is to escape dangerous situations, which makes it a form of adaptive behaviour to assure the continued existence of the individual under all circumstances—it is a kind of natural selection, the very opposite of transmigration. (p. 276)

The king sets the example of entering into his mother's womb **to be reborn**. In the Pyramid Texts the king rejoices, "It is my rebirth today, you gods…it is Nut who has borne me." Thus "the dead king has won a new life of eternal youth in the sky-goddess," and from her he will never be weaned. Even more graphic was the preparation of Osiris for his **rebirth** by being laid in a wooden cow-coffin. (p. 292)

If you are going to have either a birth or rebirth, it will require the bringing together of the elements of this earth. (p. 299)

The name of the god Atum is related to the verb *tm* "to be complete," and the nouns *tm* "everything, the universe," and *tmw* "the totality of men, everyone." This should be noted in view of Moses 1:34: "And the first man of all men have I called Adam, which is many." All the premortal spirits must pass through him as all "the totality of men" must descend from him—"many" indeed! (p. 308)

He tells how a certain brother wondered whether he was holding a true belief. One day while he was praying about it, an angel appeared to him and said he had come to show him the glory of the Father and the true way. The angel carried him up to the first heaven **but forbade him to worship the one presiding there** as he was not the Father. The same thing happened at the second heaven, and so on until the sixth, each more glorious than the last. **In the seventh heaven he worshiped the Father** who asked him whence he came. His answer: from the tribulation of the earth. In heaven he saw hosts of angels, glorious flower gardens filled with singing birds, etc., a place of joy without sorrow. He told the Father he wished to stay but was told he would have to go back to the earth again so that he could preach there the things that he had learned; but the Father granted his request to remain above a little longer. When the angel told him his time was up, he thought he had been there only two hours, but the angel told him it was actually thirty-two years, as he would find when he returned to earth. So the man mounted on the neck (*collum*) of the angel for the descent through all the heavens. Returning to earth, his report of his journey confirmed the faith of the people and strengthened the church (*secta*). This particular ascension closely parallels many after-life or near-death experiences being published abroad in our own day, in particular works by Raymond Moody and Elisabeth Kuebler-Ross (p. 384).

Final Thoughts

Joseph Smith

"And there are many among us who have many revelations, for they are not all stiffnecked. And as many as are not stiffnecked and have faith, have communion with the Holy Spirit, which maketh manifest unto the children of men, according to their faith." (Jarom 1:4)

"But behold, thus saith the Lord God: When the day cometh that they shall believe in me, that I am Christ, then have I covenanted with their fathers that **they shall be restored in the flesh, upon the earth**, unto the lands of their inheritance." (2 Nephi 10:7)

"For those that live shall inherit the earth, and those that die shall rest from all their labors, **and their works shall follow them**; and they shall receive a crown in the mansions of my Father, which I have prepared for them." (D&C 59:2)

"…they shall **return again to their own place**, to enjoy that which they are willing to receive, because they were not willing to enjoy that which they might have received." (D&C 88:32)

"Let no man be afraid to lay down his life for my sake; for whoso layeth down his life for my sake **shall find it again**." (D&C 103:27)

"Yea, we see that **whosoever will may lay hold upon the word of God**, which is quick and powerful, which shall divide asunder all the cunning and the snares and the wiles of the devil, **and lead the man of Christ in a strait and narrow course** across that everlasting gulf of misery which is prepared to engulf the wicked—**And land their souls, yea, their immortal souls, at the right hand of God** in the kingdom of heaven, to sit down with Abraham, and Isaac, and with Jacob, and with all our holy fathers, **to go no more out**." (Helaman 3:29–30)

Hugh Nibley

Here's what we've come out for. "And these are the councils of the spirit for the sons of truth while they are on the earth, and which will be the testing [*pequddah* is a *testing* or a *visitation*; somebody comes and checks up on you, etc.] of all those who walk in this way. And it is for this: for healing, for increase of peace, for length of days, for the multiplication offspring [these were not celibates out here at all; men, women, and children were buried in the cemetery together] and all the blessings of eternity, and for eternal joy and **lives [plural]** of glory, [this is *netsah*, and it's the same as the Latin word, *nieo*, meaning *to shine*, or *to be glorious*; *nitein*, shining, brilliant, the high glory], and for a crown of exaltation *middat-hadar*, with a garment of glory [*hadar* is white brilliance] in the light of the eternities." A rabbi will tell you, "Well, we don't have eternal life. Heaven is a philosophical concept." But this is the sort of language we use, isn't it? This is not orthodox Judaism. You can see why they didn't want it. It's not orthodox Christianity either— **this eternal progression thing** and getting the crowns, and being tested while you are here. Then we get to the preexistence, the plan as it was made in the beginning. (*Teachings of the Book of Mormon—Semester 1*: Transcripts of Lectures Presented to an Honors Book of Mormon class at BYU, 1988–1990 [Provo: FARMS] p. 154)

Now it's this name Joseph that they play on, but this is a characteristic thing in genealogy, and Joseph is very special. **But the fact that it should be the same Joseph, leading right down to Joseph Smith, should not surprise you.** (Ibid, p. 277)

In Mosiah 1 he is going to give them a new name and a new identity. See, **every time you get a new life or a new advancement, a new step or initiation, you get a new identity, a new persona**. When a person is born he gets christened. He is not christened until he joins the church. This is the theory in the Christian world. With us it used to be always on the eighth day, circumcision, etc. You have a new name, and when you get married you get another new name. If you get any office, you also get another new name. Then at your funeral you get another identity, etc. They go through the same ritual every time. And, of course, when you reach maturity there's a very important thing—the rites of initiation that come with maturity. In the Christian churches it's when you are confirmed, around the age of fifteen. In all primitive tribes and [other societies] when a person becomes mature—reaches manhood or womanhood—there is that rite. Then they get a new name; they are identified with another group entirely. Boys are no longer with the women, etc. They now belong to a man's *phratry*. These are the rites of puberty. **So each time you get a new name, a new identity, a new appearance, new marks, and a new title or degree.** (Ibid, pp. 448–449)

See, the Spirit of the Lord guides you. It won't promise you instant prosperity; it will guide you and give you a sense of the things you should be doing. If you don't, you are in a state of "open rebellion against God; therefore he listeth to obey the evil spirit…Therefore if that man repenteth not, and remaineth and dieth an enemy to God, the demands of divine justice…" Notice that he shifts this whole thing to the larger scale. This is on a cosmic pattern and has to do with the other world. That's where atonement takes place. That's where we return to Heavenly Father and are redeemed, bought back again. **See all that re business. You are redeemed, you are resurrected, you are raised up again, you return and go back**. Teshûvah means to return and yeshîvah, sit down once you get there.

We mentioned the reconciliation. It all has to do with going back to a prior condition that you lived in before you came here—it's very clear. As I said, the only alternative to that is a simplistic predestination which just stops everything dead cold. "The demands of divine justice do awaken his immortal soul to a lively sense of his own guilt, which doth cause him to shrink from the presence of the Lord [this is what hell is, of course], and doth fill his breast with guilt, and pain, and anguish, which is like an unquenchable fire, whose flame ascendeth up forever and ever." (Ibid, p. 459)

Now concerning that which was to come, remember, the purpose of the year festival was to determine the fortunes of the new age. It was not just launching a new year. *Year* is *gear* and *yule*, the same word as *wheel*. It means "**a turning, a revolution.**" It's the same word as *while*. The interesting thing is that in the Arabic world it's *hawl hawla*. It means "**the cycle turned, the wheel revolved**, the year went around." The Greeks call it the *enianton*, "**the here we are again.**" Jane Harrison wrote a book about that. **You come back again, and you are in a revolving circle of the time that goes on forever and ever.** (Ibid, p. 461)

They treated John the Baptist the same way. Remember, he was "the mad mullah of the desert." He dressed in camel skin and lived on wild locusts and honey. The people flocked out to see him, etc. **Josephus said an interesting thing about him**. When people asked him who [John the Baptist] was, Josephus didn't know his name. He knew all about him, but he didn't know his name was *John* because he never told anybody his name was *John*. **He said he was *Enoch*,** a very interesting thing, and they took him for Enoch Redivivus, "**the returned Enoch.**" **And, of course, Enoch is going to return with Elijah**, another one who was treated the same way. (Ibid, p. 76)

Why should the Father be jealous of the Son, or the Son jealous of the Father? This is what glory is for, to be shared. **The more it is shared, the greater the glory.** It's not like something else—giving out a little of it and not having as much left. No, his glory is this. "For behold, this is my work and my glory-to bring to pass the immortality and eternal life of man" (Moses 1:39). He brings them up, and then his glory is increased. Glory increases the more it is spread around. So this is a different concept. **He comes down himself, but he comes as a Son**. He is the Son of God. Again, we don't argue about the Christological question, the equality, etc. In coming down here and following commandments, he identifies his will with the will of the Father. He does exactly what he is told to do because he is setting the example for us. We must do the same thing; it's going to make this very clear here. **That's why he comes down here, and he is called the Son**. (*Teachings of the Book of Mormon—Semester 2:* Transcripts of Lectures Presented to an Honors Book of Mormon class at BYU, 1988–1990 [Provo: FARMS p. 82)

Verse 3: "The Father, because he was conceived by the power of God." What does that have to do with it? The status of the Father goes back to another order of existence, obviously way back there. He [the Son] was conceived by the power of God, a godly power which is not of this earth and has nothing to do with this earth at all. **This is a place where men** dwell in perishable flesh, a condition designated as "the Son." Not second rate, but completely dependent. They are identical species working on different levels. This is the whole point-we are identical species. We get this in 3 Nephi when the Lord goes and prays. It's the very same thing we have in John 13–17, showing exactly how we are identical. If the Father and the Son are one, we are one with the Son; thereby, we are one with the Father exactly as they are one. Of course, the Bible says that over and over again, and people won't believe it. They say, "John can't be that naive; this must all be just spirit." So they make John the most ghostly, the most spiritual, the most unreal of all the gospels. They say, "John is the great mystery." (Ibid, p. 83)

"And they are one God, yea, the very Eternal Father of heaven and of earth." That's a very thrilling statement to make—that we are in on that. **Then the next verse tells us that the flesh is to the spirit as the Son is to the Father, or the Father is to the Spirit as the Son is to the flesh. It's exactly alike**. **They both belong to the spiritual order of things**. The flesh is not against the spirit but "subject to the Spirit," we are told. When mortals become totally subject to God, they will have passed the test and are ready to go on. You have to be subject—that's the thing. "… the flesh becoming subject to the Spirit, or the Son to the Father, being one God, suffereth temptation, and yieldeth not to the temptation." This is saying that you belong to this same category. He came to the same category as you. He was tempted just as much as you are, etc. You don't have to give in, but we all do because that was the Fall. That's where Adam did give in. This is necessary for experience, knowing the good from the evil.

Verse 6: "And after all this, after working many mighty miracles among the children of men, he shall be led, yea, even as Isaiah said, as a sheep before the shearer is dumb, so he opened not his mouth." He left the celestial circuit to bring us into that celestial circuit, you might say (verses 6 and 7). The Lord must come down to us to arrange for our removal to a higher realm; we can't go up there to make arrangements. He must come to us to give us a chance to acknowledge him, and accept the offering, and understand what the thing is. It's a sort of martialing area here. Verse 8 tells us that it is a physical breaking of confining bonds, a barrier beyond which life ceases. The bands of death have to be broken, as we are told in 2 Nephi 9:7 . The second law would be in effect if it weren't for that. That's what Hawking talks about here. Why should the second law [have to] be broken? Why should it ever be there at all? They are all right back where they started, at square one, now. There's no limit to the power of whatever put us here. It could put other people in other places. As Voltaire said long ago, "**Once we get a person born, the idea of getting reborn is just a technical matter**." Just a matter of working out a few bugs. If you've already got him born out of nothing—**all you have to do is repeat the thing**. (Ibid, p. 84)

Mosiah 27:25: "And the Lord said unto me: **Marvel not that all mankind…must be born again**." **Notice that it's nothing less than being born all over again. We are so completely out of it when we** are here. **We cannot make the change without leaving the scene. You have to be born again**. See, there's the one world or the other; you can't mix them. It's a very hard thing, as Brigham Young said, as he tried to take the water on both shoulders. "The Latter-day Saint who tries to live in both worlds is torn apart." There's no such agony, no worse experience than that, and it happens to them here.

As it explains here, "...yea, born of God, changed from their carnal and fallen state, to a state of righteousness [a complete change], being redeemed of God, becoming his sons and daughters." They become new creatures; it's an entirely different thing, as this explains. (Ibid, p. 191)

This is one of the best-known phenomena of ancient history now. It wasn't a few years ago, but I've been yelling about it for years. As is well known, this is a stock theme. It's a rehearsing of the creation, the refounding, **the rebirth of the human race**. It's the *natalia*, it is the refounding of the kingdom, it's universal. **Everybody is reborn and receives a new name on a particular day**, which is the new year—it's gauged by the sun. And it [this ceremony] is very conspicuous in the documents, and only within the last three or four years, the anthropologists have latched onto it. Finally when they catch up to it, it has become very obvious. You can see that. And this is a very basic theme. I notice the three principal anthropologists writing about this now. They've all got into the act, and they're talking about primitive societies. This is universal. Van Gennep's theory is that society has to regenerate itself by rites of passage. **You know what a rite of passage is—the rite of passage into the other world. Then you have to get passage to come back. That's what they're talking about now**. There are two worlds. **You go to the one, and then you come back refreshed and renewed to your old world and begin a new cycle of life**.

This is what they're saying today. Well, it's been obvious for a hundred years, but they didn't notice it. They've been following Frazier instead, which is a very different pattern. Well, Van Gennep's theory is **regeneration by rites of passage. He says it sometimes takes the form of rites of death and rebirth**. And Victor Turner says the rites all apply to the society and don't affect the individual at all. The society first separates itself from its former life. That is what you do when you drive out a scapegoat, etc. You purge yourself of what you were before. **They separate themselves from their former life. Then there's what he calls the transition; and then there's the reincorporation when you come back to ordinary life and you're good for a new period**. (Ibid, p. 276)

Verse 39: "And Amulek said unto him: Yea, he is **the very Eternal Father** of heaven and of earth, and all things which in them are." He made the whole thing possible. And Hebrews 1:2 says the same thing. He **made possible the physical resurrection**. "And he shall come into the world to redeem his people." **To redeem something, as we said before, is to bring back somebody who had been there before—to bring him home again.** *Redemptio* is to buy back again. It's to buy back something that was yours before and got lost; now you buy it

back again. Well, we were with Him in the eternities before this. Now we have been separated, and then we go back again. "And he shall take upon him the transgressions of those who believe on his name; and these are they that shall have eternal life, and salvation cometh to none else." (Ibid, p. 320)

Suggested Reading

The following items from both LDS and non-LDS sources are suggested as further reading references as to their relevance to the concept of "Eternal Lives" or any pertinent associated topic. Some of this material contains concepts and ideas that have not been addresses by LDS General Authorities, and thus have not been directly approved of, nor repudiated, as possible within the scope of LDS doctrine.

All of the books noted in the references for the quotes that have been used in this book are highly recommended first for additional reading. Many of the articles below can be located at the following links:

http://maxwellinstitute.byu.edu/
http://www.sunstonemagazine.com/
http://dialoguejournal.com/

LDS Sources

Alexander, Thomas G., "The Reconstruction of Mormon Doctrine," *Sunstone,* Vol. 10, No. 5, May 1985, pp. 8–16.

Boyd, George T., "A Mormon Concept of Man," *Dialogue,* Vol. 3, No. 1, Spring 1968, pp. 57-74.

Buerger, David John, "The Fulness of the Priesthood," *Dialogue,* Vol. 16, No. 1, Spring 1983, pp. 10-44.

—"The Adam-God Doctrine," *Dialogue,* Vol. 15, No. 1, Spring 1982, pp. 14–45.

Burton, Robert P. and Webster, Bruce F., "Some Thoughts on Higher Dimensional Realms," *BYU Studies,* Vol. 20, No. 3, Spring 1980, pp. 281-296.

Cannon, Donald Q., "The King Follett Discourse: Joseph Smith's Greatest Sermon in Historical Perspective," *BYU Studies,* Vol. 18, No. 2, Winter 1978, pp. 179-192.

England, Eugene, "Perfection and Progression: Two Complementary Ways to Talk About God," *BYU Studies,* Vol. 29, No. 3, Summer 1989, pp. 31-45.

Farrell, Charles R., "The Development of the Doctrine of Preexistence, 1830–1844," *BYU Studies,* Vol. 28, No. 2, Spring 1988, pp. 1-25.

Gileadi, Avraham. *Isaiah Decoded: Ascending the Ladder to Heaven*, Hebraeus Press, 2002.

Hale, Van, "The Doctrinal Impact of the King Follett Discourse," *BYU Studies*, Vol. 18, No. 2, Winter 1978, pp. 209-225.

Hunsaker, U. Carlisle, "Soul-Making, or Is There Life Before Death?," *Dialogue*, Vol. 18, No. 3, Fall 1985, pp. 152–159.

Jeffery, Duane E., "Intersexes in Humans: An Introductory Exploration," *Dialogue*, Vol. 12, No. 3, Fall 1979, pp. 100–113.

Keller, Jeffrey E., "Is Sexual Gender Eternal?" *Sunstone,* Vol. 10, No. 11, July 1986, pp. 38–39.

Kirkland, Boyd, "Elohim and Jehovah in Mormonism and the Bible," *Dialogue*, Vol. 19, No. 1, Spring 1986, pp. 77-93.

—"Of Gods, Mortals, and Devils," *Sunstone,* Vol. 10, No. 12, October 1986, pp. 6–12.

Larson, Stan, "The King Follett Discourse: a Newly Amalgamated Text," *BYU Studies*, Vol. 18, No. 2, Winter 1978, pp. 193-208.

Ostler, Blake Thomas, Collection of Essays (estimated release 2011).

—"Clothed Upon: A Unique Aspect of Christian Antiquity," *BYU Studies*, Vol. 22, No. 1, 1982, pp. 31–45.

—"The Mormon Concept of God," *Dialogue*, Vol. 17, No. 2, Summer 1984, pp. 65–93.

—"The Idea of Preexistence in the Development of Mormon Thought," *Dialogue,* Vol. 15, No. 1, Spring 1982, pp. 59–74.

Paul, Robert, "Joseph Smith and the Plurality of Worlds Idea," *Dialogue*, Vol. 19, No. 2, Summer 1986, pp. 13-36.

Thomas, M. Catherine, *Light in the Wilderness: Explorations of Spiritual Life*, Digital Legend, 2010.

Turner, Rodney, "The Moral Dimensions of Man," *Dialogue,* Vol. 3, No. 1, Spring 1968, pp. 74-84.

Wright, H. Curtis, "A Sophic and a Mantic People," *BYU Studies*, Vol. 31, No. 3, Summer 1991, pp. 51-65.

Other Sources

Gershom, Yonassan, *Beyond the Ashes*, ARE Press, 1996.

—*From Ashes to Healing*, ARE Press, 1997.

Hornung, Eric, *Conceptions of God in Ancient Egypt: The One and the Many,* Cornell University Press, 1982.

Monroe, Robert A., *Journeys out of the Body*, Broadway Books, 2001.

—*Far Journeys*, Main Street Books, 1985.

—*Ultimate Journey*, Main Street Books, 1996.

Moody, Raymond, *Coming Back*, Bantam Books, 1991.

Morgan, Marlo, *Mutant Messages Down Under*, Harper Perennial, 1995.

Morse, Melvin, *Where God Lives*, Harper Collins, 2000.

Newton, Michael, *Journey of Souls*, Llewellyn Publications, 2001.

—*Destiny of Souls*, Llewellyn Publications, 2001.

Spalding, Baird T., *Life and Teachings of the Masters of the Far East*, DeVorss, 6 volumes, 1964.

Weiss, Brian L., *Many Lives, Many Masters*, Fireside, 1998.

—*Messages from the Masters*, Warner Books, 2000.

—*Only Love is Real*, Warner Books, 2000.

—*Through Time into Healing*, Fireside, 1993.

Woolger, Roger J., *Other Lives, Other Selves*, Bantam Books, 1988.

Index

A

A Rational Theology 81
Abel...268
Abraham 25-27, 51, 65, 67, 70-71, 86-87, 92, 103, 109, 115-116, 118, 124, 129, 141, 192, 205, 213, 238, 258, 264, 276, 317, 334, 339, 343, 351-355, 367-371, 379, 381, 385
accelerated.......................161-162, 241
accountable 293, 322
Adam 5, 22-28, 35-36, 52-54, 63, 70-71, 78, 88-89, 93-94, 104, 121, 126, 132, 142, 155, 166-168, 171-173, 176-177, 180-181, 185-186, 189-190, 198, 201-214, 227, 241, 247-248, 252, 255, 267-270, 287, 289-290, 293-300, 304-310, 327
Adam-God 212, 391
added upon...............................343, 346
advance...........27, 43, 53, 61-62, 65-66, 74-75, 80, 84, 88-89, 95, 111, 122, 165, 235, 248, 256, 277-278, 288-289, 344, 361, 386
affliction 56, 67, 73, 84, 176, 270
ageless...340
agency.............22, 83-84, 284, 314, 321, 344-345, 373
agent.132, 214, 268, 316, 322, 345-348
Ahman 181, 215
all things 6, 11, 13, 19, 33-34, 42, 51-58, 70, 88, 97-98, 103-105, 119, 125-126, 131, 137-143, 149, 153, 167, 175, 180-196, 201, 211, 235, 242-243, 251, 256, 269-270, 278-281, 290, 294, 296-297, 300-301, 308, 314, 317, 323, 366, 383, 389
Ancient of Days 14, 201-203, 206-210, 267, 300, 305-306, 358
Ancient One 211
angel.....5, 15, 23-27, 32-33, 39, 42, 52, 55, 60-61, 70, 74, 76-78, 81, 87, 93-94, 102, 104, 115-120, 124-126, 130-131, 137-138, 141, 143, 155, 168-169, 172-175, 181, 186-190, 195, 206, 220, 225, 231, 240, 246-248, 265, 269-273, 276, 279, 288-289, 291, 296-297, 323-330, 333, 340, 350-351, 358, 361, 370, 375, 383-384
annihilate / annihilation 218-222, 256,271-276, 279-280, 318
anointing 90-91, 115, 119, 244, 358-359
anthropomorphic/ism 189, 210
apostate(s).........................258, 262-266
apostle ...3, 5, 12, 19, 24-29, 36, 39, 41, 48, 61, 65, 68-70, 77-79, 88, 90, 98, 103, 109, 119-122, 126, 132-135, 143, 157-161, 171, 175-176, 179-180, 183, 186, 190-191, 194-195, 198, 205, 207, 213, 240-242, 250, 257, 262, 265-269, 271, 281-282, 284, 286, 290-291, 299-305, 337, 341-342
Apostle John 39, 48, 107, 109, 143, 157, 175, 180, 186, 190, 194, 198, 213
Apostle Matthew..5, 39 , 135, 190, 337
Apostle of / to Joseph.............132 -133
Apostle Paul.........41, 48, 79, 157, 176, 180, 186, 191, 194, 198, 290
Apostles of Jesus Christ...........24, 133
Archangel 202-206, 252, 261, 267, 300, 322, 327
are one........96, 150, 181-199, 269, 303, 358, 388
Articles of Faith...........................60, 80
ascend 42, 45, 55, 70, 78, 83, 96, 104-105, 115-120, 141, 153-154, 193, 204-205, 217, 242, 246, 253, 270, 310, 326, 387
ascension 114-120, 205, 310
ask 12-13, 21-28, 31, 50, 53, 56, 59-62, 73, 96, 116-117, 135, 139-141, 161, 179, 183, 188-189, 198, 210, 220, 232, 241, 247, 250, 254-255, 259, 263, 267, 273, 277-285, 291-293, 295, 301-302,

307-309, 325-332, 348, 352, 366, 368, 371, 373, 383, 387
Assmann, Jan...................................377
astonish / astonished 85, 124, 177, 203, 208, 286, 290, 294, 305, 340, 362, 365
Atonement......18, 27, 82, 95, 116, 150, 163, 166, 171, 180, 184, 316-317, 323, 386
attain / attainment....15, 35, 41, 52-53, 62, 66-67, 70-75, 81-83, 92, 102, 154, 178, 202, 204, 213, 252, 270, 273-274, 310
Atum 208-211, 349, 354-358, 378, 381-383
awake / awakening ..96, 154, 225, 261, 270, 279, 331, 349, 378, 387

B

Ba 377-378
Ballard, M. Russell 80, 83
Ballard, Melvin J........................80, 83
banishment 61, 234-235
Baraq'el....................................131, 375
Baurak Ale 131
be one 33, 51, 59, 149, 167, 190-193, 197, 207, 264, 269, 281, 358
becoming........1, 20, 42, 50, 55, 66, 97, 108, 115, 150, 181, 185, 187, 196, 208, 211, 269, 377, 381, 388-389
begets 79, 355, 357, 365, 368
begotten.........40, 42-43, 54, 60, 63, 68, 94, 131, 168, 180-189, 198, 203, 230, 266-268, 294-298, 308, 310, 354, 365, 373, 377, 379
below all things 104, 153, 193, 235
birth.55, 70, 74, 97, 107-108, 112, 137, 209, 234, 303, 321, 327, 339-340, 356, 363, 372, 377-383, 389
birth chamber.................................379
Black, Susan Easton....................44-45
blasphemy 32, 35, 44, 142, 177, 179, 202, 254, 262, 265, 268
blood 24, 28, 31-32, 109, 159, 191, 198, 218, 248, 251, 258-261, 266, 291, 294, 298-300, 317, 323, 328, 373
Book of Mormon 16, 95-96, 108, 119, 143, 181, 185-187, 195, 265, 290, 341-342, 355, 363, 367, 386-387
Book of Moses........................351, 365
born of 50, 74, 85, 97, 107-108, 120, 135, 139, 183, 188, 231, 260, 291, 297, 322, 339, 389

born again.....22, 50, 97, 107-108, 378, 382, 388-389
brain 66, 227, 263, 359
bring back again.......................51, 158
Brown, Hugh B................................82
Bunker, Edward 85

C

Cain 268, 359, 374
calling and election ...29, 240, 242-243
Campbell, Alexander 260
Cannon, George Q....2, 19, 65, 72, 122, 391
capacity.........35, 42-45, 55, 75, 90, 111, 166, 213, 252, 269, 277, 282, 288, 349, 379
cease to be 59, 219, 271, 274, 288
cease to learn 15, 59-60, 220
celestial kingdom 15, 64, 81, 84-85, 98, 103-105, 111-112, 166, 168, 172-173, 259, 269, 281, 289, 297
celestial robe 115
character of God................21, 41, 178, 249-254
child 48, 75, 78, 143, 168, 187, 195, 260, 268, 288, 322, 327, 355
Christ ....see Jesus Christ
Clawson, Rudger 77
clay.........22, 25, 37-38, 47, 71, 85, 166, 169, 215, 218-220, 231, 249, 255, 313-319, 332, 349
Clayton, William ..22, 25, 85, 215, 249
cleanse 66, 72, 300
climb 20, 42, 52, 226, 232, 253
Coltrin, Zebedee....23-24, 31, 198, 254
come again 123, 149, 172
come forth 51, 53, 72, 78, 119, 150, 154, 163, 259, 276, 319, 364
come to an end 219, 274-279, 334
Comforter 29, 189, 197, 316, 323
commandment(s) 6, 20, 34, 43-44, 48, 51-53, 66, 68, 73-76, 90, 124-125, 129, 137, 149, 167, 185, 217, 219, 244, 246, 257-258, 271, 331-332, 387
commune 7, 12, 250, 252, 317
communion ...7, 11, 183, 191-192, 198, 385
conceived ....113, 150, 181, 185, 187, 196 , 210, 268, 278, 339, 363, 379
condescend / condescension 7, 143, 153, 186, 195, 241
corporeal 202
cosmos..87-89, 102, 184, 345, 363, 381

INDEX

council of the gods.........210, 249, 254, 354-357, 369
Council in Heaven..342, 345, 369, 374
Council of Fifty................................215
Council of the Twelve......................66
countless 57-58, 209, 234, 377
Cowan, Richard O. 45, 98-99
Cowdery, Oliver..........................23-24
creating 36, 55, 141, 211, 234, 269, 282, 289, 310, 377
creation.........18, 43, 54, 58, 61, 79, 86, 89, 97, 102, 118, 177, 184, 188, 201-205, 209-211, 219-221, 230, 235, 250, 253, 256, 271, 278-280, 288, 291-297, 310, 321-322, 324, 329-330, 333, 339-340, 344, 352, 355-358, 361-362, 367-368, 377, 381, 389
creator............54, 82, 88, 210-211, 329, 344, 352, 360, 364, 378
crossing the plains...................104, 298
crown 40, 49, 51, 53-60, 70-71, 87, 94-95, 103-104, 112-119, 124, 133, 158, 202, 205-206, 209, 211, 214, 229, 231-232, 235, 269-270, 280, 290, 297, 299, 314, 321-325, 347, 349, 353, 356, 380, 385-386
cycle 89, 96-97, 161-162, 361, 379-380, 382, 387, 389, 392

D

damnation 12, 73, 158, 172, 204, 240, 254, 259-261, 268
damned.....12, 173, 196, 221, 240, 257, 260, 265, 269, 284, 375
Daniel 48, 138
daughters.......50, 53, 67-68, 78-81, 97, 108, 137, 172, 182, 187, 197, 208-209, 213-214, 268, 300, 324, 375, 389
David....26, 47-48, 79, 84-85, 119, 153, 188, 334
David, King of Israel........5, 21, 37, 39, 47, 111, 150, 153, 175
Dead Sea Scrolls 89, 118, 173, 340-344
death chamber................................379
decay / decaying........63, 104, 144, 219, 257, 271, 273, 275, 318, 382
decompose / decomposition 104, 218-222, 271-279
defeat 335
degenerate................................218, 232
degree to another/degree 1, 41, 59, 74, 213, 252

degree(s) of glory.....67, 69, 75, 79, 87, 111
deity.....1, 55, 57, 63, 79, 115, 176-177, 208, 211, 229, 262, 268
depraved / depravity...............226, 337
Deseret News 36, 214
destroy / destroyed 24, 28, 67, 84, 125, 151-154, 161-163, 167-169, 191, 193, 217-221, 240-241, 255, 273--279, 282, 284, 300, 314, 340, 360, 366, 369, 376
destroy death 219, 221, 276
destruction......124, 217-221, 271, 279, 294, 314, 335
devil.....36, 51, 60-61, 65, 72, 109, 123, 158, 165-166, 172-173, 189-190, 218-221, 240-242, 258-259, 269-270, 273-276, 284-286, 291, 297, 302, 317, 337, 373, 385, 392
diamond 347, 350, 369
disciples...15, 39, 50, 83, 135, 139-142, 162, 172, 193, 245-248, 267, 286, 303, 309
dismantled 361
disorganize / disorganization........104, 219-223, 235, 273-274
dispensation 11, 43, 62, 79, 114, 123, 126, 130-133, 141-142, 201, 205, 208, 229, 231, 257, 266, 287, 299, 316, 323
dissolution.................89. 219, 221-222, 256-258, 271, 277, 279, 318
divine teachings.................................21
divinity.......66, 166, 234, 255, 268, 381
Djehuty..358
Doctrine and Covenants 43, 45, 99, 131, 207, 265, 371, 375
dominion 7, 33, 53-54, 60, 65-66, 70-71, 74, 86-87, 105, 112, 167, 180, 207, 222, 241, 261, 265-266, 273, 277, 280, 284, 293, 302, 305, 310, 323, 375
door(s)............14, 16, 89, 119, 142, 240, 243-244, 248, 274, 296, 304, 322, 351, 375
drawn up 2, 75
dream / dreaming 51, 117, 169, 225-229, 232, 315, 349, 371
dregs..88, 162-163
dust ...66, 166, 173, 219, 266, 270, 276, 278, 295-296, 311, 331-332, 369, 382
dwelt in him 182, 188, 197
dynamic...376

E

eagle 349
ears to hear................20, 118, 139, 322
Eden ....see Garden of Eden
Egypt 26, 87, 89, 92, 101, 129, 151, 155, 209, 211, 339-340, 343-365, 376-383
elements 20, 25, 55-56, 63, 81, 101, 104, 115, 175, 193, 202-205, 208, 218-222, 273-274, 279, 282-297, 34, 308, 310, 318, 353, 361-363
Elias ..126, 135-142, 225, 230-234, 379
Elijah..........96, 135-141, 257, 334, 387
Eloheim / Elohim 63, 179-181, 203, 235, 250, 263, 268, 294, 308, 369, 371, 392
embryo 54, 69, 78, 81, 234, 298
endless 54, 75, 89, 158, 181, 206, 214, 218-221, 228, 230, 234, 237, 277-285, 310, 322, 376
endless life / lives 51, 54, 60, 86, 213-214, 221, 237, 280, 322
endless variety 167-168, 282, 285
endowed..........119, 138, 168, 246, 284, 326, 381
endowment...81, 89, 92, 104, 209, 211, 244, 351, 376
enlargement 68, 84, 165, 256
enlighten.........6, 14, 19, 140, 193, 222, 273, 306, 337
Enoch 26, 36, 65, 96, 101-103, 114-118, 122, 131-135, 142, 214, 236, 342-344, 375-376, 387
Ephraim 124, 154, 230, 236
episode / episodes 92, 358, 368, 376, 380
equal 547, 87, 103, 116, 119, 148-149, 168, 179, 185, 245, 265-2696, 269, 295, 340-342, 357, 371, 378
estate.........43, 55, 62, 68, 81, 208, 212, 234-235, 242, 247, 269, 291, 322-324, 343, 374
eternal existence...........54-56, 93, 262, 273, 277, 310-311
Eternal Father 53, 74, 82, 97, 143, 150, 181, 184-188, 195-196, 388-389
Eternal God 178, 182, 188, 196
eternal life...6, 8, 14, 19-20, 29, 35, 41, 44, 50, 55-58, 64, 78, 81, 83, 86, 94, 98, 121, 120, 132, 155, 165-167, 185, 190, 205, 208, 211, 213, 220-222, 226, 240, 247-252, 256, 259, 279, 292, 303, 308, 311, 324, 337, 354, 372-377, 386-387, 390

eternal lives 77, 81-86, 89, 92, 98, 102-104, 108, 112, 112, 124, 130, 137-138, 144, 154
eternal progression..............47, 49, 55, 79-86, 95, 176, 377, 382, 386
eternal worlds................19, 31, 51, 64, 104-105, 176, 206, 242, 259
eternities 58-59, 61, 94, 98, 112-113, 177, 220-221, 238, 273, 278-279, 288-289, 292, 321-322, 324, 386, 390
eternity..........1, 6, 8, 12, 15-16, 18, 26, 35, 41-42, 52-68, 75, 79, 81, 93-94, 104, 113, 122, 126, 166-167, 171, 180, 183, 201, 203, 205-206, 210-211, 214, 219-222, 225, 227-228, 252-281, 285-298, 301-305, 310, 321, 324, 342, 344, 378-385
England, Eugene 175, 391
Evans, Richard L. 82
Eve.24-28, 54, 177, 190, 202, 268, 290, 294, 298-300, 304, 358, 370, 372
Evening and Morning Star................84
everlasting burnings 41, 218, 249, 252, 261, 264
evil 11, 14, 40, 44, 51, 71, 74, 95, 103-105, 113, 125, 146-149, 158, 165, 170, 182, 186-188, 191, 196, 217-218, 239, 248, 259, 261, 274, 284-285, 293, 302, 321-323, 326-327, 330-333, 345, 354, 374, 386, 388
exalt 42, 60, 71, 85, 166, 183, 253-255, 265, 276, 288
exaltation 15, 31-32, 41-45, 51, 54-56, 60, 64, 66-73, 85-89, 94, 103, 116, 166, 173, 175, 183, 201-204, 213-214, 252-253, 271, 273-274, 293, 297, 299-300, 310-311, 316, 373, 386
exaltations 70 85, 202, 274
exaltation to exaltation 15, 41, 43, 213, 252
exist.....24, 56, 64, 66, 73, 80, 255, 264, 274-275, 279, 346
existence.........22, 42-43, 51-64, 71, 74, 79, 90, 92-98, 101, 104, 112, 130, 167, 176, 178, 185, 208, 214, 219-222, 247, 250, 253, 255, 262, 264, 271-279, 282, 288, 293, 304, 310-311, 322, 339-347, 351-360, 364, 374, 379-380, 383, 386-387, 392-392

INDEX

expand 15, 18, 34, 60, 122, 159, 289, 352, 362, 366

experience ..1, 5, 12, 22, 24, 26, 44, 52, 59, 65, 68, 73, 80-86, 94, 97, 102, 104, 108, 113-117, 167, 171, 184, 186, 189, 206, 209, 247, 261, 269, 287, 293, 304-305, 326, 330, 347, 377, 380, 388-389

express purpose 55, 167, 172, 262, 268-269, 273, 289

extension..........44, 219, 2875, 277, 382

eye(s) 7-8, 13, 20, 23-24, 33, 40, 56, 58, 60, 76, 84-86, 113, 129, 142, 154, 162, 169, 172, 177, 183, 192-193, 196, 198-199, 210, 218-219, 225-228, 234, 238, 241, 256-260, 264, 275, 282, 284-296, 318, 321-323, 343, 348, 358-359, 373-374, 380, 382

F

faith...1, 6, 11-15, 20-21, 29, 33-36, 40, 43, 49, 52-57, 60-62, 66, 69-70, 73-74, 80-83, 86, 103, 111, 122-125, 133, 154-155, 165, 167, 171-173, 176, 181, 183, 192, 202, 205, 218-219, 226, 233, 236-240, 242, 249, 259-262, 266, 269, 272-273, 276, 279, 285-287, 290-295, 299-304, 316, 323-328, 331-332, 350, 364, 376, 381, 384-385

faithful............14-15, 21, 40, 49, 52-57, 61-62, 66, 69-70, 73-74, 81, 103, 123, 125, 133, 154-155, 171, 176, 183, 202, 205, 218-219, 233, 239, 266, 269, 273, 276, 279, 287, 290-295, 299-300, 304, 316, 331-332, 350

false doctrine 65, 76

family.............35-36, 38, 42, 70-71, 92, 113-114, 167-168, 176, 178, 201-208, 214, 268, 281, 285, 293-304, 309-310, 322-323, 347-350

Father Adam 35, 70, 104, 121, 132, 155, 202-206, 214, 267, 297, 299, 304

Father and the Son....24, 56, 104, 126, 150, 181-189, 195, 197-198, 202, 205, 269-270, 311, 355-356, 373, 388

fear 5, 13, 17-18, 27, 42, 47, 61-62, 121, 137, 154, 158, 176, 225, 228, 253, 259, 264, 291, 323, 333-334

female......176-177, 182, 187, 192, 196, 353-356

find out......5-6, 22, 35, 61, 68, 94, 121, 132, 155, 177, 182, 250, 258, 289, 305, 341, 365

finite..................42, 58, 81, 84, 87, 112, 182-183, 197, 208, 226, 256, 267, 281, 360, 370

finitist 44, 93, 159, 177, 210, 345, 369

First Presidency........................66, 180

five minutes.................5, 52, 61, 247

foreknowledge...................................76

foreordained 70, 333

forever 1, 12, 25, 49, 53-54, 64-66, 82-86, 93, 96, 109, 129, 207, 217-219, 252, 260-261, 266, 271, 291, 311, 343-344, 362, 364-365, 370, 373, 381, 387

former life 88, 97, 389

forward 15, 20, 80, 88-91, 248, 270, 321, 374

freedom 221, 249, 251, 334, 381

fulness / fullness 2, 11, 18, 32-33, 40-45, 50, 53, 53, 57, 61, 68, 74, 77, 86, 94, 126, 130-133, 141, 153, 155, 158, 182, 186, 188, 192, 194, 197, 201, 213-214, 226, 231, 237, 244-245, 257, 270, 278, 289-290, 296, 297, 302, 331, 349

future........5, 15, 22, 52, 66, 74, 78, 94, 112, 115, 153, 202, 207, 210, 228, 235-236, 247, 287, 291, 316, 359-360, 378, 382

G

Gabriel.....................................137-138

Garden of Eden......190, 202-203, 207, 267-268, 297-298, 304, 347, 370

garment...........24, 47, 69, 94, 101-102, 109-120, 203, 324-325, 347-350, 376, 379, 386

gate 20, 44, 51, 57, 70, 88, 90-91, 118-119, 141, 166, 179, 183, 210, 214, 218, 238, 262-263, 330, 350-351, 364-365, 369, 379

Gazelam 131

Geb 354, 357-358

gender 63

general conference 203

generation(s)...6, 16, 31-32, 59, 64, 69, 97, 111, 120-122, 133, 141, 153, 189, 202, 208, 230, 242-244, 294, 299, 304, 323, 344, 354, 368, 389

gift(s)...6, 22, 33, 42, 45, 53, 55, 72, 81, 189, 197, 220, 234, 249, 254, 277, 284, 317, 375

gift of seeing 284
glories 29, 31, 112-113, 167, 227, 240-247
glory 1, 7, 12-15, 23, 25, 27-28, 33, 38, 41-45, 50-57, 60-62, 66-87, 90, 94, 103-105, 111-119, 131, 133, 148, 165, 172-173, 180, 182, 185, 189-193, 197-198, 201-208, 212-213, 225-231, 235, 238, 240-241, 244-245, 248, 252-261, 264-280, 285-286, 293, 297, 300, 306-307, 310, 314, 316, 321-323, 331-335, 345-349, 353, 356, 365-367, 372-374, 383-387
glory to glory.....................15, 41-42, 53
go no more out 109, 385
God himself shall come down 143-145, 150, 181, 187, 195
God the Father 7, 51, 59, 86, 180-188, 196-197, 207, 220, 248, 262-264, 287
godhead 19, 55, 60, 63, 85, 178, 186, 189, 194, 208, 246, 261
godhood...81-82
godlike 45, 63, 70, 167
godliness 5, 9, 12, 16, 20, 22, 54-55, 178, 183, 215, 235, 240-242, 251, 268, 326-327
God-Man / God-Men......................208
God-Mother 208
gods many 18 180, 183, 194, 246, 262, 290-294
good logic 255
gospel 2, 7, 14, 26, 34, 38, 41-42, 45, 53-57, 64, 72, 76-79, 83, 86, 88, 93, 102-105, 116, 133, 140-141, 161, 166, 171, 173, 185, 199, 204, 214, 234, 240, 245, 252-253, 257-260, 270-271, 278-280, 292, 297, 302, 316, 340-345, 357, 364-365, 373-375
grace 1, 23, 41-45, 55, 94, 104, 153, 158, 168, 173, 183, 188, 213, 252, 298, 340, 365-366
grace and truth 1, 42, 55, 94, 365-366
grace for grace 1, 42, 44-45, 158
grace to grace 41-45, 188, 213, 252
grade after grade 71
grade to grade....................................80
grade(s)...........52, 71, 80, 85, 183, 188, 278-279, 298, 360, 379-381
grain....48-49, 58-59, 88, 280, 327, 380
grand key....................12, 29, 190, 240
grandfather.......58, 159, 180, 204, 291, 310

grandson 180
Grant, Heber J. 77
Grant, Jedediah M. 71, 126
great God 27, 31, 409, 181, 211, 242, 251, 260, 382
great grandfather 180, 291
great secret....................29, 53, 240-241
greater things 8, 33, 89, 328
greatness 66, 153, 226, 229, 340
grinding 169, 313-315
guide(s) 19, 22, 83, 95, 118, 120, 323, 348-350, 380, 386

H

hands uplifted / upreaching / upraised....................24, 26, 214, 311
head God...................178-179, 253, 263
heaven of heavens 204, 246
Heavenly Mother 210, 350-351
heir(s) 29, 52, 63, 70, 84, 192, 201, 209-210, 213, 240, 244, 253, 265, 269, 293, 300, 321, 330, 348-349
hell...........12, 38, 41, 51, 59-63, 92, 96, 104, 117, 153-154, 168-172, 217-221, 240-241, 245-246, 252-254, 260-261, 271, 274-275, 289, 292, 315-317, 326, 331, 370, 387
hidden 5-6, 16, 102, 119, 228, 328, 331, 364, 380
hide.....................90, 150-151, 237, 328
hiding 150-151, 241, 325, 377
hierarchy...............................87-88, 215
highest heaven 114, 117-118, 120, 241
Hinckley, Gordon B. 80-82
Holy Ghost 5, 15, 33, 39, 49, 59, 81, 87, 137, 140, 167, 173, 180, 182, 187-191, 194-198, 207, 213, 218-222, 245-249, 253-254, 258-263, 267-270, 277, 280, 276-287, 316-317, 373-375
Holy Spirit.......7, 11, 13, 19, 33, 53, 66, 83, 104, 117, 120, 165, 182, 188-189 196-197, 219, 249, 256, 273, 285-286, 385
hope 29, 61, 65-68, 78, 93, 113, 130, 147, 173, 177, 186, 222, 225-226, 234, 240, 247, 259-260, 328, 335, 351, 359, 373
Horus 209, 234, 353, 357-358, 378-382

INDEX

human...........25, 28, 36, 38, 42, 52, 63,
  72-74, 78-79, 92, 97, 167-168, 176,
  206-211, 226, 229-230, 238,
  250-251, 268, 278, 281-285, 294,
  297, 299, 302, 309, 331-332,
  342-344, 352-353, 356, 360, 363,
  368-370, 375, 378, 381, 389
hundred fold 31, 51, 124, 242
Hyde, Orson.....................................222

I

I am the Father.......181-182, 187, 197,
  355
identity......65, 83, 89, 92, 95, 132, 214,
  220-221, 346, 353, 358, 364,
  376-379, 383, 386
Idumia 321-324
ignorant..........36, 52, 64, 89, 102, 184,
  247, 279, 299, 341
image.......41, 51, 68, 70, 176-177, 179,
  203, 210-212, 230, 252, 263, 342,
  349-352, 377
immortal...........69, 109, 176, 178, 208,
  228, 232, 249, 252, 255-256, 279,
  334, 342-434, 370, 385, 387
immortality.........19, 44, 50, 53-54, 78,
  83, 86, 103, 112, 166, 185, 208, 219,
  255, 269, 279, 291, 296-297, 330,
  334, 365, 372, 387
in due time 44, 50, 66, 123, 287
in the flesh..........33, 38, 42, 50, 69, 71,
  84, 104, 123, 126, 163, 168,
  203-207, 257, 268-271, 295, 303,
  310, 316-317, 323, 340, 365, 385
inclusive 98
increase......8, 17, 53-60, 64, 74, 80-84,
  88, 94, 98, 104, 176, 183-185, 206,
  214, 219-220, 272-280, 289, 324,
  328, 334, 362, 385, 387
infinite 58, 84, 87, 182, 197, 208,
  226, 256, 267, 281, 370
infinity 58, 363
inheritance................40, 49-50, 63, 70,
  90-92, 103, 124-126, 130, 161, 163,
  209, 235, 330, 350, 357, 385
initiate(s).............27, 115-116, 211, 342,
  376, 383
innumerable.....58, 172, 247, 321, 335,
  366
inquire.............6, 13, 16-17, 21, 70, 85,
  171, 222, 250-251, 270, 274, 279,
  283-284, 289, 296-297, 326
inspection 91, 211
inspiration........6, 19, 82, 84, 165, 178,
  250-251, 256

integrity..............8, 16, 21, 79, 122, 347
intelligence..............6, 13, 18-19, 32-35,
  53-56, 66, 69-70, 81-83, 86-89, 104,
  122, 165-166, 172, 176, 205,
  220-222, 227, 242, 249, 255-256,
  260, 264, 269, 273, 275, 279, 284,
  288, 291-292, 300-302, 307, 340,
  373
intelligent..... 1, 36, 64-66, 74, 87, 103,
  165-166, 172, 222, 256, 288-289,
  291-298, 345
invigorated 380
Isaiah............37, 47, 96, 114-120, 151,
  154-156, 363, 388
Israel 5, 8, 21, 35-39, 47-48, 66, 69,
  84-89, 107, 111, 115, 119-121, 124,
  129-133, 138, 141-144, 150-155,
  175, 207, 215, 222, 243, 259,
  265-267, 292-293, 300, 306,
  313-319, 326-330, 334

J

Jehovah 25, 43, 63, 130, 162,
  180-186, 207, 238, 274-276, 369,
  392
Yahovah 180, 203, 268, 294
Jeremiah.................37-38, 47, 314-319
Jesse...............................142, 154-155
Jesus Christ........1-2, 12-14, 18, 23-29,
  32-35, 40-41, 49, 51-59, 64, 70,
  74-79, 83, 121-124, 132-133, 155,
  161-162, 165-166, 179-199,
  203-206, 213-215, 220, 239-276,
  285-287, 290-296, 300-311, 316,
  355, 395
Jeu............................88, 102, 162, 184
John the Baptist 96, 135-142, 260,
  387
Johnson, Benjamin F........................86
joy........6, 13, 21, 33, 43, 60, 81-83, 94,
  104, 112-113, 137, 148-149, 153,
  172, 191-192, 197, 209, 222, 228,
  235, 313, 322, 324, 333-339, 351,
  383, 385

K

kept hid 7, 11
key word..................................25, 119
keys 7, 11, 16-21, 29, 63, 70-71,
  123, 126, 133, 137-138, 141-142,
  155, 161, 179 190, 201, 205-206,
  213-215, 240, 246-248, 251, 254,
  260, 264, 286, 296, 299, 316, 358
Kimball, Heber C. 1, 32, 34, 38, 62,
  71, 126, 127, 142, 214-215, 290, 313

king 5, 21, 37, 39, 42, 47-48, 52-55, 84, 102, 111-112, 117, 132, 137, 150-153, 175, 179, 190, 210-215, 231, 244, 249, 259, 263, 266, 294, 306, 324, 348-350, 353, 356, 360, 377, 379-383, 391-392, 397
King and Priest 213, 215
King Follett........42, 249, 259, 391-392
king of kings .52, 54-55, 112, 231, 266, 349-350
Kingdom of God 13, 29, 31-32, 35-36, 50, 55, 74, 80, 103-112, 119, 133, 166-169, 176, 182, 187, 195-196, 206-207, 214-215, 221, 240, 244-248, 259-260, 271-272, 281, 287-290, 292, 297, 299, 301
kingdom of heaven........5, 7-8, 29, 109, 119, 135, 139, 240, 316, 385
Kirtland..23
knock.........6, 11, 21-22, 241, 277, 283, 359, 376
Kolob 113, 371

L

labors ...50, 69-71, 74-75, 86, 109, 122, 158, 282-283, 385
ladder 42, 52, 242, 253
Lamb of God 143, 181, 187, 195
law.13, 23, 32, 45, 48-50, 55-57, 62-63, 81, 89, 96, 115, 135, 139, 157-162, 167, 172-173, 205, 213-214, 264, 276, 310-311, 323-326, 329-333, 364, 373, 388
let us go 144-148, 260, 275, 300, 326
level 45, 52, 87-91, 114, 185, 345, 368, 371, 378-380, 388
life eternal 6, 21, 55, 64, 104, 235, 248-250, 290, 302, 378, 382
lift..........1, 75, 120, 178, 208, 231, 234, 238, 250-251, 356
light...1, 6, 11, 13, 16-17, 24-29, 32-35, 42-45, 54, 60, 66, 74-76, 79, 82, 85-86, 90-94, 98, 103-104, 111-112, 116, 118, 121, 132, 153, 155, 162-163, 166, 172, 193, 203, 205, 226, 232-237, 240-242, 248, 268, 275-277, 285, 301, 303, 307, 318, 321, 323-324, 331-334, 342, 344, 347, 350, 360, 363, 368, 386
likeness 51, 80-81, 176-177, 199, 210, 230, 252, 264, 268, 313, 340, 365
line upon line 43, 189
Little, James A..................................214

live 14-15, 23, 40, 49, 52, 56, 64-67, 70, 74, 78, 80, 82, 84, 97, 108 112, 130, 158, 172-176, 183, 202, 211, 221, 229, 236-237, 245, 249, 277, 285, 289, 291, 298-299, 305-306, 318, 326-330, 335, 370, 376, 385, 389
living..........6, 17, 20, 43, 53, 61, 74, 77, 88, 130, 141, 159, 167, 203, 206-207, 212, 231, 233, 237, 246, 255, 260, 278, 281, 288, 290-291, 294, 298, 305-306, 330-331, 335, 341-343, 366, 370-372, 377-382
Lord of lords 52, 54-55, 112, 230, 266
lords 18, 52, 54-55, 112, 180, 183, 194, 202, 230, 246, 262, 266, 290, 292, 294
lords many 18, 180, 183, 194, 246, 262, 290, 292, 294
lords of lords....................................112
love 7, 22, 25, 33, 43-44, 56-57, 82, 94, 116, 143, 181, 186-187, 191, 195, 219, 237, 241, 261, 269, 272-276, 329, 340, 359
Ludlow, Daniel H...........................114
Lyman, Amasa................................249

M

Macdermot, Violet 161
Madsen, Truman G. 20, 44, 66, 98, 117, 135
male 176-177, 182, 187, 192, 196, 354, 356
male and female 176-177, 182, 187, 196, 356
Man of Holiness 181, 186
manifestation(s).........................33, 286
mankind 24, 35, 50, 54-56, 60, 63, 81, 89, 97-98, 108, 114, 162, 166, 177-178, 180-181, 187, 197, 203, 220, 226, 231, 239, 250, 262, 268-279, 281, 287-288, 291, 335, 373, 388
mar / marred 37, 12-124, 241, 314, 318-319
Maria..161-162
marriage / married........70, 81, 85, 95, 98, 267, 298-299, 355, 372, 386
Mary Magdalene 161
matter......35, 56, 60, 89, 202-205, 273, 294, 362-363
Maxwell, Neal A......................43, 84
McKay, David O................................79

McConkie, Bruce R. 23, 188
measure 103, 157, 192, 211, 219, 271, 324-327
Melchizedek 7, 22, 90-91, 103, 131-132, 141-142, 162, 213-214, 362
merits 79
messenger ... 16-17, 27, 61, 63, 84, 101, 135, 139, 189-190, 225, 232
Messenger and Advocate 84, 225
Messiah 43, 115, 135, 188-189, 228-232, 236, 331, 340
metamorphosis 379
Michael 87, 98, 180, 201-208, 215, 267-268, 294-295, 300, 305, 369-372, 393
midst of all kinds 165, 218
midst of eternity 61, 281, 288-289
mill 38, 169, 283, 314, 317, 319
Millennial Star 31, 71, 122, 236
missionaries 77, 350, 360
molded 313-314
more sure word 29, 240-241
Mormonism 6, 27, 60, 78, 98, 104, 114, 170, 283, 286, 319, 392
mortal ....
mortality 19, 44, 50, 53-54, 57, 71, 78, 83, 86, 103, 112, 117, 166, 185, 188, 208, 219, 229, 255-256, 269, 279, 285, 289, 291, 296-297, 330, 334, 365, 372, 387
Moses 35, 45, 65, 115, 121, 124, 129-133, 140, 142, 155, 176, 236, 295, 298, 306, 334-335, 343, 351, 355, 363, 365-368, 371-374, 383
mother of God 143, 186, 195
multiplied 334, 362
my servant 8, 13, 47-48, 51, 84, 123-125, 130-131, 142, 151, 156
mysteries 5-9, 18-22, 25, 29, 32-33, 49, 63, 86-92, 116, 132, 142, 161-163, 184, 214-215, 222, 233, 240, 244, 259, 289, 293, 352, 376-377, 380
mysteries of Godliness 5, 9, 20, 22, 215
mysteries of the kingdom 5, 7, 29, 32, 116, 142, 222, 240, 244, 289

N

Name of God 118-119, 325, 373
native element 37, 57, 59, 218-222, 276-279
natural element 275
natural selection 383

Nauvoo 34, 65, 76, 132, 175, 189, 206, 319
Nephi 28, 50, 154, 343, 375
never die 56, 71
new house 63
new identity 92, 95, 386
new life 95, 211, 377-379, 383, 386
new man 53
new name 22, 92-97, 370, 386, 389
New Testament 16, 39, 138, 199, 204, 245, 254, 262, 269, 344, 355, 364
new world 92, 184, 242, 357, 361-364, 378
Nibley, Hugh 25, 28, 86, 89, 91, 101-102, 108, 114, 173, 184, 209-210, 214, 339-341, 351, 361, 364, 376, 385
Noah 26, 65, 103, 137-139, 142, 206, 262

O

O Lord 21, 27, 37, 47, 153, 177, 329, 333, 335, 344
Oaks, Dallin H. 43
obedient / obedience 20, 38, 42-43, 53, 57, 63, 72-75, 79, 138, 193, 209, 222, 246, 293, 300, 302, 315-319, 323, 331, 343
offspring 53, 63, 68, 79, 94, 155, 183, 188, 202, 208, 268, 385
Old Testament 204, 212, 290, 342-343, 357, 367, 373
olive-trees 125, 144-147
omnipotence 229, 276
omnipotent 64, 181
omnipresent 181
omniscient 181
one body 149, 191-192, 198-199, 246
one Eternal God 182, 188, 196
one God 18, 33, 150, 168, 179-188, 191-197, 207, 246, 260, 262-264, 290-294, 388
one God to us 183
one in me 193, 197
one in us 191
Only Begotten of the Father 42-43, 183, 188-189, 198
opportunity(ies) 20, 34, 66, 73, 75, 80, 83-85, 89, 102, 112, 257, 345
opposite 51, 113, 158, 17, 218-219, 271, 274-279, 284, 289, 299, 331, 366, 383

ordained 55, 66, 70, 81, 126, 167, 178, 201, 215, 222, 231, 245, 292-293, 297, 330, 333
ordeals........14, 54, 59-60, 73, 166, 182
ordinance(s)...........5, 14-15, 32, 42, 52, 57-58, 75, 81, 88-93, 137, 141-142, 167, 184, 201, 204, 213, 243-247, 288-297, 309, 356, 359, 371, 382
organized 23-24, 35, 40, 55-56, 60, 63, 71, 104, 166-168, 176, 179, 203, 206, 219-222, 235, 255, 263, 267-279, 282, 288-299, 309-311, 317, 322, 324, 330, 361-363
Origen 88, 343-346
original sin 183
Osiris.................................210, 377-383
Ostler, Blake T. 118, 120, 392
overcome / overcometh 1, 48, 55, 70, 72, 103, 109, 120, 131, 133, 146-148, 165-166, 169, 198, 304, 322-323, 333

P

Palmer, Spencer J............................115
parable.........38, 98, 124-125, 130-131, 193, 327
Paracletes 321-323
Parry, Donald W......................115-117
passive 37-38, 218-220, 313-317
past............6, 15, 85, 112, 118-119, 138, 159, 169, 178, 222, 226, 228, 232, 235-236, 249-250, 260, 287, 316, 326, 360, 382
path 1, 11, 14, 17, 61, 67-68, 73-74, 115, 126, 153, 161-162, 219, 249, 278-279, 306, 330
path of life 153
patriarch(al).27, 67, 84, 116, 124, 132, 207, 213-214, 248, 356, 364
Paul 36, 41, 48, 51, 79, 111, 118, 126, 157, 162, 176-177, 180, 186, 191, 194, 198, 242-245, 257, 259, 262-265, 290, 297, 392
Pearl, The 101, 346-351
Pearl of Great Price, The 131, 210, 339-346, 351-368, 372-378
pearly gates 20
peer(s)..............................231, 236, 377
Penrose, Charles...............................98
perdition..........20, 38, 75, 78, 171-173, 191, 258, 332, 374
perfection 5, 20, 53, 55, 72, 75, 89, 103, 166-167, 175, 179, 209, 259-260, 263, 277, 322, 339-340, 391

permanent.......................309, 316, 382
perpetual......................79, 98, 322-323
personage(s)...........14, 24, 29, 83, 130, 179, 189, 204, 206, 246, 262, 267, 270, 306, 310
pesedj / pesedjet 354-358
Peterson, Daniel C................118, 126
pharaoh 339
phase 83, 92-94, 350, 364, 370, 374
Phelps, William W....................84-85
phenomena (on)........97, 278, 350, 389
Philip 88, 135, 143, 161, 192, 194, 342, 354, 364-365
philosophical 18-19, 94, 104, 279, 386
philosophy...........18-19, 42, 53, 59, 64, 79, 176, 228, 278, 282, 284, 288, 292
piqeakh 373-374
Pistis Sophia 87-89, 119, 132, 161-163, 214, 340, 361-362
plan......1, 27, 34-35, 42, 79, 83, 88, 95, 121, 132, 150, 155, 201, 217, 254, 258, 273, 278, 297, 326, 339-340, 357, 362, 369, 375, 386
plan of happiness 1
plan of mercy 150
plan of redemption 217
plan of salvation 42, 79, 258, 278
planet(s) 22, 78, 203, 272, 279, 282, 294, 307, 356, 361
plant / planted..................89, 125, 142, 145-148, 203, 268, 271, 294-298, 363-364
planting...............................89, 363-364
possibility(ies) 45, 68, 86, 129, 131, 171, 208, 359-360
potter 37-38, 218-221, 313-319
potter's wheel 37
pottery 221, 314
power(s)............. 11, 23, 41, 45, 56, 60, 67-68, 70-71, 81, 87, 105, 113, 119, 165, 204, 207, 229, 237, 252, 265, 271, 274, 280, 242, 284, 292, 297, 302, 310, 317, 321, 342, 356, 382
power of Elias 138
power of endless lives....................322
power of God 8, 12, 54, 77, 150, 181, 185, 187, 196, 269, 387
power of the Holy Ghost......5, 49, 188
power of the priesthood 67, 126
powers of heaven 23
Pratt, Orson 18, 63, 85, 131, 206
Pratt, Parley P...............31, 40, 63, 123, 205-206, 243

INDEX

pray 20, 22-25, 33, 83, 113, 191, 249, 264, 277, 308, 328, 334
prayer(s) 13, 21-28, 32, 67, 76-77, 80, 92, 122, 137, 181, 222, 232, 243, 247-249, 261, 272, 287, 344, 350
praying 24, 27-28, 137, 269, 383
precept(s)..............13, 43, 119, 226, 234
precept upon precept 43
predestination / predestined 96, 231, 340, 386
preexistence 74, 95, 339-340, 343-347, 351, 360, 374, 386, 391-392
preexistent........118, 210, 340, 346, 378
premortal 43, 90, 101, 383
preparatory.....104, 123, 289, 293, 297
prepared over....................................37
present.............11, 13, 15-16, 19, 22-23, 231, 35-36, 40, 42, 53, 55, 59, 69, 72, 74, 76-77, 89, 95-96, 102, 108, 112, 116, 120-121, 130-132, 141, 155, 167, 171, 184-185, 193, 205, 211, 220, 228, 235-236, 239-243, 253, 267-272, 282-289, 297, 306-307, 316, 323-324, 330, 334, 349, 359-360, 366, 380, 382, 386-387
previous life..80
priest and king 131-132, 214-215, 235
priestesses 105, 323, 325
priesthood 7, 11, 13, 16, 21-22, 27, 49, 54, 57, 64, 67, 70-71, 81, 92, 112-115, 126, 132, 138, 142, 155, 172, 206-207, 213-214, 242-246, 266, 271, 276, 281, 286, 296, 317, 358, 376, 391
priests 12, 36, 39, 41, 67, 105, 131, 140, 179, 213-214, 235, 242, 246, 252-253, 260-263, 266, 270, 276, 310, 321-323
priests and kings 131, 213, 235
principalities 61, 105, 118, 204, 207, 265, 271, 280, 292, 297, 302, 310
private information...........................66
privilege(s)........7, 12-15, 18, 23, 33-36, 56, 60, 64, 72, 92, 165, 171-172, 201-202, 251-256, 269-273, 277, 279, 293, 303
probation(s)......1, 56-59, 62, 65, 72-73, 76, 79-80, 84-86, 93, 98, 104, 126, 165-166, 188-189, 219, 234, 271, 316, 323, 343-344, 359, 375
probationary..................................1, 80
probationers 316

process 44-45, 80, 92, 94, 115, 184, 274, 288, 314, 318, 361-364, 368, 380, 383
progress............1, 31, 43-45, 52, 54, 57, 72-89, 208, 225, 262, 283, 301, 345, 377-379
progressing 65, 75, 88-89
progression 1, 25, 47, 49, 52, 55-57, 65, 69, 74, 79-86, 88, 95, 175-176, 219, 279-280, 377, 382, 386, 391, 398
progressive...............................62-63, 81
promises 50, 67-68, 70, 75, 84, 175, 257, 322, 329, 360
prophets 1, 3, 22, 24, 32, 39, 43, 70, 103, 109, 126, 135-142, 183, 188, 203-207, 240, 243-246, 29-270, 281, 284, 286, 290-291, 303, 316, 335, 341, 367, 375
prove 8, 28, 63, 79, 91, 104-105, 112, 168, 202-203, 245, 251, 256, 263, 268, 276, 296, 316, 343
Ptah 209-211, 352-358
purified 54, 72, 79, 161-162, 234
purify............7, 33, 66, 71, 81, 277, 314

Q

queen(s)............105, 209, 231, 322-324, 349, 353
quicken / quickened 11, 39-40, 47-49, 59, 84, 158, 193-194, 248
quickening 104, 212
Quinn, D. Michael 98, 215
Quorum of the Twelve 159, 222

R

rainbow 52
raise up 47, 124, 129-130, 325, 367
raised up......48, 95, 211, 241, 367, 386
rank(s)....................19, 92, 115, 162-163
realm(s) 86, 91, 96, 120, 231, 237, 322, 376, 388, 391
reap...............14, 80, 157-159, 235, 327
rebel..........95, 201, 218, 235, 258, 274, 276, 293, 314-317, 349, 386
rebellious / rebellion........95, 219, 258, 276, 314-317, 349, 386
rebirth 97, 377-383, 389
reborn 96-97, 377-383, 389
reckon................133, 211, 297-300, 371
reconciliation 80, 95, 386
reconstruction.................................391
redeem 40, 71-72, 98, 125, 130, 150, 173, 181, 183, 187, 195, 197, 202, 270, 273, 309, 317, 389

redeemed 15, 38, 50, 72, 78-79, 95, 97, 108, 151, 214, 217, 260, 281, 295, 317, 373, 386, 389
redeemer 21, 74, 82, 84, 124, 219, 274
redemption 50, 69-70, 79, 84, 114, 124-126, 129, 131, 171-172, 181, 187, 196-197, 207, 217, 220, 235, 259, 270, 293, 359
refuge 150, 241, 362, 381
regeneration 59, 97, 120, 389
reincarnation 78, 98, 346
rejuvenate / rejuvenation 377-380
renewed / renewal / renewing 49, 97, 181, 230, 237, 248, 333, 340, 376-380, 389
repent 34, 40 75, 93-94, 133, 157, 196, 272, 308, 366, 373-375
repentance 2, 40, 75, 81, 93, 153, 158, 217, 258, 260, 290, 323, 333, 335, 345, 366, 374
reshuffling 361
restoration 51, 54, 124, 137, 141-142, 154, 158, 182-183, 187, 196
restored 2, 28, 50, 157-158, 182, 188, 196, 318, 346, 382, 385
restored in the flesh 50, 385
resurrected 62, 88, 95, 118, 159, 189, 214, 296-297, 304, 337, 355, 378, 386
resurrection ...14, 16, 40-41, 48, 50-55, 58-62, 67, 70, 78, 85, 98-99, 104, 112, 116, 118, 130, 133, 159, 206, 210-213, 218-219, 222, 244-247, 252, 255, 259-261, 265, 270, 274, 279, 295-296, 299, 325, 337, 342, 356, 377, 380, 382, 389
Retreads 126, 237
revealer 12, 358
reveals 14, 16-17, 114, 167, 183, 256, 265, 273, 285, 287, 305-306
revelation(s) ...3, 5-8, 11-25, 31, 34-39, 43, 48, 52-54, 57-58, 65, 67, 70, 84-85, 98, 108-109, 121-123, 130-132, 138, 141-142, 155, 157, 165, 177, 198199, 206, 213, 215, 219, 222, 240-248, 251, 254-256, 260-266, 278, 285-287, 290, 301-308, 323, 349, 367, 385
Richards, Willard 243, 249
Rigdon, Sidney 23, 131, 252

righteous 23, 35, 51, 71, 86, 93, 101-102, 109, 114-118, 137, 153, 158, 163, 190-191, 202, 245-246, 249, 252, 268-272, 286, 327, 330-334, 375
righteousness 12, 45, 47, 50, 57, 70, 74, 81, 97, 108, 133, 151, 154-155, 176, 189, 193, 206, 217-219, 236, 248, 276, 281, 284, 324, 328, 334, 389
rite of passage 97, 364, 389
robe(s) 115-119, 133, 193, 205-207, 337, 347-350, 391-392
Roberts, B. H. 83, 207
Robinson, Joseph Lee 32, 85
rod 37, 129, 154, 221, 314
rod of iron 37
Rod of Jesse 154
role(s) 2, 43-44, 211, 231, 380
Root of Jesse 142, 155

S

sacrifice 25-28, 67-70, 82, 90, 115, 213, 232, 235, 271-272, 373
Saints 1, 14, 18-19, 21, 31-34, 36, 38, 42, 53, 56, 61, 63-64, 72-73, 76-77, 83-88, 104, 114, 116122, 126, 131, 133, 159, 161, 165-166, 169-173, 189, 192, 201, 204, 209, 215, 218-219, 243, 247-249, 258, 261, 269-275, 281, 287-288, 292-293, 299-300, 309, 314, 316-317, 324, 345
salvation ..2-3, 8, 12, 15-17, 26, 38, 42, 53, 56-59, 62, 70, 75, 77, 79, 89, 98, 104, 113, 121-122, 161, 166-167, 171-173, 176, 183, 196, 201, 203, 206, 209, 218-222, 239, 242-247, 253-260, 268-270, 273, 275, 278, 281, 285-287, 290, 302, 308, 317, 322-323, 332, 335, 370, 390
sanctification.....................................18
Satan 27-28, 53, 65, 67, 73, 79, 84, 94, 217, 219, 222, 235, 264, 273-274, 276, 284, 298, 300, 323, 344, 348, 357, 359, 366, 373-375
Savior 12, 22, 26, 29, 54, 67, 74, 76, 82, 119, 183, 189, 199, 207, 240, 257-258, 269-270, 286, 316, 365
savior in training 189
Schmidt, Carl 161
Scott, Richard G. 122
sealed 8, 29, 33, 48, 76, 81, 91, 141-142, 240, 248, 262, 349

Index

search 5, 9, 12, 20, 22, 77, 82-84, 93, 102, 153, 171, 250, 262, 287, 293, 323, 329, 377
second death 217, 219, 222, 249, 260-261, 318
secret(s)..........3-9, 16-18, 29, 41, 53, 79, 84, 89, 98, 102, 114-116, 132, 150, 154, 210, 214, 225, 227, 233, 240-242, 251, 261, 323, 339, 342, 344, 358, 367
seed(s).....49, 60, 64, 99, 124, 129, 141, 153, 192, 195, 208, 242, 268, 276, 280, 282, 288, 304, 323, 327, 355, 358, 363
seeing and knowing..........7, 33
seek / seeketh..........5-6, 11-13, 20-23, 35, 49, 53, 77, 84, 88, 90, 101, 119, 121, 123, 132, 150, 155, 167, 169, 177, 207, 227, 239-240, 251, 257-258, 272-277, 286, 293, 308, 364
seer(s) 17, 70, 129-130, 208, 233, 236, 284
self-existent 165, 255-256
serpent..........347-348, 350
servant(s) 8, 13, 25, 27, 39, 47-48, 51, 58, 79, 84-85, 119, 123-125, 130-131, 141-156, 181, 202, 215, 246, 248, 251, 287, 297, 313-319, 325, 330, 333-334, 366
Seth..........88, 209, 354, 357-358
seven heavens..........111-115, 118, 120
seventh heaven..........79, 114-119, 383
seventh *hekal*..........114
Shabako..........209, 211, 339, 354, 356-357, 363
Shabako Stone..........339, 357
shape(s) 18, 24, 38, 72, 114, 221-222, 248, 279, 307, 313-318, 337
sign(s) 22, 27-28, 48, 50, 89-91, 118-119, 173, 230, 242, 328, 331, 349-350, 370
sin(s) 22, 40, 48, 59, 75, 93, 150, 167, 171, 173, 183-184, 193, 197, 213, 218-222, 257-261, 266, 292, 316-317, 322-323, 332, 345
sisters..........22, 35, 51, 57, 67-68, 74, 76, 86, 112, 202, 205, 261, 285-286, 294, 298-300, 303, 311
Smith, George Albert..........77
Smith, Hyrum 8, 16, 85, 111, 123, 126, 175
Smith, Joseph..........5-7, 11-14, 20-21, 23-24, 29-34, 38-42, 49-52, 69, 76-79, 89, 92, 95, 98, 103, 109, 111, 121-133, 138-139, 141-143, 153-159, 165, 168-171, 175, 178-181, 186, 188-189, 193, 195, 199, 201, 205-218, 239-249, 261-262, 286, 299, 316, 321, 337, 344, 346, 351, 353, 364, 375-378, 385-386, 391-392
Smith, Joseph F. 76, 180
Smith, Joseph Fielding 355
Snow, Eliza R.........78, 86, 98, 208-209, 347
Snow, Erastus 69, 176, 184, 222
Snow, Lorenzo..........65-66, 78, 98, 113-114, 178, 183, 188, 214
Son of God 24, 29, 34, 40, 42, 44, 51, 54, 59, 67, 78, 119, 126, 150, 167, 176, 179-197, 202, 207, 220, 240, 246, 264-269, 296, 303, 310, 313, 325, 387
Son of Man 49, 114, 135, 139, 181, 186, 203-204, 246, 257, 262, 359
son of my son 209
sons 20, 38, 42, 50, 53-58, 67-70, 78-81, 94, 97, 108, 114-115, 124, 131, 166, 171-175, 182-188, 193, 197-202, 206-208, 213-214, 229, 233-234, 238, 258, 265, 268-269, 300, 321, 324-325, 334, 339, 341-342, 385, 389
son(s) of perdition 20, 38, 75, 78, 171-173, 191, 258
soul 6, 12, 20, 22, 29, 33, 43, 47, 56, 63, 66, 80, 86, 89-91, 96, 98, 101, 109, 118-119, 122, 151, 153-154, 161-163, 167-168, 212, 217, 219, 222, 226-231, 234-240, 255-258, 268, 280, 295, 308, 323, 327-328, 331-334, 337, 342-345, 362-363, 371, 377, 379-387, 392-393
sovereign(ty) 219, 231, 241, 274, 327-332
soweth..........157
space......15, 58-61, 143, 187, 195, 203, 234, 273, 276-278, 282, 284, 288, 294, 302, 307, 318, 321, 324, 359, 362-364
spark 363-364
species 166, 176, 185, 202-204, 309-311, 388
speculation 13, 20
Kimball, Spencer W. 20, 22

sphere(s) 55, 64, 66, 69, 70, 75, 112, 162, 178, 208, 226, 231, 234, 250, 268, 307, 321, 381
Spirit of God 13, 17, 19, 108, 191, 205, 246, 248, 311
spiritual body..........................189, 322
stage(s) 52, 57, 61, 81, 92, 184-185, 237, 280, 355, 368-370, 380, 383
Stapley, Delbert L...............................81
stars 78-79, 87, 193, 227, 231, 234, 236, 259, 265, 280, 321, 324, 328, 331, 334-335, 339, 361
state 8, 17, 50-53, 56-59, 62, 64, 69, 80, 84, 92, 94-97, 104, 108-109, 112, 133, 158, 166, 189, 197, 204, 212, 214, 231, 289, 299, 309, 353, 364, 370-372, 383, 389
state of existence...62, 64, 92, 214, 364
static...84, 88
stationary..................................80, 278
step by step 42-43, 88, 253
Stevenson, Edward...................85, 180
subjection 62, 72, 165, 262, 314
succession........1, 70-71, 210, 268, 322-323, 364, 377, 380
succession of lives 364
suffer........36, 39-40, 56, 112, 131, 135, 139, 153, 172, 192, 199, 217-219, 228, 258, 269, 306, 326, 329, 334-335, 341, 345, 377, 380-381
suffered......27, 40, 103, 172, 270, 330, 380
suffering 26, 32, 52, 70, 93, 104, 113-114, 166, 171, 176, 183, 221, 247, 276, 341, 345, 380
sun 62, 67, 78, 88, 92, 206, 211, 228, 236, 258, 313, 328, 331, 351, 353, 364, 370
suppressed..................................74, 341
Swanson, Vern G. 189

T

tabernacle......24, 35, 40, 54-58, 62-65, 69, 72, 76, 104, 112, 140-141, 150, 167-168, 175, 182, 188, 193, 197, 202, 218, 220, 222, 235, 239-240, 242, 248, 252, 255-256, 267-270, 274, 285, 298, 306, 310, 316, 318
tabernacle of God..........175, 193, 255, 267
Talmage, James E..............80, 343-344
Taylor, John..........18-19, 64, 103, 105, 121, 176, 180, 184, 321

temple........15-16, 62, 89, 93, 102, 109, 114-117, 137, 150, 161, 167, 183-184, 188, 191, 193, 210, 243, 246-248, 261, 277, 316, 342, 350, 355, 358, 368, 376
temptation............40, 66, 73, 150, 181, 186-187, 196, 348, 373, 388
terrible questions 346
tested 72, 80, 89-90, 93, 95, 101, 105, 190, 293, 344-345, 351, 373, 375, 386
testified 45, 129, 372
testing 94, 122, 340, 343, 351, 385
theologian(s) 268, 303, 345
theological 44, 180, 301
theology.........27, 81, 84, 209, 302-303, 358, 376, 378, 395
theory(ies) 76, 87, 95, 97, 177, 352, 355, 360, 386, 389
things of God 6, 8, 12, 15-16, 18-19, 32, 107-108, 183
throne.......22-24, 41, 48, 54, 57, 60-61, 68, 70, 78, 87, 102, 105, 113-120, 166, 175, 181, 198, 203-210, 220, 228, 230-233, 237, 251-253, 260, 265, 271, 280, 292-294, 297, 302, 305, 310, 317, 347-349, 352-358, 374-376, 380
thrown back 37-38, 219, 221, 276, 313-317, 362
time to time 29, 33, 38, 86, 177, 211, 330, 369
timeless 28, 89, 102, 173, 210, 364-365, 371
Times and Seasons 8, 180, 184, 186, 321-324
to go no more out....................109, 385
tracks...42, 253
tradition(s) 14, 20, 25, 32, 87, 117, 122, 135, 167, 183, 212, 266, 278, 282-283, 299, 317, 374-375
transformation.......115, 225, 378, 380, 383
treasure(s) 1, 89, 101-102, 118, 203, 268, 308, 333, 347, 361-364
treasury 90-91 101-102, 161-162, 364
trial(s).........1, 29, 50, 56, 67, 72-73, 83, 103-105, 111-112, 166-168, 172, 184, 230, 240, 242, 279, 298, 316-317, 343, 347-349
tried 14, 21, 28, 32, 72, 89, 97, 103, 105, 108, 167, 229, 236, 238, 296, 314, 317, 340, 389

triumph(ant).....71, 212, 235, 238-239, 242, 258-259, 266, 324, 379-380
true...5, 9, 14, 19, 27-28, 36, 38, 41-42, 49, 52-57, 62-67, 78, 81-82, 86, 98, 104, 108, 123, 126, 141, 159, 166, 171-172, 182, 187, 195, 204-205, 213, 226, 232, 235, 242-256, 260, 266-268, 272-273, 276, 278, 282-290, 296, 302, 305-310, 316, 319, 340-341, 344, 346, 369, 380, 383
true and faithful 57, 276
truth.........1, 6, 11-14, 16, 18-22, 33-36, 40-45, 55-57, 63-64, 72, 76-80, 83, 86-88, 94, 108, 111, 122, 143, 153, 166, 170-173, 177-182, 187-188, 191-197, 202-204, 207, 219, 225-237, 247-251, 255, 258-269, 272-277, 281, 284, 286, 291, 295-296, 304-305, 309, 323, 328, 331, 334, 337, 340, 346, 351, 365-366, 381, 385
Turner, Rodney................................392
two dimensional..............................374

U
unclean 131, 201, 284, 293, 311
universal redemption 171
universal salvation............79, 171, 173
universe.....19, 40, 78, 81-82, 208, 228, 302, 321, 324, 356, 362, 383
unorganized.....................297, 362-363
Urim and Thummim................25, 347

V
variety.........40, 165, 167-168, 203, 239, 282-288, 291, 293-294, 322
variety of Spirits.......................165, 239
veil 8, 14, 41, 56, 64, 70, 82, 120, 185, 203, 226-227, 231, 238, 251-253, 285-287, 316-317, 350-351
vessel 37-38, 94, 169, 313-319
vineyard.....85, 124-131, 144-150, 231, 363
vision 12-13, 16-17, 23-26, 29-32, 34, 58, 67, 70-71, 93, 115-116, 120-122, 127, 154, 171, 201, 209, 214 218, 222, 229, 231-232, 240-242, 257, 265, 270-273, 277, 284-287, 293, 350, 353, 357-359, 362-363, 373-374
visitation...............26, 94, 159, 242, 385

W
Watchers 375
Wells, Daniel H................................126
Whitney, Orson F. 32, 65, 77-79, 126, 131, 142, 225-227, 261, 379
who I am 31-32, 142, 230
whom we have to do...............202, 267, 292-293, 305
Widtsoe, John A......42, 53-54, 80, 104
Woodruff, Wilford 1, 19, 64-65, 76-78, 122, 204, 206, 239, 243, 249
wives 51, 55, 67, 98, 202, 267, 283, 295-298, 300
words of my mouth 21, 25-27
words of our mouth..........................23
works shall follow them 158, 385
worlds without end 53, 64-65, 98, 176, 261, 288-290

Y
Yahovah 180, 203, 268, 294
Yahovah Michael....................203, 294
Young, Brigham 1, 8-9, 14-15, 17-19, 22, 31, 33-37, 42, 52, 54, 59, 65, 71, 97, 103-108, 111-113, 121-127, 132-133, 155, 165, 170-171, 180, 182-184, 188, 199-208, 213-218, 222, 267, 275, 287, 289, 295, 300, 308, 315-321, 354

Z
Zacharias 137-138

Made in the USA
Coppell, TX
06 June 2023